Second Edition

Informants, Cooperating Witnesses, and Undercover Investigations

A Practical Guide to Law, Policy, and Procedure

CRC SERIES IN
**PRACTICAL ASPECTS OF CRIMINAL
AND FORENSIC INVESTIGATIONS**

VERNON J. GEBERTH, BBA, MPS, FBINA *Series Editor*

**Practical Homicide Investigation: Tactics, Procedures, and
Forensic Techniques, Fourth Edition**
Vernon J. Geberth

**Practical Homicide Investigation Checklist and Field Guide,
Second Edition**
Vernon J. Geberth

**Informants, Cooperating Witnesses, and Undercover Investigations:
A Practical Guide to Law, Policy, and Procedure, Second Edition**
Dennis G. Fitzgerald

Practical Military Ordnance Identification
Tom Gersbeck

Practical Cold Case Homicide Investigations Procedural Manual
Richard H. Walton

Autoerotic Deaths: Practical Forensic and Investigative Perspectives
Anny Sauvageau and Vernon J. Geberth

Practical Crime Scene Processing and Investigation, Second Edition
Ross M. Gardner

**The Counterterrorism Handbook: Tactics, Procedures, and Techniques,
Fourth Edition**
Frank Bolz, Jr., Kenneth J. Dudonis, and David P. Schulz

Practical Forensic Digital Imaging: Applications and Techniques
Patrick Jones

Practical Bomb Scene Investigation, Second Edition
James T. Thurman

Practical Crime Scene Investigations for Hot Zones
Jacqueline T. Fish, Robert N. Stout, and Edward Wallace

**Sex-Related Homicide and Death Investigation: Practical and Clinical
Perspectives, Second Edition**
Vernon J. Geberth

Second Edition

Informants, Cooperating Witnesses, and Undercover Investigations

A Practical Guide to Law, Policy, and Procedure

Dennis G. Fitzgerald, JD

CRC Press
Taylor & Francis Group
Boca Raton London New York

CRC Press is an imprint of the
Taylor & Francis Group, an **informa** business

CRC Press
Taylor & Francis Group
6000 Broken Sound Parkway NW, Suite 300
Boca Raton, FL 33487-2742

Printed on acid-free paper
Version Date: 20140911

International Standard Book Number-13: 978-1-4665-5458-0 (Hardback)

Visit the Taylor & Francis Web site at
http://www.taylorandfrancis.com

and the CRC Press Web site at
http://www.crcpress.com

Table of Contents

Appendix 6B: Confidential Source Establishment Report   166
Appendix 6C: Statistical Accomplishments Form   170
Appendix 6D: Source Criminal History Check   171
Appendix 6E: Source File Chronology   172
Appendix 6F: Supervisor's 60-Day Informant File Review Log   172
Appendix 6G: Defendant's Motion for Disclosure of
            Confidential Informants   173
Appendix 6H: DEA Source Debriefing Guide   175
Endnotes   192

7   **Sources of Compensation for Informants**   **199**

     7.1   Introduction   199
     7.2   Putting a Price Tag on Information   199
           7.2.1   Case Study: Informant Fire   203
     7.3   Immigration and Customs Enforcement   204
           7.3.1   Purchase of Information   204
           7.3.2   Commissions   204
           7.3.3   Personal Assistance Agreement   205
           7.3.4   Confidential Informant Expenses   205
           7.3.5   Violator/Trafficker-Directed Funds   206
           7.3.6   Undercover Businesses: Proprietary Operations 206
     7.4   Federal Bureau of Investigation   207
           7.4.1   Lump-Sum Payments   208
           7.4.2   Rewards   208
           7.4.3   Forfeiture Awards   208
           7.4.4   One-Time Non-Confidential Human Source
                   Payment   209
     7.5   Drug Enforcement Administration   209
           7.5.1   Calendar Year Cap   210
           7.5.2   Lifetime Cap   210
           7.5.3   Accountability   210
           7.5.4   Tax Responsibilities   211
     7.6   State Department Rewards for Justice   211
           7.6.1   Bureau of International Narcotics and Law
                   Enforcement: Narcotics Reward Program   211
     7.7   Central Intelligence Agency   212
     7.8   Forfeiture Awards   212
           7.8.1   Department of Justice Asset Forfeiture Fund
                   Awards   213
           7.8.2   Civil and Criminal Forfeiture   214
                   7.8.2.1   Award Type I   215
                   7.8.2.2   Award Type II   215

8   Whistleblowers: The Justice Department, the Securities and Exchange Commission, and the Commodities Futures Trading Commission   237

9   Corroboration of Informant Information   267

10   Informants and Search Warrants   313

Series Note

This book is part of a series entitled *Practical Aspects of Criminal and Forensic Investigations.*

This series was created by Vernon J. Geberth, a retired New York City Police Department lieutenant commander, who is an author, educator, and consultant on homicide and forensic investigations.

This series has been designed to provide contemporary, comprehensive, and pragmatic information to the practitioner involved in criminal and forensic investigations by authors who are nationally recognized experts in their respective fields.

Preface

Like most criminal investigators, active and retired, I owe the informants and cooperating witnesses I recruited and operated over the years for many, if not most, of the investigative successes I enjoyed. Some threatened the outcome of costly investigations. Each informant I worked with presented unique challenges.

Informants often face incredible risks for their handlers. Some try to take advantage of their relationship with law enforcement in a system ripe with opportunities for abuse. My experience with informants has been mixed. An informant saved my life during an undercover heroin operation. One of the informants I utilized was murdered in a Miami alley when she was suspected of cooperating with the police. I've had to deactivate a few informants for misconduct. The cooperating witness in a smuggling investigation I participated in had to enter the U.S. Marshals Witness Security Program because of death threats, never to be heard from again. I've helped send more than one informant to prison.

My experience with informants has proven invaluable in my later career as a criminal attorney and international criminal law advisor. Regardless, this book could not have been written was it not for the experience of working side by side in highly charged situations with an odd mix of felons, prostitutes, and con artists. Unfortunately, they all must go unnamed. I am sure they would want it that way.

Informants and cooperating witnesses have occupied commanding roles in some of the highest stakes domestic and international criminal investigations of the twentieth and twenty-first centuries. Likewise, so-called routine criminal cases generated in whole or in part through information received from informants and cooperating witnesses fill the dockets of courtrooms across the United States.

While confidential sources are an inextricable thread of the fabric of American law enforcement, their use does not come without substantial risk and controversy. There is no shortage of criticism regarding a police practice many regard as nothing less than dealing with the devil.

When properly operated, the benefits yielded from the use of cooperating individuals are substantial. Informants provide first-hand, eyewitness accounts of criminal activity. They are often in a position to provide intelligence information regarding targeted criminals and criminal organizations.

Informants are crucial in developing probable cause for search warrants and court-ordered telephone wire intercepts. The testimony of cooperating witnesses has secured the convictions of major organized crime figures. Those waging the War on Terror readily admit they couldn't accomplish their mission without informants. It's a fair assumption that the use of informants and cooperating witnesses not only will continue uninterrupted but will increase.

As valuable as informants and cooperating witnesses are to the overall mission of law enforcement, their use has proven to be extremely problematic. Many, if not most, informants are felons. They are one of the most unstable and unpredictable components of America's criminal justice system. That they would present a management challenge to police administrators, prosecutors, and informant handlers should come as no surprise. Throughout history, they have been the catalyst for police corruption, prosecutor misconduct, false convictions, and the death of officers and innocent citizens alike. The fallout from informant mismanagement has been costly in terms of dollars, destroyed careers, and lives lost.

Remarkably, informant scandals repeat themselves decade after decade. It almost seems there is no institutional memory to aid police administrators and prosecutors in avoiding informant- and cooperating witness–related embarrassments and disasters. The names of the police department, officers, prosecutors, informants, and victims are the only facts that seem to change. The root causes for the debacles are almost always the same.

In 2009, the City of Atlanta paid a 4.9 million dollar settlement to the family of a 92-year-old woman shot to death by police during the execution of an illegally obtained drug search warrant. A phantom informant, one created by officers on paper, and a search warrant obtained through perjury led to the shooting. Drugs were planted. A highly publicized cover-up followed. Three officers went to prison. Sweeping departmental reform followed.

The Atlanta episode was eerily reminiscent of a 1980s Boston Police Department phantom informant scandal. The only major difference was that in the Boston case, the phantom informant was used in 38 search warrants spanning more than a year. The scheme only came to an end when a police officer was killed during the execution of a phantom informant search warrant.

A monumental informant-inspired *fake drug* scandal that unfolded in Texas resulted in the 2010 passage of a law requiring corroboration before an informant is permitted to testify. An estimated 80 drug cases were dismissed in the wake of the scandal. Informants had devised a scheme where gypsum was substituted for cocaine. An officer was sentenced to prison. A number of law enforcement careers were destroyed. At least 25 federal civil rights lawsuits made their way through the courts. The City of Dallas taxpayers paid an estimated $8 million. The scheme used by the informants was nothing new. The con game has been used by informants across the United States for decades. The scheme never succeeds when time-tested informant control procedures are followed.

A Florida law passed in 2011 was the first governing the recruitment and operation of informants. It was in response to the murder of an informant during a botched undercover buy-bust drug operation. The legislation ended Florida law enforcement agency autonomy regarding informants. Other states are considering similar laws. The scandal cost Florida taxpayers $2.6 million.

That same year, wrongful convictions won with perjured informant testimony spurred California to pass a law requiring corroboration of jailhouse informant testimony. In 2013, the Texas legislature also passed legislation that clarifies the prosecutor's duty to disclose exculpatory evidence. An ex-prosecutor became the first in history to be jailed for allegedly withholding evidence from the defense. The wrongly convicted defendant in the case served 25 years for murder before being released.

An FBI informant scandal that took nearly three decades to come to a conclusion in 2013 has led to an estimated $2 billion in lawsuits. Two informants were alleged to have committed 19 murders while working for the FBI. Their FBI agent handler was convicted of murder and is serving life in a Florida prison. The FBI informant guidelines have been rewritten. The Bureau has discarded the term informant in favor of confidential human source.

Lax or unenforced guidelines governing the recruitment and operation of informants by police and federal agents have been blamed for many of the scandals. Prosecutors failing to abide by the ethical and procedural rules in the use of cooperating witnesses share in the blame.

Informants, Cooperating Witnesses, and Undercover Investigations is the most comprehensive examination of informant and cooperating witness practices and procedures to ever appear in one publication. It is a ready reference for the full spectrum of criminal justice professionals who face informant and cooperating witness issues.

The work also provides practical insight into undercover police practices. It expands on the first edition particularly in tactical areas including money-laundering stings, reverse undercover operations and controlled delivery investigations. Undercover tactics that have been influenced by changes in statutory and case law are examined. The informant's role in undercover operations is explored in-depth. The impact of the USA PATRIOT ACT on domestic undercover law enforcement is also examined.

Tort lawyers and criminal defense counsel will find the book a valuable resource as they prepare for trial. Well-entrenched, often antiquated informant handling practices dating back to the 1970s have been on a collision course with the realities of the twenty-first-century court room. The magnitude and frequency of monetary compensation awarded to injured parties and acquittals in criminal trials reflect judicial and jury intolerance for what is often viewed as law enforcement's institutional indifference to the risks presented by informant programs and informant handler misconduct.

Risk managers will find the work particularly helpful. The operation of informants as a high-risk police activity is often overlooked until after a disaster. Effective risk management should be proactive, not reactive.

The book relies upon controlling or pertinent Supreme Court cases; leading federal and state cases; relevant statutory law; federal, state, and local law enforcement guidelines; and time-tested training materials. Reported cases, statutes, treatises, and manuals used to establish or fortify the propositions advanced by the author are, to the best of his knowledge, accurate at the time of publication. Over time, all are subject to change and should be verified before relying upon them as precedents.

This book and any discussions set forth herein are for informational purposes only, and should not be construed as legal advice. Use of material contained in the work does not create an attorney–client relationship with the author or publisher. Please consult with an attorney with the appropriate level of experience if you have any questions.

Author

Dennis G. Fitzgerald is an attorney specializing in criminal informant and cooperating witness issues. He is a retired U.S. Drug Enforcement Administration (DEA) special agent, former City of Miami, Florida, Police vice and narcotics sergeant and police training instructor. During his law enforcement career he recruited and operated criminal informants and cooperating witnesses. He also supervised investigators under his command in their operation of informants.

Mr. Fitzgerald has conducted informant handling training for investigators and prosecutors from around the world. He served as a visiting faculty member at the Federal Bureau of Investigation's International Training Academy in Budapest, Hungary.

He was posted in Kiev, Ukraine, as the anti-corruption strategy coordinator for the Newly Independent States. A State Department funded program, he assisted several post-Soviet countries in their anti-corruption efforts. His duties included assessments of proposed legislation and regulations governing the use of informants, cooperating witnesses, undercover investigations and witness protection. He provided assistance to the Council of Europe in their reform of informant related laws and regulations.

Mr. Fitzgerald also served as the U.S. Department of Justice, Central and East European Law Initiative's criminal law liaison in Vilnius, Lithuania. He was credited with being instrumental in the creation of Lithuania's first independent anti-corruption agency, the Special Investigation Service. He assisted agency commanders in the development of innovative undercover investigative techniques, electronic surveillance and their informant and cooperating witness program.

He also provided assistance to Lithuania's Ministry of Interior in developing its witness security program, the first post-Soviet program of its kind. Both the anti-corruption agency and witness security program became models for post-Soviet and developing countries. In 2005, he was awarded the Prosecutor General's highest civilian medal for his work.

Mr. Fitzgerald is a graduate of Seattle University School of Law and Florida International University (BS criminal justice). He has published articles on informant-related issues for prosecutors, police, and defense attorneys and is the author of the *Informant Law Deskbook*. He developed the training curriculum for informant handling and undercover investigations that has been presented to thousands of investigators and prosecutors throughout the United States, South America, Central and Eastern Europe, Central Asia, and China. He is currently a trial consultant specializing in criminal cases that have relied on informants and cooperating witnesses and is an international criminal law advisor.

Not many people know very much about informants, and to many people, it's a queasy area. There is a tradition against snitching in this country. However, they don't recognize that the informant is THE, with a capital "T," THE most effective tool in law enforcement today—state, local, or federal. We must accept that and deal with it.

—Former FBI Director William Webster
(FBI Director 1978–1987)

After 40 years in our justice system, I conclude that the greatest threat to the integrity of our justice process and to its truth seeking mission—indeed, even to prosecutors themselves—comes from informers poorly chosen for their roles and then carelessly managed and handled.

—Senior Federal Circuit Judge Stephen S. Trott
(Former Assistant Attorney General, Criminal Division,
Public Integrity Section, U.S. Department of Justice,
currently serving as Senior Circuit Judge,
U.S. Court of Appeals for the Ninth Circuit.)

Historical Background

1

1.1 The Crown Jewels

Never before in history have America's law enforcement institutions relied so heavily upon informants. A presidential commission regarded human intelligence sources as the intelligence community's *crown jewels*.[1]

Since the 1960s, the government has launched three separate wars on crime: the War on the Mafia, the War on Drugs, and the War on Terror. Each of the wars has been extremely dependent on informants and cooperating witnesses. Initially meant to be foot soldiers in crime wars, informants and cooperating witnesses now occupy more commanding roles in criminal investigations across the United States.

The first war was Attorney General Robert F. Kennedy's and Federal Bureau of Investigation (FBI) director J. Edgar Hoover's War on the Mafia. Commenced in the early 1960s, it was a war that Hoover had long resisted[2]; during the 1950s, he refused to acknowledge that the Mafia even existed.

The use of informants by the FBI to fight crime was nothing new. The Bureau had relied upon informants in routine investigations since its inception. But the dealings of the Mafia were far more secretive. For all practical purposes, it was a closed society. Either it had to be infiltrated by agents, or insiders had to be recruited as informants.

The FBI's Top Echelon Criminal Informant Program was established in 1961, when Hoover instructed all Special Agents in Charge to "develop particularly qualified, live sources within the upper echelon of the organized hoodlum element who will be capable of furnishing the quality information"[3] needed to attack organized crime. Convincing a mobster to turn on his or her own was a tough sell. Violating the Mafia's code of silence, omertà, was punishable by death.

In 1978, the FBI replaced that program with the Criminal Informant Program. Its mission was to develop a cadre of informants who could assist the FBI in making cases against organized criminal enterprises. Director William Webster explained his views regarding the value of informants: "Not many people know very much about informants, and to many people, it's a queasy area. There is a tradition against snitching in this country. However, they don't recognize that the informant is THE, with a capital 'T,' THE most effective tool in law enforcement today—state, local, or federal. We must accept that and deal with it."[4]

FBI agents, under intense pressure to recruit mobsters as informants, did as they were told. Hit men, bank robbers, extortionists, loan sharks, and bookies quickly filled FBI informant files in field offices across America.

The second major offensive against crime was the War on Drugs. It continues, also with no end in sight. The war has not been cheap. The year 2010 marked the 40th anniversary of the war with a price tag of $1 trillion for the effort. Drug czar Gil Kirlikowske concedes, "In the grand scheme, it has not been successful."[5]

Regardless, the war goes on. The Obama administration's drug control budget for 2011 was $15.5 billion: $10 billion was for law enforcement.[6]

In the early years, drug traffickers and smuggling operations proved to be soft targets for infiltration by trained undercover agents. As the multibillion-dollar business of trafficking drugs has become more sophisticated, it has also become more ruthless and nearly impenetrable by outsiders. One need only look to the reign of terror inflicted by the drug cartels in Mexico for evidence that infiltration of their ranks by a police officer is far too dangerous. Informants have become law enforcement's weapon of choice when it comes to making cases against the drug cartels.[7] In effect, undercover work in that arena has been outsourced to informants.

The third war and the one with possibly the most at stake is the twenty-first century's War on Terror. It also holds the potential for profound civil liberty consequences. Guidelines were put into place to rein in the invasive techniques of the FBI's domestic counterintelligence programs of the 1960s and 1970s. Many restrictions were removed following 9/11, and an unprecedented recruiting drive for terrorism informants continues to this day. Making a case against terror suspects is the FBI's top priority.[8]

1.2   Political Weapons and Cure-Alls for Crime

The practice of employing informants to fight crime or support a cause is nothing new. Throughout history, governments have turned to informants as quick fixes for solving the crime problems of their day. With few exceptions, the wholesale use of informants as a cure-all for crime or as a political weapon has had adverse consequences.

Informants can be traced to biblical times. Moses was using informants when he dispatched twelve Israelites to "spy out the land" of Canaan, promised to them by God. History's most well-known paid informant is Judas Iscariot, the disciple who betrayed Jesus. He was paid 30 pieces of silver by Jewish religious leaders in return for leading them to Jesus. Judas identified him with a kiss. Jesus was subsequently turned over to Roman governor Pontius Pilate for crucifixion.[9]

The emperors of Rome relied upon spies and informers to forward the agenda of history's first totalitarian state.[10] Known as delatores, Rome's informants were rewarded based on the value of the information they provided. One class of informant received as much as one-fourth of the estate belonging to the accused. Fixed rewards were set for certain categories of crime. For example, information resulting in the return of a runaway slave earned the delator five pieces of gold.

The easy money brought forward a wave of informants. It was not uncommon for delatores to fabricate cases. Emperor Domitian severely punished informants who brought false accusations against innocent citizens. A warning attributed to him cautioned: "An emperor who does not punish informers encourages them."[11] At least two emperors eliminated the system of rewarding informants altogether.

1.3   Blood Money Certificates and the Reward Statutes

Seventeenth-century England was the first European country to officially solicit the services of paid informants to combat crime. Although the lessons the British learned were not pleasant ones, they provided the backdrop for the informant and reward system found today in the United States.

In 1692, the English Parliament was under intense pressure by the public, particularly the upper class, to stop the wave of robberies that were occurring throughout the countryside. Their solution was the passage of the Highwayman's Act.[12]

Better known as the Reward Statutes, the law provided for a reward of £40 (today's equivalent of $8000) to an informant who could give information leading to the capture and conviction of a thief. If more than one informant was involved, the reward was to be divided among the informants. As an added incentive, the informant could lay claim to the thief's horse, money, weapons, and any other belongings that were not stolen property. The statute apparently anticipated that the informants they would be dealing with would, in all likelihood, be criminals themselves. If their newly found source was wanted for a crime, he was also granted a royal pardon.

In the early days of the program, the rewards and the bonus pardons proved extremely successful in Britain's fight against crime. There was a marked downturn in the incidence of highway robberies. Word soon spread, and travelers returned to the road without fearing for their lives and property.

Unfortunately, the rewards proved to be a bit too tempting. A veritable army of professional criminal informants emerged, skilled in the art of blackmail, extortion, perjury, and entrapment. The rewards soon became known as blood-money certificates. Informants concocted phony cases against innocent citizens in hopes of collecting rewards and taking their unsuspecting target's property. Many of the falsely accused were executed as the result of contrived cases and false testimony by the paid informants.[13]

While the war on highway robbers was being won, the streets of London began to experience a crime wave. The most prevalent crimes were pick-pocketing and mugging. Predictably, the wealthy were the preferred targets. Trafficking in stolen goods became an extremely profitable enterprise.

In 1706, England once again looked to informants as the solution to its crime problem. A law was enacted that made it a capital offense to be found in possession of stolen property. An informant who provided evidence sufficient to convict a crook received a reward of £40.[14] A royal pardon was thrown in as an incentive to bring wanted criminals into the informant game.

1.4   Informants and Official Corruption: The Thief Taker General of Great Britain and Ireland

The lure of rewards and a justice system awash in informants had a corrupting influence on official law enforcement institutions. London's Under City Marshall, Charles Hitchin, paid £700 for appointment to his position. He then employed a network of thieves and informants to cash in on capturing felons.[15]

Before being sacked for extortion, Hitchin hired Jonathan Wild. He had begun his career as an informant of sorts, working his way into law enforcement by providing information to Hitchin regarding thieves and fences. After Hitchin was fired, Wild became known as the Thief Taker General of Great Britain and Ireland. His biographer refers to Wild as the "first modern gangster and the spiritual father of Al Capone."[16]

Wild made a fortune by corrupting the informant system of his day. He created a network of thieves who would steal valuables from the rich and famous. Once a reward surfaced for the stolen item, Wild would arrange for the return of the property to the original owner. And when an informant was no longer useful, Wild would turn him in for the £40 felon reward.

Ironically, an informant exposed his criminal enterprise, Wild was tried and sentenced to death. An outraged crowd sped the execution along by stoning him while he was on the gallows at London's infamous Old Bailey.[17]

Britain's system of rewards for information was eventually outlawed. In 1765, commentator William Blackstone said this about rewards for information: "For the truth was that more mischief hath arisen to good men by these kinds of rewards, upon false and malicious accusations of desperate villains, than benefits to the public by the discovery and conviction of real offenders."[18]

1.5   Eugene Vidocq: From Informant to Chief of the French Sûreté

Eighteenth- and nineteenth-century France also looked to informants as a solution for crime. Police inspectors of that era, the Officiers de Paix, had a network of informants who were paid for their information either in cash or with immunity from prosecution. This practice produced the era's top cop.

Eugène François Vidocq, a notorious thief and escaped prisoner, was captured by authorities based on an informant's tip. In exchange for being placed in a prison of his choice, Vidocq agreed to become what we would now refer to as a jailhouse informant. While incarcerated at the La Force prison in Paris, he obtained confessions and informed on fellow inmates for nearly 21 months.

Upon release, he was employed as a police agent and worked his way up to the rank of police inspector. Vidocq was known as a master of disguises and particularly adept at working undercover.[19] He was appointed first chief of the Sûreté[20] and commanded 28 detectives, all former criminals or informants.

Some law enforcement historians consider Vidocq to be the father of modern criminal investigation. He is credited with introducing the science of ballistics and being the first to make plaster cast impressions of footprints left at crime scenes.[21]

Victor Hugo based the two main characters in *Les Misérables*, ex-con Jean Valjean and the relentless police inspector Javert, on Vidocq and his exploits. Herman Melville quoted Vidocq in *Moby-Dick*, and the fugitive in Charles Dickens's *Great Expectations* was inspired by Vidocq's exploits. Edgar Allan Poe praised him in "The Murders in the Rue Morgue," and Honoré de Balzac's character Vautran, in *Le Père Goriot*, was also based on Vidocq.[22]

Despite his many successes, Vidocq's and his men's methods of solving crime proved controversial. He was constantly at odds with higher-ranking members of his organization. Vidocq voluntarily resigned in 1827. At 52, he became a successful businessman.

1.6   Washington, Nathan Hale, and the Culper Spy Ring

The Revolutionary War produced one of America's first undercover intelligence officers. In 1776, Continental Army Captain Nathan Hale volunteered to spy behind enemy lines in New York for General George Washington. He posed as a Dutch school teacher. Hale was captured by the British while returning to his regiment. He was promptly hanged in New York City without a trial. Legend has it that he was betrayed by a relative who had become a British informant.

Hale is considered by the U.S. intelligence community to be America's first spy. His statue is on the grounds of the CIA headquarters in Langley, Virginia. Hale is best remembered for his last words: "My only regret is that I have but one life to lose for my country."

General George Washington also recognized the value of recruiting and paying civilian operatives for information. In a letter written in February

1777, Washington offered Nathaniel Sackett, a New York political activist and merchant for the Continental Army, $50 a month to set up a network to obtain "the earliest and best intelligence of the designs of the enemy."[23]

Washington tasked Benjamin Tallmadge with the responsibility of setting up a group of cooperators to pass along information about British troop movements in and around New York City. The group was known as the Culper Spy Ring.[24] Spy chief Tallmadge introduced code numbers, invisible ink, dead drops, and false names for his assets.[25]

Farmers, merchants, and tavern owners proved to be indispensable Revolutionary War sources of information. Anna Strong, a Long Island resident, alerted the Culper Spy Ring by hanging a black petticoat on her clothesline accompanied by varying numbers of white handkerchiefs to transmit secret messages.[26]

Washington's miraculous victory over superior British forces is credited in part to his ability to out spy the British.[27] In 1777, General George Washington told an aide, "The necessity of procuring good intelligence is apparent and need not be further urged—all that remains for me to add is that you keep the whole matter as secret as possible." In 1779, Washington cautioned members of his intelligence service that the identities of their spies "should be kept profoundly secret, otherwise we not only lose the benefits desired from [their espionage], but may subject him to some unhappy fate."[28]

1.7   The Civil War, Slaves as Undercover Operatives, and the Lincoln Law

From the onset of the Civil War, President Abraham Lincoln recognized that he was operating at a distinct disadvantage without an intelligence service. Washington, DC, was saturated with informers working for the Confederacy's spy service, known as the Signal Bureau. It seemed the Union had no secrets that Confederate informants and operatives were not privy to.

Lincoln sought out Scottish-born detective Allan Pinkerton to fill the Union's intelligence void. The owner of a successful detective agency whose motto was "We Never Sleep," Pinkerton became the chief of intelligence for the Army of the Potomac. It became his company's dual mission to gather intelligence on the Confederate Army and neutralize the effectiveness of their informants and spies.[29] Many of the detectives he employed had checkered pasts. Some were nothing more than hired guns or informants carrying Pinkerton badges.

Pinkerton began his own informant recruiting drive focusing on the weak links of the Confederacy. There was no shortage of Confederate Army deserters ready to sell out and provide intelligence information to Pinkerton. War profiteers were easy to recruit. They were working both sides of the conflict and were for sale to the highest bidder.

But Pinkerton recognized that the individuals with the most insight into the inner workings of the Confederacy were current and former slaves. They were present during strategic military planning sessions and were also in attendance at social gatherings attended by the Confederacy's Who's Who. They also had a stake in the outcome of the war.[30]

Two of Confederate president Jefferson Davis's slaves began providing the Union with information from the onset of the war.[31] William A. Jackson, Davis's coachman, reported to his Union handlers what he heard during high-level strategy sessions between Davis and his generals.[32]

Mary Touvestre was a freed slave who worked in Norfolk for a lead engineer involved in the building of the *U.S.S. Merrimac*, the Confederacy's first ironclad warship. She managed to steal a set of the plans and successfully smuggle them to the Department of the Navy in Washington.[33]

Lincoln also sought out informants to bring down wartime corporate profiteers. Arms manufacturers were supplying the army with defective rifles and unreliable ammunition. Livestock suppliers were delivering lame horses and mules. Manufacturers supplied boots that fell apart when exposed to the elements. Despite the fact that armies fight on their stomachs, suppliers routinely delivered spoiled rations unfit to eat.[34]

Lincoln viewed the corporate thieves as more threatening to the Union cause than turncoats. The president was quoted as saying, "Worse than traitors in arms are the men who pretend loyalty to the flag, feast and fatten on the misfortunes of the nation while patriotic blood is crimsoning the plains of the South and their countrymen are moldering in the dust."[35]

The president recognized that it would take the promise of enormous rewards to turn a rich business insider into an informant. In 1863, Congress passed the False Claims Act. More commonly known as the Lincoln Law, it provided for rewards of 50% of the amount of damages recovered by the government from corrupt defense suppliers. A version of the law survives to this day. Known as the Federal False Claims Act,[36] the law turns countless corporate whistleblowers into millionaires.

1.8   Police Departments, Detective Bureaus, and Informants

Following the Civil War, Pinkerton's National Detective Agency, with its single-eye logo, stayed busy. The logo gave birth to a new term for private detectives: private eye. His agency was hired by banks, stagecoach lines, and train companies plagued by armed robbers. His detectives, relying upon information from their informants, went after the notable crooks of the day, including Jesse James, Butch Cassidy, the Sundance Kid, and the Hole in the Wall Gang.

Cities of the era began to rely upon uniformed police officers as their primary deterrent to crime.[37] If a crime occurred in their presence, they were expected to respond. Other than that, they were primarily passive when it came to crime prevention and detection. A police officer using an informant was the exception rather than the rule.

Late-nineteenth-century police departments became more sophisticated as the crimes they investigated became more complex. Detective bureaus emerged to meet the challenge.

The appearance of plainclothes officers had unintended consequences. The ability of police to move about with some degree of anonymity allowed for a far more casual interaction of officers with criminals and informants. Leaving the uniform in the closet opened up new avenues for intelligence gathering. It also presented new opportunities for corruption. It seemed that mixing good police officers with the dregs of society produced a lethal cocktail.

1.9   Emergence of Federal Law Enforcement Agencies

The emergence of federal law enforcement agencies as a deterrent to crime was late in coming. The U.S. Marshals Service, established in 1789, was delegated the duty to execute federal judicial writs. The United States Postal Service established the Office of Inspection in the late 1830s. Far from being a law enforcement agency, it outsourced most of its work to Pinkerton. Today, the agency is known as the United States Postal Inspection Service.

Following the Civil War, counterfeiting became the crime of the day. The Treasury Department responded with the creation of the Secret Service Division. The law creating the Secret Service was waiting for Abraham Lincoln's signature the night he was assassinated.

The Secret Service became the first federal law enforcement agency other than the United States Marshals Service. Both agencies soon became the catchalls for investigating every federal crime on the books. It was not until the 1901 assassination of President William McKinley that the Secret Service was tasked with providing protection for the president and his family.

In 1924, Attorney General Harlan Fiske Stone established the Bureau of Investigation, forerunner of the Federal Bureau of Investigation, and named J. Edgar Hoover as its first director. Stone was apprehensive about giving an agency such broad investigative powers. He posited, "There is always the possibility that a secret police may become a menace to free government and free institutions because it carries with it the possibility of abuses of power which are not always quickly apprehended or understood."[38] As a precaution, Stone made the new agency part of the Department of Justice. Hoover reported directly to the United States attorney general.

It was not long before the public was bombarded with headlines about the new law enforcement agency. The articles named, and often glamorized, the bad guys of the Prohibition and Depression Era. "Baby Face" Nelson, Bonnie and Clyde, "Pretty Boy" Floyd, Ma Barker, Al "Scar Face" Capone, and John Dillinger became household names. On rare occasions, so did the names of the informants responsible for their capture.

1.10   John Dillinger and the Lady in Red

Possibly, the first FBI informant to be exposed by the press was responsible for stopping a long-running, one-man interstate crime wave. In the 1930s, FBI agent Melvin Purvis was constantly one embarrassing step behind in his attempts to capture the Great Depression's Robin Hood, bank robber John Dillinger. That was until he recruited informant Anna Sage. An illegal alien with access to Dillinger, Sage was promised that in return for her assistance she would be allowed to remain in the United States and that she would not be deported to her native Romania. Believing Purvis's promise, she agreed to escort Dillinger to the Clark Gable gangster movie, *Manhattan Melodrama*. Purvis instructed her to wear a distinctive red dress and walk with Dillinger from the theater lobby to the sidewalk when the movie ended. Dillinger was summarily shot to death by Agent Purvis. Sage would be forever known as the Lady in Red. The FBI reneged on its deal with Sage, and she was deported to Romania.[39]

1.11   Unlikely Informants: Mirroring
the Cause of Their Day

Investigative reporters, thanks in part to the Freedom of Information Act, have helped to unmask some rather unlikely undercover operatives and informants. Each was sought out by the government to help win the crime war or cause of their day.

1.11.1   Julia Child and the Office of Strategic Services

Like Washington and Lincoln, many of President Franklin Roosevelt's wartime successes could be attributed to information obtained by citizen operatives. During World War II, the Office of Strategic Services (OSS) became the United States' first secret centralized intelligence agency. President Roosevelt tasked the OSS with the mission of obtaining information about the German war machine worldwide.

Thousands of pages of formerly secret documents were recently released from the U.S. national archives. The documents described a spy agency that aggressively recruited as many as 24,000 actors, athletes, academics, journalists, and lawyers to act as operatives. In concert with military agents and other members of the intelligence community, their mission was to seek out intelligence information about the Nazis' war effort. They were assigned throughout the world.

Members of the OSS who later became well-known public figures include the following:

Author Thomas Braden[40] (*Eight Is Enough*)
Author–chef Julia Child[41]
Film director John Ford[42]
Supreme Court Justice Arthur Goldberg[43]
Actor Sterling Hayden[44]
Historian Arthur Schlesinger, Jr.[45] (special assistant to President John F. Kennedy).

Prior to the release of the documents from the archives, former OSS members were sworn to secrecy and were not allowed to discuss their wartime experiences.[46]

1.11.2 Ronald Reagan

In the late 1930s and well into the 1950s, the fear of Communists infiltrating American society became the cause célèbre of the day. In 1938, the creation of the House Un-American Activities Committee (HUAC) was seen as the weapon of choice to ferret out communists and their cronies. HUAC's mission extended well into the 1950s.

One of the first anticommunist salvos was directed at the Hollywood film community by Senator Joseph McCarthy. He had long suspected the movie industry of being a safe haven for communists and began a series of relentless inquiries that eerily resembled witch hunts. Directors, writers, and actors found themselves in the crosshairs of not only the committee but the FBI.

The senator found a powerful ally in FBI director J. Edgar Hoover. A fervent anticommunist, he pulled out all the stops in the hunt for communists by sanctioning burglaries, illegal wiretaps, and the leaking of official-looking false documents that named names and destroyed careers. Countless members of the film industry were called to testify and be grilled by the HUAC. Some of those who refused to cooperate found themselves behind bars for contempt of Congress and became known as the Hollywood Ten. Others found themselves blacklisted for merely having been called by the committee; once they were tagged as communists or communist sympathizers, their careers were over.[47]

If the FBI was going to find Hollywood communists, it needed Hollywood sources, and so agents began the remarkably easy task of recruiting informants from within the film community.

Actor Ronald Reagan[48] was one of at least 18 informants used by the FBI to gauge Communist infiltration in the film industry during the 1940s. Reagan was explicitly identified as confidential informant "T-10" on page 40 of a lengthy Bureau report. Dated December 19, 1947, it was entitled "Communist Infiltration of the Motion Picture Industry."[49] The report was released to the *San Jose Mercury News* in 1985 in response to Freedom of Information requests.

According to the *Mercury News* article (quoting FBI documents), Reagan, identified as "T-10," kept agents informed about pro-Communist influences in the Screen Actors Guild and other Hollywood organizations. The reports described how he and his first wife, actress Jane Wyman, had provided the FBI with the names of actors who they believed were pro-Communist.[50]

The documents showed that Reagan, who was then president of the guild, disagreed with the tactics of the House Un-American Activities Committee, which was attempting to rid the movie industry of Communists.[51] In one interview with the FBI, Reagan criticized the attempts of a committee of producers and actors to fire Communists from film work.[52]

1.11.3 Gerald Ford

The 1963 assassination of President John F. Kennedy generated a spate of conspiracy theories. It also brought the FBI a great deal of criticism, including allegations that FBI director Hoover was somehow involved in covering up facts surrounding the shooting.

A retired FBI agent and author of *The Bureau: My Thirty Years in Hoover's FBI* alleged that Gerald Ford became an FBI informant following the assassination. Ford's assignment was to provide Hoover with information about the activities of staff members of the Warren Commission. The commission, created by President Lyndon B. Johnson, was directed to "ascertain, evaluate and report upon the facts relating to the assassination."[53]

According to the agent, "Hoover was delighted when Gerald Ford was named to the Warren Commission. The director wrote in one of his internal memos that the Bureau could expect Ford to 'look after FBI interests,' and he did, keeping us fully advised of what was going on behind closed doors. He was our man, our informant, on the Warren Commission."[54]

An Associated Press account claimed that Congressman Ford "secretly advised the FBI that two of his fellow members on the Warren Commission doubted the FBI's conclusion that John F. Kennedy was shot from the sixth floor of the Texas Book Depository in Dallas."[55]

Ford reported to a senior FBI official about internal panel disputes over hiring staff, Chief Justice Earl Warren's timetable for completing the final report on the assassination, and what panel members said about the Bureau. In return, Assistant FBI director Cartha "Deke" DeLoach confidentially advised Ford of FBI director J. Edgar Hoover's position on panel disputes, discussed where leaks were coming from, and, with Hoover's personal approval, loaned him a Bureau briefcase with a lock so he could securely take the FBI report on the 1963 assassination with him on a ski trip.[56]

1.11.4   Sara Jane Moore: Would-Be Assassin

Ironically, Sara Jane Moore, President Ford's would-be assassin, was an FBI informant who had been reporting on extremist groups in the San Francisco Bay Area during the early 1970s. On September 22, 1975, she fired a shot from a .38 revolver at Ford as he was leaving a San Francisco hotel. She missed the president when an ex-marine in the crowd saw the gun as she was taking aim and pushed her arm into the air. Moore was sentenced to life in prison but was paroled in 2008 after serving 32 years of her sentence. She was 77 years old when released. In a 1988 interview with the *San Jose Mercury News*, she explained that she thought she would be killed when her identity as an informant became public. The article quoted her as saying, "I was going to go down anyway. If the government was going to kill me, I was going to make some kind of a statement."[57]

The FBI claimed to have deactivated Moore approximately 4 months before she attempted to shoot Ford.[58]

1.11.5   Ernest Withers: The Original Civil Rights Photographer

The bloody civil rights era of the 1960s was a magnet for the attention of the FBI. Hoover considered Dr. Martin Luther King, the Southern Christian Leadership Conference, and civil disobedience as threats to national security. He was convinced King was in league with Communists. The need for informants within his organization was viewed as critical.

It was not until 2010 that a clerical error in the processing of a Freedom of Information release revealed just how deep the FBI was into the Reverend King's organization. In September 2010, Memphis's *Commercial Appeal* published the results of a nearly 2-year investigation. It revealed that Ernest Withers, a man who became known as the Original Civil Rights Photographer, was paid FBI informant number ME 338-R.[59]

Historian Athan Theoharis called Withers's work for the FBI an "amazing betrayal. It really speaks to the degree that the FBI was able to engage individuals within the civil rights movement. This man was so well trusted."[60]

1.11.6   Gregory Scarpa: The Grim Reaper and Mississippi Burning Revisited

For most Americans, the 1964 disappearance and murder of civil rights workers Michael Schwerner, Andrew Goodman, and James Chaney[61] at the hands of the Ku Klux Klan (KKK) would probably be lost to history were it not for the 1988 movie *Mississippi Burning*. The trio of activists were beaten, shot, and buried in an earthen dam near Philadelphia, Mississippi, on June 21, 1964.

The dam was by no means a shallow grave: These bodies were never meant to be found. Heavy equipment was employed by the killers to eliminate the possibility of a chance discovery of their remains, and two of the Klansmen were the local sheriff and one of his deputies. It seemed like the perfect crime.

It was a rogue black FBI agent whom the *Mississippi Burning* filmmakers credited with cracking the case. In the script, the case reached a dead end, and the agent was sent to Mississippi to rough up witnesses. The fiction was nowhere near as interesting as reality: the truth remained an FBI secret for more than 40 years.

The mystery of how the case was solved came out during the 2007 murder trial of a retired FBI agent.[62] He was alleged to have leaked the identities of four informants to Gregory Scarpa, a Mafia enforcer[63] and mob hit man. Scarpa was also the FBI agent's informant. The agent was the former head of the FBI's New York Colombo family C-12 organized crime squad.

His acumen in dealing with mobsters and mob informants earned him the nickname Mr. Organized Crime. The agent fit the part: he was a flashy dresser and soon he even began talking like a mobster.[64]

He was sent to the FBI Academy to train new agents in the art of informant handling. He would open his course by telling trainees: "I have two college degrees and my vocabulary has degenerated to four-letter words, and if that bothers you—fuck you."[65] Some of his fellow agents openly worried that Mr. Organized Crime had gotten too close to the mob.

The agent's most prized informant was Gregory Scarpa. Known on the street as the Grim Reaper, he was a paid FBI Top Echelon informant. He worked for the Bureau for nearly three decades and made his control agent an FBI star.

Scarpa was also one of the mob's most ruthless killers. Primarily involved in gambling and extortion, he eliminated anyone who crossed him. Not satisfied with one of his killings, he told a friend, "I'd like to dig him up and shoot him again."[66] Lore has it that he shot one of his victims off of a ladder while the man was stringing Christmas lights on his home.[67] One associate described him as "an absolutely fearless man who enjoyed killing, and enjoyed vengeance, and enjoyed the subtlety. He would smile at a guy, take him out to dinner, and blow his brains out."[68]

Over the years, Scarpa openly bragged that he had a source within law enforcement who fed him information in return for bribes. He referred to the source as his girlfriend.[69] In 1992, Scarpa was arrested for racketeering and three murders. There was nothing his handler could do to save him. He pled guilty to two murders and was sentenced to 10 years in prison.

He died in prison in 1994, never implicating Mr. Organized Crime. Even after Scarpa's death, the corruption rumors surrounding his FBI handler persisted.[70]

Despite an investigation, no charges were brought against the handler; the FBI transferred him out of New York, and he retired 2 years later.

It was not until 2006 that the state prosecutor's office in Brooklyn finally put a case together. The state's primary witness was Scarpa's longtime girlfriend; the second witness was a retired FBI agent who had been assigned to the C-12 squad and was convinced his former colleague was corrupt. The third witness was one of Scarpa's jailed henchmen ready to trade testimony for a sentence reduction.

The prosecutor alleged the agent's leaks to his snitch in return for bribes had led to the gangland-style murders of four informants. He called the affair "one of the worst cases of law enforcement corruption in the history of this country."[71]

It was a lengthy trial complicated by rumors that one of the prosecutor's female investigators had fallen in love with the jailed mob informant looking for leniency. Letters were allegedly intercepted by guards showing a scheme between the investigator and the snitch to obtain his sperm so she could be impregnated.[72]

The former agent was acquitted after testimony by Scarpa's girlfriend fell apart but not before she told the story of her trip to Mississippi in the 1960s.

In the weeks following the slayings of the three civil rights activists, the case was at a standstill. Agents had suspects, but nobody would talk. FBI director J. Edgar Hoover was under pressure from the White House and Attorney General Robert Kennedy to solve the case and to solve it quickly. Drastic measures needed to be employed.

Scarpa's girlfriend testified that in the weeks following the murders, she had accompanied him on a trip to Philadelphia, Mississippi. Once they checked into their hotel, she recalled that an FBI agent came to their hotel room and gave Scarpa a gun. In addition, he provided the identity and address of a Klansman believed by the Bureau to know where the civil rights workers were buried. FBI agents had interviewed him and other suspects without success. The Ku Klux Klan had erected a wall of silence.

Scarpa visited the suspect's appliance shop and bought a television set before beginning the task of extracting information. According to testimony from the girlfriend, he persuaded the Klansman to disclose the location of the three bodies by "putting a gun in the guy's mouth and threatening him."[73]

Scarpa related what he learned from the Klansmen to his FBI handler. The girlfriend testified that the unidentified agent returned to their hotel room, gave Scarpa a large sum of money, took the gun, and left the room.[74] The bodies of the civil rights workers were recovered 44 days after their disappearance.

Nearly four decades later, the trial judge, having seen Scarpa's FBI files and hearing the girlfriend's testimony, was stunned. That, along with other investigative shortcomings, brought the retired agent's trial to an abrupt end. Before dismissing the case against the retired agent, he berated the FBI: "That a thug like Scarpa would be employed by the federal government to beat witnesses and threaten them at gunpoint to obtain information regarding the deaths of civil rights workers in the South in the early 1960s is a shocking demonstration of the government's unacceptable willingness to employ criminality to fight crime." He accused the FBI agent of "making a deal with the devil."[75]

Historians believe that the deaths may have led to the passage of the 1964 Civil Rights Act.

Seven KKK members were convicted for their role in the murders. Two were acquitted because of a hung jury; one of them was Edgar Ray Killen. The case against Killen lay dormant until he was retried in 2005 at the age of 85. He was convicted on three counts of manslaughter and sentenced to 60 years in prison.

In February 2010, Killen filed a multimillion-dollar lawsuit in the U.S. District Court against the FBI and the Mississippi Attorney General's Office. He claimed that the FBI's use of Scarpa violated his rights to a fair trial.[76]

1.11.7   The Dalai Lama

During the early years of the Cold War, the U.S. intelligence community was aggressively recruiting sources in its efforts to undermine communist governments. Declassified intelligence documents indicate that the Dalai Lama was one of those sources.

Documents published by the State Department in August 1998 reported that from the late 1950s until 1974, the Dalai Lama received $180,000 a year from the CIA for his assistance.[77] According to the *Los Angeles Times*, a CIA memo dated January 9, 1964, itemized the payments: "Support of 2,100 Tibetan guerrillas based in Nepal: $500,000. Subsidy to the Dalai Lama: $180,000." The *Times* journalist described the memo as listing several other costs, arriving at a final figure of $1,735,000.[78] He speculated that "the memo was written to help justify continued funding for the clandestine operation."[79]

CIA support did not stop there. The *Los Angeles Times* also reported that the CIA provided training for Tibetan guerrillas at "a covert military site in Colorado, 'Tibet Houses' in New York and Geneva, Switzerland, educational opportunities for Tibetan operatives at Cornell University and supplies for reconnaissance teams."[80]

A *New York Times* article reported that the Dalai Lama's administration acknowledged receiving $1.7 million a year from the CIA during the 1960s. The administration denied that the Dalai Lama pocketed any of the money for his own use from the $180,000-a-year stipend.[81]

1.11.8   Timothy Leary: The Most Dangerous Man in America

Former Harvard Professor Timothy Leary, once described by President Richard Nixon as "the most dangerous man in America," was an FBI informant. While serving time in 1970 for possession of LSD, members of the radical guerrilla group the Weathermen aided him in escaping from prison. Probably best known for telling the world to "tune in, turn on, drop out," Leary successfully fled the United States, hiding out in Switzerland until he was extradited. Freedom of Information Act (FOIA) releases revealed he agreed to give the FBI information regarding the Weathermen in exchange for an early release from prison. The FBI code-named him Charlie Thrush. No one was ever arrested as a result of Leary's information.[82]

1.11.9   Former New York Yankees Owner

It was not until after George Steinbrenner's death in July 2011 that the FBI was willing to answer FOIA requests from journalists concerning a chapter of the New York Yankees' owner's secret life. The nearly 800 pages[83] of released documents confirmed a decades-old rumor: from 1976 to 1987, Steinbrenner had assisted the FBI in national security and criminal investigations.[84]

Countless news articles followed the FOIA release. Most accounts fell short of referring to Steinbrenner as an informant, but in a released FBI memo from 1988, the bureau said that it "support[ed] the contention that George Steinbrenner has provided the FBI with valuable assistance."[85]

Steinbrenner, like most sources, had a motive for assisting the FBI. He needed a big favor: a presidential pardon. He had gotten sucked in by the prosecution fever of the Watergate era and drawn more than his share of the attention of Watergate special prosecutor Archibald Cox over a campaign contribution to the Nixon campaign. In August 1973, Cox tasked FBI director Clarence Kelley with making sure Steinbrenner's case received "the same, immediate and preferred handling"[86] as the other headline-grabbing cases that continued to blossom from the Watergate scandal.

Throughout the ensuing investigation, Steinbrenner remained adamant that he had committed no crime. He insisted that if any crime had occurred, it was the fault of bad advice from his corporate counsel. By 1974, it became clear that the cards were stacked against Steinbrenner: he ultimately pled guilty to illegally authorizing corporate contributions to President Richard Nixon and to obstructing justice.[87]

There was never really a chance Steinbrenner would have gone to prison. It seemed to many at the time that the government simply wanted him on its Watergate wall of shame. For Steinbrenner, the $15,000 fine did not matter; it was the sting of being a convicted felon.

Compounding his embarrassment, Major League Baseball Commissioner Bowie Kuhn suspended Steinbrenner from baseball for 2 years, saying he was "ineligible and incompetent."[88]

The 800 pages of released FBI documents leave little doubt about Steinbrenner's frame of mind regarding the conviction. In 1987 he explained,

"Everybody has dents in his armor. That's something I have to live with."[89] His only way to erase the felony was a presidential pardon.

FOIA reports indicate that he made his first petition for a pardon in 1979. Although the reports were radically redacted, one made reference to his assisting the FBI in a terrorist-related matter.[90] Steinbrenner was not granted a pardon.

He continued on as an FBI source, with two reports from the early 1980s referring to his participation in "an undercover operation" and in an investigation described only "as a sensitive security matter."[91]

News stories following the FOIA release reveal that Steinbrenner was going to allow the FBI to use Yankee Stadium[92] as a lure for an elaborate sting operation. It seems the stadium was to be the backdrop for the arrest of scores of New York mobsters running a gambling operation.[93] Unfortunately for Steinbrenner, another venue was used, "as it was more adaptable for the purpose intended."[94]

It was no secret that the felony was a thorn in the executive's side. He persisted in his efforts to obtain a pardon. In a 1987 petition for a presidential pardon that followed his first rejection, one of his lawyer's letters submitted in support of the petition reminds the Justice Department of his assistance: "Mr. Steinbrenner knows that he placed the lives of his family and himself in jeopardy through being involved in a terrorist matter. He knows he made the right decision because the agents stated this information was very valuable to the United States."[95]

A 1988 FBI memo backed up Steinbrenner's case for a pardon. An unidentified agent wrote that he "supports the contention that George Steinbrenner has provided the FBI with valuable assistance."[96]

On January 20, 1989, President Reagan had at least three celebrities seeking pardons: industrialist Armand Hammer, heiress and Symbionese Liberation Army bank robber Patty Hearst, and George Steinbrenner. Only one of them won the lottery: Steinbrenner's pardon was one of former FBI informant President Ronald Reagan's last official acts.[97]

1.11.10   General Manuel Noriega

The War on Drugs, declared in the late 1970s and going full steam by the early 1980s, ushered in an unprecedented informant-recruiting drive. Among some of the more interesting informants of the era was General Manuel Noriega. The former Panamanian head of state during the 1980s was a longtime Central Intelligence Agency asset and an informant for the Drug Enforcement Administration and the FBI. His nickname at the State Department was Rent-a-Colonel.[98]

A Senate subcommittee came to the following conclusion: "It's clear that each U.S. government agency which had a relationship with Noriega turned a blind eye to his corruption and drug dealing, even as he was emerging as a key player on behalf of the Medellín Cartel." The subcommittee concluded that Noriega established the hemisphere's first "narcokleptocracy."[99]

On February 4, 1989, Noriega was indicted for drug trafficking by a federal grand jury in Miami, Florida. The general ignored the indictment, which led to the 1990 invasion of Panama by U.S. troops. A dramatic 2-week standoff at the Vatican embassy in Panama City ended with his surrender.

Noriega stood trial in Miami, was found guilty, and served a 17-year prison term.[100] In May 2010, he was extradited to France, where he was found guilty of money laundering and sentenced to 7 years in prison.[101] A French court granted 77-year-old Noriega a conditional release, and he was returned to Panama in December 2011 to begin serving a 20-year sentence for crimes committed while in office.[102]

1.12   The War on Drugs and Terror

The War on Drugs has produced an unprecedented number of informants and cooperating witnesses. The success of the recruiting drive is attributed in part to significant monetary rewards for informants and dramatic sentence reductions for cooperating witnesses. Those waging the War on Terror have adopted many of the same recruiting methods used in the drug war and have developed new methods unthought-of before 9/11.

1.13   A Valuable but Dangerous Tool

Informants have played a valuable role in assisting those responsible for fighting the crime wars and causes of their day. Those pressed into service by Washington, Lincoln, and Roosevelt were genuine heroes. Individuals continue to step forward and assist their governments without any thought of receiving recognition or payment.

The seventeenth-century British informants working for blood-money certificates and framing innocent citizens were taking advantage of a system ripe for abuse. Similar schemes continue to this day. There seems to be endless supply of con artists, miscreants and mercenaries coming forward as informants, ready to test the limits of the criminal justice system and the honesty and integrity of informant handlers.

Corrupt law enforcement officials like Jonathan Wild continue to be exposed in every country that uses informants. However, they are a distinct minority, thanks in part to advances in training, reform of informant guidelines, and new laws designed to govern a covert facet of law enforcement that has had a long history of abuse.

Endnotes

1. Commission on the Intelligence Capabilities for the United States Regarding Weapons of Mass Destruction, 2005, p. 380.
2. Sifakis, C., *The Mafia Encyclopedia*. New York: Checkmark Books, 1999.
3. House Committee on Government Reform, Everything Secret Degenerates: The FBI's Use of Murderers as Informants, 3rd Report, H.R. Rep. No. 108–414 at 454 (2004).
4. FBI Director 1978–1987.
5. "After 40 years, $1 trillion, U.S. War on Drugs Has Failed to Meet Any of Its Goals," Associated Press, May 13, 2010.
6. Ibid.
7. Thompson, G., "U.S. Agencies Infiltrate Drug Cartels Across Mexico," *The New York Times*, October 24, 2011.
8. *Domestic Investigations and Operations Guidelines,* Federal Bureau of Investigation, October 15, 2011.
9. Matthew 26:15, 27:3–5.
10. Kirsh, J., God Against the Gods, Viking Compass, Mar. 2004: The Roman empire of late antiquity has been characterized as the first totalitarian state in history, and the Roman emperors were able to call on the expert services of an imperial bureaucracy that included spies, informers, inquisitors, torturers, and executioners.
11. Suetonius, The Twelve Caesars (XII Domitian, 9).
12. William and Mary, C.8.
13. Howson, G., *Thief Taker General*. New York: St. Martin's Press, 1985.
14. 5 Anne C. 31.
15. Howson, G., *Thief Taker General*. New York: St. Martin's Press, 1985.
16. Ibid.
17. Ibid.
18. Blackstone, W., *Commentaries on the Laws of England,* Vol. 4, p. 325, 1765. See Langbein, J.H., "Shaping the eighteenth-century criminal trial: a view from the Ryder Sources," U. Chi. L. Rev. 50(1), 106–114, 1983. See also W. Holdsworth, *A History of the English Law,* Vol. 13, p. 395, 1952. See also Howson, *Thief Taker General*. New York: St. Martin's Press, 1985.
19. Eugène François Vidocq, *Memoirs of Vidocq, The Principal Agent of the French Police*. Philadelphia: T.B. Peterson and Brothers, 1859.
20. The Sûreté, founded in 1812 by Eugène François Vidocq, was the model for the present-day Scotland Yard, the FBI, and other criminal investigation organizations. It is now the French national police.
21. Edwards, S., *The Vidocq Dossier: The Story of the World's First Detective*. Boston: Houghton Mifflin, 1977; Stead, P.J., *VIDOCQ, Picaroon of Crime*. New York: Roy Publishers, 1945.
22. Lotter, K., Vidocq Society of Philadelphia, January 23, 2008, vidocq.org.
23. Superville, D., "Museum Exposes Sneaky History," Associated Press, July 16, 2002.
24. Rose, A., *Washington's Spies: The Story of America's First Spy Ring*. New York: Bantam Books, 2006.
25. Wilcox, J., Revolutionary Secrets: The Secret Communications of the American Revolution, nsa.gov (National Security Agency website), 2011.

26. Weber, R. E., Masked Dispatches: Cryptograms in Cryptology in American History, 2nd ed., Center for Cryptologic History, National Security Agency, 2002, nsa.gov.
27. "The Culper Spy Ring," www.history.com/topics/culper-spy-ring.
28. Fleming, T., "George Washington, Spymaster," *American Heritage Magazine*, February/March 2000, Vol. 51, Issue 1.
29. Pinkerton, A., *The Spy of the Rebellion*. Chicago: A.G. Nettleton and Company, 1883.
30. Markle, D. E., *Spies and Spy Masters of the Civil War*. New York: Hippocrene Books, 1995.
31. Rose, P.K., The Civil War: Black American Contributions to Union Intelligence, CIA Directorate of Operations.
32. Fishel, E. C., *The Secret War for the Union*, Houghton Mifflin. Boston: 1996, p. 440.
33. P.K. Rose, *The Civil War: Black American Contributions to Union Intelligence*, CIA Directorate of Operations.
34. Lahman, L. D., "Bad Mules: A Primer on the Federal False Claims Act," *Oklahoma Bar Journal*, 76 Okla. B.J. 901 (2005).
35. Quote attributed to Lincoln as he pressed to have the False Claims Act passed by Congress, date unknown.
36. Federal False Claims Act, 31 USC 3729–3733.
37. Doherty, P. (City of Miami Police Chief, Ret.), *The Miami Police Worksheet, A Glimpse of Miami Law Enforcement Past and Present*, Xlibris Press, 2012, p.16. Organizing the Force, describing the need for uniformed police officers as a deterrent to criminals.
38. *New York Times*, May 10, 1924; cited in U.S. Senate, Final Report of the Senate Select Subcommittee to Study Governmental Operations with Respect to Intelligence Activities [the Church Committee], Book II (1976).
39. May, A. and Bardsley, M., John Dillinger, *Crime Library*, trutv.com.
40. Elaine Woo, "Tom Braden Dies at 92; Former CIA Operative Became Columnist and Talk Show Co-Host," *Los Angeles Times*, April 4, 2009.
41. "Julia Child Cooked Up Double Life as Spy," NBC News, August 14, 2008.
42. "John Ford Spy," *All Things Considered*, NPR, February 26, 1995.
43. Andrea Stone, "Famous Personnel Included in Opened OSS Spy Files," *USA Today*, August 14, 2008.
44. Ibid.
45. Bret Blackledge, "Documents: Julia Child Notable among 24,000 OSS Spies," *The Huffington Post*, August 14, 2008.
46. *See* "Recipe for Intrigue: Julia Child's Spy Career," CBS News, August 14, 2008.
47. Schrecker, E., *Many Are the Crimes: McCarthyism in America*. New Jersey: Princeton UP, 1999.
48. Rosenfeld, S., *Subversives: The FBI's War on Student Radicals, and Reagan's Rise to Power*. New York: Farrar, Straus and Giroux, 2012.
49. Herhold, S., "Reagan Acted As an Informant for the FBI," *San Jose Mercury News*, August 25, 1985.
50. Ibid.
51. Ibid.
52. Ibid.

53. Sullivan, W. C., *The Bureau: My 30 Years in Hoover's FBI.* 1979.

54. Ibid.

55. Associated Press, "Ford FBI Informant on Warren Report," August 10, 2008, quoting from released records from Ford's FBI files; see *Houston Chronicle*, "Gerald Ford FBI informant," August 9, 2008.

56. Sniffen, M. J., "Ford Told FBI Panel's Doubts on JFK Murder," *The Washington Post*, August 9, 2008.

57. Elias, P., "Woman Who Tried To Shoot Ford Released," *USA Today*, January 1, 2008.

58. Ibid.

59. Brown, R., "Civil-Rights Photographer Was Spy for FBI, Files Show," *The New York Times*, September 14, 2010.

60. Ibid.

61. Mitchell, J., "Klansman Got Away with Murder," *Clarion-Ledger*, December 27, 1998.

62. Author's note: The agent was acquitted; his name has been intentionally omitted.

63. Colombo crime family.

64. Lance, P., *Cover-Up.* New York: Regan Books, 2004.

65. Danne, F., "The G-Man and the Hit Man," *The New Yorker*, December 16, 1996.

66. Capeci, J., *Jerry Capeci's Gangland,* Penguin Group, 2003.

67. Danne, F., "The G-Man and the Hit Man," *The New Yorker*, December 16, 1996.

68. Ibid.

69. Ibid.

70. The FBI's Compliance with the Attorney General's Investigative Guidelines, Office of the Inspector General, Case Study 2, at 85," September 2005.

71. Hayes, T., "'Sopranos' Echo at Ex-FBI Agent's Trial," *USA Today*, September 18, 2007.

72. Celona, L., "DA Boots Prober–Turned-Mob-Sweetie," *New York Post*, February 19, 2007.

73. "Witness: FBI Used Mob Muscle to Crack '64 Case; Woman Says Gangster Ex-Boyfriend Was Recruited by FBI to Find KKK Victims," Associated Press, October 29, 2007.

74. Ibid.

75. Hayes, T., N.Y. judge: "FBI Made a Deal with the Devil," *USA Today*, November 2, 2007.

76. Lengel, A., "Lawsuit Says FBI Used Mafia Help in 1964 Probe," *AOL News*, February 26, 2010.

77. Backman, M., "Behind the Dalai Lama's Holy Cloak," *The Age, Business Day*, May 23, 2007; see also J. Mann, "CIA Papers Detail 1960s Payments to Dalai Lama," *Los Angeles Times*, September 16, 1998.

78. Mann, J., "CIA Papers Detail 1960s Payments to Dalai Lama," *Los Angeles Times*, September 16, 1998.

79. Ibid.

80. Ibid.

81. "Dalai Lama Group Says It Got Money from CIA," World News Briefs, *The New York Times*, October 2, 1998.

82. Gumbel, A., Timothy Leary was an FBI informer, *The Independent*, (British) June 29, 1999.

83. Frommer, F. J. and Yost, P., "Steinbrenner Helped FBI Before Winning Pardon," *The Huffington Post*, May 10, 2011.
84. Sielski, M., "The Original Undercover Boss," *The Wall Street Journal*, May 10, 2011.
85. Frommer, F. J. and Yost, P., "Steinbrenner Helped FBI Before Winning Pardon," *The Huffington Post*, May 10, 2011.
86. Ibid.
87. Ibid.
88. "FBI Files on Steinbrenner Released," Associated Press, December 25, 2010.
89. Sandomir, R., "Pursuing Pardon, Steinbrenner Aided FBI," *The New York Times*, May 9, 2011.
90. DeLissio, J., "Before Getting His Presidential Pardon, George Steinbrenner Helped the FBI," *New York Magazine*, 9, 2011.
91. Ibid.
92. Sielski, M., "The Original Undercover Boss," *The Wall Street Journal*, May 10, 2011.
93. Sandomir, R., "Pursuing Pardon, Steinbrenner Aided F.B.I.," *The New York Times*, May 9, 2011.
94. Sielski, M., "The Original Undercover Boss," *The Wall Street Journal*, May 10, 2011, quoting an excerpt from FBI documents.
95. Ibid.
96. Fromme, F. J. and Yost, P., "Steinbrenner Helped FBI Before Winning Pardon," *The Huffington Post*, May 10, 2011.
97. Johnson, J., "Steinbrenner Pardon by Reagan For '72 Election Law Violations," *The New York Times*, Jan. 20, 1989.
98. Kempe, F., *Divorcing the Dictator: America's Bungled Affair with Noriega*, New York: G.P. Putnam's Sons, 1990.
99. Drugs, Law Enforcement and Foreign Policy, United States Government Printing Office, December 1988, p. 3.
100. Landers, K., "Noriega Fails to Block Extradition," *ABC News*, January 10, 2008.
101. "Noriega Sentenced to Seven Years in Prison in France," *The New York Times*, July 16, 2010.
102. Wilkinson, T., "An Extradited Noriega Returns to Panama," *Los Angeles Times*, December 11, 2011.

Informants, Cooperating Witnesses, and Sources Defined

2

2.1 Introduction

Informants and cooperating witnesses (CWs) have occupied commanding roles in some of the highest-stakes domestic and international criminal investigations of the twentieth and twenty-first centuries. Likewise, so-called routine criminal cases generated in whole or in part through information received from cooperating individuals fill the dockets of courtrooms across the United States.[1]

The benefits yielded by the use of cooperating individuals are substantial. Informants provide first hand, eyewitness accounts of criminal activity. They are often in a position to provide intelligence information regarding targeted criminals and criminal organizations. Informants are crucial in developing probable causes for search warrants and court-ordered telephone intercepts. The testimony of CWs has secured the convictions of major organized crime figures.

The risks associated with the use of cooperators are also substantial. Informants have been known to commit perjury, plant evidence, entrap targets of investigation, and commit murder. They have also proved to be a catalyst for corruption at every level of law enforcement.

A former assistant attorney general (AAG) tried to explain to Congress who occupies the often ill-defined role of an informant and why they cooperate with law enforcement:

> [S]ome informants are responsible citizens who report suspected criminal activities without any hope of return. In the middle, other informants live in the midst of the criminal underworld and inform largely for cash. Still others, at the other pole, are charged with serious crimes and cooperate with law enforcement officials in return for the hope or promise of leniency.[2]

The AAG chose to label the good citizen sources of information as informants and placed them alongside money-motivated mercenaries and criminals. It's not unusual. Many law enforcement officers, prosecutors, defense attorneys, and judges use the generic term "informant" and attach it to any individual providing information to the authorities. Many law enforcement professionals have found the overgeneralization to be problematic.

A study conducted by the Independent Commission Against Corruption in Australia described why clarity in terms used to identify the various types of cooperators is essential:

> [Current] definitions do not always assist those who deal with informants to identify those in respect to whom there need to be special rules. Most raise more questions than they answer. It is vital that definitions are clear, unambiguous and as objective in their interpretation as possible. Badly or subjectively defined terms will inevitably result in informants who should be subject to the rigors of special rules escaping the net. The definitions should be able to be usefully applied by operational officers. Lack of precision will also allow those case officers who, for various reasons including motives of impropriety, do not wish to register a person as an informant, a way out of the registration process by claiming that the person did not come within the definition.[3]

Failure to provide a definition that distinguished between CWs and confidential informants (CIs) became a critical concern for the Federal Bureau of Investigation (FBI) in the late 1980s. At the time, the identities of valuable informants were being compromised in criminal trials. A memorandum to all special agents provides a historical background for the need to distinguish between a CI and a CW: "Historically, individuals who would normally meet the definition of a cooperative witness (CW) were 'opened' as informants and later testified in court. This resulted in routine disclosures of CW/informant's identities in open court, which has caused continuing erosion of the Criminal Informant Program. By their testimony in court, CWs had the title of 'informant' unnecessarily attached to them. When the need arose to protect the true informant, the courts are not as disposed to rule in the FBI's favor because of the number of previous 'routine' disclosures of CW/informant identities in connection with testimony at trial."[4]

2.2   Informant, Cooperating Witness, or Good Citizen?

As the FBI learned, how a source is categorized is more than an exercise in semantics. A source's classification may allow a great deal of latitude in how far the agency can go in protecting the individual's identity. It also has a direct bearing on how their information will be utilized and how much scrutiny their information deserves. Corroboration of information is done in recognition that informants and CWs frequently lie to both their control agents and prosecutors and may commit perjury if given the opportunity.[5]

As a result, the information and testimony obtained from paid sources or criminal informants should be received with far more caution than a tip received from a concerned citizen. A pattern jury instruction illustrates the point:

> The testimony of some witnesses must be considered with more caution than the testimony of other witnesses. For example, a paid informer, or a witness who has been promised that he or she will not be charged or prosecuted, or a witness who hopes to gain more favorable treatment in his or her own case, may have a reason to make a false statement because he wants to strike a good bargain with the Government. So, while a witness of that kind may be entirely truthful when testifying, you should consider that testimony with more caution than the testimony of other witnesses.[6]

2.2.1   Confidential Informant

A CI is any individual who provides useful and credible information to a law enforcement agency regarding criminal activities and from whom the law enforcement agency expects or intends to obtain additional useful and credible information regarding such activities in the future, pursuant to an agreement that the agency will seek not to disclose the person's identity.[7]

CIs are often operated in a manner that prevents them from providing evidence that could make them a witness in a later prosecution. They are used for intelligence-gathering purposes only. Since they will not testify in court, an agency can usually preserve their anonymity.[8]

2.2.2   Cooperating Witness

The distinction between a CI and a CW is often blurred. An accused hit man turned CW described how he saw the difference: "One's got the courage to stand on the stand (the CW); the other ones are doin' it behind your back and droppin' dimes (CIs)."[9]

Unlike CIs, CWs are expected to testify in legal proceedings. That is often where the distinction between a CW and an informant ends. CWs are often used as operatives in long-term undercover investigations. These are the individuals portrayed in films wearing wires and tape-recording meetings with bad guys. Those tapes become evidence and, consequently, the CW becomes a witness, and his or her identity may be subject to disclosure in any legal proceedings that result.[10]

CWs typically have written agreements with an assistant U.S. attorney or state prosecutor that spell out their obligations and their expectations of future judicial or prosecutive consideration.[11] Their substantial assistance[12] can result in a reduced prison sentence, known as a downward departure, or charges being dropped completely.

Much like their informant counterparts, it is not unusual for CWs to work undercover for protracted periods in the furtherance of a criminal investigation.

It is safe to assume that nearly all CWs are accused criminals. They are literally working for their freedom. If they don't deliver information that results in arrests or the seizure of money or property, they will probably go to prison.

2.2.3   Sources of Information: The Good Citizen

Persons who provide information without an ulterior motive are generally referred to as sources of information. A source provides information to a law enforcement agency only as a result of legitimate routine access to information or records. Unlike what is often the case with CIs and CWs, a source does not collect information by means of criminal association with the subjects of an investigation. He or she is not a criminal. Sources can obtain their information only in a manner consistent with applicable law.[13]

2.3   Autonomy of Terms

2.3.1   State and Local Police Agencies

The vast majority of informants and CWs are recruited and controlled by members of the United States' 18,000 state and local police agencies. Nearly every significant criminal investigation undertaken by police involves the services of an informant, a CW, or a citizen source. However, local and state law enforcement agencies would not be the place to look for uniformity in terms used to define cooperators.

2.3.1.1   Florida

In Florida, there should be no confusion in any courtroom or police station regarding a definition for the term "confidential informant." The legislature made sure of this in 2009 with the passage of "Rachel's Law."[14] This new statute regarding CIs was passed following the murder of Rachel Morningstar Hoffman in Tallahassee, Florida. Hoffman, an informant, was shot to death during a botched controlled purchase of cocaine and firearm investigation (see Chapter 8).

The *Guidelines for Florida State and Local Law Enforcement Agencies in Dealing with Confidential Informants,* issued in March 2009, defined a CI as follows:

Any person who by reason of his or her familiarity or close association with suspected or actual criminals

1. Can make a controlled buy or controlled sale of contraband, controlled substances, or other items material to a criminal investigation or
2. Can or does supply regular or constant information about suspected or actual criminal activities to a law enforcement agency or

3. Can otherwise provide information important to ongoing criminal intelligence gathering or criminal investigative efforts and who is, through such efforts, seeking to improve his or her status in the criminal justice system

A person's improved status in the criminal justice system may include, but is not limited to, avoiding an arrest, a reduction or modification of a sentence imposed or to be recommended to be imposed on him or her, or a reduction or modification of charges pending or anticipated to be placed against him or her, and the person's association or cooperation with law enforcement must remain unknown to those about whom the information is provided or with whom one or more transactions occur.

2.3.1.2 Miami, Florida

The City of Miami Police Department wasted no time coming into compliance with the new law. The department regulates the use of confidential informants and confidential sources (CSs) through departmental orders[15] that govern the activities of the Criminal Investigations Unit. The department revised its order governing the use of CIs/sources on August 1, 2009.[16]

The City of Miami Police Department's new departmental order defines a CI as a person who cooperates with a law enforcement agency confidentially to protect the person or the agency's intelligence gathering or investigative efforts and

1. Seeks to avoid arrest or prosecution for a crime, or mitigate punishment for a crime in which a sentence will be or has been imposed, and
2. Is able, by reason of his or her familiarity or close association with suspected criminals, to make a controlled buy or controlled sale of contraband, controlled substances, or other items that are material to a criminal investigation
3. Supplies regular or constant information about suspected or actual criminal activities to a law enforcement agency or
4. Otherwise provides information important to the ongoing criminal intelligence gathering or criminal investigative efforts

The order went further than the legislation required by defining a *confidential source*. A CS is a person who cooperates with a law enforcement agency confidentially to protect the person or the agency's intelligence gathering or investigative efforts and

1. Is *not* seeking to avoid arrest or prosecution for crime, or mitigate punishment for a crime in which a sentence will be or has been imposed
2. Is compensated and

3. Is able, by reason of his or her familiarity or close association with suspected criminals, to make a controlled buy or controlled sale of contraband, controlled substances, or other items that are material to a criminal investigation; supply regular or constant information about suspected or actual criminal activities to a law enforcement agency; or otherwise provide information important to ongoing criminal intelligence gathering or criminal investigative efforts.[17]

The difference between the two categories is clear. CIs are attempting to avoid arrest or prosecution through cooperation. CSs are paid and do not have charges pending.

2.3.1.3 Denver, Colorado

In contrast to the City of Miami Police Department is the Denver Police Department. The term *informant* is used to identify all individuals who provide information to the department. Informants are further categorized as follows:

1. Participating informant: an informant acting under the specific direction of a primary control officer with command approval
2. Nonparticipating informant: an informant whose cooperation may be sporadic or irregular and is accomplished independent of the officer's guidance (e.g., hotel clerk, airline receptionist, and security guard)

Participating informants are classified as follows:

Class 1: persons who have a serious criminal record (i.e., felony offenses, which include, but are not limited to, robbery, sexual assault, aggravated assault, assault to a peace officer, etc.) or have a known propensity for violence.

Class 2: persons who do not have a criminal record or known propensity for violence, or persons with criminal records for offenses other than those described with respect to class 1 participating informants (i.e., burglary, theft, drug offenses, etc.), or persons with a reputation for involvement/association with the criminal element.[18]

2.3.1.4 California Police Officer Standards and Training

The *California Police Officer Standards and Training Manual* defines an informant as any person who provides information to an investigator.[19] This definition can include criminals, victims of crime, police dispatchers, and police officers. The manual cautions readers to consult individual police agency manuals for specific regulations, reminding the readers that individual departments in California have variations in policy.[20]

2.4   Federal Law Enforcement Agencies

Uniformity in informant programs or terms will not be found within federal law enforcement agencies. The closest to anyone in charge of the federal informant network is the person in charge of the Department of Justice (DOJ), the attorney general (AG) of the United States.[21]

The DOJ employs more than 25,000 FBI, Drug Enforcement Administration (DEA), and Bureau of Alcohol, Tobacco, Firearms, and Explosives (ATF) special agents. Each of the DOJ agents is required to aggressively recruit and operate informants and CWs.

The Department of Homeland Security (DHS), which is not a DOJ agency, employs more law enforcement personnel than the FBI, DEA, and ATF combined. The DHS has a vibrant informant program that very likely dwarfs the size of its DOJ competitors.

Although the FBI, DEA, and DHS constitute the troika of informant-dependent federal law enforcement agencies, they don't have a monopoly on federal informants. There are 44 other federal agencies and 64 offices of inspector general, all with law enforcement responsibilities. Their agents are also expected to recruit informants in the course of their investigations.

2.4.1   Federal Bureau of Investigation

On May 31, 2013, the FBI had a total of 35,902 employees. This includes 13,785 special agents, the only employees permitted to recruit and operate sources. The agents have broad investigative responsibilities covering more than 250 federal crimes. The FBI has concurrent jurisdiction with the DEA over drug offenses covered by the Controlled Substances Act. As might be expected, the two agencies often compete for the same cases, informants, and CWs.

Since the inception of the FBI in 1908, informants have played major roles in the investigation and prosecution of a wide variety of federal crimes. The FBI's Top Echelon Criminal Informant Program was established in 1961 when FBI Director J. Edgar Hoover instructed all special agents in charge (SACs) to "develop particularly qualified, live sources within the upper echelon of the organized hoodlum element who will be capable of furnishing the quality information" needed to attack organized crime.

In 1978, the FBI replaced that program with the Criminal Informant Program. Its mission was to develop a cadre of informants who could assist the FBI's investigation of federal crimes and criminal enterprises. Informants have become integral to the success of many FBI investigations of organized crime, public corruption, the drug trade, counterterrorism, and other initiatives.[22]

2.4.1.1 *Confidential Human Sources*

A barrage of front-page FBI informant scandals, the events of 2001, and a Congressional investigation[23] into the FBI's use of murderers as informants have been the catalyst for dramatic changes in the way the FBI refers to its sources. In 2006, the term informant was discarded and replaced with a new term: *confidential human source* (CHS). The sources are operated under the FBI's post-9/11 Directorate of Intelligence.

A CHS is defined as any individual who is believed to be providing useful and credible information to the FBI for any authorized information collection activity; from whom the FBI expects or intends to obtain additional useful and credible information in the future; and whose identity, information, or relationship with the FBI warrants confidential handling.[24] The term *CHS* replaced the terms *cooperating witness, confidential informant,* and *asset* as terms used to identify cooperators covered under FBI policy.[25]

The *Attorney General's Guidelines Regarding the Use of FBI Confidential Human Sources*[26] govern the utilization of CHSs. An executive assistant FBI director told a Senate committee that the guidelines marked a pivotal milestone in accomplishing the FBI's new one-source concept.[27] Two manuals complement the AG's guidelines: the *Confidential Human Source Policy Manual* (policy manual) and the *Confidential Human Source Validation Standards Manual* (validation manual). The policy manual governs source administration including compliance with the AG's guidelines, whereas the validation manual standardizes the FBI's source-validation review process. The manuals, along with the new AG guidelines, took effect on June 13, 2007.[28]

CHSs are further categorized as follows:

Senior leadership source: a CHS who is in a position to exercise significant decision-making authority over, or to otherwise manage and direct, the unlawful activities of the participants in a group or organization involved in unlawful activities that are nationwide or international in scope or deemed to be of high significance to the FBI's criminal investigative priorities, even if the unlawful activities are local or regional in scope.

High-level government or union source: a CHS who is either (1) in relation to the federal government or the government of a state, the chief executive, the official next in succession to the chief executive, or a member of the legislature; or (b) a president, the secretary/treasurer or vice president of an international or national labor union, or the principal officer or officers of a subordinate regional entity of an international labor union.

Privileged or media source: a CHS who is under the obligation of a legal privilege of confidentiality (physician, attorney, or clergy) or affiliated with the media.

Long-term sources: a CHS who has been registered for more than 5 consecutive years.

Sources requiring special approval include federal or state prisoners, probationers, parolees, and supervised releasees; and current or former participants in the Witness Security Program.[29]

As a matter of historical reference, prior to the CHS program the FBI defined an informant as any person or entity who furnished information to the FBI on a confidential basis.[30] Informants were categorized according to the type of information they provided:

1. Organized crime (OC)
2. General criminal (C): those providing information concerning investigations into matters of a general criminal nature
3. Domestic terrorism (DT): those providing information concerning investigations into persons or groups involved in terrorist activities within the United States, such as bombings and other criminal terrorist activities
4. White-collar crime (WC): those providing information concerning violations falling within the white-collar crime program
5. Drugs (D): those providing information concerning investigations falling within the drug program
6. International terrorism (IT)
7. Civil rights (CR)
8. National Infrastructure Protection/Computer Intrusion Program (NI)
9. Cyber crime (CC)
10. Major theft (MT)
11. Violent gangs (VG)

2.4.1.2 Whistleblowers

Whistleblowers, also known as relators, are mentioned here because the FBI is routinely called on by DOJ attorneys to investigate corporate fraud involving federal funds. Many of these cases come to the DOJ via whistleblowers. Agents are called on to investigate and develop information from whistleblowers.

Whistleblowers are individuals who file suit under the Federal False Claims Act (FCA) on behalf of the United States. The suits are often referred to as a "qui tam" action. Claims under the FCA are filed by persons with insider knowledge of false claims, which usually involve military or health-care spending. Federal funding must be involved and the alleged fraud must be substantial. If the lawsuit is successful, the whistleblower is entitled to between 15% and 25% of the recovery made by the DOJ. The identity of the whistleblower, while frequently kept secret in the early stages of the investigation, is fully disclosed as the case moves to court (see Chapter 8).

2.4.2   Drug Enforcement Administration

The U.S. DEA is an investigative agency within the DOJ. The mission of the DEA is to enforce the controlled-substances laws. The DEA investigates criminal organizations and principal members of organizations involved in the growth, manufacture, or distribution of controlled substances appearing in or destined for illicit traffic in the United States.

The DEA employs approximately 5000 special agents, 500 diversion investigators, 800 intelligence research specialists, and 300 chemists. The DEA employees who are authorized to recruit and operate sources are referred to as special agents. Their job classification within the DEA is criminal investigator.

The agency has 226 offices organized in 21 divisions throughout the United States and 86 offices in 67 countries around the world. The DEA's annual budget in fiscal year (FY) 2012 was $3 billion. From FY 2005 through December 2011, the DEA claims to have seized approximately $19.3 billion in revenue from drug trafficking organizations, making it a nearly self-sustaining agency.

The DEA's policy and procedures regarding sources are contained in the *DEA Agents Manual*.[31] The DEA has discarded the term *informant* from its manual and now uses the term *confidential source* or *CS*.

2.4.2.1 Confidential Source

A CS is a person who, under the direction of a specific DEA agent and with or without the expectation of compensation, furnishes information on drug trafficking or performs a lawful service for the DEA in its investigation of drug trafficking.

Three criteria must be met to establish a person as a DEA CS:

1. The person is in a position to measurably assist the DEA in a present or future investigation.
2. To the extent a prudent judgment can be made, the person will not compromise DEA interests and activities.
3. The person will accept the measure of direction necessary to effectively utilize his or her services.[32]

The term *confidential source* applies to the individuals discussed in Sections 2.4.2.1.1 through 2.4.2.1.3.

2.4.2.1.1 Defendant Confidential Source   A defendant CS is as discussed in Section 2.4.5 but subject to arrest and prosecution for a federal offense or a defendant in a pending federal or state case. He or she expects compensation for his or her assistance in the form of either judicial or prosecutive consideration, or compensation in some other form.[33]

Only individuals who are believed to be able to furnish reliable enforcement information or lawful services and who are believed to be able to maintain the confidentiality of DEA interests and activities may be used as a defendant/CS. The approval of the appropriate U.S. attorney or other prosecutor shall be obtained prior to an agent seeking the cooperation of or utilizing a defendant/CS.[34]

2.4.2.1.2 Restricted-Use Confidential Source   A CS who meets any of the following criteria is considered a "restricted-use CS" and subject to special authorization:

1. Persons less than 18 years of age may only be utilized with written consent of parent or legal guardian.[35]
2. Persons on probation or parole (federal or state) require approval from the SAC. The SAC is responsible for establishing procedures to obtain permission from appropriate officials within the SAC's area of responsibility.

2.4.2.1.3 Federal Prisoners   Where the person intended for use as a CS is currently a federal prisoner, and the intended utilization will require temporary furlough or transfer from his or her detention site or the use of consensual monitoring devices, it is necessary to obtain prior DOJ approval.[36]

2.4.2.2   *Source of Information*

The DEA applies the term "source of information" to a person or organization, not under the direction of a specific agent, who provides information without becoming a party to the investigation itself (e.g., a business firm furnishing information from its records; an employee of an organization who, through the routine course of his or her activities, obtains information of value to the DEA; or a concerned citizen who witnesses an event of interest to the DEA). The term *confidential source* does not apply to sources of information.

Should a person who would otherwise be considered a source of information become a continuing active part of an investigation, then his or her status should be shifted to that of a CS. A source of information that seeks financial compensation or becomes a recipient of an award from the Assets Forfeiture Fund must be established and assigned a code number only for the purpose of payment.

Generally, a person or an organization fitting this definition can be identified by name in investigative reports. However, if there is cause to preserve anonymity, yet the circumstances do not warrant establishing the source as an informant, the term *source of information* may be used. Sources of information are identified in an administrative memorandum attached to the investigative report.[37]

2.4.3   Department of Homeland Security

The U.S. Immigration and Customs Enforcement (ICE) is the largest and the primary investigative arm of the DHS. It was established on March 1, 2003, as part of the post-9/11 government reorganization. Its predecessor agency was the U.S. Customs Service.

The ICE Homeland Security Investigations (HSI) directorate investigates immigration crime; human smuggling; smuggling of narcotics, weapons, and other contraband; financial crimes; cyber crime; and export enforcement issues. In addition to criminal investigations, the HSI oversees the agency's international affairs operations and intelligence functions. The HSI consists of more than 10,000 employees, of whom 6,700 are special agents assigned to more than 200 cities throughout the United States and 47 countries around the world. HSI special agents possess broader investigative powers than any of their federal counterparts. In 2003, the informants working for U.S. Customs Service agents moved to the ICE along with their handlers.

2.4.3.1   Confidential Source

In 2008, the ICE discarded the term *informant* in favor of the blanket term *confidential source*.[38] The ICE defines a CS as an individual who reports information to the ICE regarding possible violations of law or other information in support of law enforcement investigations and activities. Before being identified as a CS, the individual must be properly documented.

2.4.3.2   Non-Confidential Sources

Non-confidential sources include federal, state, local, tribal, territorial, or foreign government personnel or law enforcement officers and members of the public acting in either their personal or their professional capacities.

2.4.4   Internal Revenue Service

The Internal Revenue Service (IRS) is the federal agency that collects taxes and enforces the internal revenue laws. The IRS is the *only* federal agency with jurisdiction to investigate criminal violations of the Internal Revenue Code.[39] The IRS has concurrent investigative jurisdiction with other federal agencies for money laundering and some bank-secrecy-act violations.

The investigative arm of the IRS is the Criminal Investigation Division (CID). The CID is staffed by special agents who are expected to recruit and operate informants. The CID special agents have the same criminal investigator job classification as other federal law enforcement agencies and are empowered to make arrests and carry firearms.

The IRS has launched an aggressive informant recruiting campaign to identify and prosecute tax evaders. The agency's website is quite specific about what it is looking for in its search for informants. The service wants "solid information, not an educated guess or unsupported speculation."

The IRS manual uses three terms for its sources: *CIs*, *CWs*, and *sources of information*.[40]

2.4.4.1   Confidential Informant

A CI is any individual who provides useful and credible information to a special agent regarding criminal activities and from whom a special agent expects or intends to obtain additional useful and credible information regarding such activities in the future. Individuals who act at the direction of a special agent face the potential of any type of retaliation as a result of their cooperation with the IRS, expect their identity to remain confidential, or receive payment or other compensation are considered CIs. Federal prisoners and former or current members of the Witness Security Program can be documented as CIs.[41]

2.4.4.2   Cooperating Witness

CWs differ from CIs in two significant ways. They do not expect their identity to be kept confidential, and they agree to testify in court or administrative proceedings. There can be no expectation of confidentiality with a CW.

2.4.4.3   Source of Information

Sources of information are individuals who do not meet the definition of a CW or CI. An example would be a person who telephones or visits an IRS office to provide information but will not be directed in the future by the IRS to secure evidence. Another example is an individual who is paid for information or evidence that he or she secured independently.

Federal, state, and local law enforcement officials and other governmental officials, acting within the scope of their authority, who provide information to the IRS can also be considered sources of information. However, if the official provides information with respect to corruption within his or her own agency, such as the acceptance of bribes by police officers, the official is considered either a CW or a CI.

2.4.5   Central Intelligence Agency

The Central Intelligence Agency (CIA) is charged with the responsibility of collecting intelligence information relating to the security of the United

States. It is not a law enforcement agency and reports to the National Security Council. Since September 11, 2001, the focus of CIA activity is on terrorism.

In recent decades, its mission has crossed into areas of responsibility thought to be reserved by the FBI, DEA, and ICE, most notably in the areas of drug trafficking and money laundering. Highly publicized misadventures involving drug trafficking in Central and South America confused the intelligence-gathering responsibilities of the CIA with the law enforcement responsibilities of other agencies.[42]

2.4.5.1   Assets

Within the CIA, individuals whom law enforcement agencies routinely refer to as informants are known as assets. The assets are often referred to as agents. The information they collect for the CIA is referred to as human intelligence or HUMINT (not to be confused with signal intelligence [SIGINT], imagery intelligence [IMINT], measurement and signature intelligence [MASINT], telemetry intelligence [TELINT], and electronic intelligence [ELINT]).[43]

2.4.5.2   Defectors

The CIA also recruits defectors. The agency defines a defector as an individual who has committed treason; that is, a person who first accepted identification with a regime and then betrayed his or her allegiance to cooperate with a hostile foreign intelligence service.[44]

One investigative journalist described the value of defectors to the U.S. intelligence community: "Over the years, defectors have given Washington the kind of vital information no billion-dollar satellite or supercomputer ever could. Three al-Qaida defectors, for instance, provided crucial testimony against four associates of Osama bin-Laden involved in the 1998 embassy bombings in East Africa. A Russian defector led the government to FBI spy Robert Hanssen. And in 1987 a Taiwanese defector spilled secrets about Taiwan's nuclear weapons program that helped avoid a conflict with China." A senior CIA official told the journalist, "Some of the information is pure gold."[45]

2.4.5.3   Case Officers

The CIA employees who manage assets, collect intelligence, and work in the field are known as case officers.[46] Case officers are taught "tradecraft," or how to collect information and how to recruit and manage assets at the CIA's Camp Peary Training Center. Known as "the farm," the facility is located on a 9275-acre tract near Williamsburg, Virginia.

While performing their duties overseas, case officers often operate under diplomatic cover as state department officials or economic officers assigned to American consulates. Former CIA Director Admiral Stansfield Turner provided an insightful job description for case officers: "The clandestine service calls for unusual sacrifice. It is not just the anonymity but the lack of credit for what you do. People know you're Joe Jones. They think you are second secretary or some other position in some government bureau, but you never get very high, you are never the top person. You are always undercover doing a different job, and to others who don't know what you are really doing, it appears you're not very successful."[47]

2.4.5.4   NOCs: No Official Cover

Some case officers do not operate under official cover and are referred to as NOCs, since they have no official cover. NOCs are the most covert CIA employees. They work abroad without diplomatic immunity and often appear to be working for a commercial enterprise.

2.5   International Criminal Justice Community

The War on Terror and the growth of transnational organized crime, namely, trafficking in weapons, humans, and drugs, have dramatically increased the international law enforcement community's dependence on informants. The wars have also increased the level of interaction between foreign and U.S. law enforcement agencies. The lack of clarity in the terms used for cooperators has been a source of debate.

2.5.1   Council of Europe

In February 2003, the Council of Europe's[48] Multidisciplinary Group on International Action against Terrorism (GMT) met to discuss terror informants. It identified the protection of witnesses and *pentiti*,[49] an Italian term that roughly translates to informant, involved in terrorism cases as one of the priorities of the Council of Europe. The group's work became bogged down over terminology used to distinguish between the types of sources.

The GMT conducted a survey on legislation and practice regarding both witnesses and informants in member and observer states. They found a lack of clarity in terms of reference in member states for those individuals who cooperated with the authorities. This lack of clarity was particularly profound in the states that had been part of the Soviet Union.

Post-Soviet member states had suffered at the hands of the Committee for State Security (KGB), notorious for their citizen spy network. The infamous Stasi, East Germany's former ministry for state security, maintained files on one-third of East Germany's population. Files seized following the fall of the Berlin Wall showed that friends, business associates, husbands, wives, and other family members were regularly reporting on each other to the Stasi. All telephone calls from abroad were monitored by the Stasi.

One group of researchers estimates that 1 in 50 East Germans collaborated with the Stasi as informants. Another group estimates that the Stasi employed 620,000 people as informants. It was one of the highest per-capita penetrations of a population by an intelligence service in history. The Stasi exceeded the informant saturation of Stalinist Russia and Nazi Germany.[50] Stasi's reign of informant-generated terror operated from 1945 until the fall of the Berlin Wall in 1989.

Taking the sensitivity of the informant issue into account, the GMT adopted a final report that contained recommendations for definitions for cooperators that would be appropriate for an international instrument for witness protection.[51] The definitions included the ones discussed in Sections 2.5.1.1 and 2.5.1.2.

2.5.1.1   Collaborator of Justice

Any person who faces criminal charges, or has been convicted of taking part in a criminal association or a criminal organization of any kind, or in offences of organized crime, but who agrees to cooperate with criminal justice authorities, particularly by giving testimony about a criminal association or organization or about any offence connected with organized crime or other serious crimes is a *collaborator of justice*.

2.5.1.2   Witness

Any person who possesses information relevant to criminal proceedings about which he or she has given and/or is able to give testimony (irrespective of his or her status and of the direct or indirect, oral or written form of the testimony in accordance with national law) and who is not included in the definition of *collaborator of justice* is a *witness*.

2.5.2   United Nations

UN programs have had considerable impact on the international criminal justice community. The work of the United Nations Office on Drugs and Crime (UNODC) is guided by the UN standards and norms on crime prevention and criminal justice. The UN standards and norms are sets of nonbinding rules, principles, and guidelines relating to different aspects of criminal justice. Most of the UN standards and norms are resolutions adopted by the General Assembly or the Economic and Social Council.

The *UN Handbook on Practical Anticorruption Measures for Prosecutors and Investigators,* issued in Vienna in September 2004, addresses the issue of defining terms of reference for informants and other sources of information.

The authors of the handbook felt that distinguishing between the types of sources that investigators rely on would facilitate the internal administration of an investigative agency.

The handbook classified information sources by the nature and extent of the cooperation they provide to investigators. Generally, it divides sources into three categories:

> CIs are likely to be persons who are themselves engaged in criminal activities or associated with persons who are. The various motivations for someone to act as a CI include revenge, financial gain, or the desire to further a beneficial relationship with the investigator. CIs are often paid by law enforcement agencies, and their relationship with investigators is expected to be a continuing one. Their status as an informant and the information they provide are kept absolutely confidential, and thus (unlike a CW) they are not expected to testify in court or otherwise participate publicly in any prosecution.
>
> CSs are those who provide information obtained by virtue of their lawful employment. For example, a hotel employee with access to registration records or a travel agent with knowledge of travel plans would usually be classified as CSs.
>
> The motivation for a CS's cooperation with law enforcement may stem from a sense of public duty, a friendship with a law enforcement officer, or the sheer excitement derived from assisting the police clandestinely. CSs are normally not paid for their assistance, and they require a lower level of management by investigators. For their protection, these sources will often ask that the information they provide be used discreetly or that a formal and open request for the information they have given be made by the agency if the information is to become part of judicial proceedings or a matter of public record. Special care must be taken where a country has privacy or data protection laws, and attention must be paid to the fact that the employment of the source will probably be at risk.
>
> CWs are sources who assist law enforcement officials in a confidential manner but who are expected eventually to be witnesses in public judicial proceedings. CWs may be involved in the corrupt dealings under investigation or be closely associated with the activities. A CW sometimes acts as an operative of the police in an undercover investigation and may need to know aspects of the investigative plan.
>
> The motivation to act as a CW can include the same factors that influence a CI, that is, revenge, financial gain, and leniency in punishment or nonprosecution for prior criminal acts. The distinguishing characteristic of CWs is the fact that their identity and cooperation with law enforcement will ultimately be publicly disclosed. Accordingly, these types of sources can require relocation or other special protection by law enforcement when their role becomes public.

Endnotes

1. See *The Federal Bureau of Investigation's Compliance with the Attorney General's Investigative Guidelines Special Report*, Office of the Inspector General, September 2005.
2. Hearings before the Subcommittee on Administrative Practice & Procedure of the Senate Committee on the Judiciary 95th Cong. 40 (1978) (Testimony of Philip B. Heymann, Assistant Attorney General, Criminal Division, Department of Justice). The complex relationship between the FBI and its informants is also described in *United States v. Doe*, No. 96 Cr. 749 (JG), 1999 WL 243627 (E.D.N.Y. April 1, 1999).
3. Independent Commission against Corruption, *Police Informants, A Discussion Paper on the Nature and Management of the Relationships Between the Police and Their Informants*, ISBN 0-7310-0289, May 1997. The Independent Commission against Corruption is an independent agency of the Government of New South Wales, Australia, responsible for attacking government corruption.
4. Memorandum to All Special Agents in Charge Re: Cooperative Witness Program Interim Guidelines, from William S. Sessions, April 10, 1990. Incorporated by reference into the *FBI Manual of Investigative Operations and Guidelines*, Part 1, section 270–1 (3).
5. See *Illinois v. Gates*, 462 U.S. 213 (1983).
6. Pattern Jury Instructions of the District Judges Association of the Eleventh Cir. Crim. Cases, Special Instruction No. 1.1 (1985). See *United States v. Hernandez-Escarsega*. 886 F.2d 1560, 1574–75, (9th Cir. 1989), *cert. denied*, 497 U.S. 1003, 110 S. Ct. 3237, 111 L. Ed. 2d 748 (1990).
7. See *Standards on Prosecutorial Investigations, ABA Criminal Justice Standards*, Section 2.4, and *Department of Justice Guidelines Regarding the Use of Confidential Informants*.
8. See *Roviaro v. United States*, 353 U.S. at 62, 77 S. Ct. at 628–29 (1957); see *FBI's Manual of Investigative Operations and Guidelines* (MIOG) § 137–3.
9. John, M., "The time capsule of mob lingo at the Whitey Bulger trial," quoting Martorano in 60-minute interview, Associated Press, June 23, 2013.
10. *Brady v. Maryland*, 373 U.S. 83, 87, 80 3 S. Ct. 1194, 10 L. Ed. 215 (1963).
11. See Hughes, G., *Agreements for Cooperation in Criminal Cases*, 45 VAND. L. REV. 1 (1992); Ian Weinstein, Regulating the Market for Snitches, 47 BUFF. L. REV. 563 (1999); George C. Harris, Testimony for Sale: The Law and Ethics of Snitches and Experts, 28 PEPP. L. REV. 1 (2000); Daniel C. Richman, Cooperating Clients, 56 OHIO ST. L.J. 69 (1995).
12. U.S.S.G. § 5K1.1.
13. See *Department of Justice Guidelines Regarding the Use of Confidential Informants*, § I.B.8 at B-9.
14. Fla. Stat. § 914.28 (2010).
15. See Departmental Order 9, Chapter 12.
16. See Official Bulletin #2009-52, June 30, 2009.
17. Departmental Order 9, Chapter 12.
18. *Denver Police Department Operations Manual*, Revised 7/08, 307.01, Informant Categories and Classification.

19. See Santiago, M. R., Comment, *"The Best Interests of the Child"—Scrutinizing California's Use of Minors as Police Informants in Drug Cases*, 31 McGeorge L. Rev. 777, 778 (2000) (the brutal murder of a juvenile informant led to reform legislation in California).

20. See California Commission on Peace Officer Standards and Training (POST), Specialized Investigators' Basic Course Workbook Series Student Materials, *Learning Domain 62 Case Management and Sources of Information, Version 2. Developing Informants* [62.03.EO1, 62.03.EO2, 62.03.EO3, 62.03.EO4].

21. See Title 28, United States Code, Sections 509, 510, and 533. See also *Department of Justice Guidelines Regarding the Use of Confidential Informants.* The guidelines provide definitions for sources.

22. *The Federal Bureau of Investigation's Compliance with the Attorney General's Investigative Guidelines Special Report*, Office of the Inspector General, September 2005.

23. House Committee on Government Reform, *Everything Secret Degenerates: The FBI's Use of Murderers as Informants, 3rd Report*, H.R. Rep. No. 108-414 at 454 (2004), also available at www.gov/hreports/108-414.html.

24. *The Attorney General's Guidelines Regarding the Use of FBI Confidential Human Sources* was signed on December 13, 2006 and supersedes the *FBI Manual of Investigative Operations and Guidelines* (MIOG). Section 137 had governed the bureau's Criminal Informant Program. The MIOG defined an informant as any person or entity who furnishes information to the FBI on a confidential basis. The manual had defined a CW as an individual whose relationship with the government is concealed until testimony is required at trial and who, on a continuing basis and under the direction of an agent, contributes substantial operational assistance to the resolution or direction of a case through active participation in the investigation.

25. *Confidential Human Source Policy Manual*, Appendix C: Legal Authorities.

26. *Attorney General Guidelines Regarding the Use of FBI Confidential Human Sources* took effect on December 13, 2006; *Confidential Human Source Policy Manual* and the *Confidential Human Source Validation Standards Manual* took effect on June 13, 2007. It was revised and reissued on March 26, 2010.

27. Testimony of Willie T. Hulon, executive assistant director, National Security Branch FBI, before the Senate Select Committee on Intelligence, Washington, DC, October 23, 2007.

28. Ibid.

29. *Attorney General's Guidelines Regarding the Use of FBI Confidential Human Sources*, December 13, 2006.

30. *MIOG* §137-3.

31. *DEA Agents Manual.* (Author's note: four versions of the *DEA Agents Manual* have been issued since 1998. The DEA is in the process of rewriting a new manual. All references to the manual are taken from the latest version of the manual available to the author.)

32. *DEA Agents Manual*, Ch. 66.

33. Ibid.

34. Ibid.

35. See Blair, J., "Ethics of Using Juvenile Informants," *Christian Science Monitor*, April 14, 1998.

36. *DEA Agents Manual*, Ch. 66.
37. Ibid.
38. Federal Register: December 9, 2008 (Volume 73, Number 237) [Page 74729–74732].
39. *Internal Revenue Service Manual*. Part 9. Criminal Investigation, Chapter 4. Investigative Techniques, Section 2. Sources of Information.
40. Quote from www.irs.gov, Whistleblower-Reward.
41. *IRS Manual* 9.4.2.5.1.1 (03-15-2007).
42. Pincus, W., "CIA Wonders Why Young Spies Are Quitting—Fighting Drugs Rather Than Cold War, Some Say Thrill Is Gone," *Washington Post*, November 26, 1996.
43. The following is taken directly from the FBI Directorate of Intelligence home page: "Various kinds of intelligence—military, political, economic, social, environmental, health, and cultural—provide important information for policy decisions. Many people view intelligence as gathered through secret or covert means. Although some intelligence is indeed collected through clandestine operations and known only at the highest levels of government, other intelligence consists of information that is widely available. There are five main ways of collecting intelligence that are often collectively referred to as 'intelligence collection disciplines' or the 'INTs':

"Human intelligence (HUMINT) is the collection of information from human sources. Beyond U.S. borders, HUMINT is generally collected by the CIA, but it is also collected by other U.S. components abroad. The collection may be done openly, as when FBI agents interview witnesses or suspects, or it may be done through clandestine or covert means (espionage). Within the United States, HUMINT collection is the FBI's responsibility. Although HUMINT is an important collection discipline for the FBI, we also collect intelligence through other methods, including SIGINT, MASINT, and OSINT.

"Signals intelligence (SIGINT) refers to electronic transmissions that can be collected by ships, planes, ground sites, or satellites. Communications Intelligence (COMINT) is a type of SIGINT and refers to the interception of communications between two parties. U.S. SIGINT satellites are designed and built by the National Reconnaissance Office, although conducting U.S. signals intelligence activities is primarily the responsibility of the National Security Agency (NSA). The FBI collects SIGINT through authorized wiretaps and other electronic intercepts of information.

"Imagery intelligence (IMINT) is sometimes also referred to as photo intelligence (PHOTINT). One of the earliest forms of IMINT took place during the Civil War, when soldiers were sent up in balloons to gather intelligence about their surroundings. IMINT was practiced to a greater extent in World Wars I and II when both sides took photographs from airplanes. Today, the National Reconnaissance Office designs, builds, and operates imagery satellites, whereas the National Geospatial-Intelligence Agency is largely responsible for processing and using the imagery.

"Measurement and signatures intelligence (MASINT) is a relatively little-known collection discipline that concerns weapons capabilities and industrial activities. MASINT includes the advanced processing and use of data gathered from overhead and airborne IMINT and SIGINT collection systems.

"Telemetry intelligence (TELINT) is sometimes used to indicate data relayed by weapons during tests, whereas electronic intelligence (ELINT) can indicate electronic emissions picked up from modern weapons and tracking systems. Both TELINT and ELINT can be types of SIGINT and contribute to MASINT."

44. Bradford, H., *Westerfield, Inside the CIA's Private World*. Yale University Press, Connecticut, 1995.

45. Pasternak, D., "Squeezing Them, Leaving Them," *U.S. News*, July 8, 2002.

46. Davis, F., "Agent Tells Tale of CIA Defect in Drug War," *Miami Herald*, September 18, 1997.

47. Weiner, T., "In Latest Turncoat Scandal, CIA Assumes the Worst," *International Herald Tribune*, November 21, 1996. See also Gup, T., "Nameless Stars of the CIA," *Washington Post*, October 1, 1997.

48. An international organization promoting cooperation between all countries of Europe in the areas of legal standards, human rights, democratic development, and the rule of law, representing 47 countries with 820 million citizens.

49. Plural for *pentito*, an Italian term for a person who collaborates with the judicial system to assist in an investigation.

50. "Stasi Informant Loses Court Privacy Battle," *The Local* (Germany's news in English), April 22, 2008, estimates that 620,000 people were employed by the Ministry of State Security as informants.

51. Council of Europe, Committee of Ministers, Recommendation of the Committee of Ministers to member states on the protection of witnesses and collaborators of justice (adopted by the Committee of Ministers on April 20, 2005 at the 924th meeting of the ministers' deputies).

Motivations for Cooperation

3

3.1 Introduction

A federal judge sentencing a key cooperating witness in the trial of mafia boss John Gotti told those in attendance at the hearing that he considered the man's decision to cooperate and testify a "leap from one social planet to another."[1] It is vital for the recruiting agent to accurately determine a prospective informant's true motivation for taking that leap. Failure to accurately gauge an informant's motivation has led to the deaths and serious injuries of innocent citizens,[2] false arrests,[3] wrongful convictions,[4] lawsuits,[5] scandals,[6] and destroyed law enforcement careers.[7]

The prosecutor must also be cognizant of what brought the individual into his relationship with law enforcement.[8] Federal Judge Stephen Trott urges prosecutors to "assess the motivation of the witness. Why did he decide to cross over? You must understand why he has turned in order to keep him on your side once he has crossed over. This understanding will keep you from making mistakes caused by thinking you have to be friendly and generous to keep him on the team. Normally he will stay with you so long as the carrot he seeks is still in the future."[9]

Many defense attorneys fail to understand the importance of determining the motivation of the cooperating witness as they examine the case against their client. It is crucial in developing an effective trial strategy.[10]

Motivations for cooperation will generally fall into one or more of several categories, including money, fear, revenge, threats from criminal associates, special consideration while incarcerated, ego, threats of deportation, repentance, and civic duty.

3.2 Money

Money is probably the easiest motivation to understand. Rewards for information have been sanctioned by the courts on the grounds of public policy interests and in recognition that money loosens lips.[11] Informants in this category are often referred to as mercenaries.

The concept of paying for information is not a new one and not unique to the United States. In 1706, England enacted laws governing rewards in

45

response to the growing problem of what today would be called buying and receiving stolen property. A "receiver" or fence,[12] although considered an accessory after the fact, if convicted would be sentenced to death as a capital felon. An informer who provided evidence sufficient to convict the fence received both a reward of £40 and a royal pardon.[13]

Today, informing can be a profitable enterprise.[14] Thanks in part to press reports, leaked information, and federal statutes governing rewards, we know that federal informants are paid handsomely for their efforts.[15] Many earn millions of dollars during their stints as informants.[16] One FBI (Federal Bureau of Investigation) secretary responsible for preparing the paperwork for informant payments was so outraged at the size of the rewards being paid as compared to her salary that she refused to process the payment paperwork.[17]

Informants motivated by money view their work as a productivity-based enterprise contingent upon success.[18] The sums paid by federal, state, and local agents following successful investigations would suggest that a majority of agents also share that opinion.[19] Multi-defendant cases, particularly those resulting in significant asset forfeiture, will result in a correspondingly greater award.[20]

One long-term Drug Enforcement Administration (DEA) informant made millions during his years with the agency. *Newsweek* magazine named him "King of the Drug Busters."[21] A photograph of the well-dressed informant accompanied the article.

The confidential informant (CI) enjoyed a 16-year relationship with the DEA and at one time was considered one of its most valuable informers. He worked in 12 of the DEA's 22 domestic field offices. Earning more than $2.2 million from the DEA[22] and nearly that much from other law enforcement agencies, he may have grossed more than $4 million[23] during his career as an informant.[24] In 2000, the DEA identified him as its second-highest-paid informant but refused to identify its highest-paid CI or how much he was paid.[25]

The informant was responsible for providing evidence that led to the arrests of 445 drug dealers.[26] His record for drug seizures was equally impressive. One journalist claimed DEA records showed that the CI was responsible for the seizure of tons of cocaine, heroin, and methamphetamines.[27]

In terms of measuring and informant's productivity and determining what he is paid, the DEA regards asset seizures as a top priority. The "King of the Drug Busters" excelled at forfeitures. His cases brought in approximately $6 million in seized assets, including numerous weapons and vehicles.[28]

The money-motivated informants are usually the most willing to follow the directions of their handlers.[29] They understand that productive sources get paid. Unproductive informants do not. Problems can arise when information becomes scarce and the informant needs money. He may fabricate accounts of criminal activity or entrap his target in an effort to make a money-making case.

3.3   Fear

Fear is the catalyst for many criminals to transition into informants.[30] It is also an example of a motive that may not be initially offered as the true reason for becoming an informant, particularly for alpha males. The prospective informant's fear is usually driven by

- Fear of arrest
- Fear of imprisonment
- Fear of social stigma arising from arrest or imprisonment
- Fear of criminal retribution
- Fear of separation from family
- Fear of arrest of family member(s)[31]

The fear of being arrested as the result of an encounter with a police officer should not be difficult to understand. The United States has the highest incarceration rate in the world. At the close of 2010, 1 out of every 201 U.S. residents was behind bars in a state or federal prison.[32] With 743 per 100,000 of our population held as prisoners—the highest per capita prison population in the world—we eclipsed the incarceration rates of China's 615 per 100,000 and Russia's 118 per 100,000 residents.[33] We have less than 5% of the world's population but nearly 25% of the world's prison population.[34] At the close of 2010, 4.9 million residents of the United States were either on parole or probation.[35]

3.4   Revenge

Many are motivated to become informants by a need to exact revenge.[36] Business associates, ex-spouses, fellow members of a criminal organization, or members of a rival gang are the usual targets.

Ex-paramours can be motivated by either fear, revenge, or a combination of both. The emotional fallout from a divorce can be a powerful motivator for an ex-spouse to come forward with information. Their motive should not be discounted, but their accounts must be closely scrutinized. One court recognized that a society can ill afford to throw away the evidence produced by the fallings-out, jealousies, and quarrels of those who live by outwitting the law.[37]

Business associates may seek revenge by providing law enforcement with damaging evidence against a former partner or competitor. Tips are important to the Internal Revenue Service (IRS) and are often received from disgruntled employees, competitors, unpaid creditors, or angry neighbors.

The fear and the revenge-motivated informants should be immediately debriefed and their information evaluated. It is not unusual for disputes to be resolved and the burning desire for revenge extinguished.

While the informant's value is being evaluated, a threat assessment should be conducted. If there is a substantiated risk of harm present, some measure of protection should be provided to the individual during the evaluation period.

3.4.1   Case Study: Joe Dogs and Operation Home Run

Fear coupled with a desire to exact revenge is how an informant known as "Joe Dogs," nicknamed for his love of dog racing, found himself cooperating with the government. Dogs was a mid-level bookie and loan shark who fell behind in paying his debts to a local mobster. He received an unexpected late fee: a baseball-bat beating that left him close to death. Angry and in fear for his life, he agreed to cooperate with the FBI in a sting operation.

The informant helped set up a phony gambling club in Riviera Beach, Florida, run by the FBI. The sting investigation was code-named Operation Home Run. At great risk to himself, the informant wore a concealed recorder for more than a year, collecting valuable evidence.

Joe Dogs provided testimony in several trials that dismantled a major illegal gambling operation and sent dozens to prison, including a corrupt police chief. Fear coupled with a desire for revenge motivated a career criminal to deliver to the FBI what money could never have bought. Joe Dogs, if still alive, is believed to be in the Witness Security Program.[38]

3.5   The Jailhouse Informant and Incentivized Testimony

Correctional facilities, particularly federal institutions, have become informant mills. Some prisons are known as "cheese factories"[39] for their ability to turn inmates into informants or "rats." Inmates with valuable criminal information or fabricated accounts of crime compete with each other to win the ear of a detective or federal agent. They've coined slogans for the practice: "Don't go to the pen, send a friend" and "If you can't do the time—just drop a dime."[40]

The jailhouse informant plays an important yet controversial role within the criminal justice system. Many "cold cases," those that have gone unsolved for many years, are solved by jail cell "confessions" given by the perpetrator or an accomplice to a fellow inmate. Recently committed crimes are also solved when a newly incarcerated prisoner confides in his cellmate the details about his latest crime.[41] The jailhouse informant will generally channel his information either by telephone or through a corrections officer to an interested detective in exchange for consideration peculiar to the informant's needs.

Depending on what stage their case is at, informing is their only hope for a favorable recommendation for bond, probation, parole, or a sentence reduction.[42] Absent that option, the jailhouse CI wants to make his period of incarceration as tolerable an experience as possible. As a member of a jail or prison population, the corrections staff fulfills his immediate needs. They can control nearly all facets of his environment. He can do "easy time" or "hard time." In most cases, he probably views even the best day in jail as "hard time."

Prisoners have a lot of time on their hands, most of it spent trying to figure a way out of jail. The forced confinement of some of America's most cunning criminals has turned prisons into informant think tanks. Federal agents and detectives alike are constantly being outwitted by streetwise jailhouse informants who promise agents a big case. The case is usually the result of a confession from a fellow inmate.

Federal prosecutors are taught: "The most dangerous informant of all is the jailhouse snitch who claims another prisoner has confessed to him, and the snitch now stands ready to testify in return for some consideration in his own case. Sometimes the snitch is telling the truth, but more often they invent testimony out of the air and stray details. This is why O.J. Simpson's lawyers asked that he be in solitary quarters while in the Los Angeles County Jail. They knew any prisoner who got close to him might manufacture incriminating statements."[43]

Jailhouse informants are resourceful. When "confessions" are not available, they can make themselves invaluable in ongoing investigations occurring outside the prison walls.

One jailhouse informant demonstrated to 60 Minutes reporters his skill in obtaining evidence by telephone. He had been a witness in more than a dozen Los Angeles County felony investigations, several of them murder cases.[44]

Without ever leaving a hotel room, and with reporters present, the informant obtained key information regarding a murder. He posed as a deputy sheriff, a deputy district attorney, and a Los Angeles Police Department detective in a flurry of calls to assorted county offices. The informant talked an array of officials into disclosing the victim's cause of death, when the shooting occurred, and the age and race of the victim. He was even told about the existence of multiple gunshot wounds to the deceased's thighs. In the course of his telephone calls, he collected enough details about a criminal case to fabricate a believable cellmate confession.

The informant then arranged for himself and a selected fellow prisoner to be transported in the same vehicle to court—enabling him the chance to appear to be in position to converse with his target and solicit a jailhouse confession.[45] The 60 Minutes TV segment helped spur an extremely critical probe of the jailhouse informant phenomenon occurring in L.A. County's correctional facilities.

3.5.1 DNA and the Innocence Project

Advances in the use of DNA evidence have been a blow to jailhouse informants. In 1992, the Innocence Project was established by the Benjamin

Cardozo School of Law and functions to exonerate with DNA evidence those who have been wrongly convicted.

The project has proven that more than 15% of "solved" death penalty cases resulted in the conviction of an innocent man.[46] This translates to 38 innocent people sitting on death row.[47] All of the wrongly convicted were victims of an informant lying to detectives and committing perjury at trial. The convictions were overturned only because DNA testing exonerated the men with irrefutable physical evidence.

A spokesperson for the project was frank in his assessment of the results of their work: "DNA exonerations have shown that snitches lie on the stand. To many, this is not a surprise. Testifying falsely in exchange for an incentive—either a sentence reduction or an early release—is often the last resort for a desperate inmate. For someone who is not in prison already but who wants to avoid being charged with a crime, providing false testimony may be the only option."[48]

One judge, while not condoning jailhouse informant perjury, understood exactly why it happens: "It is difficult to imagine a greater motivation to lie than the inducement of a reduced sentence."[49]

The Innocence Project's findings confirm that for both police and prosecutors, making a case and winning at trial are the primary objective. The project's findings also confirmed what many defense lawyers had long suspected: "In some cases, snitches or informants come forward voluntarily, often seeking deals or special treatment. But sometimes law enforcement officials seek out snitches and give them extensive background on cases—essentially feeding them the information they need to provide false testimony."[50]

3.5.2   Police Targeting Suspect Prisoners

Controversy surrounding the jailhouse informant arises when he is instructed by police to obtain information from a targeted prisoner. The problem is compounded when, at the direction of detectives, he is strategically placed by the correction staff in close proximity to the target.

The most comprehensive examination of the jailhouse informant phenomenon was conducted by a Los Angeles County Grand Jury.[51] Although the term *jailhouse informant* was used in their report, the California Penal Code[52] refers to this category of cooperating individuals as "in-custody informants," defining them as "a person other than a codefendant, percipient witness, accomplice, or coconspirator whose testimony is based upon statements made by the defendant while both the defendant and the informant are held within a correctional institution."[53]

Whether or not true, many incarcerated informants believe that law enforcement officials have directly or indirectly solicited them to actively secure incriminating statements from fellow inmates. Some informants in the Los Angeles Grand Jury investigation claimed that various law enforcement officials supplied them with information about crimes, so they (the informants) could fabricate a defendant's confession.

The Grand Jury determined that inmates were planted by jail authorities with or near criminal defendants in high-profile cases with instructions to obtain information and confessions. If true, the risk of serious Fifth[54] and Sixth Amendment[55] violations should have been apparent to prosecutors and police.[56]

In exchange for providing evidence for the prosecution, informants expected significant benefits from the government. Based on this expectation, informants supplied information favorable to the prosecution, often irrespective of its truth.

The Grand Jury reported that the benefits to a jailhouse informant could range all the way from as little as added servings of food up to the ultimate reward, release from custody. According to an officer at the central jail, inmates who provided information about problems within the jail might have been rewarded with an extra phone call, visits, food, or access to a movie or television.

A former high-ranking official with the California Department of Corrections described what he believed motivates a jailhouse informant:

> [Informants] want something ... and I don't know anybody that has ever come forward with information inside of a prison or criminal justice system that didn't want something for himself or for some friend of his.

The Grand Jury findings determined that the Los Angeles Sheriff's Department failed to establish adequate procedures to control improper placement of inmates, with the foreseeable result that false claims of confessions or admissions would be made. It also found that the Los Angeles County District Attorney's Office failed to fulfill the ethical responsibilities required of a public prosecutor by its deliberate and informed declination to take the action necessary to curtail the misuse of jailhouse-informant testimony.

3.6 Repentance

Informants often claim they are cooperating to repent for past crimes or wrongdoings.[57] They are usually criminals who have turned away from crime but retain access to information of importance to the police.[58] Many CI handlers doubt informants who claim repentance as their motivation, and that if it exists, it is often short-lived.

The skilled investigator can capitalize on the potential for repentance with individuals who otherwise would refuse to cooperate.[59] Fear of going to prison spurs many to claim sorrow for past transgressions or a newfound belief in God as their motive for volunteering to cooperate. However, it is seldom their only motive for becoming an informant.[60]

One of the most publicized accounts of a repentant informant is that of former New York City Detective Robert Leuci, glamorized in the book and movie *Prince of the City*.[61] Detective Leuci, alleged to have been a corrupt officer, became a valuable witness for the Knapp Commission's investigation into corruption within the New York City Police Department during the 1970s.

Many involved in the case claimed "the Knapp Commission had nothing on Leuci, but he didn't know it,"[62] inferring he came forward out of an unfounded fear of punishment. Those close to Leuci believe he viewed himself as a good police officer who seemed to genuinely regret the misdeeds he committed while a detective.

The conversion of Detective Leuci from corrupt detective to cooperating government witness is credited to the skills of a Knapp Commission prosecutor and former assistant district attorney. He was successful in recruiting the repentant detective, and he said, "If Leuci would cooperate, he could wipe his own slate clean."[63]

3.7   Burning Bridges and Starting a New Life

A close cousin to the repentant informant is the individual who wants to start a new life by wiping out any possibility of returning to their life of crime. It has been suggested by some that burning bridges by becoming an informant can be the first step toward rehabilitation. Their reasoning is that cooperation with the government, even by former career criminals, can provide a chance to begin anew.[64] Like the repentant informant, they may retain access to information of importance to the police.

3.7.1   Case Study: The DEA's Princess

Princess, the great-granddaughter of a famous Colombian politician,[65] had been married to a major Colombian cocaine trafficker. She came to the DEA because "she was trying to get out of the drug business and was looking for monetary gain."[66]

An unknown quantity, Princess had to be tried out in the field before agents could accept her as an informant. Her recruiting agent recalled her debut:

> It's kind of a strange situation. We were asking her at that point to gain our confidence by doing a small cocaine deal. We were looking for possibly one or two or three or four, five kilograms of cocaine. And she basically kept on telling us she couldn't do that. And we kept on saying, "Well, why?" We were getting ready to say okay, we're going to forget about this whole thing, it's not worth the aggravation, because if she can't do five kilos, what's she going to do for us?[67]

And what we didn't realize at the time was actually what she was capable of doing.... We asked her for five; she said no, she can't do it. And then she said, "Because I'm much bigger than that. People think that it would be disrespecting for me to ask for [just] five kilos." Well, we felt that, you know, she wasn't telling us the truth; she couldn't have been that big. And basically, within a couple weeks we found out that she was.[68]

Nearly overnight, Princess set up a 400-kilo cocaine deal with a kilo of heroin thrown in for good measure. At the time, the drugs were worth $60 million.

Princess was signed up as informant number SGS-92-X003. During the course of her work as an informant, she traveled undercover to Colombia, Switzerland, Costa Rica, Ecuador, Spain, Italy, and Canada. She posed as a wealthy art dealer and money launderer who could move millions in drug money to safe havens through legitimate business accounts. The accounts belonged to fictitious companies set up by the DEA for laundering dirty money. The DEA ultimately seized nearly $22 million as a result of Princess's work (see Chapter 6).

3.8   Excitement and the James Bond Syndrome

Individuals motivated by a desire for excitement often view becoming an informant as an outlet for their fantasies. Police officers describe these informants as "007s" or suffering from the "James Bond Syndrome."[69]

The "007" is usually difficult to utilize and control. He may possess valuable information or criminal connections but is often detached from reality. Many of this type see themselves as characters from television, movies, or novels.

The "007" may dress as if in costume, attempting to look like a fictional character. Some purchase a fake police badge, false or official-appearing identification, and may carry a firearm, all in violation of his informant agreement. He is not beyond telling people that he works for the government. He may impersonate his agent handler by using the agent's business cards.

Obviously, all informant information must be questioned and corroborated. However, the "007's" information deserves even more attention. He may grossly exaggerate his account of criminal activity or completely fabricate his information.[70]

3.9   Police Buff

The "police buff"[71] is motivated by a strong desire to be a police officer but for a variety of reasons is unable or unwilling to enter the law enforcement profession. Many "buffs" are disqualified due to physical restrictions or lack of formal education. Some are unable to survive a background investigation due to a bad credit record, poor employment history, or an arrest record.

It is not unusual for "police buffs" to already have a successful civilian career but become bored. "Buffs" will often become the neighborhood crime watch captain or join community police organizations.

Although well intentioned, the "police buff" is generally not a productive informant. He is not involved in criminal activity and has little to offer a handler.

3.10   Perversely Motivated Informants aka Double Agents

The perversely motivated informant[72] initiates his relationship with law enforcement to further his own criminal ambitions.[73] In becoming an informant, his objective may include learning how the agency conducts its investigations or to identify its undercover agents, informants, and targets of investigation.[74] He may be using the police to eliminate his drug competitors or an informant.[75] Criminal organizations have directed individuals to infiltrate a police department or agency as an informant to further their own criminal agenda.[76] Bona fide information may be provided by the informant to divert attention away from their operation.

Immigration and Customs Enforcement (ICE) informant ranks were compromised in 2008 when a Juarez Cartel hitman known as Dorado was dispatched to El Paso, Texas. He easily became an ICE informant working for a control agent with a track record for operating cartel CIs. The agent had recently recruited Daniel Galena, a cartel lieutenant who had fled to El Paso from Juarez after being wrongfully identified as an informant in a Mexican newspaper. He had agreed to work with Immigration and Customs Enforcement (ICE) in exchange for immigration assistance and some measure of protection.

Within weeks of El Dorado's activation as an informant, Galena was followed to his upscale home located on the same block as the El Paso police chief's house. He was shot eight times at point-blank range with a .45-caliber semiautomatic pistol. Neighbors reported hearing shouting in Spanish just before shots were fired. The shooter was so close to Galena that two of the eight slugs had enough punch left over to rip through his chest and exit his body. One bullet embedded itself in the wall of a neighbor's home. Another struck a parked car.[77]

The chief of police heard the shots from his backyard. According to the chief, "He got shot up close. Whoever did it wanted to make sure it was known that it was for payback."[78] Hidalgo earned the distinction of being the first Mexican cartel boss assassinated on U.S. soil.

Dorado was arrested by local police 2 months after the murder. He immediately identified himself as an ICE informant and demanded that his control agent be contacted.

Detectives learned that Dorado had managed to track Galena's cell phone and had been stalking his victim for weeks before the murder. How he obtained the phone information remains a mystery. Dorado had employed an 18-year-old U.S. Army private to commit the murder. He flipped soon after his arrest and is cooperating with prosecutors as they prepare for Dorado's capital murder trial.[79]

3.11 Altruism

Some informants come forward out of a concern for the welfare of others.[80] While altruism as a motive for cooperating is frequently claimed, it is seldom the case, and the recruiting agent should proceed with caution. That is not to say that informants driven by altruism do not exist.

Ted Kacznski, better known as the Unibomber, enjoyed a nearly 2-decade mail bombing reign of terror, killing 3 and maiming 23 other victims. Despite leaving valuable evidence behind, agents were never close to identifying and making a case on the Unibomber. The investigation was one of the most costly in FBI history.[81]

It was not until the Bureau put a $1 million reward on the Unibomber's head that the case started getting new leads. Kacznski would probably still be sending bombs had his brother not reported him to the FBI.[82] According to his brother, the reward was not what motivated him to come forward. He wanted to put an end to his brother's bombing spree and get him help. He insisted that the money would be given to the families of the bombing victims to help ease their pain.

Several members of the House of Representatives attempted to pass a bill exempting the reward from taxation. The bill did not pass, and the IRS taxed the reward.[83]

3.11.1 Case Study: Altruism or Money?

An American FBI informant who aided Britain's domestic intelligence service, MI5, was instrumental in bringing terrorism charges against Michael McKevitt, the alleged leader of the Real IRA (Irish Republican Army),[84] for a deadly 1998 car bombing in Omagh, Northern Ireland. The bomb killed 29 and injured more than 200 people.

The informant, a former truck driver, told an interviewer he became an informant for "moral" reasons. He claimed his success as an infiltrator began when he "went to the bars and hung out with the right people." He was quoted as saying he was "a whore who worked for anybody," although he later claimed he was only being "facetious."[85]

After successfully infiltrating the IRA as its chief fundraiser in the United States, he spent more than 3 years collecting damaging evidence and ultimately testifying against McKevitt. The IRA leader was convicted in 2009 for executing the most lethal attack in Northern Ireland's history. McKevitt's conviction was the first under Britain's new law against directing terrorism.[86]

Depending on which news source you believe, the informant was paid somewhere between $1.25 million[87] and €5 million.[88] He is alleged to have been given a new identity by the FBI, relocated, and paid a stipend of $12,000 a month.[89] He also owns a new $400,000 house. An Irish news source claims there is no official record of who paid for the home.[90]

3.12   Ego

Ego drives many to become informants. Some have had successful careers but are motivated by unrealized goals. Historically, pilots,[91] executives, former members of the military,[92] and other professionals have proven to be members of the ego-driven category. Money often enters into the picture, but ego is usually their driving force.

The ego-driven informant can easily be mistaken for the police buff or the 007. While they may share some of the same characteristics, the ego-driven informant should not be dismissed before being evaluated. If accepted as an informant or cooperating witness, the control agent should exert every effort to maintain the upper hand in his dealings with the source. The informant may well be shrewder and possibly better trained than the handler.

3.12.1   Case Study: FBI Day of Terror Informant

Dwarfed by the magnitude of 9/11 was the earlier 1993 World Trade Center (WTC) bombing and the ensuing FBI investigation into what was dubbed the Day of Terror plot. Followers of Sheikh Abdel-Rahman, better known as "the blind sheikh," had planned to blow up the Holland and Lincoln Tunnels, the U.N. General Assembly building, and the FBI's New York Field Office at 26 Federal Plaza.

The terrorist cell was successfully infiltrated by a former Egyptian army intelligence officer turned FBI informant. Since his arrival in the United States, he had worked as a department store security guard and other low-paying unskilled positions. By all accounts, he was underemployed and unhappy with job prospects in the United States.

Under the original FBI plan, the informant would help the plotters build the WTC bomb but at the last minute substitute the explosives with fake powder. According to the CI, an FBI supervisor "came and messed it up"[93] by removing him from the investigation. The conspirators went ahead without him, and the actual bomb was assembled, delivered in a rental truck, and detonated.

Almost immediately after the bombing, the informant called one of his handlers to express his outrage. In broken English he told the agent: "We was start already building the bomb, which is went off in the World Trade Center. It was built, uh, uh, uh, supervising, supervision from the bureau [FBI] and the DA [district attorney] and we was all informed about it. And we know that the bomb start to be built. By who? By your confidential informant. What a wonderful great case. And then he [the FBI supervisor] put his head in the sand and said, oh no, no, no that's not true, he is a son of a bitch, okay." The conversation, like at least 70 others with agents, was secretly recorded and retained by the informant.[94]

Still eager to vent, the CI wanted to complain to FBI headquarters about the missteps in the WTC case. However, he recalled being told by a New York agent, "I don't think that the New York people would like to take things out of the New York office to go to Washington, D.C."[95] his handler appeared to agree with her informant's account in her testimony: "Well, of course not, because they don't want to get their butts chewed."[96] Conversations covertly recorded by the informant revealed his handler's frustration with her FBI supervisors, whom she referred to as "gutless" and "chicken shits." [97]

The informant later testified against those accused of the bombing. He received $1.5 million for thwarting the plot and was allegedly admitted into the federal Witness Security Program.

3.13   Fear of Deportation and Visas

The wars on drugs and terror have focused vast government resources on enforcing the immigration laws. The inception of ICE's Secure Communities Program[98] in 2008 has made the fear of deportation following an arrest or the threat of an arrest a powerful motivation for aliens in search of a visa to become informants. Visas are discussed at length in Chapter 4, "Recruiting Informants."

3.14   The Unwitting Informant

The unwitting informant[99] is not motivated by a desire either to help the police or to improve his own situation. Instead, he is unwittingly passing along criminal intelligence information to law enforcement.

His involvement generally begins after being befriended by an undercover agent or an informant. This is usually not by accident. The unwitting informant has been identified as possessing information about targeted criminal activity. He may be a member of an ongoing conspiracy and have valuable information about the criminal enterprise.

Once the relationship with the unwitting informant is established, the undercover agent uses his refined skills as an interrogator to extract as much information from the source as possible. Obviously, this must be done without raising suspicion, often an extremely delicate and sometimes dangerous task.

The CI usually capitalizes on a relationship that existed with the "unwitting" before his own involvement with the police. Very often, the informant will claim the information he obtains from the "unwitting" as his own, and the true source will remain unknown to the control agent.

Information obtained from an unwitting informant can be extremely reliable. He may be actively involved in the criminal venture he is discussing with the agent or informant and relaying firsthand information about a crime that is still in the planning stage. All information received, however, must be corroborated by the agent to maximize its value to the investigation and ensure its reliability.[100]

3.15   The Good Citizen informant

Good citizens getting involved in the fight against crime is nothing new. The year 2010 marked the 30th anniversary for "McGruff the Crime Dog." The cartoon bloodhound's caricature and motto, "Take a Bite out of Crime," has most recently been used in an awareness program against identity theft. Neighborhood Crime Watch signs are intended to tell criminals that neighbors are watching out for neighbors and will not hesitate to call the police if they observe something suspicious.

Passive anti-crime awareness programs aimed at soliciting information from ordinary citizens have proven their value. The programs pose no risk to the good citizen reporting crime being mislabeled as an informant. However, the government's aggressive approach to getting *ordinary citizens* involved in the War on Terror[101] does not come without risk. The unprecedented interaction between government agents and private citizens can become seductive. The pressure on agents to transform good citizens into informants or agents of the state is always present.[102]

3.15.1   Good Citizen or Agent of the State?

The citizen informant is motivated by a belief that there is a civic duty to report crime and suspicious activity occurring in his community to the police.[103] They often come forward with valuable information that may be used to initiate or further an ongoing criminal investigation and is generally treated as reliable.[104]

The citizen informant should neither receive nor be offered any form of compensation by police in return for his information. Unlike those informants with ulterior motives for cooperating with police, his "reward" is a sense of personal satisfaction for his contribution.

Their information is often used as probable cause in an affidavit for a search warrant. The affiant must affirmatively set forth circumstances that would allow a neutral magistrate to determine the informant's status as a citizen informer.[105]

The prosecutor is not required to establish either the credibility of the citizen informant or the reliability of his information.[106] The identity of the informant need not be disclosed.

Informant tips vary greatly in their value, credibility, and reliability.[107] If a police officer intends to utilize an informant's information in an affidavit, the details he provides should be corroborated if possible.[108] For example, a report of suspicious activity occurring repeatedly at particular times of the night would merit surveillance to determine if criminal activity was in fact being committed.[109]

However, if an unquestionably honest citizen comes forward with a report of criminal activity, which if fabricated would subject him to criminal liability, rigorous scrutiny of the basis of his knowledge is unnecessary.[110] Conversely, even if there was some measure of uncertainty[111] or suspicion of the citizen informant's motive, the more explicit and detailed description of alleged wrongdoing, along with a statement that the event was observed firsthand, entitle his tip to greater weight than might otherwise be the case.[112]

Many citizen informants occupy positions and occupations that enable them to provide "expert" information to the police. Law enforcement agencies actively encourage individuals in businesses utilized by criminals to report their suspicions.[113]

The DEA, ICE, and local police departments routinely contact employees of hotels near airports to enlist their assistance.[114] They are instructed to be suspicious of the following: guests paying for their rooms with cash, requesting adjoining rooms, refusing maid service for several days, ordering room service and rarely leaving their rooms, heavy telephone activity both incoming and outgoing, and receiving visitors at all hours of the day and night. The described behavior is indicative of drug dealing by hotel guests.

Long before September 11, 2001, airline employees had been taught to regard as suspicious cash purchases of one-way tickets by passengers with little or no luggage.[115] At that time it was drugs, not terror, that increased interaction between government agents and members of the private sector. Today, most major airports have a DEA Special Agent or plainclothes police officers assigned to the facility.

Real estate sales agents and rental agents in coastal communities are routinely contacted by investigative agencies. It is not uncommon for smugglers to either purchase or rent waterfront property to facilitate an off-loading of drugs or illegal immigrants.

Indoor marijuana-growing operations and clandestine laboratories both rely on goods and services available from legitimate businesses. In the case of growing operations, large amounts of growing medium and fertilizer are needed as well as planting containers, lights, and drip irrigation systems. Commercial outlets offer information to law enforcement agencies that is routinely investigated and developed.

The government's aggressive approach to getting "ordinary citizens" involved in law enforcement[116] can transform an otherwise good citizen informant into a cooperating individual with full informant status. The widely publicized willingness of the government to pay for information or to share in the proceeds of seized property is the leading cause of such transformations. An otherwise well-intentioned citizen may believe he is entitled to a reward for performing his civic duty.

The commercial shipping industry offers an example of the influence rewards have had. By the late 1970s, the movement of narcotics through the U.S. mail reached epidemic proportions. The U.S. Customs Service joined forces with the U.S. Postal Inspection Service and increased its enforcement efforts to stop the trend. Postal employees were instructed in the methods used to package and conceal drugs and the characteristics of postal patrons involved in criminal activity. Controlled deliveries and search warrants resulted from their tips, and well-publicized arrests followed.

Traffickers, also resilient and resourceful, moved to less risky methods of moving their product, particularly for domestic movements of packages.[117] Commercial delivery companies such as UPS, Federal Express, and the airlines all began to appear as an attractive option to the traffickers. They were particularly appealing because they were not a governmental entity: no postal inspectors = less risk.[118]

In the normal course of business, employees of package companies began discovering drug shipments, either when containers were broken or contents were legitimately examined.[119] Lost luggage, for example, is routinely opened and examined by airline employees to identify the owner in furtherance of the legitimate interests of the airline. If contraband is discovered, it is a private search.[120] A wrongful search or seizure by a private party does not violate the Fourth Amendment.[121]

The DEA began responding to the commercial discoveries and initiated an "awareness program." Agents met with and instructed the carrier employees of what to look for and whom to call when a discovery was made.

Predictably, discoveries of contraband by employees increased as more "legitimate" inspections by employees occurred. The bond between government agents and the employees grew. Had the searches been solely to assist the government agents, they may have been classified as governmental intrusions.[122]

The increasing interaction between government agents and the shippers did not immediately raise Fourth Amendment concerns. The court, in *United States v. Gumerlock,* addressed the issue.

While a certain degree of governmental participation is necessary before a private citizen is transformed into an agent of the state, de minimis or incidental contacts between the citizen and law enforcement agents before or during the course of a search or seizure will not subject the search to Fourth Amendment scrutiny. The government must be involved either directly as a participant or directly as an encourager of the private citizen's actions before we deem the citizen to be an instrument of the state.[123]

The requisite degree of governmental involvement in the inspections would require proof of more direct knowledge and acquiescence in the search. There appeared to develop a "gray area" between the extremes of overt governmental participation in a search and the complete absence of such participation.[124]

The "gray area" became somewhat better defined when an airfreight employee became "suspicious" of a package's contents. He opened the package, inspected its contents, discovered drugs, *but* admitted that he knew a reward was a possibility for his find when he contacted the DEA. There was no legitimate business need or duty present in the employee's actions, and he was found to be acting as an "agent" of the government.

In *United States v. Walther*, the court recommended that resolutions of cases falling within the "gray area" could best be resolved on a case-by-case basis with the consistent application of certain general principles. In determining whether an individual has become an "instrument or agent" of the government, two critical factors in the analysis are (1) the government's knowledge and acquiescence, and (2) the intent of the party performing the search.[125]

The court recognized the value of citizen informants in its decision by concluding,

> We do not by this opinion diminish the duty of any private citizen to report possible criminal activity, nor do we frown upon the use of paid informants. We merely hold that the government cannot knowingly acquiesce in and encourage directly or indirectly a private citizen to engage in activity that it is prohibited from pursuing where that citizen has no motivation other than the expectation of reward for his or her efforts.[126]

The DEA has required agents to refer to citizen informants in their reports as "sources of information."[127] Should a source of information seek financial compensation or become the recipient of an award from the Asset Forfeiture Fund, then he must be established and assigned a code number for purposes of payment. The source of information, however, is not considered by the DEA to be a confidential source in this type of situation, even though he received payment.[128]

Citizen informants are usually kept confidential to ensure their safety and encourage others to come forward with information. Generally, members of business organizations fitting the definition of source of information in DEA investigations are identified by name in investigative reports. However, if there is a need to preserve anonymity, but circumstances do not merit establishing the source as an informant, the term *source of information* is used. The source is fully identified in an internal memorandum that is attached to the original investigative report.[129]

3.15.2   Post-9/11 Law Enforcement and the Good Citizen

The value of the good citizen and citizen awareness programs in the War on Terror was validated on May 2, 2010, in Times Square. A T-shirt vendor spotted smoke coming from a parked SUV. The vehicle was laden with explosive material. The bomb had been ignited but did not explode. Two days later, police arrested a Pakistani-born U.S. resident on board a flight bound for Dubai. The vendor recited the "See Something, Say Something" public awareness campaign slogan for the media when interviewed.

In 2008, nearly 2000 tips credited to the program were called in to police. The New York City Police Department has established computer databases for terrorism-related information reported by private citizens. A total of five arrests are tied to the tips. Two of the arrests were terrorism-related, one for possessing bomb-making devices and one for conspiring to carry out a terrorism-related crime.

New, federally funded anti-terror citizen awareness programs bring agents into contact with thousands of potential informant candidates from all professions. The pool of new sources to draw information from is almost limitless. So is the potential of turning otherwise well-intentioned citizens into agents of the state.[130] Even more chilling is their loss of anonymity. If an arrest is made because of the source's involvement, his or her identity is no longer a secret.[131]

Endnotes

1. Remark made by Federal Judge Leo Glasser taken from the transcript of Sammy "The Bull" Gravano's 1994 sentencing hearing.
2. See *U.S. v. Salemme*, 91 F.Supp.2d 141 (D. Mass. 1999) (Wolf, J.)
3. Caniglia, J., "Informant Lies About Drug Deals," *Plain Dealer*, December 20, 2007.
4. Koran, M., "Sidebar: Cases Raise Concerns About Informant Testimony," *Wisconsin Watch*, November 24, 2013.
5. See *McIntyre v. U.S.* 477 F.Supp.2d 54, 98 (D. Mass. 2006); LEXIS 63217.
6. House Report 108–414, "Everything Secret Degenerates, The FBI's Use of Murderers as Informants," February 2, 2004.
7. Turner, K., "DEA agent indicted on perjury, civil rights charges; pleads not guilty," *Cleveland Plain Dealer*, May 13, 2009; Krouse, P., "Jury Acquits DEA Agent on All 18 Charges Related to Drug Investigation," *Cleveland Plain Dealer*, February 5, 2010.
8. See *United States v. Bernal-Obeso*, 989 F.2d 333 (9th Cir. 1993). See *United States v. Wallach*, 935 F.2d 445 (2nd Cir. 1991).

9. Trott, S.S., Senior Circuit Judge, United States Court Of Appeals, *The Use of a Criminal as a Witness: A Special Problem*, Lecture Supplement, October 2007.

10. See *United States v. Kinkle*, 631 F. Supp. 423. 425 (E.D. Pa., 1986).

11. See *United States v. Murphy*, 41 U.S. (16 Pet.) 203 (1842); *United States v. Walker*, 720 F.2d 1527 (11th Cir. 1983); *United States v. Valle-Ferrer*, 739 F.2d 545 (11th Cir. 1984).

12. A person who knowingly sells stolen property.

13. 5 Anne C.31.

14. See *United States v. Shearer*, 473 U.S. 52 (1985).

15. Department of Justice Guidelines Regarding the Use of Confidential Informants, III B. 4. See also *DEA Agents Manual*, Ch. 6612.43.

16. Murr, A., "King of the Drug Busters," *Time Magazine*, July 3, 2000, (informant paid $2.2 million by DEA). See Smith, M., "Rampant use of informants in drug cases coming under fire," *Houston Chronicle*, August 6, 2000 (U.S. Customs informant paid $2.2 million in money laundering case). See *also* Krikorian, G., "Arrest May Lead to FBI Changes," *Los Angeles Times*, April 11, 2003 (FBI informant paid $1.7 million).

17. FBI agent statement dated May 7, 2001, in Plaintiff's "Motion for Justice" in Bari/Cherney civil rights lawsuit filed against the FBI and Oakland Police, Case #C-91—1057CW (JL).

18. Green, F., "Telling on Cheats: How to Profit by Putting the IRS on the Tax Frauds Trail," *San Diego Union-Tribune*, March 29, 1998, p. 11.
    United States v. Cervantes-Pacheco, 826 F.2d 310 (5th Cir. 1987), overruling *Williamson v. United States*, 311 F.2d 441 (5th Cir. 1962). See also *United States v. Edenfield*, 995 F.2d 197 (11th Cir. 1993).

19. Messina, L., "Criminals Earn Cash, Beat Rap by Becoming Drug Informants," *Charleston Sunday Gazette–Mail*, May 10, 1998.

20. *Informants and Undercover Investigations, Contingent-Fee Arrangements*, January 1992, p. 19, Department of Justice, Office of Justice Programs, Bureau of Justice Assistance.

21. Murr, A., "King of the Drug Busters," *Newsweek*, July 3, 2000.

22. Ibid.

23. *Bennett v. Drug Enforcement Administration*, 55 F. Supp.2d 36 (1999).

24. Smith, M., "Search for Truth in Tangled Tale," *Houston Chronicle*, February 21, 2000.

25. Ibid.

26. Murr, A., "King of the Drug Busters," *Newsweek*, July 3, 2000.

27. Meyers, J., "DEA Put on Grill Over Lies by Mole," *Los Angeles Times*, March 5, 2000.

28. Smith, M., "Search for Truth in Tangled Tale," *Houston Chronicle*, February 21, 2000.

29. "Drug Informants: Motives, Methods and Management," *FBI Law Enforcement Bulletin*, 62(9), September 1993, p. 11.

30. Ibid., p. 10.

31. New South Wales Independent Commission against Corruption 1993, *Police Informants: A Discussion Paper on the Nature and the Management of the Relationship between Police and Their Informants*, ICAC, Sydney.

32. U.S. Department of Justice, Bureau of Justice Statistics, NCJ 236096.

33. International Centre for Prison Studies, April 16, 2011.
34. Liplak, A., "U.S. Prison Population Dwarfs That of Other Nations," *The New York Times*, April 23, 2008.
35. U.S. Department of Justice, Bureau of Justice Statistics, NCJ 231674.
36. *Cooperating Individual Management*, U.S. Department of Justice, DEA Office of Training, Quantico, VA.
37. *On Lee v. United States*, 343 US 747, 756 (1952).
38. Iannuzzi, J., *Cooking on the Lam*, Simon & Schuster, New York (2005).
39. "Madoff Not Diagnosed with Cancer," Reuters, August 24, 2009. Butner Medium Federal Correctional Institution is known as a "cheese factory," a nickname alluding to the many federal informants, or "rats," incarcerated there.
40. Scheck, B., Neufeld, P., and Dwyer, J., *Actual Innocence: Five Days to Execution and Other Dispatches*, Doubleday, New York (2000). ("If you can't do the time just drop a dime" and "Don't go to the pen—send a friend" attributed to notorious jailhouse informant Leslie Vernon White).
41. See *Illinois v. Perkins*, 196 U.S. 292, 110 S. Ct. 2394, 2397 (1990).
42. Hoffman, B.C., Rule 35(b) of the federal rules of criminal procedure: balancing the interests underlying sentence reduction, *Fordham Law Review*, 52(2), 1983.
43. See Trott, S.S., Senior Circuit Judge, United States Court Of Appeals, *The Use of a Criminal As a Witness: A Special Problem*, Lecture Supplement, October 2007.
44. Soble, R., "Figure in Jail Informant Probe Sentenced to Prison," *Los Angeles Times*, June 15, 1989.
45. "Investigation of the Involvement of Jail House Informants in the Criminal Justice System in Los Angeles County," *Los Angeles County Grand Jury*, June 26, 1990.
46. Scheck B. C. and Neufeld P. J., Innocence Project, Benjamin N. Cardozo School of Law, New York (1992).
47. *The Snitch System: How Incentivized Witnesses Put 38 Innocent Americans on Death Row*, The Innocence Project, Center on Wrongful Convictions, Chicago, IL (2005).
48. Ibid.
49. *U.S. v. Cervantes-Pacheco*, 826 F.2d 310.
50. *The Snitch System: How Incentivized Witnesses Put 38 Innocent Americans on Death Row*, The Innocence Project, Center on Wrongful Convictions, Chicago, IL (2005).
51. "Investigation of the Involvement of Jail House Informants in the Criminal Justice System in Los Angeles County," *Los Angeles County Grand Jury*, June 26, 1990.
52. California Penal Code § 1127(a).
53. Tarlow, B., "Silence May Not Be Golden: Jailhouse Informers and the Right to Counsel," *Champion Magazine,* May 2005.
54. U.S. Constitution, Amendment V. The Fifth Amendment privilege against compulsory self-incrimination draws with it the right to have counsel present during custodial interrogation.
55. U.S. Constitution, Amendment VI. The Sixth Amendment guarantees that "In all criminal prosecutions, the accused shall enjoy the right … to have the assistance of counsel for his defense."

56. See *Miranda v. Arizona,* 384 U.S. 436, 469, 86 S. Ct. 1602, 1625, 16 L. Ed. 2d 694 (1966).
57. Harney, M. and Cross, J.C., *The Informer in Law Enforcement,* 1968, ISBN 0398007829.
58. New South Wales Independent Commission Against Corruption 1993, *Police Informants: A Discussion Paper on the Nature and the Management of the Relationship between Police and Their Informants,* ICAC, Sydney.
59. Orecklin, M., "Oh, My God! Get Martha on the Phone," *Time,* February 16, 2004.
60. "Drug Informants: Motives, Methods and Management," *FBI Law Enforcement Bulletin,* 62(9), September 1993, p. 11.
61. Daly, R., *Prince of the City, The True Story of a Cop Who Knew Too Much,* Houghton Mifflin, Boston, MA (1978), p. 10.
62. Dershowitz, A.M., *The Best Defense,* Random House, New York (1982), p. 324.
63. Ibid.
64. Parker, R., "Confidential Informants and the Truth Finding Function," *Cooley Law Review,* 4, 1986, pp. 565–73.
65. Clarke, L., "The DEA and the Princess: A Tale of Risk and Reward," *Miami Herald,* January 24, 2009.
66. Ibid.
67. *SGS-92-X003 v. U.S.,* No. 97-579C (Filed under Seal January 27, 2009) from testimony of recruiting agent.
68. Ibid.
69. Payne, B.K. and Gainey, R.R., *Drugs and Policing: a Scientific Perspective,* Charles C. Thomas Publishing, Springfield, IL (2005).
70. Ibid.
71. Miller, J.M., "Becoming an Informant," *Justice Quarterly,* 28(2), 2011, pp. 203–220.
72. New South Wales Independent Commission Against Corruption 1993, *Police informants: A discussion paper on the nature and the management of the relationship between police and their informants,* ICAC, Sydney identifies *perverse motives* to include the desire to use the police to the detriment of the police by, for example: "framing" a police officer; "framing" an associate; getting confidence of police so as to misdirect, or mislead, them; getting confidence of police so as to obtain information on police activities, interests.
73. "Drug Informants: Motives, Methods and Management," *FBI Law Enforcement Bulletin,* 62(9), September 1993.
74. *Informant Interaction.* U.S. Department of Justice, DEA. See Report shows FBI missed Chinese spy, Mark Sherman, Associated Press, May 24, 2006.
75. Caldwell, A.A., "Slain Cartel Leader Said to Be U.S. Informant," Associated Press, July 27, 2009.
76. "Drug Informants: Motives, Methods and Management," *FBI Law Enforcement Bulletin,* 62(9), September 1993, p. 11.
77. Caldwell, A.A., "Slain Cartel Leader Said to Be U.S. Informant," Associated Press, July 27, 2009.
78. "Juarez Cartel Member Murdered in El Paso," *KTSM News,* July 28, 2009.
79. "U.S. Soldier Charged in Mexico Cartel Killing," Associated Press, August 11, 2009.

80. Levinson, D., *Encyclopedia of Crime and Punishment*, Volume 1, Sage, Thousand Oaks, CA, 2002.
81. Chase, A., "Harvard and the Making of the Unibomber," *The Atlantic Monthly*, June 2000.
82. Brooke, J., "Unabomber's Kin Collect Reward of $1 Million for Turning Him In," *New York Times*, August 21, 1998.
83. Rosenberg, E., "Big Tax on Brother's Reward for Unabomber," *San Francisco Examiner*, October 8, 1998.
84. "Keeping the Dissidents at Bay," *The Economist*, August 8, 2003.
85. Breen, S., "All Eyes on the Spy from the FBI," *Irish Times*, July 3, 2003.
86. Offenses Against the State Act 1998.
87. Ibid.
88. "FBI Agent to Tell How He Infiltrated the Real IRA," *The Sunday Evening Post Online, Independent* (Dublin), August 4, 2002.
89. Breen, S., "All Eyes on the Spy from the FBI," *Irish Times*, July 3, 2003.
90. "FBI Agent to Tell How He Infiltrated the Real IRA," *Sunday Evening Post Online, Independent*, (Dublin), August 4, 2002.
91. Hopsicker, D., *Barry and the Boys: The CIA, the Mob and America's Secret History*, Trine Day, Waterville, OH, 2006; See "Ex-Customs Informant Gets Life for Smuggling Cocaine," Associated Press, April 22, 1999.
92. Lance, P., *Triple Cross, How Bin Laden's Master Spy Penetrated the CIA, the Green Berets, and the FBI*, HarperCollins, New York, 2008.
93. Blumenthal, R., "Tapes Depict Proposal to Thwart Bomb Used in Trade Center Blast," *New York Times*, October 28, 1993.
94. Bovard, J., *Terrorism and Tyranny: Trampling Freedom, Justice and Peace to Rid the World of Evil*, Palgrave MacMillan, New York, 2003.
95. Ibid.
96. Ibid.
97. Lance, P., *Triple Cross*, HarperCollins, New York, 2007.
98. The ICE website describes the Secure Communities Program as "a simple and common sense way to carry out ICE's priorities. It uses an already-existing federal information-sharing partnership between ICE and the Federal Bureau of Investigation (FBI) that helps to identify criminal aliens without imposing new or additional requirements on state and local law enforcement."
99. See *Slade v. The Commonwealth of Virginia*, Record No. 1524-03-1, May 18, 2004 (unwitting informant gives confidential informant source for cocaine).
100. See *Henley v. United States*, 406 F.2d 705, 706 (5th Cir. 1969).
101. Hoffman, L., "Be on Terror Alert, Americans Urged," *Seattle Post Intelligencer*, May 19, 2003. The nation's domestic terrorism watchdog disseminated an "information bulletin" it hoped will perk up ordinary Americans' anti-terrorism antennas and, perhaps, stop an attack before it occurs.
102. See *U.S. v. Gumerlock*, 590 F.2d 794, 800 (9th Cir.) (en banc), cert. denied, 441 U.S. 948, 99 5. Ct. 2173, 60 L. Ed. 2d 1052 (1979).
103. See *Chambers v. Maroney*, 399 U.S. 42, 46–47 (1970); *Jaben v. United States*, 381 U.S. 214, 224 (1965).
104. See *United States v. Cova*, 585 F. Supp. 1187 (ED. Mo., 1984).
105. See *People v. Hetrick*, 590 N.Y.S.2d 183, 185–86, 604 N.E.2d 732 (N.Y., 1992).
106. See *State v. Purser*, 828 P.2d 515, 517 (Utah App.1992).

107. See *Adams v. Williams*, 407 U.S. 143, 147, 92 5. Ct., 1921, 1924, 32 L. Ed 2d 612 (1972).
108. *Illinois v. Gates*, 462 U.S. 213, 241 (1983); *Draper v. United States*, 358 U.S. 307 (1959).
109. See *United States v. Alexander*, 559 F.2d 1339, 1344 (5th Cir. 1977); *McCray v. Illinois*, 386 U.S. 300, 87 5. Ct. 1056, 18 L. Ed. 2d 62 (1967); *Bourbois v. United States*, 530 F.2d 3 (5th Cir. 1976); *Jones v. United States*, 362 U.S. 257, 271, 80 5. Ct. 725, 735 (1960).
110. See *Adams v. Williams*, 407 U.S. 143 (1972).
111. See *Davis v. State*, 447 S.E.2d 68, 70 (Ga. Ct. App., 1994); *Rynearson v. State*, 950 P.2d 147, 150–52 (Alaska Ct. App., 1997).
112. *Illinois v. Gates*, 462 U.S. 213, 103 5. Ct. 2317, 2330 (1983).
113. See *United States v. Cangiano*, 464 F.2d 320 (2nd Cir. 1972).
114. See *United States v. Reed*, 810 F. Supp. 1078, 1080 (9th Cir. 1992).
115. See *United States v. Ortiz*, 714 F. Supp. 1569 (C.D. Cal, 1989).
116. Hoffman, L., "Be on Terror Alert, Americans Urged," *Seattle Post Intelligencer*, May 20, 2003.
117. See *United States v. Pierce*, 893 F.2d 669 (5th Cir. 1990); *United States v. Blackwell*, 127 F.3d 947 (10th Cir. 1997).
118. See *United States v. Edwards*, 602 F.2d 458 (1st Cir. 1979).
119. See *United States v. Sanders*, 592 F.2d 788 (5th Cir. 1979), *rev'd*, 447 U.S. 649, 100 5. Ct. 2395 (1980); *Burdeau v. McDowell*, 256 U.S. 465, 41 5. Ct. 574, 65 L. Ed. 1048 (1921); *United States v. Lamar*, 545 F.2d 488 (5th Cir. 1977); *United States v. Blanton*, 479 F.2d 327 (5th Cir. 1973); *Barnes v. United States*, 373 F.2d 517 (5th Cir. 1967).
120. See *United States v. Gomez*, 614 F.2d 643 (9th Cir. 1979).
121. See *Walther v. United States*, 447 U.S. 649, 100 5. Ct. 2395, 65 L. Ed. 2d 410, 417 (1980).
122. See *Corngold v. United States*, 367 F.2d 1 (9th Cir. 1966) (en banc).
123. 590 F.2d 794, 800 (9th Cir.) (en banc), *cert. denied*, 441 U.S. 948, 99 5. Ct. 2173, 60 L. Ed. 2d 1052 (1979).
124. *United States v. Sherwin*, 539 F.2d 1 (9th Cir. 1976) (en banc).
125. 652 F.2d 788 (9th Cir. 1981).
126. Ibid.
127. *DEA Agents Manual*, Ch. 66.
128. Ibid.
129. Ibid.
130. See *U.S. v. Gumerlock*, 590 F.2d 794, 800 (9th Cir.) (en banc), *cert. denied*, 441 U.S. 948, 99 S. Ct. 2173, 60 L. Ed. 2d 1052 (1979).
131. See *U.S. v. Walther*, 652 F.2d 788 (9th Cir. 1981).

Recruiting Informants

4

4.1 Introduction

The ability to effectively recruit informants is perhaps the most frequently encountered skill possessed by successful police officers, detectives, and federal agents. Remarkably, relatively little formal training is provided on the subject of cultivating and recruiting informants. Instead, agents and police officers alike are often left to rely on experience and common sense as they search out potential informants.

The importance of the informant recruitment process is often overlooked. As a veteran prosecutor, now a federal judge, warned, "After 40 years in our justice system, I conclude that the greatest threat to the integrity of our justice process and to its truth seeking mission—indeed, even to prosecutors themselves—comes from informers poorly chosen for their roles and then carelessly managed and handled."[1]

Informants are an extremely valuable law enforcement tool and the secret to the successful conclusion of many criminal investigations.[2] The Drug Enforcement Administration (DEA), in the course of an official investigation into its informant program, claimed it could not accomplish its mission without confidential informants (CI).[3]

Admitting to reliance on informants does not diminish the value of crime-scene investigations and the collection of extremely valuable physical evidence. But often at crime scenes there is no evidence to collect, and when evidence does exist it sometimes leads nowhere. In many cases, informants are responsible for a suspect's ultimate arrest.[4]

Crimes like armed robberies aren't "solved" as one might imagine. Most detective work is either looking for or waiting for someone to tell an investigator what happened before an arrest can be made. That "someone" is usually an informant. Although the source's tip may not be enough for an arrest, it can provide enough information or leads for the case to be exceptionally cleared[5] and closed.

The same holds true for organized crime and drug and terrorism investigations. Although dogged detective work may be required, most complex conspiracy investigations are successful only through the use of informants and cooperating witnesses.

The DEA emphasizes to new agents during basic training that recruiting and operating confidential sources will be an intrinsic part of their duties. They are instructed that "the use of informants in drug enforcement is so fundamental as to be considered the single most elemental technique available to the Special Agent. As such, it is essential that the successful drug enforcement agent develop and continuously expand the skills required to develop, maintain, and utilize these vital human resources."[6]

4.2   Outsourcing Undercover Work

In the not-so-distant past, it was routine for agents and police officers to assume undercover roles to penetrate criminal organizations. It's a role increasingly being taken over by informants. The protracted use of law enforcement officers in long-term undercover operations has proved to be extremely dangerous, controversial, and costly.

Investigators continue to work undercover, but most of the dirty work associated with covert operations has in a sense been outsourced to informants. A veteran gang investigator for the Los Angeles County Sheriff Department noted, "Despite what you might have seen on TV or the movies, law enforcement today almost never uses undercover officers to infiltrate dangerous criminal organizations. Yes, they use electronic surveillance tactics, but they need informants, confidential sources, cooperating witnesses, and snitches."[7]

The use of informants in lieu of undercover agents has its drawbacks. Their guile and ruthlessness, the very attributes that make them desirable as informants, also make them difficult to control. One veteran DEA agent explained, "Informers are running today's drug investigations, not the agents. Agents have become so dependent on informers that the agents are at their mercy."[8]

4.3   Pressure to Recruit Informants

Federal Bureau of Investigation (FBI) agents are expected to recruit quality informants immediately following graduation from the FBI Academy. An excerpt from the *FBI Manual of Investigative Operations and Guidelines* explains:

> Each Agent involved in investigative activity is obligated to develop and operate productive informants. Those Agents who cannot develop productive informants must overcome the lack of informants through some other substantial contribution, such as the continued development during investigative assignments of Cooperative Witnesses. The proper operation of informants is a basic skill that requires dedication and ingenuity. The success each Agent enjoys normally depends on the strength of the Agent's personality and resourcefulness exercised in obtaining information.[9]

One agent described the importance recruiting informants had in his career in this way: "Informant development and informant handling was my specialty throughout most of my FBI career. I worked OC [organized crime] for approximately sixteen of my twenty-two years. I worked, handled, developed, or attempted to develop literally hundreds of individuals as informants. I handled seven Top Echelon [TE] informants including a Mafia member informant ... I received two cash-incentive awards for my work with informants. My two letters of censure from the FBI, neither of which I am ashamed, was because of overzealousness in my informant work."[10]

4.4   Recruiting Guidelines

As valuable as informants may be to the overall mission of law enforcement, their use has proved to be extremely problematic. Informants have been the direct cause of police corruption, false convictions, and the death of officers and innocent citizens alike. Lax or nonexistent guidelines governing the recruitment and operation of informants have been blamed for the scandals.

The FBI has had its share of informant-related scandals. One prompted a congressional investigation. In 2004, the House Committee on Government Reform issued a damning report entitled *Everything Secret Degenerates: The FBI's Use of Murderers as Informants.*[11] The scandal stemmed, as the title suggests, from the FBI's recruitment of murderers as informants.

During the recruiting stage, the FBI is supposed to consider the following factors[12] in determining an individual's suitability to become an informant:

1. Whether the person appears to be in a position to provide information concerning violations of law that are within the scope of authorized FBI investigative activity
2. Whether the individual is willing to voluntarily furnish information to the FBI
3. Whether the individual appears to be directed by others to obtain information from the FBI
4. Whether there is anything in the individual's background that would make him or her unfit for use as an informant
5. Whether the nature of the matter under investigation and the importance of the information being furnished to the FBI outweigh the seriousness of any past or contemporaneous criminal activity of which the informant may be suspected
6. Whether the motives of the informant in volunteering to assist the FBI appear to be reasonable and proper

7. Whether the information that the informant can provide could be obtained in a more timely and effective manner through other sources or by a less intrusive means
8. Whether the informant is sufficiently reliable and trustworthy, and whether there is an adequate means by which to verify his or her truthfulness
9. Whether the individual appears to be willing to conform to FBI and attorney general guidelines regarding his or her operation
10. Whether the FBI will be able to adequately monitor and control the activities of the informant
11. Whether his or her use as an investigative technique will intrude on privileged communications or inhibit the lawful association of individuals or the expression of ideas
12. Whether the use of the informant could compromise an investigation or subsequent prosecution that may require the government to move for a dismissal of the case

4.5   Realities of the Law Enforcement Profession

Once an officer leaves the police station or an agent leaves the federal building, he or she is very much on their own. Self-motivation, strength of character, and common sense are the only reliable guidance available as he or she interacts with the cast of characters who inhabit the streets and who may hold potential as informants.

Discretion, particularly the discretion to arrest or not arrest an individual, is perhaps their greatest power. This power also serves as an extremely effective informant-recruiting tool.

4.6   Working Off a Charge: The Quid Pro Quo of the Street

The nation's 800,000 police officers are the gatekeepers of the justice system. They are also the members of the criminal justice system most frequently encountered by criminals. Officers are granted broad discretion in determining whom to arrest and whom to release. It's a subjective decision often influenced by a suspect's willingness to become an informant and the story he or she has to tell.

Offering an arrested individual or one facing imminent arrest the opportunity to cooperate as a way to mitigate his or her situation is the technique most frequently used to recruit an informant. The suspect knows that once the criminal justice system ball starts rolling, it is difficult to stop. The suspect also knows that informally negotiating away criminal liability with a police officer in exchange for promised cooperation[13] can halt the arrest process. It is a get-out-of-jail-free card regularly cashed in by accused criminals across the United States. Some continue working as informants for protracted periods out of fear that charges will be filed unless they continue to provide information.

After the fear factor subsides and if rapport is established with the recruiting officer, informants recruited in this fashion very often continue supplying information. Petty criminals, usually those plying the so-called victimless crimes like pimping, prostitution, and small-time drug dealing, may be given an unofficial free pass to work the street during their recruiter's shift. Their identities and assistance never become known to the department employing the police officer. If arrested by another officer, informants use their recruiter's name in the hope that it will help their situation.

On the street, it's known as working off a charge, flipping, rolling over, cutting a deal, or doing the right thing. These are the terms for a process that, for cops and criminals alike, streamlines the criminal justice system. It's meted out daily in alleys, squad cars, and in the confines of police interrogation rooms. Remarkably, the practice goes without a legal term. Quite often, the entire process begins with a field interrogation[14] or a stop and frisk[15] designed to give the impression of escalating into an arrest situation.

Cutting a deal removes the players that many officers view as impediments to getting their job done: defense attorneys, prosecutors, and judges. It may be far more effective to make a deal directly with the criminal on the street.

There is an endless stream of suspects who have contact with police each day, though only a fraction enters the criminal justice system as defendants. However, every person who finds himself or herself being field-interrogated or arrested holds the potential of becoming a new informant.

An old police expression sums up the dilemma a field interrogation that seems to be escalating to arrest presents to potential informants: "You might beat the rap, but you won't beat the ride."[16] An officer can make it clear to the suspect that failure to cooperate will land him or her in jail for a crime he or she may or may not have committed. Some officers are willing to resort to creative writing, otherwise known as perjury, to justify the arrest.

4.7 Fabricating Probable Cause and Perjury

A 2011 study conducted in New Jersey found that on occasion police fabricated facts following arrests that were made without probable cause:

> In such cases, the officer(s) reported facts necessary to establish reasonable suspicion for a stop and then probable cause for an arrest. The officer(s) reported those facts as if they occurred before the arrest, denying the facts as

they actually occurred. Said differently, the police reports in question create an impression that officers undertook an illegal search or seizure, discovered contraband, and then created an account of the facts that legally justified their actions. At the time the arrest was made, the totality of the circumstances were already known, and by working backwards, officers were able to fill in the previously unknown gaps that existed before they acted. Under these circumstances officers must perjure themselves first in the official report, then again at the Grand Jury, then again in open court by testifying to a fact pattern where the ordering of the events are not accurate, or at least the facts as reported were not known to them *before* they took action.[17]

4.8   Fighting the Charges

Although the suspect might win in court, he or she is still going to take the ride to jail. Beating the rap is another matter.

If he or she has the money to post bail, he or she will get out and hire a lawyer. Many do not have money for bail and must remain in custody until their case is called. At this point, their only hope is to be released on their own recognizance. Much depends on what the arresting officer wrote in his or her arrest report. Many find it a good time to reconsider becoming an informant.

Most defendants, particularly those charged with a federal violation, are initially denied bond prior to trial.[18] Federal judicial officers deny bond if it is determined that a release will not reasonably ensure the appearance of the person as required or will endanger the safety of another person[19] or the community.[20] Most defendants seem to fit this description and stay in jail until trial. Cooperation will almost always result in a favorable recommendation by the prosecutor for a bond or recognizance release.

If the defendant decides to fight the charges, he or she gets a public defender. Known in prison circles as the "public pretender," they are often inexperienced lawyers just beginning their legal careers. This is not always the case. Some are top-notch professionals who have chosen to serve indigent clients, foregoing the lucrative private practice. Regardless, most are overworked, underpaid, and, regrettably, often the quickest to plead their client guilty. It's the price paid by the accused for not accepting the pitch to cooperate.

Obviously, not everyone stopped by police and briefly questioned, or even subjected to a stop and frisk,[21] becomes an informant. However, the New York City Police Department does keep records on the number of individuals who are stopped and questioned by police based on little more than a hunch. From 2004 through 2009, there were three million street stops of "suspicious subjects" in New York City.[22] Only 1 in 10 of those stopped was arrested.[23] Most of those questioned were young black and Hispanic males.[24] All had the opportunity to receive the informant-recruiting pitch. There is no indication of how many became informants.

We do not know how many stop-and-frisk encounters escalate into the arrest of the suspect. But we do know how many people actually have the jail door close behind them. According to the FBI,[25] more than 12 million people were arrested in 2012.[26]

4.9   Timing the Recruiting Effort

Timing is critical when attempting to flip an arrestee. One drug informant recounted being told by agents immediately following his arrest that "[t]here was a red, white and blue bus coming down the road and there was one seat left on it, and if I didn't get on it, it would run me over."[27]

At the moment of arrest, the suspect is unnerved, confused, frightened, angry, and/or experiencing a combination of these emotions. Their fight-or-flight rush has drained them, so whichever option they pick, the result is the same. He or she has likely stared down the barrel of a Glock pistol and been thrown to the ground, handcuffed, searched, and placed in the back of a police car.

If he's been through the system before, he knows exactly what awaits him: transportation to the nearest jail to be fingerprinted, photographed, and strip-searched; have his body cavities probed; and be sprayed down for lice. He'll be placed in the "bullpen"[28] with other inmates where one open toilet serves all. His physical stature and demeanor will determine whether or not he's raped. If he's new to the system, and the police are interested in turning him, they will graphically describe what awaits him.

The most important thing to the arresting officer is that the individual hasn't "lawyered up"[29] yet, as a request for a lawyer often stops the flipping process dead in its tracks.[30] The arrest goes forward, a prosecutor is assigned, and a defense attorney enters the picture. This is not to say that deal-making opportunities have evaporated; it just becomes more complicated when an attorney is retained or appointed.[31]

If the suspect's arrest was designed to recruit him or her,[32] the takedown should have occurred discreetly and without fanfare. If not, word of the arrest spreads quickly on the street, and once he is booked into jail, his value as an informant rapidly diminishes. His criminal associates will learn of the arrest, usually through bail bondsmen, defense attorneys, or jail personnel, which is indicative of how far and quickly courthouse gossip spreads.

News of the arrest damages the defendant's future value as an informant, as his criminal associates know how the system works and will keep their distance from him. An arrest can be the scarlet letter[33] of the streets.

Cutting a deal is a straightforward pitch: become an informant, "make a few cases," and it will be as if the crime you committed never happened—no jail, no bail bondsman, no defense attorney, no trial, and no record. Agree and you are *unarrested*.

Making a case usually translates to going undercover and, in most cases, purchasing drugs or other contraband from friends or criminal associates, with the transactions being secretly recorded. The contraband and tape recordings become evidence for later prosecution of the target, and they may also be used to convince the new target to cooperate.

If a deal with the new target isn't cut, the individual is arrested and booked into jail. In extreme cases, the detective may "snitch jacket" the defendant. Snitch jacketing[34] is accomplished by planting false information with the jail population or corrections staff that labels the defendant as an informant. The consequences for the inmate can be devastating.[35]

4.10 Squeezing Suspects

Police "squeeze" prospective defendant informants by threatening to file additional charges or counts related to their pending case if they do not become an informant or cooperating witness.[36] Many of the targets are incarcerated, and the threat of snitch jacketing may also be mentioned as an added incentive to cooperate.

One informant described how squeezing occurs: "They made me an offer I couldn't refuse. Are you with us or against us? I imagined another indictment for racketeering, or organized crime, with a minimum of life, which means 25 years or more, and me without a lawyer, broke and more cooked than fish in a pan, in other words, fried."[37]

Those who succumb find themselves in a form of legal limbo. The newly minted informant's immediate future is determined by his or her control officer. Play by the rules and perform to the officer's satisfaction, and additional charges are not filed. Fail to live up to the control agent's expectations, and all deals are off. The irony is that the unfiled charges used as leverage may not exist.

4.11 Cultivating Informants

Investigators often use creative recruiting strategies for individuals not subject to arrest. The recruiting officer's experience usually dictates the effectiveness of the effort. As a result of intelligence information received from informants or as a judgment based on experience, the investigator believes that with the correct amount of pressure or persuasion a person can be convinced to become an informant.

The pressure may take the form of either a hint of a pending arrest or the very direct threat of prosecution for a crime. Agents may offer to back off from their investigation into the prospective informant's own criminal operation in return for cooperation.[38] Regardless, the suspect does not know the extent of his or her exposure to prosecution.

The method selected for exerting the pressure varies and is limited only by the imagination, experience, and skill of the investigator. Generally, it will take the form of a chance encounter on the street, an unannounced visit to the target's home or workplace, or requesting the individual to come to the investigator's office. Often, however, the subject may be left to contemplate his future with the agent's telephone number as the only way out.[39]

4.12   Offering Protection

Recruiters are skilled at capitalizing on a variety of incentives when flipping criminals. Fear often tops the list, with a desire for revenge coming in a close second. Even members of the hierarchy of criminal organizations are vulnerable to fear-based recruiting pitches. A promise of a lifetime of protection in the federal Witness Security Program (WITSEC) can provide the leverage to seal a cooperation deal. WITSEC satisfies an informant's desire to live and protect his family. At the same time, it allows him to exact revenge in the form of testimony on his source of peril.

A comedy of mafioso errors demonstrates the power of WITSEC as a recruiting tool. In August 1990, two corrupt New York Police Department (NYPD) detectives who moonlighted as mob hit men and later earned the title "Mafia Cops"[40] had valuable inside police information for a ranking mobster. They tipped off the Luchese crime boss known as "Little Al"[41] that fellow capo Bruno Facciolo was a government informant. The information turned out to be a windfall for the FBI, producing a pair of unlikely informants.

A contract on the turncoat's life was issued almost immediately. Facciolo was stabbed; shot through both eyes; and, to make sure the job was done, shot one more time in the head. To send the message home that ratting on the Mafia wasn't tolerated, a dead canary was stuffed in Facciolo's mouth.[42] The killing and the gory details were all over the news. Mobsters thinking about informing had to have taken note of the choreographed murder.

Several months after the Facciolo killing, Little Al got an unexpected visit from two FBI agents. He'd soon learn that an informant reported that one of his management decisions didn't go over well with Mafia higher-ups. The agents told him he was marked for death after botching the murder of "Big Pete,"[43] a former Luchese captain who was believed to have turned informant. It was Little Al's job to neutralize the alleged defector. The kill order went out, but something went wrong. Big Pete was shot 12 times, but he miraculously survived to make it to the witness stand in a wheelchair. Doctors credited his survival to his 500-lb. girth. Little Al failed to do a follow-up on the botched hit. That omission proved to be a life-altering mistake.

As a further warning to Big Pete to stop snitching, his wife's life was threatened by mobsters. As it turned out, Pete was not an informant. Having been charged with racketeering, he merely pleaded guilty to lesser charges to avoid a long sentence. Although it had all the earmarks of an informant deal, Big Pete had not crossed the line.

His shooting, coupled with the death threats against his wife, made him a prime target for an informant-recruiting pitch by the FBI. Big Pete succumbed and became a government witness in a bid-rigging case that involved three New York crime families. During testimony in one of the trials, he claimed to have undergone a "transformation from a violent criminal to a man with a conscience." He was asked by the prosecutor, "What was it sir that caused this transformation?" Big Pete replied, "I was shot twelve times."[44] In return for his testimony, he received no prison time for racketeering and was awarded WITSEC protection for himself and his family.[45]

The FBI agent who issued the warning to Little Al recalled: "When we told him there was a contract out on him, all he said was 'OK'."[46] Several days later, almost as if on the bureau's schedule, he appeared at the FBI office in Westchester, New York. He agreed to begin cooperating in return for protection.

Little Al was far from being a run-of-the-mill informant. He has testified in trials for nearly two decades, bringing down the mob hierarchy in countless cases. His 2006 testimony was instrumental in putting away the NYPD Mafia Cops for life for eight mob-ordered murders.[47]

4.13   Walk-In Informant

Whereas some informants have to be cultivated before being successfully recruited, others volunteer information. The term "walk-in informant" does not describe a recruiting technique. Rather, it literally depicts how the informant's relationship with law enforcement began: the individual walked into the police department or federal agency field office to offer his services as an informant. Since no arm-twisting or inducement brought them in, their motives should be suspect.

These individuals merit discussion because they were not sought out by the law enforcement agency as potential informants. The walk-in may have his own agenda and pose an unexpected risk to his handler and the recruiting agency.

Local police narcotics units generally assign a detective to meet with and screen walk-ins. Often, they are unstable individuals imagining criminal activity where none exists. Although the temptation may be great to dismiss walk-ins as a waste of time, very often they provide worthwhile information. Once their information is evaluated as being of value, the informant is assigned to a detective or an agent for further development.

"Operation Swordfish," the DEA's first and arguably most successful international money laundering case, owed much of its success to a walk-in. The lead informant in the case was previously unknown to the DEA. He simply arrived at its doorstep offering information and services.[48] A total of 61 arrests were made at the conclusion of Swordfish.

4.14   Historical Cases

Federal agencies encourage agents in search of new informants and cooperating witnesses to examine old or closed cases.[49] Interviewing an incarcerated defendant can lead to either a new investigation or the indictment of additional defendants and reopening the closed case.

Often referred to as historical cases, the task of examining the cases is usually left to new agents without informants. Defendants already serving time for their participation in a conspiracy ordinarily will no longer have a legal privilege to refuse to testify.[50]

Prisoners serving their sentences and wishing to become informants often contact agents. Those defendants who rejected the offer to provide substantial assistance at the time of their arrest or pending trial often have a change of heart after beginning to serve their sentence. In prison, the term "getting on the bus" for a trip to court (to testify) is a frequent topic among inmates hoping for a reduced sentence.[51]

Inmates who do not flip may continue to be the target of recruitment efforts by agents. They will pressure him with the threat of further prosecution if he refuses to cooperate.

4.15   Illegal Aliens and Snitch Visas

Federal agents and police seeking to recruit legal and illegal aliens who are facing the threat of arrest have an incredible weapon at their disposal: deportation. Under a new Immigration and Customs Enforcement (ICE) policy announced in December 2012, agents may issue detainers for those convicted or charged with a felony; with three or more misdemeanor convictions, excluding traffic offenses and other minor crimes; and whose misdemeanors are more serious, such as offenses involving violence or driving under the influence.

The *Los Angeles Times* reported that of the more than 230,000 people deported since the ICE program's inception, about 30% were convicted of a crime no more serious than a misdemeanor. The message delivered while attempting to recruit an alien in legal trouble is straightforward: become an informant and your immigration problems are resolved.

Those with immigration problems who are approached by agents seeking information and refuse to cooperate are often arrested and held for deportation. Two Islamic religious leaders, one in Miami, Florida, and one in New York City, were at this writing in court contesting deportation. Both claim the move to deport them was prompted when they refused to become FBI informants.[52] The Muslim American Society Immigrant Justice Center is representing several other Muslims fighting deportation based on similar claims of resisting pressure to become FBI sources.

Most aliens who become informants or cooperating witnesses are promised legal residency at the conclusion of their work.[53] Many are promised nondeportation or other immigration benefits.[54] The deals are seldom reduced to writing. Some informants find themselves fighting deportation when their relationship with the government comes to an end.[55]

4.15.1 S Visas

S visas, informally known as "snitch visas," have become a powerful informant-recruiting tool. The visas allow federal, state, and local investigators and prosecutors to offer witnesses and informants an avenue through which they can maintain nonimmigrant status in the United States in exchange for their cooperation in investigations and prosecutions of criminal organizations and terrorist activities.

The S visa was created in response to the 1993 bombing of the World Trade Center. Congress amended the Immigration and Nationality Act to include the new "S" nonimmigrant visa category for alien witnesses and informants. The visas became part of the Violent Crime Control Act of 1994.[56]

The provision establishing the S visa program was originally set to expire on September 13, 1999; ironically, Congress extended it until September 13, 2001. About 2 days after the events of 9/11, Senator Edward Kennedy introduced legislation providing permanent authority for the S visa program. Both the Senate and the House passed the law by unanimous consent within 2 days.[57]

The Justice Department wasted no time in its push to recruit potential terrorist informants. On November 29, 2001, Attorney General John Ashcroft announced the "Responsible Cooperators Program." It was an unprecedented informant-recruiting drive that sought out all non-U.S. citizens present in the United States or who sought to enter the United States to come forward to the FBI with any valuable information they had to aid the war on terrorism. In return, the Department of Justice promised to assist the informants in obtaining S visas.[58]

According to the former head of the National Security Division of the Justice Department during the Bush administration, "The essence of the S visa is there's people who are in the U.S. who you would want their cooperation in the context of a criminal case, and you can gain them status in the U.S. so they can live here and work here and even have a path toward becoming a lawful permanent resident if they are granted an S visa."[59] The only individuals specifically excluded from consideration are Nazis or perpetrators of torture or genocide.

A former federal prosecutor and immigration official characterized what is expected of informants aspiring to gain an S visa: "The evidence that is provided by these criminal defendants and terrorists has to be *extraordinary.*"[60] She recalled, "When I was a prosecutor, I remember that almost every foreign national that was a defendant in one of my cases wanted this visa."[61]

4.15.2   S-5 Visas and Criminal Investigations

The provision for S visas includes two categories: S-5 and S-6 visas. The S-5 visa may be granted to a foreign national who has been determined by the attorney general to possess critical, reliable information concerning a criminal organization or enterprise.

The alien must be willing to supply or must have supplied the information to federal or state law enforcement authorities, or to a federal or state court. The attorney general must also determine that the alien's presence in the United States is essential to the success of an authorized criminal investigation or to the successful prosecution of an individual involved in a criminal organization or enterprise. The number of witnesses or informants granted S-5 status is capped at 200 per year. The limit has never been met.

4.15.3   S-6 Visas and Terror Investigations

The S-6 visa may be granted to an alien who the attorney general and the secretary of state have determined to possess critical, reliable information concerning a terrorist organization, operation, or enterprise and who is willing to supply or have supplied information to federal law enforcement authorities or to any federal court. Both the attorney general and the Secretary are required to determine that the alien has been or will be placed in danger as a result of providing information. The number of informants granted S-6 visas is capped at 50 per year.

An enticing aspect of both S-5 and S-6 visa programs is their generous treatment of the informant's family members. Spouses, married or unmarried children, and parents are awarded S-7 visas. There is no limit on the number of S-7 visas the government can issue.

To get the process started, a federal law enforcement officer operating an alien informant must complete the six-page Interagency Alien Witness and Informant Record application.[62] The law enforcement agency making the application is responsible for the alien from the time of their admission until their departure from the United States. Every three months, the control agent is required to complete a quarterly report detailing the informant's whereabouts and activities for the Justice Department's Criminal Division.

Moreover, the agent must certify that he or she will be responsible for controlling the informant and monitoring his activity.[63]

4.15.4   T Visas and Federal Human Trafficking Investigations

The T visa[64] differs significantly from the S visa in that it is considered a victim witness classification.[65] It is designated for those who are or have been victims of severe forms of human trafficking, including commercial sexual exploitation and forced labor.[66] The T visa allows victims to remain in the United States to assist federal authorities in the investigation and prosecution of human trafficking cases.

The T visa was originally designed for victims and witnesses in federal prosecutions. That isn't necessarily a bar for local prosecutors and law enforcement officers seeking to use the visa as an informant-recruiting tool. They can assist the witness in applying for the visa with a Form I-914, "Application for T Nonimmigrant Status." As an added incentive, the recruiting investigator or prosecutor can promise to submit a law enforcement endorsement form.[67] The endorsement is encouraged by the ICE.

To qualify for the visa, applicants must have complied with all reasonable requests for assistance in the investigation and prosecution of trafficking crimes and would suffer extreme hardship involving unusual and severe harm on removal.[68] A prospective T visa applicant with a criminal record is not barred from consideration.[69]

T visas expire 4 years from the date of approval. The visa may be extended if law enforcement officials certify that the alien's presence is necessary to assist in the investigation or prosecution of trafficking crimes. After 3 years of continuous presence in the United States, the alien can apply for permanent residence.[70]

T visa recipients are eligible to be certified for refugee benefits.[71] The benefits can include housing assistance, cash assistance, Medicaid, and other social services. They are also eligible for employment authorization by the ICE. Once a T visa is granted, a victim can apply for permanent residence in the United States. An alien who has applied or been granted a T visa may apply for admission of certain immediate family members.[72]

4.15.5   U Visas and State and Non-Federal Trafficking Prosecutions

The U visa[73] can also be used as an informant- and cooperating witness–recruiting tool in the investigation of crimes related to human trafficking.[74] To become eligible for the visa, the individual must have assisted, be currently assisting, or be likely to assist in the investigation and/or prosecution of a criminal case.[75] Crimes covered include violations of state and local laws. Consequently, state prosecutors as well as state and local law enforcement officers can offer assistance in obtaining the U visa in exchange for cooperation and testimony.[76]

Congress limited the amount of U visas to 10,000 per fiscal year. Once a U visa is granted, a recipient can apply for permanent residence after 3 years. An alien who has been granted a U visa may apply for admission of immediate family members.

4.15.6   Continued Presence

Continued presence (CP) is a temporary immigration status that allows victims of human trafficking to remain in the United States during the ongoing investigation into the human trafficking–related crimes committed against them. CP is initially granted for 1 year and may be renewed in 1-year increments.[77] Aliens granted CP are allowed to work while in the United States.

4.15.7   Significant Public Benefit Parole and Ongoing Criminal Investigations

Significant public benefit parole (SPBP) may be utilized by federal, state, and local prosecutors and investigators to bring alien informants, cooperating witnesses, and defendants (who are otherwise inadmissible) into the United States to assist with ongoing investigations, prosecutions, or other activities "necessary to protect national security and that are beneficial to the United States."[78] An alien is initially paroled into the United States for a specified time ranging from 1 day to 1 year. Individuals granted SPBP have been used undercover in federal drug investigations.

Parole does not constitute a formal admission to the United States and confers only temporary authorization to be present in the country. In extremely limited cases, the alien's immediate family members may also be admitted who are at risk due to the principal parolee's cooperation with a law enforcement agency.[79] SPBP requests for family members require the law enforcement agency to submit a threat assessment. Employment authorization may also be granted.[80]

4.15.8   Deferred Action

There is no statutory definition of deferred action (DA), but federal regulations provide a description: "[D]eferred action [is] an act of administrative convenience to the government which gives some cases lower priority."[81] Basically, DA means the government has decided that it is not in its interest to arrest, charge, prosecute, or remove an individual for a specific, articulable reason.

Two distinct types of DA requests are made to ICE by prosecutors and investigators: those seeking DA based on sympathetic facts and a low-enforcement priority, and those seeking DA based on their status as important cooperating witnesses in an investigation or prosecution.

DA does not confer any immigration status on an alien, nor is it in any way a reflection of an alien's immigration status. The fact that an alien has been granted DA does not preclude the ICE from commencing removal proceedings at any time against him or her.

Requests for DA can be made by federal, state, and local law enforcement agencies. The alien cooperating witness need not be in custody when the request is made. DAs are granted for a specific period of time but can be terminated at any time by the ICE.

4.15.9   Administrative Stay of Removal

Administrative stay of removal (ASR) is a discretionary tool that permits ICE to temporarily delay the removal of an alien. ICE will stay the removal of an alien in two limited circumstances: (1) where immediate removal is not practicable or proper, or (2) where the alien is needed to testify in the prosecution of a case involving a violation of federal or state law.[82]

4.15.10   Breaking Visa Promises

Informants in several highly publicized cases report that police and federal agents, particularly ICE agents, fail to deliver on their promise to apply for cooperation-related visas. Several informants have been arrested and slated for deportation despite having served as informants or cooperating witnesses. Two were spared when pleas to a congressman were heard, and a rare bill was passed granting them legal status.[83]

Headlines like "Informants for Feds Face Deportation: Immigrant Siblings Say Government Reneged on Promise of Special Visa"[84] and "ICE Burns Informants Across the Country"[85] sum up the claims of broken promises alleged to have been made by federal agents when recruiting informants. It is important to remember that only ICE can grant visas and is not bound by promises regarding nondeportation or any immigration benefits made by other law enforcement agencies or prosecutors.[86]

4.17   Recruiting Terror Informants

Historically, recruiting members of ideologically driven movements and organizations as informants has proved more difficult than flipping common criminals. The benchmark of a botched attempt at recruiting an ideologue as an informant culminated in a bloodbath followed by costly civil litigation.

Randall Weaver first came to the attention of the U.S. Secret Service in 1985. According to one of the organization's paid informants, he had ties to the Aryan Nations, a violent white supremacist group. The CI told his handlers that Weaver had a large cache of illegal weapons and ammunition hidden at his mountaintop home.[87]

The chain of events leading to what became known as "the siege at Ruby Ridge" began as a failed attempt to recruit Weaver as an informant for the Bureau of Alcohol, Tobacco, Firearms, and Explosives (ATF). Weaver, a former member of the U.S. Army's special forces, had moved to northern Idaho with his wife to begin living an uncomplicated life.

In October 1989, at the direction of ATF agents, the informant brought two shotguns to Weaver, offering to pay him for sawing off the barrels. The informant secretly recorded that conversation and the one when the sawed-off shotguns were delivered. The ATF now had a chargeable offense to use as leverage in its recruitment of Weaver as an Aryan Nations informant.[88] The informant was paid $5000 for his work and was promised more if Weaver was convicted.

In June 1990, ATF agents, without having obtained an indictment, arranged for a chance meeting with Weaver outside a Sandpoint, Idaho, motel. After he was shown photographs of the shotguns and given the opportunity to listen to a tape recording of the sale, he was offered a deal: inform on the Aryan Nations, and the case against him would go away.[89]

Weaver declined their offer, refusing to become an informant. On December 13, 1990, six months after the failed recruitment effort, he was indicted for manufacturing and possessing an unregistered firearm.[90] The agent in charge of obtaining the warrant had told the prosecutor that Weaver was a convicted felon, suspected of robbing banks in Montana. Neither allegation was true,[91] but the recruiting drive was still in play.

Weaver was arrested and was again offered the opportunity to become an informant. Resisting the pressure, he used his home to secure bond for his release and wanted a trial.

The effort to recruit Weaver found its way into the federal courthouse. The U.S. magistrate told him that if he was convicted at trial, his home would be forfeited to pay the cost of his court-appointed lawyer. That was a lie, but it was one that Weaver believed. He left court under the impression that if he failed to win his case he'd lose the only thing he owned.[92] He and his family would be homeless. The pressure to flip was intense.

Weaver didn't show up on the appointed date for trial. A U.S. probation officer had written Weaver a letter giving him the wrong date to appear in court.[93] A warrant for his arrest was issued.

Attempts to arrest Weaver at his mountaintop home were a catastrophe: on the first attempt to arrest Weaver in August 1992, his 13-year-old son, Sammy, and his yellow Labrador retriever were shot and killed by a deputy U.S. marshal. Weaver wouldn't give up, and a weeklong siege of his residence by government agents commenced. In the siege, Weaver's wife, Vicki, holding their infant daughter, was shot and killed by an FBI sniper. Weaver and a visiting friend were also seriously wounded by sniper fire. Both were taken into custody and held without bond until trial.

A jury acquitted Weaver of the firearms charges. Weaver sued the FBI in federal court. The government reluctantly awarded $3.1 million to what was left of the Weaver family in an out-of-court settlement.

The arrest and prosecution of Weaver probably cost more than the settlement. Putting the handcuffs on Weaver required the following:

- 52 FBI hostage-rescue team members
- 60 Marshals Service Special Operations Group personnel
- 41 FBI Special Weapons and Tactics Team members
- 3 ATF special agents
- 8 Marshals Service management personnel
- 15 marshals directly involved in the Ruby Ridge crisis
- 4 FBI negotiators
- 43 Idaho state police officers
- 26 members of other law enforcement agencies
- 31 FBI field office personnel
- 17 FBI laboratory personnel
- 30 other persons involved with the prosecution, including personnel from the U.S. Attorney's Office and U.S. Probation Office

4.18   The New FBI: A Global Counterintelligence Organization

A November 2004 secret directive from the White House to the FBI demanded more terror informants. It cited "human source development and management"[94] as a top priority for the FBI's counterterrorism program.

The Uniting and Strengthening America by Providing Appropriate Tools Required to Intercept and Obstruct Terrorism (USA PATRIOT) Act, passed shortly after 9/11, had officially put the FBI in the business of fighting terror. Instead of the traditional crime-fighting bureau created by J. Edgar Hoover, Director Robert Mueller was expected to transform the FBI into a global counterintelligence organization. At the same time, the bureau was expected to unearth United States–based Muslim-led terror plots, nipping them in the bud while they were still in the planning stages. This was a tall order for a law enforcement agency without language-capable agents and with very few Muslim informants. Even as late as 2006, the number of Muslim agents was estimated to be approximately a dozen out of the bureau's 12,664 agents.[95]

The new FBI also launched a domestic surveillance program that can target people engaging in political activity, nonviolent protests, and civil disobedience, otherwise known as domestic advocacy.[96] The initiation of the program followed the October 2001 passage of the USA PATRIOT Act.[97] The act created the new crime of "domestic terrorism," allowing the surveillance and investigation of individuals engaged in conduct "involv[ing] acts dangerous to human life" to "influence the policy of a government by intimidation or coercion."[98] Political rallies and public events are not off-limits to FBI agents or their confidential human sources.

Testimony from John Lewis, the FBI's deputy assistant director for counterterrorism, before a Senate panel in May 2005 informed senators that environmental and animal rights militants posed the most serious domestic terrorist threat to the United States. The Animal Liberation Front and the Earth Liberation Front (ELF) were of greatest concern for the bureau. His report cited more than 150 pending investigations.[99] He gave the FBI credit for more than 1200 criminal indictments since 1990.[100]

Senate Environmental Committee Chairman James Inhofe compared the two groups to al-Qaeda. He based the comparison on their dependence for outside money to accomplish their goals. He singled out People for the Ethical Treatment of Animals (PETA) as one of their major fundraisers.[101]

On September 10, 2007, in an address to the Senate, FBI Director Robert Mueller weighed in on the internal threat. This time, he gave the threat a name: "single issue groups/domestic terrorism." Domestic terrorists include white supremacists, anarchists, and ecoterrorists.[102] Each of the groups has drawn the attention of terror investigators in search of informants.

It is highly unlikely that the FBI will be sending special agents to PETA meetings. Documents obtained through a Freedom of Information request by the American Civil Liberties Union (ACLU) prove the point. An FBI report showed that the bureau cultivated a "well-insulated PETA insider to attend a meeting to gain credibility within the animal rights movement."[103] In this case, "PETA insider" translates to an informant.

Using a paid informant, not an undercover agent, was how the government was able to secure a 2007 conviction against a California ELF activist—the largest FBI victory against the ELF since the organization was designated a domestic terrorism threat.

The conviction was based primarily on the evidence collected by and testimony from an informant known as "Anna." She was a young woman from Florida. By the time Anna was in her early twenties, she was already a veteran FBI informant.

As early as 2004, the FBI had deployed Anna throughout the United States with instructions to infiltrate anarchist protest groups.[104] In an affidavit filed in one case, the FBI claimed that Anna "provided information that has been utilized in at least twelve separate anarchist cases" and that her "information has proved accurate and reliable."[105] A defense attorney involved in one of those cases was clear about what he viewed as Anna's key to successfully penetrating protest groups. He claimed that her forte was identifying "radical" young men and women and "getting them" to fall in love with her.[106]

4.19   Recruiting Political Infiltrators

In the year running up to the 2008 Republican National Convention (RNC), the Joint Terrorism Task Force (JTTF) in the Twin Cities, Minnesota, had a mission: recruit informants to infiltrate groups of demonstrators. It was only natural for FBI agents and local detectives assigned to the JTTF to farm University of Minnesota students for potential informants. One target was a sophomore; it was thought that he might go for the standard recruiting pitch. He was accused of spray-painting the interior of a campus elevator and had charges pending in court. He might agree to cooperate in exchange for his charges being dropped. The student refused to be identified when he took his story to the local newspaper. He went by the name of Carroll.[107]

The University of Minnesota police sergeant who cracked the vandalism case developed the plan to flip Carroll. He telephoned the student and invited him to meet at a local coffee shop.[108] He assured him that the meeting had nothing to do with the case.

The coffee-shop meeting was more than Carroll expected. The sergeant arrived accompanied by a woman who identified herself as JTTF FBI Special Agent Maureen Murphy.[109] Carroll wondered how his spray-painting caper had become a federal case. The FBI agent was there for another purpose. She spent nearly 30 minutes trying to recruit him as a paid informant. She needed someone to show up at "vegan potlucks" throughout Twin Cities and work his way into the confidence of RNC protesters.[110]

Carroll explained, "She told me that I had the perfect 'look' and that I had the perfect personality—they kept saying I was friendly and personable—for what they were looking for."[111]

Carroll declined the offer. According to his account, the FBI agent took it in stride, saying "Well, if you change your mind, call this number" and left one of her cards on the table.[112]

4.20   Not New Territory: COINTELPRO

Surveillance of domestic advocacy groups is nothing new to the FBI. It was the order of the day from 1956 through at least 1972. Civil rights groups and anti–Vietnam War groups were their primary targets.[113] During this time, the FBI disregarded First Amendment free speech and Fourth Amendment privacy protections and operated the controversial Counter Intelligence Program. Better known as COINTELPRO, the program targeted organizations that were considered to have politically radical elements. The FBI's official mission statement said that the effort was aimed at "protecting national security, preventing violence, and maintaining the existing social and political order."[114]

The FBI investigated and infiltrated headline-grabbing organizations like the Weathermen and Students for a Democratic Society.[115] Both advocated the overthrow of the U.S. government. Other targeted groups included the Ku Klux Klan,[116] Socialist Workers Party, Black Panthers, and American Nazi Party. All were heavily infiltrated by FBI agents and their informants.

Despite their commitment to nonviolence, civil rights groups did not go unnoticed by the FBI. The NAACP, National Lawyers Guild, and American Friends Service Committee were targets of investigation, infiltration, and harassment.

The Southern Christian Leadership Conference, headed by Martin Luther King, Jr., probably consumed more FBI film, wiretap tape, and man-hours than any other civil rights group. The FBI was convinced that King had links to Communists. The bureau considered him the "most dangerous and effective Negro leader in the country."[117]

King's group was heavily infiltrated by informants and was the subject of constant wiretapping and electronic surveillance. His Atlanta home was bugged for more than 2 years.[118]

The bureau's wiretapping was intended to give the FBI "a complete analysis of the avenues of approach aimed at neutralizing King as an effective Negro leader."[119] The FBI's presence was so intrusive that Andrew Young, a major figure in the civil rights movement, testified that his colleagues referred to themselves as members of the "FBI's golden record club."[120] Young later became a member of Congress, the mayor of Atlanta, and an ambassador to the United Nations.

During a Senate probe[121] of the King surveillance, the man in charge of the FBI's war against King was unrepentant. William Sullivan, deputy director of the FBI, told the committee, "No holds were barred. We have used [similar] techniques against Soviet agents. [The same methods were] brought home against any organization against which we were targeted. We did not differentiate. This is a rough, tough business."[122] The FBI was never able to directly link King to Communists.

COINTELPRO would probably still be a secret and be conducting business as usual had it not been for the efforts of the Citizen's Committee to Investigate the FBI. In 1971, members of the group burglarized the FBI office in Media, Pennsylvania. The burglars removed volumes of secret files that detailed the FBI's domestic spying activity and released them to the press.[123]

COINTELPRO's secret mission statement was discovered among the files. It directed FBI agents to "expose, disrupt, misdirect, discredit, or otherwise neutralize"[124] the activities of suspect movements and their leaders. Undercover tactics included infiltration of organizations by agents and paid informants, psychological warfare, and harassment.

Abuse of the legal system and officially tolerated violence were tools frequently used by the bureau to destabilize or destroy targeted organizations.

Local police departments across the United States, particularly those in cities known for political activism, such as New York, Chicago, Los Angeles, and Miami, were drawn into the investigations. Departments with aggressive intelligence-gathering capabilities like the NYPD's Bureau of Special Services began amassing dossiers on members of groups advocating political or social change.

In 1975, the country was reeling from the revelations that came out of the Watergate scandal. A Senate subcommittee,[125] known as the Church Committee (headed by Senator Frank Church), investigated COINTELPRO.[126] Among its many findings, it concluded, "Too many people have been spied upon by too many government agencies and too much information has been collected." (Revelations from documents leaked in 2013 revealed that Senator Church had been the subject of National Security Agency surveillance while he was investigating the FBI.[127])

The committee also found that the FBI, operating primarily through secret informants, used other intrusive investigative techniques. Wiretaps, microphone "bugs," surreptitious mail openings, and break-ins swept in vast amounts of information about the personal lives, views, and associations of American citizens.

The committee was extremely critical of the information-gathering methods used by the FBI. Members found that "many of the techniques used [by the FBI] would be intolerable in a democratic society even if all of the targets had been involved in violent activity, but COINTELPRO went far beyond that ... the Bureau conducted a sophisticated vigilante operation aimed squarely at preventing the exercise of First Amendment rights of speech and association, on the theory that preventing the growth of dangerous groups and the propagation of dangerous ideas would protect the national security and deter violence."[128]

4.21   Operation CHAOS and the CIA's Family Jewels

The fallout from COINTELPRO was widespread. It brought on congressional investigations focused on illegal domestic spying by the Central Intelligence Agency (CIA). The probes, part of an initiative known as the Rockefeller Commission, were ordered by President Gerald Ford. Together with the House's Pike Committee and the Senate's Church Committee, they produced a 693-page report entitled "Report to the President by the Commission on CIA Activities within the United States." The investigation revealed that the CIA routinely violated the rules of its charter regarding domestic spying from the 1950s well into the 1970s.

On December 31, 1974, CIA Director William Colby released a classified document to the Justice Department enumerating 18 violations. The classified list became known as "the Family Jewels." In 1981, President Reagan issued an executive order restricting the CIA from conducting any further domestic spying within the United States.[129]

The Family Jewels remained secret until June 26, 2007, when a Freedom of Information Act (FOIA) request by the privately funded National Security Archive was unexpectedly answered. A highly redacted version of hundreds of pages of reports revealed numerous violations of the CIA charter, including an assassination plot against Fidel Castro.[130] Straight from pulp fiction, poison pills were provided to two U.S. gangsters with access to Castro by a former FBI agent at the direction of CIA agents. Break-ins within the United States, the wiretapping of two syndicated columnists, and the physical surveillance of investigative reporter Jack Anderson were reported.[131] Opening of mail sent by U.S. citizens to the Soviet Union and China and dosing unwitting Americans with LSD also figured prominently among the Family Jewels.

The FOIA release also disclosed details of the CIA's Operation CHAOS, a clandestine operation aimed at antiwar dissidents and civil rights activists protesting throughout the United States. The program ran from 1967 until 1973. More than 300,000 names were entered into the CHAOS computer index. From those names, more than 7000 detailed dossiers of American citizens, known at the CIA as personality files, were completed. More than 3000 reports detailing the activities of individuals and their organizations were compiled by CIA agents assigned to CHAOS.[132]

The findings of the Rockefeller Committee had the same effect on the CIA that the Church Committee's conclusions had on the FBI: unwanted congressional oversight and drastic revision of operational guidelines.

Following the recommendations of the committees,[133] Congress passed the Foreign Intelligence Surveillance Act of 1978 to curtail intelligence-gathering operations directed at individuals within the United States. Under the microscope of the Senate, the FBI voluntarily discontinued COINTELPRO-style domestic surveillance. The CIA was believed to have followed the FBI's lead.

4.22 Domestic Terror Human Source Recruiting and Domain Management

Director Robert Mueller's new FBI turned to the CIA for assistance in launching an unprecedented terror informant–recruiting drive. In the end, the bureau persuaded one of the CIA's deputy directors to join the FBI. A 20-year CIA veteran, he was formerly the second-in-command of counterterrorism analysis in the CIA's Counterterrorist Center. The FBI appointed him national security branch associate executive assistant director. Shortly after, the bureau launched a program known as "Domain Management."[134] It is a computer-based effort to ethnically map America, locating Middle Eastern/Muslim communities for surveillance, infiltration, and informant-recruiting efforts.

Using commercially available marketing software, immigration records, and census data, the FBI identified Muslim communities throughout the United States in an effort to more effectively direct its agents in search of ethnically correct informants. *The New York Times* reported that the former CIA official hired by the FBI "displayed a map of the San Francisco area, pocked with data showing where Iranian immigrants were clustered—and where, he said, an F.B.I. squad was 'hunting'."[135]

It is no secret that the FBI continues to aggressively recruit Muslim informants, usually those with immigration problems. Not all prospects take the offer. Those who don't may regret their decision.

4.23   Targets of Opportunity

A 35-year-old Los Angeles man, a naturalized citizen from Afghanistan, had the bad luck to be visiting his neighbor's house when the FBI came crashing through the door with a search warrant. After the dust settled, an FBI agent made him a straightforward offer: come to work for the bureau as an informant or your life will be made "a living hell."[136] He refused.

A few weeks later, the Afghani man was arrested on charges of perjury, procuring naturalization unlawfully, using a passport procured by fraud, and making false statements. A search warrant was executed on his home. In court, an FBI agent said the man had discussed terrorist plots with an undercover informant.[137]

The immigration arm of the Department of Homeland Security, ICE, was tapped by the FBI to assist in identifying Middle Eastern men most likely to succumb to an informant-recruiting offer: those subject to deportation. Those who agree to become informants will have help at their deportation hearing: an FBI agent. He will tell the immigration judge how critical the potential deportee is to national security. The FBI request is almost always successful.

Immigrant informants are often promised legal residency at the conclusion of their undercover work. The government has been known to disregard the terms of nondeportation agreements,[138] and the immigrant may once again find himself standing before an immigration judge, this time without an FBI agent by his side.[139]

Not all terror informants are working under the threat of deportation. Many are motivated strictly by money. They are paid from the FBI's $3.3 billion counterterrorism budget.[140]

4.23.1   No-Fly and Selectee List

Investigative reporting articles from around the world indicate that the FBI is using what is known as the "no-fly list" as an informant-recruiting tool.

Passengers who are denied boarding claim that they are interviewed by FBI agents who attempt to recruit them as informants. While many of the travelers are from foreign nations, several U.S. citizens also claim to have been targeted for arm twisting–style recruitment efforts.

The ACLU is suing the attorney general of the United States, alleging that FBI agents sought to exploit their traveling clients' fear, desperation, and confusion when they were most vulnerable and to coerce them into working as informants. The suit argues that barring individuals from flying without due process is unconstitutional. There are now 13 plaintiffs; none have been charged with a crime, told why they are barred from flying, or given an opportunity to challenge their inclusion in the no-fly list. Another suit filed on behalf of a traveler by the Center for Constitutional Rights claims the "defendants [FBI] sought to exploit the draconian burden posed by the No Fly List—including the inability to travel for work, or to visit family overseas—in order to coerce him into serving the FBI as a spy with American Muslim communities and places of worship."[141]

The no-fly and selectee lists are subsets of the federal government's consolidated watch list, the Terrorist Screening Database. Meant to identify potential terrorists who could threaten commercial aviation, individuals on the list either are prevented from boarding an aircraft or receive additional physical screening prior to boarding an aircraft.[142] The list is said to contain the names of approximately 20,000 people, identified because the government has reasonable suspicion to believe they are connected to terrorism.[143]

4.24 NYPD Counterterrorism Bureau and Recruiting Terror Informants

Following 9/11, the NYPD began an aggressive search for terror informants. The department also began laying the groundwork for the new Counterterrorism Bureau. The prevailing opinion within the department held FBI incompetence in the handling of actionable intelligence at least partly responsible for the success of the attack on the World Trade Center.[144]

Police leaders saw a proactive, world-class anti-terror intelligence unit as the only way to avert another attack. Their existing intelligence unit was ill equipped and too bogged down in interdepartmental feuding to take on the challenge. The federal government could no longer be counted on to protect the city from future terror attacks. NYPD detectives would be dispatched anywhere in the world to prevent another 9/11.

Historically, combating terror is not new territory for the NYPD. Manhattan has been the target of terror threats since the early 1900s.[145] Neither is stretching jurisdictional boundaries or sending detectives abroad to further NYPD's interests.

In 1909, Police Commissioner Theodore Roosevelt assigned Detective Lieutenant Giuseppe "Joe" Petrosino to hunt down fugitives in Palermo, Italy. Petrosino had earned notoriety in the department with the creation of the Italian Squad. He assembled a team of Italian-American detectives to work undercover against the Black Hand Gang, the precursor to today's Italian Mafia. He became the first NYPD officer to be officially sent abroad.

Petrosino also became the first of New York's finest to be killed in the line of duty on foreign soil.[146] Lured to Palermo's city center by an informant, Petrosino was shot to death by three gunmen.

It was clear that for the NYPD to get back into the international intelligence world, the department would need a federal mentor. Commissioner Raymond Kelly saw it this way: "I knew we had to do business differently. I thought we had to get some people with a fresh outlook and with federal experience to help us."[147]

The NYPD took the FBI's lead and bought what it needed from the intelligence unit's $62 million budget. The department hired a 35-year CIA veteran to head the newly created NYPD Counterterrorism Bureau as deputy commissioner of intelligence.

It was the first time that a municipal police department attempted to enter the international intelligence arena as a major force. The executive director of the Center on Law and Security at New York University remarked, "It really makes the NYPD into its own freestanding law enforcement agency. In a way, the city has its own state department."[148]

Commissioner Kelly explained his reasoning for the move: "I knew we couldn't rely on the federal government. I know it from my own experience. We're doing all the things we're doing because the federal government isn't doing them. It's not enough to say it's their job if the job isn't being done. Since 9/11, the federal government hasn't taken any additional resources and put them here."[149]

NYPD's new deputy commissioner of intelligence is credited by the press as being the main architect of the intelligence-gathering protocols now employed by the NYPD. Journalists quoted him as saying, "It's like starting the CIA over in the post-9/11 world. What would you do if you could begin it all over again? Hah. This is what you would do."[150]

Soon after the deputy commissioner's appointment, an unprecedented training opportunity presented itself at the CIA's Camp Perry. Known as "the farm," it's a 10,000-acre former military base located near Williamsburg, Virginia. An NYPD detective was dispatched to attend the Basic Operations Course with CIA trainees to learn tradecraft, the skills used by spies deployed abroad.[151] Once trained, he could pass on what he had learned from the CIA to fellow counterterrorism detectives.

No cost was spared in preparing the headquarters for the new counterintelligence unit. A journalist who visited the secret facility described it as "gleaming and futuristic." He noted electronic maps, LED news tickers, international time walls, and the latest in computer and electronic audio equipment. In the facility's Global Intelligence Room, 12 flat-screen TVs broadcast news from around the world via satellite. The 24/7 facility is secured with bulletproof glass, antiballistic Sheetrock, and backup generators.[152] Rumors place the facility at the Brooklyn Army Terminal.

4.24.1   Informant-Recruiting Infrastructure: The Terrorist Interdiction Unit and Mosque Crawlers

The Terrorist Interdiction Unit (TIU) was formed. The TIU is tasked with recruiting, developing, and handling terror informants. There is no undercover work here—men and women assigned to the TIU are ordered to search for prospective informants. With the entire NYPD uniform division at their disposal, special emphasis was placed on keeping tabs on street interrogations and arrests of Middle Eastern men made by patrol officers. Indeed, the word was out department-wide that special emphasis should be placed on stopping and questioning individuals from countries commonly associated with terrorism.

Flipping an arrested suspect, or one who thinks he's subject to arrest, particularly one who fears deportation, is a TIU interview priority. Everybody who comes under TIU scrutiny is debriefed with an eye toward flipping the individual. A veteran NYPD detective interviewed by reporters explained, "When someone is arrested who might be useful to the intelligence unit—whether because he says something suspicious or because he is simply a young Middle Eastern man—he is singled out for extra questioning. Intelligence officials don't care about the underlying charges; they want to know more about his community and, ideally, they want to put him to work."[153]

The New York City Taxi and Limousine Commission would seem like an unlikely venue in the hunt for prospective terror informants. That was until someone in the Counterterrorism Bureau discovered the obvious. As is true in many other major U.S. cities, a disproportionate number of taxi licenses in New York are held by Pakistanis. Taxi licenses are hard to come by in New York and often obtained fraudulently. A Pakistani driver in fear of having his license revoked would probably be more inclined to become an informant than to reject a TIU cooperation pitch.[154]

Informants developed by the TIU are deployed based on ethnicity. Their assignment is to frequent places like mosques, bookstores, coffee shops, or any other place where people of similar ethnicities congregate. When they encounter someone espousing radical sentiments, it's their job to attempt to befriend the individual and see where conversation takes them. These informants have been unceremoniously named "mosque crawlers."[155]

4.24.2   The Demographic Unit and Ancestries of Interest

The new Demographic Unit (DU) was established. According to Associated Press investigative reporters, the unit is composed of 16 multilingual officers assigned to an office located at the Brooklyn Army Terminal. The unit has compiled a list of 28 countries, almost all of them Muslim, that it found had "ancestries of interest." Most, if not all, of the countries have citizens who have immigrated to the United States and reside in New York City.[156] Much as with the FBI's Domain Management project, it is up to the DU to pinpoint ethnic neighborhoods throughout the city. The logic is simple: undercover officers and informants of Pakistani descent are deployed in Pakistani neighborhoods, officers of Egyptian descent are sent to neighborhoods with concentrations of Egyptian immigrants, and so forth.

4.24.3   The Special Services Unit and Rakers

The Special Services Unit (SSU) was thus formed. The SSU is an undercover squad staffed almost entirely of young, bilingual Muslim or Arab officers. Members of the squad have been instructed to "rake the coals, looking for hot spots"[157] in their search for terror suspects. SSU officers soon became known as "rakers."[158]

Members of the SSU may never experience a day in a police uniform. Instead, they are recruited into the SSU almost immediately after being hired and don't attend the traditional police academy. Rather, they are trained in a special program developed by the Counterterrorism Bureau that emphasizes self-defense, the use of weapons, surveillance, and undercover safety.[159] For some, their cover is so deep that they are instructed to keep their work a secret from family members.[160]

Collectively fluent in Arabic, Bengali, Hindi, Punjabi, Fujianese, and Urdu, they are given assignments that are ethnically based on the findings of the DU.[161] And yet, a former NYPD intelligence detective dismissed the notion that the department was engaging in ethnic profiling. He told an investigative reporter, "It's not a question of profiling. It's a question of going where the problem could arise. And thank God we have the capability. We have the language capability and the ethnic officers. That's our hidden weapon."[162]

Not very much was known about mosque crawlers or rakers until the defendant in the 2004 Herald Square subway station terror prosecution did the unexpected: instead of cutting a deal with prosecutors and pleading guilty, the 24-year-old Pakistani immigrant whom the government claimed was the mastermind of the plot took his case to trial. This meant open access to witnesses for the prosecution, including the informant and the undercover detective responsible for making the case.

The informant, his identity exposed in court, gave a rather grim account of his experience as an NYPD mosque crawler. Following the trial, the source who helped make the case expressed his regrets over becoming an informant. He told a *CBS News* reporter, "I got damaged, big-time. I'm in a bad situation."[163]

The 51-year-old CI was recruited in 2003 when members of the TIU made a routine visit to the Egyptian-born naturalized American citizen's home. It's likely they were directed to the residence through the work of the DU. In a move better known in police circles as a "cold call," the detectives were there to deliver an informant-recruiting pitch. They walked away with a new CI. He was to be paid for his work.

The new recruit agreed to visit mosques in Staten Island and Brooklyn. His orders were simple: listen for talk of jihad, or holy war. When he asked the detectives to be a bit more specific, they said, "'OK, go to pray and see if things are going on.' I asked, 'Like what?' They said, 'Like radical—the theoretical conversations, just to keep your eyes and ears open.'"[164]

For 13 months during 2003 and 2004, the CI made more than 500 uneventful visits to mosques. This was until his handler steered him in the direction of an Islamic bookstore. It was adjacent to a mosque in Brooklyn. An SSU undercover officer had met a young Pakistani clerk who worked there who might be worth some attention.[165]

The clerk and the informant became friends. When the Pakistani learned that the CI had a degree in nuclear engineering, their conversations turned to explosives.[166] Almost everything was recorded. Soon there were enough taped conversations about blowing up bridges and the 34th Street Herald Square station to bring charges against the Pakistani. The clerk was arrested.

The case went to trial. The NYPD informant was called as the government's star witness. The CI's identity had to be disclosed during his testimony. As an informant, he was finished.

The defense argued that it was a clear case of entrapment.[167] The informant was an agent provocateur. The jury didn't believe it. The Pakistani was sentenced to 30 years in prison.

Having his identity disclosed in court was not what the informant had bargained for. He told reporters that one of the conditions of his cooperation was to keep his real name a secret.[168] That of course could not happen. The minute his handlers instructed him to start taping conversations, he was in the business of collecting evidence. If an arrest was made, he would likely be named as a witness for the government if the case went to trial.

The informant was bitter: "It's been hurting me. Everybody believes that I am a cheater."[169] Although he has not received any direct threats, he has been told by friends that his life is in danger.[170] As a precaution, he was moved to another part of the United States. Press accounts said that the informant was paid a total of $100,000 over the 3-year period that he was visiting mosques.[171]

The Bangladeshi undercover NYPD detective responsible for dispatching the snitch to the bookstore was also called to testify. Unlike the informant, he was allowed to use a pseudonym. During cross-examination, a few interesting facts emerged, in spite of vigorous objections made by the prosecutor, about the job description and background required of rakers. It was the rookie's first time on the witness stand, and his supervisors were understandably concerned about his performance. NYPD's deputy commissioner for legal matters, the department's highest-ranking lawyer, was present during much of his testimony.[172]

The detective explained that he had been 7 years old when he and his family moved from Bangladesh to the United States. He had graduated from the John Jay College of Criminal Justice and entered the NYPD Police Academy in July 2002. It was 3 months into the 6-month police academy training when he was recruited by the Counterterrorism Bureau and assigned to the SSU.[173]

During testimony, the young detective described his first assignment. Just 3 weeks after being plucked from the police academy, he was sent to Bay Ridge, Brooklyn, where he lived undercover for 2 years. He described himself as being a "walking camera." He added, "I was told to act like a civilian—hang out in the neighborhood, gather information." His orders were "never to push for information but to 'take a back seat' and 'observe, be the ears and eyes'."[174]

In the years following the Herald Square trial, the Counterterrorism Bureau has managed to keep its undercover SSU detectives off the witness stand. Failure to insulate its Bangladeshi detective from becoming a witness was a tactical blunder.

4.25   NYPD International

Detectives assigned to the NYPD Counterterrorism Bureau are now posted in Tel Aviv, London, Toronto, Montreal, Singapore, and Lyon. They recruit and deploy their informants worldwide.[175]

Police Commissioner Raymond Kelly told journalists questioning the practice, "The NYPD has a great brand overseas. There's high expectations that come with these postings and we want to meet it, so that means a very careful selection process on our end."[176]

Endnotes

1. Trott, S.S., "The Successful Use of Snitches, Informants, Coconspirators, and Accomplices as Witnesses for the Prosecution in a Criminal Case" (January 1984). Former Assistant Attorney General Criminal Division, Public Integrity Section, U.S. Department of Justice, currently serving as Federal Judge, 9th Circuit Court of Appeals.
2. See Law Enforcement Confidential Informant Practices: Joint Hearing Before the Subcommittee on Crime, Terrorism, & Homeland Sec. and the Subcomm. on the Constitution, Civil Rights, and Civil Liberties of the Commission on the Judiciary House of Representatives, 110th Cong. 76–78 (2007) [hereinafter Joint Hearing] (statement of Ronald E. Brooks, President, National Narcotic

Officers' Association Coalition) ("In the vast majority of the thousands of ... investigations that I have conducted or supervised there would not have been a successful conclusion had it not been for the information provided or access gained through the use of an informant.").

3. See *The Drug Enforcement Administration's Payments to Confidential Sources Audit Report*, July 2005, Office of the Inspector General.

4. See *United States v. Bernal-Obeso*, 989 F.2d 331, 334–35 (9th Cir. 1993) ("[O]ur criminal justice system could not adequately function without information provided by informants ... .").

5. In the FBI's Uniform Crime Reporting (UCR) Program, law enforcement agencies can clear, or "close," offenses in one of two ways: by arrest or by exceptional means. In certain situations, elements beyond law enforcement's control prevent the agency from arresting and formally charging the offender. When this occurs, the agency can clear the offense exceptionally.

6. *Cooperating Individual Management*, at 1, U.S. Department of Justice, Drug Enforcement Administration Office of Training, Quantico, Virginia.

7. Valdenar, R., "Cultivating Effective Gang Informants," *Police Magazine*, December 5, 2012.

8. Natapoff, A., quoting retired DEA Special Agent Celerino Castillo, in "Bait and Snitch, The High Cost of Snitching for Law Enforcement," *Slate*, December 12, 2005.

9. *FBI Manual of Investigative Operations and Guidelines* (MIOG), § 137-2(3).

10. FBI agent statement dated May 7, 2001, in Plaintiff's "Motion for Justice" in Bari/Cherney civil rights lawsuit filed against the FBI and Oakland Police, Case #C-91—1057CW (JL).

11. House Committee on Government Reform, *Everything Secret Degenerates: The FBI's Use of Murderers as Informants*, 3rd *Report*, H.R. Rep. No. 108-414 at 454 (2004), also available at www.gov/hreports/108-414.html.

12. *Attorney General Guidelines Regarding the Use of Confidential Informants*, I.B.9, B-9; II.D.3-6, B-20-22.

13. Natapoff, A., "Snitching: The Institutional and Communal Consequences," 73 *University of Cincinnati Law Review*, 2004, Loyola Law School, Los Angeles.

14. Field Interrogation: general on-the-scene questioning of a person about a crime or other general questioning of witnesses in the fact-finding process, provided that the person being questioned has not been taken into custody nor has been deprived of his freedom of action in any significant way (Chicago Police Department general order GO4-O3).

15. See *Terry v. Ohio*, 392 U.S. 1, 885 S. Ct. 1868, 20 L. Ed. 2nd 889.

16. Earl, J., "You Can Beat the Rap, But Not the Ride: Bringing Arrests Back into Research on Repression," In Coy, P.G., ed., *Research in Social Movements, Conflicts and Change*, Vol. 26, Emerald Group Publishing, Bingley, UK, 2005.

17. *An Exploratory Study of the Use of Confidential Informants in New Jersey*, a report commissioned by the American Civil Liberties Union of New Jersey in partnership with the Criminal Law Reform Project of the American Civil Liberties Union, John Jay College of Criminal Justice, City University of New York, June 2011.

18. See *United States v. Gebro*, 948 F.2d 1118, 1121 (9th Cir. 1991).

19. 18 USC § 3142 (f).

20. 18 USC § 3142 (e); see *United States v. Medina*, 775 F.2d 1398, 1402 (11th Cir. 1985); *United States v. Fortna*, 769 F.2d 243, 250 (5th Cir. 1985); *United States v. Motamedi*, 767 F.2d 1403, 1406–07 (9th Cir. 1985); and *United States v. Chimurenga*, 760 F.2d 400, 405–06 (2d Cir. 1985).
21. See *Terry v. Ohio*, 392 U.S. 1, 885 S. Ct. 1868, 20 L. Ed. 2nd 889.
22. Baker, A., "Patterson Is Urged to Veto Bill to Pare the Stop and Frisk Data Base," *The New York Times*, July 3, 2010.
23. Ibid.
24. Natapoff, A., "Snitching: The Institutional and Communal Consequences," 73 *University of Cincinnati Law Review*, 2004.
25. See *Uniform Crime Report and FBI's Crime in the United States*, annual report documenting arrest statistics.
26. Ibid., 12,196,959 arrests in 2012.
27. Lyons, D. and Garcia, M., "Felon's Testimony May Have Backfired in Willie, Sal Case," *Miami Herald*, February 26, 1996, at B1.
28. A large cell where prisoners (people awaiting trial or sentence, refugees, or illegal immigrants) are confined together temporarily.
29. Retained an attorney.
30. See *Miranda v. Arizona*, 384 U.S. 436, 470 (1966) (establishing minimum standards by which police officers must inform suspects of their constitutional rights). Chief Justice Warren wrote in *Miranda v. Arizona*, "[t]he presence of counsel at the interrogation may serve several significant subsidiary functions as well … . With a lawyer present the likelihood that the police will practice coercion is reduced, and if coercion is nevertheless exercised the lawyer can testify to it in court." *Id.* Even as the Supreme Court later narrowed the holding of *Miranda*, the notion of coercion has remained central. See *Colorado v. Connelly*, 479 U.S. 157, 159, 170 (1986) (holding that coercive police conduct precludes a finding of voluntariness in the context of confessions).
31. Weinstein, I., "Regulating the Market for Snitches," 47 *Buffalo Law Review*, 563, 593 (1999); See Richman, D.C., "Cooperating Clients," 56 *Ohio State Law Journal*, 69, 89 (1995) ("Even for the most knowledgeable defendant, the decision to cooperate will be a leap into the unknown. In this situation, the advice of a defense attorney will be critical, perhaps dispositive").
32. Topping, R., "Lawsuit Takes on Use of Informants by Cops," *Newsday*, December 4, 1996. Lawsuit alleging deliberate police misconduct in building a drug case designed to induce an individual to become an informant.
33. The term *scarlet letter* has been used as a noun to refer to any method that would brand a person in some negative manner.
34. See *The FBI: A Comprehensive Reference Guide*, Oryx Press, Phoenix, AZ, 1999, indicating snitch jacketing was used by the FBI in the 1960s and 1970s during COINTELPRO (jacket refers to file folder).
35. See Case #SACV10-00102-JVS, U.S. District Court, Central District of California. Suit filed by inmate claiming he was beaten and stabbed after law enforcement officer leaked his identity as an informant to the prison population.
36. *An Exploratory Study of the Use of Confidential Informants in New Jersey*, a report commissioned by the Criminal Law Reform Project of the John Jay College of Criminal Justice, City University of New York, June 2011. Legal coercion: police squeeze criminal defendants by threatening them with additional charges or counts related to their own cases if they do not cooperate by becoming CIs.

37. "The Impossible Victory," *Miami New Times*, February 29, 1996.
38. See *United States v. Simpson*, 813 F.2d 1462, 1469 (9th Cir. 1987).
39. See *United States v. Ryan*, 548 F.2d 782,788–789 (9th Cir. 1976).
40. McShane, L., "Mafia Cops Louis Eppolito and Stephen Caracappa Sentenced to Life in Prison," *New York Daily News*, March 6, 2009; see Guy Lawson, G., and Oldham, W., *The Brotherhoods*, Pocket Books, New York, 2006.
41. Last name omitted.
42. McShane, L., "Ex-Mob Boss Now a Devastating Informant," Associated Press, 2006.
43. Last name omitted.
44. Lubasch, A., "Witness in Bid Rigging Case Tells of Mob Threat to His Wife," *The New York Times*, September 17, 1991.
45. Lubasch, A., "Witness in Bid Rigging Case Tells of Mob Threat to His Wife," *The New York Times*, September 17, 1991.
46. Rabb, S., "Mob Boss Said to Have Fled over Botched Assassination," *The New York Times*, October 3, 1991.
47. Stevens, C., "NYPD's Notorious Mafia Cops Sentenced to Life," CNN, March 6, 2009.
48. McClintick, D., "*Swordfish*," Random House, New York, 1993.
49. *Cooperating Individual Management*, at 1, U.S. Department of Justice, Drug Enforcement Administration Office of Training, Quantico, Virginia.
50. See *U.S. Attorneys Manual*, 9-27.610(B) (l) (a).
51. Fed. R. Crim. P. 35(b).
52. Vitello, P. and Semple, K., "Muslims Say F.B.I. Tactics Sow Anger and Fear," *The New York Times*, December 17, 2009.
53. See *Rosciano v. Sonchik*, No. 01-CV-00472, 2002 WL 32166630, at *7 (D. Ariz. September 9, 2002).
54. See 28 CFR 0.197; see also Melody, C., *Trading Information for Safety: Immigrant Informants, Federal Law Enforcement Agents, and the Viability of Non-Deportation Agreements*, Washington Law Review Association, Seattle, WA, 2008.
55. Kahn, C., "The Case of a Confidential Informant Gone Wrong," National Public Radio, February 11, 2010. See Hyde, J., "House of Death," *Dallas Observer*, March 8, 2007.
56. 8 USC § 1101(a) (15) (S).
57. S.1424.
58. Individuals cannot self-petition for an S visa. The sponsoring law enforcement agency (LEA) initiates the application and submits it to its headquarters for approval. Before submitting the application to Department of Justice, Office of Enforcement Operations, all federal, state, and local LEAs must first obtain the signature of the U.S. attorney with jurisdiction over their district to endorse the application.
59. Johnson, C., "Snitch Visa: Tool to Get Terrorism Suspects Talking," National Public Radio, July 16, 2010, quoting Patrick Rowan.
60. Ibid.
61. Ibid.
62. Form I-854, Part B, Law Enforcement Agent Certification.
63. Ibid.
64. T nonimmigrant status.
65. Victims of Trafficking and Violence Protection Act (TVPA) of 2000, Pub. L. No.106-386, 114 Stat. 1464, (2000).

66. See 22 USC § 7101, 8 CFR § 214.11(a).
67. Form I-914, Supplement B, Declaration of Law Enforcement Officer for Victim of Trafficking in Persons.
68. See INA § 101(a) (15) (T), 8 USC § 101(a) (15) (T).
69. See INA § 212 (d) (13).
70. http://www.uscis.gov.
71. Benefits are obtained through the U.S. Department of Health and Human Services, Office of Refugee Resettlement.
72. Family members are known as derivatives, which are otherwise admissible, and accompany or allowed to join the principal alien.
73. Victims of Trafficking and Violence Protection Act (TVPA) of 2000. Pub. L. No.106-386, 114 Stat. 1464, (2000).
74. Crimes covered but not limited to include rape; torture; trafficking; incest; domestic violence; sexual assault; abusive sexual contact; prostitution; sexual exploitation; female genital mutilation; being held hostage; peonage; involuntary servitude; slave trade; kidnapping; abduction; unlawful criminal restraint; false imprisonment; blackmail; extortion; manslaughter; murder; felonious assault; witness tampering; obstruction of justice; perjury; or attempt, conspiracy, or solicitation to commit any of the aforementioned crimes.
75. The Trafficking Victims Protection Act enhanced the protection of victims by increasing access to legal counsel and providing better information to the victims on assistance programs.
76. The witness must self-petition for a U visa by submitting Form I-918, "Petition for U Nonimmigrant Status," directly to USCIS. A law enforcement certification is required on Supplement B of Form I-918 pursuant to 8 CFR § 214.14(c) (2).
77. 22 USC § 7105(c) (3); Trafficking Victims Protection Reauthorization Act (TVPRA), 2008.
78. INA § 212 (d) (5) (A), 8 USC § 1182(d) (5) (A).
79. See O'Neil, H., "Siblings Face Deportation After Work for Feds As ICE Informants," Associated Press, February 13, 2010.
80. DHS SPBP Parole Template, Law Enforcement Agency certification, agency memorandum and record checks for immigration and criminal history.
81. See 8 CFR § 274a.12(c) (14).
82. INA § 241(c) (2) (A), 8 USC § 1231(c) (2) (A).
83. O'Neill, H., "Undercover Informant Facing Deportation Wins Stay," Associated Press, February 19, 2010.
84. Ibid.
85. *San Diego Examiner*, February 28, 2010.
86. 28 CFR 0.197—Agreements, in connection with criminal proceedings or investigations, promising nondeportation or other immigration benefits.
87. *Department of Justice Report on Internal Review Regarding the Ruby Ridge Hostage Situation and Shootings by Law Enforcement Personnel*, §2(a), "Statement of Facts" (Lexis Counsel Connect). See also *Ruby Ridge: Report of the Subcommittee on Terrorism*, Technology and Government Information of the Senate Committee on the Judiciary Hearings, Sept. 6–19, 1995, report published on February 1996.

88. Ibid. at 2(c).
89. Ibid. at 2(d).
90. Ibid.
91. Jackson, R.L., "Ruby Ridge Informant Denies Entrapping Weaver," *Los Angeles Times*, September 9, 1995.
92. Reese, C., "Senate Turns in Sparkling Performance on Ruby Ridge Hearings," *Orlando Sentinel Star*, September 17, 1995.
93. Ibid.
94. Bartosiewicz, P., Deploying Informants, "The FBI Sting's Muslims," *The Nation*, July 29, 2012.
95. Shane, S. and Bergman, L., "F.B.I. Struggling to Reinvent Itself to Fight Terror," *The New York Times*, October 10, 2006.
96. *A Review of the FBI's Investigation of Certain Domestic Advocacy Groups,* Office of Inspector General, September 2010.
97. USA PATRIOT Act of 2001 (Uniting and Strengthening America by Providing Appropriate Tools Required To Intercept and Obstruct Terrorism).
98. 18 USC 2331.
99. Hsu, S.S., "FBI Papers Show Terror Inquiries into PETA; Other Groups Tracked," *Washington Post*, December 20, 2005.
100. Frieden, T., *FBI, ATF Address Domestic Terrorism*, CNN.com, May 19, 2005.
101. Ibid.
102. Testimony from Robert S. Mueller, III, Director, Federal Bureau Investigation, before the Senate Committee on Homeland Security and Government Affairs, September 10, 2007.
103. Hsu, S.S., "FBI Papers Show Terror Inquiries into PETA; Other Groups Tracked," *Washington Post*, December 20, 2005.
104. Petroski, W., "FBI Infiltrated Iowa Antiwar Group Before GOP Convention," *Des Moines Register*, May 17, 2009.
105. Van Bergen, J., "FBI Confidential Informant Also Said to Be Provocateur," *The Raw Story*, June 8, 2006.
106. Ibid.
107. Snyders, M., "Moles Wanted: In Preparation for the Republican National Convention, The FBI Soliciting Informants," *Minneapolis City Pages*, May 21, 2008.
108. Ibid.
109. Name changed.
110. Snyders, M., "Moles Wanted: In Preparation for the Republican National Convention, The FBI Soliciting Informants," *Minneapolis City Pages*, May 21, 2008.
111. Ibid.
112. Ibid.
113. Author's note: the FBI and local police surveilled and infiltrated a number of activist groups prior to and during the 1972 Democrat and Republican nominating conventions in Miami Beach, Florida. The author was a supervisor in charge of one of the local police intelligence-gathering teams. Copies of police reports generated by the teams were forwarded to the FBI.
114. *Final Report of the Select Committee To Study Governmental Operations with Respect to Intelligence Activities*, United States Senate, April 23, 1976.

115. Author's note: The Weathermen, or Weather Underground, comprised a radical spin-off of the 1960s' student activist group Students for a Democratic Society (SDS). The SDS was known for its nonviolent protests on college campuses throughout the United States. The Weather Underground formed alliances with more radical and violent groups like the Black Panthers.
116. May, G., *The Informant: The FBI, the Ku Klux Klan, and the Murder of Viola Liuzzo*, Yale University Press, 2005.
117. Christensen, J., "FBI Tracked King's Every Move," CNN, March 31, 2008, quoting transcripts of released FBI memos.
118. *Final Report of the Select Committee to Study Governmental Operations with Respect to Intelligence Activities*, United States Senate, April 23, 1976 (under authority of the order of April 14, 1976: Dr. Martin Luther King, Jr., Case Study, herein after Select Committee Report).
119. Ibid.
120. Select Committee Report, testimony from Andrew Young, February 19, 1976.
121. Select Committee Report, testimony from William Sullivan, former assistant director, FBI, November 1, 1975.
122. Ibid.
123. Churchill, W. and Wall, J.V., *The Face of COINTELPRO*, South End Press, Brooklyn, NY, 1990.
124. Senate Select Committee to Study Governmental Operations with Respect to Intelligence Activities (1975).
125. Ibid.
126. Ibid.
127. Cassidy, J., "When the NSA Spied on Art Buchwald," *The New Yorker*, September 26, 2013. Citing recently declassified documents, the NSA even spied on two prominent senators, Frank Church, the Idaho Democrat who headed the Senate Foreign Relations Committee, and Howard Baker, the Tennessee Republican who would go on to serve as Ronald Reagan's chief of staff.
128. Citing recently declassified documents, the NSA even spied on two prominent senators, Frank Church, the Idaho Democrat who headed the Senate Foreign Relations Committee, and Howard Baker, the Tennessee Republican who would go on to serve as Ronald Reagan's chief of staff.
129. *Report to the President by the Commission on CIA Activities within the United States* the Rockefeller Commission, June 1975.
130. Smith, B., "How the CIA Enlisted the Chicago Mob to Put a Hit on Castro," ChicagoMag.com, November 18, 2007.
131. Hersh, S., "Huge CIA Operation Reported in U.S. against Anti-War Forces, Other Dissidents in Nixon Years," *New York Times*, December 22, 1974.
132. See CIA home page for full report regarding "Family Jewels."
133. Senate Select Committee to Study Governmental Operations with Respect to Intelligence Activities, Final Report, S. REP. NO. 755, 94th Cong., 2d Sess. (1976).
134. Knefel, J., "Is the FBI's Domestic Spying Out of Control?" *Rolling Stone Magazine*, September 19, 2013.
135. Ibid.
136. McLaughlin, E., "FBI Planting Spies in U.S. Mosques, Muslim Group Says," CNN, March 20, 2009.

137. Ibid.
138. See *Rosciano v. Sonchik*, No. 01-CV-00472, 2002 WL 32166630 (D. Ariz. September 9, 2002).
139. Melody, C., *Trading Information for Safety: Immigrant Informants, Federal Law Enforcement Agents, and the Viability of Non-Deportation Agreements*, Washington Law Review Association, Seattle, WA, 2008.
140. Aronson, T., "The Informants," *Mother Jones News*, September/October 2011 issue prepared with the assistance of the Investigative Reporting Program at the University of California, Berkeley.
141. *Latif et al. v. Holder.*
142. *Role of the No-Fly and Selectee Lists*, Office of the Inspector General, July 20, 2009.
143. "FBI Accused of Using No-Fly List to Recruit Informants," ALL-GOV.com, October 8, 2013.
144. Horowitz, C., "The NYPD's War on Terror," *New York Magazine*, February 2, 2003.
145. Dickey, C., *Securing the City: Inside America's Best Counterterror Force—The NYPD*, Simon & Schuster, New York, 2009.
146. Ibid.
147. "The NYPD's War on Terror," *The New Yorker*, September 2011.
148. Sostek, A., *Taking Action, New York's State of Mind: Out of the Twin Towers' Ashes, NYPD Is Building a World-Class Terror-Fighting Machine*, Manhattan Institute for Policy Research, New York, October 2004.
149. Schiller, J., *Avoid Terrorist Attacks*, CreateSpace, Seattle, WA, 2010.
150. Goldman, A., "CIA Key in NYPD's Post-9/11 Spying," Associated Press, August 11, 2011.
151. Goldman, A. and Apuzzo, M., "What's the CIA Doing at NYPD? Depends Whom You Ask," Associated Press, October 17, 2011.
152. Description taken in part from the article by Horowitz, C., "The NYPD's War on Terror," *New York Magazine*, February 2, 2003.
153. "NYPD CIA Anti-Terror Operations Conducted in Secret for Years," *Huffington Post*, August 24, 2011.
154. Goldman, A. and Apuzzo, M., "Inside the Spy Unit That NYPD Says Doesn't Exist," Associated Press, August 31, 2011.
155. Suarez, R., '*Mosque Crawlers,' 'Rakers' Monitoring U.S. Muslims for NYPD*, PBS, February 28, 2012.
156. Goldman, A. and Apuzzo, M., "Inside the Spy Unit That NYPD Says Doesn't Exist," Associated Press, August 31, 2011.
157. Goldman, A., "CIA Key in NYPD's Post-9/11 Spying," Associated Press, August 2011.
158. Suarez, R., '*Mosque Crawlers,' 'Rakers' Monitoring U.S. Muslims for NYPD*, PBS, February 28, 2012.
159. Raschbaum, W.K., "Detective Was 'Walking Camera' among City Muslims, He Testifies," *New York Times*, May 19, 2006.
160. Hays, T., "NYPD Undercover Unit Key in NJ Terror Arrests," *Miami Herald*, June 8, 2010.
161. Ibid.
162. Goldman, A. and Apuzzo, M., "CIA Teaches Spy Tricks to NYPD," Associated Press, August 24, 2011.

163. Keteyian, A., Hirschkorn, P., Rey, M., *The Cost of Cooperation: A Confidential Informant Who Helped Break Up a Terror Plot Opens Up*, CBS Evening News Investigative Unit, September 14, 2006.
164. Ibid.
165. Ibid.
166. Shulman, R., "The Informer: Behind the Scenes, or Setting the Stage," *Washington Post*, May 29, 2007.
167. Ibid.
168. Ibid.
169. Ibid.
170. Ibid.
171. Keteyian, A., *The Cost of Cooperation: A Confidential Informant Who Helped Break Up a Terror Plot Opens Up*, CBS Evening News Investigative Unit, September 14, 2006.
172. Raschbaum, W. K., "Detective Was 'Walking Camera' among City Muslims, He Testifies," *New York Times*, May 19, 2006.
173. Ibid.
174. Ibid.
175. Shorn, D., *Inside the NYPD's Anti-Terror Fight*, 60 Minutes, March 19, 2006.
176. "NYPD in Israel: Police Department Opens Branch in Kfar Saba with Lone Detective," *Huffington Post*, September 6, 2012.

Plea-Bargaining, Substantial Assistance, and Downward Sentencing Departures

5

5.1 Introduction

Suspects who resist informant recruitment efforts on the street are often arrested. Once taken into custody, the wheels of the criminal justice system begin to turn. The broad discretion granted to the police officer over the fate of the suspect is greatly diminished. The prosecutor and his discretionary powers now govern the course the defendant's case takes. That does not mean efforts to enlist the cooperation of the defendant are over.

5.2 Law Enforcement Officers and Plea Negotiations

Following arrest, agents can promise an arrestee only that in exchange for cooperation he or she will make a favorable recommendation to the prosecutor. The Drug Enforcement Administration (DEA), for example, requires the approval of the appropriate prosecutor (federal, state, or local) before seeking the cooperation of a defendant.[1] The prosecuting attorney has sole authority to decide whether or not to prosecute the case.

The Federal Bureau of Investigation (FBI) agents offer prospective cooperating witnesses (CWs) a similar message by explaining, "The FBI on its own cannot promise or agree to any consideration by a Federal Prosecutor's Office or a court in exchange for your cooperation, since the decision to confer any such benefit lies within the exclusive discretion of the [prosecutor] and the Court. However, the FBI will consider (but not necessarily act upon) a request by you to advise the appropriate [prosecutor] or Court of the nature and extent of your assistance to the FBI."[2]

The defendant may or may not be "Mirandized" during postarrest interviews. Streetwise individuals may refuse to cooperate without the advice of counsel. Once a suspect invokes his right to have counsel present during a custodial interrogation, all questioning should cease until counsel is present.[3]

The McDade Amendment,[4] signed into law on October 21, 1998, placed restrictions on the conduct of federal prosecutors and the law enforcement officers who work for them regarding contact with represented defendants. It requires prosecutors and their agents to conform to and be subject to state laws, local bar rules, and local federal court rules governing attorneys and their investigators.[5] Once a suspect is represented by counsel, custodial and noncustodial questioning should cease unless the defendant's attorney is present.

5.3   Prosecutorial Discretion

The power a prosecutor wields in flipping a defendant cannot be overstated. According to the chief deputy prosecuting attorney in Little Rock, Arkansas's state court, "We make a charging decision. We don't always charge. The options we have are to charge a felony, to send it back to the police for more investigation, to reduce it to a misdemeanor, or to mark it DNF, 'Do not file'."[6] If a defendant is willing to cooperate, his case may never reach the courtroom.

A former Memphis politician caught up in a 2006 FBI corruption sting described why he flipped following his arrest this way: "It's kind of like TV. They take you into a room, and in my case it was a nice hotel room, and they basically scare the heck out of you and you have ten minutes to decide—do you want to bring in other people involved that you know about or do you want to spend twenty years in prison. Well, I'm sixty-five. It took me about half an hour to figure it out and probably some of the people involved who were mad at me for doing this, it wouldn't have taken them that long really."[7]

In return for delivering to the FBI a corrupt city councilman (substantial assistance), the prosecutor told the judge at sentencing that the politician's substantial assistance was "timely, supportive and extensive."[8] He received 6 months instead of a 20-year sentence. It was a generous six-level reduction from what the federal sentencing guidelines called for.

5.4   Plea Bargaining: Let's Make a Deal

Taking a criminal case from arrest to trial is nearly a thing of the past. As the U.S. Supreme Court recognized in 2012, "[n]inety-seven percent of federal convictions and ninety-four percent of state convictions are the result of guilty pleas."[9] Guilty "pleas account for nearly 95% of all criminal convictions. The reality is that plea bargains have become so central to the administration of the criminal justice system that plea bargains are not an adjunct to the criminal justice system; it *is* the criminal justice system."[10]

One judge described the plea system in this manner: "The mandatory minimum is mandatory only from the perspective of judges. To the parties, the sentence is negotiable. Did a marginal participant in a conspiracy really understand that a 10-kilo deal lay in store? A prosecutor may charge a lesser crime, if the minor player offers something in return. Let's make a deal. Does the participant have valuable information; can he offer other assistance?

Congress authorized prosecutors to pay for aid with sentences below the floor. Let's make a deal."[11]

During plea-negotiating sessions, state and federal prosecutors alike may offer one or a combination of inducements to encourage a defendant to plead guilty and become a CW. These may include any of the following:

- Promises to dismiss one or more charges.
- Reduction of offenses to lesser included charges.
- An assurance that there will be a recommendation or an agreement not to oppose the defendant's request for a particular sentence (with the understanding that such recommendation or request is not binding upon the court).
- The prosecutor will agree that a specific sentence is the appropriate disposition of the case.
- An offer of immunity.
- An agreement by the prosecutor to forgo prosecuting a witness's family member.
- An agreement not to forfeit property.
- The return of forfeited property.

If it is a federal criminal case, the most sought after assurance aside from a dismissal of charges is that the prosecutor will file a 5K1[12] motion informing the judge that the defendant has provided substantial assistance.[13]

5.5   Risk of Trial: An Innocence Problem

Criminal trials have become the exception rather than the rule. The incentives for a criminal defendant to plea bargain and plead guilty have never been greater. One observer believes plea bargaining has an "innocence problem," inferring that even innocent people plead guilty to avoid the risk of trial. The writer explained that "the incentives for defendants to plead guilty are greater than at any previous point in the history of our criminal justice system[,]" and "today, the incentives to bargain are powerful enough to force even an innocent defendant to falsely confess guilt in hopes of leniency and in fear of reprisal."[14]

The National Center for State Courts in Williamsburg, Virginia, found that the percentage of felonies taken to trial in nine states with available data fell to 2.3% in 2009, from 8% in 1976. The vast majority of the remaining cases were resolved through negotiated pleas.

A defendant who insists on a trial despite any merit to his case is a true gambler. Some simply want to roll the dice with a jury of their peers. After all, 12 people randomly selected for jury duty will decide the defendant's fate. But by going to trial, the accused runs the risk of stirring the ire of the judge.

Judges encourage cooperation deals because doing so spares them the time and expense of a jury trial. It is called judicial economy. If every defendant went to trial, the criminal justice system would become unmanageable.

Judges want their calendars to be cleared of cases that could have been resolved through a plea deal. When the guilty verdict is finally handed down, the defendant is often given a longer sentence than he was offered by the prosecutor before trial. If he thinks the sentence is retaliation for putting the judge and jury to all the trouble of a trial, he may be correct. Some judges even announce their disdain for a needless trial at sentencing.[15]

One study reported, "US constitutional jurisprudence offers scant protection from prosecutors who are willing to pressure defendants into pleading [guilty] and punish those who insist on going to trial. Courts do not view defendants as unconstitutionally coerced to forego their right to a trial if they plead guilty to avoid a staggering sentence. Nor do they consider defendants to have been vindictively punished for exercising their right to trial when prosecutors make good on their threats to seek much higher mandatory penalties for them because they refused to plead."[16]

5.5.1   Drug Cases and the Gun Bump

Going to trial can be risky, particularly for those arrested for a federal drug crime, and drug cases flood the dockets of courts throughout the United States.[17] In 2012, the average sentence for federal drug defendants convicted after trial was three times higher (16 years) than that received after a guilty plea (5 years and 4 months). Among first-time drug defendants facing mandatory minimum sentences who had the same offense level and no weapon involved in their offense, those who went to trial had almost twice the sentence length of those who pled guilty (117.6 vs. 59.5 months).[18]

If a firearm was involved during the alleged drug crime, the so-called gun bump applies. It can increase the sentence anywhere from 5 to 25 years.[19] Prior felony drug convictions can dramatically increase a mandatory minimum drug sentence.[20]

5.6   The United States Sentencing Guidelines and Prosecutorial Discretion

Federal criminal defendants in the 1970s and early 1980s had little reason to become informants or CWs. First offenders and those accused of less serious crimes, including drug offenses, could receive probation or a hand-slap sentence of several years. It all depended on the judge's sentencing practices and his mood on the day of sentencing.

The U.S. Parole Commission could be expected to reduce the sentence by at least 50%. A defendant could do his time and return to the street and his illicit business with his criminal reputation intact, never having become a CW.

Some defendants did become CWs, usually those afraid to do even 1 day in jail. Others rolled over only after skillful recruiting efforts by experienced and persevering agents. But when word got out that they cooperated, their lives were turned upside down.

The U.S. Sentencing Guidelines (USSGs) changed the criminal mind-set on cooperating. The days of the stand-up guy who is willing to keep his mouth shut, take his lumps in court, and go to prison are a thing of the past. Omertà—the code of silence—is routinely violated. Within the criminal community, cooperation is expected and often tolerated.

For instance, in 2007, a "Chicago Outfit" crime boss was the target of the FBI's Operation Family Secrets. He was tried along with 13 other members of the Chicago mafia. His crew was alleged to have committed 18 murders.[21] One of the FBI's chief CWs was one of the bosses' sons. He testified in exchange for a reduced sentence, becoming the first son in a mob trial to take the witness stand against his father. The mobster was found guilty and sentenced to life in prison.[22] In an interview, the son told a journalist, "I'm a cooperating witness, I'm a turncoat, I'm a bad son, whatever you want to call me, but I don't feel that I'm a rat."[23] The son wrote a book about his life in the Chicago Outfit and wearing a wire for the FBI during conversations with his father.

During the summer of 2010, a 93-year-old Colombo underboss was tried for extortion in U.S. District Court in Brooklyn, New York. The government had flipped a surprising witness. The senior mobster, a onetime financial backer for the porn classic *Deep Throat*, had boasted of killing 60 people during his career. None of his victim's bodies were ever found. He was never charged with murder. A journalist reported that investigators caught him on tape in 2006 describing his favorite recipe for disposing of bodies: "Dismember victim in kiddie pool. Cook body parts in microwave. Stuff parts in garbage disposal. Be patient. He explained that 'Today, you can't have a body no more. It's better to take that half an hour, an hour, to get rid of the body than it is just to leave the body in the street.'"[24] He was found guilty of extortion, not murder, and sentenced to 8 years,[25] a potential life sentence.

The government's primary witness was one of his sons.[26] He testified that the FBI was giving him a chance to change his life, referring to his addiction to drugs.[27] He later wrote a book about his life in a mob family.[28]

5.7 Shifting the Balance of Power in the Court

For over two decades, the USSGs shifted the balance of power in the courtroom, putting the prosecutor in the commanding role when it imposed severe minimum mandatory sentences. That did not sit well with federal judges.

In 2003, Supreme Court Justice Anthony M. Kennedy weighed in on the subject: This "transfer of sentencing discretion from a judge to an Assistant U.S. Attorney, often not much older than the defendant, is misguided." It "gives the decision to an assistant prosecutor not trained in the exercise of discretion and takes discretion from the trial judge..., the one actor in the system most experienced with exercising discretion in a transparent, open, and reasoned way."[29]

With the advent of the guidelines, life sentences for many accused of committing felonies became a distinct possibility.[30] Overnight, 20 years behind bars suddenly became a light sentence. Parole and early release for "good behavior" became a thing of the past. At the same time, the guidelines stripped judges of their power to arbitrarily reduce a defendant's sentence based on gut feelings, moral compass, or compelling pleas for leniency.[31]

5.7.1   *Booker v. United States*

Two years following Justice Kennedy's admonishment, the power of the federal prosecutor was dealt a setback. It was a result of the Supreme Court's 2005 decision in *Booker v. United States*.[32] The court had found a constitutional defect in the federal sentencing scheme that raised Sixth Amendment concerns. In essence, the court found that the sentencing guidelines resulted in harsher sentences based solely on facts found by the judge instead of the jurors. The result meant that for federal judges, the USSGs were now advisory instead of mandatory.

Federal District Court judges now have discretion in rendering sentences. The *Booker* Court did not throw out the guidelines altogether. Instead, federal judges must "consult those Guidelines and take them into account when sentencing" along with other factors including the nature and circumstances of the crime.

5.8   Substantial Assistance and Downward Departures

Unlike most legal documents, the message behind the USSGs was very simple to understand: Cooperate by providing "substantial assistance" in the prosecution of another criminal or suffer the sentencing consequences. The assistance runs the gamut from going undercover and collecting evidence in an ongoing investigation to testifying against close friends, criminal associates, and even family members.

5.9   Case Study: Sammy "The Bull" Gravano

Fear of life in prison probably motivated Sammy "The Bull" Gravano, one of the nation's most notorious criminals, to cut a deal with agents and federal prosecutors. He confessed to taking part in 19 murders. As part of a sentencing deal,[33] he was granted immunity from prosecution for the killings and pled guilty to a racketeering charge. All he had to do in return was testify against his boss, John Gotti, the head of the Mafia's Gambino crime family.

The press had nicknamed Gotti the "Teflon Don." A veteran of several federal jury trials, he was acquitted each time. Charges did not seem to stick until Gravano became a CW. Gotti received a life sentence and died in prison.

The judge in the Gotti trial was obviously impressed with the days of testimony he heard from Sammy "The Bull." Before rendering his sentence, Federal Judge Leo Glasser stood up for Gravano's decision to become a CW. During the sentencing hearing, the judge said that he regarded Gravano's decision to testify as "the bravest thing I have ever seen." That was not all. Judge Glasser told those present for the sentencing hearing, "I can't recall seeing any reference to Gravano that wasn't preceded by words such as *rat, snitch, turncoat* or some other pejorative word. Would we view it in the same way if, for example, a member of the World Trade Center bombing conspiracy informed on his fellow conspirators, the perpetrators of that disaster? Who, in that context, has Gravano informed against? Is assisting the government to bring major criminals to book a contemptible thing? Is it somehow less commendable because the informant is or was himself a member of that band of criminals? And yet who can provide the information necessary to convict if not one privy to that information?"

In Judge Glasser's opinion, "There has never been a defendant of his stature in organized crime who has made the leap he has made from one social planet to another. There has never been a defendant whose impact on organized crime and the suffocating hold of that criminal octopus upon industry and labor that has been so important and so extensive."[34]

In return, Gravano received a downward departure in his sentence for substantial assistance. He was sentenced to only 5 years in prison. It worked out to a little more than 3 months per murder.

He served his time in one of the Federal Bureau of Prisons' minimum-security lockups reserved for CWs and informants. Known collectively as "rat prisons," they are the Bureau of Prisons' contribution to the Witness Security Program.

On release in 1995, Gravano was placed in the U.S. Marshals' Witness Security Program, relocated to Arizona, and given a new identity. He underwent plastic surgery at his own expense to ensure his anonymity.

Gravano quickly became the benchmark the government would never want to exceed. He went public, writing a book called *Underboss* with author Peter Maas. His new face was plastered all over the cover. He also granted televised interviews with ABC's Diane Sawyer. Gravano was now officially out of the Witness Security Program.

Gravano's freedom was short-lived. In 1998, he became involved in the lucrative business of selling large quantities of ecstasy. His celebrity status quickly led to his arrest by Arizona drug agents. In 2002, he was convicted of possession and distribution of ecstasy and sentenced to 19 years in Arizona state prison.

Gravano's bad luck did not stop at the prison's gate. Shortly after beginning to serve his time, he was successfully sued by the families of his 19 victims. Royalties from his book *Underboss* now go directly to a trust account controlled by the Attorney General of Arizona for distribution to the family members of Gravano's victims.[35]

5.10 Minimum Mandatory Sentences

Advisory or not, for a criminal facing the prospect of prosecution, particularly for drug crimes, the guidelines still resemble a menu. Look up the crime and see exactly how much time behind bars it may cost you.[36] They are the starting point, and federal judges are known for handing out stiff sentences.[37]

One 24-year-old defendant failed to consult the menu before appearing in a Los Angeles federal courtroom for sentencing. When he learned that under the guidelines he was looking at a 20-year prison sentence, he tried to run out of the courtroom. According to the *Los Angeles Times*, U.S. District Judge Dickran Tevrizian bolted over his bench with his black ropes flowing, dashed after the defendant, and nabbed him with a hammerlock. According to the judge, "I felt like a young man. I'm fifty years old. This guy is twenty years old." The judge was a former member of the USC gymnastics team.[38]

Federal defendants, or those facing indictment, should know what their sentence range will be during the first meeting with their attorney. Indeed, the arresting agent, in his first attempt to recruit the prospective informant, probably detailed exactly how much time the guidelines' sentencing tables said the defendant faced. It is also likely he provided a vivid account of what a future in prison holds. Agreeing to offer substantial assistance by way of becoming a CW is offered as the only way out.

5.11 Section 5K1.1

Section 5K1.1 of the USSGs provides, "Upon motion of the government [the prosecutor] stating that the defendant has provided substantial assistance[39] in the investigation or prosecution of another person who has committed an offense, the court may depart from the guidelines."[40] The hope of a 5K1 sentence departure seems to have provided federal agents and prosecutors with a nearly inexhaustible supply of CWs to draw on.

The assistance has to be *substantial*, not just lip service or idle rumors about another criminal. Wearing a wire and going undercover for government agents, collecting damaging evidence, and testifying against another criminal are examples of substantial assistance.

At least one in six defendants is awarded a 5K1 letter from prosecutors saying he or she gave substantial assistance during an investigation.[41] Most prosecutors insist that the defendant plead guilty to some offense. According to a U.S. Attorney in Birmingham, Alabama, using 5K1s "puts a lot more scores on the board a lot quicker."[42]

The sentencing reductions are significant. Federal defendants who flip can receive sentences that are nearly half the minimum mandatory required by the USSGs.[43] It is quite an incentive to testify against friends, family, or criminal associates.[44]

5.12   In-Camera Hearing and Sealing

The court must state for the record the reasons for reducing a sentence for substantial assistance under §5K1.1.[45] Criminal organizations took note of that anomaly and began attending hearings and searching court files for information. Investigations were compromised and CWs were placed in needless danger. Today the hearing can be done *in camera* and under seal to protect the safety of the defendant or to avoid disclosure of an ongoing investigation.[46]

5.13   Case Study: White-Collar Criminals

The October 2001 Enron scandal led to the bankruptcy of the Enron Corporation and the destruction of Arthur Andersen, one of the five largest audit and accounting partnerships in the world. Shareholders lost $11 billion when shares fell from $90 to less than $1 in approximately one month. At the time it was the largest corporate bankruptcy in U.S. history.

Former chairman Kenneth Lay, along with the company's former president and its former chief accounting officer (CAO), were charged with fraud and conspiracy. The case was set for trial in early 2006, and the three codefendants were set to stand trial together. It was a rare show of solidarity.

That was, until their chief financial officer (CFO) reached a deal with prosecutors.[47] In exchange for pleading guilty to one count of securities fraud, he was sentenced to 5½ years and was never called to testify.

At trial, the company's former president was convicted on 19 counts and received a 24-year sentence. Lay was convicted on 10 counts but died shortly after the trial.

Enron's CFO could not lay claim to the best sentencing deal in corporate fraud history for very long. WorldCom, once the second-largest long-distance telecommunications company in the United States after AT&T, filed for bankruptcy in July 2002. The bankruptcy followed the discovery of an $11 billion accounting scandal. WorldCom's CFO was alleged to have been the chief architect of one of the biggest frauds in U.S. history.

Striking an even better deal with prosecutors than Enron's CAO, the former CFO at WorldCom received a 5-year sentence[48] instead of the 27 years in prison he faced. He pled guilty to conspiracy, securities fraud, and false financial filings.

At sentencing he told the court he was "ashamed and embarrassed. I made horrible decisions. It was a misguided effort to save the company—I ask for leniency so I can get back to my family as soon as possible."[49]

The lenient sentence was in return for information and testimony that resulted in the conviction of WorldCom's CEO for the $11 billion fraud. The former CFO testified that the CEO repeatedly instructed him to "hit the numbers" to meet the expectations of Wall Street. The former CEO received a term of 25 years in prison, one of the most severe sentences ever given in a white-collar criminal case.[50]

In January 2012, the Enron and WorldCom CWs may have felt cheated when they learned of the incredible cooperation deal landed by a trader for the Galleon Group, one of the world's largest hedge-fund management firms. The trader-turned CW was facing up to 25 years for conspiracy and securities fraud before agreeing to cooperate and pleading guilty as charged.

The CW's cooperation led to the biggest probe of insider trading ever launched by federal prosecutors. He wore a wire on numerous occasions during more than 2 years of working undercover for federal agents and prosecutors.[51] Evidence collected by the CW, coupled with his testimony, netted prosecutors the conviction of the Galleon Group's cofounder and nine others connected to the investigation. Federal prosecutors called the CW's help "nothing short of extraordinary."[52]

In return, the CW received 3 years' probation, was fined $500,000, and was ordered to perform 300 hours of community service. At the conclusion of the sentencing hearing, U.S. District Judge Richard Sullivan remarked, "Mr. [deleted], you have your life back. I think you've earned it by virtue of the work you've done over the last five years."[53]

The CW told Judge Sullivan, "These last four years have been humbling and humiliating. I am ashamed of the bad decisions that I made back in 2002, which haunt me to this day."[54]

The lenient sentence drew the attention of commentators. One wrote, "The justice system probably can't crack big cases without the cooperation of unsavory characters, and giving [the CW] favorable treatment is justified up to a point. But even for the best information, letting confessed felons like him essentially off the hook is too high a price to pay."[55]

5.14 Big Fish versus Little Fish

In multi-defendant criminal cases, it is often a race to see who can cut a deal first. Quite often, the outcome flies in the face of fairness. The bigger criminals with more to offer tend to benefit most from cooperation.

Federal Judge Stephen Trott reminds prosecutors to make agreements with "little fish" only to get "big fish." He explains "a jury will understand this approach, but they may reject out of hand anything that smacks of giving a fat deal to a 'big fish' to get a 'little fish.' It will offend their notion of basic fairness and play into the hands of the defense."[56] Unfortunately, the USSGs often allow the big fish out of the net, leaving the little fish behind.

In *United States v. Brigham*[57] the case took a frustratingly illogical twist when the least culpable defendant in a major cocaine prosecution was sentenced. A mere lookout with no information of value to trade, he received a 10-year minimum mandatory sentence. The boss who cooperated got 7 years. The judge summed up the dilemma: "Bold dealers may turn on their former comrades, setting up phony sales and testifying at ensuing trials. Timorous dealers may provide information about their sources and customers. Drones of the organization—the runners, mules, drivers and lookouts—have nothing comparable to offer. They lack the contacts and trust necessary to set up big deals, and they know little information of value. Whatever tales they have to tell, their bosses will have related. Defendants, unlucky enough to be innocent, have no information at all.... The more serious the defendant's crimes, the lower the sentence—because the greater his wrongs, the more information and assistance he has to offer to a prosecutor."[58]

The facts surrounding a routine smuggling case demonstrates the point. Shortly after dawn, an Immigration and Customs Enforcement (ICE) aircraft based out of the Homestead Air Reserve Base located south of Miami, Florida, spotted two boats. The 26-foot SeaVee fishing boat and a 24-foot Four Winds pleasure boat were headed west from Bimini, Bahamas, toward the coast of Florida. There was nothing creative about the route; it was the same one favored by sports fishermen and smugglers alike. ICE headquarters in Miami dispatched three high-speed patrol boats from West Palm Beach and Fort Lauderdale to stop the boats for inspection.

As the pleasure boats approached the Port Everglades Inlet, they were intercepted by the ICE patrol boats and boarded by agents who discovered 26 bales containing 380 kg of cocaine and 487 lb. of marijuana. The agents arrested Henry Rudolf, age 56, and Charles Pilchard, age 45.[59] Both were residents of South Florida.[60]

The men were separated following their arrests. Both were eager to cooperate. However, it quickly became clear that Pilchard was the brains behind the operation. Rudolph was just a boat handler who had been promised a big payday by Pilchard. Later that same evening, Pilchard agreed to participate in what is known as a controlled delivery of the intercepted drugs. Accompanied by an undercover DEA agent, he met with Neko Symonette,[61] the intended recipient of the load. Neko provided them with a minivan that was to be loaded with cocaine and marijuana. Pilchard and the agent departed and returned a short time later to a predetermined location with the dope. The Bahamian was arrested.[62]

From the onset of the investigation it was apparent that Pilchard was farther up the food chain than his codefendant. Only Pilchard got credit for cooperation, and he received an 11-year sentence. Because anything Rudolf knew came from Pilchard, he was not offered a cooperation deal and was sentenced to nearly 20 years in prison.

5.15   Drug Defendants and the Safety Valve

Lower-level drug defendants can escape harsh sentences through what is known as the federal safety valve exception to the drug mandatory minimums.[63] As should be noted, the defendant cannot remain silent regarding the facts surrounding his case and receive favorable sentencing consideration.

Instituted in 1994, it is a strict five-part test that when met allows for a reduced sentence. Each of the following criteria must be met:

1. No one was harmed during the offense.
2. The offender has little or no history of criminal convictions.
3. The offender did not use violence or a gun.
4. The offender was not a leader or organizer of the offense.
5. The offender told the prosecutor all that they know about the offense.

If the court is satisfied that each of the terms is met, a sentence below the minimum mandatory can be applied.

5.16   Reducing Cooperation Agreements to Writing

Cooperation agreements are agreements between the prosecutor and otherwise culpable individuals who provide the government with assistance useful to an investigation in exchange for benefits.[64] Written cooperation agreements are frequently employed by both federal and state prosecutors. Some are case specific and drafted to reflect the needs of the investigation. Others, like those employed by the Broward County, Florida State Attorney's

Office, are boilerplate documents where the only variables are the names of the defendant and his attorney.[65] (See Appendix 5D.)

Whether the document is referred to as a substantial assistance agreement or cooperation agreement, the writing should serve to clarify from the beginning of the relationship what performance the government expects from the CW. It should also leave no doubt about the severity of the consequences for failure to perform.

Substantial assistance agreements also serve as a yardstick against which the pace of a CW's cooperation is measured.[66] When drafting the agreement, care should be taken to guard against placing undue pressure on a defendant to produce cases.

A CW should not be required, in an allegorical sense, to deliver the head of a specific individual to the prosecutor on a silver platter.[67] The cooperation agreement in one DEA case was described by the court as "a remarkable document, the likes of which neither [the judge] nor the prosecutor nor the three defense lawyers" had ever seen. It required in part that:

> The prosecutable cases contemplated by this agreement include purchases of narcotics from the above named persons. These purchases must be corroborated to the satisfaction of the office of the county attorney. At the discretion of the investigating officers, the defendant may make introductions of undercover narcotics officers for the purpose of making above said purchases. Corroboration will be sufficient if such introductions result in successful purchases of controlled narcotics. The defendant must, within 30 days of the signing of this agreement, accomplish 2 purchases each from the California connections (specified target's name) and the Texas connection (unnamed), a total of 4 purchases
>
> A prosecutable case may also include providing information which results in a seizure by search warrant which results in evidence sufficient, in the opinion of the office of the county attorney, to charge one or more of the above listed persons with charges relating to possession of controlled substances with the intent to distribute.[68]

The risk of perjury or entrapment by the CW is too great when his only hope to stay out of prison is to seal the fate of another individual with a prosecutable case. The agreement in question clearly provided an incentive for the informant to frame his designated targets.[69]

The agreement should contain a reasonable time frame for the promised cooperation to occur. If an unreasonably short amount of time is granted for the informant's performance, perjury or entrapment of an investigative target may result. Failing to include when performance by the informant must occur may impede an investigation. Informants seem inclined to postpone their cooperation until the latest possible time, usually shortly before trial or sentencing.

Cooperation agreements can be a two-edged sword for the prosecutor. The existence of the agreement may support the witness's credibility by demonstrating his or her interest in testifying truthfully. The agreement may also hold the potential of impeaching the witness's credibility by showing his or her interest in testifying as the government wishes, regardless of the truth.

Offering too attractive a deal or too many deals to a CW can backfire on the prosecutor.[70] In the high-profile drug trafficking trial of two Miami drug kingpins, the government presented 27 eager witnesses from U.S. prisons to testify against the defendants. That testimony failed to persuade the jury, and the defendants were found not guilty.[71]

5.17   Proffers, Non-Prosecution Agreements, and Immunity

Some cooperation agreements cover onetime statements by the CW, whereas others contemplate continuing active cooperation. Instances in which the CW is to make a onetime statement can have one of two focuses: (1) the CW wants to share information, but asks for immunity before sharing it; or (2) the CW wants a benefit—promise of non-prosecution, a reduced charge, or sentence reduction—and is willing to make a statement to get it.[72] Judge Stephen Trott made the following observation:

> The first problem that usually arises is the "catch 22" situation where you want to know exactly what the witness has to offer before committing yourself to a "deal." But the witness—even though desirous of cooperating—is afraid to talk for fear of incriminating himself unless he is promised something first. When you get into such a situation, never buy a pig in a poke! If you first give a criminal absolute immunity from prosecution or commit to a generous deal and then ask him what he knows, the probability is that you will get nothing but hot air. *Remove the witness' incentive to cooperate and you will lose all the fish, both big and little.* Never forget that almost always they are cooperating because you have them in a trap. Open the door too early and their willingness to cooperate will evaporate.[73]

5.18   Queen for a Day

Proffers or queen-for-a-day letters are written agreements between federal prosecutors and the target of a criminal investigation.[74] The proffer makes it possible for the potential CW to tell the government about his crimes without fear that his own admissions will be used against him later. (See Appendix 5A.)

The queen-for-a-day[75] session is usually an oral presentation attended by the target, his or her attorney, the federal prosecutor, and the case agent. They are there to measure up the target for credibility and to hear what he or she has to offer in the way of cooperation. A great deal rides on how forthcoming she is with information. This is not necessarily a tell-all session. It is a chance for the target to offer her audience pieces of valuable information.

If the prosecutor and the case agent are convinced that the target is of value as either a witness or in an ongoing investigation, they move on to stage two. The prosecutor and target, usually with assistance of counsel, will enter into either a written plea agreement or an immunity agreement.[76]

If no deal is reached, the target is free to leave. Although nothing said can be used against her, the government is free to use the information gained to further their investigation. The target may be indicted at a later date.

5.19   Non-Prosecution Agreements

Entering into a non-prosecution agreement in exchange for the individual's cooperation is often a last resort for the prosecution. Factors to be considered are the importance of the case, the expected value of the cooperation sought, and the relative culpability and criminal history of the individual.

Reasons for considering non-prosecution agreements vary, but usually fall into one of four following categories:

1. There may be no effective means of obtaining the person's timely cooperation short of entering into a non-prosecution agreement.
2. The person may be unwilling to cooperate fully in return for a reduction of charges.
3. The delay in bringing the person to trial might jeopardize the investigation or prosecution of the case in which his cooperation is sought.
4. It is impossible or impractical to rely on the statutory provisions for compulsion of testimony or the production of evidence.

Two examples illustrate the need for considering a non-prosecution agreement. The cooperation sought from the individual is assistance in an ongoing investigation. Although his testimony may one day be needed, his value to the government is in developing evidence in a proactive manner under the direction of the government. Time-sensitive cases involving the statute of limitations, the Speedy Trial Act, or the need to bring evidence to the grand jury may not permit a timely application for a court order to compel testimony.[77]

The attorney for the government should exercise extreme caution to ensure that his non-prosecution agreement does not confer "blanket immunity" on the witness. He should attempt to limit his agreement to non-prosecution based on the testimony or information provided. Such an agreement has advantages over an agreement not to prosecute on the basis of independently obtained evidence if it later appears that the person's criminal involvement was more serious than it originally appeared to be. It also encourages the witness to be as forthright as possible, because the more he reveals, the more protection he will have against a future prosecution. To further encourage full disclosure by the witness, it should be made clear in the agreement that the government's decision to not prosecute is conditioned upon the witness's testimony or production of information being complete and truthful and that failure to testify truthfully may result in a perjury prosecution.[78]

5.20 Immunity

The U.S. Attorney can also compel a witness to testify or provide other information regardless of their assertion of the Fifth Amendment privilege against compulsory self-incrimination.[79] The method is reserved for those persons who have either refused or likely to refuse to cooperate based on that privilege.[80] At trial, compelled testimony may provide a tactical advantage to the prosecution. The witness's testimony is forced from him, not bargained for. Defense efforts to portray the witness as a person who has "cut a deal" with the government will have little credibility when presented to a jury.

Prosecutors obtain immunity for witnesses either pursuant to the federal immunity statute[81] or by an agreement.[82] It is helpful to keep this in mind to avoid becoming confused by a number of other terms frequently used to describe immunity, such as *formal, informal, use, transactional, letter,*[83] *desk, pocket,* and *act-of-production immunity.*[84]

Before obtaining a compulsion order, the attorney for the government should weigh all relevant considerations, including the following:

- Importance of the investigation or prosecution to effective enforcement of the criminal laws.
- Value of the person's testimony or information to the investigation or prosecution.
- Likelihood of prompt and full compliance with a compulsion order, and the effectiveness of available sanctions if there is no such compliance.
- Person's relative culpability in connection with the offense or offenses being investigated or prosecuted, and his or her criminal history.
- Possibility of successfully prosecuting the person before compelling his or her testimony.
- Likelihood of adverse collateral consequences to the person if he or she testifies or provides information under a compulsion order.[85]

A witness who refuses to testify or to produce information following the issuance of an order of compulsion[86] may be found in either civil contempt[87] or criminal contempt.[88] Confinement is limited to the life of the court proceeding or the term of the grand jury, but in no event may the confinement exceed 18 months.[89]

Individuals already serving a prison sentence are not immune to the criminal penalties for contempt. If they refuse to testify following a compulsion order, their sentence may be interrupted while they serve their intervening sentence for contempt.[90]

Judge Trott had this warning for prosecutors to consider before offering an immunity deal:

> In this perilous world, "character" and "credibility" aren't just interesting issues in a book about evidence—they become the pivotal win-or-lose elements in the prosecution's case, from start to finish. How these witnesses are managed and how these issues are approached and handled may determine the success or failure of the case. In this vein, the prosecutor on occasion will surprisingly discover that his or her own personal integrity is on the line, and this is not a laughing matter. It is neither helpful to a prosecutor's case nor very comforting personally to have the defense arguing to the court and jury, for example, that you, as a colossal idiot, have given immunity to the real killer in order to prosecute an innocent man.[91]

5.20.1   Case Study: Immunity and a Federal Case That Imploded

FBI informant Fannie "Patsy" Beard's days were numbered when the prosecution turned over its evidence to defense lawyers. They were representing members of a Richmond, Virginia, street gang known as the Brick Yard Boys. Among the exhibits the government planned to use at trial was a DVD of Beard purchasing $100 worth of crack from a gang member. She had worn a hidden camera while making the buy. There was no mistaking that she was an FBI informant.

Complicating matters for Beard, her home address was on the DVD. The prosecutor called it "a colossal blunder." He later told a reporter, "For obvious reasons, you don't want a defendant to learn the identity of a confidential informant."[92]

This was not the first time information had made it to the street identifying Beard as an informant. Earlier in the month, she was called as a government witness in the prosecution of another drug dealer. Defense attorneys were quoted as saying, "Numerous witnesses from the community have confirmed that Beard's status as a working informant was common knowledge. Likewise, word of the existence of the video of Beard's buy from one of the gang leaders travelled like wildfire through the community."[93]

The FBI knew Beard was in danger. They gave her $7800 to move out of town for a while. According to testimony by one of her FBI agent handlers,

"She didn't want to move from Richmond. She just said she wasn't going to have people selling drugs make her move."[94]

Just after midnight on December 2, 2006, Beard was lured from her apartment into an alley below her window. She was shot eight times in the back and once in the abdomen with a .40 caliber pistol.[95]

Beard's killing spurred an intensive FBI investigation. Two men were quickly arrested and charged with the informant's murder.

One of the men had been through the system before and began cooperating almost immediately. He named his partner as the shooter and agreed to testify in exchange for immunity. He was immunized and the prosecution began building its case against the shooter.

It was a mistake. According to defense attorneys for the two, it was a "federal case that imploded." A jailhouse informant reported that the informant who was granted immunity bragged about killing Beard. The confidential informant (CI) recounted details about the crime that only the killer could have provided.[96] Prosecutors had charged the wrong man with murder and had granted the killer immunity.

The U.S. Attorney for the district was forced to drop the murder charges against both men. One of the defense lawyers stated, "Unfortunately, the government had already struck an astonishingly lenient deal with [one of the defendants], a deal with the devil."[97]

At this writing, no one has been prosecuted for Beard's murder. The court files regarding the case have been sealed. Had it not been for the work of an investigative journalist with the *Richmond Times-Dispatch*,[98] the entire fiasco would have remained a courthouse secret.

5.21 Prisoners and Rule 35

A Rule 35 motion is filed by a federal prosecutor on behalf of a prisoner already serving his sentences in return for substantial assistance.[99] It is for those who have a change of heart regarding cooperating with the government following conviction. It asks the court to reduce a previously imposed sentence based on a prisoner's substantial assistance.

Rule 35 allow the judge to impose a sentence reduction below the statutory minimum sentence.[100] The reason for the sentence reduction can be provided *in-camera* and under seal for the safety of the CW or to avoid disclosing an ongoing investigation.[101]

5.22 Surrogate and Third-Party Cooperation

Some defendants have nothing of value to offer the government in exchange for a downward sentencing departure.[102] Others cannot cooperate with the government because of very real threats against themselves or members of their family. Individuals in both predicaments have become extremely resourceful. Some have resorted to recruiting surrogates, usually family members, friends, or associates, who can provide information or produce cases and become CWs or informants on their behalf.[103]

The defendant may try to act as a middleman, receiving the information and passing it on to his agent handler for action. Some act as an intermediary and introduce the prospective informant to the agent for evaluation and utilization.

The brokered information or informant, if valuable, will garner the defendant favorable consideration at sentencing. The proxy or surrogate informant, however, may receive nothing in return for his services.

Not all courts or U.S. Attorneys Offices are receptive to the services of a surrogate. One court instituted a four-part test for determining whether a motion for sentence reduction may be based on third-party assistance. The following questions must be answered in the affirmative:

1. Did the defendant play a material role in requesting, encouraging, facilitating, or persuading a third party to provide substantial assistance to the prosecution?
2. Was the defendant a motivating factor for the third party to provide substantial assistance to the prosecution?
3. Did either the defendant or the third party act with any impermissible motivation that undermines the court's confidence in the integrity of the substantial assistance process or the information provided?
4. Are there any other circumstances that weigh against granting the substantial assistance motion?[104]

The surrogate scheme, although resourceful, can be dangerous for the proxy informant. One desperate defendant in Miami recruited eight CWs for the government. It did not go over well with the targets of the investigation. The defendant and his brother were shot to death in retaliation. Four other people connected to the case were also shot.[105]

Surrogates are not a twenty-first-century phenomenon. The 1992 prosecution of General Manuel Noriega apparently relied upon the testimony of a surrogate CW. *Newsweek* magazine reported that "a Cali Cartel lawyer offered Noriega's prosecutor a deal: if the government would cut the prison sentence of a Cali trafficker (half brother of a Cali Cartel boss), the cartel would produce a witness to nail Noriega."[106]

Without asking too many questions, the government agreed, and the relative's sentence was cut by 9 years. All sides understood the need for secrecy. It was later learned that the witness was paid $1.2 million by the cartel for his testimony. It was also learned that his alternative to testifying was not a lengthy prison sentence, it was a threat. In Mexico, such an arrangement is referred to as a choice, *entrela plata el plombo*, that is, "the choice is between silver and lead."[107]

5.23   Sentence Reduction Scams and Schemes

5.23.1   Rent-a-Rat

An Atlanta attorney and his investigator, a former smuggler, formed a business that exploited the potential Rule 35 held for prisoners. Both men knew the cooperation system and its potential for exploitation.

The attorney had represented his investigator in the late 1980s. He was facing a lengthy prison sentence for drug smuggling. The attorney worked out a deal with the DEA and FBI. The smuggler agreed to work as an informant and wound up spending only 4 years in prison.[108] His attorney became known as being "among the elite of Atlanta criminal defense lawyers."[109]

Their business was known as Conviction Consultants.[110] The pair aided convicts in search of sentence reductions.[111] The problem for some inmates was that their information just was not good enough to satisfy federal agents.

The attorney and his nonlawyer partner came through for prisoners in need of information. They sold actionable criminal information to their jailed clients. Some prisoners were reported to have paid as much as $225,000 for information.[112] Once the inmate received the information, it was committed to memory and a story rehearsed to satisfy agents. The local defense bar referred to the business as "Rent-a-Rat."[113]

As might be expected, federal agents finally got wind of the scheme through an informant. Investigators learned that the pair culled valuable information from the files of other federal criminal investigations.[114]

Both men were arrested for tax evasion and obstruction of justice. The lawyer's investigator knew the drill. He immediately rolled over and became a CW against his partner.[115] The attorney pled guilty to one count each of tax evasion and obstruction of justice and agreed to surrender his license to practice law.[116] His investigator got a hand slap sentence.

5.23.1.1   *5K1s and the Cartel of Snitches*

A federal informant from Miami, Florida devised a sentence reduction scheme during the late 90s that ran for nearly a decade. He used the promise of 5K1sentence reductions to convince one hundred and fourteen major Colombian cocaine traffickers to become cooperating witnesses and informants. Colombian drug kingpins called the plan the "Programs de Resociallacion de Narcotraficantes" or the Narcotics Traffickers

Rehabilitation Program. Detractors called it the Cartel of Snitches.[117] While no firm evidence exists, the government alleged that the informant was paid hundreds of millions of dollars by traffickers.

The program, while achieving some measure of success, became extremely dangerous, both for the informant and some of the traffickers who became participants. At least one trafficker enrollee was murdered in Colombia. The program also drew the attention of FBI corruption investigators. FBI agents executed a search warrant on a DEA agent's office, seizing records and other evidence. The reputations of DEA agents, federal prosecutors and federal judges who became involved in the "program" were tarnished. The informant was arrested, although never convicted of a serious crime relating to the scheme.[118]

The FBI investigation alleged that the informant and an accomplice, also an informant, solicited huge cash payments from traffickers to arrange phony cooperation deals. Excerpts from an FBI affidavit explain the scheme: "From at least as early as May 1999, [the informant] and others have been obstructing justice and laundering money through a scheme devised to circumvent the United States justice system, by taking money, both in cash and in the form of wire transfers, which is known to [the informant] to be the proceeds of illegal narcotics trafficking, from federally indicted and as yet unindicted narcotics traffickers, in order to bribe members of the United States Justice Department, United States Customs Service agents, and Drug Enforcement Administration agents to arrange phony cooperation deals to insure that the traffickers do not receive sentences of imprisonment. [The informant] advises them that for a substantial fee, typically millions of dollars, they can bribe members of the U.S. Justice Department and Federal Agents.

"[The informants] represent to the traffickers that the federal officials will agree to the traffickers' release on bond and agree to credit phony cooperation to the traffickers to reduce their possible jail sentences. [The informants] typically promise the traffickers that they will not serve a single day in jail. [The informants] further arrange for the traffickers to surrender their own money or a load of cocaine (which they own), to agents of the DEA with whom they are working, making it appear as though the money and the narcotics belong to another drug trafficking organization. The fee [the informant] charges each trafficker to enter the program depends on their ability to pay. More successful traffickers are charged a larger fee. According to sources who have spoken with several of these drug traffickers, [the informant's] fees have ranged from $6,000,000 to $100,000,000."

The Narcotics Traffickers Rehabilitation Program no longer exists. The informant was allegedly blacklisted by the DEA. Agents involved in the scheme claimed they were duped and endured years of adverse employment actions. Most were vindicated.

In 2007, the informant sued the government for $28,500,000. That is the sum he settled on for unpaid rewards for his actions as head of the program.

The informant's version of how the Narcotics Traffickers Rehabilitation Program differs dramatically from the FBI account. What follows is taken from his lawsuit[119]:

During the late 1990s, the Plaintiff became a documented confidential informant for the Federal Bureau of Investigation and later, for the Drug Enforcement Administration.[120] According to his attorney, he was not a traditional informant and his methodology was anything but parochial.

The informant would play the role of an intermediary, or broker, between Colombian drug traffickers. Some were completely unknown (and thus, unidentified) to U.S. law enforcement. Others were already identified by their real names or nicknames as "suspects" by U.S. law enforcement. Others were already indicted for drug trafficking and/or money laundering charges in various federal districts across the United States.[121]

The informant approached several Colombian targets in Colombia, South America, and attempted to convince them that it would be better for them to anticipatorily negotiate their criminal exposure with the United States. He explained the advantages of striking a deal in advance rather than waiting until an investigation and/or an indictment and/or an arrest and/ or an extradition to the United States might result against them. Many of the targets welcomed the suggestion and decided to participate in the informant's plan.[122]

The informant educated the Colombian targets on their criminal exposure by connecting them with various experienced American federal criminal defense lawyers, one being a former federal prosecutor. All of these lawyers were based out of Miami, Florida.[123] Naturally, it made sense for the Colombian targets to listen to the informant and the American lawyers, and, if then interested in proceeding with the plan/program, to have legal representation secured before embarking on this plan/program. The Colombian targets needed legal counsel to "navigate" them through the federal criminal justice system. If the Colombian targets ultimately negotiated a deal, they would need lawyers to handle the entire gamut of initial appearance, bond, plea colloquy, presentence investigation report, and sentencing.[124]

Once the informant introduced the American lawyers to the Colombian targets, the lawyers would then get retained and then take over as legal representatives for the Colombian targets and further deal with a group of U.S. law enforcement agents and prosecutors, handpicked to work out deals for the Colombian targets. A particular U.S. Attorney for the Southern District of Florida became the coordinator of this "recruiting effort."

Generally, the plan/program required the Colombian targets to meet with FBI and/or DEA agents in Panama. The purpose of the initial part of the meeting was for introductions to be made between the Colombian targets (and their lawyers) on one side and the federal agents on the other side. Subsequently, the meetings took the form of debriefings, all with a view toward negotiating plea agreements between the targets and the United States. There were many of these types of meetings in Panama over a period of several years. Several FBI and DEA agents were involved in this plan/program that grew exponentially over the years.[125]

As indicated, some of these Colombian targets were not even under investigation at the time. Some were under investigation in various (early, midrange, or advanced) stages. Others were already under indictment in the United States. Depending on the then legal status of each Colombian target and the level of his or her "cooperation" with U.S. law enforcement each Colombian target would, in varying degree, reach a "sweetheart deal" (in varying degrees of course) and then receive, in some instances, an "S" Visa—to prevent his/her/their deportation back to his/her/their home country: Colombia.[126]

Cooperation included grand jury testimony, trial testimony, the recruitment of other Colombian targets, and voluntary forfeitures. Voluntary forfeitures included "plan participants" making their own bank accounts and huge personal cashes of cocaine available for seizure by DEA. These forfeitures became known as "positives" and were considered as substantial assistance at sentencing.

According to the lawsuit, the plan/program was extremely successful. All in all, the informant convinced and successfully recruited about 114 Colombian targets to enter into the program. Twenty-five participants were fugitives at the time of negotiating the deals.[127] From 2000 until 2007, there were 35 Colombian targets who reached deals with the United States. A list identifying these individuals was attached to the lawsuit.[128]

The informant's lawyer described the economic and noneconomic benefits to the United States in bringing all of these Colombian targets to justice as "mind-boggling." He explained in the lawsuit that "United States obtained over a hundred federal drug convictions. Much of the cooperation of the Colombian targets itself resulted in other investigations, prosecutions and convictions—something akin to a 'domino effect.' In varying degrees, these targets forfeited cash, real estate, jewelry, and art in an estimated total amount somewhere between $250 million and $500 million."[129]

The informant's attorney placed the value of the 114 cases, based on $250,000 per case at $28,500,000. At this writing the case has yet to be resolved.[130]

5.23.1.2 *Defense Attorney Windfall*

The biggest cash beneficiary of the USSGs is the criminal defense lawyer. The threat of harsh prison sentences in state courts and the strict federal sentencing guidelines were a windfall for the defense bar. Six-figure, money-up-front, nonrefundable fees, particularly in federal drug cases, are the rule, not the exception. In most cases, the accused are merely hiring a conduit to a cooperation deal.[131]

Those lawyers with the gumption to go to trial and who have wealthy clients who can afford the cost can do very well. The defense attorney who represented Colombian drug baron Fabio Ochoa in 2003 received more than $5 million for going to trial, despite the guilty verdict. According to Ochoa's attorney, "It was difficult to get a fair trial in Miami."[132]

Some lawyers demand an obscenely high fee when they promise a trial with no intention of ever seeing the first juror. Instead, they rush to the prosecutor, begging for a cooperation deal. It is called *bleed 'em and plead 'em.*[133]

Appendix 5A: U.S. Attorney's Ground Rules Letter Regarding Proffer

To: Informant's Attorney

From: United States Attorney

Date:

RE: *United States v. (client)*

Dear Mr.   ,

Through you, your client has informed the government that he would like to plead guilty and cooperate with the government in the subject case and in the investigation of future cases, with a view toward obtaining a favorable sentence in the subject case. Let me outline the ground rules of your client's cooperation.

The government requires from your client a completely truthful written statement of his involvement in this case and the involvement of the other participants therein, including his codefendant. He also must provide complete and truthful information regarding any other criminal activity of which he has personal knowledge. This office agrees that no statements made by (client) in any written proffer or debriefing pursuant to this letter will be offered into evidence against him as part of the government's direct case in any criminal proceeding. However, the government remains free to make derivative use of the information derived from your client directly or indirectly for the purpose of obtaining leads to other evidence. Such information may be used against (client) in any subsequent prosecution. Your client expressly waives any right to claim that such evidence should not be introduced because it was obtained as a result of his statements. This provision is specifically imposed to preclude the necessity of a *Kastigar* hearing in any proceeding in which such evidence is to be used against your client.

Further, the government may use statements made by your client in any written proffer or debriefing and all evidence, derived directly or indirectly for the purpose of impeachment of cross-examination, if (client) testifies at any trial or hearing, and/or in any rebuttal case against him in a criminal trial in which he is a defendant or a witness.

No additional promises, agreements, or conditions have been entered into other than as set forth in this letter, and none will be entered into unless in writing and signed by all parties. This letter does not confer any derivative use immunity or transactional immunity upon your client. If the foregoing accurately reflects the understanding and agreement between this office and your client, it is requested that (client) and yourself execute this letter as provided below.

Very truly yours,
UNITED STATES ATTORNEY
BY:_____

ASSISTANT UNITED STATES ATTORNEY

ACKNOWLEDGMENT
I have received this letter from my attorney, John Smith, have read it and discussed it with him, and I hereby acknowledge that it fully sets forth my understanding and agreement with the office of the United States Attorney for the Southern District of Florida. I state that there have been no additional promises or representations made to me by any official of the United States Government or by my attorney in connection with this matter.
Dated: _____
DEFENDANT
Witnessed by: _____
COUNSEL FOR DEFENDANT

Appendix 5B: Cooperating Witness Agreement and Waiver

I, _____, acknowledge that I have been advised of and fully understand my Constitutional rights to remain silent and to an attorney, including, but not limited to, the following rights:
1. That I have a right to remain silent.
2. That anything I say can and will be used against me in a criminal prosecution, pursuant to and limited by the terms of this Agreement.
3. That I have a right to the presence of an attorney to assist me prior to questioning and to be with me during questioning if I so desire.
4. That if I cannot afford an attorney I have a right to have an attorney appointed for me prior to questioning at no cost to myself.

I further acknowledge that no one has used any sort of violence or threats or any promise of immunity or benefit whatsoever to encourage me to answer questions, and that no representations have been made to me other than the representations set forth in this Agreement.

My consent to cooperate with the investigation of _____ is limited to consent to derivative use of my statements, and to the direct use of my statements for impeachment and to the direct use of my statements in actions against myself for violations of any of the terms of this Agreement. I do not consent to any other direct use of my statements made pursuant to this Agreement against myself. I agree that the State may use any information, leads, evidence, or witnesses supplied by me, i.e., any "fruits" of my cooperation, in any way.

This interview is being conducted so that the State is made aware of all information I have in the matter of_____. At this point, I understand that the State makes no promises or benefits regarding any future plea negotiations or sentencing recommendations in [pending case].

I enter into this Agreement in the hope that my cooperation will be considered as a mitigating circumstance by the State in any future plea negotiations in [pending case]. However, I acknowledge that the State retains complete discretion in plea negotiations and sentencing recommendations and that the State has no power to assure that the Court will even consider any particular mitigating circumstances or sentencing recommendations. I agree that any favorable action by the State as a result of my cooperation is contingent on the State's evaluation of the truthfulness, completeness, and usefulness of my cooperation and that the State's judgment in all respects is final and binding upon me. In particular, I agree that any untruthfulness on my part will disqualify me from any benefit due to my cooperation whatsoever.

This Agreement and Waiver is to cover all statements made by me and/or actions taken by me at the request of the undersigned Interviewer(s) commencing at the time this Agreement and Waiver is signed by the Interviewer(s) and continuing until rescinded in writing by me or until superseded by another written Agreement or until the commencement of the trial in [pending case], whichever occurs first.

_____ _____
Date and Time Signature of Witness

_____ _____
Date and Time Witness's Attorney, if any

_____ _____
Date and Time Interviewer

_____ _____
Date and Time Interviewer

Appendix 5C: Prosecutor's Ground Rules Letter to Attorney for Cooperating Witness

IT IS HEREBY AGREED between the State of _____ and _____, that in return for pleading guilty to Possession of a Narcotic Drug, a class four felony, *with* probation available, which is currently pending in cause number _____, before the Superior Court of _____ County, that _____ will perform all of the conditions listed in this agreement:

1. That he will execute a standard _____ County Informant's agreement and abide by the conditions set forth therein.
2. That he will provide control agents with introductions to drug dealers and/or information that will enable the control agent to obtain search warrants resulting in a total of [ ] cases. A case shall be defined as involving at least [ ] kilos of cocaine or heroin.
3. That he has 180 days from the first of _____ in which to complete these [ ] introductions.
4. That he understands that, if possible, he shall not be required to testify unless he has become a material witness in a case.
5. That he agrees that if the State determines that he is a material witness, he shall testify truthfully at all proceedings required by the prosecutor including, but not limited to, interviews, pretrial motions, trials, retrials, or any other proceeding that the State deems necessary. He further agrees that all such testimony shall be truthful and that failure to testify truthfully will, at the prosecutor's discretion, result in felony charges of perjury being filed and/or this agreement being revoked and the original charges being reinstated and prosecuted to the fullest extent of the law. He further understands and agrees that the State has this right even though he may have been found guilty and sentenced. The prosecutor shall have sole right to determine whether the terms and conditions set forth have been breached.
6. He understands that if the full terms of this agreement are not completed, the attorney for the State shall determine what credit will be given for the parts that were completed.

Failure to abide by any of the conditions set forth in this agreement will result, at the discretion of the State, in revocation of the agreement and resumption of prosecution on the original charges.

I have read and understand the terms of the agreement set forth above and agree to the conditions set forth. Signed this _____ day of _____, 2_____.

_____
DEFENDANT

I have discussed the terms set forth in the agreement with _____ and believe that he understands the terms and conditions contained in the agreement. Signed this ____ day of _____,2___.

_____
ATTORNEY FOR DEFENDANT
I hereby bind the State of _____ to the terms and conditions set forth in the
above agreement. Signed this _____ day of _____, 2____.

_____
DEPUTY COUNTY ATTORNEY

Appendix 5D: Substantial Assistance Agreement

In the Circuit Court of the Seventeenth Judicial Circuit
In And For Broward County, Florida
State of Florida, Plaintiff

vs.

Defendant

SUBSTANTIAL ASSISTANCE AGREEMENT

As part of entering into this Substantial Assistance Agreement, I, [defendant's name] understand and agree to the following conditions:

1. I must enter a plea of guilty to the charges in this case. I cannot enter a plea of no contest or nolo contendere. My plea of guilty will be open to the court without any promises having been made as to what sentence I might receive. The court will set a sentencing date in the future. The substantial assistance must be rendered by the time of the sentencing date. The State will consent to one sentencing continuance if I need additional time and I have complied with all of the conditions of this Agreement. It is up to the court to decide whether to continue the sentencing date. If I have not complied with all the terms and conditions of this Agreement as determined by the State, the State will advise the court that I am in violation of this Agreement and the State thereafter will not move the court to reduce the sentence, pursuant to F.S. Section 93.135(4) or 921.0026(2)(i). Any assistance I provide to the police after I have violated this Agreement will not be considered in determining substantial assistance.
2. I agree and understand that the failure to do anything lawfully asked by law enforcement or by the State Attorney's Office is a violation of this agreement.
3. I agreed to provide a sworn truthful deposition, statement, or testimony if requested. As part of this Agreement, if determined necessary by a court or the State, I must testify truthfully in any statement, deposition, or trial.

I further agree that the State will determine if my statement, deposition, or testimony is truthful. Failure to testify truthfully is a violation of this Agreement.

4. I agreed to submit to a polygraph examination of requested. I agree not to take any other polygraphs prior to taking the test requested by the State Attorney's Office. By entering into this Agreement I stipulate to the qualifications of the examiner and the results of the polygraph. If the examination indicates any deception concerning the substantial assistance rendered, the State will not move for substantial assistance, and I will be bound by my previously entered plea of guilty. I agree that if I take any polygraph not requested by the State Attorney's Office or law enforcement, I am in violation of this Agreement.

5. I agree and understand that the violation of a court order including the conditions of bond is violation of this Agreement.

6. I agree that the commission of any new criminal offense during the pendency of this Agreement, including any traffic criminal offense, is a violation of this Agreement. I further understand that it will not be necessary that I be convicted of this new offense to violate this Agreement and that is a violation of this Agreement if the State determines that probable cause exists that the new criminal offense was committed.

7. I agree and understand that the possession of illegal drugs, unless under the direction and supervision of a police officer in furtherance of a criminal investigation, is a violation of this Agreement.

8. I agree to cooperate with law enforcement, including contacting the lead detective a minimum of three times a week or more if requested and to abide by all the terms and conditions of police supervision. Failure to do so is a violation of this Agreement.

9. I agree and understand that acting without being authorized and monitored by law enforcement as a violation of this Agreement.

10. I agree to only deal with people that have been verified by law enforcement to be involved in criminal activity.

11. I agree that it is my responsibility to provide substantial assistance if I am unable to do so or otherwise violate this Agreement I cannot withdraw my plea.

12. I understand that in order for the State to request substantial assistance my assistance must result in a prosecutable case or cases in an amount deemed sufficient by the State. It will be in the prosecutor's sole discretion to decide if I have provided substantial assistance. This is a unilateral decision and is not subject to review by the court.

13. I agree and understand my case has been available for review as a public record, including being available on the Internet. I understand my attorney may ask the court to seal the change of plea proceedings, and portions of the Clerk of the Court's Internet website which references my plea of

guilty. However, whether the change of plea proceeding is sealed or not, it remains my responsibility to perform substantial assistance and that the failure of portions of my case to be sealed on the Internet or in any other manner will not excuse my failure to perform substantial assistance.

14. I understand I will not know the State's recommendation to the court until sentencing. The court will determine what sentence is imposed. I stand even if I provide substantial assistance, the State may recommend to the court, prison, community control, county jail or probation. I also may be sentenced as a habitual offender if qualified.

15. I understand the State will consider any assistance rendered to law enforcement, if any, since the time of my arrest in this case. However, should I violate any provisions of this Agreement, no credit will be given.

16. I agree that I violate any of the terms, conditions, or understandings of any paragraph of this Agreement in any way, or fail to provide substantial assistance as determined by the State, I will not be given credit for any assistance that was previously provided and cannot withdraw my plea. I understand I will be subject to immediate revocation of my bond or release status, and my case will proceed to sentencing on my open plea. I further agree that if I violate any of the terms, conditions, or understandings in each paragraph of this substantial assistance Agreement that the State may seek an ex parte warrant from a court that revokes my release. I further understand that by violating any of the terms of this Agreement I am subjecting myself to be sentenced to the maximum penalties as described in this Agreement.

17. I agree that our entire understanding is contained in this document and tape recording and that no other promises have been made by anyone relating to this Agreement or sentencing.

18. I understand that by entering into this Agreement I am giving up my right to be tried by a jury, the right to compel witnesses on my behalf, the right to confront and cross-examine witnesses, the right not to be compelled to incriminate myself, and the right to appeal all matters relating to the judgment, including the issue of guilt or innocence. I further understand that pleading guilty may subject me to deportation if I am not a US citizen. Furthermore, if I have been previously convicted of a sexually violent offense or a sexually motivated offense the plea may subject me to involuntary civil commitment as a sexually violent predator upon completion of the sentence. I further understand that if I am convicted of a Trafficking or Conspiracy to Traffic in Drugs offense, I must be adjudicated guilty, pursuant to F.S. 893.135(3). I further understand that if convicted pursuant to F.S. 322.055, of possession or sale of, trafficking in, or conspiracy to possess, sell or traffic in a controlled substance, my driver's license will be revoked.

19. I understand there may be danger involved to myself in assisting the police. No one has pressured me into entering this Agreement and I am entering this Agreement freely and voluntarily and with the advice of counsel.

20. The State reserves the right to withdraw from this Agreement if I fail to enter a guilty plea within seven (7) days from the date this Agreement was signed. This Agreement becomes binding on the parties upon the court's acceptance of the defendant's guilty plea to the charges.

_____

Defendant   Date

_____

Attorney for Defendant   Date

_____ _____

Assistant State Attorney   Date

Endnotes

1. *DEA Agents Manual*, Ch. 66.
2. See Attorney General's Guidelines Regarding the FBI's Use of Confidential Human Sources.
3. *Miranda v. Arizona*, 384 U.S. 436, 474, 86 S. Ct. 1602, 1628, 16 L. Ed. 2d 694 (1966).
4. 28 U.S.C. 530B.
5. The ABA's Model Rule of Professional Conduct 4.2 prohibits communication with a witness about the particular matter on which he is being represented without the consent of his counsel. Many states have similar ethical standards for their attorneys. For example, the California Bar's Rules for Professional Conduct tracks the language of the ABA Rule 4.2. Thus, beginning upon the moment of indictment at the latest, a prosecuting attorney has a duty under ethical rules to refrain from communicating with represented defendants.
6. Leveritt, M., "Snitches: Death Undercover," *Arkansas Times*, February 28, 2007.
7. Baker, J., "FBI Informant Gets 6 Months for Money Laundering," *Memphis Flyer*, June 18, 2008; see also DEA Press Release, "Memphis City Councilmen and Former Shelby County Commission Candidate Charged," December 4, 2006.
8. US Sentencing Guidelines §5K1.1. Substantial Assistance to Authorities: Upon motion of the government stating that the defendant has provided substantial assistance in the investigation or prosecution of another person who has committed an offense, the court may depart from the guidelines.
    1. The appropriate reduction shall be determined by the court for reasons stated that may include, but are not limited to, consideration of the following:
        a. The court's evaluation of the significance and usefulness of the defendant's assistance, taking into consideration the government's evaluation of the assistance rendered

b. The truthfulness, completeness, and reliability of any information or testimony provided by the defendant
c. The nature and extent of the defendant's assistance
d. Any injury suffered, or any danger or risk of injury to the defendant or his family resulting from his assistance
e. The timeliness of the defendant's assistance

9. *Missouri v. Frye*, 132 S.Ct. 1399, 1407 (2012).
10. Ibid.
11. *U.S. v. Brigham*, 977 F.2d 317 (7th Cir. 1992).
12. Government's Motion for Reduction in Sentence Pursuant to U.S.S.G. 5K1.1
13. §5K1.1 Sentencing Guidelines.
14. Dervan, L.E., "Bargained Justice: Plea-Bargaining's Innocence Problem and the Brady Safety-Valve," *2012 Utah L. Rev.* 51, 64, 56 (2012) (citing research literature to state "it is clear that plea-bargaining has an innocence problem."
15. Markham, J., "Improper Consideration at Sentencing of a Defendant's Decision To Go to Trial," North Carolina Criminal Law, UNC's School of Government Blog, December 15, 2010, citing cases where judge's statements at sentencing indicate disdain for defendant's decision to go to trial.
16. "An Offer You Can't Refuse: How US Federal Prosecutors Force Codefendants to Plead Guilty, "*Human Rights Watch*, 2013, ISBN 978 1 62313 0824. (Hereinafter, "An Offer You Can't Refuse").
17. In fiscal year 2012, out of a total of 26,560 federal drug cases, 24,736, or 93%, involved drug trafficking; the remainder were cases for simple possession and use of a communications facility to facilitate a drug offense. Federal Sentencing Statistics by District, Circuit & State for Fiscal Year 2012, http://www.ussc.gov/Data_and_Statistics/Federal_Sentencing_Statistics/State_District_Circuit/2012/index.cfm
18. "An Offer You Can't Refuse."
19. 18 U.S.C. §924(c).
20. 21 U.S.C. §841(b)(1).
21. Warmbir, S., "Calabrese: No Time To Kill People," *Chicago Sun-Times*, August 17, 2007.
22. *Operation Family Secrets*, National Public Radio, November 14, 2011; Robinson, M., "Mob Hit Man Frank Calabrese, Sr. Gets Life in Prison," *Huffington Post*, June 29, 2009.
23. Goudie, C., "Peek Inside Former *Mobster's New Book*," *ABC News*, March 4, 2011.
24. "'The Oldfather', 93, Sentenced to 8 Years," *The Telegraph*, January 14, 2011.
25. "Mob Boss, 93, is Jailed for Eight Years over Strip Joint Extortion—But Judge Tells Him He'll Be Out to Celebrate His 100th Birthday if He Behaves," *The Daily Mail*, January 23, 2011.
26. Lengel, A., "Modern Mobsters Still Follow Dad into the Mafia," AOLnews, February 5, 2011.
27. Fisher, J., "Mobster Gets into Heated Fight Outside a Brooklyn Courtroom," *New York Post*, June 10, 2010.
28. Capeci, J., "Turncoat Son, Death Behind Bars," *Huffington Post*, June 1, 2010.
29. Kennedy, A.M., "Speech at the American Bar Association Annual Meeting in San Francisco," August 9, 2003.

30. For example, pursuant to 21 U.S.C. §§ 841(b) (1) (A) and 960(b) (1), a statutory range of 10 years to life applies to offenses involving at least: 1 kilogram of heroin, 5 kilograms of cocaine (powder), 280 grams of cocaine base, 1000 kilograms of marijuana or 1000 plants, 50 grams of actual methamphetamine or 500 grams of mixture or substance.

31. 18 U.S.C. 3553.

32. 543 U.S. 220, 125 S. Ct. 738, 160 L.Ed. 2d 621, 2005 U.S. It is in violation of the Sixth Amendment right to trial by jury to allow a judge to enhance a sentence using facts not reviewed by a jury.

33. USSG 5K1.1.

34. From transcript of Gravano's 1994 sentencing.

35. Smith, G.B., "Sammy Bull's Book Bucks Will Go to Victims," *Daily News*, August 25, 2001.

36. U.S. Sentencing Comm'n, Mandatory Minimum Penalties in the Federal Criminal Justice System (October 2011) (Mandatory Minimum Report), http://www.ussc.gov/Legislative_and_Public_Affairs/Congressional_ Testimony_ and_Reports/Mandatory_Minimum_Penalties/20111031_RtC_Mandatory_ Minimum.cfm.

37. Report on the Continuing Impact of *United States v. Booker* on Federal Sentencing, United States Sentencing Commission (Dec. 2012) finding: The sentencing guidelines have remained the essential starting point in all federal sentences and have continued to exert significant influence on federal sentencing trends over time. The most stable relationship between the guidelines and sentences imposed occurred in some of the most frequently prosecuted offenses, including drug trafficking, immigration, and firearms offenses.

38. Sobel, R.L., "Judge Vaults Rail, Helps Nab Escaping Defendant," *Los Angeles Times*, April 16, 1991.

39. A sentence is reduced for substantial assistance under Section 5K1.1 of the U.S. Sentencing Guidelines and Rule 35 of the Federal Rules of Criminal Procedure.

40. USSG Section 5K1.1.

41. Cohen, L.P., "Split Decision: Federal Cases Show Big Gap in Reward for Cooperation," *The Wall Street Journal*, November 29, 2004.

42. Ibid.

43. USSG Commission, *Sourcebook of Federal Sentencing Statistics,* Table 30 for 2000—50.3%, 2001—50%, 2002—50%, 2003—49.9%, 2004—48.5%, 2005— 50%, 2006—47.8%, 2008—47.8%, 2009—48.9%.

44. See *Departure and Variance Primer,* Prepared by the Office of General Counsel U.S. Sentencing Commission June 2013.

45. 18 U.S.C. § 3553(c).

46. A hearing is said to be *in camera* when it is heard before the judge in his or her chapters or when spectators are not in the courtroom.

47. Elkind, P., "The 'Pillsbury Doughboy' Jumps the Fence," *Fortune*, December 28, 2005.

48. "Ex-WorldCom CFO Gets 5 Years," *CBS News*, August 11, 2005.

49. "Ex-WorldCom Finance Chief Jailed," *BBC News*, August 11, 2005.

50. "Sullivan Gets Five Years for WorldCom Raw," Associated Press, August 11, 2005.

51. Van Voris, B., "Ex-Galleon Trader Who Led U.S. to Probe Rajaratnam Gets Probation," Bloomberg.com, January 20, 2012.
52. Ibid.
53. Ibid.
54. Ibid.
55. "Insider Trading Snitch Got Off Too Lightly," *Thomson Reuters News & Insight*, January 23, 2012.
56. Trott, S.S., "The Successful Use of Snitches, Informants, Coconspirators, and Accomplices as Witnesses for the Prosecution in a Criminal Case" (January 1984). Former Assistant Attorney General Criminal Division, Public Integrity Section, U.S. Department of Justice, currently serving as Federal Judge, 9th Circuit Court of Appeals.
57. *U.S. v. Brigham*, 977 F.2d 317 (7th Cir. 1992).
58. Ibid.
59. Names changed.
60. Cohen, L.P., "Split Decision: Federal Cases Show Big Gap in Reward for Cooperation," *The Wall Street Journal*, November 29, 2004.
61. Name changed.
62. "Three Individuals Charged in Large-Scale Cocaine and Marijuana Importation Ring," DEA News Release, January 28, 2004.
63. 18 U.S.C. § 3553(f) and U.S.S.G § 5C1.2.
64. ABA Standard 2.5 Cooperation Agreements and Cooperating Individuals and Organizational Witnesses.
65. Florida Statute 921.186 Substantial Assistance. Notwithstanding any other law, the state attorney may move the sentencing court to reduce or suspend the sentence of any person who is convicted of violating any felony offense and who provides substantial assistance in the identification, arrest, or conviction of any of that person's accomplices, accessories, coconspirators, or principals or of any other person engaged in criminal activity that would constitute a felony. The arresting agency shall be given an opportunity to be heard in aggravation or mitigation in reference to any such motion. Upon good cause shown, the motion may be filed and heard in camera. The judge hearing the motion may reduce or suspend the sentence if the judge finds that the defendant rendered such substantial assistance.
66. *Informants and Undercover Investigations*, U.S. Department of Justice, Bureau of Justice Assistance Police Executive Research Forum, 1992.
67. *United States v. Medina-Reyes*, 877 F. Supp. 468, 475 (S.D. Iowa 1995).
68. Ibid.
69. Ibid.
70. See Keneally, K., "White Collar Crime, at a Loss for an Explanation," *Champion Magazine*, November 1998; See also Glaberson, W., "Ruling against Testimony-for-Leniency Jolts Court System," *New York Times*, October 27, 1998. *Cf. United States v. Singleton*, 165 F.3d 1297, 1301 (10th Cir. 1999).
71. *United States v. Falcon*, 91-6060-CR. See "Felon's Testimony May Have Backfired in Willie, Sal Case," *Miami Herald*, Feb. 26, 1996, 1, 6B. Author's Note: The foreman and one other juror in the case accepted cash bribes for the verdict and were later prosecuted.

72. *Informants and Undercover Investigations*, 16, U.S. Department of Justice, Bureau of Justice Assistance, Police Executive Research Forum, November 1990.
73. Trott, S.S., "The Successful Use of Snitches, Informants, Co-conspirators, and Accomplices as Witnesses for the Prosecution in a Criminal Case" (January 1984). (Former Assistant Attorney General Criminal Division, Public Integrity Section, U.S. Department of Justice, currently serving as Federal Judge, 9th Circuit Court of Appeals.)
74. Tarlow, B., "Queen for a Day: Proffer Your Life Away," *Champion Magazine*, March 2005.
75. *Queen for a Day* was a popular 1950s daytime game show where several women contestants would compete against each other to become queen for a day. The winner would be crowned and rewarded with prizes and trips. Her dreams to become a queen, if only for one day, were fulfilled.
76. See Trott, S.S., "The Successful Use of Snitches, Informants, Co-conspirators, and Accomplices as Witnesses for the Prosecution in a Criminal Case" (January 1984). (Former Assistant Attorney General Criminal Division, Public Integrity Section, U.S. Department of Justice, currently serving as Federal Judge, 9th Circuit Court of Appeals).
77. *U.S. Attorneys Manual*, 9-27.000.
78. See *Kastigar v. United States*, 406 U.S. 458–459. *Federal Grand Jury Practice*, Chapter Eight, "Immunity Procedures and Practice," U.S. Department of Justice, Criminal Division.
79. U.S. Constitution, Amendment V.
80. See *U.S. Attorneys Manual*, 9-23.000. See also *United States v. Balsys*, 118 S. Ct. 2218 (1998).
81. 18 USC § 6001, enacted in 1970 and upheld by the Supreme Court in *Kastigar v. United States*, 406 U.S. 441, 453, 92 S. Ct. 1653, 32 L. Ed. 2d 212 (1972).
82. Even if it is not practicable to obtain the desired cooperation pursuant to an "informal use immunity" agreement, the attorney for the government should attempt to limit the scope of the agreement in terms of the testimony and transactions covered, bearing in mind the possible effect of his agreement on prosecutions in other districts. See *U.S. Attorney Manual*, 9-23.000, "Witness Immunity."
83. Non-statutory immunity is often referred to as letter immunity or pocket immunity. *Federal Grand Jury Practice*, U.S. Department of Justice, Criminal Division, January 1993.
84. See *United States v. Doe*, 465 U.S. 605, 612–614 (1984) for Doe immunity.
85. *U.S. Attorneys Manual*, 9-23.000.
86. 18 USC § 6002. See *Kastigar v. United States*, 406 U.S. 441, 460–461, 92 S. Ct. 1653, 32 L. Ed. 2d 212 (1972).
87. 28 USC § 1826.
88. 18 USC § 401, and Fed. R. Crim. P. 42.
88. *U.S. Attorneys Manual*, 9-23.000; 28 USC § 1826.
89. *United States v. Liddy*, 510 F.2d 669, 672–673 (D.C. 1974), *cert. denied*, 420 U.S. 980 (1975); See also *In re Liberatore*, 574 F.2d 78 (2nd Cir. 1978).

91. Trott, S.S., "The Successful Use of Snitches, Informants, Coconspirators, and Accomplices as Witnesses for the Prosecution in a Criminal Case" (January 1984). (Former Assistant Attorney General Criminal Division, Public Integrity Section, U.S. Department of Justice, currently serving as Federal Judge, 9th Circuit Court of Appeals.)

92. Green, F., "FBI Informant's Slaying Goes Unpunished," *Richmond Times-Dispatch*, September 12, 2008.

93. Green, F., "Sentencing Hearing Today in '06 Slaying," *Richmond Times-Dispatch*, December 16, 2008.

94. Green, F., "Prosecutors Seek Stiff Drug Sentence," *Richmond Times-Dispatch*, December 18, 2008.

95. Ibid.

96. Green, F., "Slaying Will Not Lengthen Sentence," *Richmond Times-Dispatch*, January 21, 2009.

97. Green, F., "Sentencing Hearing Today in '06 Slaying," *Richmond Times-Dispatch*, December 16, 2008.

98. Ibid.

99. A Rule 35 motion is a motion filed by a prosecutor under the authority granted by Rule 35(b) of the Federal Rules of Criminal Procedure.

100. Federal Rules of Criminal Procedure, Rule 35 (b).

101. 2011 Federal Sentencing Guideline Manual, Chapter 5, Part K, Commentary.

102. Pursuant to 18 U.S.C. § 3553(e) and U.S.S.G. § 5K1.1, for a downward sentencing departure.

103. See *United States v. Doe*, 870 F. Supp. 702 (E.D. Va. 1994).

104. *United States v Lander*, No. CR 11-4098 MWB, Northern District of Iowa, Western Division, October 23, 2012.

105. "Slain Informant Recruited Drug-Case Witnesses," *Miami Herald*, June 25, 1993, p. B1. See *United States v. Nichols*, 606 F.2d 566, 569 (5th Cir. 1979).

106. Katel, P., "A Deal with the Devil: Did Feds Use the Cali Cartel to Get Noriega?" *Newsweek*, October 30, 1995, p. 59.

107. Ibid.

108. Heller, E., "Road to Ruin," *Fulton County Daily Report*, May 15, 1997.

109. Heller, E., [Attorney] "Battles to the End," *Fulton County Daily Report*, April 25, 1997.

110. Moushey, B., "Selling Lies," *Pittsburgh Post-Gazette*, November 30, 1998.

111. USSG Rule 35 (b).

112. Moushey, B., "Selling Lies," *Pittsburgh Post-Gazette*, November 30, 1998.

113. Ibid.

114. Ibid.

115. Ibid.

116. Heller, E., "[Name deleted] Case Wasn't Pretty," *Fulton County Daily Report*.

117. Abams, D., "Dr. B and Group 43," *St. Petersburg Times*, May 4, 2003.

118. "DEA Informants Swindled Druglords? Millions in Cash Allegedly Taken," *Miami Herald*, May 21, 2000.

119. *Vega v. United States*, U.S. Court of Federal Claims, 07-685, Sept. 21, 2007. Hereinafter "Lawsuit."

120. Within the meaning of Title 19 U.S.C. §1619. (lawsuit paragraph 1). According to the lawsuit, the plaintiff became an informant in 1996 or 1997.

121. Lawsuit, In the Federal Court of Claims, Case No. 07-685, September 21, 2007; paragraph 6.
122. Ibid.; paragraph 8.
123. Ibid.; paragraph 9.
124. Ibid.; paragraph 10.
125. Ibid.; paragraphs 13 and 14.
126. Ibid.; paragraph 15.
127. Ibid.; paragraph 16.
128. Ibid.; paragraph 17.
129. Ibid.; paragraph 18.
130. Adams, D., "Dr. B. and Group 43," *St. Petersburg Times*, May 4, 2003.
131. The American Bar Association (ABA) Model Code of Profession Responsibility, EC-7-7 provides that "a defense lawyer in a criminal case has the duty to advise his client fully on whether a particular plea to a charge appears to be desirable." New York's Code of Professional Responsibility has similar provisions regarding plea bargaining.
132. "Colombian Drug Kingpin Convicted of Charges He Rejoined the Drug Trade," CNN, May 29, 2003.
133. See ABA R.

Documentation, Registration, and the Confidential Source File

6

6.1 Introduction

Procedures for documenting new informants can vary dramatically between agencies.[1] Some police departments require as little as a criminal background check to determine if the informant has a criminal record or is a fugitive before approving his use.[2] The departmentally required documentation may be nothing more than an index card kept in the control agent's desk. On the other end of the spectrum is the Federal Bureau of Investigation (FBI). It requires an Initial Suitability Report & Recommendation that requires agents to explore at least 17 areas that may disqualify a potential informant.[3] The process can take months to accomplish. The complexity of the documenting process can be indicative of how many times the department has been involved in an informant-related law suit or scandal.

A comprehensive informant registration and approval system begin the process of asserting departmental control over the use of informants. It also assists in assessing the risk associated with operating an informant. Risk assessment as applied to informants is the continual identification and analysis of relevant adverse factors that are weighed against the potential benefits of using a confidential source.[4] An effective informant program should require the law enforcement agency to periodically assess the productivity[5] and risk associated with each source it utilizes.[6]

6.2 Resistance to Documenting Informants

Control begins by requiring that all informants be documented and registered with the law enforcement agency before their use by any officer will be authorized. Resistance to institutional control over sources can be expected and is not a new phenomenon. It can be traced to the proprietary approach over informants taken by many control agents: in their opinion, they own the informant. However, the prevailing official view is that the informant belongs to the department.[7]

The International Association of Chiefs of Police and the Bureau of Justice Assistance described the difficulties a proprietary approach to informants by agents can create in the documentation process.

Investigators may be reluctant to maintain department files on informants they use. They may fear that potential informants will not participate if they know records of their activities will be on file. They may not believe departmental security procedures will be effective in protecting their informant's identity—and may fear that incompetent or corrupt law enforcement personnel will gain access to their informant's name. Some may fear that a supervisor or another investigator will destroy a trust relationship built with a considerable investment of effort and time or "steal" the informant for his own use.[8]

There may be justification for the fear factor. Four FBI informants were murdered during the 1980s after their identities were leaked to killers by a corrupt FBI agent. The murderers were both FBI informants. The FBI agent was their handler.[9] In 2009, a veteran Immigration and Customs Enforcement (ICE) agent was alleged to have been querying law enforcement computer databases in an effort to identify informants for Mexican drug traffickers. He pleaded guilty to charges of leaking sensitive law enforcement information and was sent to prison.[10]

6.2.1   Operating Unregistered Informants

Despite the requirement that informants be registered, many officers continue to operate undocumented sources. They have been referred to by some as hip-pocket or informal informants: an unregistered informant who provides tips to police. By operating without documentation, there is little or no risk that the source's identity will ever be disclosed. However, informants seldom work for free; they expect something in return. Because an unregistered informant cannot be paid with official funds, officers may be tempted to pay them with favors or contraband, including drugs.[11]

Former FBI director William Webster called hip-pocket informants an "occasion for mischief."[12] Two "informal informant" cases were cited in an Office of Inspector General's report. In one case, an FBI Special Agent resigned while under investigation for having an inappropriate relationship with an informant and the agent's effort to make the informant's relative an informal informant. In another case, an FBI agent was suspended for having an inappropriate relationship with an unregistered informant, failing to properly document the individual as a confidential informant (CI), and failing to arrange for the arrest of the source after discovering there was an outstanding warrant for her arrest.[13]

Theft of informants is often raised as a reason to resist the documenting process and can be a valid concern. For decades, local police have complained that federal law enforcement agencies lure informants away from police departments with the promise of bigger rewards. Joint federal/local task forces have provided the setting for the informant thefts to occur. It starts by requiring that all informants used by a federal task force be registered as a task force informant. As an example, Drug Enforcement Administration (DEA) Task Forces require informants be documented as DEA Task Force informants and given a DEA code number.

A Bureau of Alcohol, Tobacco, Firearms, and Explosives Task Force-agreement recognized and addressed the concern. An excerpt from the task force memorandum of understanding explains:

> Informants developed by Task Force Officers may be registered as informants of their respective agencies for administrative purposes and handling. The policies and procedures of the participating agency with regard to handling informants will apply to all informants that the participating agency registers. In addition, it will be incumbent upon the registering participating agency to maintain a file with respect to the performance of all informants or witnesses it registers.[14]

6.3   Informant File

Agencies differ on terms for the informant's file, often dependent on the title they assign to their cooperators.[15] For the purposes of this discussion, the file will be referred to as the confidential informant file.[16]

The CI file is generally kept by the law enforcement agency in a safe or a Mosler-style combination safe/file cabinet. Those individuals with the combination are generally command-level personnel. The safe or cabinet when unattended is usually locked.

Informant files should be segregated from all other investigative files. Access to the file is generally restricted to the informant's control agent, supervisor, or others who can show a legitimate need to inspect the file. Many agencies, including the DEA,[17] have sign-out logs that record the date and time the file was removed, who removed the file, and when it was returned. The DEA assigns an agent designated as Confidential Source Coordinator to maintain the files.

6.3.1   Code Numbers and Code Names

The primary method used to keep an informant's identity confidential is to assign a code number or a code name. The code number system is more common, but some agencies issue both.

The number or name is used in both investigative reports and internal memoranda that document the informant's activity. Receipts for payment made to the informant for information and expenses will also bear the code number and may be signed by the informant with his code name.

Agencies that use both code names and numbers do so for security and as a matter of convenience in dealing with their sources. Keeping the informant's true identity a secret from others in the police department or agency is not uncommon.

6.4   Documentation Data Format

The process used in documenting an informant can vary drastically between agencies.[18] Depending on a department's size and sophistication in handling informants, the questionnaire used for documentation can be the size of an index card or it may be several pages in length, similar to a complete background investigation.[19] Most agencies use a form of their own design that is completed by the recruiting agent and witnessed by a second agent. It is forwarded to a supervisor for review and approval.

The format followed for documentation will include some or all of the following data and may require additional information:[20]

1. *Informant's true name and all known aliases*

The informant's true name must be obtained for purposes of completing a criminal background check. Some agencies, including ICE, allow CIs to adopt assumed names both for future identification and payment purposes. The informant's true name is maintained in an agencies' primary CI file.

Aliases are often as valuable as true names for identification purposes. Many CIs have been arrested, prosecuted, and incarcerated under an alias. Hyphenated names are often used interchangeably. Nicknames should also be included in the informant file. Many informants are known to their associates only by their nicknames. Having their nicknames can be a valuable piece of information when attempting to locate an informant who is avoiding contact with his handler or is wanted for a crime.

2. *Residence/business address or addresses and telephone numbers*

All residences used by the informant should be recorded, including the CI's parents', siblings', and paramour's home addresses. The information is extremely helpful in locating the informant during periods when he wishes to conceal his location, usually before trial. Recording business addresses accomplishes the same purpose.

Obtaining *all* telephone numbers used by the CI serves a purpose other than communication. They also provide intelligence information concerning the criminal contacts the informant has outside of his dealings with his control agent. The CI's number (s) may appear on subpoenaed toll records of criminal targets other than those he is working on with police. His number may also appear on pen registers or touch-tone decoders or be phoned during a wiretap investigation.

3. *Personal description, including date and place of birth*

Biographical data are necessary to secure a complete criminal background check of the informant. The informant's place of birth can also provide investigative leads in determining the informant's whereabouts. Tattoos are also an indelible indication of present or past gang affiliations.

4. *Fingerprints and current photograph of the informant*

Many informants object to having their fingerprints and photographs taken. Unless the informant has a verified FBI number (because of a previous arrest or fingerprint submission), there can be no excuse for not fingerprinting the informant. Fingerprinting informants serves several administrative purposes, although its primary goal is to fully identify the individual and learn the full extent of his criminal record.

Informants who object to being photographed may resent the idea of having a mug shot taken. They also fear that the photo will be circulated and their involvement as a CI will be exposed to others. As with fingerprints, there is no excuse for not photographing the CI. Law enforcement agencies routinely request a CI's driver's license photographs from state driver's license bureaus. They are in color and generally of good quality. Photos can also be obtained surreptitiously.

Photos, as with fingerprints, serve a valid law enforcement purpose. Informants routinely commit crimes while working as informants. They often "turn" on their agent handler, setting him up for armed robbery during a drug deal or exposing him to other danger. Both photographs and fingerprints assist in fully identifying the CI and can aid in his apprehension. They can also help in identifying the CI's remains in the event of death.

5. *Employment history; if unemployed, current source of income*

The informant may possess special skills that could increase his value to the agency. Informants with boat captain and pilot licenses are routinely recruited as CIs.

Like many criminals, some informants have never held a job. Unexplained income can be an indicator that the informant is involved in illegal activity. That is to be expected. The reality is that most informants are criminals, and the money paid to them by law enforcement is usually not enough to sustain their lifestyle or drug habit.

6. *Social Security number*

Social Security numbers are contained in numerous computer indexes outside of the government. They are a valuable investigative tool in tracking the activities of the informant and are available to law enforcement.

7. *Past activities (criminal or criminally associated)*

Each informant must be fully debriefed by the recruiting agent. The nature and extent of the debriefing varies with the individual informant's background, whether he is a long-time associate of criminals or has information pertaining to one criminal event.

Agencies whose focus is restricted to particular crimes such as the DEA and ATF are encouraged to explore all areas of criminal activity in the debriefing of informants. Information developed outside their area of responsibility should be disseminated to the appropriate agency "unless there is a valid reason not to do so."[21]

8. *FBI number, state and local criminal ID numbers*

Informants routinely attempt to conceal their criminal histories from their agent handlers. Lies by an informant about his criminal record can be relevant evidence at later trials concerning the informant's credibility.[22] A serious felony record could cause a jury to completely disregard the informant's testimony and possibly to conclude that the government's entire case is suspect.[23]

9. *Who the informant knows in the criminal world is an indicator of his potential value to police. The names of his associates should be checked in the databases available to the agent. Criminal reputation and known associates*

There is a great deal of criminal intelligence information collected by federal, state, and local police agencies. Much of the information is stored in computer databases and is readily accessible to agents. There is no "central clearinghouse" for all criminal intelligence files.

Some of the systems available to agents include

a. *The National Crime Information Center (NCIC).* The NCIC is a telecommunications system operated by the FBI. The system is accessible to various federal, state, and local law enforcement agencies throughout the country. An NCIC query will provide a criminal history and determine whether the informant is a fugitive.

b. TECS (not an acronym) is the updated and modified version of the former Treasury Enforcement Communications System. TECS is owned and managed by the U.S. Department of Homeland Security's component of U.S. Customs and Border Protection (CBP). TECS is an information-sharing platform, which allows users to access different databases that may be maintained on the platform or accessed through the platform, and the name of a system of records that include temporary and permanent enforcement, inspection, and operational records relevant to the anti-terrorism and law enforcement mission of CBP and numerous other federal agencies that it supports. TECS not only provides a platform for interaction between those databases and defines TECS users but also serves as a data repository to support law enforcement "lookouts," border screening, and reporting for CBP's primary and secondary inspection processes.

c. *Narcotics and Dangerous Drugs Information System (NADDIS).* NADDIS is the DEA's computerized information system. All intelligence and criminal-related information collected by the agency and memorialized in an investigative report (DEA 6) finds its way into the NADDIS system. If the informant's name, telephone number, addresses, or vehicle license plate number appeared in a report prepared by the DEA, it would be found in NADDIS.

   d. *State Record Repositories.* Each state operates a central criminal history record repository that receives case processing information contributed by law enforcement agencies, prosecutors, courts, and correction agencies throughout the state.[24] These repositories compile the information into comprehensive criminal history records or "rap sheets," as they are often called. Rap sheets are made available to criminal justice personnel, for authorized purposes, by means of statewide telecommunication systems.

Maintenance of such central repositories relieves local and state criminal justice agencies of the need to maintain expensive and duplicate information systems that attempt to compile comprehensive offender records. They need maintain only systems that support their own case-processing needs and can rely on the state central repositories for information about the processing of cases in other agencies.[25]

All 50 states, Puerto Rico, and the District of Columbia have established central repositories for criminal history records.

10. *Military*

Military records for personnel discharged from all branches are maintained at the National Personnel Records Center, St. Louis, Missouri.

11. *Citizenship*

ICE maintains records pertaining to noncitizens. The records are maintained up until the time the alien becomes a naturalized citizen.

12. *Parole and probation*

Each agency has its own guidelines pertaining to the use of informants on parole or probation.[26] Conversely, many state parole and probation commissions have their own policy on probationers or parolees working as informants. An investigative agency ignoring the requirements of a parole or probation department risks violating the terms of the informant's release. Probation files may hold information bearing upon the credibility of an informant and be discoverable.[27]

13. *Brief résumé of information furnished in the past, including the following:*

   a. *Reliability of information provided.* Many agencies maintain a log of all instances in which the informant has provided reliable information. In jurisdictions applying the *Aguilar-Spinelli*[28] two-prong test: the basis of knowledge or "underlying circumstances" is the first prong, and reliability or veracity is the second prong of the test. Logging reliability is essential in those jurisdictions. In 1983, the Supreme Court abandoned the two-prong test in *Illinois v. Gates,*[29] adopting a totality-of-the-circumstances analysis.

    b. *Date and value of information furnished.* Some agencies log all official reports generated because of an informant's information. The number of arrests, amount of contraband seized, money or property forfeited, and monies paid to the source are noted.

    c. *Whether the informant will testify in open court.* Agencies differ on their policies concerning the testimony of informants. Many local agencies have clauses in their informant agreements stating that they will recommend dismissal of a prosecution if the CI must testify.

Federal agencies attempt to keep informants off the witness stand but warn prospective CIs that they may have to testify.[30] There is no fixed rule on withholding the identity of the informant once a case goes to trial (see Appendix 6G).[31]

    d. *Identity of other agencies to which the informant is currently supplying information.* Agencies should not use informants who are simultaneously working with another agency. It is difficult, if not impossible, for the CI to effectively and loyally serve two agencies at the same time. Federal and state agencies routinely use informants in joint investigations, but the CI is controlled by the recruiting agency.

14. *Reason for becoming an informant (if known)*

The informant's true motive for cooperating must be determined and documented. It allows any future agents who may come in contact with the informant to understand why he is cooperating or what is at stake if he fails to perform.

15. *Whether the informant has been declared unsatisfactory (blacklisted aka blackballed).*[32]

An informant who is deactivated for misconduct or unreliability is considered blacklisted. Blacklisting alerts any DEA agent making inquiries about a prospective informant that he has been declared unreliable and should not be used.

16. *If the informant is or has been enrolled in the U.S. Marshal's Witness Security Program (see Chapter 14, The Witness Security Program).*

17. *A statement as to whether the informant has shown any indication of emotional instability, unreliability, or of furnishing false information*

Needlessly placing an undercover officer in the company of an unstable or dangerous informant should be avoided. A comprehensive background investigation may determine that the informant was "black balled" by another agency for misconduct and deactivated.

An informant who has previously committed perjury in court should not be utilized. False testimony is the strongest form of impeachment.[33] If the informant has a reputation as a liar, there is little sense in expending time, effort, and money in his utilization.[34]

18. *The nature of the information or service to be supplied*

If a specific investigative activity has been identified, it should be included here.

The CI file maintained by the police department or federal agency will usually contain only agreements between the control agent and the informant. It will be signed by the control agent, the CI, usually one witness, and a supervisor. Although agreements between the prosecutor and the informant may exist, they do not necessarily find their way into the CI's file maintained by the law enforcement agency. Those agreements are generally retained in the prosecutor's file.

19. *Financial or other arrangements agreed to or expected by the informant in return for providing information or services*

Any written agreements or personal service contracts should be incorporated into the informant's file. Some agencies use a performance agreement that outlines what cooperation the law enforcement agency expects from the informant. It may also state what the informant can expect in return for that cooperation (see Appendix 6C).

6.4.1   Tax Responsibilities

There is no requirement for the paying agency to notify the Internal Revenue Service (IRS) of the payments made to an informant. The Code of Federal Regulations does not require IRS notification for "a payment to an informer as an award, fee, or reward for information relating to criminal activity but only if such payment is made by the United States, a State, Territory, or political subdivision thereof, or the District of Columbia."[35]

6.5   Informant Conduct Agreements

The Informant Conduct Agreements contain the rules that an informant must follow while working for the police. It should not be confused with personal assistance agreements or contracts that outline what cases are expected from the informant and what he may expect in return for his cooperation.

The effectiveness of an informant contract agreement is open to debate. One MS-13 gang-member-turned-informant violated the most significant terms of his agreement, notably by committing violent crimes and drug dealing. When the centerpiece witness was asked at trial about the violations, he testified, "I honestly didn't pay much attention" when the rules governing his conduct were read to him.

In testimony before Congress in May 2002, FBI Director Mueller argued that requiring agents to read "verbatim instructions" to their informants, "written in often intimidating legalese, [was] proving to have a chilling effect, causing confidential informants to leave the program."[36]

While the agreement that follows is the one employed by ATF, some or all of its contents are found in conduct agreements used by many federal, state, and local law enforcement agencies. (Comments in italics are the author's.)

Bureau of Alcohol, Tobacco, Firearms and Explosives Informant Agreement

1. This confirms the agreement entered into between the Bureau of Alcohol, Tobacco, Firearms and Explosives (ATF) and (informant's name). *Comment: This item is meant to ensure that the informant cannot claim any other promises were made outside of the Informant Agreement. CSs routinely claim promises including immunity from prosecution[37] and awards/rewards.*

2. ATF has asked me to assist in an official investigation. In furtherance of this investigation, I agree to (describe activity that the informant or cooperating witness or subject will be doing for ATF). *Comment: This item is intended to clearly identify what the control agent expects from the informant.*

3. ATF has assigned Special Agent _____ to serve as the controlling agent in this investigation. It is imperative that I maintain contact with Special Agent _____ and advise him/her of my activities and abide by his/her instructions. *Comment: It must be made clear at the beginning of the informant–control agent relationship exactly who is in charge. By the time he has been recruited he will have probably met several agents and has already decided who is the weakest. The agent who has been designated control agent has to make clear that he is the only point of contact and is the agent the informant has to report to. In-house, an alternate agent is usually designated in the event the control agent is unavailable. The alternate's name is made available to the informant when those occasions occur.*

4. I will not participate in any unlawful activities except in so far as ATF determines that such participation is necessary to this investigation and ATF expressly authorizes such acts in advance. I understand that any violation of the law not expressly authorized by ATF may result in my prosecution. *Comment: The informant is cautioned to not break the law unless authorized. The control agent has to leave no question in the informant's mind that he will be prosecuted if arrested while not working under the direction and control of ATF. Justice Department law enforcement agencies can obtain authorization for informants to participate in Otherwise Illegal Activity[38] (see Chapter 10).*

5. I will not initiate any plans to commit criminal acts. Further I understand I will not induce any individual to commit a crime that he or

she has no predisposition to commit. *Comment: Informants are often accused of being agent provocateurs,*[39] *creating crime where crime otherwise would not exist. It is a defense strategy routinely employed in drug and terror cases. Every effort should be made to target investigative resources on high-value targets of investigation.*

6. I will not attempt to be present during conversations between individuals under criminal indictment or their attorney. If I am inadvertently present and learn of defense plans or strategy, I am not permitted to report such conversations without prior approval from the United States Attorney's Office. *Comment: The control agent is to explain what constitutes a privileged lawyer/client communication to the informant and expect him to comprehend the concept.*[40]

7. While I will be working closely with ATF for purposes of this investigation, I understand I am not a law enforcement officer, employee, or agent of ATF and I will not hold myself out to be such. *Comment: Remarkably, some informants get so taken by their role as an informant that they will impersonate a law enforcement officer. So-called police buffs discussed earlier will obtain badges, official-looking identification, and handguns. Some have been known to use their control agent's business card and impersonate the agent. The* Seattle Times *reported an informant triggered a citywide "officer needs help" call in June 2011 when, during a fight with an alleged drug dealer, he told the manager of a North Seattle motel he was a federal agent. The manager called 911, prompting officers to rush to the motel. The informant was later sentenced to 10 years in prison after admitting he sexually abused an 18-year-old woman who was held against her will for days inside a South Seattle motel that was being paid for by the ATF.*[41]

8. I understand information I provide to ATF may be used in a criminal proceeding. All legal means available will be used to maintain the confidentiality of my identity but I may be required to testify before a grand jury and that any subsequent hearing and trial. I understand that I have an obligation to provide truthful information and testimony, and that any deliberate false statements or testimony will subject me to criminal prosecutions. *Comment: This admonition is meant to dispel any hopes of anonymity that the informant may hold and to protect the agency from suit. An informant sued the FBI for $39,980,000, claiming they improperly disclosed his name in the prosecution of Colombian drug dealers.*[42]

9. If, as a result of being a cooperating witness, it is determined by ATF that my life or that of any member of my immediate family may be in danger, ATF will, with my permission, apply to the Department of Justice (DOJ) to admit me to the witness security program. I understand that the final decision is made solely by, and at the direction of, the DOJ and not ATF. *Comment: Informants have claimed that agents*

have promised witness protection and later been denied admission to the Witness Security Program. There have been lawsuits filed by disgruntled informants claiming to have been abandoned after receiving threats related to their work as an informant (see Chapter 14).

10. I will in no way reveal the confidential and sensitive nature of this investigation. Further, I will not undertake any publication or dissemination of any information or material that results from this investigation without the prior express authorization of the ATF. *Comment: Much to the displeasure of their recruiting agency, informants have sold their stories as books and screenplays.[43] While this warning has little hope of enforceability, the recruiting agency may refuse to honor future rewards if the informant goes public with his story.*

11. ATF will reimburse me for expenses incurred that are deemed by ATF to be reasonable and in furtherance of this investigation. I understand that any monetary or other type of reward given to me by ATF, either for services rendered or information provided, must be declared as other income on any income tax return I may be required to file. *Comment: Informants are instructed that monies paid as rewards/awards are to be treated as income and reported on their tax returns. Federal law enforcement agencies do not report payments made to informants to the IRS.*

12. I understand that any monetary or other type of reward given to me by ATF will not be contingent upon the prosecution, conviction, or punishment of individuals. *Comment: The Attorney General's Informant Guidelines forbid payments to informants contingent upon the conviction or punishment of any individual.[44]*

13. I understand that any monetary or other type of reward given to me by ATF will not be contingent upon my testimony in court or other hearings. *Comment: The control agent is expected to dispel the notion that rewards and other payments are based on the successful prosecution of the target of investigation. It is a difficult task when informants learn during their work leading up to trial that rewards are based on productivity, "a more you give the more you get" mentality. The task is further complicated when dealing with cooperative witnesses (CWs). For a CW to obtain a downward departure in his sentence, he must provide substantial assistance in the investigation and prosecution of another person.*

14. I understand that ATF cannot guarantee me any rewards, payments, or other compensation based on the outcome of any judicial actions. *Comment: Rewards based on the conviction or punishment of any individual are prohibited by the Attorney General's Guidelines. That does not mean that an informant cannot be paid any funds related to a case following the conviction of an investigative target. In the case of rewards related to civil forfeiture, no disbursement to an informant can be made until the case makes its way through the courts.*

Informants have filed suit claiming they were owed rewards. In 2008, a former FBI/DEA informant claimed responsibility for over one hundred drug convictions based on his efforts.[45] He also claimed the government seized between $250 and $500 million in forfeited cash, real estate, jewelry, and art. He claimed he was entitled to an award of 25% of the appraised value of the forfeited properties, subject to a $250,000 limitation per case.[46]

15. I will not engage in witness tampering, witness intimidation, entrapment, or the fabrication, alteration, or destruction of evidence. *Comment: The informant is warned that witness tampering, witness intimidation and fabrication, alteration, or destruction of evidence are all crimes and will not be tolerated. For agents, the greatest challenge in this warning is explaining entrapment to the informant in a manner that he will understand.*

16. I understand if I'm cooperating with ATF in exchange for consideration on my pending case, at my request, ATF will advise the prosecuting office (s) of the nature and extent of my cooperation.[47] *Comment: This item is included for cooperating witnesses. They are operated in much the same manner as informants. As a general rule, CWs are not paid with the exception of being reimbursed for out-of-pocket expenses. They are providing substantial assistance in hopes of receiving a downward departure in their sentence. It is not unusual for CWs to continue working after their criminal case is resolved with their classification changed.*

17. I understand I may not enter into any contract or incur any obligations on behalf of the U.S. government, except as specifically instructed and approved by ATF. *Comment: It is not unusual for informants utilized in protracted investigations, particularly sting operations, to enter into government-approved undercover business leases. Item 16 is meant to ensure that all leases/contracts are approved by the control agent.*

18. No promises or representations have been given to me regarding my alien status and/or my right to enter or remain in the United States. *Comment: Many non-citizen informants are working in hopes of receiving a green card or other immigration benefit, usually an S visa. Agents are instructed to advise non-citizen informants that Immigration and Customs Enforcement is the only agency that can grant visas. Agents are permitted to assist the informant in obtaining a visa by making their cooperation known to ICE and completing the required paperwork (see Chapter 4, Section 4.15).*

Signature and Date _____
Witness and Date _____
ATF Special Agent _____
ATF Form 3252.2
Revised May 2007

6.6   The Miami-Dade Police Department

The Miami-Dade Police Department utilizes a much shorter form than ATF. It covers many of the same points. A notable addition is their strict prohibition against the informant carrying a weapon while working with the police and the liability waiver.

Miami-Dade Police Department

INFORMATION SOURCE LIABILITY WAIVER FORM

I, _____, have volunteered to be an information source of the Miami-Dade Police Department. In exchange for allowing me to be an information source, I agree to the conditions herein.

- I have been instructed and I understand that as an information source of the Miami-Dade Police Department, I do not have permission to violate any local, state, or federal laws, and I further understand that I do not have police powers of any kind. I am not a police officer, nor an employee of the Miami-Dade Police Department, and will not represent myself as a police officer at any time. Should I violate any laws, I understand I will get no special treatment or consideration because I am an information source for the Miami-Dade Police Department. I consent to my fingerprints being taken for the purpose of positive identification.
- I also understand that I am specifically not authorized by the Miami-Dade Police Department to carry or use any weapons or firearms.
- I further agree that the determination of the amount of any payment for assistance in these investigations shall be determined by, and rests in the sole discretion of, the Miami-Dade Police Department. Any payment which I receive for my services in connection with any investigation shall be the full and complete payment to which I am entitled for those services; I shall have no other or further claim against the above-mentioned agency, nor any of its agents, officers or employees or the political subdivisions employing them, in connection with my payment for my services.
- I hereby release and forgo any and all rights and/or claims of any kind, legal or equitable, against the Miami-Dade Police Department, as well as all of its agents, officers and employees and the political subdivisions employing them, whether acting in their official or individual capacities, from any and all liability for any injury or loss of any kind that I may suffer in any way connected to or arising from my assistance with these investigations, including those resulting

from any negligent acts or omissions by myself, or any officer, agent, or Miami-Dade Police Department employee. Liability for any negligent, willful, or illegal acts of the Information Source, which acts were undertaken without prior express approval of the Miami-Dade Police Department, are the sole responsibility of the Information Source.

Finally, I hereby acknowledge that I have read and understand this agreement, and sign it freely and voluntarily.

Information Source Signature _____ Witness _____

Date_____   Date_____

Witness_____ Juvenile Parent/Guardian_____

Date_____   Date_____

6.7   Confidential Informant File Content

All reports relating to a particular cooperating individual are kept in the CI's individual file. The CI files maintained by most agencies contain some or all of the following reports or information:

- Confidential Informant (CI) Establishment Report[48]
- CI acknowledgement of guidelines and instructions
- Departmentally required warnings/admonishments
- CI Agreement
- CI payment and benefit receipts (reflects all payments of cash and other items of value given to the CI including immigration benefits)
- Case initiation reports, investigative reports generated by CI activity and CI debriefing reports
- FBI fingerprint card[49]
- Current photograph
- Copy of driver license
- Handwriting sample
- Rap sheets (State and FBI)
- Administrative correspondence
- Quarterly and annual supervisory reports
- CI chronology sheet briefly describing activity regarding the CI
- Identity of informant secondary officer (serves as CI contact when control officer is unavailable)
- CI reliability reports (some agencies track instances of reliable information attributed to the CI)
- Concealed transmitter and recording consent forms
- Deactivation report

- Original CI statements.[50] (*Comment: Some agencies require that a written statement be taken from the informant if he has provided information or has participated in an activity in which he may be required to testify. The informant is usually told by his control agent that the statement will serve as his "report" of what occurred. It should be taken immediately or soon after the police activity and should be a fresh recollection of what the informant saw, heard, and said. In reality, the procedure is a precaution the agency takes in the event the informant decides to deny his role in the investigation. It is not always followed. Some informants refuse to sign a statement. DEA has a provision "where taking a statement may adversely impact an investigative outcome, the procedure may be waived if all relevant information is reported in a DEA 6"[51] investigative report. Very often the statement is prepared by the control agent for the informant's signature. There is seldom an ulterior motive for this method of obtaining the statement. Some CIs are illiterate and have no idea what they have signed.*)*

6.8   Supervisor Approval and Oversight

Agencies differ on the level of supervisory approval required before a prospective informant is activated for use in the field. Once activated, the DEA, for example, requires first-line supervisors to perform quarterly and annual management reviews of each active CI. ICE and the FBI have a similar requirement.

Face-to-face interviews of the informant by the control agent's supervisor do occur and are usually triggered when the informant's rewards meet or exceed certain predetermined amounts and lifetime caps. It is the responsibility of the supervisor to approve any payment made to an informant. It is also the supervisor's responsibility to be alert for any "danger signals" in the agent–informant relationship. Random audits, reviews, and interviews of informants and control agents are recommended.[52]

Supervisory reviews are not fail-safe. A Justice Department Office of Inspector General's review of 120 FBI informant files found over 85% of the files examined contained violations of internal informant-handling guidelines, most beginning at the early stages of the informant–agent relationship. Among the chief violations were the failure of agents to caution informants about the "limits of their activities," the "failure to report unauthorized illegal activity" by their informants, and the issuance of "retroactive approvals" for illegal acts the informants had already committed. The report attributed the violations to "inadequate training at every level."[53]

6.9   Documentation and Disclosure: *Brady* and *Giglio*

Failures during the early stages of the CS's documentation can result in defense claims of prosecutorial misconduct and allegations of *Brady*[54] and *Giglio*[55] violations. It is during the registration process that damaging and potentially disqualifying information is often uncovered.

Brady requires the government to provide the defense with all evidence favorable to the defendant that is material to guilt or punishment. *Giglio* requires the prosecutor to disclose not only CS misconduct but also undisclosed promises of leniency or immunity. A prosecutor cannot get around *Brady* or *Giglio* through willful ignorance or allowing the control agent to compartmentalize information about a CS.[56]

The prosecutor must insist that his case agents fully explore the backgrounds of their sources and report all that is found in the CS file to avoid the potential for *Brady* errors.[57] In one case, DEA agents unwittingly used an informant who was responsible for two murders.[58] In another case, DEA agents utilized an informant, reported to be one of its highest-paid sources, who was alleged to have repeatedly lied on the witness stand about his criminal history.[59] Communication errors within DEA were blamed for the perjured testimony. The agency ordered a review of procedures for informant handling.

The Office of Inspector General launched an investigation into the FBI's failures to reveal Brady information. Their investigation found: When the FBI fails to afford the required notice, fails to document activities or events involving informants in accordance with the Confidential Informant Guidelines, or is not candid with prosecutors concerning informant-related issues, the informants or other subjects of criminal prosecutions may claim that the government's failure to provide exculpatory or impeachment information arising from the informant's activities amounts to a violation of their constitutional rights. This was illustrated in *United States v. Blanco*,[60] in which the court held that the government "wrongly suppressed" impeachment information about a CI in violation of *Brady*[61] and *Giglio*[62] during a narcotics prosecution. In particular, the court ruled that the government had suppressed information pertaining to the special immigration treatment provided to the CI by the Immigration and Naturalization Service for his work with the DEA. The court found that the DEA was well aware of the informant's immigration status, and the government affirmatively represented that the informant's sole reward for work was monetary compensation, but it was not clear whether the prosecutor knew of the informant's immigration status, because the DEA had been reluctant to provide information to the prosecutor. As a result, the appellate court issued an order requiring the district court to order the government to reveal all informant-related information.[63] See Appendix 6G.

6.10   Protecting Sources, Parallel Construction and Discovery

The reliability of the discovery process was dealt a setback in mid-2013, when Reuters learned from a 2005 IRS document about "parallel construction" report writing and DEA's Special Operations Division (SOD). Parallel construction is a form of creative writing used by a law enforcement officer. Its purpose is to protect a source of information from being disclosed in a report by recreating the events that lead to a discovery of contraband or an arrest.

According to Reuters, the SOD is an intelligence-gathering arm of the DEA specializing in funneling information from overseas National Security Agency (NSA) intercepts, domestic wiretaps, informants, and a large DEA database of telephone records to authorities nationwide to help them launch criminal investigations of Americans. The DEA phone database is distinct from NSA databases.[64]

The IRS document explained that the "Special Operations Division has the ability to collect, collate, analyze, evaluate, and disseminate information and intelligence derived from worldwide multi-agency sources, including classified projects. SOD converts extremely sensitive information into usable leads and tips which are then passed to the field offices for real-time enforcement activity against major international drug trafficking organizations."[65]

Parallel construction in this case was a method of eliminating SOD as the source. When actionable information from SOD was received, the agent in receipt of the lead was expected to "clean up" the information and devise an alternative method of reporting the source of information and in effect create a new paper trail.

The IRS document offered further details on parallel construction: "Usable information regarding these leads must be developed from such independent sources as investigative files, subscriber and toll requests, physical surveillance, wire intercepts, and confidential source information. Information obtained from SOD in response to a search or query request cannot be used directly in any investigation (i.e. cannot be used in affidavits, court proceedings or maintained in investigative files)."[66]

The journalist reporting the story asked two senior DEA officials about the practice and was told, "Parallel construction is a law enforcement technique we use every day. It's decades old, a bedrock concept." A former agent described it a bit differently, saying, "It's just like laundering money—you work it backwards to make it clean."

When a federal prosecutor in Florida learned about parallel construction, he told the journalist, "I was pissed. Lying about where the information came from is a bad start if you're trying to comply with the law because it can lead to all kinds of problems with discovery and candor to the court."

6.11   Phantom Informants

Comprehensive documentation and informant file systems also serve to verify the existence of the source to prosecutors and police managers. Creating informants rather than recruiting informants has been an allegation made by defense attorneys for decades. Prosecutors and police alike have routinely dismissed these claims as a defense smoke screen designed to mandate an evidentiary hearing to disclose an informant's identity.[67]

The unfortunate truth is that some police officers do "invent" their informants. Agents are able to obtain search warrants by attributing fictitious accounts of criminal activity in affidavits to a nonexistent "reliable informant." Police officers who lie under oath privately refer to the practice as "testilying."[68]

In 2006, 92-year-old Kathryn Johnston became a victim of a phantom informant when she was murdered by Atlanta police during a no-knock search warrant. Shot six times in a hail of over 40 bullets, she was handcuffed as she lay dying. Three officers were hit by friendly fire.[69]

An FBI investigation into the shooting revealed that all of the probable cause recited in the Johnston affidavit was false.[70] The informant was a phantom; he did not exist. The controlled buy never occurred. The drugs "purchased" by the phantom were supplied by the police, seized during an earlier arrest. Money used for the purported buy was pocketed by the affiant police officer. Drugs found in the Johnston home were planted by members of the raid team, seized in an earlier, unrelated investigation.[71]

Four detectives involved in the case[72] were found guilty of a multitude of crimes.[73] The victim's family received a $4.9 million out-of-court settlement.[74]

6.11.1   Long History of Phantoms

The Johnston case was not an aberration. Phantom informants have been used to obtain search warrants for decades.[75]

A notable example was uncovered during a Boston Police Department search warrant scandal in the 1980s. A "reliable informant's" account of drug dealing was used to support an affidavit for a search warrant filed by a Boston Police detective. During the execution of the warrant, the affiant's partner was shot and killed by the occupant of the residence.

The gunman was arrested shortly after the shooting and charged with the murder of the officer. The defendant's attorney began a diligent investigation of the case and discovered discrepancies in the affidavit and search warrant regarding the informant.

Attempts by homicide detectives to locate the informant failed. At one point in the investigation, the detectives claimed the informant had been killed in a drug dispute. "The detectives said they could not find the informant, nor did they have any idea of where to locate him or anything about his background, even though the affidavits showed the detective and the informant had met more than 120 times."[76] The defense team traced the informant to 38 other affidavits. An independent investigation conducted by the Suffolk County District Attorney found 50 warrants using that same informant in a one-year period.

In January 1990, the lead detective testified in a preliminary hearing that the informant never existed. He also testified that his superiors had told him to "use this form affidavit because it contains everything we need to get over constitutional hurdles to have a good search warrant."[77]

The court wrote:

> This case shows that some police officers will lie and will lie further in an effort to cover up the initial lie. This is a case, in which defense counsel ... has uncovered contemptible and disgusting misconduct by police officers in blatant violation of their sworn duties.[78]

Illustrating that the Boston case was not unusual, the *National Law Journal* reported the following instances of fabricated informants:

> In 1993, in Waltham, outside Boston, seven drug convictions were thrown out when two investigators admitted they had fabricated the existence of informants to obtain warrants. "The detectives had gone into an apartment without a warrant, searched the house carefully and found drugs and money," says Peter A. Bella, a former Waltham, MA, prosecutor who represented one of the defendants. "The detectives then created an imaginary informant and attributed all the information to him, (then) went to a judge to get their search warrant."
>
> In 1991, a Los Angeles Sheriff's Sergeant testified in the trial of six drug cops he supervised that in the mid-1980s the squad made up informants for search warrants and, in one case, fed a CI information and paid him to appear before a judge to repeat the details
>
> In 1991, a former Metro-Dade County police officer in Miami, Florida cooperated with federal prosecutors and testified in a racketeering trial of four other cops that he had stated falsely on search warrant affidavits that his information came from CIs "known for previous reliability." In fact, they did not exist. The former officer testified that he needed warrants to break into drug dens, where he stole thousands of dollars and drugs. In one of the cases, two officers not involved in the home invasion by warrant scheme were shot by occupants of the house as they assisted in making entry. The corrupt officer was placed on five years' probation.[79]

The phantom informant may also become a paid informant. To further the ruse, the detective can withdraw funds to pay his source for the controlled buys. The reward money is pocketed by the detective. The money withdrawn for the purchase of evidence is also pocketed. The drugs that are placed into evidence were not purchased; they are usually stolen from other crime scenes.

The documenting of sources makes the use of a phantom informant difficult if not impossible to accomplish. In the *Lewin* case, investigators determined that the "informant handler" had intentionally failed to follow police procedure concerning identification, supervision, and payment of informants. The incident led the Boston Police Department to revise their informant guidelines.

Appendix 6A: Source Identification Card

NAME (Last, First, Middle)   SOURCE NO.

A/K/A*:
   1)_____ 2)_____
ADDRESS:_____

                        (Street-P.O. Box-Apt., etc.)

(City)   (State)   (Country)
(ZIP)
DOB: / / / POB:

SSN: / / D/L:

DESCRIPTION: RACE/SEX: _____/_____ _____
HGT: _____'_____ __WGT: _____
EYES: _____ HAIR: _____ _____
SCARS / MARKS: _____

NCIC: _____ TECS: _____
OTHER _____
MOTIVATION: _____EXPERTISE: _____

Reporting Officer / Alternate Officer - Date Documented
*A/K/A — Also Known As.

Appendix 6B: Confidential Source Establishment Report

DEA Form 512

U.S. Department of Justice
Drug Enforcement Administration

Privacy Act Information

The following Privacy Act Statement must be read or shown to the confidential source beforehand. Collection of personal history information is authorized under Title 21, U.S. Code. Your supplying of identifying personal information is voluntary. This information is an element used to create a record of your cooperation. However, failure to provide the information requested may disqualify you from becoming a confidential source.

1. Name (Last, First, Middle)
2. No.
3. Source Date of Birth (MM/DD/YY)
4. Alias Name
5. Alternate Date of Birth
6. NADDIS No.
7. FBI No.
8. Social Security No.
9. Misc. Numbers (e.g., TECS; DRUG-X; Registrant, CSS No., etc.)
10. Place of Birth (City, State/County)
11. Citizenship (Country)
12. Alien Status
    Illegal
    Legal (Alien Registration No.)
13. Race
    Black
    White
    Native American
    Unknown
    Asian-Pacific Islander
14. Ethnicity
15. Sex
    Male
    Female
16. Color Hair

17. Height
18. Occupation
19. Color Eyes
20. Weight
21. Address (No., Street, Unit, City, State/Country, Zip Code)
22. Identifying Characteristics (Scars, tattoos, marks, physical defects, etc.)
23. Telephone Number (including Area Code)
24. Employer Name and Address
25. Employer Telephone Number (including Area Code)
26. Passport No.
27. Issue Date
28. Issuing Country
29. Expiration Date
30. Name on Passport
31. Driver's License No.
32. Issuing State/Country
33. Expiration Date
34. Name on License
35. FAMILY INFORMATION
    a. (Last, First, Middle Name)
    b. Age
    c. Address (No., Street, Unit, City, State/Country)
    d. Phone Number
    Father
    Mother
    Spouse
    Companion
    Paramour
    Children
    Other Relatives (Name) (Relationship)
36. Confidential Source Type (Check one)
    Regular
    Defendant
    Restricted Use
    Other (Nonhuman) *Author's note: Wiretaps often produce information that must be acted upon. To preserve the secrecy of the wiretap's existence, they may be assigned an informant number.*
37. Confidential Source Action (Check one)
    Original
    Supplemental
    Reactivation

38. Source Type Qualification
(Brief statement of situation qualifying the Source Type)
39. Confidential Source System (CSS) Check Coordinator
(Name and Date Checked)
CSS Results
Negative
System Hit
CS Number(s)
40. Type of Cooperation (Brief statement on proposed cooperation: Include case number and NADDIS number if any)
41. Source Declared Unsatisfactory (8812.63)
Yes
CS Number
Date
No
42. Unsatisfactory CS Reestablished
Yes
No
Date
OC Approval Date
43. Is (has) Source (been) Enrolled in U. S. Marshals WITSEC?
Yes
CS Number
Date
No
44. CS Status (Check one)
Probationer or Prisoner (Name of Approving Official)
Parolee (Name of Approving Official)
Date Approved:
(Check one) Fed. State
45. Criminal History Check—NADDIS: NCIC, Computerized Criminal History
(CCH).
Interstate Identification Index (III); and INTERPOL (6612.26)
(Submit copies of positive & negative results along with DEA-202)
Date inquiry Performed
Criminal History Yes/No
Active Warrant (s) Yes/No
(Do not proceed with approval process without discharging warrant.)
Agency Name
Agency Willing to Extradite Yes/No

46. Interpol Check Name & Telephone No. of Interpol Contact, Date Performed, Results (i.e., negative)
47. Prosecutor Approval If Defendant Source
Prosecutor Name:
Area Code and Telephone Number:
Judicial District:
Date of Approval:
48. Cooperation Agreement included Yes/No
49. Two (2) Photographs included Yes/No
50. DEA-105, Criminal Inquiry
Request for FD - 249, Fingerprint Cards *(3 cards)*
51. DEA—6. Initial Debriefing Report Included Yes/No
52. Telephonic Approval *(Date)*
GS/RAC received telephonic approval for CS establishment by SAC/CA
(Name) Via ASAC/ACA *(Name)*
53. Remarks
54a. HQS, Command Center System Coordinator Issuing Number:
54b. Coordinator's Name
54c. Date
55a. Agent/Officer Name *(Print or Type)*
55b. Signature Date
56a. Coagent/Officer Name *(Print or Type)*
56b. Signature
56c. Date
57a. Supervisor Name *(Print or Type)*
57b. Signature
57c. Date
58a. ASAC Name *(Print or Type)*
58b. Signature
58c. Date Concur Yes No
59a. Assoc. SAC Name *(Print or Type)*
59b. Signature
59c. Date Concur Yes No
60a. SAC Name *(Print or Type)*
60b. Signature
60c. Date Approved Yes No

Appendix 6C: Statistical Accomplishments Form

Criminal Informant/Cooperative Witness (CI/CW)

1. Number of Subjects Arrested:
   a. Controlling Agency _____
   b. Other Federal Agencies _____
   c. State and Local Agencies _____
2. Number of Subjects/Victims Identified and/or Located:
   a. Controlling Agency _____
   b. Other Federal Agencies _____
   c. State and Local Agencies _____
3. Number of Investigative Matters Initiated:
   a. Controlling Agency _____
   b. Other Federal Agencies _____
   c. State and Local Agencies _____
4. Number of Disseminations Based Upon CI/CW Information: _____
5. Number of Violent Acts Prevented: _____
6. Number of Times CI/CW Information Used in Title III
   (telephone intercept) Affidavits:
   a. Controlling Agency _____
   b. Other Federal Agencies _____
   c. State and Local Agencies _____
7. Number of Times CI/CW Information Used in Search
   Warrant Affidavits:
   a. Controlling Agency _____
   b. Other Federal Agencies _____
   c. State and Local Agencies _____
8. Number of Times CI/CW Information Used in Obtaining
   Complaint/Information/Indictment:
   a. Controlling Agency _____
   b. Other Federal Agencies _____
   c. State and Local Agencies _____
9. Merchandise Recovered (Value)
   a. Controlling Agency _____
   b. Other Federal Agencies _____
   c. State and Local Agencies _____
10. Asset/Property Seized (Value at Time of Seizure):
    a. Controlling Agency _____
    b. Other Federal Agencies _____
    c. State and Local Agencies _____

11. Monetary Value of Asset/Property Actually Forfeited
    to Government: $ ___
12. Number of Convictions Obtained as a Result of Information
    Furnished by CI/CW or as a Result of other Significant Operational
    Assistance Furnished:
    a. Controlling Agency   ___
    b. Other Federal Agencies   ___
    c. State and Local Agencies   ___
13. Number of Times Undercover Agent or Other Law Enforcement
    Officer Introduced into an Investigative Matter by CI/CW:
    a. Controlling Agency   ___
    b. Other Federal Agencies   ___
    c. State and Local Agencies   ___
14. Drugs Recovered (Wholesale Value):
    a. Controlling Agency   ___
    b. Other Federal Agencies   ___
    c. State and Local Agencies   ___
15. Number of Consensually Monitored Conversations CI/CW partici-
    pated in:
    a. Controlling Agency   ___
    b. Other Federal Agencies   ___
    c. State and Local Agencies   ___

Appendix 6D: Source Criminal History Check

Source Number:_____
Controlling Agent:_____

Agencies Checked	Date Checked	Negative	Positive
STATE:	_____	_____	_____
LOCAL:	_____	_____	_____
NADDIS:	_____	_____	_____
TECS:	_____	_____	_____
NCIC:	_____	_____	_____
CRIMINAL HISTORY:	_____	_____	_____

CONTROLLING AGENT SIGNATURE: _____
If Positive, the Printout Is Attached in Sealed Envelope _____
Indicate State/Agency Queried for Criminal History

Appendix 6E: Source File Chronology

SOURCE NUMBER: _____
CONTROLLOING AGENT: _____

DATE OF ACTIVITY	DESCRIPTION OF ACTIVITY
_____	_____
_____	_____
_____	_____
_____	_____
_____	_____
_____	_____
_____	_____
_____	_____
_____	_____
_____	_____
_____	_____
_____	_____

Appendix 6F: Supervisor's 60-Day Informant File Review Log

Date:	Initials:	Date:	Initials:
Remarks:		Remarks:	
Date:	Initials:	Date:	Initials:
Remarks:		Remarks:	
Date:	Initials:	Date:	Initials:
Remarks:		Remarks:	
Date:	Initials:	Date:	Initials:
Remarks:		Remarks:	
Date:	Initials:	Date:	Initials:
Remarks:		Remarks:	

Date:	Initials:	Date:	Initials:
Remarks:		Remarks:	

Date:	Initials:	Date:	Initials:
Remarks:		Remarks:	

Date:	Initials:	Date:	Initials:
Remarks:		Remarks:	

Date:	Initials:	Date:	Initials:
Remarks:		Remarks:	

Date:	Initials:	Date:	Initials:
Remarks:		Remarks:	

Appendix 6G : Defendant's Motion for Disclosure of Confidential Informants

IN THE UNITED STATES DISTRICT COURT FOR THE DISTRICT OF XXXXX

UNITED STATES

v.

Defendant

DEFENDANT'S MOTION FOR DISCLOSURE OF CONFIDENTIAL INFORMANTS

Defendant, by and through undersigned counsel, in accordance with the decisions in *Roviaro v. United States*, 353 U.S. 53 (1957),[80] *Brady v. Maryland*, 373 U.S. 83 (1963)[81] and *United States v. Eniola*, 893 F.2d 383, 388 (D.C. Cir. 1990),[82] moves this honorable Court for the entry of an Order directing the government to furnish counsel for the accused with the name, address, and present location of any informant, confidential informant, informer, confidential source, special employee, source of information, cooperating individual, or witness (hereinafter referred to as "informant"), paid or unpaid, of any governmental agency or unit, state or federal, who supplying or who had supplied information or performed any role whatsoever which formed the background for, or resulted in the search warrant in this case or the indictment against the accused.

Specifically, the accused requests that the Court direct the attorney for the government to furnish counsel for the accused with the following information concerning any such potential government witness:

1. Whether any informant was a user of any controlled substances or was a distributer of controlled substances, and, if so, the complete nature and extent of his drug use and trafficking.
2. Whether any informant has, since becoming an informant, continued to use or distribute any controlled substances, and, if so, the dates, times, places and recipients of such distributions.
3. Whether any informant was suspected, apprehended, or convicted of any crime(s) at any time during which he/she agreed to gather information on behalf of the United States Government.
4. What crimes or other breaches of law (including jurisdiction and case number) have such informant(s) committed or were suspected of having committed at any time during which he/she agreed to gather information or testify on behalf of the United States Government.
5. Whether any potential or actual criminal charges against any informant were abandoned, altered, or otherwise disposed of upon agreement with any such informant to gather information or testify on behalf of the United States Government.
6. What financial arrangements existed or exist between any informant and the agencies of the United States, the District of Columbia, or any other sister state, and the amount of money that has been paid to the informant.
7. The names, addresses and criminal records (including juvenile records) of any informant to be called as a witness for the United States Government.
8. The substance of any plea bargain(s) entered into by the informant and any agency of the United States, the District of Columbia, or any other state, and the authority for any such plea bargain(s).
9. The substance of any agreements made by the United States, the District of Columbia, or any other state with any informant not to charge crimes, and the authority for any such agreements.
10. Information tending to show bias and/or prejudice on the part of any informant.
11. Information tending to show that any informant has made contradictory or inconsistent statements relative to this case or any related case.
12. Information tending to show that any informant suffered from any material defect in perception, memory, veracity or articulation during any time period relevant to the witness' testimony in this case.

Respectfully submitted,

_____
Defense Attorney Signature

_____
Date

Appendix 6H: DEA Source Debriefing Guide

Prepared by the Drug Enforcement Administration, Intelligence Division, with the advice and assistance of the Intelligence Community.

Preface

The DEA Intelligence Division has updated this *Source Debriefing Guide* to assist debriefers in formulating questions concerning international and domestic drug trafficking.

The *Source Debriefing Guide* is a source document used to supplement the skills and knowledge of debriefers in the technical areas of drug production, smuggling, and distribution. Information gained from responses to the questions in this *Guide* can provide tactical, operational, and strategic intelligence for drug law enforcement activities.

It is not expected that every person interviewed, whether defendant, suspect, or witness, will supply information about all aspects of the drug traffic. A series of general questions provided in Part One of this *Guide* is designed to identify the areas of knowledge of the person being debriefed. It is recommended that all of the general questions be posed first.

Part Two of the *Guide* consists of eight subject sections, each with specific questions that may be asked to develop information on relevant subjects. Using the general questions in Part One, the debriefer can then identify specific areas of knowledge and refer to the relevant set of questions in Part Two.

Should the interviewee's answers to the general and specific questions indicate extensive technical or area knowledge on his or her part, it is recommended that technical debriefing assistance be requested from DEA elements or other Federal agencies with in-depth knowledge of the subject.

Drug traffickers often are aware of other criminal activity, such as burglary, robbery, homicide, etc. You should make note of any knowledge of these activities for later referral to other agencies.

This publication was revised to include additional guidance on precursor and essential chemicals, evolving financial practices, and the increasing use of computers among drug traffickers.

Part One: Drug Trafficking (General)

1. Which illegal drugs have you used, sold, transported, or have knowledge of? When? Are there "brands" or trade names on the drugs? Specify and explain:
   - Heroin
   - "Black Tar"
   - Morphine Base
   - Opium
   - Cocaine hydrochloride
   - "Crack"
   - Hashish
   - Hashish Oil
   - Marijuana
   - Amphetamines
   - Barbiturates
   - LSD
   - PCP
   - Other Drugs (specify)

2. Who is the source of supply? Where is this person located? Where did this person obtain the drugs? Who are the U.S. distributors? Who are the foreign distributors?

3. Who else is involved in the trafficking of these drugs?

4. Do you know of any locations where drugs are cultivated, manufactured, processed, or stored? (See Part Two: Section I, A and B; and Section II, A and B).

5. Do you have any knowledge of the smuggling of drugs across the U.S. Border? If so, where are the entry points? (See Part Two: Section I, C.) Do you know about smuggling across other international borders? Is this for end use or for transit purposes?

6. Do you have any knowledge of methods used to transport drugs? (See Part Two: Section IV.)

7. Describe the method of concealment, type of conveyance, and persons involved in drug smuggling. (See Part Two: Section IV.)

8. Are false documents used to conceal the identity of smugglers or couriers? How are these documents obtained? How are they falsified, and by whom? What type of documents are used?

9. What are the prices and purities of the drugs when they enter the United States? Do you know the prices and purities at other stages of the trafficking?

10. Have you ever seen or been told of opium poppy, coca, cannabis, or mescal cultivation either in or outside the United States? (See Part Two: Section I.)

11. Do you have any knowledge of heroin, cocaine, hashish, "crack," or dangerous drugs laboratories within or outside the United States? (See Part Two: Section II or III.)

12. Who finances the drug trafficking operations?

13. How are drugs paid for? Is the money paid up front, or are the drugs sold on consignment or exchanged for other goods? If payment is in currency, identify which country's currency. If payment is by exchange, identify the exchange goods.

14. How are funds used to pay for the drugs being moved? By cash? Letter of credit? Bank deposits? Bank wire transfer? International checks? Or, traditional "underground" banking systems? (See Part Two: Section VI.)

15. Do you know how or where the proceeds of any drug transactions have been hidden or invested? Who controls laundered drug funds?

16. Do you know the associates or businesses of any drug trafficker?

17. Do you have knowledge of any drug transactions?

18. What types of ledgers, journals, classified ads, computers, bulletin boards, or other documents or mechanisms are used to manage drug transactions? Are codes used?

19. Are you familiar with any areas of the United States or of the world? Describe those areas. Have you ever lived in those areas? When? For how long?

20. Do you know of any other smuggling activity into or out of the United States? Are drugs exchanged for other goods? Do you know of any non-U.S. international smuggling activity?

21. Is there any exchange of one drug for another? For example, cocaine for heroin? Are weapons being traded for narcotics? Identify the sources and recipients of the weapons and the drugs. (See Part Two: Section VII.)

22. Is there any official corruption involved? By whom? Paid by whom? How much? For how long? With which major traffickers are they associated? (See Part Two: Section VII.)

23. Have you been involved in or do you have any knowledge of any non-drug criminal activity? Give dates of involvement. Identify the crime category, the type of operation, and the level of operation.
    Crime Categories:
    - Contraband smuggling, sexual assault, prostitution, pornography, weapons or explosives violations, stolen property or vehicle, forgery, fraud, or other.

    Types of Operation:
    - Smuggling, financing, wholesaling, or other.

    Levels of Operation:
    - Syndicate, international foreign based, international domestic based, national, local, other.

24. What is the principal ethnic group involved in the drug activity? What syndicates or organizations, multi-national or national, are involved? Will the traffickers deal outside their own group or organization?
25. What language(s) do you speak?
26. What special skills do you have? Are you a pilot? Radio operator? Chemist? Photographer? Money launderer? Other?
27. Have you ever worked as a confidential informant? For whom? Give dates and current status.
28. Have you ever been confined in prison or any other institution? Give names, dates, locations, and reasons for confinement.

Part Two: Drug Trafficking (Specific)

Section I. Opium–Heroin–Morphine Base, Coca–Cocaine–"Crack," and Marijuana–Hashish–Hashish Oil

A. Sources
  1. Where are the opium poppy, cannabis, or coca cultivation fields? Give geographic coordinates, names of roads, and local name for the area. Identify landmarks.
  2. Identify the owners and cultivators of the fields, their residences, telephone numbers, and associates.
  3. When are the fields planted and harvested?
  4. How many harvests are there per year?
  5. What yield is expected and obtained from the fields? How many opium poppy bulbs per plant? Does this yield vary with the harvest season if there is more than one?
  6. What is the size of the field? How many plants per square meter or hectare? (1 hectare = 2.47 acres)?
  7. What are the arrangements between owners and cultivators?
  8. Specify and explain the support for growing areas including:
     • Water sources and irrigation methods used,
     • Chemicals and fertilizers used, and
     • How seeds and other supplies are obtained and paid for.
  9. Is the opium gum, coca leaf or paste, or cannabis stored at the field or moved? If moved, how? Where? When? By whom? And to whom?
  10. Are the fields protected? If so, by police? Military? Government officials? Guerrillas? Or, others? Are the protectors armed? Do the fields have electronic surveillance devices? Are the fields booby-trapped? Are attempts made to hide or disguise fields? If so, how?

11. Do the local authorities know of the fields? Have they previously destroyed them? When? If not, why not? Identify the local authorities.

B. Laboratories

1. What are the geographic coordinates and locations of laboratories?
2. Are the laboratories at or near the fields? How are the labs built, and how is equipment brought in?
3. What equipment is used at the lab? Are the labs mobile? How large are they?
4. What chemicals are used? Where do they come from? What else do you know about the chemicals?
5. Describe and name the chemist(s). How is he trained? By whom? Does the chemist have any other interests in the operation?
6. Who finances the laboratory? How?
7. What security measures are used?
8. Is the heroin or cocaine dyed, diluted, or adulterated?
9. Does the laboratory operate continually? If not, does it operate only when an order is received? Only at harvest time? Or, on some other schedule?
10. How are orders and instructions received or passed? Is there a telephone? Two-way radio? Electronic teletype? Computer? Or, contact point? Identify telephone number, radio call sign, teletype address, computer password, codes, or contact point.
11. What conveyances are used? Describe the type, ownership, drivers, and transportation routes.
12. How many people are involved in the operation of the lab? What are their names and identities? How often is the lab moved? Who decides when to move the lab?
13. What are the hours of operation of the lab? How many days a week is it in operation?
14. Are records maintained regarding drug production and distribution?
15. What else do you know about the lab and its operations?

C. Transportation and Storage

1. How is the product moved? Does the buyer pick up the product at the lab? At the growing field? Or, at some other point?
2. Who are the backers, financiers, and protectors? Identify the principals' family members and relationships.
3. Are any other persons or groups involved? What routes and contact points do they utilize?

4. What nationalities, ethnic groups, religious organizations, criminal syndicates, or other groups do the couriers belong to? Are they males or females, adults, or children?

D. Obtaining or Moving Drugs
   1. How is contact made for the order, delivery, pickup, security, and transfer of drugs, etc.?
   2. What communications methods are used? If telephones, faxes, or beepers, what are the numbers? If radios are used, what call signs and frequencies are used? If written messages or cables, what addresses? If signals or couriers, what are the details? If computers, what are the passwords? What kind of computers are used? What software or computer programs are used?
   3. Do the traffickers employ any communications security? Do they utilize communications centers? Who controls them?
   4. What counterintelligence methods are used by the traffickers?
   5. Are controllers used to monitor drug movements? How do they get their instructions?
   6. How are couriers recruited and by whom?
   7. Are periodic reports made on the progress of the shipment? If so, to whom and by what means?
   8. What ports or places of entry are used for these shipments? Why?
   9. What methods are used to conceal shipments? Describe and explain. Are the shipments transferred within a country to other means of movement or concealment? Describe.
   10. Are false documents involved in the shipments? Describe these documents and identify the supplier.
   11. Who knows when the shipments are en route and the methods being used? Identify fully.
   12. When is payment made? In advance or upon delivery to intended recipient? or at some other time? Are the same people involved in payment and movement of the drugs? Are payments made in cash or by wire transfer, bank draft, in products, or in some other form? Are drugs exchanged one for another? Are drugs exchanged for weapons?
   13. Identify any business (wittingly or unwittingly) involved in the traffic. Describe the extent of this involvement.
   14. Are there any package markings used to identify recipients? Are the markings related to the seller as well as to the recipient or buyer? Describe the packaging and the markings.
   15. Who packages the drugs and where are they packaged? Are they ever repackaged at any point?

Section II. Dangerous Drugs

A. Sources
  1. What drugs are involved? Which chemicals are used?
  2. What is the finished form of the drug, e.g., powder? Crystal? Liquid? Capsule? Tablet? Blotter? Or, other?
  3. Were you a courier? How are arrangements made to pick up the drug? Are children being used as couriers?
  4. How do you get the drugs, e.g., from street sellers? From a minor or major distributor? Or, directly from the lab?
  5. From whom and how are they obtained? By direct or indirect contact through a second or third party? Is the supplier associated directly with the manufacturer?
  6. How much do the drugs cost? How much can they be sold for? How much for greater or lesser quantities? Who is buying and using the drugs?
  7. How are the drugs distributed, e.g., personal pickup or delivery? U.S. Mail? UPS? Or, other kinds of shipment? What are the names of distributors and sellers?
  8. Can you obtain samples? Make purchases? Introduce someone?
  9. Give names of people financing the operation. Do they take part in the actual physical transactions? Is anyone else involved in any way?
  10. Do you know the location or address of the lab? Who owns and operates the lab? Who are the chemists? Who is financing the lab?
  11. Are the drugs intended for U.S. consumption? What proportion goes where?
  12. In the case of mescaline or peyote and similar drugs, where are the plants located or grown? Who is "harvesting" the crop? Where do they bring the raw material?
  13. How are the drugs or chemicals smuggled? Describe in detail.
  14. Do you have any other knowledge concerning drugs, diluents, or chemicals used to make drugs?

B. Illicit Laboratories
  1. How many people are involved in the operation of the lab? What are their identities? Where is the lab located? How often is the lab moved? Who decides when the lab is to be moved?
  2. What are the lab's hours of operation? How many days a week does it operate? What quantity of the drug is produced?
  3. What type of equipment is used? Describe the type, capacity, and quantity of equipment in use at the lab, for example, pill press, mixing equipment, etc.

4. Who supplies the equipment? Who installs the equipment? How is it powered?

5. What manufacturing process is used? Is more than one process used? What formulas are used? Do you have or can you get the formula?

6. What chemicals are used? Where did they come from? How were they obtained? Where are the chemicals stored? What method is used to divert the chemicals from any legitimate source? Give the name of firms, country of origin, and method of operation, e.g., the use of brokers, false invoices, and transshipments to other countries.

7. How are the drugs packaged, e.g., in plastic bags? Bundles? Jars? Bottles? Or, packages? How many dosage units or hits in a package? Describe them. Where does the packaging come from? (Follow same questions as for chemicals, #6.)

8. What payment, paperwork, equipment dealers, brokers, and company names are used? Describe. (Follow same questions as for chemicals, #6.)

9. What diluents are used? Are the same ones always used? (Follow same questions as for chemicals, # 6.)

10. Do you have or can you obtain samples?

11. To whom is the drug distributed after sale? In what form? What do they do with it?

12. Are any of the suppliers or laboratories involved in manufacturing illicit drugs? Are any of these drugs being diverted?

13. Do these labs have security systems? What methods or weapons are available to defend the labs?

14. How are the equipment and chemicals disposed of?

C. Diversion of Legitimate Drugs

1. How are the drugs obtained? By prescription from physicians? Dispensed without a prescription? Excessive quantities of over-the-counter medications dispensed by pharmacists? Or, directly from physicians? Identify the physicians and pharmacists involved.

2. Are any records falsified by legitimate handlers to cover illicit distribution? How? Are fraudulent names used on dispensing records?

3. Are the drugs stolen? Give details: By whom? From whom? How? Where? When?

4. How is payment made for the prescription? Does it differ according to the controlled substance obtained?

5. How often can you get a prescription and for which drugs? How many dosage units are prescribed per prescription?

6. Is the physician part of a conspiracy?
7. Are the drugs sold by a pharmacist without a prescription? What volume? What price? What form?
8. Will the pharmacist sell one or many prescriptions at a time? How large a volume will he or she prescribe or sell?
9. Does the pharmacist prepare a phony prescription to cover the transaction?
10. Does he provide illegal refills for a legitimate prescription?
11. Are real or fictitious names used? If fictitious, how are these names obtained?
12. Does the physician perform an examination? If an examination is performed, what is the procedure?
13. Does the physician know that the controlled substances he dispenses or prescribes are not for legitimate use?
14. Will the physician sell one or numerous prescriptions at a time? How large a volume will he or she prescribe or sell?
15. Does the physician identify the pharmacist who will fill the prescriptions?
16. Is the transaction documented in a record and, if so, how is it recorded and maintained?
17. If the physician sells directly, where are the drugs obtained and in what quantities? Are drug samples involved in the diversion?
18. Does the physician require a person to take or administer the drug in his presence?
19. What other drugs are available from the source?
20. If the drugs are obtained from a wholesaler or manufacturer, at what point are they diverted? If in finished form, are the lot numbers available?
21. Are the employees or the owners involved?
22. Is the diversion by employee theft? If so, how was security breached?
23. Is the diversion covered by falsification of records?

Section III. Detailed Laboratory Questions

A. Chemicals and Equipment
  1. What kinds of drugs are being produced? What is the main drug? What other kinds of drugs can be made in the lab? What is the production capacity?
  2. List all the chemicals being used in the lab. For each chemical, list the following:
     • Chemical name
     • Amount of chemical

- Size and type of container
- Company or manufacturer name on the label
- Where was each chemical purchased or otherwise obtained?
- Was it a local company or source?
- Ordered from out of town?
- Imported from another country?
- What was the unit cost?
- What was the total cost?

3. List all the equipment used at the lab, e.g., glassware, tubing, heating mantles, vacuum pumps, hydrogenators, pill presses, and other equipment. List the brand names or manufacturer names. Where was the equipment purchased or obtained? What did it cost?
4. What else do you know about the chemicals and equipment?
5. What are the sources of the laboratory equipment, chemicals, labor, etc.?

B. Production
1. During what hours and how often is the lab operated?
2. What processes are used to make the drugs? Are there formulas? Directions? Or, a cookbook? How long does it take to make a batch? What does the finished product look like? What is done with it? How are old chemicals and equipment disposed of, e.g., thrown out in the trash? Poured down the drain? Poured into a lake or stream? Or, buried?
3. What chemicals are used? Where do the chemicals come from? How are the chemicals obtained? Where are the chemicals stored? What method is used to divert the chemicals from any legitimate source? Give the name of firms, country of origin, and method of operation, such as the use of brokers, false invoices, transshipment to other countries, etc. What else do you know about the chemicals?
4. What safety equipment is in the lab, e.g., fire extinguishers? Fire alarms? Or, oxygen masks?
5. Is the laboratory protected from or by the police? Military? Or, Guerrillas? If so, by whom? Are there armed guards? Are there electronic surveillance devices or booby traps installed? Are there locks? Bars? Alarms? Guard dogs? Radio scanners? Guards? Lookouts? Or, weapons?
6. Is the lab also used for any legitimate purpose, e.g., commercial production? Student teaching? Research? Experiments?
7. What else do you know about the laboratory and the production of drugs? How much is the chemist paid?

C. Marketing
1. What records are kept? Can you obtain copies? Are the records coded? Do you know the codes used?
2. How is the product packaged? Shipped? Or, stored? Is the product marked? What is the meaning of the marking?
3. To what extent do local marketing conditions influence the use or modifications of operating procedures? For example:
   Heroin produced in Southeast Asia is deliberately made fluffy in consistency because operators are paid off in volume of product, rather than weight. (Knowledge of such local customs would enable more accurate estimates to be made of the country or region of origin of subsequent seizures or purchases.)
4. What else do you know about the marketing of these drugs?

Section IV. Detailed Smuggling and Transportation Questions

A. Smuggling
1. Do you have direct knowledge of any drug smuggling? If so, how did you acquire this knowledge?
2. What kind of drug is being smuggled?
3. Where is the drug smuggling occurring? Give detailed locations, Identify trans-shipment points, if any. Does ownership of drugs change after transshipment or staging points?
4. Who is involved? Is this person a runner for someone else? If so, for whom? Who are the lieutenants of the drug smuggling group?
5. How is the drug smuggling done? Give details of any special devices or procedures used by the drug smuggler.
6. How are the smuggling means acquired and from whom?
7. How often does the drug smuggling occur? Is there a pattern?
8. Is any border official involved? Who? How is he paid off? How much? By whom?
9. Who else knows about this drug smuggling?
10. When did you first learn about it? How long has it been going on?
11. Is there a fixed fee for couriers? Is payment made in cash? Merchandise? Drugs? Or, stolen goods?
12. Are any of these shipments co-op ventures? Are "insurance" schemes involved to reduce risk or loss?
13. Do you know of special instructions concerning crossing points? Times to cross? Cover stories? Backup arrangements for delivery, etc.?
14. Have you knowledge of any seizures which have taken place? Can you attribute these seizures to a specific organization?

B. Transportation

Cars, Trucks, Campers

1. Are you aware of any pattern of transportation of drugs by car? Truck? Or, camper? Describe.
2. Which drugs are being moved?
3. Who is involved? Identify with names, addresses, or locations, aliases, and associates.
4. What routes are used? Identify pickup points, transshipment points, stash points, and delivery points. Are the same routes used each time?
5. Has any vehicle been modified in any way to carry drugs? Describe in detail.
6. Where and by whom was the modification made?
7. How much is earned per shipment? How often?
8. How long has this system been active?

Air — Private Planes

9. Which drugs are being transported by private aircraft?
10. Who is the pilot? Does he own the plane? If not, who owns the plane? Is he a contract pilot? For whom? Who was the broker for the purchase of the plane?
11. Is the plane rented? From whom?
12. What is the make of the plane? If unknown, how many engines does it have? What color is the aircraft? What is the tail number? Has the tail number been altered?
13. How much is carried per shipment? How are the drugs packaged? Are drug shipments owned by only one person or more than one?
14. How often are the drugs transported? Is there a pattern?
15. Does the plane or ground crew have any special equipment?
16. Where is the pickup point? Identify by name of field, city, farm, or other location. Give directions to that point.
17. Where is the shipment delivered? To whom?
18. Are pilots or ground crews armed? With what type of weapons?
19. Is the organization involved in airdrop activities? Where do the airdrops occur: over land or at sea? What are the names or numbers of pickup vessels?
20. Has the aircraft been modified for airdrop activities? How does the crew contact vessels or ground crews?
21. What happens to the shipment once it leaves the plane? Identify and give the license numbers of any ground vehicles used. Identify ground crews or drivers.
22. Where is the ultimate destination of the shipment? Who are the recipients?

23. What are the air smuggling routes? Are there drug transshipment points? Where are the staging areas for the aircraft?
24. Are any special techniques used to avoid detection? Specify. Do the smugglers know the locations of drug enforcement radars?
25. Who owns or operates the landing fields?

Air — Commercial Aircraft

26. Which couriers or runners are using commercial planes to transport drugs? Identify by name and give description. Do the couriers travel alone or in groups?
27. Are aliases or false passports used? Give details. Who provides the false passports? Is there any nationality which is preferred?
28. Identify airport and city at both departure and arrival point. Why are these airports used? Have others been used? Why?
29. What drugs are transported? In what quantities? And how often?
30. How are they concealed? By body carry? In cargo? Or, in the aircraft? Where in the aircraft?
31. How frequent are the shipments? Is there a pattern?
32. Identify the airline and the person or group responsible for shipment of the drugs. For whom are they intended? Which flights do couriers prefer, e.g., red-eye or nonstop?
33. Describe any methods known for shipping drugs concealed in cargo. Are there particular times during which couriers fly, e.g., rush hours or weekends?
34. Identify any airport or airline personnel involved.
35. How are airline tickets purchased? How are they paid for? By cash? Credit card? Or, other?
36. Describe any special techniques used to avoid customs or other airport security.
37. Are false documents used for shipping? Explain. Who provides them?
38. How are the drug shipments delivered to the intended receiver by the courier(s)?

Boats and Ships — General

39. How are on-loads, transits, and off-loads coordinated?
40. With whom does the vessel communicate? When? Which radio frequencies are used? Does the vessel communicate with aircraft? What are the alternate plans in the event of communications breakdown?
41. Where does the vessel obtain fuel and provisions?
42. What do you think the risk of interception is?

43. What intelligence and guidance do you receive prior to sailing?
44. What do you know of maritime law enforcement operations and methods?
45. How many smuggling trips have you made?
46. Do you transit directly or travel near the coasts of foreign countries en route? Which countries?
47. If a rendezvous is missed, what are the alternate plans?
48. Which ports or anchorages are considered to be safe havens?
49. Do smuggling vessels transit the Panama Canal?
50. What is the destination of a courier after a drop off?
51. Do you ever see any aircraft overflying you? Do you report it? To whom? How?

Boats and Ships — Private

52. Describe and identify any private boats used to transport drugs. Are there established procedures for breakdown? Repair? Rescue? Or, replenishment? How common are breakdowns?
53. Who owns the boat or ship? Where is it kept? Identify the crew members. Who is the major dealer involved?
54. What drugs are transported onboard? In what quantities? What are the source countries?
55. Are the drugs concealed aboard the boat? Where?
56. What ports, harbors, marinas, or coastal areas are used to load and off-load the drugs? What sort of vessels do you off-load to?
57. What specific routes are used by maritime smugglers?
58. What techniques are used to avoid detection? Does the boat have special equipment or hidden compartments? Describe.
59. How often is the boat used for drug smuggling? Is there any pattern? How close do smuggling vessels travel to each other? Are there vessel holding areas en route?

Boats and Ships — Commercial

60. What commercial ships are being used to transport drugs? Identify vessel names, voyage numbers and direction, routing, and the shipping line involved. Are the officers of the shipping company involved?
61. Are any ship's officers or crew members involved? Identify them.
62. Where are the drugs loaded and off-loaded? Are freight forwarders or consolidators used? Who and where?
63. Are false shipping documents used? Who provides them? Were shipping charges prepared? How and by whom?
64. What special procedures and techniques are used to avoid detection? drop-offs? or pickups? Are the drugs shipped directly or transshipped through other countries?

65. How frequently are shipments made? Is there a pattern?
66. Are any port officials or workers involved? Identify them.
67. Is the shipping agent involved? Identify the shipping agent.
68. Who hires the crew?
69. In what country is the ship registered?
70. What is the name of the ship? Is the name of the ship altered at sea?
71. What is the radio frequency of the ship? Call sign? Code used?
72. Are cargo containers used to conceal the drugs? Are they rented or owned? What are the container numbers?
73. Provide information from the bill of lading to include number, shipper, consignee, description of cargo, and persons to be notified when shipment arrives.
74. How are the drugs transported to the ship? If transported in advance of the ship's arrival, where are the drugs stored?

Section V. Persons Apprehended at a Border While Smuggling Drugs

A. Drugs
1. How many times have you crossed the border with drugs? Where did you cross the border? When (times, dates)? Are these preferred times and places? Was anyone with you?
2. What routes did you follow?
3. How are drugs supposed to get through the border checkpoints? Are there any advance or following vehicles escorting the drugs? Were the escorts armed? Did you encounter any law enforcement activity en route? Did you use countersurveillance?
4. What was the drug involved? What is the average amount of drugs you have carried across the border?
5. How much did it cost? How much were you paid to smuggle it? How much have you been paid in the past? From whom did you get the money? Where and when did you get the money?
6. How many accomplices do you have?
7. Do you make drug smuggling trips alone or in groups? Describe any acts of complicity on the part of officials or authorities.
8. Where are the drugs going?
9. How much will the drugs sell for?
10. Do you know anyone else smuggling drugs across the border? Tell what you know about times, locations, vehicles or trains, compartments, involvement of officials, etc.
11. Describe any techniques of concealing drugs known to you. What modifications such as false compartments are made to the vehicles?

12. Are you selling drugs? How much are you being paid for it? How much have you received in the past?

13. Do you know of any staging areas or stash sites on either side of the border?

B. Drug Traffickers

1. From whom did you obtain the drug? For whom are you moving or selling the drug? Describe the trafficking organization and the members you are involved with. Are you related by blood or class to these members?

2. Where, when, and in what place did you obtain the drug?

3. To whom would you sell the drug?

4. Do you have more than one source-of-supply? Who is your current source-of-supply? How many times have you been supplied by this person?

5. What quantity are you moving per week? Identify the location of the source of supply. Name and describe him or her.

6. Do you know any other customers of your source of supply?

7. To whom do they sell? Where do they make their sales? Who is involved in the sale? Describe them.

8. How were you recruited to smuggle or sell drugs?

Section VI. Financial

A. Transportation of Funds

1. How are drug payments made? Are the drugs paid for in advance or are they shipped on consignment?

2. How are drug payments and proceeds moved?

3. What are the domestic or international routes used to move money?

4. What methods of concealment are used?

5. Is there any particular pattern to the movement of funds? A particular day of the week, airline, etc.?

6. In what currency are drug payments made? What denominations?

B. Money Laundering Activities

1. What countries are drug monies laundered to or through? Why are these countries preferred?

2. Which U.S. cities are drug monies laundered to or through?

3. What laundering techniques are employed?

4. What banks are used to secure drug monies? Are bank officials witting?

5. Who are the major money launderers?

6. How many people are involved with your group in laundering monies? What type of people or businesses are involved?

7. What is the rate charged by the money launderer?

8. What financial instruments are used to launder monies?
   _____ Cash
   _____ Wire Transfer
   _____ Checks
   _____ Money Orders
   _____ Letters of Credit
   _____ Traditional underground instruments
   _____ Others?

C. Asset Identification
   1. What assets are held by members of the organization and where are they located?
   2. Do members of the organization hold assets in their names or in nominee names? Explain.
   3. What types of business investments do members of the organization make and where are they located?
   4. Are computers used to record activities? What kind of computers are used? What software or computer programs are used?
   5. Are money counting machines used? What type and model?
   6. What type of financial records and books are retained by the organization?
   7. Have you knowledge of any asset seizures? Can you attribute these seizures to a specific organization?

Section VII. Corruption and Terrorism

The primary use of this *Source Debriefing Guide* is to collect information which will lead to the prosecution of major drug traffickers and their organizations as well as to the forfeiture of assets. Information pertaining to drug smuggling methods, routes, and trends as well as to growing areas, refining techniques, and so on, is of significant interest to all federal drug enforcement agencies and can help them to better allocate or deploy their resources.

On occasion, a cooperating individual will claim to have knowledge of an activity of significant interest to the security interests of the U.S. Government, which may or may not relate directly to a drug violation. The following questions will assist the debriefer in some of these situations.

A. Official Corruption
   1. What is the nature of the official involvement? Are government officials taking advantage of their positions to profit from the drug trade?
   2. Is cooperation with U.S. law enforcement efforts used as a cover for drug-related activities?
   3. What firsthand knowledge does the informant have concerning this issue?

B. Foreign Government Involvement in Drug Trafficking
   1. What is the nature of the involvement? Is it a government official or is it part of a government policy?
   2. How does the informant know? Who told him? How reliable was his source of information?
   3. What services are provided to drug traffickers? Are traffickers of all nationalities treated the same? How much do the services cost? What is done with the proceeds?

C. Exchange of Drugs for Weapons
   1. Who supplies the drugs?
   2. Who furnishes the weapons? What type of weapons?
   3. How do you know that this has occurred?
   4. What were the weapons to be used for? What was the destination of the weapons?

D. Involvement of Terrorist and Insurgent Groups in the Drug Trade
   1. What is the extent of involvement by terrorist or insurgent groups? Direct? Indirect? Or, through extortion?
   2. What evidence, other than allegations, do you have to support this information?
   3. Is there a direct exchange of drugs for weapons?

Conclusion

The above topics are not areas in which all sources of information need to be questioned. The debriefer should, however, be sensitive to the need to fully explore areas of drug-related activity that go beyond the primary investigative goal. These are sensitive issues which, while they may not affect prosecutions, may shed new insights into areas of concern for policymakers.

The DEA Intelligence Division should be contacted immediately for assistance whenever it appears that a cooperating individual has information which falls into these general categories. If appropriate, other federal agencies shall be consulted.

Endnotes

1. The term used for documenting an informant varies between agencies. The FBI refers to the procedure as validation. The DOJ Guidelines uses the term *registering.*
2. *United States V. Bernal-Obeso,* 989 F.2d 331, 333 (9th Cir. 1993) (undercover agents utilizing an informant not knowing that he had murdered two people).
3. The following is taken from *The Federal Bureau of Investigation's Compliance with the Attorney General's Investigative Guidelines Special Report* (September 2005) Office of the Inspector General. The items were taken from the FBI CI Guidelines, replaced by the *Confidential Human Source Validation Manual* (March 26, 2010)

and *Confidential Human Source Policy Manual* (September 2, 2007): FOIA releases of the CHSVM and CHSPM are heavily redacted; however, there is no indication that any of the following are no longer part of the CHS validation process:

   a. whether the person is a public official, law enforcement officer, union official, employee of a financial institution or school, member of the military services, a representative or affiliate of the media, or a party to, or in a position to be a party to, privileged communications (e.g., a member of the clergy, a physician, or a lawyer);

   b. the extent to which the person would make use of his or her affiliations with legitimate organizations in order to provide information or assistance to the [FBI], and the ability of the [FBI] to ensure that the person's information or assistance is limited to criminal matters;

   c. the extent to which the person's information or assistance would be relevant to a present or potential investigation or prosecution and the importance of such investigation or prosecution;

   d. the nature of any relationship between the CI and the subject or target of an existing or potential investigation or prosecution, including, but not limited to, a current or former spousal relationship or other family tie, and any current or former employment or financial relationship;

   e. the person's motivation in providing information or assistance, including any consideration sought from the government for this assistance;

   f. the risk that the person might adversely affect a present or potential investigation or prosecution;

   g. the extent to which the person's information or assistance can be corroborated;

   h. the person's reliability and truthfulness;

   i. the person's prior record as a witness in any proceeding;

   j. whether the person has a criminal history, is reasonably believed to be the subject or target of a pending criminal investigation, is under arrest, or has been charged in a pending prosecution;

   k. whether the person is reasonably believed to pose a danger to the public or other criminal threat, or is reasonably believed to pose a risk of flight;

   l. whether the person is a substance abuser or has a history of substance abuse;

   m. whether the person is a relative of an employee of any law enforcement agency;

   n. the risk of physical harm that may occur to the person or his or her immediate family or close associates as a result of providing information or assistance to the [FBI]; and

   o. the record of the [FBI] and the record of any other law enforcement agency (if available to the FBI) regarding the person's prior or current service as a CI, Cooperating Defendant/Witness, or Source of Information, including, but not limited to, any information regarding whether the person was at any time terminated for cause.

4. Executive Summary, *DEA's Payments to Confidential Sources,* Office of Inspector General Audit Division, 2005.

5. Appendix 6C.

6. Executive Summary, The DEA's Payments to Confidential Sources, *USDOJ,* Office of Inspector General, Audit Division, May 2005; DEA could improve its risk management in the following areas: (1) initial suitability reporting and recommendations, (2) categorization of confidential sources, (3) continuing

suitability reporting and recommendation, (4) review of long-term confidential sources, and (5) maintenance of impeachment information.

7. *Confidential Informant Model Policy*, International Association of Chiefs of Police, National Law Enforcement Policy Center.
8. *Confidential Informants, Concepts and Issues Paper*, IACP National Law Enforcement Policy Center.
9. House Report 108–414, "Everything Secret Degenerates, The FBI's Use of Murderers as Informants," February 2, 2004.
10. Anglen, R., "Guilty Plea by Ex-ICE Agent Shocks Many," *Arizona Republic*, December 12, 2009.
11. Baker, A., "Drugs for Information Scandal Shakes up New York Police Task Force," *New York Times*, January 20, 2008.
12. Webster, W., "Sophisticated Surveillance: Intolerable Intrusion of Prudent Protection," *Washington University Quarterly*, Vol. 63, Number 3, 1985. See Aaronson , T., "The Informants," *Mother Jones*, October 2011.
13. *FBI Compliance with Attorney General Guidelines, Special Report*, September 2005, Office of the Inspector General.
14. MOU between the City of Salem, Oregon and ATF, Council agenda item # 4.3 (e), June 14, 2010.
15. The *Attorney General Guidelines Regarding the Use of Confidential Informants* uses the term "Confidential Informant," while the DEA uses the term "Confidential Source." Both terms refer to any individual who provides useful and credible information to a Department of Justice (DOJ) law enforcement agent regarding criminal activities, and from whom the law enforcement agent expects or intends to obtain additional useful and credible information regarding such activities in the future.
16. Seattle Police Department Manual, Section 6.130, 3/20/2013, referring to file as Confidential Informant File.
17. DEA Agent Manual Ch. 66.
18. Appendix 6B, "Confidential Source Establishment Report DEA Form 512."
19. Appendices 6A and 6B.
20. Format has been used by Bureau of Alcohol, Tobacco, Firearms and Explosives.
21. *DEA Agents Manual*, 6612.32(C).
22. Fed. R. Evid. 608(b).
23. *United States v. Bernal-Obeso*, 989 F.2d 331, 336 (9th Cir. 1993).
24. *Use and Management of Criminal History Record Information: A Comprehensive Report*, U.S. Department of Justice, Bureau of Justice Statistics, Office of Justice Programs.
25. *Criminal History Record Information: Compendium of State Privacy and Security Legislation*. U.S. Department of Justice, Office of Justice Programs, Bureau of Justice Statistics.
26. *United States v. Trevino*, 89 F.3d 187 (4th Cir. 1996); *Pennsylvania v. Ritchie*, 480 U.S. 39 (1987); *United States v. Figurski*, 545 F.2d 389 (4th Cir. 1975).
27. See Brady v. Maryland, 373 U.S. 83 (1963). See also *United States v. Strifler*, 851 F.2d 1197 (9th Cir. 1988). See also *Moore v. Kemp*, 809 F.2d 702 (11th Cir. 1987).
28. *Aguilar v. Texas*, 378 U.S. 108 (1964); *Spinelli v. United States*, 393 U.S. 410 (1969).
29. *Illinois v. Gates*, 462 U.S. 213 (1983).

30. See *United States v. Kojayan,* 8 F.3d 1315 (1993).

31. See *Roviaro v. United States,* 353 U.S. 53 (1957).

32. *DEA Agent Manual* Ch. 66.

33. *Bagley v. Lumpkin,* 798 F.2d 1297 (9th Cir. 1986). See also *United States v. Cohen,* 888 F.2d 770, 776–777 (11th Cir. 1989).

34. *Mesarosh v. United States,* 352 U.S. 1, 9, 14. (1956). The court reversed convictions when it was learned that the informant had told numerous lies about his background in earlier trials. The court said that the informant's reputation as a liar "tainted" any conviction obtained with his testimony.

35. 26 CFR 1.6041-3(l), April 2012 Edition of the Code of Federal Regulations, Internal Revenue Service, Treasury.

36. Bartosiewicz, P., "Deploying Informants, the FBI Stings Muslims: Behind Nearly Every 'Foiled Terror Plot' Lurks a Government Informant Sent to Entrap Hapless Young Muslim Men," *The Nation,* June 13, 2012.

37. *U.S. v. Salemme,* 195 F.Supp.2d 243 (D. Mass. 2001). Stephen Flemmi claimed he was immune from prosecution based on his FBI informant agreement.

38. The Attorney General's Guidelines Regarding the Use of Confidential Informants.

39. Aronson, T., "The Informants," *Mother Jones News,* September/October 2011.

40. Attorney General's Guidelines, IV. D (1).

41. Carter, M., "Former Seattle ATF Supervisor Indicted in Embezzlement Case," *Seattle Times,* November 21, 2013.

42. *Doe V. United States,* 58 F. 3d 494, 495 (1995).

43. Mass, P., *Underboss, Sammy the Bull Gravano's Story of Life in the Mafia,* Harper Collins, NY, 1997.

44. The Attorney General's Guidelines Regarding the Use of Confidential Informants.

45. *Vega v. United States,* No. 07-685C, June 12, 2008.

46. 28 U.S.C. § 1619.

47. USSG 5K1.1.

48. See Appendix 6B, DEA Form 512. The form has over 60 boxes that require the agent to obtain information from and about a prospective informant. Beyond name, date, place of birth, Social Security number, and address, it also requires that the informant's criminal history be fully investigated.

49. FBI Form FD-249.

50. *DEA Agent Manual* Ch. 66.

51. Ibid.

52. Guidelines for Establishing and Operating Gang Intelligence Units and Task Forces, U.S. Bureau of Justice Assistance, October 2008.

53. FBI Compliance with Attorney General Guidelines, Special Report, September 2005, Office of the Inspector General.

54. *Brady v. Maryland,* 373 U.S. 83, 87, 83 S. Ct. 1194, 10 L. Ed. 215 (1963).

55. *Giglio v. United States,* 405 U.S. 150, 92 S. Ct. 763 (1972).

56. *Carey v. Duckworth,* 738 F.2d 875, 878 (7th Cir. 1984).

57. Request for Disclosure of Confidential Source Information
    1. Name of confidential source
    2. Total amount paid to the confidential source in the instant case
    3. Total amount paid to the confidential source by law enforcement agency in all cases

  4. All benefits and other consideration paid or granted to the confidential source in return for the confidential source's cooperation
  5. The confidential source's criminal record
  6. Oral or written agreements between the law enforcement agency and the confidential source
  7. Any statements generated by the confidential source
  8. Impeachment and information known to the law enforcement agency about the confidential source
58. *United States v. Bernal-Obeso*, 989 Fd 2d 331 (9th Cir. 1993).
59. Wagener, D., "DEA Reactivates Fired Informant," *USA Today*, June 5, 2013.
60. 392 F.3d 382 (9th Cir. 2004)
61. 373 U.S. 83 (1963).
62. 405 U.S. 150 (1972).
63. *The Federal Bureau of Investigation's Compliance with the Attorney General's Investigative Guidelines, Chapter Three*: The Attorney General's Guidelines Regarding the Use of Confidential Informants (Redacted), Office of the Inspector General, September 2005.
64. Shiffman, J., "U.S. Directs Agents to Cover Up Program Used to Investigate Americans," *Reuters*, August 5, 2013.
65. Ibid.
66. Ibid.
67. See *Franks v. Delaware*, 438 U.S. 154, 171 (1978).
68. Zuckoff, M. and O'Neill, G., "'Testilying' Reporting Plan Set Up," *Boston Globe*, December 27, 1997.
69. Evans, B., "Shooting Draws Questions From Lawmakers," Associated Press, March 3, 2007.
70. Visser, S., "Ex-Cop: Officers Routinely Lied to Obtain Search Warrants," *Atlanta Journal-Constitution*, May 8, 2008.
71. Department of Justice Press Release, "Atlanta Police Officers Plead Guilty to Civil Rights Conspiracy: Defendant was Sergeant over Narcotics Team," May 24, 2008.
72. "2 Plead Guilty in Atlanta Police Shooting Death; Manslaughter Pleas Come after Three Officers Indicted for Killing Elderly Woman," Associated Press, April 26, 2007; See Balko, R., "Botched Raids Not Rare," *Atlanta Journal Constitution*, December 6, 2006; See also Katel, P., "The Trouble with Informants," *Newsweek*, January 30, 1995, at 1, 48.
73. Department Of Justice Press Release, "Atlanta Police Officers Plead Guilty to Civil Rights Conspiracy," May 24, 2008.
74. Stirgus, E., "No-Knock Victim's Family Seeks Deal," *Atlanta Journal Constitution*, November 22, 2008.
75. Testimony of Professor Alexandra Natapoff before the House of Representatives Joint Hearing on Law Enforcement Confidential Informant Practices, July 19, 2007. ("The Atlanta police could invent an informant to get a warrant because the culture of snitching assured them they would never have to produce an actual person in court.")
76. Curriden, M., "Secret Threat to Justice," *Natl. L. J.*, 1, 29 (February 20, 1995) quoting Defense Attorney Max Stern.

77. *Commonwealth v. Lewin,* 405 Mass. 566, 542 N.E.2d 275 Mass. (1989).
78. Ibid.
79. Curriden, M., "Secret Threat to Justice," *Natl. L. J.,* 1, 29 (February 20, 1995)
80. *Roviaro v. United States,* 353 U.S. 53 (1957).
81. *Brady v. Maryland,* 373 U.S. 83 (1963).
82. *United States v. Eniola,* 893 F.2d 383, 388 (D.C. Cir. 1990).

Sources of Compensation for Informants

7

7.1 Introduction

Compensating informants for their services is an inextricable component of our criminal justice system. The courts have accepted that it is sometimes necessary to compensate an informant before he will agree to undertake the often dangerous task of an undercover investigation. One judge explained, "Few would engage in a dangerous enterprise of this nature without assurance of substantial remuneration."[1] It is simply unreasonable to expect the government "to depend exclusively upon the virtuous in enforcing the law."[2]

Putting officers and agents in the position of rewarding their informants financially has its risks. The practice has been the catalyst for corruption and unfounded allegations of police misconduct. The theft of informant funds by police is a recurring subject of internal affairs investigations worldwide.

The Drug Enforcement Administration (DEA), Immigration and Customs Enforcement (ICE), and the Federal Bureau of Investigation (FBI), leaders in the use of paid informants, have adopted their own philosophies and methods for compensating their sources. All three allot funds from their annual appropriation for informant payments. Each agency also uses funds derived from criminal and civil forfeiture to reward their informants.

State and local police agencies also pay informants from monies allotted from their departmental operating funds. Departments also pay their informants from funds derived from forfeitures arising under state law. Since 1984, many police agencies participate in the "sharing" of federal forfeiture proceeds obtained from cooperative investigative efforts. Those funds are also used for informant payments.

7.2 Putting a Price Tag on Information

There is no fixed rule for how the amount paid to an informant is determined. Much depends on the quality of the information provided, the law enforcement agency, its size, budget, sophistication, and geographic location.[3] As one experienced Washington, DC, informant explained, "I get paid for bodies, for results. It's business with me. I ain't getting rich. I'm paying my bills. Warrants have been issued on my word alone. I've done three to four hundred search warrants."[4] Most sources are not getting rich from their work with police. One hundred dollars per controlled buy is not unusual.[5]

There is no fixed rate or schedule governing how much a source is paid. The absence of a formula for calculating an informant's payment for services can create tension between the informant and the control agent. For some CIs, there seems to be no logic in how the amount of their payment was determined. Even the sum paid for a controlled search warrant purchase of evidence can change from day to day. The amount can be tied to a departmental budget cut. If budget money dries up at the end of the fiscal year, informants may not get paid what they expect. Conversely, if an agency has not exhausted its informant funds by the end of the fiscal year, agents are encouraged to inflate informant payments.

Some police informants are paid significant sums. An investigative journalist in South Florida wrote in 2012, "Snitches can haul in riches." He cited the case of one City of Sunrise Police Department informant. In 5 years she has assisted police in 63 drug sting investigations. She has been paid $806,640.[6] Her cases have netted the police department over $5 million in cash and forfeited vehicles. That is far from the experience of most informants (see Table 7.1).

Table 7.1 Breakdown of payments to Sunrise police informant

Cash Seized	Value of Cars Seized	Total Assets Seized	Amount Paid to Informant	Percent Paid to Informant
$34,800	$25,675	$60,475	$1,000	1.7%
$0	$4,300	$4,300	$1,500	34.9%
$45,000	$0	$45,000	$1,000	2.2%
$23,833	$6,145	$29,978	$4,800	16.0%
$26,278	$0	$26,278	$5,200	19.8%
$108,700	$9,952	$118,652	$39,740	33.5%
$25,114	$4,669	$29,783	$2,500	8.4%
$31,000	$2,388	$33,388	$6,000	18.0%
$185,985	$4,604	$190,589	$37,000	19.4%
$0	$5,028	$5,028	$1,500	29.8%
$5,000	$2,439	$7,439	$1,000	13.4%
$44,000	$15,456	$59,456	$4,000	6.7%
$40,000	$4,000	$44,000	$4,000	9.1%
$29,000	$0	$29,000	$6,000	20.7%

Table 7.1 Breakdown of payments to Sunrise police informant (*Continued*)

$15,000	$0	$15,000	$3,000	20.0%
$241,627	$12,067	$253,694	$56,000	22.1%
$20,695	$0	$20,695	$4,500	21.7%
$30,300	$18,015	$48,315	$6,000	12.4%
$111,135	$2,594	$113,729	$22,000	19.3%
$43,860	$26,070	$69,930	$9,000	12.9%
$12,000	$6,434	$18,434	$2,400	13.0%
$28,750	$0	$28,750	$2,500	8.7%
$73,825	$17,785	$91,610	$14,700	16.0%
$22,000	$0	$22,000	$1,500	6.8%
$22,535	$4,216	$26,751	$6,900	25.8%
$10,155	$13,967	$24,122	$2,500	10.4%
$25,111	$0	$25,111	$5,000	19.9%
$25,149	$2,803	$27,952	$5,000	17.9%
$14,145	$7,497	$21,642	$3,000	13.9%
$410,000	$0	$410,000	$85,000	20.7%
$47,832	$7,197	$55,029	$10,000	18.2%
$349,943	$0	$349,943	$7,500	2.1%
$62,600	$5,415	$68,015	$13,000	19.1%
$85,000	$32,580	$117,580	$2,500	2.1%
$38,500	$1,681	$40,181	$6,500	16.2%
$45,725	$17,739	$63,464	$5,200	8.2%
$106,107	$23,161	$129,268	$16,000	12.4%
$26,094	$14,909	$41,003	$5,200	12.7%
$84,700	$2,300	$87,000	$13,000	14.9%
$41,100	$0	$41,100	$8,000	19.5%
$18,000	$9,476	$27,476	$5,000	18.2%
$10,506	$6,724	$17,230	$2,000	11.6%
$18,000	$0	$18,000	$1,400	7.8%
$12,097	$11,643	$23,740	$1,000	4.2%
$39,000	$0	$39,000	$7,800	20.0%
$26,600	$8,898	$35,498	$5,000	14.1%
$28,398	$9,100	$37,498	$5,000	13.3%
$19,513	$4,669	$24,182	$4,300	17.8%
$108,311	$27,131	$135,442	$20,500	15.1%
$15,000	$13,439	$28,439	$3,000	10.5%
$21,000	$20,159	$41,159	$4,000	9.7%
$14,065	$68,903	$82,968	$1,500	1.8%

(*Continued*)

Table 7.1 Breakdown of payments to Sunrise police informant (*Continued*)

Cash Seized	Value of Cars Seized	Total Assets Seized	Amount Paid to Informant	Percent Paid to Informant
$100,000	$26,015	$126,015	$20,000	15.9%
$166,344	$19,101	$185,445	$31,000	16.7%
$22,000	$12,613	$34,613	$4,000	11.6%
$438,732	$0	$438,732	$72,000	16.4%
$19,000	$19,756	$38,756	$2,000	5.2%
$24,000	$10,000	$34,000	$2,500	7.4%
$83,000	$21,541	$104,541	$5,500	5.3%
$214,466	$11,152	$225,618	$47,000	20.8%
$16,909	$24,061	$40,970	$1,500	3.7%
$83,318	$32,309	$115,627	$7,000	6.1%
$290,690	$7,885	$298,575	$7,000	2.3%

Source: Megan O'Matz and John Maines, "Cops, Cash and Cocaine: How Sunrise police make millions selling drugs," *Sun Sentinel*, Fort Lauderdale, FL, Oct. 7, 2013.

The amount paid to an informant is based on the value of the information they provide. The following items are considered when determining payments made to an informant.[7]

- Significance of the investigation.
- Degree of assistance rendered by the informant.
- Did the informant provide general or specific information?
- Was the informant responsible for initiation of the case?
- Was the information available from other informants?
- What length of time was spent by the informant in assisting in the investigation?
- Did the informant participate in consensual monitoring activities?
- Were undercover agents introduced by the informant?
- What was the potential risk of violence toward the informant?
- What was the value of seized and forfeited property obtained as a result of the informant's cooperation?
- What other substantial accomplishments are attributable to data supplied by the informant, that is, arrests, convictions, violent acts prevented, Title IIIs (wiretaps) generated, search warrants executed, and so on?
- In how many consensually monitored and recorded conversations did the informant participate?

- Will the informant testify if deemed appropriate, and what is the potential for future investigative contributions?
- Was the informant able to continue his/her normal job while working for the department?
- Did the informant suffer any financial losses as a result of the cooperation?

7.2.1 Case Study: Informant Fire

Mohamed Temani,[8] a Yemeni FBI terrorism informant, was not satisfied with the payment he received for his undercover work. The *Washington Post* reported that he was growing despondent over the way his FBI handlers had failed to honor promises regarding how much he would be paid and help with obtaining citizenship.[9] The promises were allegedly made when he was recruited. Unable to resolve the conflict in-house, the informant took a dramatic approach to draw President Bush's attention to his dispute with the FBI.

According to the informant, it was the attacks on 9/11 that motivated him to work for the FBI. He claimed to have met with FBI agents in New York where he volunteered information about al-Qaeda financiers operating in Yemen who supplied money, arms and recruits to mujahedeen fighters. He was registered as a confidential human source and assigned code number C11. On at least three occasions, the FBI sent him to Yemen on intelligence-gathering missions.[10]

In January 2003, the informant became a key player in a FBI sting operation conducted in Frankfurt, Germany.[11] A *New York Times* journalist described the case: "The transcripts by federal prosecutors depict a scene that could be out of a B-movie. In a German hotel room bugged by American agents, a Yemeni sheik was murmuring about jihad, a federal agent was posing as a former Black Panther eager to give millions to terrorists, and a roundish Yemeni man with a checkered past was egging on the others in his new role as one of the United States government's favorite—and best-paid—informers."[12]

The source was extremely disappointed with how much he had been paid. The *Post* reported, "He [the informant] volunteered that the FBI paid him $100,000 in 2003. But he said he had been expecting much more because he said some agents told him he would 'be a millionaire.' He also hadn't received the permanent residency he had been promised."[13]

At 2:05 PM on November 16, 2004, the fifty-two-year-old informant went to the White House with a note for President Bush. After being turned away by Secret Service officers, he set himself on fire. He had soaked his overcoat with gasoline prior to arriving at Pennsylvania Avenue.[14] Guards extinguished the flames and he was taken to the hospital in serious condition.

Following his recovery he told a journalist, "It is my big mistake that I have cooperated with FBI. The FBI have already destroyed my life and my family's life and made us in a very danger position . . . I am not crazy to destroy my life and my family's life to get $100,000."[15]

An FBI spokesman refused to discuss Mr. Temani's claims or the incident, saying, "We don't have a policy on revealing who is a cooperator or informing witness."[16]

7.3   Immigration and Customs Enforcement

U. S. Customs, the predecessor agency of ICE, has been paying its sources for over two centuries. In addition to informant payments and rewards from ICE's annual budget, the agency pays its informants moiety, meaning a share of the proceeds of goods forfeited by customs.[17]

ICE informants receive funds from special agents for the purchase of evidence (PE) and payments for information (PI). ICE agents use a Confidential Source Payments and Benefit Transaction Receipt form 293. The form can also be used to memorialize receipt of immigration benefits.

The amount of the payment and the reason for the payment appears on the form. Informants are required to sign form 293. The receipt is also signed by the agent making the payment and one witness.

Form 293 also bears the name and signature of the supervisor authorizing the payment. Supervisors are required to personally meet with informants. One of the triggering events for a supervisory meeting with an informant is when a threshold amount is paid. The supervisor is required to confirm that the informant has received the payments his case file reflects.

7.3.1   Purchase of Information

POI is defined as a payment to an informant for information or services provided to ICE in connection with an investigation. The funds come from ICE's annual operations budget. The amount of the payment is determined by the control agent and his supervisor. How much is paid is based on a variety of factors. For example, informants involved in money laundering investigations are often called upon to make undercover currency pickups from traffickers during currency pickup operations. Although the amount of the POI is often based on a percentage of the sum picked up, the POI payment is not being paid from those funds.[18]

Informants can also be paid from the proceeds of a certified undercover operation. The POI payments are posted in the Customs Undercover Fundamental Financial System.[19]

7.3.2   Commissions

Compensation paid to an informant by a target of investigation during an undercover operation in the form of commissions, points, brokerage fees, and monies of a similar nature are collectively referred to as "commissions." The commissions are often recurring and can amount to significant payments over the duration of an undercover operation.

ICE explains the reasoning behind allowing informants to retain their commissions: "In order to initiate long-term investigations, ICE must identify, cultivate, and retain assistance from confidential informants (CIs) who are intimately involved in these criminal organizations. The credibility and potential of these CIs and the positions, roles, and relationships they establish are directly related to the commissions that they receive."[20]

7.3.3 Personal Assistance Agreement

A personal assistance agreement (PAA) is an agreement between a CI and a Special Agent in Charge (SAC) that details the general activities and responsibilities expected of the CI, places limitations upon his or her behavior, and states the amounts and methods of compensation that the CI could expect to receive if he or she adheres to the provisions of the agreement. The principal reason for a PAA is to limit the government's liability arising out of an informant's activities in connection with an undercover operation or investigation. A PAA is required when a CI actively participates in an undercover activity associated with an undercover operation and he or she receives commissions, profits, or bonuses as a result of services rendered in furtherance of that operation. A PAA is not necessary when a CI is providing information or participating only on a casual basis (see Appendix 7D).[21]

7.3.4 Confidential Informant Expenses

Funds given to a CI to further an investigation are considered expenses and not considered when calculating the amount paid to the informant during an investigation. Expenditures related to activities of a CI are calculated as expenses of an operation when they

- Are necessary for the conduct of the operation
- Are primarily for the conduct of the government's mission (providing only incidental benefit to the CI)
- Are incurred by the CI in direct support of the undercover operation.

Expenses are not income for a CI and need not be documented on a CF-293. However, they must be approved and documented.

The *ICE Handbook* explains that at times, expenditures might facilitate the operation, yet provide the CI a significant benefit that is incidental to the needs of the government. Such expenses will be considered POI and documented accordingly. For example, if a CI's boat required a satellite location system for an operation, the cost of the system will be considered POI and therefore count toward the threshold levels of the CI. Otherwise, the satellite system is government property and must be removed at the conclusion of the operation.[22]

7.3.5   Violator/Trafficker-Directed Funds

Informants are often provided with funds by the target of investigation with the understanding that the funds are to be used in a specific way for the benefit of the violator or to further illegal activity. Those funds are classified as trafficker-directed funds and not considered as conveying a benefit to the informant. See *SGS-92-X003 v. U.S.*, No. 97-579C.

7.3.6   Undercover Businesses: Proprietary Operations

Informants are often assigned to serve in undercover companies known as a proprietary.[23] There are two types of proprietary operations: those that engage only in illegal activities and those that engage in both legal and illegal business transactions. CIs may profit from the operation of businesses established to further an undercover operation and often enter into written agreements with their control agency (see Appendix A). Known in some law enforcement agencies as churning investigations, the businesses can generate millions of dollars. One ATF informant made an estimated $4.9 million while working in a proprietary operation[24] (see Chapter 10).

The *ICE Handbook* defines a proprietary as "an undercover company or undercover operation that is established exclusively to engage in business transactions with targets of investigation to support an illegal activity and will not seek to do business with the general public and whose relationship with ICE is concealed from third parties." As applied to ICE undercover operations, the definition of operating "on a commercial basis" will include activities by undercover operatives who engage only in otherwise illegal business as well as activities of undercover operatives who engage in both legal and illegal business transactions.[25] For example, a cooperating individual or undercover agent who is established in an apartment to provide the service of illegally exporting munitions would be considered a proprietary undercover business. This will enable the SAC to seek the business exemption required to acquire services and property, as well as perform other necessary transactions in a covert manner outside the federal acquisition requirements, when necessary."[26]

The *Handbook* cautions that undercover business activities that are both of a legal and illegal nature and which might engage in business with the general public are considered to be sensitive. The type of proprietary that engages in business with the general public is discouraged but not prohibited.

7.4 Federal Bureau of Investigation

Thanks in part to press reports, leaked information, and federal statutes governing rewards, we know that FBI informants are paid handsomely for their efforts. Some are paid $100,000 or more per year, and many earn millions of dollars during their relationship with the government.[27] One FBI secretary responsible for preparing the paperwork was so outraged at the size of the informant payments as compared to her salary that she refused to process the reward paperwork.[28]

FBI confidential human sources (CHSs) are paid for services and expenses. Payments to CHSs "shall be commensurate with the value of services rendered by gathering information or by their active involvement in FBI investigations.[29] The amount paid to an established CHS is established at the beginning of the fiscal year and automatically renewed each year.[30] If the allotted amount is exceeded, a request for enhanced spending authority is submitted[31] for enhanced spending authority. The request must be accompanied by the amount requested and supporting justification. The CHS manual recommends that all CHS payments for services should be made after the services are rendered. Payments for services are not to be characterized and submitted as a payment for expenses and vice versa.

Agents are instructed to advise their CHSs that payments are considered taxable compensation by the Internal Revenue Service. They also must warn that the FBI has an obligation to report such compensation payments, upon request by the IRS, for income tax purposes." However, there is no requirement for any paying agency to notify the Internal Revenue Service of a payment to an informant.[32]

After obtaining approval for a CHS payment, the case agent, or any FBI agent, obtains a payment check from the FBI draft office. The agent may cash the check or otherwise convert it to another form of payment to provide the CHS.[33]

Payments to a CHS who may have to testify must be coordinated with the federal prosecuting attorney (FPO) participating in the conduct of the investigation. If the FPO objects, no payment can be made until the dispute has been resolved through appropriate channels.

The CHS manual specifies that "under no circumstances shall any payment be contingent upon the conviction or punishment of any individual."[34] The manual also instructs case agents (CA) "in determining the way to classify a particular payment as a service or an expense to a CHS, the CA should not consider whether or not that classification might result in a basis for impeachment at trial."[35]

7.4.1   Lump-Sum Payments

Lump-sum payments to a CHS may be paid from the FBI headquarters' (HQ's) budget unit. A request for a lump-sum payment may be made at the conclusion of any investigation in which the CHS has made significant contributions to FBI investigative matters. The amount paid is based on the merits of the case and whether the CHS has not previously been compensated for those contributions. The following issues must be addressed in any request for a lump-sum payment:

- Title and character of the case to which the CHS contributed information
- Significance of investigation
- Justification for lump-sum payment (must be for assistance not previously compensated)
- Whether the CHS suffered any financial loss (not previously compensated) as a result of his/her cooperation
- Total amount of services and total amount of expenses paid to the CHS
- If the CHS is to testify or has testified, state whether the assigned FPO concurs with the payment
- Value of seized or forfeited property obtained as a result of his/her cooperation
- Whether the CHS has received or would be nominated for an award or nominated for a payment resulting from forfeited assets
- Whether the CHS has or will receive any payment for services or expenses from any other law enforcement agency(s) in connection with the information or services that he/she provided to the FBI[36]

7.4.2   Rewards

A CHS may also accept rewards offered as a result of their assistance. Reward shall be commensurate with the value of the CHS's information or assistance. Approval is required if it is necessary to disclose the CHS's identity as terms for receiving the reward. If it is necessary for an agent to receive the reward on behalf of the CHS to protect the CHS's identity, the agent shall document receipt of the reward and release the reward to the CHS after obtaining a witnessed receipt.[37]

7.4.3   Forfeiture Awards

A CHS may receive an award from a forfeiture investigation even if he/she has already been compensated for an action or for providing information that led to the forfeiture. However, any such award shall be offset by any previous PI or assistance that led to the seizure, excluding expense payments. If the forfeited property is being placed into official use, the appraised value would be used to determine the award.[38]

7.4.4   One-Time Non-Confidential Human Source Payment

Only one payment may be made to any individual who has provided information to the FBI in furtherance of an FBI investigation and who has never been opened as a CHS. The payment must be approved in advance by the SAC.[39]

7.5   Drug Enforcement Administration

The DEA is authorized by law to pay its confidential sources (CS) for information.[40] Funds given to an informant are classified as payments for information and purchase of evidence.

According to the *DEA Agents Manual*,[41] "When an informant assists in developing an investigation, either through supplying information or actively participating in it, he may be paid for his services either in a lump sum or in staggered payments."[42] "DEA can also pay an informant a commission based upon some percentage of the value of the cases he provides. However, the following precautions are recommended:

1. CS paid on a commission basis should be instructed in advance concerning the law of entrapment;
2. The fee arrangement should be discussed with the CS in detail; there should be no gaps in understanding the terms of the arrangement;
3. The usual instructions to the CS, the details of the fee arrangement and the entrapment instructions should be provided to the informant in writing at the beginning of the operation;
4. Every effort should be made to maximize the control and supervision of the CS;
5. Every effort should be made to corroborate the CS's statements concerning his activities;
6. Payments should be completed before the CS testifies; and
7. We should be prepared to give reasons why it is necessary to use informants in this unusual manner."[43]

Control agents are not permitted to make any promise to a CS regarding the amounts of payments he or she might receive for their assistance. Although CSs can be advised that they may be eligible to receive payment for their services, they must also be advised that any decision to compensate them is at the sole discretion of DEA management. Any deviation from this policy must be approved in writing by the appropriate Senior Executive Service (SES) manager.[44]

All payments of DEA-appropriated funds to a CS are documented on a DEA form 103. Payments for different purposes including information/services, expenses, reward, award, or for security purposes must be made on a separate DEA 103. The remarks section of form 103 must contain a brief synopsis of the basis of justification for the payment (see Appendix 7A).

Agents are advised that under no circumstances will the CS be presented with a DEA 103 that does not have the payment amount typed or printed on the form[45] prior to the informant's signature. The admonition is intended to remove the temptation of having the informant sign a blank receipt allowing the agent to enter any amount at a later date. That has been the most common ploy used in the theft of CS funds by agents.

Undercover expenses necessary to further an investigation are often incurred. They can include the rental of vehicles, hotel rooms, meals, and beverages. Depending on the length and complexity of the case, the expenditures can prove costly. Although they may directly benefit the informant, they are not necessarily reflected in the overall amount an informant has been paid. If charged by the control agent as an investigative expense, it is not chargeable as either PE or PI. The sums will not be reported in a manner that will reduce the informant's PI potential. Those sums might not be reflected in informant payment disclosures made at trial. The nondisclosure of the payments to the defense can give rise to allegations of *Brady*[46] violations.

In addition to the DEA 103, an entry reflecting an informant payment must be made on the Informant Payment Record.[47] The payment record is one of the first forms seen when opening the informant's internal file and reflects all payments made to the CI.

7.5.1   Calendar Year Cap

All payments with DEA appropriated funds will be included in the CS's Lifetime (LT) and Calendar Year (CY) Caps. The CY cap for payments to a CS is currently $100,000,[48] and calculated from January 1 through December 31. Authority to increase the CY cap must be approved based on a memorandum submitted by the appropriate SES level manager to DEA HQ. Requests for increases are recommended in increments of $50,000.[49]

7.5.2   Lifetime Cap

The LT Cap for payments to a CS is $200,000. Authority to increase the LT Cap must be made by the appropriate SES manager via memorandum to DEA HQ that justifies raising the cap. The request for increase should be made in increments of $100,000.

7.5.3   Accountability

An Office of Inspector General audit of the DEA Confidential Source program revealed that the agency could not accurately account for its informant payments. According to the report, the DEA did not have an effective system to account for and to reconcile all confidential source payments. The report stated the agency had no way to determine how much an informant working for multiple DEA offices had actually been paid.[50]

7.5.4 Tax Responsibilities

The DEA issued the following notice to all of its Special Agents regarding instructions that must be given to confidential sources concerning federal income tax and rewards, awards, and payments for information: *The controlling Special Agent will advise all cooperating individuals that they must file federal income tax returns to include all payments, awards, and rewards paid to them by the DEA. In addition, the controlling Special Agent will advise the cooperating sources that all payments must be reported as "other income" on their federal income tax returns, and it will be their responsibility to obtain receipts and other supporting documentation to offset the legitimate expenses from income for possible audit by the Internal Revenue Service. Special Agents will advise all cooperating sources that their tax liability is a matter strictly between them and the Internal Revenue Service. Special Agents will remind cooperating individuals of this policy when any payment is made.*[51]

7.6 State Department Rewards for Justice

The U.S. government's response following the events of September 11, 2001, left no doubt that an unprecedented price tag had been put on information regarding terrorism. Never before in history had a government launched such an aggressive worldwide attempt to enlist the aid of paid informants. As an example, the U.S. Treasury and State Departments jointly sponsor the "Rewards for Justice" program. The program offers up to $25 million for information about individuals or organizations that finance terrorism and that leads to an arrest or conviction or the dismantling of a terrorist financing system. According to former Secretary of State Colin L. Powell, the program "gives us millions of additional pairs of eyes and ears to be on the lookout. It puts informants in every place a terrorist might try to operate or hide."

7.6.1 Bureau of International Narcotics and Law Enforcement: Narcotics Reward Program

The Bureau of International Narcotics and Law Enforcement Affairs (INL), known colloquially at the State Department as "Drugs and Thugs,"[52] is an outfit known to be generous: Up to $5 million per tip/per head is offered for information leading to the arrest *and/or* conviction of major narcotics traffickers who operate outside of but send drugs into the U.S.[53] The reward program is operated in coordination with the biggest stakeholders in the Drug War: the DEA, Department of Homeland Security, ICE, and the FBI.

The 50 leaders of the Fuerzaz Armadas Revolucionarias de Colombia (Revolutionary Armed Forced of Colombia) command the largest rewards. The organization stands accused of smuggling more than $25 billion worth of cocaine worldwide. The United States has the dubious distinction of being the organization's biggest customer.[54]

7.7   Central Intelligence Agency

The Central Intelligence Agency (CIA), while not a law enforcement agency, is possibly the leader in both the number of informants operated and the amounts paid for information. Known as assets, CIA informants often gather intelligence information that crosses over into the law enforcement responsibilities of other federal agencies.[55]

No one outside of the CIA knows exactly how much the agency pays its informants. The covert world of "black programs" is essentially free of oversight and public scrutiny. The annual CIA "black budget" is secret.[56]

It was not until July 2010 that the *Washington Post* opened a small window on the world of CIA informant payments. An unnamed U.S. official admitted that the CIA had paid an Iranian nuclear scientist $5 million for information concerning his country's nuclear program. According to the scientist, CIA agents offered him $50 million to remain in America.[57] The payment was made from a CIA program referred to as *Brain Drain*, an operation designed to induce high-value foreign scientists to defect to the United States.[58] The Iranian defector returned to Iran claiming to be a double agent.

The unnamed U.S. official used as a source for the article was candid about how the CIA puts a price on information and how the money is paid: "The support is keyed to what the person has done, including how their material has checked out over time. You don't get something for nothing."[59] The source for the *Post* article implied that the payment was not in a lump sum but put into long-term investments: "You basically put together a long-term benefits package," one that would sustain the defector over a lifetime in the United States.[60] According to the article, promises of resettlement and reward money are the two primary inducements used by the CIA to recruit informants inside "hard target" countries such as North Korea and Iran.[61]

7.8   Forfeiture Awards

The private sector has begun paying significant sums for information from informants. Privately funded rewards from businesses range from 7-Eleven's

$25,000 reward for information concerning robberies of its stores to Microsoft's Antivirus Reward Fund of $5 million.

Crime Stoppers International is an example of a unique partnership between community-based organizations, the media, and law enforcement. Beginning in 1976 with one chapter in Albuquerque, New Mexico, it now has approximately 1200 programs in 20 countries, including the United States, Canada, the United Kingdom, Australia, and South Africa. Central America and the Caribbean are also represented.

Crime Stoppers solicits tips from anonymous call-in informants who are willing to trade information for money. Rewards are only paid for tips that lead to the arrest and indictment of people charged with felony offenses. Unlike informants in the federal system, Crime Stoppers informants do not walk away as millionaires.

Offering cash rewards, insulating the call-in informant from the police, and promising anonymity have proven extremely successful. The Crime Stoppers website reports the following impressive statistics:

Cases cleared: 1,092,920
Arrests made: 625,381
Rewards paid: $98,804,944
Value of property recovered: $1,612,786,650
Value of drug seized: $6,052,955,993
Total dollars recovered (1976 through August 2006): $7,665,742,643

Crime Stoppers claims a conviction rate of approximately 95%.[62]

7.8.1 Department of Justice Asset Forfeiture Fund Awards

The Assets Forfeiture Fund was created by the Comprehensive Crime Control Act of 1984[63] to be a repository of the proceeds of forfeitures under any law enforced and administered by the Department of Justice (DOJ).[64] Annual revenues deposited into the Assets Forfeiture Fund (AFF) from the liquidation of forfeited assets increased from $500 million in 2003 to $1.8 billion in 2011, in part due to an increase in prosecutions of fraud and financial crimes cases. With more than $1 billion in forfeited assets deposited into the AFF every year since 2006, the Asset Forfeiture Program generates substantial revenue for the DOJ.[65]

The AFF's mission has as its primary strategic goal to enforce Federal laws and prevent and reduce crime by disrupting, damaging, and dismantling criminal organizations through the use of civil and criminal forfeiture. The program attempts to remove those assets that are essential to the operation of those criminal organizations and punish the criminals involved by denying them the use of the proceeds of their crimes.[66]

The DEA, the FBI, and the Bureau of Alcohol, Tobacco, and Firearms are authorized to pay cooperating individuals awards from the DOJ AFF.

The AFF 2012 annual performance budget explained its need and appreciation for informants:

> Awards payable from the Fund directly support law enforcement efforts by encouraging the cooperation and assistance of informants. The Fund may also be used to purchase evidence of violations of drug laws, Racketeering Influenced and Corrupt Organizations (RICO), and criminal money laundering laws. Payment of awards to sources of information creates tremendous motivation for individuals to assist the government in the investigation of criminal activity and the seizure of assets. Many cases would be impossible to bring to trial without the information from cooperating individuals. Even when the government has reason to believe criminal activity is occurring, an inside informant can facilitate the cost-effective deployment of investigative resources to obtain the greatest results.

PIs (listed in the budget as awards for information leading to forfeiture) for FY 2011 were $11,300,000. In FY 2012, informants were paid $11,500,000 from AFF funds.[67] PE expenses for 2011 were $8,800,000. In 2012 the amount spent on evidence purchases was $8,690,000.[68] At this writing, the 2013 estimate for PIs and PEs was $20,079,000.[69]

7.8.2   Civil and Criminal Forfeiture

There are two types of forfeiture available to the government: civil forfeiture and criminal forfeiture. In civil forfeiture, property used or acquired in violation of law is confiscated; criminal forfeiture is imposed as part of the defendant's punishment following conviction. Although the procedures followed in the two types of forfeiture are very different, the result is the same. If the government prevails, which is usually the case, the rights, title, and interest in the property reverts to the United States. The proceeds from the sale of the forfeited assets such as real property, vehicles, businesses, financial instruments, vessels, aircraft, and jewelry are deposited into the AFF and are used to further law enforcement initiatives including payments to informants.

Under the AFF's Equitable Sharing Program, proceeds from sales are shared with the state and local law enforcement agencies that participated in the investigation that led to the forfeiture of the assets. State and local agencies also use the funds for payment to informants. From FY 2003 through 2011, DOJ has shared over $3.2 billion in cash and property with more than 9200 state and local law enforcement agencies.[70]

The U.S. Marshals Service administers the AFF by managing and disposing of the property seized and forfeited.

Awards paid from the AFF to CIs are not charged against either agency's operating budget but reimbursed from the AFF.[71] Other contributors to the fund include the U.S. Marshals Service, the U.S. Attorneys' Offices, the Department of State's Diplomatic Security Service, and the Bureau of Alcohol, Tobacco, Firearms, and Explosives.

There are two types of awards paid from the AFF:

7.8.2.1 Award Type I

An award payment of up to $250,000 may be paid to a cooperating individual for either assistance or information that relates directly to violations of

- The criminal drug laws of the United States
- Money laundering offenses covered by 18 USC §§ 1956 and 1957[72]
- Reports on domestic coins and currency transactions covered by 31 USC §§ 5313 and 5324[73]
- Section 60501 of the Internal Revenue Code of 1986[74]

While information or assistance qualifies an individual for an award, the DEA recommends that asset seizure should be a factor taken into consideration when recommending the amount of the reward.

7.8.2.2 Award Type II[75]

Awards for information or assistance leading to a civil or criminal forfeiture are available under 28 USC § 524(c)(1)(C). Awards are asset-specific. To qualify, a cooperating individual must provide original information that result in the seizure and forfeiture of one or more assets. The award may not exceed the lesser of $500,000 or 25% of the amount realized by the United States from the forfeited property.

Cooperating individuals are eligible for more than one award if their information results in several seizures under the same investigative case number. The information pertaining to each seizure must be separate and distinct. The application for separate awards under the same case number has to clearly explain the unique character of the information.

The amount of the award is determined by the amount realized by the government. That amount is defined as the gross receipts of the forfeiture, either cash or proceeds of sale, less management expenses attributable to the seizure and forfeiture of the property. In the event the property is retained for official use, for example, an aircraft put into service by the FBI, the amount realized for award purposes is the amount realized by the United States from the property forfeited and is the value of the property at the time of the seizure less any management expenses paid from the fund. The net figure is used as the basis for calculating the award.

Awards under 524(c)(l)(B) and (C) are discretionary in nature.[76] The DEA requires that the application for the award originate in a memorandum from the Special Agent in Charge to the Assistant Administrator for Operations. The memorandum must address ten items:

1. The type of award, either 524(c)(l)(B) or 524(c)(l)(C)
2. Amount requested by the award applicant, if an amount is claimed
3. Recommended amount or percentage proposed by the Special Agent in Charge
4. Cooperating individual code number
5. Seizure number for the asset claimed against
6. Amounts received by the CI in the same investigation
7. Whether the CI will receive funds from any other agency as a result of the investigation under consideration
8. Whether the individual desires to be paid by check or cash
9. The significance of the CI's information or assistance in the investigation and the resulting asset seizure
10. Whether the CI is requesting more than one award under the same case number; a complete explanation must describe how seizures are separate and distinct from each other

7.8.3   Calculating Informant Forfeiture Awards

There is little doubt concerning how much an informant *may* expect if he or she is the sole source responsible for a seizure of property. It *may* not exceed the lesser of $500,000 or 25% of the amount realized by the United States from the forfeited property.

The first published account of how an informant's award was actually calculated came in a GAO report in 2012.[77] In that case, the informant was only partially responsible for a forfeiture that netted the government $1.6 million. According to the report,

> In the course of our review, DOJ officials provided examples of these qualitative factors. For example, if a state or local law enforcement agency provided a helicopter, drug-sniffing dog, or a criminal informant to an investigation, DOJ would consider these contributions to be unique or indispensable assistance. In one case we reviewed, a local law enforcement agency that participated in a joint investigation with federal agents would have received 7.4 percent in equitable sharing based on the work hours it contributed to the investigation. However, the agency also provided information obtained from a confidential source that led to the seizure and provided a helicopter for aerial surveillance. As a result, its final sharing determination was adjusted upward from 7.4 percent to 12 percent. If the net proceeds of the forfeiture are $1.6 million once all investigative and forfeiture-related expenses have been paid, the resulting equitable sharing payment made to the law enforcement agency will increase from $118,400 to $192,000.[78]

The GAO report, focusing on transparency in the process of determining the amount an award should be or the amount shared with a local police department, could find little rationale in the decision-making process.[79]

7.9   Informant Lawsuits

Informants have sued federal agencies and their handlers over disputes concerning the amount of their award payments.[80] The claims generally relate to issues of breach of contract, negligent misrepresentation, and fraud. Nearly all plaintiff informants claim that their control agent promised them one fourth of the amount of money seized during an investigation or one-fourth of the value of the property forfeited.[81] The informants argue that they had an implied-in-fact contract that promised a 25% commission.

The essence of many of the disputes is centered on the language in the DOJ AFF provisions. Agents may either mistakenly or deliberately communicate a "flat rate of 25%" to their informants. They may also give the impression that they are the decision maker as to how much is paid. In reality, it is the Special Agent in Charge (in DEA cases) who makes a recommendation concerning the amount to DEA HQ. A high-ranking HQ official evaluates the case and decides how much the informant will be paid.[82]

7.9.1   The DEA Princess Suit

A $33 million lawsuit was filed against the DEA for breach-of-contract by an informant code-named "Princess." Heard in the Washington, DC, Court of Federal Claims in 2009, the suit was initially kept under seal.

Princess was seeking rewards she claimed were promised her during a money laundering operation called Operation Princess. She was paid *only* approximately $1.85 million.[83] Depending on whom you believe, a reward of up to 25% of the funds seized during the money laundering operation could have worked out to nearly $15 million. Princess was also seeking damages for the DEA's failure to protect her while she was working undercover in Colombia.

The court found that evidence at trial established that Princess had an implied-in-fact contract with DEA but not for a set commission. Rather, the head of DEA's Ft. Lauderdale office promised to pay the Princess her salary, expenses, and rewards or commissions of "up to" 25% of her seizures subject to the approval of high level government officials. Under this contract, which the court found was demonstrated by the parties' course of performance, the informant's supervising DEA agent could pay her up to $25,000 per quarter but only *recommend* rewards or commissions above that amount. Higher-ups at DEA and/or the DOJ had to approve additional payments. The Court found that given the nature of the agreement, the Princess was not entitled to any more commissions, rewards, or awards from the money laundering operation.[84]

The Princess case is still winding its way through the court system—still under seal. This time the court will only hear her claim for damages. Evidence produced at trial established that Princess went above and beyond the call of duty.[85]

Her control agent sent Princess on a money laundering and cocaine-trafficking mission to Cali, Colombia, allegedly without following DEA procedures. During the mission, Princess was kidnapped by guerillas brandishing machine guns and hand grenades, thrown into the trunk of a car, and taken to a jungle hideaway.

Still in possession of her purse, she ate her telephone book. She testified: "It took me like one day, one day and a half to eat it, because I had to eat those pages. But I had all the information…. So I had to eat all of that so that nobody would get to the information because I figure they better kill me but no information is going to be released."[86]

She was held for more than three months in a windowless, dirt-floor room where she slept on a straw mattress. It wasn't until another DEA informant came through with $350,000 that she was finally released. According to a DEA account, "The Princess's release was effected through a highly confidential source of the Bogota office. This confidential source risked and utilized numerous associates and personal assets to aid DEA in getting the Princess back."[87]

Princess's claim for damages asserts that the ordeal left her with multiple sclerosis and bipolar disorder. She might do well to remember what DEA agents once told her the agency initials stand for: "Don't Expect Anything."[88]

7.10   Pressure to Seize Forfeitable Assets

There is a great deal of pressure put on the Justice Department's FBI, DEA, and ATF agents worldwide to go after forfeitable assets. The same is true for agents within the Treasury Department and the Department of Homeland Security's ICE Division. Their informants are told in no uncertain terms to focus their energies on targets with seizable assets.

The Bureau of Alcohol, Tobacco, and Firearms is known as ATF: the initials officially stand for *alcohol, tobacco, and firearms*. Since the advent of forfeiture, the agency unofficially uses the initials to remind their agents to "Always Think Forfeiture." The agency is notorious for ruthlessly seizing ill-gotten gains.

In April 2006, ATF agents in Tacoma, Washington, filed a sealed (secret) seizure warrant for property belonging to two jailed drug dealers who were awaiting trial.[89] The two men were spirited from their Federal Detention jail cells and taken to the U.S. Marshals Office in Tacoma, where the warrant was served.

The ATF agents had a court order allowing them to take their prisoners to a dentist in Seattle to have gold-decorated teeth pulled out of their mouths. The agents alleged in their warrant that the teeth were known as "grills" or "grillz" and could be worth as much as $25,000. As authority for their estimate they cited the website gangstagold.com.

Following a flurry of phone calls to their lawyers the men were able to get a reprieve from the dentist. Their lawyers insisted the teeth were permanently affixed.

A Seattle forfeiture defense attorney was in disbelief. He told a Seattle Times reporter, "I've been doing this (defending forfeiture cases) for over 30 years and I have never heard of anything like this. It sounds like Nazi Germany when they were removing the gold teeth from the bodies, but at least then they waited until they were dead."[90]

The flap over the grillz did nothing to the bravado surrounding the agency's "Always Think Forfeiture" mind-set. It was not until May 2008 that ATF's slogan caused the agency to do some explaining.[91] An Idaho Congressman learned that the ATF had ordered 2000 Leatherman style–pocket knives engraved with "Always Think Forfeiture" on one side and "ATF—Asset Forfeiture" on the other side.[92] The knives were meant for distribution to state and local police officers attending a ATF-hosted asset forfeiture training sessions. Money from the AFF was earmarked to pay for the knives. The congressman was not amused.

Shortly after the story broke, a ATF spokesman said, "Because it has caused concern among the public, we are no longer utilizing that slogan in our training sessions."[93]

7.11 State and Local Pressure for Forfeitable Assets

State and local law enforcement officers are not exempt from the pressures of superiors to send out informants and to bring in forfeitures. The Canton, Michigan, Police Department is a small department with only sixty-four officers. It has a forfeiture unit staffed by a few detectives who seized $343,699 in 2008. The sergeant in charge of the unit was bluntly honest about the motive behind police forfeiture: "Police departments right now are looking for ways to generate revenue, and forfeiture is a way to offset the costs of doing business. You'll find that departments are doing more forfeitures than they used to because they've got to—they're running out of money and they've got to find it somewhere."[94]

7.12 Kickbacks, Corruption, and Informant Payments

Award shakedown schemes have sent control agents to prison. The amounts that agents sell out for are remarkably low. The account that follows offers insight into the practice.

7.12.1 U.S. Customs Agent Takes Share of Informant Forfeiture Award

The agent worked with an informant who provided assistance to the Customs Service in criminal investigations. One of the agent's duties was to monitor and assess the work of the informant. During a period of several years, the informant received a number of payments from the Customs Service as compensation for his services as informant. On one or more occasions, the informant expressed gratitude for the agent's assistance by observing that both he and the agent had engaged in hard work for which the informant would receive substantial compensation, but for which the agent only would receive his salary. The informant offered to share with the agent a portion of his earnings from the Customs Service. The agent nominated the informant for a large payment, which represented a portion of the value of certain assets forfeited as a result of information provided by the informant. The agent then initiated a telephone conversation with the informant in which he asked the informant for money. During August 1992, the informant went to San Francisco to receive the payment. The agent personally gave the informant a U.S. Treasury check in the amount of $110,875. While riding in a government-owned vehicle, the informant attempted to hand the agent an envelope with $4000 in cash. The agent responded that the informant should drop the envelope in the car because he could not accept the cash directly. The informant left the money in the car and the agent recovered it.

The agent pled guilty pursuant to a plea agreement to a charge of a criminal violation of 18 U. S. C. 209, illegal supplementation of salary. Under the plea agreement, the agent agreed to the imposition of a fine of $4000 by the Court, to not seek employment with any Federal, state, or local law enforcement Agency, and to pay a special assessment of $25. In exchange for these agreements, the United States agreed to move to dismiss the indictment charging the agent with a violation of 18 U. S. C. 201(c)(1)(B) and not to prosecute him for any other criminal offense relating to his receipt of $4000 from the informant.[95]

7.12.2 Press Release: Former ICE Agent Pleads Guilty in Kickback, Obstruction Scheme

According to a proffer during a change of plea hearing, the defendant was employed as a Special Agent with the U.S. ICE, Office of Investigations (ICE-OI), and was assigned to the Miami office. The former agent was assigned to an investigative group that focused on human smuggling organizations based domestically and internationally.[96]

In 2004, the defendant was the controlling agent of a CI, who provided significant information regarding human trafficking organizations based in Ecuador. As part of on going investigations, the CI agreed to introduce defendant to members of the various human smuggling organizations. ICE agreed to financially compensate the CI for his services. As the alien smuggling investigations progressed, however, defendant asked the CI for certain financial favors. For example, in late 2004, defendant instructed the CI to deliver $300 to defendant's girlfriend in Ecuador. In addition, the CI gave defendant a gold bracelet valued at $800, and obtained cellular telephones for defendant's girlfriend in Ecuador, as requested by defendant. The source of funds for the gifts and money were the funds that the CI received from his official activities on behalf of ICE-OI. From late 2004 until January 2006, defendant received a 10% commission based on the $125,000 total payment he received for his undercover work with ICE-OI.

In addition, defendant solicited gratuities from a second CI, A.W., who also provided ICE with intelligence regarding human trafficking organizations operating in Ecuador and other foreign countries. On May 19, 2005, defendant solicited a kickback payment from A.W., who complied and paid defendant $3000. On June 3, 2005, defendant again asked A.W. for another payment and A.W. paid the defendant $4000.[97]

The defendant pled guilty to charges of receiving a gratuity by a public official,[98] and was sentenced to 2 years in prison, the maximum for the offense. He was spared the $250,000 fine the sentence carried. The 52-year-old agent was eligible for retirement at the time of his arrest.

7.12.3 Drugs for Information: Noble Cause Corruption

Remarkably, there is a belief held by some that police can give narcotics to their informants in lieu of cash. Police are prohibited from paying informants with drugs or other contraband. There is no evidence to indicate that any police department or federal agency condones the use of paying for informant services with drugs.

However, the unauthorized practice of rewarding CIs with narcotics does occur. A drugs-for-information scandal led to the January 2008 arrest of two Brooklyn, New York narcotics detectives and the transfer of four high-level supervisors. The officers were accused of paying informants with cocaine seized from earlier raids that were not logged in as evidence. There was no self-enriching motive uncovered to account for the officer's conduct. One senior officer interviewed by the press attributed their conduct to laziness. There were funds available for informant payments; it was simply easier to give them drugs.[99]

Appendix 7A: Drug Enforcement Administration Voucher for Purchase of Evidence/Payment for Information/Services

I GENERAL (complete for all submissions)
1. Claimant
2. Group No.
3. Office
4. Case No.
5. G-DEP Code
6. Purpose of Submission (check one)
   __Purchase of evidence
   __Payment for Information/Services Evidence

II PURCHASE OF EVIDENCE complete as appropriate)
7. Exhibit No.
8. Amount Expended $_____
9. Description of Exhibit (same as DEA Form 7/7a):
   *Drug & Non-Drug Evidence Forms

III PAYMENT FOR INFORMATION/SERVICES (complete as appropriate)
10. Purpose (check one)
    __Information/Services
    __Security
    __Reimbursement of Expenses
11. Source of Funds (check one)
    __PE/PI (Purchase of Evidence/Information)
    __AFF (Asset Forfeiture Fund) _____
    __Trafficker Directed/Generated Proceeds
12. Basis for Payment (Brief narrative of reason for payment)
13. I certify that I received payment in the amount of $____ in U. S. currency or the equivalent amount in another currency. (Sign last copy only) Code Number____
    Date_____

IV CERTIFICATION (complete for all submissions)
14. PURCHASER/PAYOR (Signature)_____
    Type or Print Name _____ Date_____
15. WITNESS (Signature, only for III above) _____
    Type or Print Name _____ Date_____
16. CLAIMANT (Signature, if different from 14 above)
    _____
    Type or Print Name_____ Date_____
17. SUPERVISOR (Signature) _____
    Type or Print Name_____ Date_____

V ACCOUNTING CLASSIFICATION (see instructions)

FUND CITATION AMOUNT $_____
Fiscal Officer (Signature) _____
Type or Print Name _____Date_____

Appendix 7B: Statistical Accomplishments Form

Criminal Informant/Cooperative Witness (CI/CW)

1. Number of Subjects Arrested:
    a. FBI ____
    b. Other Federal Agencies ____
    c. State and Local Agencies ____
2. Number of Subjects/Victims Identified and/or Located:
    a. FBI ____
    b. Other Federal Agencies ____
    c. State and Local Agencies____
3. Number of Investigative Matters Initiated:
    a. FBI____
    b. Other Federal Agencies____
    c. State and Local Agencies____
4. Number of Disseminations Based Upon CI/CW Information:____
5. Number of Violent Acts Prevented:____
6. Number of Times CI/CW Information Used in Title III Affidavits:
    a. FBI____
    b. Other Federal Agencies ____
    c. State and Local Agencies____
7. Number of Times CI/CW Information Used in Search Warrant Affidavits:
    a   FBI____
    b. Other Federal Agencies____
    c. State and Local Agencies____
8. Number of Times CI/CW Information Used in Obtaining Complaint/ Information/Indictment:
    a. FBI____
    b. Other Federal Agencies____
    c. State and Local Agencies____
9. Merchandise Recovered (Value)
    a. FBI____
    b. Other Federal Agencies____
    c. State and Local Agencies____

10. Asset/Property Seized (Value at Time of Seizure):
    a. FBI____
    b. Other Federal Agencies ____
    c. State and Local Agencies____
11. Monetary Value of Asset/Property Actually Forfeited to Government:
    $_____
12. Number of Convictions Obtained as a Result of Information Furnished by CI/CW or as a Result of other Significant Operational Assistance Furnished:
    a. FBI____
    b. Other Federal Agencies ____
    c. State and Local Agencies____
13. Number of Times Undercover Agent or Other Law Enforcement Officer Introduced into an Investigative Matter by CI/CW:
    a. FBI____
    b. Other Federal Agencies____
    c. State and Local Agencies____
14. Drugs Recovered (Wholesale Value):
    a. FBI____
    b. Other Federal Agencies____
    c. State and Local Agencies____
15. Number of Consensually Monitored Conversations CI/CW participated in:
    a. FBI____
    b. Other Federal Agencies____
    c. State and Local Agencies____

Appendix 7C: Statutes Enforced by Federal Investigative Agencies That Permit Equitable Sharing with State and Local Agencies

The guidelines for participating in the sharing process grant the Attorney General authority to share federally forfeited property seized pursuant to federal statutes with participating state and local law enforcement agencies. The exercise of that authority is *discretionary*. The Attorney General is not required to share property in any case. Those statutes include:

8 USC § 1324(b)
    Civil forfeiture of conveyances that have been used in the attempted or accomplished smuggling of aliens into the United States or transportation of illegal aliens within the United States.

17 USC § 509

Civil forfeiture of specific property that has been used to illegally manufacture, reproduce or distribute phonograph records or copies of copyrighted materials.

18 USC § 512

Civil forfeiture of automobiles and parts involved in specific prohibited conduct.

18 USC § 545

Civil forfeiture applicable to merchandise imported contrary to law.

18 USC § 1955

Civil forfeiture of property used in an illegal interstate gambling business.

18 USC §§ 1956/1957

Money laundering offenses.

18 USC § 981

Civil and criminal forfeiture provisions—property representing gross receipts of money laundering section is subject to seizure and forfeiture.

18 USC § 1961

Racketeer Influenced and Corrupt Organizations (RICO)—upon conviction, property constituting or derived from proceeds of racketeering shall be forfeited.

18 USC § 2253, 18 USC § 2254, 18 USC § 1467

Child Protection Act of 1984, Sexual Exploitation of Children—visual depictions, equipment used to manufacture or reproduce child pornography, and property derived from a violation of this Act may be seized and forfeited under the Customs laws.

18 USC § 2513

Civil forfeiture of certain property used to illegally intercept wire, oral, or electronic communications.

19 USC § 1436

Seizure and forfeiture of merchandise not properly reported (including monetary instruments per amendment to 19 USC § 1401. Definition of "merchandise" or any conveyance used in connection with a violation of this section.

19 USC § 1462

Civil forfeiture is authorized for any article, the importation of which is prohibited, the container or vehicle.

19 USC § 1497

Penalties for failure to declare include seizure and forfeiture of undeclared articles as well as controlled substances and civil penalty equal to the value of the article or 200% of street value of a controlled substance.

19 USC § 1584

Penalties for falsity or lack of manifest includes provision permitting forfeiture if penalty is unpaid.

19 USC § 1586

Any vessel, merchandise, or cargo associated with the unlawful unloading or transshipment is subject to seizure and forfeiture.

19 USC § 1587

Vessel and cargo aboard may be subject to seizure and forfeiture.

19 USC § 1588

Merchandise transported between U.S. ports via foreign ports is subject to seizure and forfeiture.

19 USC § 1590

Aviation Smuggling—authorizes seizures and forfeitures of vessels and/or aircraft used in connection with or aiding or facilitating a violation of this section.

19 USC § 1592

Merchandise entered, introduced, or attempted to be entered or introduced by false or fraudulent means may be seized in limited circumstances and forfeited if the monetary penalty is not paid.

19 USC § 1594

Seizure of conveyance—conveyances subject to seizure and forfeiture to secure payment of Customs penalties. Common carriers are subject to seizure and forfeiture in limited situations.

19 USC § 1595

Searches and seizures through civil warrant expanded to cover any article subject to seizure (not just imported merchandise), for example, to seize conveyances, monetary instruments, and other evidence of Customs violations.

19 USC § 1595

Forfeitures—authorizes forfeiture of conveyances aiding or facilitating importation, introduction, or transportation of articles contrary to law.

19 USC § 1703

Vessels and aircraft built or fitted out for smuggling and their cargo shall be seized and forfeited.

21 USC § 333(e)(3)

A conviction under this section of the Food Drug and Cosmetic Act for distribution of Human Growth Hormones, or for possession with intent to distribute Human Growth Hormones, shall be considered a felony violation of the Controlled Substances Act for the purposes of forfeiture under 21 USC § 848 Continuing Criminal Enterprise (CCE)—upon conviction, profits, interest in and everything affording a source of influence over the enterprise shall be forfeited.

21 USC § 853
  Criminal forfeiture.
21 USC § 857
  Civil forfeiture of drug paraphernalia.
22 USC § 401
  Arms, munitions, or other articles exported in violation of law and conveyances used in exporting or attempting to export shall be seized
  and forfeited.
31 USC § 5317(b)
  Authorizes forfeiture of monetary instruments being transported in
  situations where reports required by 31 USC § 5316 are not filed or
  contain material omissions or misstatements. Provision as amended
  by the Anti-Drug Abuse Act of 1986 includes a "tracing" provision,
  for example, seizure and forfeiture of any property traceable to unreported or misreported instruments.
50 USC App. § 16
  Trading with the Enemy Act—any property or conveyance concerned
  in a violation of this Act shall be forfeited.
50 USC App. § 2410
  Export Administration Act—upon conviction, any property associated
  with the violation shall be forfeited.

Appendix 7D: Personal Service Agreement

This agreement made this (date), between [Law Enforcement Agency] and
Source Number _____, hereinafter called Source, and the [Law Enforcement
Agency], specifies various terms and conditions as follows:

Responsibilities of the Parties

Source, a Confidential Informant, will assist [Law Enforcement Agency] in
the gathering of evidence concerning the criminal activities of _____
_____.

Source agrees, at the direction and under the supervision of [Law Enforcement
Agency], to meet with designated individuals and to make or have made by
Law Enforcement Officers consensual video, oral, electronic, and/or wire
recordings of such meetings, including consensually monitored telephone
conversations. Further, Source will provide written authorization to [Law
Enforcement Agency] to monitor and record such meetings and conversations prior to such monitoring/recording.

Source understands that [Law Enforcement Agency], by entering into this
agreement, makes no promises or agreements with regard to any court action

now pending or which may be pending in the future concerning Source. Source acknowledges that his/her entering into this agreement with [Law Enforcement Agency] is completely voluntary, and that he/she is under no coercion or pressure from [Law Enforcement Agency] to participate in this undercover operation.

Source will not participate in any unlawful activities without the express approval of [Law Enforcement Agency]. Any such unauthorized action may subject him/her to any applicable civil and/or criminal sanctions.

Source agrees, when directed by [Law Enforcement Agency], to furnish the information in his/her possession, custody, or control, which he/she received during the course of, relating to, the activities covered by this agreement. Source agrees that, if requested by [Law Enforcement Agency], he/she will testify fully and truthfully in any judicial proceedings necessary. Source agrees to be available for reasonable and necessary periods for preparation in connection with any such testimony.

Source understands that his/her role as Source does not convey any authority to carry a firearm and that he/she is not an agent, employee, partner, member of a joint venture, associate, or officer of [Law Enforcement Agency]. In accordance with guidance from [Law Enforcement Agency], Source will neither identify himself/herself nor hold himself/herself out to be an agent, employee, partner, member of a joint venture, associate, or officer of [Law Enforcement Agency], and he/she will not use his/her association with [Law Enforcement Agency] to resolve personal matters.

Source will not initiate any plans to commit criminal acts, nor will he/she initiate or participate in any acts of violence. If the Source is asked to participate in any act of violence or learns of such plans, he/she will attempt to discourage those plans or acts and will promptly notify [Law Enforcement Agency]. In accordance with guidance from [Law Enforcement Agency], Source further agrees that he/she will not take action to entrap any person as part of his/her assistance to [Law Enforcement Agency].

Source shall have no authority, actual or implied, to obligate and/or bind [Law Enforcement Agency] to any contract and/or obligation; any contract or obligation so made is the sole obligation of the Source and not of [Law Enforcement Agency]. Source will take no action in furtherance of an operation or business activity to be conducted by [Law Enforcement Agency] without the prior approval of [Law Enforcement Agency].

It is understood that [Law Enforcement Agency], at its sole discretion, will control all investigative matters, including any decision to terminate action taken in furtherance of this activity.

Compensation

Source understands that only reasonable expenses approved in advance by the appropriate officials of [Law Enforcement Agency] may be reimbursed. In the event that Source fails to obtain the approval of [Law Enforcement Agency] prior to incurring reasonable expenses, [Law Enforcement Agency] in its sole discretion may nonetheless reimburse the Source.

Nothing in this agreement precludes Source from applying for an award as provided by law.

Nothing in this agreement precludes [Law Enforcement Agency] in its sole discretion from making a Purchase of Information/Evidence payment to Source for evidence, information, or assistance provided by Source, during or upon completion of the investigation. The decision whether to pay and, if so, in what amounts are within the complete and full discretion of [Law Enforcement Agency].

Source understands and acknowledges that payments to Source from [Law Enforcement Agency], including those identified herein, may constitute taxable income and, if taxable, it is his/her responsibility to report them as such to the appropriate Federal, State and local taxation authorities.

[Law Enforcement Agency] will compensate Source $_____ per month for the Source's full-time services in connection with the above-mentioned investigation for the duration of this agreement.

Source agrees to immediately advise [Law Enforcement Agency] of any deferred or future compensation anticipated by Source from activities arising out of this agreement and circumstances surrounding such deferred or future compensation.

The [Law Enforcement Agency] in no way obligate itself to pay Source any monies for compensation for services or for expenses related to this agreement except as expressly provided herein. Furthermore, [Law Enforcement Agency] may, without liability to Source, at any time and for any reason decided not to engage in any transaction, contract, or sale, or to terminate any transaction, contract, or sail in progress under this agreement.

Liabilities of the Parties

Liability for any negligent act of [Law Enforcement Agency] employees will be borne by the [Law Enforcement Agency] in accordance with applicable law. Liability for any acts of the Source which are undertaken without prior express approval of [Law Enforcement Agency] are the sole responsibility of the Source.

It is further expressly understood that [Law Enforcement Agency] assumes no responsibility or liability for any business loss, income loss, or harm to business reputation which may result to Source as a result of Source's assistance to [Law Enforcement Agency] in this investigation.

Confidentiality

Source will not reveal the confidential and sensitive nature of the investigation or identify any undercover [Law Enforcement Agency] agents or employees unless authorized in advance by [Law Enforcement Agency]. Source will not undertake any publication or dissemination of any information or material that results from, or is related to, this agreement and/or [Law Enforcement Agency]'s investigation without prior written authorization of [Law Enforcement Agency]. Source further understands and agrees not to discuss or in any manner disclosed this agreement or any of its contents without prior written authorization of [Law Enforcement Agency].

Source agrees to take polygraph examinations as requested by [Law Enforcement Agency].

Duration of Agreement

Source understands this assistance will be for an unspecified period of time not to exceed one year from the date of this agreement. Source understands that his/her assistance may be terminated at any time at the sole discretion of [Law Enforcement Agency].

Source agrees to the terms of this agreement may be changed at any time, in writing, upon the mutual agreement of Source and [Law Enforcement Agency]. This agreement contains the entire understanding between the parties hereto and supersedes all prior written or oral agreements between them respecting the subject matter of this agreement unless otherwise provided herein. They're in our present nations, agreements, arrangements, or understandings, oral or written, between the parties hereto relating to the subject matter of this agreement which are not fully expressed herein.

By their signatures below, the parties acknowledge that they have read, understand and will abide by the foregoing statements.

_____
Source

_____   _____
Control Agent Date   Witness   Date

Endnotes

1. *United States v. Reynoso-Ulloa*, 548 F.2d at 1338 n. 19.
2. *United States v. Richardson*, 764 F.2d 1514, 1521 (11th Cir. 1985).
3. See *Confidential Funds: Model Policy*, International Association of Chiefs of Police, National Law Enforcement Policy Center; *Confidential Fund: Concepts and Issues Paper*, International Association of Chiefs of Police, National Law Enforcement Policy Center.
4. Cherkin, J., "I'm a professional informant," *Washington City Paper*, July 11, 2008.
5. *Tennessee v. McMurray*, No. E2012-02637-CCA-R3-CD. Filed December 16, 2013; informant paid $100 for each controlled buy.
6. Cops, Cash and Cocaine, *Sun Sentinel*, October 21, 2013.
7. Several of the items were obtained from an Internal FBI memorandum to Special Agents regarding payments to informants, date of issue unknown.
8. Name changed
9. Caryle Murphy, "Terror informant ignites himself near White House," *Washington Post*, Nov. 16, 2002.
10. See Glaberson, W., "Terror case hinges on wobbly key player," *The New York Times*, Nov. 27, 2004.
11. Ibid.
12. Ibid.
13. Murphy, C., "Terror Informant Ignites Himself near White House," *Washington Post*, Nov. 16, 2002.
14. Ibid.
15. Ibid.
16. Ibid.
17. The "moiety acts" of the eighteenth century were statutes designed to encourage citizens to report crime by authorizing payment of half the fines collected by the government.
18. *ICE Handbook*, Section 7.7.4 Currency Pick-up Operations.
19. *ICE Handbook*, Section 7.5.2, provides that:
A. the approval levels do not exceed the current delegated authority for standard POI payments;
B. the approval process outlined in the Interim ICE Informants Handbook is followed;
C. the information obtained and the resulting enforcement activities were in direct support of the operation which generated the proceeds;
D. the transaction is properly posted in Customs Undercover Fundamental Financial System (CUFFS);
E. the Information/Evidence Transaction Receipt (CF-293)
    1) is processed and filed in accordance with standard policy;
    2) includes the TECS II program code for the operation making payment;
    3) is annotated "Paid With Proceeds"; and
    4) the copy that is normally sent to the National Finance Center is included in the operation's financial records.
20. *ICE Handbook*, Section 7.6 Commissions.

21. *ICE Handbook*, 6.7 Personal Assistance Agreement (PAA), see former Customs Directive 4210-017, "Personal Assistance Agreements with Confidential Informants," dated December 12, 2001.
22. Ibid.
23. A sole proprietorship, partnership, corporation, or other business entity operated on a commercial basis, which is owned, controlled, or operated wholly or in part on behalf of third parties.
24. *Audit of the Bureau Of Alcohol, Tobacco, And Firearms and Explosives' Use of Income Generating Undercover Operations*, U.S. Department Of Justice Office of the Inspector General Audit Division, Audit Report 13-36, September 2013.
25. *ICE Handbook*; See 19 U.S.C. 2081 and 8 U.S.C. 1363a.
26. Federal Acquisition Regulations (FAR): The term refers to those regulations that govern the normal procurement procedures that agencies of the U.S. Government must follow when acquiring property or leasing space. Undercover operations of the ICE may be specifically exempted from these requirements if they are certified under the provisions of 19 U.S.C. 2081(a)(1) and 8 U.S.C. 1363a(a) and such acquisition outside the FAR is necessary to protect the safety and security of the operation.
27. Attorney General's Guidelines Regarding the Use of Confidential Informants, III B. 4.
28. FBI agent statement dated May 7, 2001, in Plaintiff's "Motion for Justice" in Bari/Cherney civil rights lawsuit filed against the FBI and Oakland Police, Case #C-91—1057CW (JL).
29. *Confidential Human Source Policy Manual* (herein after CHSP Manual), FBI POLO7-0004-D1, Revised 2007. Section 17.3.1 Payments to Confidential Human Sources.
30. CHSP Section 17.1
31. Request is submitted to the FBI headquarter substantive unit.
32. 23.26 CFR l.604l-3(2)(n).
33. CHSP Section 17.5. Paying a Confidential Human Source.
34. CHSP Section 17.2 Prohibitions
35. CHSP Section 17.2 Prohibitions
36. CHSP Section 17.9. Lump-Sum Payments.
37. CHSP Section 17.12. Rewards.
38. CHSP Section 17.13. Forfeiture Awards.
39. CHSP Section 17.19. One-Time Non-Confidential Human Source Payment.
40. Authority to pay "awards for information or assistance directly relating to violations of the criminal drug laws of the United States" is set forth in 28 USC 524(c)(l)(B).
41. *DEA Agents Manual* Chapter 66, Payments for Information and/or Active Participation.
42. *DEA Agents Manual* cited in *SGS-92-X003 v. U.S.*, No. 97-579C (Filed under Seal January 27, 2009).
43. Ibid.
44. Ibid.

45. DEA form numbers are subject to change.
46. *Brady v. Maryland,* 373 U.S. 83, 87, 83 S. Ct. 1194, 10 L. Ed. 215 (1963).
47. DEA form 356, Confidential Source Payment Record.
48. Amount subject to change.
49. Cap information obtained from a 2012 FOIA release made by DEA. At that time the requestor was advised that the *DEA Agents Manual* was in the process of being rewritten.
50. *DEA Payments to Confidential Sources,* Office of Inspector General Audit, U.S. Department of Justice, 2005.
51. *DEA Agents Manual,* Ch. 66
52. Rogin, J., "House Staffer Moves to 'Drugs and Thugs' Bureau," *The Cable,* January 7, 2010.
53. Narcotics Reward Program, Target Information, Department of State website.
54. DEA Public Affairs, March 22, 2006.
55. Davis, F., "Agent Tells Tale of CIA Defectors in Drug War," *Miami Herald,* September 18, 1997.
56. Weiner, T., *Blank Check: The Pentagon's Black Budget,* Warner Books, New York, NY, 1990.
57. Miller, G., "CIA Paid Iranian $5 Million for Nuclear Information," *Washington Post,* July 15, 2010.
58. Ibid.
59. Ibid.
60. Ibid.
61. Ibid.
62. See http://www.crimestoppers.com.
63. P.L. 98–473, October 12, 1984.
64. 28 U.S.C. 524(c).
65. GAO Asset Forfeiture Report 2012, p. 38.
66. The United States currently has a Mutual Legal Assistance Treaty (MLAT) that facilitates forfeiture cooperation with 62 countries. In addition, more than 172 countries are parties to the Vienna Drug Convention, 153 countries are parties to the United Nations Convention against Transnational Organized Crime, and 143 countries are parties to the U.N. Convention Against Corruption. The U.S. is a party to all of these conventions, which contain forfeiture cooperation provisions and encourage jurisdictions to have mechanisms for asset sharing and/or asset repatriation.
67. U.S. Department of Justice Assets Forfeiture Fund Performance Budget FY 2012.
68. Ibid.
69. U.S. Department of Justice Assets Forfeiture Fund Performance Budget FY 2013.
70. GAO Asset Forfeiture Report 2012.
71. 28 USC § 524.
72. 18 USC § 1956; 18 USC § 1957.
73. 31 USC § 5324.
74. 28 USC § 524(c)(1)(B)
75. 28 USC § 524(c)(1)(C)

76. 28 USC § 524(c)(1)(b).
77. GAO, *Justice Asset Forfeiture Fund, Transparency of Balances and Controls over Equitable Sharing Should Be Improved,* July 12, 2012.
78. GAO Report at page 30: In the cases we reviewed, the net proceeds had not yet been determined. Until the asset has been sold, and all forfeiture expenses—such as storage and advertising—have been paid, DOJ does not know the net proceeds that will ultimately be paid in each case. For this reason DOJ agencies identify a percentage (as opposed to a dollar amount) when making equitable sharing recommendations.
79. GAO Report at page 33: In the absence of documenting work hours or the rationale for making adjustments to sharing percentages, deciding authorities have limited means to verify the basis for equitable sharing decisions. Agency headquarters officials have reported that altogether, DEA, ATF, and FBI reviewed a total of 52,034 equitable sharing requests in fiscal year 2011, and 113 of these requests went to AFMLS for review and approval. As a result, agency headquarters officials note that they have limited resources to verify the basis for each and every equitable sharing determination.
80. See *Perri v. United States,* 53 Fed. Cl. 381 (2002), in which a former FBI informant claimed unsuccessfully that the United States breached a promise to pay him 25 percent of any sums forfeited in an investigation in which he assisted.
81. *DEA Agents Manual,* Ch. 66. See *Perri v. United States,* 53 Fed.Cl. 381 (2002).
82. *DEA Agents Manual,* Ch. 66. Note: The authority to pay an award of $250,000 or more *shall not be delegated* to any person other than the Deputy Attorney General, the Associate Attorney General, the Director of the Federal Bureau of Investigation, or the Administrator of the Drug Enforcement Administration. 19 USC § 1619(2) states the Secretary [Treasury] may award and pay such person (informant) an amount that does not exceed 25% of the net amount so recovered.
83. Clark, L., "The DEA and the Princess: A Tale of Risk and Reward," *Miami Herald,* January 24, 2009
84. *SGS-92-X003 v. U.S.,* No. 97-579C (Filed Under Seal January 27, 2009).
85. Ibid.
86. Ibid.
87. Ibid.
88. Clark, L., "The DEA and the Princess: A Tale of Risk and Reward," *Miami Herald,* January 24, 2009; Princess explaining to reporter, "The other agents kept telling me, 'It's the DEA. It stands for Don't Expect Anything.'"
89. U.S. District Court, Western District of Washington, In the Matter of the Seizure of Removable Dental Appliances Commonly Known as Grills, Case # 06-5064M.
90. Clarridge, C., "2 Suspects Keep Flashy Smiles," *Seattle Times,* April 7, 2006, quoting Richard Troberman, past president of the Washington Association of Criminal Defense Lawyers and an expert on forfeiture law.
91. Crombie, N., "Idaho Lawmaker Says He Prompted AFT to Ditch Controversial slogan," *The Oregonian,* May 17, 2008.
92. Ibid.
93. Ibid.

94. Hunter, G., "Money Raised by Metro Detroit Agencies Increases 50% in Five Years," *The Detroit News*, citing $20.62 million seized by police 2003–2007.

95. *Encyclopedia of Ethical Failure*, Department of Defense Office of General Counsel Standards of Conduct Office, Updated July 2013.

96. Text from Press Release: U.S. Attorney's Office Southern District of Florida, Former ICE Agent Pleads Guilty in Kickback, April 3, 2009.

97. Ibid.

98. In violation of Title 18, U.S.C. § 201(c)(1)(B).

99. Baker, A., "Drugs for Information Scandal Shakes up New York Police Task Force," *The New York Times*, January 20, 2008.

Whistleblowers
The Justice Department, the Securities and Exchange Commission, and the Commodities Futures Trading Commission

8

8.1 Introduction

The Justice Department relies upon white-collar informants known as relators or whistleblowers in the fight against corrupt corporate contractors. In a sense, whistleblowers are allowed to take the law into their own hands. Under the False Claims Act (FCA),[1] relators can file lawsuits on behalf of the government against persons or corporations who have defrauded the government by submitting false claims for payment for services or materials. As a monetary incentive for insiders to come forward, the whistleblower is eligible to receive anywhere from 15% to 30% of the amount recovered by the government as his reward.[2] Not traditionally viewed as informants per se, whistleblowers have reaped significant rewards through *qui tam* lawsuits.[3]

Whistleblowers are not new entrants to the informant community. In the fourteenth century, the royal courts of England encouraged aggrieved parties to initiate legal actions on behalf of themselves and the king. However, it was not until the sixteenth century that Parliament enacted qui tam statutes that invited informers who had suffered no personal financial loss to sue on behalf of the king and share in the fines collected by the government.[4] *Qui tam* is taken from a Latin phrase "*qui tam pro domino rege quam pro seise*," meaning "who as well for the king as well for himself sues in this matter."[5]

Today's American whistleblowers trace their history more directly to the passage of the Civil War–era Civil False Claims Act.[6] Also known as the Lincoln Law or the Informant Act, it was passed to expose profiteers preying on the Union Army and to recover government funds. In effect, it privatized the process. The law allowed informants, or relators, to sue price-gougers on their own in what are still known as qui tam lawsuits. The practice continues to this day.

The Civil False Claims Act was substantially amended by the False Claims Amendments Acts of 1986.[7] The action was spurred in part by 1980s whistleblower revelations that the Defense Department was paying $900 for toilet seats and $500 for hammers. Fraud in federal programs, procurement, and in the payment of obligations owed to the government was not the exception, it was nearly the rule.

The amendments were intended by Congress to create substantial monetary incentives for individuals who are aware of fraud against the government to step forward without fear of corporate reprisals or government inaction. The changes in the FCA substantially reduced the level of proof needed to nail a corporate profiteer and extended the statute of limitations.[8]

The FCA provides in part that any person who, with "actual knowledge, in reckless disregard or in deliberate ignorance of the truth," submits a false or fraudulent claim to the U.S. Government for payment or approval, or who makes or uses a false record or statement to avoid an obligation to pay money to the government, is liable to the government for a civil penalty of not less than $5,000 and not more than $10,000 for each claim, plus three times the amount of the damages sustained by the government because of the false claim. The act allows any person having knowledge of a false or fraudulent claim against the government to bring an action in federal district court for himself and for the U.S. Government and to share in any recovery. If the government declines to intervene after investigating the claim, the law's qui tam provision encourages individuals to pursue their own lawsuits.[9]

The relator must file a disclosure statement with the government before going forward with a lawsuit. If the action moves forward, it then goes into stealth mode. The lawsuit is filed under seal to ensure that only the government knows of the claim and has time to investigate the allegations before the corporate target can conceal evidence.[10]

The secrecy period is also meant to give the government enough time to evaluate the case and to determine whether or not to intervene. If the department decides in favor of intervention, it takes over prosecution of the whistleblower's case. The act allows for an initial sealing period of 60 days; however, courts can extend the period if the government can show cause for the extension.[11]

Cases have remained under seal for years to allow for investigation. The government lawyers have a nearly unlimited pool of investigative resources at their disposal to make a case against an investigative target. They have Federal Bureau of Investigation (FBI) agents to conduct interviews and review internal government documents often stamped top secret. Government attorneys can apply for court-ordered wiretaps of a corporate target's telephone. The FCA also has the Civil Investigative Demand at their disposal. It is similar to but far more effective than a subpoena[12] and is one of the FCA's most powerful investigative tools.

Once the government decides to intervene, the case is unsealed and taken over by attorneys assigned to the Department of Justice Civil Division with the assistance of local U.S. Attorneys. The corporate wrongdoer is served with papers, and the identity of the whistleblower is divulged. Although the whistleblower and his attorneys remain involved, the federal attorneys control the litigation, including the power to settle the case. If the government takes over prosecution of the action and wins,[13] the whistleblower can receive 15% to 25% of the proceeds of the action or settlement of the claim.[14]

If the government does not proceed with an action, the relator and his lawyer are entitled to go forward on their own. If they win, they are entitled to no less than 30% of the proceeds of the action or settlement. The reward is paid out of the proceeds.

The relator is entitled to recover reasonable expenses, including attorney's fees and costs, if the court finds them to have been necessary to further the lawsuit. All such expenses, fees, and costs are charged against the defendant.[15]

Out-of-court settlements of FCA cases are routine but do not occur overnight. Protracted pretrial maneuvers are to be expected. The lawyer's lament, "When you are in trial you are in trouble," was never truer than with FCA cases. For the corporate defendant, these are high-stakes cases. An FCA allegation has been called the civil law equivalent of the death penalty for a contractor.[16] Going to trial and losing exposes the corporate client to a host of nightmarish outcomes: penalties, treble (triple) damages, and suspension or debarment from further contracting with the government.

The threat of either penalty creates intense pressure to resolve matters by settlement rather than by taking the risk of trial. It is not only in the movies that a runaway jury, eager to teach corporate America a lesson, renders a verdict meant to cripple a company.

Government lawyers are empowered to settle the case if the recovery is "fair, adequate, and reasonable." The relator is notified of proposed settlements, and if he objects he is given an opportunity to be heard by the court.[17]

For government contractors, settlements are the path of least resistance and least exposure. Since 2003, Northrop Grumman and the government have settled three whistleblower lawsuits. One was in 2003 for $111 million. It was alleged that Northrop overcharged the government on space projects. A company spokesman commenting on the settlement said it "expressly denied any liability for violating the False Claims Act."[18]

The second settlement was in 2009 for $325 million, the largest by a defense contractor in a whistleblower case. It was alleged that a company bought by Northrop in 2002 had supplied faulty electronic components for military and intelligence-gathering satellites.[19]

The third whistleblower action settled in 2010 for $12.5 million. The company was alleged to have neglected to test electronic parts for military aircraft navigation systems. In an article by the *L.A. Times*, Northrop declined to say whether it agreed with the allegations, but a company spokesman said it "fully cooperated with the government's investigation ... and is pleased that the matter is now behind us."[20]

From 1986 through 2006, the total amount recovered by the government under the FCA was approximately $18 billion. Whistleblower lawsuits were responsible for $11 billion of that amount. During that period informants received approximately $1.8 billion in rewards.[21]

The largest sum awarded in a single case followed a government settlement in June 2003 when Healthcare Corporation of America (HCA) was accused of improperly billing Medicare for hundreds of millions of dollars. The government received $631 million from the settlement. The three whistleblowers received a combined total of $151,591,500.[22]

One of the whistleblowers donated a portion of his reward to the Montana State University College of Business to establish an entrepreneurship program. He had been fired from HCA when he questioned the company's practice of keeping two sets of books.[23]

8.2   The Securities and Exchange Commission

The Bernie Madoff investment scandal left many wondering why the Securities and Exchange Commission (SEC) had not launched an investigation into his 20-plus-year Ponzi scheme.[24] For over a decade, *Wall Street* insiders suspected that the phenomenal gains he was delivering to his investors were impossible to achieve legally.[25] In the end, he bilked thousands of investors out of an estimated $65 billion.[26] On June 29, 2009, he was sentenced to 150 years in prison.[27]

Following the scandal, the SEC initiated what it calls a "whistleblower program." In effect, it is an informant program with few similarities to the Justice Department's FCA program. The SEC now pays informants rewards of up to 10% from civil penalties assessed for insider trading. Since 2012, over $14 million in rewards have been paid to whistleblowers.

The Dodd-Frank Wall Street Reform and Consumer Protection Act (the Dodd-Frank Act),[28] signed into law on July 21, 2010, offers enticing reward provisions for insider-trading whistleblowers. The act allows the SEC to compensate whistleblowers who provide original information leading to an action by the commission that result in penalties of more than $1 million. In those instances, the SEC may reward the whistleblower with up to 30%, in total, of the monetary sanctions imposed in the action or related actions (see Appendix 8C).

The bounties are paid out of the newly created SEC Investor Protection Fund. The program is self-funded, paying sources with monies collected from SEC enforcement actions.

The law promises whistleblower confidentiality, stating that all information provided to the commission by a whistleblower shall be confidential and privileged as an evidentiary matter.[29] Notably, the bill removes from judicial review any agency decisions on whistleblower payments.

In the run-up to passage of the new law, the SEC's Inspector General was looking forward to rewards as a solution to the whistleblower void. He told reporters "It looks like a big focus will be in creating a new incentive structure so folks will come forward to the SEC when they know something. We know people knew things about Madoff, but we don't know why they didn't come to us."[30]

In February 2012, the SEC went to Hollywood for assistance to promote their insider trader whistleblower recruiting drive. They turned to Michael Douglas, winner of an academy award for 1987's *Wall Street*, to do a public service announcement (PSA). In the PSA he tells viewers "In the movie *Wall Street* I played Gordon Gekko, who cheated to profit while innocent investors lost their savings. The movie was fiction but the problem is real," He explains, "Our economy is increasingly dependent on the success and integrity of the financial markets. If a deal looks too good to be true, it probably is." Prospective informants are given instructions on how to channel their information.[31]

The whistleblower recruiting drive was officially launched on September 10, 2012. It has been productive. Fifty-eight informants reported *Wall Street* quality information to the Commission's Whistleblower Office (WBO) during 2012.[32] The SEC's first payment to a whistleblower was made in August 2012 and totaled approximately $50,000.[33] In August and September 2013, more than $25,000 was awarded to three whistleblowers who helped the SEC and the U. S. Department of Justice halt a sham hedge fund, and the ultimate total payout in that case once all sanctions are collected is likely to exceed $125,000.

In October 2013, the SEC announced an award of more than $14 million to a whistleblower whose information led to an SEC enforcement action that recovered substantial investor funds. The award was the largest made by the SEC's whistleblower program to date.

The whistleblower, who did not wish to be identified, provided original information and assistance that allowed the SEC to investigate an enforcement matter more quickly than otherwise would have been possible. Less than 6 months after receiving the whistleblower's tip, the SEC was able to bring an enforcement action against the perpetrators and secure investor funds.

Sean McKessy, chief of the SEC's Office of the Whistleblower, gave the following statement: "While it is certainly gratifying to make this significant award payout, the even better news for investors is that whistleblowers are coming forward to assist us in stopping potential fraud in its tracks so that no future investors are harmed. That ultimately is what the whistleblower program is all about."[34]

8.3   Commodities Futures Trading Commission: Misappropriation and Ponzi Schemes

The Commodities Futures Trading Commission (CFTC) is a little-known enforcement entity. Its mission is to protect market users and the public from fraud, manipulation, and abusive practices related to the sale of commodity and financial futures and options—and now, over-the-counter derivatives. Today it looks to whistleblowers, probably well-placed insiders, lured by the promise of lottery-size rewards as a way of accomplishing its mission statement.

Madoff-style ponzi schemes are expected to be one of the primary targets of the CFTC. They are not crimes that are called in to 911. The best way to describe a Ponzi scheme is to read the description provided by the Chairman of the CFTC. It is taken from his book *Ponzimonium: How Scam Artists Are Ripping off America*[35]:

> Ponzi schemes, named after Charles Ponzi, are scams in which early "investors" are given supposed returns paid through funds provided by later investors. Typically, an investment is made and then some "profits" are paid out, prompting the investor to assume that his or her money has increased in value. In actuality, the perpetrators of these schemes—Ponzi and Madoff—take the money for themselves. The legal term for this kind of taking is "misappropriation."
>
> As new investors enter the fraud, supposed returns are offered continually to initial investors, and many times are accompanied by fake account statements. This continues until new money stops flowing in and the investors want their money back. During the 2008 economic downturn, people needed their money back at the same time that there were no new investors. Many "house of cards" scams have fallen and the perpetrators of the swindles have been caught. Charles Ponzi ran these types of scams in the U. S. until he was deported to Italy, his birthplace, in 1934 as an "undesirable alien."
>
> While this [Madoff's] may have been the largest swindle ever, scores and scores of Ponzis of all sizes and values continue to be unearthed. There have never been more of these scams, and they are occurring all over the world.

The FBI claims an unprecedented number of informants have been coming forward since the new Commodity Exchange Act was unveiled in 2011.[36] It is understandable. Informants with information about illicit trading of items sold on the commodities futures markets stand to earn millions. The CFTC FY 2012 budget boasted $99,996,749 in its Customer Protection Fund available for awards.[37]

Investigative techniques once reserved for drug dealers and the mafia have been turned on traders. Undercover informants, cooperating witnesses, and wiretaps are now being used against an industry described by the FBI as "undercover resistant."[38] An investigative journalist reported that agents have "tracked mobile phone calls, instant messaging and social media to collect evidence."[39]

Commodities fraud investigations have earned dramatic operational names once reserved for international drug cases. Operation Perfect Hedge took down the billionaire founder of the Galleon Group.

The FBI and the CFTC are not reticent about giving credit for the success of Perfect Hedge. An insider's cooperation led to the biggest probe of insider trading funds ever launched by federal prosecutors. The trader, facing federal charges, wore a wire on numerous occasions during more than 2 years of working with federal agents.[40] Evidence collected by the cooperating witness, coupled with his testimony, netted prosecutors the conviction of the Galleon Group's co-founder. Nine executives, traders, and consultants were also arrested for insider trading and related crimes. Federal prosecutors called the informant's help *nothing short of extraordinary.*[41]

But cooperating witnesses, working under the threat of going to prison, were not going to be enough to put a dent into insider trading. Solid insider tips were needed from a lock-jawed industry. Substantial rewards were settled on as the way to recruit informants.

As part of the informant recruiting program, a CFTC website was launched that included the 15 most asked questions regarding the program. The list included the following:

8.3.1   Who Can Be a CFTC Whistleblower?

A whistleblower can be anyone from a fraud victim or an investor, a trader or market observer, all the way up to corporate insider or officer.[42] Unlike the Internal Revenue Service whistleblower program, persons convicted of a crime related to the conduct being reported is ineligible for a reward.[43]

The tip must be what the CFTC refers to as *original information.* That is, information not already known to the Commission that is derived from a whistleblower's independent knowledge and not generally known or available to the public. It can also be information that is a result of independent analysis of information by the whistleblower that may be publicly available but which reveals information that is not generally known. The whistleblower must be the *original source* of the information and able to prove it in the event that someone else steps forward with the same or similar tip.[44]

A tip that leads the CFTC to open a new examination or investigation, re-open a previously closed investigation, or pursue a new line of inquiry in connection with an ongoing investigation resulting in a successful enforcement action based at least in part on the whistleblower's information can result in an award. A whistleblower *might* also be eligible for an award if his or her information relates to an ongoing examination or investigation, and it significantly contributes to the success of an enforcement action.[45]

Whistleblowers working for a company with an internal compliance process are under no obligation to report internally to be eligible for a whistleblower award. They are free to submit their information directly to the CFTC.[46]

8.3.2 Will the CFTC Keep My Identity Confidentiality?

The CFTC offers this assurance regarding confidentiality:

> Whether or not you seek anonymity, we are committed to protecting your identity. For example, we will not disclose your identity in response to requests under the Freedom of Information Act. As a general rule, we treat information learned during the course of an investigation—including the identity of our sources—as non-public and confidential.
>
> There are, however, limits on our ability to shield your identity. For example, in an administrative or court proceeding, we may be required to produce documents or other information that would reveal your identity. In addition, as part of our ongoing investigatory responsibilities, we may use information you have provided during the course of our investigation. In appropriate circumstances, we may also provide information, subject to confidentiality requirements, to other governmental or regulatory entities.[47] (See appendices 8A through 8C).

Appendix 8A: The False Claims Act: 31 U.S. Code §3729

Pub. L. 113-75.

(a) Liability for Certain Acts.—
(1) In general.— Subject to paragraph (2), any person who—
(A) knowingly presents, or causes to be presented, a false or fraudulent claim for payment or approval;
(B) knowingly makes, uses, or causes to be made or used, a false record or statement material to a false or fraudulent claim;
(C) conspires to commit a violation of subparagraph (A), (B), (D), (E), (F), or (G);
(D) has possession, custody, or control of property or money used, or to be used, by the Government and knowingly delivers, or causes to be delivered, less than all of that money or property;
(E) is authorized to make or deliver a document certifying receipt of property used, or to be used, by the Government and, intending to defraud the Government, makes or delivers the receipt without completely knowing that the information on the receipt is true;
(F) knowingly buys, or receives as a pledge of an obligation or debt, public property from an officer or employee of the Government, or a member of the Armed Forces, who lawfully may not sell or pledge property; or

(G) knowingly makes, uses, or causes to be made or used, a false record or statement material to an obligation to pay or transmit money or property to the Government, or knowingly conceals or knowingly and improperly avoids or decreases an obligation to pay or transmit money or property to the Government,is liable to the United States Government for a civil penalty of not less than $5,000 and not more than $10,000, as adjusted by the Federal Civil Penalties Inflation Adjustment Act of 1990 (28 U. S. C. 2461note; Public Law 104–410 [1]), plus 3 times the amount of damages which the Government sustains because of the act of that person.

(2) Reduced damages.— If the court finds that—

(A) the person committing the violation of this subsection furnished officials of the United States responsible for investigating false claims violations with all information known to such person about the violation within 30 days after the date on which the defendant first obtained the information;

(B) such person fully cooperated with any Government investigation of such violation; and

(C) at the time such person furnished the United States with the information about the violation, no criminal prosecution, civil action, or administrative action had commenced under this title with respect to such violation, and the person did not have actual knowledge of the existence of an investigation into such violation,the court may assess not less than 2 times the amount of damages which the Government sustains because of the act of that person.

(3) Costs of civil actions.— A person violating this subsection shall also be liable to the United States Government for the costs of a civil action brought to recover any such penalty or damages.

(b) Definitions.—For purposes of this section—

(1) the terms "knowing" and "knowingly"—

(A) mean that a person, with respect to information—

(i) has actual knowledge of the information;

(ii) acts in deliberate ignorance of the truth or falsity of the information; or

(iii) acts in reckless disregard of the truth or falsity of the information; and

(B) require no proof of specific intent to defraud;

(2) the term "claim"—

(A) means any request or demand, whether under a contract or otherwise, for money or property and whether or not the United States has title to the money or property, that—

(i) is presented to an officer, employee, or agent of the United States; or

(ii) is made to a contractor, grantee, or other recipient, if the money or property is to be spent or used on the Government's behalf or to advance a Government program or interest, and if the United States Government—

(I) provides or has provided any portion of the money or property requested or demanded; or

(II) will reimburse such contractor, grantee, or other recipient for any portion of the money or property which is requested or demanded; and

(B) does not include requests or demands for money or property that the Government has paid to an individual as compensation for Federal employment or as an income subsidy with no restrictions on that individual's use of the money or property;

(3) the term "obligation" means an established duty, whether or not fixed, arising from an express or implied contractual, grantor-grantee, or licensor-licensee relationship, from a fee-based or similar relationship, from statute or regulation, or from the retention of any overpayment; and

(4) the term "material" means having a natural tendency to influence, or be capable of influencing, the payment or receipt of money or property.

(c) Exemption From Disclosure.— Any information furnished pursuant to subsection (a)(2) shall be exempt from disclosure under section 552 of title 5.

(d) Exclusion.— This section does not apply to claims, records, or statements made under the Internal Revenue Code of 1986.

Appendix 8B: False Claims Act Relator Share Guidelines

Section 3730(d)(1) of the False Claims Act (FCA), 31 U. S. C. §§ 3729-33, provides that a qui tam relator, when the Government has intervened in the lawsuit, shall receive at least 15 percent but not more than 25% of the proceeds of the FCA action depending upon the extent to which the relator substantially contributed to the prosecution of the action. When the Government does not intervene, section 3730(d)(2) provides that the relator shall receive an amount that the court decides is reasonable and shall be not less than 25% and not more than 30%.

Items for Consideration for a Possible Increase in the Percentage

- The relator reported the fraud promptly.
- When he learned of the fraud, the relator tried to stop the fraud or reported it to a supervisor or the Government.
- The qui tam filing, or the ensuing investigation, caused the offender to halt the fraudulent practices.
- The complaint warned the Government of a significant safety issue.
- The complaint exposed a nationwide practice.
- The relator provided extensive, first-hand details of the fraud to the Government.
- The Government had no knowledge of the fraud.
- The relator provided substantial assistance during the investigation and/or pretrial phases of the case.

- At his deposition and/or trial, the relator was an excellent, credible witness.
- The relator's counsel provided substantial assistance to the Government.
- The relator and his counsel supported and cooperated with the Government during the entire proceeding.
- The case went to trial.
- The FCA recovery was relatively small.
- The filing of the complaint had a substantial adverse impact on the relator.

Items for Consideration for a Possible Decrease in the Percentage

- The relator participated in the fraud.
- The relator substantially delayed in reporting the fraud or filing the complaint.
- The relator, or relator's counsel, violated FCA procedures: (a) complaint served on defendant or not filed under seal; (b) the relator publicized the case while it was under seal; (c) statement of material facts and evidence not provided.
- The relator had little knowledge of the fraud or only suspicions.
- The relator's knowledge was based primarily on public information.
- The relator learned of the fraud in the course of his Government employment.
- The Government already knew of the fraud.
- The relator, or relator's counsel, did not provide any help after filing the complaint, hampered the Government's efforts in developing the case, or unreasonably opposed the Government's positions in litigation.
- The case required a substantial effort by the Government to develop the facts to win the lawsuit.
- The case settled shortly after the complaint was filed or with little need for discovery.
- The FCA recovery was relatively large.

Appendix 8C: Form TCR: Tip, Complaint or Referral

OMB APPROVAL

OMB Number: 3235 0686

Expires: . . . . . . August 31, 2014

Estimated average burden

hours per response. 1

UNITED STATES
SECURITIES AND EXCHANGE COMMISSION
Washington, DC 20549

FORM TCR
TIP, COMPLAINT OR REFERRAL

A. INFORMATION ABOUT YOU			
COMPLAINANT 1:			
1. Last Name		First	M.I.
2. Street Address			Apartment/ Unit #
City	State/ Province	ZIP/ Postal Code	Country
3. Telephone	Alt. Phone	E-mail Address	
4. Occupation		Preferred method of communication	
COMPLAINANT 2:			
1. Last Name		First	M.I.
2. Street Address			Apartment/ Unit #
City	State/ Province	ZIP/ Postal Code	Country
3. Telephone	Alt. Phone	E-mail Address	
4. Occupation		Preferred method of communication	
B. ATTORNEY'S INFORMATION (If Applicable - See Instructions)			
1. Attorney's Name			
2. Firm Name			
3. Street Address			
City	State/ Province	ZIP/ Postal Code	Country
4. Telephone	Fax	E-mail Address	

SEC 2850 (8/11)

C. TELL US ABOUT THE INDIVIDUAL OR ENTITY YOU HAVE A COMPLAINT AGAINST

INDIVIDUAL/ENTITY 1:

1. Type: ☐ Individual ☐ Entity

If an individual, specify profession:

If an entity, specify type:

2. Name

3. Street Address			Apartment/ Unit #
City	State/ Province	ZIP/ Postal Code	Country
4. Phone	E-mail Address	Internet Address	

INDIVIDUAL/ENTITY 2:

1. Type: ☐ Individual ☐ Entity

If an individual, specify profession:

If an entity, specify type:

2. Name

3. Street Address			Apartment/ Unit #
City	State/ Province	ZIP/ Postal Code	Country
4. Phone	E-mail Address	Internet Address	

D. TELL US ABOUT YOUR COMPLAINT

1. Occurrence Date (mm/dd/yyyy):   /   /   2. Nature of complaint:

3a. Has the complainant or counsel had any prior communication(s) with the SEC concerning this matter?   YES ☐   NO ☐

3b. If the answer to 3a is "Yes," name of SEC staff member with whom the complainant or counsel communicated

4a. Has the complainant or counsel provided the information to any other agency or organization, or has any other agency or organization requested the information or related information from you?   YES ☐   NO ☐

4b. If the answer to 4a is "Yes," please provide details. Use additional sheets if necessary.

4c. Name and contact information for point of contact at agency or organization, if known

5a. Does this complaint relate to an entity of which the complainant is or was an officer, director, counsel, employee, consultant or contractor? YES ☐   NO ☐

5b. If the answer to question 5a is "Yes," has the complainant reported this violation to his or her supervisor, compliance office, whistleblower hotline, ombudsman, or any other available mechanism at the entity for reporting violations?   YES ☐   NO ☐

5c. If the answer to question 5b is "Yes," please provide details. Use additional sheets if necessary.

5d. Date on which the complainant took the action(s) described in question 5b (mm/dd/yyyy):   /   /

6a. Has the complainant taken any other action regarding your complaint?   YES ☐   NO ☐

6b. If the answer to question 6a is "Yes," please provide details. Use additional sheets if necessary.

7a. Does your complaint relate to a residential mortgage-backed security?   YES ☐   NO ☐
7b. Type of security or investment, if relevant

7c. Name of issuer or security, if relevant	7d. Security/Ticker Symbol or CUSIP no.

8. State in detail all facts pertinent to the alleged violation. Explain why the complainant believes the acts described constitute a violation of the federal securities laws. Use additional sheets if necessary.

9. Describe all supporting materials in the complainant's possession and the availability and location of any additional supporting materials not in complainant's possession. Use additional sheets, if necessary.

10. Describe how and from whom the complainant obtained the information that supports this claim. If any information was obtained from an attorney or in a communication where an attorney was present, identify such information with as much particularity as possible. In addition, if any information was obtained from a public source, identify the source with as much particularity as possible. Attach additional sheets if necessary.

11. Identify with particularity any documents or other information in your submission that you believe could reasonably be expected to reveal your identity and explain the basis for your belief that your identity would be revealed if the documents were disclosed to a third party.

12. Provide any additional information you think may be relevant.

E. ELIGIBILITY REQUIREMENTS AND OTHER INFORMATION

1. Are you, or were you at the time you acquired the original information you are submitting to us, a member, officer or employee of the Department of Justice, the Securities and Exchange Commission, the Comptroller of the Currency, the Board of Governors of the Federal Reserve System, the Federal Deposit Insurance Corporation, the Office of Thrift Supervision; the Public Company Accounting Oversight Board; any law enforcement organization; or any national securities exchange, registered securities association, registered clearing agency, or the Municipal Securities Rulemaking Board?

YES ☐   NO ☐

2. Are you, or were you at the time you acquired the original information you are submitting to us, a member, officer or employee of a foreign government, any political subdivision, department, agency, or instrumentality of a foreign government, or any other foreign financial regulatory authority as that term is defined in Section 3(a)(52) of the Securities Exchange Act of 1934 (15 U.S.C. §78c(a)(52))?

YES ☐   NO ☐

3. Did you acquire the information being provided to us through the performance of an engagement required under the federal securities laws by an independent public accountant?

YES ☐   NO ☐

4. Are you providing this information pursuant to a cooperation agreement with the SEC or another agency or organization?

YES ☐   NO ☐

5. Are you a spouse, parent, child, or sibling of a member or employee of the SEC, or do you reside in the same household as a member or employee of the SEC?

YES ☐   NO ☐

6. Did you acquire the information being provided to us from any person described in questions 1 through 5?

YES ☐   NO ☐

7. Have you or anyone representing you received any request, inquiry or demand that relates to the subject matter of your submission (i) from the SEC, (ii) in connection with an investigation, inspection or examination by the Public Company Accounting Oversight Board, or any self-regulatory organization; or (iii) in connection with an investigation by the Congress, any other authority of the federal government, or a state Attorney General or securities regulatory authority?

YES ☐   NO ☐

8. Are you currently a subject or target of a criminal investigation, or have you been convicted of a criminal violation, in connection with the information you are submitting to the SEC?

YES ☐   NO ☐

9. If you answered "yes" to any of the questions 1 through 8, use this space to provide additional details relating to your responses. Use additional sheets if necessary.

F. WHISTLEBLOWER'S DECLARATION

I declare under penalty of perjury under the laws of the United States that the information contained herein is true, correct and complete to the best of my knowledge, information and belief. I fully understand that I may be subject to prosecution and ineligible for a whistleblower award if, in my submission of information, my other dealings with the SEC, or my dealings with another authority in connection with a related action, I knowingly and willfully make any false, fictitious, or fraudulent statements or representations, or use any false writing or document knowing that the writing or document contains any false, fictitious, or fraudulent statement or entry.

Print name

Signature   Date

G. COUNSEL CERTIFICATION (If Applicable—See Instructions)

I certify that I have reviewed this form for completeness and accuracy and that the information contained herein is true, correct and complete to the best of my knowledge, information and belief. I further certify that I have verified the identity of the whistleblower on whose behalf this form is being submitted by viewing the whistleblower's valid, unexpired government issued identification (e.g., driver's license, passport) and will retain an original, signed copy of this form, with Section F signed by the whistleblower, in my records. I further certify that I have obtained the whistleblower's non-waiveable consent to provide the Commission with his or her original signed Form TCR upon request in the event that the Commission requests it due to concerns that the whistleblower may have knowingly and willfully made false, fictitious, or fraudulent statements or representations, or used any false writing or document knowing that the writing or document contains any false fictitious or fraudulent statement or entry; and that I consent to be legally obligated to do so within 7 calendar days of receiving such a request from the Commission.

Signature   Date

Privacy Act Statement

This notice is given under the Privacy Act of 1974. This form may be used by anyone wishing to provide the SEC with information concerning a possible violation of the federal securities laws. We are authorized to request information from you by various laws: Sections 19 and 20 of the Securities Act of 1933, Sections 21 and 21F of the Securities Exchange Act of 1934, Section 321 of the Trust Indenture Act of 1939, Section 42 of the Investment Company Act of 1940, Section 209 of the Investment Advisers Act of 1940 and Title 17 of the Code of Federal Regulations, Section 202.5.

Our principal purpose in requesting information is to gather facts in order to determine whether any person has violated, is violating, or is about to violate any provision of the federal securities laws or rules for which we have enforcement authority. Facts developed may, however, constitute violations of other laws or rules. Further, if you are submitting information for the SEC's whistleblower award program pursuant to Section 21F of the Securities Exchange Act of 1934 (Exchange Act), the information provided will be used in connection with our evaluation of your or your client's eligibility and other factors relevant to our determination of whether to pay an award to you or your client.

The information provided may be used by SEC personnel for purposes of investigating possible violations of, or to conduct investigations authorized by, the federal securities law; in proceedings in which the federal securities laws are in issue or the SEC is a party; to coordinate law enforcement activities between the SEC and other federal, state, local or foreign law enforcement agencies, securities self regulatory organizations, and foreign securities authorities; and pursuant to other routine uses as described in SEC-42 "Enforcement Files."

Furnishing the information requested herein is voluntary. However, a decision not to provide any of the requested information, or failure to provide complete information, may affect our evaluation of your submission. Further, if you are submitting this information for the SEC whistleblower program and you do not execute the Whistleblower Declaration or, if you are submitting information anonymously, identify the attorney representing you in this matter, you may not be considered for an award.

Questions concerning this form maybe directed to the SEC Office of the Whistleblower, 100 F Street, NE, Washington, DC 20549, Tel. (202) 551-4790, Fax (703) 813-9322.

Submission Procedures

- After manually completing this Form TCR, please send it by mail or delivery to the SEC Office of the Whistleblower, 100 F Street, NE, Washington, DC 20549, or by facsimile to (703) 813-9322.

- You have the right to submit information anonymously. If you are submitting anonymously and you want to be considered for a whistleblower award, however, you *must* (1) be represented by an attorney in this matter and (2) complete Sections B and G of this form. If you are not submitting anonymously, you may, but are not required to, have an attorney. If you are not represented by an attorney in this matter, you may leave Sections B and G blank.

- **If you are submitting information for the SEC's whistleblower award program, you *must* submit your information either using this Form TCR or electronically through the SEC's Tips, Complaints and Referrals Portal, available on the SEC web site at https://denebleo.sec.gov/TCRExternal/index.xhtml.**

Instructions for Completing Form TCR:

Section A: Information about You

Questions 1-4: Please provide the following information about yourself:

- Last name, first name, and middle initial

- Complete address, including city, state and zip code

- Telephone number and, if available, an alternate number where you can be reached

- Your e-mail address (to facilitate communications, we strongly encourage you to provide your email address),

- Your preferred method of communication; and

- Your occupation

For more than two complainants, use additional sheets as necessary to provide the required information for each complainant.

Section B: Information about Your Attorney. Complete this section only if you are represented by an attorney in this matter. You must be represented by an attorney, and this section must be completed, if you are submitting your information anonymously and you want to be considered for the SEC's whistleblower award program.

Questions 1-4: Provide the following information about the attorney representing you in this matter:

- Attorney's name

- Firm name

- Complete address, including city, state and zip code

- Telephone number and fax number, and

- E-mail address

Section C: Tell Us about the Individual and/or Entity You Have a Complaint Against. If your complaint relates to more than two individuals and/or entities, you may attach additional sheets.

Question 1:   Choose one of the following that best describes the individual or entity to which your complaint relates:

- **For Individuals**: accountant, analyst, attorney, auditor, broker, compliance officer, employee, executive officer or director, financial planner, fund manager, investment advisor representative, stock promoter, trustee, unknown, or other (specify).

- **For Entity**: bank, broker-dealer, clearing agency, day trading firm, exchange, Financial Industry Regulatory Authority, insurance company, investment advisor, investment advisor representative, investment company, Individual Retirement Account or 401(k) custodian/administrator, market maker, municipal securities dealers, mutual fund, newsletter company/investment publication company, on-line trading firm, private fund company (including hedge fund, private equity fund, venture capital fund, or real estate

fund), private/closely held company, publicly held company, transfer agent/paying
agent/registrar, underwriter, unknown, or other (specify).

Questions 2-4: For each subject, provide the following information, if known:

- Full name
- Complete address, including city, state and zip code
- Telephone number,
- E-mail address, and
- Internet address, if applicable

Section D: Tell Us about Your Complaint

Question 1:   State the date (mm/dd/yyyy) that the alleged conduct began.

Question 2:   Choose the option that you believe best describes the nature of your complaint. If you are
                 alleging more than one violation, please list all that you believe may apply. Use additional
                 sheets if necessary.

- Theft/misappropriation (advance fee fraud; lost or stolen securities; hacking of account)
- Misrepresentation/omission (false/misleading marketing/sales literature; inaccurate,
  misleading or non-disclosure by Broker-Dealer, Investment Adviser and Associated
  Person; false/material misstatements in firm research that were basis of transaction)
- Offering fraud (Ponzi/pyramid scheme; other offering fraud)
- Registration violations (unregistered securities offering)
- Trading (after hours trading; algorithmic trading; front-running; insider trading,
  manipulation of securities/prices; market timing; inaccurate quotes/pricing information;
  program trading; short selling; trading suspensions; volatility)
- Fees/mark-ups/commissions (excessive or unnecessary administrative fees; excessive
  commissions or sales fees; failure to disclose fees; insufficient notice of change in fees;
  negotiated fee problems; excessive mark-ups/markdowns; excessive or otherwise
  improper spreads)
- Corporate disclosure/reporting/other issuer matter (audit; corporate governance; conflicts
  of interest by management; executive compensation; failure to notify shareholders of
  corporate events; false/misleading financial statements, offering documents, press
  releases, proxy materials; failure to file reports; financial fraud; Foreign Corrupt Practices
  Act violations; ongoing private transactions; mergers and acquisitions; restrictive legends,

including 144 issues; reverse stock splits; selective disclosure – Regulation FD, 17 CFR 243; shareholder proposals; stock options for employees; stock splits; tender offers)

- Sales and advisory practices (background information on past violations/integrity; breach of fiduciary duty/responsibility (IA); failure to disclose breakpoints; churning/excessive trading; cold calling; conflict of interest; abuse of authority in discretionary trading; failure to respond to investor; guarantee against loss/promise to buy back shares; high pressure sales techniques; instructions by client not followed; investment objectives not followed; margin; poor investment advice; Regulation E (Electronic Transfer Act); Regulation S-P, 17 CFR 248, (privacy issues); solicitation methods (non-cold calling; seminars); suitability; unauthorized transactions)

- Operational (bond call; bond default; difficulty buying/selling securities; confirmations/statements; proxy materials/prospectus; delivery of funds/proceeds; dividend and interest problems; exchanges/switches of mutual funds with fund family; margin (illegal extension of margin credit, Regulation T restrictions, unauthorized margin transactions); online issues (trading system operation); settlement (including T+1 or T=3 concerns); stock certificates; spam; tax reporting problems; titling securities (difficulty titling ownership); trade execution.

- Customer accounts (abandoned or inactive accounts; account administration and processing; identity theft affecting account; IPOs: problems with IPO allocation or eligibility; inaccurate valuation of Net Asset Value; transfer of account)

- Comments/complaints about SEC, Self-Regulatory Organization, and Securities Investor Protection Corporation processes & programs (arbitration: bias by arbitrators/forum, failure to pay/comply with award, mandatory arbitration requirements, procedural problems or delays; SEC: complaints about enforcement actions, complaints about rulemaking, failure to act; Self-Regulatory Organization: failure to act; Investor Protection: inadequacy of laws or rules; SIPC: customer protection, proceedings and Broker-Dealer liquidations;

- Other (analyst complaints; market maker activities; employer/employee disputes; specify other).

Question 3a: State whether you or your counsel have had any prior communications with the SEC concerning this matter.

Question 3b: If the answer to question 3a is yes, provide the name of the SEC staff member with whom you or your counsel communicated.

Question 4a: Indicate whether you or your counsel have provided the information you are providing to the SEC to any other agency or organization.

Question 4b: If the answer to question 4a is yes, provide details.

Question 4c: Provide the name and contact information of the point of contact at the other agency or organization, if known.

Question 5a: Indicate whether your complaint relates to an entity of which you are, or were in the past, an officer, director, counsel, employee, consultant, or contractor.

Question 5b: If the answer to question 5a is yes, state whether you have reported this violation to your supervisor, compliance office, whistleblower hotline, ombudsman, or any other available mechanism at the entity for reporting violations.

Question 5c: If the answer to question 5b is yes, provide details.

Question 5d: Provide the date on which you took the actions described in questions 5a and 5b..

Question 6a: Indicate whether you have taken any other action regarding your complaint, including whether you complained to the SEC, another regulator, a law enforcement agency, or any other agency or organization; initiated legal action, mediation or arbitration, or initiated any other action.

Question 6b: If you answered yes to question 6a, provide details, including the date on which you took the action(s) described, the name of the person or entity to whom you directed any report or complaint and contact information for the person or entity, if known, and the complete case name, case number, and forum of any legal action you have taken. Use additional sheets if necessary.

Question 7a: Check the appropriate box regarding whether your complaint relates to residential mortgage-backed securities.

Question 7b: List the following options that you believe best describes the type of security or investment at issue, if applicable:

- 1031 exchanges
- 529 plans
- American Depositary Receipts
- Annuities (equity-indexed annuities, fixed annuities, variable annuities)
- Asset-backed securities
- Auction rate securities
- Banking products (including credit cards)
- Certificates of deposit (CDs)
- Closed-end funds
- Coins and precious metals (gold, silver, etc.)

- Collateralized mortgage obligations (CMOs)
- Commercial paper
- Commodities (currency transactions, futures, stock index options)
- Convertible securities
- Debt (corporate, lower-rated or "junk", municipal)
- Equities (exchange-traded, foreign, Over-the-Counter, unregistered, linked notes) Exchange Traded Funds
- Franchises or business ventures
- Hedge funds
- Insurance contracts (not annuities)
- Money-market funds
- Mortgage-backed securities (mortgages, reverse mortgages)
- Mutual funds
- Options (commodity options, index options)
- Partnerships
- Preferred shares
- Prime bank securities/high yield programs
- Promissory notes
- Real estate (real estate investment trusts (REITs))
- Retirement plans (401(k), IRAs)
- Rights and warrants
- Structured note products
- Subprime issues
- Treasury securities
- U.S. government agency securities
- Unit investment trusts (UIT)
- Viaticals and life settlements
- Wrap accounts
- Separately Managed Accounts (SMAs)
- Unknown
- Other (specify)

Question 7c: Provide the name of the issuer or security, if applicable.

Question 7d: Provide the ticker symbol or CUSIP number of the security, if applicable.

Question 8:   State in detail all the facts pertinent to the alleged violation. Explain why you believe the facts described constitute a violation of the federal securities laws. Attach additional sheets if necessary.

Question 9:   Describe all supporting materials in your possession and the availability and location of additional supporting materials not in your possession. Attach additional sheets if necessary.

Question 10:   Describe how you obtained the information that supports your allegation. If any information was obtained from an attorney or in a communication where an attorney was present, identify such information with as much particularity as possible. In addition, if any information was obtained from a public source, identify the source with as much particularity as possible. Attach additional sheets if necessary.

Question 11:   You may use this space to identify any documents or other information in your submission that you believe could reasonably be expected to reveal your identity. Explain the basis for your belief that your identity would be revealed if the documents or information were disclosed to a third party.

Question 12:   Provide any additional information you think may be relevant.

Section E: Eligibility Requirements

Question 1:   State whether you are currently, or were at the time you acquired the original information that you are submitting to the SEC, a member, officer, or employee of the Department of Justice; the Securities and Exchange Commission; the Comptroller of the Currency, the Board of Governors of the Federal Reserve System, the Federal Deposit Insurance Corporation, the Office of Thrift Supervision; the Public Company Accounting Oversight Board; any law enforcement organization; or any national securities exchange, registered securities association, registered clearing agency, the Municipal Securities Rulemaking Board

Question 2:   State whether you are, or were you at the time you acquired the original information you are submitting to the SEC, a member, officer or employee of a foreign government, any political subdivision, department, agency, or instrumentality of a foreign government, or any other foreign financial regulatory authority as that term is defined in Section 3(a)(52) of the Securities Exchange Act of 1934.

> • Section 3(a)(52) of the Exchange Act (15 U.S.C. §78c(a)(52)) currently defines "foreign financial regulatory authority" as "any (A) foreign securities authority, (B) other governmental body or foreign equivalent of a self-

regulatory organization empowered by a foreign government to administer or enforce its laws relating to the regulation of fiduciaries, trusts, commercial lending, insurance, trading in contracts of sale of a commodity for future delivery, or other instruments traded on or subject to the rules of a contract market, board of trade, or foreign equivalent, or other financial activities, or (C) membership organization a function of which is to regulate participation of its members in activities listed above."

Question 3:   State whether you acquired the information you are providing to the SEC through the performance of an engagement required under the securities laws by an independent public accountant.

Question 4:   State whether you are providing the information pursuant to a cooperation agreement with the SEC or with any other agency or organization.

Question 5:   State whether you are a spouse, parent, child or sibling of a member or employee of the SEC, or whether you reside in the same household as a member or employee of the SEC.

Question 6:   State whether you acquired the information you are providing to the SEC from any individual described in Questions 1 through 5 of this Section.

Question 7:   State whether you or anyone representing you has received any request, inquiry or demand that relates to the subject matter of your submission in connection with: (i) an investigation, inspection or examination by the SEC, the Public Company Accounting Oversight Board, or any self-regulatory organization; or (ii) an investigation by Congress, or any other authority of the federal government, or a state Attorney General or securities regulatory authority?

Question 8:   State whether you are the subject or target of a criminal investigation or have been convicted of a criminal violation in connection with the information you are submitting to the SEC.

Question 9:   If you answered "Yes" to any of questions 1 through 8, provide additional details relating to your response.

SECTION F: Whistleblower's Declaration.

You must sign this Declaration if you are submitting this information pursuant to the SEC whistleblower program and wish to be considered for an award. If you are submitting your information anonymously, you must still sign this Declaration, and you must provide your attorney with the original of this signed form.

If you are not submitting your information pursuant to the SEC whistleblower program, you do not need to sign this Declaration.

SECTION G: COUNSEL CERTIFICATION

If you are submitting this information pursuant to the SEC whistleblower program and are doing so anonymously, your attorney must sign the Counsel Certification section.

If you are represented in this matter but you are not submitting your information pursuant to the SEC whistleblower program, your attorney does not need to sign the Counsel Certification Section.

Endnotes

1. False Claims Act, 31USC §3729.
2. Drew, C., "Military Contractor Agrees to Pay $325 Million to Settle Whistleblower Lawsuit," *The New York Times*, April 3, 2009.
3. Weinberg, N., "The Dark Side of Whistleblowing," *Forbes*, March 14, 2005.
4. See *U.S. v. Stephens*, 529 US 765 for discussion.
5. Sir William Blackstone, Commentaries on the Laws of England 161.
6. Act of March 2, 1863, Ch. 67, Section 6, 12 Stat. 698.
7. 31 USC §§3729-32, as amended, Pub. L. 99-562, 100 Stat. 3153(1986).
8. 31 USC §3731(b).
9. 31 USC §3730(4) (6).
10. 31 USC §3732(b) (2).
11. 31 USC §3730(b) (3).
12. 31 USC §3733.
13. 31 USC §3730(C).
14. See Shaw, D., "Whistleblower's Case Serves as Cautionary Tale," *Seattle Times*, February 8, 1998. When the federal government collected a $325 million fine from SmithKline Beecham last year for Medicare fraud, the Department of Justice praised whistleblower Robert Merena as crucial to the case. Today, after Merena spent 4 years working with federal investigators in Philadelphia, the Justice Department is balking at paying him.
15. 31 USC§ 3730.

16. Latham, L.D., "Bad Mules, A Primer on the False Claims Act," *Oklahoma Bar Journal*, Vol. 76, No. 12, April 9, 2005.
17. 31 USC§3730(c)(2)(B).
18. "Northrop Grumann Pays to Settle Federal Lawsuit," Reuters, June 9, 2003.
19. Drew, C., "Military Contractor Agrees to Pay $325 Million to Settle Whistleblower Lawsuit," *The New York Times*, April 3, 2009.
20. Hennigan, W.J., "Northrop Grumman to Pay $12.5 Million to Settle Whistleblower Suit," *Los Angeles Times*, June 24, 2010.
21. Amounts taken from U.S. Department of Justice False Claims Act statistics.
22. "The Top 100 False Claims Act Settlements," *Corporate Crime Reporter*, December 30, 2003.
23. *Taking an Ethical Stand: The Story of Two Whistleblowers*, University of Wisconsin, Previous Years, March 11, 2008.
24. "A Ponzi scheme is a fraudulent investment operation that pays returns to its investors from their own money or the money paid by subsequent investors, rather than from profit earned by the individual or organization running the operation." Wikipedia.
25. *The Man Who Figured Out Madoff's Scheme*, CBS News, February 27, 2009.
26. Bray, C., "Madoff Pleads Guilty to Massive Fraud," *The Wall Street Journal*, March 2, 2009.
27. *Bernard Madoff Gets 150 Years Behind Bars for Fraud Scheme*, CBS News, June 29, 2009.
28. Pub. L.111-203, H.R. 4173, July 21, 2010.
29. Section 21F, Securities Whistleblowers Incentives and Protection.
30. Chew, R., "Calling All Whistleblowers! The SEC Wants You," *Time*, February 24, 2009.
31. To file a tip or complaint: http://www.cftc.gov/ConsumerProtection/FileaTiporComplaint/index.htm
32. Since fiscal year 2010, the SEC brought more than 100 enforcement actions against nearly 200 individuals and 250 entities for carrying out Ponzi schemes. In these actions, more than 65 individuals have been barred from working in the securities industry. The SEC also has worked closely with the U.S. Department of Justice and other criminal authorities on parallel criminal and civil proceedings against Ponzi scheme operations (SEC Homepage).
33. From August 12, 2011, through September 30, 2011, 334 whistleblower tips were received by the SEC.
34. Press Release, SEC Awards More Than $14 Million to Whistleblower, October 1, 2013.
35. Chilton, B., Ponzimonium, How Scam Artists Are Ripping off America. Published by Commodity Futures Trading Commission (CFTC) www.cftc.gov
36. Pub. L.111-203, H.R. 4173, July 21, 2010, Section 21F of the Security Exchange Act.
37. Commodities Futures Trading Commission Annual Report, October 12, 2012.
38. McCool, G., "FBI Sees More Hedge Fund Trading Probe Informants," Reuters, Febraury 27, 2012.
39. Ibid.
40. Van Voris, B., "Ex-Galleon Trader Slain Who Led U.S. to Probe Rajaratnam Gets Probation," Bloomberg.com, January 20, 2012.

41. Ibid.
42. Rules 165.2(p),165.3.
43. Rules 165.5(a),165.6.
44. Rule 165.2(k)-(l).
45. Rule 165.2(i).
46. Rule 165.2(i)(3).
47. Rule 165.4.

Corroboration of Informant Information 9

9.1 Trust but Verify

Doveryai no proveryai, trust but verify, is an old Russian proverb. It was used by the former Committee for State Security (KGB) as a warning to its agents to guide them in their dealings with informants. A veteran KGB agent and former station chief in Denmark called the admonition "a verification of good intentions."[1] The proverb is not new. It dates back to ancient Rome's intelligence-gathering activities but with a slight twist. The Roman admonition was *Trust in the Gods but verify.*[2] Both the Roman and Russian versions, while softer than American law enforcement's warning of *never trust an informant*, deliver the same message.[3]

Unconditional trust of an informant can be dangerous. The majority of informants operate without a moral compass, share few, if any, of the values of their handlers, and are motivated only by self-interest. Their information must be corroborated before being acted upon. One commentator warned, "The cooperating witness is probably the most dangerous prosecution witness of all. No other witness has such an extraordinary incentive to lie. Furthermore, no other witness has the capacity to manipulate, mislead, and deceive his investigative and prosecutorial handlers."[4]

Information received from a paid informant merits critical examination. No information means no reward. Informants "with nothing to sell sometime embark on a methodical journey to manufacture evidence and to create something of value, setting up and betraying friends, relatives, and cellmates alike. Frequently, and because they are aware of the low value of their credibility, criminals will even go so far as to create corroboration for their lies by recruiting others into the plot."[5]

The courts expect the police to question and verify the truthfulness of information brought in by their paid informants and cooperating witnesses. The Supreme Court in *Illinois v. Gates*[6] emphasized the value it placed on the "corroboration of details of an informant's tip by independent police work." Many states have enacted statutes requiring corroboration.[7]

Failure to corroborate an informant's information can have devastating consequences on an innocent citizen's life. Homeowner Donald Carlson was shot and seriously wounded during the execution of a search warrant on his Poway, California, home.[8] The probable cause for the search warrant was the result of information provided by an informant who was considered unreliable by at least two law enforcement officers involved in the case. He had claimed that a massive amount of cocaine guarded by armed men was concealed in the Carlson residence.

Customs agents failed to recognize warning signals that indicated that the informant's accounts were either seriously flawed or false.[9] Corroboration through investigation did not occur. The government settled the case for $2.75 million.

Accounting for the failure to adequately corroborate the informant's claims, an unidentified Customs agent told a reporter,

> "I'm not saying we willfully violate people's rights. It's just that you get caught up in the whirlwind, where the only thing that's important is to make seizures and you end up cutting corners."[10]

9.2   Traditional Investigative Methods to Cutting-Edge Technology

Corroboration is a corner that cannot afford to be cut.[11] The amount of investigation is case-specific.[12] Some of the investigative avenues open to investigators range from the simple to the complex.[13]

9.2.1   Physical Surveillance

The reliability of an untested informant's tip can be verified or corroborated through independent investigation by law enforcement officers.[14] Surveillance is perhaps the most valuable of the traditional investigative methods. Verifying the information can also serve to safeguard the identity of an informant.

A tip concerning a Florida drug smuggling conspiracy received from a previously untested informant demonstrated the value of surveillance.[15] Following the initial tip, agents began the time-consuming task of verifying the informant's account and developing investigative leads.

The case consumed nearly 2 weeks of investigation. Surveillance enabled agents to observe an off-loading of drugs unfold before them.[16] Several arrests and a significant seizure of drugs followed.

In ruling favorably for the government in a motion to disclose the identity of the informant, the court noted, "The information furnished by the informant had to be corroborated by substantial information gathered by extensive surveillance in order to provide probable cause. The suspicious activity observed during this surveillance that suggested criminal conduct was necessary to provide probable cause. Under these circumstances, appellants had no right to compel disclosure of the informant's identity."[17]

The objectives of surveillance include the following:

- Determine whether a violation exists
- Identify co-conspirators
- Obtain evidence
- Determine an informant's reliability
- Corroborate an informant or undercover agent's testimony
- Protect agents and informants while acting in an undercover capacity
- Develop probable cause

Types of surveillance employed:

- Foot surveillance teams (employed in urban settings)
- Vehicle
- Aerial
- Fixed observation point
- Still photographs
- Audio
- Video
- GPS[18]

9.2.2 Consensual Telephone Recordings

An informant who reports a fruitful, unsupervised encounter with a target of investigation to his control agent may be met with skepticism. A recorded telephone call made under the supervision of the control agent may assist in corroborating his account.

Consensual telephone intercepts are routinely used as a method of documenting a conversation between a criminal target and an informant. Several U.S. Supreme Court cases have held that consensual interceptions or recordings do not violate the Fourth Amendment.[19]

Consensually monitored telephone conversations initiated by an informant to a criminal target should occur at the direction and supervision of his control agent. A good rule to follow is that all conversations between the confidential informant (CI) and potential defendants during the conduct of an investigation should be recorded. Such a policy prevents the defense from charging that the government selectively recorded only favorable evidence and ignored evidence showing the defendant's innocence.

The equipment used to consensually record a telephone conversation is not complex. Informants are often provided equipment to record unsupervised incoming telephone calls from the target. They should be instructed by their control agents to record all calls received from the target.

CIs should not initiate telephone calls to the target unless directed to do so by their control agents. All calls should be recorded. This practice avoids the selectively taped argument used by the defense at trial: the government recorded only conversations favorable to their case. It also allows the agent to maintain control over the investigation.[20]

Most state courts[21] and legislatures[22] adhere to the one-party consent provisions of Title III.[23] Many states require a warrant or have imposed statutory[24] or constitutional restrictions.[25]

Police agencies complying with their individual state's regulations are often required to complete formal requests for permission to consensually record conversations. Police agencies often enforce internal regulations regardless of state regulations. The practice is designed to maintain internal control over the use of electronic surveillance equipment and the actions of their officers.

9.2.3 Concealed Transmitters and Recording Devices

Consensual undercover of face-to-face conversations between an informant and a target of investigation are obtained by either of two methods:

1. Placing a concealed transmitter on or about the person consenting to the electronic surveillance.
2. Providing a concealable recording device that can be activated by the consenting party.[26]

Concealed transmitters allow the conversation to be both overheard and recorded at a remote location. A recording device does what its name implies: provides a recording of the conversation. The recording is maintained as evidence and used at trial. Admissibility of the recording requires a showing of authenticity and accuracy. It is unnecessary for the witness used to introduce the exhibit to understand how the transmitter or recorder operated or how the tape recording was produced.[27]

9.2.3.1 Concealed Transmitters

Police and prosecutors often refer to concealed transmitters as *body bugs, body wires,* or simply as a *wire.*[28] Manufacturers refer to the equipment as a body transmitter.[29] Concealed transmitters are utilized primarily for agent or informant safety. Surveillance agents monitoring transmissions can react to events as they occur.

A surveillance agent trained in the operation of the receiver monitors the transmitted conversation. His duties include activating the internal tape recorder and advising surveillance agents about what is occurring during the monitored meeting. It is his responsibility to alert agents to assist the informant or undercover agent if he is in danger. The monitoring agent should not be assigned any other duties that might distract him from the equipment. Communication with surveillance agents is via radio or cellular telephone. Additional portable receivers are also available, allowing surveillance agents to simultaneously monitor the transmitter. There are no communication capabilities in the equipment allowing contact with the person wearing the transmitter.

Informants and undercover agents have often complained that "wearing a wire" is uncomfortable and makes them more apprehensive while meeting with a target. Many law enforcement instructors warn that the mere fact that an individual is wearing a "wire" puts them in a life-threatening situation if a criminal target discovers the device.

New designs housing the equipment have made the body wires nearly undetectable. One application has the transmitter and antenna concealed in a man's belt. The transmitter is in the buckle, and the belt has an embedded antenna. The length of the belt provides extended transmission capabilities.

Conversations can also be monitored by transmitters that are not concealed on the consenting party.[30] There is no requirement that the monitoring equipment be on the person of the informant or undercover agent.[31] New technology has made the equipment nearly undetectable.

If the transmitter or recorder is not on the consenting party's person, he is not to leave the device activated while he is not present. It must be turned off to avoid the possibility of intercepting nonconsensual private conversations occurring between other people in his absence.[32]

Concealed transmitters should not be used when the only desired result is to obtain a recording for evidentiary purposes. The equipment is usually employed as a safety measure for the undercover agent or informant wearing the device. Transmitters frequently malfunction for a variety of reasons, including lack of training for the operator[33] in the equipment's use, interference by steel buildings, and radio frequency interference caused by power lines, other radios, and electronic equipment in use in the area.

9.2.3.2 Video Surveillance

Consensual video surveillance, or the use of closed circuit television[34] (CCTV), is not regulated by Title III,[35] does not violate the Fourth Amendment, and, therefore, no court order is required.[36]

Federal law regulates only the interception or recording of wire and oral communications.[37] As a result, if only a video recording is produced[38] and the subject has no reasonable expectation of privacy, the statute does not apply.[39] If the informant consents to the videotaping[40] and the criminal target has no reasonable or justifiable expectation of privacy,[41] the audio portion of the tape is admissible as a consent surveillance exception.[42]

Video surveillance is frequently used in hotel rooms rented by the control agent to conduct narcotics transactions between an informant and a trafficker. Provided there is a consenting party with authority over the video-surveilled area, the video recording is allowed.[43] Fourth Amendment principles apply only to a surreptitious video recording of an individual with an expectation of privacy.[44] As with consensual tape recording with a device not worn by the informant, no videotaping can occur if the informant leaves the room and others are still present (see Appendices 9A and 9B).

The video recording is maintained as evidence for use at trial. Admissibility of the recording requires a showing of authenticity and that the video accurately depicts the recorded scene or events.[45] It is unnecessary for the witness used to introduce the exhibit to understand how the video recorder operated or how the images were produced.[46]

9.2.4 Personal Computers and Network Investigative Techniques

The FBI has demonstrated that a personal computer can be converted into both an audio and video surveillance device. All of the PC's data is also vulnerable to extraction.

Surreptitiously installed data-extraction software is delivered to the target's computer by the FBI's team of hackers. Known as "network investigative techniques," the software has the capacity to activate the computer's built-in camera, search the computer's hard drive, randomly access memory and other storage media, and to generate latitude and longitude coordinates for the computer's location. The captured sound and images are transmitted to FBI agents as the activity occurs.[47] The only reliable method to disable the surveillance is to disable the Internet connection.

9.2.5 Global Positioning System Devices

Global positioning system (GPS) devices can also be used to corroborate an informant's account of a target's movement.[48] The type of GPS unit frequently used for surveillance are those that broadcast a vehicle's real-time speed, direction, and positioning of the vehicle live every few seconds (see Appendix 9C).

A passive GPS, also known as a data logger, records the exact position of the vehicle for later retrieval, usually with a computer. The GPS unit is concealed in the vehicle's fenders, grill, or bumpers. Some are attached magnetically to the frame of the vehicle.[49]

9.2.6 Polygraphing Informants

An informant's information cannot always be corroborated by traditional investigative means. The polygraph can offer the investigator an opportunity to verify and confirm an informant's information, particularly when efforts to corroborate his information prove unsuccessful. While the instrument should not be used as a substitute for investigation,[50] often the mere mention of the polygraph is enough to elicit the truth. It is known as *fluttering*.[51] The candidate for testing becomes frightened by the instrument. A U.S. attorney general once explained, "Look—we know it's often wrong, but watching that needle jump is scary, and it's our best way for police to get confessions."[52]

A polygraph or lie-detector examination is a procedure used to determine whether a subject shows the physiological and psychological reactions that are believed to accompany intentional attempts to deceive. It records changes in cardiovascular, respiratory, and electrodermal patterns. The results are used for the purpose of rendering a diagnostic opinion regarding the honesty or dishonesty of an individual.[53]

Polygraph examinations used in criminal investigations are specific-issue examinations that are administered to subjects, witnesses, or informants to (1) detect and identify criminal suspects; (2) verify information furnished by an informant or a witness to establish or corroborate credibility; (3) obtain additional information leading to new evidence or identification of additional suspects, witnesses, or locations; and (4) to elicit confessions. The Federal Bureau of Investigation (FBI), Drug Enforcement Administration (DEA), Bureau of Alcohol, Tobacco, Firearms, and Explosives (ATF), and the Office of Inspector General (OIG) conduct and use polygraph examinations as a tool in criminal investigations.[54]

9.2.6.1 FBI Counterterrorism and Counterintelligence Investigations

Polygraphs are used during FBI investigations into suspected security breaches (espionage) or foreign or domestic terrorist threats to national security. Known as specific-issue polygraph examinations, they may be administered to the subjects, witnesses, or informants associated with the incident or threat under investigation. The FBI is the only department component that conducts and uses polygraph examinations in counterintelligence and counterterrorism operations.

Other Justice Department agencies that employ the polygraph include the following:

9.2.6.2 Office of Enforcement Operations

The Office of Enforcement Operations (OEO)[55] uses the results of polygraph examinations primarily to evaluate prisoner-witnesses seeking entry into the Witness Security Program (WITSEC). The FBI conducts most of the examinations, but the OIG and the Secret Service have also conducted them for OEO. Although rare, OEO has also asked the FBI and OIG to polygraph informants in undercover operations to verify their truthfulness.

9.2.6.3   Public Integrity Section

The Public Integrity Section prosecutes public corruption cases nation-wide, typically working with the law enforcement agencies, especially the FBI and the OIG community, to investigate alleged crimes. The Public Integrity Section uses polygraph examinations to verify the truthfulness of cooperating witnesses and informants, as well as the subjects of criminal investigations.

9.2.6.4   The Witness Security Program and the Polygraph

The U.S. Marshals Witness Security Program (WITSEC) frequently employs the polygraph. Administered by the U.S. Marshals Service (USMS), WITSEC is populated by cooperating witnesses and informants in need of long-term protection. WITSEC is a two-tier program: relocated witnesses and incarcerated witnesses. The prisoner portion of the program is handled in conjunction with the Federal Bureau of Prisons (BOP) (see Chapter 14).

All BOP prisoners seeking entry into the WITSEC Program are required to take polygraph examinations to determine whether they can be placed in a BOP Protective Custody Unit. The BOP has seven Protective Custody Units, so-called prisons with in prisons, that house inmates. The BOP uses polygraph examinations as a tool for maintaining the security of prisoner-witnesses and helping to determine whether an inmate seeking admission to the WITSEC Program intends to harm another WITSEC Program inmate. If prisoner-witnesses fail the polygraph examination, they may or may not be accepted into the WITSEC Program. If they fail, but are still accepted into the program, they may not be housed in a Protective Custody Unit.

The BOP also requires prisoner-witnesses in the WITSEC Program to take a polygraph examination before leaving a BOP facility. The purpose of the second polygraph is to deter prisoner-witnesses from sharing information about other WITSEC inmates. According to BOP, prisoner-witnesses know they have to undergo a polygraph and, if they believe a polygraph examination would detect this activity, they may be less likely to share information about other inmates.

9.2.6.5   WITSEC Security Breaches

Non-incarcerated WITSEC candidates are not required to undergo a polygraph as a prerequisite for admittance to the program. However, once admitted, a polygraph examination may be required. That can be the case when a security breach is reported. On occasion, a relocated protected witness will claim that his new identity has been compromised, but the USMS cannot independently corroborate the breach. Security breaches necessitate a costly relocation process, often requiring a new identity for the primary witness and his family. The USMS has found that some reported breaches are false, the claims being made by witnesses unhappy with their new home or the part of the country selected by the USMS for relocation.

In those cases, the USMS will request that the witness take a polygraph examination as a means of confirming that a security breach has really occurred before the USMS permanently relocates the witness for their safety. The USMS uses the examinations to deter protected witnesses from falsely claiming they are in danger because they want to move. The USMS claims that witnesses who believe that a polygraph examination would detect deception are less likely to make false claims. Witnesses will often admit to the security breach or their false claims of a security breach with the threat of a polygraph examination. Refusing to take a polygraph examination could result in ejection from the program.

9.2.7   Telephone Records

Telephone toll records and subscriber information are valuable investigative tools and can be utilized to corroborate information received from an informant. It has been held that no constitutional prohibition is violated by their disclosure to a law enforcement agency.[56]

The *U.S. Attorney E-Discovery Bulletin* demonstrates the potential phone records hold for investigators: "The world currently has 6.9 billion people and 5 billion cell phones, an increase from the 3 billion cell phones in 2007. Statistics demonstrate that cell phones outnumber personal computers three to one.[57] Today, 77 percent of North Americans, 58 percent of Europeans, 11 percent of Africans, and 29 percent of the world's population use the Internet. Mobile computing will define the future. People will rely primarily on their cell phones and tablet computers such as iPads to maintain a constant connection to the Internet for communicating, socializing, working, collaborating, shopping, paying for purchases, banking, sharing files, and finding information."[58]

Law enforcement access to the transactional records and information from telephone service provider is regulated by law.[59] Subpoenas for cellphone data require specificity in terms.[60]

The procedures followed by federal agencies to obtain the information include

1. An administrative subpoena or grand jury subpoena
2. A warrant issued under the Federal Rules of Criminal Procedure
3. A court order for such disclosure, as long as the government entry shows that there is reason to believe the records or other information sought are relevant to a legitimate law enforcement inquiry
4. Consent of the subscriber or customer to such disclosure

The requesting agency is not required to notify the subscriber that his telephone records have been subpoenaed. Telephone companies have their own policies on notifying their customers of the record request. A subpoena can request, but not require, that a company delay notification. The request generally contains the following language:

> Pursuant to an official criminal investigation being conducted by the requesting agency of a suspected felon, we request that your company furnish on *(date)* toll record information pertaining to *(name)* for the period *(month, day, year)* through *(month, day, year)* inclusive, and that you not disclose the existence of such request for a period of 90 days from the date of its receipt. Any such disclosure could impede the investigation being conducted and thereby interfere with enforcement of the law.

A court order can prevent the service provider from notifying the customer.

9.2.8   Pen Registers and Trap-and-Trace Devices

Pen registers and trap-and-trace devices are frequently used by investigators as an investigative tool, particularly in drug investigations. They are considered a noncontent surveillance tool as opposed to devices that capture content, such as a telephone wiretap. The orders for both devices contain time limits for their use, usually 30 days, but those limits are routinely extended. Both devices are often used in anticipation of obtaining an order for a telephone wiretap and used to support the probable cause in the application for the court order (see Appendices 9E through 9H).

A great deal of intelligence information can be obtained from both devices.[61] Commercial software is on the market to assist in the analysis of the data collected.

The pen register captures every number dialed from a telephone keypad. The devices are installed in or near the investigator's office and permits he or she to view telephone activity from or to a suspect's telephone as it is occurring. Authority for use of either device requires a court order, but the threshold is less than probable cause or even reasonable suspicion. All that needs to be established is that "the information likely to be obtained by such installation and use is relevant to an ongoing criminal investigation."[62] The relaxed standard stems from the legal theory that a caller has no reasonable expectation of privacy when he dials a telephone number.[63]

A pen register records the telephone number dialed from a specific telephone as it is dialed. It is defined as a device or process that records or decodes dialing, routing, addressing, or signaling information transmitted by an instrument or facility from which a wire or electronic communication is transmitted.[64]

A trap-and-trace device identifies the telephone number dialing a specific telephone. It is defined as "a device or process which captures the incoming electronic or other impulses which identify the originating number or other dialing, routing, addressing, and signaling information reasonably likely to identify the source of a wire or electronic communication, provided, however, that such information shall not include the contents of any communication."[65]

9.2.9 Mail Covers

A mail cover[66] is the process by which a nonconsensual record is made of any data appearing on the outside cover of any sealed or unsealed class of mail. Mail covers are routinely used by law enforcement and are permitted by law to obtain information to

- Protect national security
- Locate a fugitive
- Obtain evidence of commission or attempted commission of a crime
- Obtain evidence of a violation of a postal statute
- Assist in the identification of property, proceed, or assets for forfeiture under law

The Office of the Postal Inspection Service regularly reports the recorded information to the requesting agent.

Except for mail covers ordered to locate fugitives or subjects engaged in activities involving national security, mail covers remain in effect for 30 days. At the expiration of 30 days, the requesting authority must provide a statement of the investigative benefit of the mail cover and the anticipated benefits expected to be derived from its extension.[67]

9.2.10 Credit Card and Financial Records

Informants often provide information regarding the travel of a criminal target. Credit-card charges recorded on billing statements can often corroborate that information. Although cash transactions have been the criminal's preferred method of doing business, an increasingly cashless society has encouraged credit-card use. Airline travel, hotel stays, and restaurant visits are all memorialized once a credit card is used. The evidence can be invaluable in a conspiracy investigation.

A variety of methods are used to obtain credit-card numbers. Informants may be in a position of trust that enables them to report the account numbers. Mail covers reveal bills arriving at the target home or business. Although their contents may not be examined, a request to the billing company may reveal account information.

Informants also may have information regarding financial institutions utilized by the target. The Right to Financial Privacy Act governs obtaining financial records and credit card records from a financial institution.[68]

Access to financial records regarding a customer may be gained from a financial institution by any of the following six methods:

1. Pursuant to the prior written consent of the customer
2. Pursuant to a search warrant
3. Pursuant to an administrative subpoena

4. Pursuant to a formal written request
5. Pursuant to a judicial subpoena
6. Pursuant to a grand jury subpoena

In federal investigations, requests for financial records are generally conducted with the assistance of the U.S. Attorney's Office.

9.2.11   Trash Pulls

Many law enforcement agencies employ an investigative technique known as a "trash pull."[69] Agents retrieve garbage before its normal collection. Suspects who have successfully avoided detection by other investigative methods often throw valuable evidence into their garbage.

Trash searches routinely yield receipts, bills containing credit card numbers, and bank-account information providing investigative leads. Narcotics dealers discard packaging material containing traces of controlled substances. Clandestine laboratory operators also dispose of original containers of precursors, chemicals used to process illicit drugs, and traces of the final product.

Whether the Fourth Amendment[70] protects a trash can is governed by the Katz test,[71] also referred to as the reasonable expectation of privacy test. That expectation of privacy exists only if

- An individual actually expects privacy.
- His expectation is reasonable.

The investigator must collect trash after it has been discarded or deposited for routine pickup. Jurisdictions vary in their treatment and acceptance of trash pulls.[72] However, it has been held that there is no reasonable expectation of privacy for trash after it has been placed out for pickup.[73]

9.2.12   Cameras

The movements of a suspect reported by an informant can be corroborated by public or private sector surveillance systems. A *U.S. Attorney Bulletin* told prosecutors, "Employers and governments are deploying cameras in a wide range of public areas–streets, highways, stores, offices, campuses, and malls. These cameras digitally *record* peoples' faces, behaviors, and license plates. Defendants and the public are creating an enormous trove of potential evidence using cell phone cameras, Facebook, Flickr, Picasa, and YouTube. Soon, investigators using facial recognition software, artificial intelligence software, and other tools will mine that data to reconstruct defendants' actions."[74]

9.3 Corroboration through Electronically Stored Information

A 2011 *U.S. Attorney Bulletin* described the potential that electronically stored information holds for criminal investigators as they collect evidence and corroborate information obtained from informants. "Defendants use digital technologies to plan, communicate, purchase supplies, keep records, conduct transactions, and collect their ill-gotten gains. The more defendants use digital technology, the more their digital trails grow. Consequently, the digital revolution is great news for law enforcement because digital devices and systems are designed to *record* information. They record a cornucopia of information that proves what defendants were doing, whom they did it with, and what they were thinking. A defendant's own emails, texts, internet searches, and browser histories—all *recorded* in digital formats for investigators to find lawfully and analyze—are proof of actions, identity, intent, motive, and conspiracy."[75]

Digital technology is changing how crimes will be committed. How will con men find and defraud their victims? Facebook. Where will bank robbers—at least the ones who still rob brick and mortar banks—find maps and photos and plan their getaway? Google. How will the defendants who rob virtual banks commit their crimes? They will commit their crimes at home in their bathrobes with no mask or gloves because all they need is the Internet. How will defendants demonstrate their consciousness of guilt? By attempting to delete their digital footprints from their cell phones and Internet browsers or by creating false digital personas. Defendants habitual use of technology to commit crimes will leave an extensive trail of *recorded* data about their actions and motives that investigators may lawfully collect and analyze.[76]

9.3.1 E-communications

The Bulletin emphasizes the value of E-communications:

Increasingly, social and commercial relationships will be based upon digital interactions. In 2005, Facebook had five million accounts. Today there are 500 million Facebook accounts. In 5 years, maybe 2 billion accounts or more? Today, cell phone users in the United States send almost 5 billion text messages *per day*.[77] How will murderers track their victims? Facebook. Where will defendants conspire? Facebook and text messages. Where will defendants brag? Facebook, text messages, or Twitter, which has grown to 200 million accounts since 2006. Facebook and Twitter are simply examples of today's technology. They may dominate the market for years or new technologies and services may replace them, but the digital evidence will exist somewhere.[78]

9.3.2   Tracking and "Push Marketing"

The *Bulletin* added,

> To enable tracking and 'push marketing,' GPS chips, radio-frequency iden-
> tification (RFID) chips, and other sensors are being embedded everywhere,
> including cell phones, iPads, employee badges, personal and rental cars
> (electronic toll collection, OnStar), freight containers, passports, and prod-
> ucts. Tied to the internet, they track and record the movements of people and
> things, leaving behind a trail for investigators to reconstruct. Digital market-
> ing and new technologies may inadvertently aid law enforcement. For exam-
> ple, people will sign up for a cell phone application that allows restaurants and
> retailers to send, or 'push,' discount coupons to the customer's phone as the
> customer comes nearby. Investigators can lawfully collect that data to deter-
> mine whether a suspect was in that area.[79]

9.4   Law Enforcement Online

Online resources exclusive to law enforcement can also be used to corroborate an informant's information. Law Enforcement Online (LEO) is the latest
example of pooling investigative information through secure databases.

LEO is a secure, Internet-based, information-sharing system for agencies
around the world that are involved in law enforcement, first response, criminal justice, anti-terrorism, and intelligence. With LEO, members can access
or share sensitive but unclassified (SBU) information anytime and anywhere.
LEO members shared over 50,600 unclassified criminal activity and intelligence documents in FY2011.

LEO members can corroborate informant information through a variety
of databases,[80] including the following:

9.4.1   National Data Exchange

The National Data Exchange (N-DEx) is a criminal justice information-
sharing system that provides nationwide connectivity to disparate local, state,
tribal, and federal systems for the exchange of information. N-DEx provides
law enforcement agencies with a powerful investigative tool to search, link,
analyze, and share information on a national basis to a degree never before
possible.[81]

N-DEx allows participating agencies to detect relationships between
people, places, things, and crime characteristics; to link information across
jurisdictions; and to "connect the dots" between apparently unrelated data
without causing information overload. This capability occurs primarily in the
realm of structured data but can also include unstructured data. In addition,

N-DEx provides contact information and collaboration tools for law enforcement agencies that are working on cases of mutual interest.

Ownership of data shared through N-DEx remains with the law enforcement agency that provided it. N-DEx supplies controls to allow law enforcement agencies to decide what data to share, who can access it, and under what circumstances. It allows agencies to participate in accordance with applicable laws and policies governing dissemination and privacy.[82]

9.4.2   U.S. Marshals Joint Automated Booking System

The U.S. Marshals Joint Automated Booking System (JABS) contains information on criminal offenders who have been arrested and booked by a federal, state, or local agency, which consists of biographical data, place, date and time or arrest and jail location, charge, armed description, sentenced or unsentenced and health status, case agent names, notes and observations concerning the subject, substance use or abuse, precautionary warnings, names of acquaintances, and court records.

The primary purpose of JABS is to enable federal, state, and local agencies that conduct arrests and/or booking activities to store such data in regional repositories. JABS eliminates duplication efforts among multiple law enforcement agencies participating in a single booking/arrest. It permits law enforcement to learn of the arrest and apprehension of fugitive by another agency in that region, to verify the identity of an arrestee, to obtain identifying data that will assist in surveillance and wiretap activities in the event the arrestee becomes a fugitive subsequent to booking, and to assist other judicial/law enforcement agencies in obtaining such information.[83]

9.4.2.1 Intelink

Intelink is an integrated intelligence-dissemination and collaboration service, which facilitates the sharing of information. Millions of documents and hundreds of databases are available online through Intelink.

The Intelink intelligence network links information in the various classified databases of the U.S. intelligence agencies (e.g., FBI, CIA, DEA, NSA, USSS, NRO) to facilitate communication and the sharing of documents and other resources. Intelink-S, the secret-level variant of Intelink, has begun to expand rapidly in scope and reach. As the intelligence support medium for Global Command and Control System and law enforcement activities, Intelink-S is expected to become the principal growth area for intelligence products and services. Its customer base will be extraordinarily diverse, eventually encompassing all areas of U.S. government operations that can benefit from integrated intelligence support and collaboration.[84]

9.4.2.2 Regional Information Sharing Systems Network

The Regional Information Sharing Systems (RISS) Program supports federal, state, and local law enforcement efforts to combat criminal activity that extends across jurisdictional boundaries. Six RISS centers currently provide member law enforcement agencies nationwide with a broad range of intelligence exchange and related investigative support services.

RISS centers focus primarily on violent crime, terrorism, gang activity, organized crime, and drug trafficking. The RISS Program is the only multi-jurisdictional criminal intelligence system operated by and for state and local law enforcement agencies. The six RISS centers now serve nearly 6000 federal, state, and local law enforcement agencies in the 50 states, the District of Columbia, Puerto Rico, Guam, the U.S. Virgin Islands, Australia, England, and the Canadian provinces.[85]

9.4.2.3 National Gang Intelligence Center

The FBI established the National Gang Intelligence Center, or NGIC, in 2005. The NGIC integrates gang intelligence from across federal, state, and local law enforcement on the growth, migration, criminal activity, and association of gangs that pose a significant threat to the United States. It supports law enforcement by sharing timely and accurate information and by providing strategic/tactical analysis of intelligence. Located just outside Washington, D.C, the NGIC is manned by analysts from multiple federal agencies. The databases of each component agency are available to the NGIC, as are other gang-related databases, permitting centralized access to information. The NGIC is co-located with the Safe Streets Gang Unit and the MS-13 National Gang Task Force.[86]

9.4.2.4 Homeland Security Information Network

Homeland Security Information Network is a comprehensive, nationally secure web-based platform able to facilitate SBU information sharing and collaboration between federal, state, local, tribal, private sector, and international partners.

9.5 Intelligence Work Product and Fusion Centers

The amount of intelligence information gathered by the FBI and other federal, state, and local law enforcement agencies has overwhelmed traditional methods of handling information. Informants are responsible for much of the intelligence information collected by law enforcement agencies.

There are basically three categories of intelligence information that is collected:

1. *Criminal Intelligence.* Information compiled, analyzed, and/or disseminated in an effort to anticipate, prevent, or monitor criminal activity.
2. *Strategic Intelligence.* Information concerning existing patterns or emerging trends of criminal activity designed to assist in criminal apprehension and crime control strategies, for both short- and long-term investigative goals.
3. *Tactical Intelligence.* Information regarding a specific criminal event that can be used immediately by operational units to further a criminal investigation, plan tactical operations, and provide for officer safety.[87]

The Department of Homeland Security (DHS) and the Department of Justice (DOJ) decided that a regional approach to managing intelligence information would be required. The answer was fusion centers.

The general public knows very little about fusion centers. According to the Fusion Center Guidelines, the centers are a collaborative effort of two or more agencies that provide resources, expertise, and information to the center with the goal of maximizing the ability to detect, prevent, investigate, and respond to criminal and terrorism activity.[88]

The guidelines describe the centers as an effective and efficient mechanism to exchange information and intelligence, maximize resources, streamline operations, and improve the ability to fight crime and terrorism by merging data from a variety of sources.[89] They are not federal entities. Many are operated under the umbrella of a state law enforcement agency but are federally funded.

Despite their autonomy, the government sees fusion centers as a conduit for implementing portions of the National Criminal Intelligence Sharing Plan. The NCISP is an intelligence-sharing initiative that links the computer databases of local, state, regional, and tribal law enforcement agencies with those of the U.S. federal government.[90] Fusion center guidelines were created by the United States DHS and the DOJ. The stated purpose of the guidelines was to address the intersection of law enforcement, intelligence, public safety, and the private sector.[91]

Fusion centers would not have flourished without federal grants. Fusion centers are eligible for several types of DHS and DOJ grant programs, including the DHS's State Homeland Security Program and the Urban Area Security Initiative. DHS's FY 2009 Homeland Security Grant Program designated "Maximizing Information Sharing via the National Network of Fusion

Centers" a national priority. DHS alone has provided more than $254 million from FY 2004 to FY 2007 to state and local governments to support the centers.

As of July 2009, there were 72 fusion centers located throughout the United States. Not all are on an equal security clearance footing: fewer than a third are allowed access to material deemed secret. The DHS Fusion Center website announced, "The Homeland Security Data Network (HSDN), which allows the federal government to move information and intelligence to the states at the secret level, is deployed at 27 fusion centers. Through HSDN, fusion center staff can access the National Counterterrorism Center (NCTC), a classified portal of the most current terrorism-related information."[92]

More than 250 FBI personnel are currently assigned to 58 of the fusion centers. Security clearances have been obtained for 520 state and local law enforcement officers assigned to the centers.[93]

Sixteen of the 58 fusion centers in which the FBI is involved are co-located with the FBI's Field Intelligence Groups (FIGs). FIGs provide an intelligence link to the Joint Terrorism Task Forces, FBI headquarters, and the U.S. intelligence community. Among the ways the FBI makes national intelligence more readily available to state, tribal, and local law enforcement agencies is through the LEO network.[94]

Since 2002, the FBI claims to have produced and disseminated more than 266 timely threat assessments and situational-awareness bulletins. They are "geared toward state, local, and tribal law enforcement highlighting the tactics and vulnerabilities of international and domestic terrorist groups, as well as potential indicators of terrorist activity." Eighty percent of the assessments and bulletins issued in FY 2007 were produced jointly with the DHS.[95]

9.6 Corroboration through Public Record Sources

Information obtained from an informant about a subject of an investigation can be verified and expanded upon electronically through sources available from outside of the law enforcement community. Public records are invaluable tools that can both corroborate an informant's account and provide leads for expanding an investigation.

Skilled investigators[96] routinely examine information from the following public record sources. Much of the information is available online:

ASSESSOR'S OFFICE
    Owner (s) of property
    Address of property
    Parcel number
    Legal description

Recorder's docket/page number
Full cash value of property and land
Purchase price
Last purchase date
Type of land
Personal property records

BANKRUPTCY COURT
Name of person or business filing bankruptcy
Bankruptcy filing type
Date filed
Case number
Creditors
Detail of claims, motions, and judgments

CITY BUSINESS LICENSE
Name of business
Type of business (corporation, sole proprietor, etc.)
Business classification
Owners/officers
Date started
Reported monthly sales revenue
Current status

CORPORATION COMMISSION
Name of business
Name (s) of officers/directors
Addresses of officers/directors
Date officers/directors took office
Statutory agent
Articles of incorporation
Annual reports with balance sheets
Shareholders' names
Business description
Address of business

CRISS-CROSS DIRECTORY
Cross-reference phone numbers with addresses and names

LIBRARY
Business statistics (Dunn & Bradstreet, etc.)
Newspaper articles
Out-of-state phone books

Professional directories (attorneys, etc.)
Maps

MOTOR VEHICLE DEPARTMENT
Driver's license information
Vehicle data by VIN, title, person, registration, plate number, make/model/year, lien holder, status of registration

RECORDER'S OFFICE
Recorded documents by name
Affidavit of Value (contains owner/seller, sales price, date of purchase, etc.)

SECRETARY OF STATE
Trade names
Application for trade names
UCC statements
Business information

STATE EMPLOYMENT
Quarterly wage reports by social security number
Employer information
Business information

SUPERIOR COURT
Civil and criminal case history by name or date filed
Divorce decrees
Calendar listing

TREASURER'S OFFICE
Party (s) responsible for paying taxes on property, delinquent taxes, amount of taxes

UTILITIES
Person (s) responsible for payment of utilities
Employer information
Social security number
Previous address
References

VOTER REGISTRATION
Name, address and phone number of registered voter
Birth date and place of birth
Occupation
Date of registration
Party affiliation

9.6.1   Case Study: Corroboration and the
Castro Cocaine Connection

The chances that a Florida Keys cocaine smuggler could have his photograph taken with Hillary Clinton and Al Gore at the White House and another one taken in Cuba with Fidel Castro in Cuba during the same year were slim. But that is what a smuggler and would-be informant accomplished in 1996.

The picture with Clinton and Gore was easy to explain. The smuggler contributed $20,000 to the Democratic National Committee and was invited to the White House for a fund-raising dinner. The photo with Castro was a more interesting story.

It was the same year the smuggler and two accomplices, a Colombian national and Key West fisherman, were caught by DEA in Miami with three tons of cocaine and 30 boxes of Cuban Cohiba cigars. When agents searched the smuggler's car, they discovered the wallet-sized color photograph of the man with the Cuban dictator and members of his staff.[97] He was taken into custody immediately, and the questions that followed were predictable.

The smuggler had no intention of going to prison. In exchange for his freedom he could deliver DEA a dictator that would put their last political catch, Manuel Noriega, to shame: Fidel Castro. DEA bosses from Miami to Washington, DC, were immediately alerted. Cases like this not only made careers, they made agents famous. The investigation became a priority and moved forward.

The DEA had long believed that the waters surrounding Cuba, and the island nation itself, were a safe haven for drug traffickers. The smuggler-turned-informant claimed he could prove it. He could take DEA all the way back to 1993 when he was first contacted by a Cali cartel kingpin. The cartel planned to send a cocaine-laden freighter into Cuban waters for off-loading to smaller boats. They would be met by the smuggler's fishing boats. From the protected waters of Cuba, the rest of the trip through the Florida Straits would be simple. The informant described three Cuban-protected cocaine off-loading operations that went without a hitch.

The smuggler explained that the photograph of him taken with Castro was shot in November 1995 during the planning stages for bringing in the January 9 load he was caught with. He had witnesses to corroborate his story. His codefendants, the Colombian national and the Key West fisherman, had also flipped. They both backed up the story about being in Cuba during the last off-loading operation.

The *Miami Herald* reported that the smuggler from the Keys was in fact in Cuba with a group of Cuban-American businessman. They were looking to cut an oil exploration deal with Castro. The informant's attorney related his client's account of the meeting with the dictator: "Castro pulled me aside. He knew everything about me. He knew about the business I had in the Keys. He knew about the restaurant I had just opened in Key West. He knew I was in the stone crab business. He asked me what I paid my waitresses." He even asked the smuggler to bring stone crabs on his next visit.[98]

To set the hook even deeper, the informant was alleged to have persuaded the Key West fisherman arrested with him to tell agents and prosecutors that a Cuban patrol boat shadowed the last off-loading operation. That little detail tied the Castro government to Colombian drug trafficking.

The case against Castro didn't remain a secret for very long. At one point in the investigation, the *Miami Herald* reported that "sources familiar with the investigation say that the evidence against Castro is already greater than the evidence that led to the drug indictment of former Panamanian strongman Manuel Antonio Noriega in 1988."[99] A story ran in the United Kingdom with the headline "Castro Implicated in Massive Cocaine Smuggling Operation."[100]

From the start, DEA was far from being the only federal agency involved in the investigation. It went straight to the highest levels of government. If the United States was going to name Fidel Castro an international drug trafficker, they had better be sure of their facts and their witnesses. They now had three smugglers-turned-informants all working toward the same goal: freedom. Their man in the photo with Castro was center stage. The Colombian and the Key West fisherman needed to be squeezed a little tighter to make sure the case was airtight.

In late July, the *Herald* quoted the smuggler's attorney as saying he noticed "a chill in the air."[101] In August, the federal prosecutor and DEA agents called for a meeting with the informant and his attorney. The boat captain had changed his story. He had told investigators that the smuggler had put him up to telling the Cuban gunboat story. It never really happened.

According to the federal prosecutor in charge of the case, "It's not just lying about the gunboat. It's getting someone else to lie about it. Not only did he lie, he elicited somebody to lie for him. If somebody lies about details, how do you start sorting out what's lies and what's not lies."[102]

Under pressure from prosecutors and agents, the smuggler ultimately folded: no gunboat, no deal with Castro. There also was never a U.S. invasion of Cuba to arrest Fidel Castro on drug charges.

There was also no reduced sentence. The smuggler was sentenced to 19 years in prison. He later denied having told the boat captain to lie about the Cuban patrol boat.[103] The Castro cocaine connection, if there ever was one, remains unsolved.

Appendix 9A: Application for Video Surveillance

APPLICATION FOR AN ORDER AUTHORIZING THE
INTERCEPTION OF VISUAL, NON-VERBAL CONDUCT AND
ACTIVITIES BY MEANS OF CLOSED CIRCUIT TELEVISION

A. Pursuant to Rule 41(b) of the Federal Rules of Criminal Procedure, the United States of America by and through _____, United States Attorney for the District of_____,and_____, an Assistant United States Attorney for said District, hereby makes application to this Court for an order authorizing the interception and recording of visual, non-verbal conduct and activities by means of closed circuit television occurring within the following premises: (set forth a particularized description of the premises to be surveilled.) The factual basis for the granting of this application is set forth in the attached affidavit of, which is incorporated by reference herein.

B. Also attached to this application is a letter from the Director (or the Senior Associate Director or Associate Director), Office of Enforcement Operations, Criminal Division, United States Department of Justice, authorizing the making of this application for visual surveillance by means of closed circuit television.

C. The attached affidavit of _____ reflects that there is probable cause to believe:

1. The premises known as _____ _____ located at _____, are being and will continue to be used by (name the interceptees), to commit offenses involving (list the violations).

2. The visual, nonverbal conduct and activities of the above-named individual(s) will be obtained through interception by means of closed circuit television at these premises and that such conduct and activities will provide:

   a. information indicating the precise nature, scope, extent and methods of operation of the participants in the illegal activities referred to above,

   b. information reflecting the identities and roles of accomplices, aiders and abettors, co-conspirators, and participants in the illegal activities referred to above, and

   c. admissible evidence of commission of the offenses described above.

3. Installation of electronic visual surveillance equipment may require surreptitious entry into the premises (by breaking and entering, if necessary).

4. Normal investigative procedures have been tried and failed or reasonably appear unlikely to succeed, if tried, or appear to be too dangerous to employ.

5. On the basis of the attached affidavit of and allegations contained in this application,

IT IS HEREBY REQUESTED that this Court authorize Special Agents of the (name the investigative agency/agencies) to intercept and record by means of closed circuit television visual, non-verbal conduct and activities of (name the interceptees) and others as yet unknown within the premises known as _____,
located at _____, concerning offenses, involving (list the violations).

IT IS REQUESTED FURTHER that such interception not automatically terminate when the type of visual, nonverbal conduct described above has first been obtained but continue until conduct is intercepted that reveals: (1) the manner in which the above-named described offenses are being committed; (2) the precise nature, scope, and extent of the above-described offenses, and, (3) the identity and roles of accomplices, alders and abettors, co-conspirators, and participants, or for a period of thirty (30) days from the date of this order, whichever is earlier.

IT IS REQUESTED FURTHER that Special Agents of the (name the investigative agency/agencies) be authorized to enter the above-described premises surreptitiously, covertly, and by breaking and entering, if necessary, in order to install, maintain and remove electronic visual surveillance equipment used by the (name the investigative agency/agencies) to intercept and record visual, non-verbal conduct occurring within the foregoing premises.

IT IS REQUESTED FURTHER THAT this order require that it be executed as soon as practicable and that interception be conducted in such a manner as to minimize interception of visual, non-verbal conduct which is not criminal in nature, and that the order terminate upon attainment of the authorized objectives or at the end of thirty (30) days from the date of the order, whichever is earlier.

IT IS REQUESTED FURTHER that surveilling agents be authorized to spot monitor the premises to ascertain whether any of the aforementioned persons are present inside the premises.

When such persons are found to be present, the agents will continue the interception as to conduct that involves the designated offenses.

When it is determined that none of the named interceptees nor any person subsequently identified as an accomplice who uses the premises to commit or converse about the designated offense(s) is inside the premises, interception of visual, non-verbal conduct will be discontinued.

IT IS REQUESTED FURTHER that, in accordance with 18 U.S.C. 3103a(b), this Court's order delay notification of the execution of the order for a period not to exceed ninety days (or some lesser period) because there is reasonable cause to believe that providing immediate notification would seriously jeopardize the investigation. Such period of delay may thereafter be extended by the court for good cause shown.

Dated: _____, 20__

Respectfully submitted,

_____

Assistant United States Attorney

Electronic Surveillance Manual, Procedures and Forms, U.S. Department of Justice, Electronic Surveillance Unit, revised June 2005.

Appendix 9B: Order for Video Surveillance

ORDER AUTHORIZING THE INTERCEPTION OF VISUAL,
NON-VERBAL CONDUCT AND ACTIVITIES

Application under oath having been made before me by
_____, Assistant United States Attorney for the
_____, District, for an order authorizing the interception
and recording of visual, non-verbal conduct and activities pursuant to Rule
41(b) of the Federal Rules of Criminal Procedure and full consideration having been given to the matters set forth therein, the Court finds:

A. There is probable cause to believe that _____ and others
   as yet unknown have committed and are committing offenses
   involving (list the offenses).
B. There is probable cause to believe that particular visual, non-verbal
   conduct and activities concerning these offenses will be obtained
   through the interception for which authorization is herewith applied.
   In particular, visual, non-verbal conduct and activities will concern
   the (characterize the offenses).
C. Normal investigative procedures have been tried and failed, reasonably appear unlikely to succeed if tried or continued, or are too
   dangerous.
D. There is probable cause to believe that the premises (located at)
   (known as) have been and are being used by and others as yet
   unknown, in connection with the commission of the above-stated
   offenses.

WHEREFORE, IT IS HEREBY ORDERED that the (name of the investigative agency/agencies) is authorized, to intercept and record the visual,
non-verbal conduct and activities of (name interceptees) and others as yet
unknown, concerning the above-described offenses at the premises located at
(location). Such interception shall not terminate automatically when the type
of conduct/activity described above in paragraph (B) has first been observed
but shall continue until the conduct or activity is intercepted that reveals the
manner in which (name the interceptees), and others as yet unknown participate in the specified offenses and reveals the identities of (his)(their) coconspirators, their methods of operation, and the nature of the conspiracy, or for
a period of (state the time period not to exceed 30 days), whichever is earlier.

IT IS ORDERED FURTHER that special agents of the (name of the
investigative agency/agencies) are authorized to enter the foregoing premises
surreptitiously for the purpose of installing, maintaining, and removing any
electronic monitoring devices utilized pursuant to the authority granted by
this order.

PROVIDING THAT, this authorization to intercept visual, non-verbal conduct and activities shall be executed as soon as practicable after the signing of this order and shall be conducted in such a way as to minimize the interception of conduct and activities not otherwise subject to interception, and must terminate upon attainment of the authorized objective or, in any event, at the end of (not to exceed 30) days.

IT IS ORDERED FURTHER that, in accordance with 18 U.S.C. 3103a (b), notification of the execution of this order be delayed for a period not to exceed ninety days (or some lesser period) because there is reasonable cause to believe that providing immediate notification would seriously jeopardize the investigation. Such period of delay may thereafter be extended by the court for good cause shown.

_____

JUDGE

Date: _____

Electronic Surveillance Manual, Procedures and Forms, U.S. Department of Justice, Electronic Surveillance Unit, Revised June 2005.

Appendix 9C: Affidavit for Search Warrant for Tracking Device

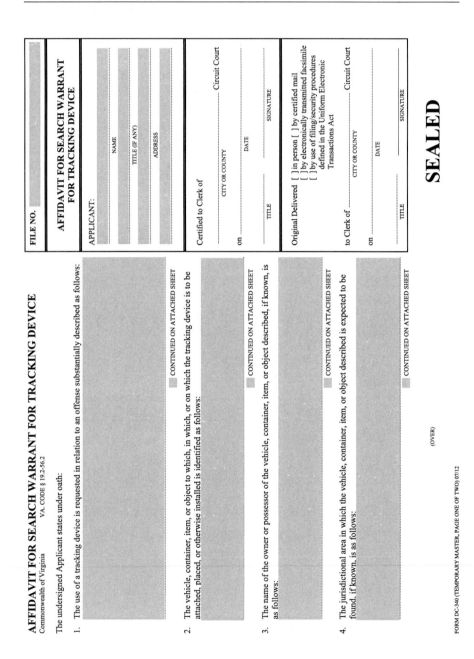

5. The county or city where there is probable cause to believe the offense for which the tracking device is sought has been committed, is being committed, or will be committed is as follows:

6. Probable cause exists that the information likely to be obtained from the use of a tracking device will be evidence of the commission of the offense, and the material facts constituting the probable cause for the issuance of the search warrant are:

7. ▢ I have personal knowledge of the facts set forth in this affidavit OR

8. ▢ I was advised of the facts set forth in this affidavit in whole or in part, by a person whose credibility or the reliability of the information may be determined from the following facts:

9. The law-enforcement agency conducting the investigation is as follows:

The statements above are true and accurate to the best of my knowledge and belief.

_____
TITLE OF APPLICANT

_____
SIGNATURE OF APPLICANT

Subscribed and sworn to/affirmed before me this day.

_____
DATE AND TIME

[ ] CLERK   [ ] MAGISTRATE   [ ] JUDGE

FORM DC-340 (TEMPORARY MASTER, PAGE TWO OF TWO) 04/12

Appendix 9D: Cellphone (Mobile Device) Search Warrant Affidavit

This sample warrant affidavit is intended for those situations where the sole subject of the search is a portable electronic device, such as a cell phone, Blackberry, or PDA. Of course, language from this sample could be included in an affidavit for a search of computers where a search scene may include both kinds of devices.

****

IN THE MATTER OF THE SEARCH OF:

CASE NUMBER: _____

APPLICATION AND AFFIDAVIT FOR SEARCH WARRANT

Detective [Name] of the [Law Enforcement Agency], who is currently assigned to [office/squad], being of lawful age and first duly sworn upon my oath, states as follows:

1. I am submitting this Affidavit in support of an application for a warrant to search and seize the following portable electronic device: [DESCRIBE DEVICE HERE].
2. I am a detective with the [Law Enforcement Agency], and have been so employed for approximately [   ] years.
3. During my career as a detective for [Law Enforcement Agency], I have participated in the execution of 100 search warrants.
4. Because this affidavit is being submitted for the limited purpose of securing a warrant, I have not included each and every fact known to me concerning this investigation. I have set forth only the facts that I believe are necessary to establish probable cause to believe that the portable electronic device described above [is evidence of violations of...] [is contraband] [is the fruit of a violation of...] [was used in committing violations of...] [and/or contains evidence/contraband/fruits/instrumentality of violations of...].

Summary of Relevant Technology

[If the exact brand and model of the device is known, identify the device as such and tailor a description of its specific capabilities here. Often this information is available from the manufacturer or online. Otherwise, insert one or more of the following generic descriptions as necessary depending on target of warrant.]

Blackberry

"Blackberry" is a brand of handheld wireless electronic communications devices made by Research in Motion. Blackberries generally enable users to send email, make and receive telephone calls, access the Internet, and organize appointments and contact information. Certain Blackberries can also send instant messages, take digital pictures or moving video, or store and play digital music or video files. Blackberries may also contain GPS technology for determining the location of the device.

Cell Phone

A cellular telephone or mobile telephone is a handheld wireless device used primarily for voice communication through radio signals. These telephones send signals through networks of transmitter/receivers called "cells," enabling communication with other cellular telephones or traditional "land line" telephones. A cellular telephone usually includes a "call log," which records the telephone number, date, and time of calls made to and from the phone.

In addition to enabling voice communications, cellular telephones now offer a broad range of capabilities. These capabilities include, but are not limited to: storing names and phone numbers in electronic "address books;" sending, receiving, and storing text messages and email; taking, sending, receiving, and storing still photographs and moving video; storing and playing back audio files; storing dates, appointments, and other information on personal calendars; and accessing and downloading information from the Internet. Cellular telephones may also include global positioning system (GPS) technology for determining the location of the device.

Digital Camera

A digital camera is a device that records still and moving images digitally. Digital cameras use a variety of fixed and removable storage media to store their recorded images. Images can usually be retrieved by connecting the camera to a computer or by connecting the removable storage medium to a separate reader. Removable storage media include various types of flash memory cards or miniature hard drives. Most digital cameras also include a screen for viewing the stored images. This storage media can contain any digital data, including data unrelated to photographs or videos.

Portable Media Player

A portable media player (or "MP3 Player" or iPod) is a handheld digital storage device designed primarily to store and play audio, video, or photograph files. However, a portable media player can also store any digital data, such as word processing documents, even if the device is not designed to access such files. Some portable media players can use removable storage media. Removable storage media include various types of flash memory cards or miniature hard drives. This removable storage media can also store digital data. Depending on the model, a portable media player may have the ability to store very large amounts of electronic data and may offer additional features such as a calendar, contact list, clock, or games.

PDA, for example, iPhone

A personal digital assistant, or PDA, is a handheld electronic device used for storing data (such as names, addresses, appointments, or notes) and utilizing computer programs. Some PDAs also function as a wireless communication device and are used to access the Internet and send and receive e-mail. PDAs usually include a memory card or other removable storage media for storing data and a keyboard and/or touch screen for entering data. Removable storage media include various types of flash memory cards or miniature hard drives. This removable storage media can store any digital data. Most PDAs run computer software, giving them many of the same capabilities as personal computers. For example, PDA users can work with word-processing documents, spreadsheets, and presentations. PDAs may also include global positioning system (GPS) technology for determining the location of the device.

Pager

A pager is a handheld wireless electronic device used to contact an individual through an alert, or a numeric or text message sent over a telecommunications network. Some pagers enable the user to send, as well as receive, text messages.

Summary of the Investigation

Describe investigation *and the device's role in the offense*. Establish probable cause that the relevant electronic device is

- Evidence of a crime
- Contraband
- The fruit of a crime
- An instrumentality of a crime
- Or that the device is a storage container for evidence, contraband, fruits, or instrumentalities
- If the device both contains evidence, contraband, fruit, or instrumentalities AND is *itself* evidence, contraband, fruit, or instrumentality, be sure to describe both roles

Also Note: As indicated above, there obviously must be a connection between the crime and the evidence sought with probable cause to believe the e-device will contain such evidence. However, where appropriate and accurate and as part of the "connection," the law enforcement officer can state that such e-device is frequently used by persons engaged in such criminal conduct—as per the below example:

Upon his arrest by the Police Department, Smith was found to be in possession of 2 cell phones: a Motorola T-Mobile phone with a built-in digital camera and a Motorola "Boost" Mobile phone. Officer Jones of the Police Department advised me that Smith had talked on the cell phone during the traffic stop referred to above. Further, CI #1 has advised me that Smith was frequently using the cell phones to speak to persons throughout the trip from Phoenix to New York. These 2 cell phones are now in the custody of the Police Department after having been seized incident to arrest of the defendant Smith.

Based on my training and experience and discussion with other officers, it is known that persons who smuggle and transport drugs frequently use cell phones to maintain contact with his associates during travel and also use cell phones to contact persons where the drugs are destined. This frequently occurs due to the transient nature of these smuggling operations and because members of these conspiracies frequently travel and require coordination of their movements in order to pick up and drop off drugs at designated times and places.)

If the device is being seized only as a container of evidence, contraband, fruit or instrumentality, insert the following 2 paragraphs to justify seizing the device and searching it off-site. (If the device itself is [evidence] [contraband], [fruit of crime] or an [instrumentality of the crime], it is already subject to seizure.)

Based on my knowledge and training and the experience of other agents with whom I have discussed this investigation, I know that in order to completely and accurately retrieve data maintained in [identify device] hardware or software, to ensure accuracy and completeness of such data, and to prevent the loss of the data either from accidental or intentional destruction, it is often necessary that the [device], related instructions in the form of manuals and notes, as well as the software utilized to operate such a device, be seized and subsequently processed by a qualified specialist in a laboratory setting.

Analyzing electronic handheld devices for criminal evidence is a highly technical process requiring expert skill and a properly controlled environment. Such devices utilize a vast array of different operating systems, software, and set-ups. The variety of hardware and software available requires even experts to specialize in some systems and applications. Thus it is difficult to know prior to the search which expert possesses sufficient specialized skill to best analyze the system and its data. No matter which system is used, however, data analysis protocols are exacting scientific procedures, designed to protect the integrity of the evidence and to recover even "hidden," erased, compressed, password-protected, or encrypted files. Since electronic evidence is extremely vulnerable to tampering or destruction (both from external sources or from destructive code imbedded in the system as a "booby trap"), a controlled environment is essential to its complete and accurate analysis. Furthermore, there are often no software tools designed for forensic searches of particular handheld devices. Thus, searching for and retrieving data from a [device] can be even more complicated than searching a computer, even if the device has a much smaller memory capacity than a computer. For the foregoing reasons, the [device] will be removed from the searched premises if the agent deems it necessary in order to conduct an efficient, complete, secure, and accurate search of the device.

Analysis of Electronic Data

Searching [the device] for the evidence described above may require a range of data analysis techniques. In some cases, it is possible for agents to conduct carefully targeted searches that can locate evidence without requiring a time-consuming manual search through unrelated materials that may be commingled with criminal evidence. For example, agents may be able to execute a "keyword" search that searches through the files stored in a computer for special words that are likely to appear only in the materials covered by a warrant. Similarly, agents may be able to locate the materials covered in the warrant by looking for particular directory or file names. In other cases, however, such techniques may not yield the evidence described in the warrant. Criminals can mislabel or hide files and directories; encode communications to avoid using key words; attempt to delete files to evade detection; or take other steps designed to frustrate law enforcement searches for information. These steps may require agents to conduct more extensive searches, such as scanning areas of the device's memory not allocated to listed files, or opening every file and scanning its contents briefly to determine whether it falls within the scope of the warrant. In light of these difficulties, your affiant requests permission to use whatever data analysis techniques appear necessary to locate and retrieve the evidence described above.

Conclusion

_____
Detective

Sworn to before me and subscribed in my presence this day of

_____
HONORABLE JUDGE   Date

Appendix 9E: Application for Trap and Trace/Pen Register

APPLICATION

Name
_____,
an Assistant United States Attorney, being duly sworn, hereby applies to the Court for an order authorizing the installation and use of a (pen register) (trap and trace device) on (telephone line or other facility). In support of this application I state the following:

1. Applicant is an "attorney for the Government" as defined in Rule 1(b)(1) of the Federal Rules of Criminal Procedure, and, therefore, pursuant to Section 3122 of Title 18, United States Code, may apply for an order authorizing the installation of a (trap and trace device) (pen register).

2. Applicant certifies that the (investigative agency) is conducting a criminal investigation of (name targets) and others as yet unknown, in connection with possible violations of (list violations); it is believed that the subjects of the investigation are using (telephone line or other facility), (listed in the name of (if known) or leased to (if known) and located at (if known) _ in furtherance of the subject offenses; and that the information likely to be obtained from the (pen register) (trap and trace device) is relevant to the ongoing criminal investigation in that it is believed that this information will concern the aforementioned offenses.

3. Applicant requests that the Court issue an order authorizing the installation and use of (a pen register to record or decode dialing, routing, addressing, or signaling information transmitted by [identify the targeted instrument or facility from which a wire or electronic communication is transmitted]), (and) (a trap and trace device to capture the incoming electronic or
other impulses which identify the originating number or other dialing, routing, addressing, and signaling information reasonably likely to identify the source of a wire or electronic communication), for a period of (enter time period, not to exceed 60) days, provided, however, that such information shall not include the contents of any communication.

4. The applicant requests further that the order direct the furnishing of information, facilities, and technical assistance necessary to accomplish the installation of (the pen register) (and/or) (trap and trace device) as provided in Section 3124 of Title 18.

5. (If trap and trace requested) The applicant requests further that the order direct that the results of the trap and trace device be furnished to the officer of a law enforcement agency, designated in the court order, at reasonable intervals during regular business hours for the duration of the order.

6. With regard to the requirement of Section 3121(c) of Title 18 that the (investigative agency) use technology reasonably available to it that restricts the recording or decoding of electronic or other impulses to the dialing, routing, addressing, and signaling information utilized in the processing and transmitting of wire or electronic communications so as not to include the contents of any wire or electronic communications, the (investigative agency) is not aware of any such technology.

WHEREFORE, it is respectfully requested that the Court grant an order for (enter time period, not to exceed 60) days authorizing the installation and use of (a pen register) (trap and trace device), and directing the (communications service provider) to forthwith furnish agents of the (investigative agency) with all information, facilities and technical assistance necessary to accomplish the installation of the (trap and trace device) (pen register).

I declare under penalty of perjury that he foregoing is true and correct.
EXECUTED ON_____, 20__

Applicant_____

Signature_____

Electronic Surveillance Manual, Procedures and Forms, U.S. Department of Justice, Electronic Surveillance Unit, Revised June 2005.

Appendix 9F: Order for Trap and Trace/Pen Register

ORDER

This matter having come before the Court pursuant to an application under oath pursuant to Title 18, United States Code, Section 3122 by _____, an attorney for the Government, which requests an order under Title 18, United States Code, Section 3123, authorizing the installation and use of a (pen register) on (telephone line or other facility), the Court

finds that the applicant has certified that the information likely to be obtained by such installation and use is relevant to an ongoing criminal investigation into possible violations of (list violations) by (list targets, if known), and others as yet unknown.

IT APPEARING that the information likely to be obtained by a (pen register) (trap and trace device) installed on (telephone Line or other facility), (listed in the name of [if known_____]) (leased to [if known_____]), (and located at_____[if known]_____), is relevant to an ongoing criminal investigation of the specified offenses,

IT FURTHER APPEARING that [conform to application statement] with regard to the limitation in Section 3121(c) of Title 18 concerning pen register technology, the (investigative agency) does not have technology reasonably available to it that restricts the recording or decoding of electronic or other impulses to the dialing, routing, addressing, and signaling information utilized in the processing and transmitting of wire or electronic communications so as not to include the contents of any wire or electronic communications.

IT IS ORDERED, pursuant to Title 18, United States Code, Section 3123, that (investigative agency) is authorized to install and use, anywhere within the United States, on (telephone line_____ or other facility) (a pen register to record or decode dialing, routing, addressing, or signaling information) (and) (a trap and trace device to capture the incoming electronic or other impulses which identify the originating number or other dialing, routing, addressing, and signaling information reasonably likely to identify the source of a wire or electronic communication) for a period of (enter time period, not to exceed 60) days; and

IT IS ORDERED FURTHER, pursuant to Section 3123(b)(2) of Title 18, that upon the request of (attorney for the Government or an officer of the law enforcement agency authorized to install and use the pen register), (provider of wire or electronic communication service, landlord, custodian, or other person) shall furnish such (investigative or law enforcement officer) forthwith all information, facilities, and technical assistance necessary to accomplish the installation of the pen register unobtrusively and with a minimum of interference with the services that the person so ordered by the court accords the party with respect to whom the installation and use is to take place, (and) (if trap and trace ordered) that upon the request of (attorney for the Government or officer of the investigative agency authorized to receive the results of the trap and trace device), (provider of a wire or electronic communication service, landlord, custodian, or other person) shall install such device forthwith on the appropriate line _____or other facility and shall furnish (investigative or law enforcement officer) all additional information, facilities and technical assistance including installation and operation of the device (including the installation of Caller ID service on telephone line or other facility) unobtrusively and with a minimum of interference with the services that the person so ordered by the court accords the party with respect to whom the installation and use is to take place. The results of the trap and trace device shall be furnished to the (officer of a law enforcement agency, designated in the court order), at reasonable intervals during regular business hours for the duration of the order.

IT IS ORDERED FURTHER that the (investigative agency) will reasonably compensate the provider of a wire or electronic communication service, landlord, custodian, or other person who furnishes facilities or technical assistance for such reasonable expenses incurred in providing such facilities and assistance in complying with this order.

IT IS ORDERED FURTHER, pursuant to Section 3123(d) of Title 18, that this order and the application be sealed until otherwise ordered by the Court, and that the person owning or leasing the line or other facility to which the pen register or a trap and trace device is attached or applied, or who is obligated by the order to provide assistance to the applicant, not disclose the existence of the (pen register) (trap and trace device), or the existence of the investigation to the listed subscriber, or to any other person, unless or until otherwise ordered by the Court.

UNITED STATES MAGISTRATE (or DISTRICT) JUDGE

Date

Electronic Surveillance Manual, Procedures and Forms, U.S. Department of Justice, Electronic Surveillance Unit, Revised June 2005.

Appendix 9G: Application for Order Permitting Government to Use Its Own PenRegister/Trap and Trace Equipment (Triggerfish/Digital Analyzer or Similar Device)

APPLICATION

____, an Assistant United States Attorney, being duly sworn, hereby applies to the Court for an order authorizing the installation and use of a pen register to identify the Electronic Serial Number (ESN) and Mobile Identification Number (MIN) of a cellular telephone (being used by _(if known)_) (within a (color, make, model of vehicle) (bearing state license plate number)). In support of this application I state the following:

1. Applicant is an "attorney for the Government" as defined in Rule 1(b)(1) of the Federal Rules of Criminal Procedure, and, therefore, pursuant to Section 3122 of Title 18, United States Code, may apply for an order authorizing the installation of a trap and trace device and pen register.
2. Applicant certifies that the United States Drug Enforcement Administration is conducting a criminal investigation of (name targets (if known) and others as yet unknown), in connection with possible violations of Title , United States Code, Section(s); it is believed that the subjects of the investigation
   are using a cellular telephone within a (color; make, model of vehicle) (bearing state license plate number)) in furtherance of the subject offenses; and that the information likely to be obtained from the pen register is relevant to the ongoing criminal investigation.
3. Applicant requests that the Court issue an order authorizing the installation and use of a pen register for a period of (enter time period, not to exceed 60) days.

WHEREFORE, it is respectfully requested that the Court grant an order for (enter time period, not to exceed 60) days authorizing the installation and use of a pen register.

I declare under penalty of perjury that the foregoing is true and correct.
EXECUTED ON _____ _____, 20 ____

_____
Applicant

Electronic Surveillance Manual, Procedures and Forms, U.S. Department of Justice, Electronic Surveillance Unit, Revised June 2005.

Appendix 9H: Order Permitting Government to Use Its Own Pen Register/Trap and Trace Equipment (Triggerfish/Digital Analyzer or Similar Device)

ORDER

This matter having come before the Court by an application under oath pursuant to Title 18, United States Code, Section 3122 by _____, an attorney for the Government, which requests an order under Title 18, United States Code, Section 3123, authorizing the installation and use of a pen register to identify the Electronic Serial Number (ESN) and Mobile Identification Number (MIN) assigned to a cellular telephone (being used by _____ (if known)) (within a (color, make, model of vehicle), bearing (state license plate number)), the Court finds that the applicant has certified to the Court that the information likely to be obtained by such installation and use is relevant to an ongoing criminal investigation into possible violations of Title, United States Code, Sections ___by (list targets (if known) and others as yet unknown).

IT IS ORDERED, pursuant to Title 18, United States Code, Section 3123, that the (investigative agency) is authorized to install and use, anywhere within the United States, a pen register to identify the ESN and MIN of a cellular telephone (being used by (if known)) (within a (color, make, model of vehicle), bearing state license plate number _____)), for a period of (enter time period, not to exceed 60) days; and

IT IS ORDERED FURTHER, pursuant to Section 3123(d) of Title 18, that this order and the application be sealed until otherwise ordered by the Court.

_____

UNITED STATES MAGISTRATE (or DISTRICT) JUDGE

_____

Date

Electronic Surveillance Manual, Procedures and Forms, U.S. Department of Justice, Electronic Surveillance Unit, Revised June 2005.

Endnotes

1. Germani, C., "Russian Spying Game Ongoing," *Baltimore Sun*, November 24, 1996.
2. Sheldon, Col. R. M., *A Guide to Intelligence from Antiquity to Rome*, Taylor and Francis Publishing, Boca Raton, FL, 2004.
3. Snow, R.L., *Terrorists Among Us: The Militia Threat*, at 11, Da Capo Press (2002) (An unwritten but ironclad rule exists in law enforcement … never trust an informant); Settle, R., *Police Informers: Negotiation and Power*, at 196, Federation Press (Australia) (1995) (Never trust any criminal, more particularly, never trust an informant); Dorn, N., *Trafficker: Drug Markets and Law Enforcement*, at 23 Routledge Publishing 1992(Great Britain) (never trust an informant).
4. Gershman, B.L., *Witness Coaching by Prosecutors*, 23 Cardozo L. Rev. 829, 847 (2002); See also *Crawford v. United States*, 212 U.S. 183, 204 (1909).
5. *Commonwealth of N. Mariana Islands v. Bowie*, 243 F.3d 1109, 1123-24 (9th Cir. 2001).
6. 462 U.S. 213, 241 (1983). See *Draper v. United States*, 358 U.S. 307 (1959); *United States v. Garcia*, 528 F.2d 580, 587 (5th Cir. 1976).
7. Alaska Stat. § 12.45.020 (Michie 2004); Ark. Code Ann. § 16-89-111E (Michie 2003); Cal. Penal Code § 111 (Deering 2003); GA. Code Ann. § 24-4-8 (2003); Nev. Rev. Stat. § 175.291 (2004); N.Y. Crim Proc. § 60.22 (Consol. 2004); Okla. Stat. title 22 § 742 (2004); OR. Rev. Stat. § 136.440 (2003). Eighteen states require corroboration of an accomplice's testimony. See also, *Humber v. State*, 466 So. 2d 165 (Ala. Crim. App. 1985) (citing statute); *State v. Shaw*, 37 S.W.3d 900, 903 (Tenn. 2001) ("In Tennessee, a conviction may not be based solely upon the uncorroborated testimony of an accomplice").
8. *Carlson v. United States*, 93-953G. See *State v. Shaw*, 37 S.W. 3d 900, 903 (Tenn. 2001).
9. Jones, D. and Eldridge, E., "Archer Daniels Informant Faces Charges," *USA Today*, January 16, 1997.
10. Alvord, J., "Snitches, Licensed to Lie?" *San Diego Union Tribune*, May 30, 1995.
11. Tulsky, F.N., "Evidence Casts Doubt on Camarena Case Trials; Probe Suggests Perjury Helped Convict Three in DEA Agent's Murder," *Los Angeles Times*, October 26, 1997. See Kassin, S.M., "Human Judges of Truth, Deception and Credibility: Confident but Erroneous," 23 *Cardozo L. Rev.* 800 (2002).
12. Kessler, R.E., "Ex-Informant Sentenced for Perjury in Pan Am Flight 103 Hoax," *Miami Herald*, May 17, 1998.
13. Leen, J., "Castro Drug Probe Collapses in Heap of Dead ends, Lies," *Miami Herald*, November 24, 1996.
14. *United States v. Mendoza*, 547 F.2d 952 (5th Cir.) *cert. denied*, 431 U.S. 956 (1977); *United States v. Tuley*, 546 F.2d 1264 (5th Cir.) *cert. denied*, 434 U.S. 837 (1977); *United States v. Brennan*, 538 F.2d 711 (5th Cir.) *cert. denied*, 429 U.S. 1092 (1976); *United States v. Anderson*, 500 F.2d 1311 (5th Cir. 1974). *See United States v. One 1967 Cessna Aircraft*, 454 F. Supp. 1352 (C.D. Cal. 1978).
15. *United States v. Alexander*, 559 F.2d 1339, 1342 (5th Cir. 1977). *See also United States v. Luck*, 560 F. Supp. 258 (N.D. Ga., 1983).

16. 559 F.2 1343.
17. 559 F.2 1344. See *McCray v. Illinois,* 386 U.S. 300 (1967); *Bourbois v. United States,* 530 F.2d 3 (5th Cir. 1976).
18. Willing, R., "Surveillance Gets a Satellite Assist," *USA Today,* June 10, 2004.
19. See *On Lee v. United States,* 343 U.S. 747, *reh'g denied,* 344 U.S. 848 (1952); *Lopez v. United States,* 373 U.S. 427, *reh'g denied,* 375 U.S. 870 (1963); *United States v. White,* 401 U.S. 745, *reh'g denied,* 402 U.S. 99, *on remand,* 454 F.2d 435 (7th Cir. 1971), *cert. denied,* 406 U.S. 962 (1972); *United States v. Caceres,* 440 U.S. 741, 79-1 U.S. Tax Cas. (CCH) 9294, 43 A.F.T.R. 2d (P-H) H 79-872 (1979) (*endorsing White* plurality).
20. Waldman, B., "As Sheik Omar Case Nears End, Neither Side Looks Like a Winner," *Wall Street Journal,* September 22, 1995.
21. See *Smithey v. State,* 269 Ark. 538, 602 S.W.2d 676, 679 (1980); *State v. Del Vecchio,* 191 Conn. 412, 464 A.2d 813, 823 (1983); *State v. Grullon,* 212 Conn. 195, 562 A.2d 481, 486–488 (1989); *State v. Tomasko,* 238 Conn. 253, 681 A.2d 922 (1996); *Humphrey v. State,* 231 Ga. 855, 204 S.E.2d 603, *cert. denied,* 419 U.S. 839 (1974); *Mitchell v. State,* 239 Ga. 3, 235 S.E.2d 509, *appeal after remand,* 142 Ga. App. 802, 237 S.E.2d 243 (1977); *Green v. State,* 250 Ga. 610, 299 S.E.2d 544 (1983); *State v. Lee,* 67 Haw. 307, 686 P.2d 816, *reconsideration denied,* 744 P.2d 780 (Haw., 1984); *State v. Jennings,* 101 Idaho 265, 611 P.2d 1050 (1980); *State v. Couch,* 103 Idaho 205, 646 P.2d 447, 449 (App., 1982); *Lawhorn v. State,* 452 N.E.2d 915 (Ind., 1983), *habeas corpus proceeding,* 620 F. Supp. 98 (N.D. Ind., 1984); *State v. Reid,* 394 N.W.2d 399, 405 (Iowa 1986); *State v. Johnson,* 229 Kan. 42, 621 P.2d 992, 994 (1981); *State v. Roudybush,* 235 Kan. 834, 686 P.2d 100, 107–109 (1984); *State v. Petta,* 359 So. 2d 143, 145 (La., 1978); *State v. Bellfield,* 275 N.W.2d 577 (Minn., 1978); *Lee v. State,* 489 So. 2d 1382 (Miss., 1986); *State v. Engleman,* 634 S.W.2d 466, 477 (Mo., 1982); *State v. Brown,* 232 Mont. 1, 755 P.2d 1364, 1368–1369 (1988); *State v. Manchester,* 200 Neb. 41, 367 N.W.2d 733, 735 (1985); *State v. Kilgus,* 128 N.H. 577, 519 A.2d 231, 238–241 (1986); *People v. Lasher,* 58 N.Y.2d 962, 447 N.E.2d 70, 460 N.Y.S.2d 522 (1983); *State v. Levan,* 326 N.C. 155, 388 S.E.2d 429, 437–438 (1990); *Ferguson v. State,* 644 P.2d 121, 123 (Okla. App., 1982); *State v. Ahmadjian,* 438 A.2d 1070,1079–1082 (R.I., 1981); *State v. Woods,* 361 S.W.2d 620 (S.D., 1985); *State v. Braddock,* 452 N.W.2d 785, 788 (S.D., 1990); *Stroup v. State,* 552 S.W.2d 418 (Tenn. App.), *cert. denied,* 434 U.S. 955 (1977); *State v. Erickson,* 36 Utah Adv. Rep. 3, 722 P.2d 756 (1986); *Cogdill v. Commonwealth,* 219 Va. 272, 247 S.E.2d 392, 12 A.L.R.4th 406 (1978); *Blackburn v. State,* 290 S.E.2d 22, 32 (W. Va., 1982); *Auclair v. State,* 660 P.2d 1156, 1158 (Wyo.), *cert. denied and app. dism'd,* 464 U.S. 909 (1983).
22. See 18 USC § 2511(C)(2). See also Ariz. Rev. Stat. Ann. § 13-3005; Cal. Penal Code. § 633; 11 Del. Code. Ann. § 1336(c) (2); Haw. Rev. Stat. § 803-42(b)(3); Idaho Code § 18-6702(2)(C); Iowa Code § 727.8; Minn. Code § 626A(2)(2); Neb. Rev. Stat. § 86-701(2); N.H. Rev. Stat. Ann. § 570-A:2, II(d); Ohio Rev. Stat. § 2933.52(B)(3) & (F)(2); 13 Okla. Code § 176.4(4); S.D. Codified Laws Ann. § 23A-35A-20; Texas Code Crim. Proc. art. 18.20 § 17(3); Utah Code Ann. § 77-23a-4(2) (b); Va. Code Ann. §§ 19.2-61 et seq.; Wyo. Code § 7-3-602(b) (iv).
23. 18 USC § 2511(c)(2).

24. See Nev. Rev. Stat. §§ 179.410 et seq.; N.J. Stat. Ann. § 2A:156A-4(c); N.M. Stat. Ann. §§ 30-12-11; *Arnold v. State*, 94 N.M. 381, 610 P.2d 1210 (1980); 19802 CCH Trade Cases H 63318; Or. Rev. Stat. § 165.540(l)(a); *State v. Underwood*, 293 Or. 389, 648 P.2d 847 (1982); 18 Pa. Cons. Stat. Ann. § 5704; Wash. Rev. Code § 9.73.090(2); *State v. Fjermestad*, 14 Wash. 2d 828,791 P.2d 897, 902 (1990).

25. See *State v. Glass*, 583 P.2d 872 (Alaska, 1978), *on rehearing*, 596 P.2d 10 (Alaska, 1979), *overruled on other grounds by Juneau v. Quinto*, 684 P.2d 127 (Alaska, 1984); *Thiel v. State*, 762 P.2d 478, 483–484 (Alaska App., 1988); Fla. Stat. Ann. § 934.03(2)(C); *State v. Tsavaris*, 394 So.2d 418 (Fla., 1981), *appeal after remand*, 414 So. 2d 1087 (Fla. App., 1982), *petition denied*, 424 So. 2d 763 (Fla., 1983); *Hoberman v. State*, 400 So. 2d 758 (Fla., 1981); Mass. Gen. Laws. Ann. Ch. 272 § 99B4; *Commonwealth v. Blood*, 400 Mass. 61, 507 N.E.2d 1029, 1044 (1987); *Commonwealth v. Penta*, 423 Mass. 546, 669 N.E.2d 767 (1996); *Commonwealth v. Thorpe*, 384 Mass. 271, 424 N.E.2d 250, 258–259, 27 A.L.R.4th 430, *cert. denied*, 454 U.S. 1147 (1981).

26. See 18 USC § 2511(2)(c).

27. See *State v. McNear*, 343 S.W. 3d 703, 705 (Mo. Ct. App. S.D. 20110.

28. See *United States v. Zuber*, 899 F. Supp. 188 (D. Utah, 1995).

29. National Institute of Justice, Technology Assessment Program, *Surveillance Receivers and Recorders*, NIJ Standard 0222.00.

30. See *United States v. Yonn*, 702F.2d 1341 (11th Or. 1983); *United States v. Bennett*, 538 F. Supp. 1045 (D.P.R., 1982).

31. 18 USC § 2511(2)(c).

32. Title III of the Omnibus Crime Control and Safe Streets Act of 1968, as amended by the Electronic Communications Privacy Act of 1986 (ECPA). See *United States v. Padilla*, 520 K2d 526 (1st Cir. 1975); *U.S. Attorneys Manual*, Ch. 9.

33. See *United States v. Shabazz*, 724 F.2d 1536 (11th Cir. 1984); *United States v. Hughes*, 658 F.2d 317 (5th Cir. 1981), *cert. denied*, 455 U.S. 922 (1982); *United States v. Greenfield*, 574 F.2d 305 (5th Cir.) *cert. denied*, 439 U.S. 860 (1978); *United States v. Corel*, 622 F.2d 100 (5th Cir. 1979), *cert. denied*, 455 U.S. 943 (1980).

34. See *Thompson v. Johnson County Community College*, 930 F. Supp. 501 (D. Kan. 1996) (college's warrantless use of CCTV to monitor locker area of storage room for thefts and weapons was constitutional).

35. See *Electronic Surveillance Manual, Procedures and Forms*, U.S. Department of Justice, Electronic Surveillance Unit, Revised June 2005.

36. *United States v. Jackson*, 213 F.3d 1269 (10th Cir. 2000). FBI installed remotely controlled cameras on the tops of telephone poles overlooking defendants' residences, and also used a "video car equipped with three hidden cameras, two VCRs and a transmitter to record and listen to conversations in and around the car with the consent of an informant who was a party to those communications); See *United States v. Cox*, 836 F. Supp. 1189 (D. Md. 1993) (cooperating defendant consented to video monitoring of motel room, was in the room at all times, and the surveillance did not pick up any words nor actions that were outside the consenting party's hearing and sight).

37. See *United States v. Torres,* 751 F.2d 875, 880 (7th Cir. 1984), *cert. denied,* 470 U.S. 1087 (1985); *United States v. Williams,* 124 F.3d 411 (3rd Cir. 1997).

38. See *Technologically-Assisted Physical Surveillance Standards,* American Bar Association.

39. See *United States v. Biasucci,* 786 F.2d 504, 508 (2nd Cir. 1986); *United States v. Koyomejian,* 970 F.2d 536 (9th Cir.1992), *cert. denied,* 117 S. Ct. 617 (1993); *United States v. Falls,* 34 F.3d 674, 680 (8th Cir. 1994). See *United States v. Chen,* 979 F.2d 714, 717 (9th Cir. 1992).

40. See *United States v. Allen,* 513 F. Supp. 547 (W.D. Okla., 1981); *Hoback v. State,* 286 Ark. 153, 689 S.W.2d 569, 571 (1985); *People v. Knight,* 288 111. App. 3d 232, 327 N.E.2d 518, 521–522 (1975).

41. See *United States v. Myers,* 692 F.2d 823, 859 (2nd Cir. 1982), *cert. denied,* 461 U.S. 961 (1983); *United States v. Felder,* 572 F. Supp. 17 (E.D. Pa.), *aff'd,* 722 F.2d 735 (3rd Cir. 1983).

42. 18 § 2511(2) (c) and (d).

43. See *United States v. Laetividal-Gonzalez.,* 939 F.2d 1455, 1461 (11th Cir. 1991); *United States v. Cox,* 836 F. Supp. 1189, 1198 (D. Md., 1993).

44. See *State v. Casconi,* 766 P.2d 397 (Or. App.1988).

45. See *U.S. v. Capers,* 708 U.S. F. 3d 1286 (11th Cir. 2013).

46. See *State v. McNear,* 343 S.W. 3d 703, 705 (Mo. Ct. App. S.D. 20110.

47. Timberg, C. "FBI's Search for 'Mo,' Suspect in Bomb Threats, Highlights Use of Malware for Surveillance," *Washington Post,* Dec. 6, 2013; See Case No. 12-SW-05685-KMI, U.S. District Court for the District of Colorado, December 11, 2013, for an example of an FBI "network investigative technique" affidavit for the search of a computer and installation of malicious software.

48. The Global Positioning Scanner, or GPS, receives signals from satellites that allow the unit to map its location via longitude and latitude.

49. See *U.S. v. Jones,* 565 U.S. (2012); tracking device on a vehicle and using GPS device to monitor the vehicle's movements constitutes a search under the Fourth Amendment.

50. "Polygraph Policy Model for Law Enforcement," *FBI Law Enforcement Bulletin,* June 1987, p. 12.

51. "The Pentagon`s Flutter Drill," *The Chicago Tribune,* January 12, 1985.

52. Safire, W., "Lying Lie Detectors," *New York Times,* October 10, 2002.

53. Employee Polygraph Protection Act of 1988, Pub. L. 100-347, Sec. 1, 29 U.S.C. § 2001.

54. *Use of Polygraphs in the Department of Justice,* OIG Report, September 2006. From FY 2002 through 2005 (the last years available), the four agencies conducted a total of 8356 polygraph examinations of informants, suspects, and witnesses.

55. OEO provides U.S. Attorneys Offices with assistance on wiretaps, subpoenas, witness security, and prisoner transfers.

56. See *Smith v. Maryland,* 442 U.S. 735 (1979).

57. BBC News, www.bbc.co.uk/news (July 9, 2010).

58. Introduction to E-Discovery, *United States Attorney Bulletin,* U.S. Department of Justice, Volume 59, Number 3, May 2011.

59. 18 USC § 2703(c).

60. ESN is an acronym for "Electronic Serial Number." An ESN uniquely identifies cellular telephone instruments. IMSI is an acronym for "International Mobile Subscriber Identity." Every mobile phone that uses GSM format has a SIM (Subscriber Identity Module) card that is installed or inserted into the mobile phone handset. The SIM card contains the IMSI, which is a nondialable number programmed on a microchip on the SIM card. It is the IMSI that is used to uniquely identify a subscriber to the GSM mobile phone network. The IMSI number is unique to that SIM card and is never reassigned. Thus, if the target exchanges his cell phone for an updated model and/or changes his phone number but retains his SIM card, the IMSI will remain the same. The IMEI (International Mobile Station Equipment Identity) is similar to a serial number and uniquely identifies the telephone handset itself. The SIM is a card, sometimes called a "smart" card, that can be installed or inserted into certain cellular telephones containing all subscriber-related data. This facilitates a telephone call from any valid cellular telephone, since the subscriber data rather than the telephone's internal serial number is used to complete the call.

A cell site is located in a geographic area within which wireless service is supported through radio signaling to and from antenna tower(s) operated by a service provider. Cellsites are located throughout the United States. Cellular telephones that are powered on will automatically register or re-register with a cellular tower as the phone travels within the provider's service area.

61. Digital analyzers/cell site simulators/triggerfish and similar devices may be capable of intercepting the contents of communications and, therefore, such devices must be configured to disable the interception function, unless interceptions have been authorized by a Title III order.

62. 18 U.S.C. §3123(a)(1).

63. See *Smith v. Maryland*, 442 U.S. 735 (1979).

64. 18 U.S.C. §3127(3).

65. 18 U.S.C. §3127(4).

66. 39 C.F.R. § 233.3 Mail Covers.

67. Ibid.

68. 12 USC §3401.

69. "The Use of Garbage to Establish Probable Cause for Granting Valid Search Warrants," *Police Chief Magazine,* June 2010.

70. U.S. Constitution, Amendment IV.

71. *Katz v. United States,* 389 U.S. 347 (1967).

72. See *United States v. Segura-Baltazar,* 448 F.3d 1281 (11th Cir. 2006).

73. *California v. Greenwood,* 486 U.S. 35 (1988).

74. Introduction to E-Discovery Issue of the *United States Attorney Bulletin,* U.S. Department of Justice, Volume 59, Number 3, May 2011.

75. Ibid.

76. Ibid.

77. Ibid.

78. Ibid.

79. Ibid.

80. Information that follows is taken directly from the cited web pages.

81. N-DEx description taken directly from Law Enforcement Online.

82. Verbatim from FBI Homepage, See FBI Information Sharing Report 2011.
83. Verbatim from U.S. Marshal Service Homepage.
84. Description verbatim from Federation of American Scientists, Intelligence Resource Program Homepage.
85. Description verbatim from U.S. Department of Justice Office of Justice Programs Bureau of Justice Assistance Homepage.
86. Verbatim from FBI National Gang Intelligence Center.
87. *Intelligence-Led Policing: The New Intelligence Architecture*, NCJ 210681, September 2005.
88. Fusion Center Guidelines, August 2006.
89. Ibid.
90. Institute for Intergovernmental Research.
91. Fusion Center Guidelines, August 2006.
92. Fusion Center Guidelines: Law Enforcement Intelligence, Public Safety, and the Private Sector: Executive Summary.
93. Ibid.
94. Ibid.
95. Ibid.
96. Contributed by William Riley and Steven Kiraly, Private Investigators, Riley and Kiraly, Miami, Florida).
97. Leen, J., "Castro Drug Probe Collapses in Heap of Dead Ends, Lies," *Miami Herald,* November 24, 1996.
98. Ibid.
99. Leen, J., "Traffickers Tied Castro to Drug Run," *Miami Herald*, July 25, 1996.
100. Davidson, P., "Castro Implicated in Massive Cocaine Smuggling Operation," *Independent*, July 26, 1996.
101. Ibid.
102. Leen, J., "Castro Drug Probe Collapses in Heap of Dead Ends, Lies," *Miami Herald,* November 24, 1996.
103. Ibid.

Informants and Search Warrants

10

10.1 Introduction

Agents routinely receive information from informants regarding criminal activity and the location of contraband. The illegally possessed items are usually available for sale to trusted customers, including informants. The investigation that follows develops information intended to establish probable cause[1] to support the issuance of a search warrant[2] and often involves an informant making a controlled purchase of evidence, also referred to as a controlled buy.

A controlled buy is the purchase of controlled substances or other contraband by a confidential informant (CI) from a target offender,[3] which is initiated, managed, or overseen by law enforcement personnel.[4] When conducted properly, the steps followed can eliminate the risk of a search warrant being executed on the wrong location. It also reduces the opportunities for informant misconduct, including the planting of evidence and theft of official funds.

Issuing magistrates, prosecutors, police managers, and defense counsel are very often misinformed when it comes to how informants must be managed in controlled-purchase investigations. Yet employing informants for use in obtaining a search warrant is usually one of the first lessons taught to new detectives and agents. The technique has been utilized in both untaxed liquor cases and drug investigations since the 1930s.

A search warrant is issued on a showing of probable cause[5] to believe that the legitimate object of a search is located in a particular place.[6] The controlled buy[7] allows the detective to send his informant into the premises, purchase an exhibit of evidence from the target, make observations[8] of other items of evidentiary value while at the location, and return to his handler with the evidence and his information.

The task of the issuing magistrate is simply to make a practical, commonsense decision whether, given all the circumstances set forth in the affidavit before him, "there is a fair probability that contraband or evidence of a crime will be found in a particular place."[9] Most magistrates, although required to be neutral, detached, and capable of determining whether probable cause exists for the requested search warrant,[10] are usually predisposed to issue the warrant. Little, if anything, is asked about the informant. A chief magistrate in Georgia recalled,

> I know for sure that neither myself nor any of the magistrates under me have ever required to know the identity of the informer, and I've never heard of that happening, but maybe we should.[11]

The informant's handler should orchestrate the controlled purchase in a prescribed manner. Following established procedures assist in ensuring that the informant is being truthful in his account of where the illegal items he obtained during the controlled buy are located. Following procedure also minimizes the opportunity for an informant's misconduct and reduces acts of omission by the control agent during the operation.

Controlled buys are also a method of reviving "stale" information.[12] The U.S. Supreme Court requires that for probable cause information to support the issuance of a search warrant, "the proof must be of facts so closely related to the time of the issue of the warrant as to justify a finding of probable cause at that time."[13]

10.2   Wrong-Door Raids

So-called *search warrant* cases have been an effective weapon in the War on Drugs. Historically, search warrants have been the staple of police departments conducting investigations with limited manpower or financial resources. The cases are usually cost-effective and produce quick results. Drugs are seized, arrests are made, drug dens are closed, and in some cases property is forfeited.

The number of federal search warrants relying exclusively on an unidentified informant has increased dramatically in the last three decades. Unfortunately, the ease of obtaining a search warrant has had unintended consequences. During the last 20 years, police have killed at least 40 innocent people while conducting wrong-door raids.[14] According to a study by the Cato Institute, "Because of shoddy police work, over reliance on informants, and other problems, each year hundreds of raids are conducted on the wrong addresses, bringing unnecessary terror and frightening confrontation to people never suspected of a crime." The Institute called the botched paramilitary police raids "an epidemic of isolated incidents."[15] Revolutionary War patriot James Otis, an outspoken critic of British "writs of assistance," believed that search warrants placed "the liberty of every man in the hands of a petty officer."[16]

There have been at least three investigations of botched search warrant raids that offer far more troubling explanations. The blame is placed on the following:

1. Willful disregard for police SOP's governing the use of informants[17] and conducting controlled buys[18]

2. Police use of "cookie-cutter" affidavits containing boilerplate language from a computer program[19]
3. Blatant lies in search warrant affidavits[20]
4. Police creating phantom informants[21]
5. Police supplying drug exhibits "purchased" by a phantom informant[22]
6. Police planting drugs in homes when no drugs are discovered during a search[23]

Remarkably, the botched raid on 92-year-old Kathryn Johnston's home that resulted in her murder (discussed in Chapter 6) was the direct result of all of the above examples of police malpractice.[24]

10.3 Controlled Search-Warrant Buys

The controlled search-warrant buy[25] is the investigative technique used to corroborate[26] the CI's claim that contraband is located at a particular location. The controlled buy is also referred to as an undercover buy,[27] a controlled informant buy,[28] or an informant buy.[29]

Although the rules may vary slightly between law enforcement agencies,[30] what follows should be standard police practice for controlled buys:

- Fully identify and document the informant.[31]
- Thoroughly debrief the CI.[32]
- Search the CI and his vehicle, if used to travel to the targeted location.[33]
- Provide CI with buy money and install recorder or transmitter.[34]
- Follow CI to the buy location.[35]
- Observe the CI enter and exit the targeted premises.[36]
- Follow CI directly to a prearranged location for a meeting that occurs immediately after the buy.[37]
- Collect evidence and electronic equipment from the CI.[38]
- Search the CI and vehicle again for any contraband or money.[39]
- Debrief the informant and obtain a written and signed statement.[40]

The procedure corroborates the informant's account of the events occurring before, during, and after the controlled purchase of evidence. The practice also ensures that the police, not the informant, identify the residence or business to be raided. Each step must be followed. There should be no shortcuts.[41]

The events are recounted in the affidavit in support of the search warrant and sworn to by the affiant officer. The procedure allows the issuing magistrate to determine how the informant came by his information and/or evidence and how the affiant corroborated the account.[42]

10.3.1   Initial Informant Debriefing: Never Trust an Informant

Before initiating the controlled buy, the control agent must conduct a complete debriefing of the informant. The initial interview begins the process of evaluating the value and veracity[43] of the source. During the interview, it is imperative that the officer remember the number one rule in informant handling: NEVER TRUST AN INFORMANT.[44]

All meetings with CIs should be attended by a second officer.[45] Informants have proven to be the leading cause of integrity complaints against agents. Nothing leaves an officer more vulnerable to allegations of wrongdoing than meeting with or paying a cooperating individual alone. The second agent minimizes the risk of unfounded accusations being made by a disgruntled informant.[46]

10.3.2   Determine Informant's Motivation

The investigator must determine what motivated[47] the informant to come forward with information.[48] When a spouse or paramour informs on a partner, revenge as a motive should be suspected.[49] The CI could be attempting to use the police as a lever in a domestic quarrel or a custody dispute. An informant holding a grudge and with access to the targeted location could easily plant drugs to further his or her own agenda.

A Lowell, Massachusetts, police informant looking for work with the state police was arrested after bragging to recruiting detectives that he was good at "planting stuff." He described planting a gun in one defendant's car and 29 g of cocaine in another individual's vehicle's gas cap shortly before bringing the crimes to the attention of police.[50] Both men were arrested. Neither had a criminal record. One was a pharmacist, and the other a licensed practical nurse.

An investigation of the informant's work with police resulted in 17 cases being dropped. A federal civil rights lawsuit was filed in U.S. District Court against the city of Lowell, and a veteran Lowell police officer alleging "systematic failure to supervise confidential informants within its police department."

10.3.3   Corroboration

Following the debriefing, the value of the CI's information should be assessed by the control agent's supervisor. Many agencies maintain a log of all instances in which the informant has provided reliable information. The case will move forward if the criminal conduct described by the informant meets the agency's requirements for initiating an investigation.

10.3.4 Identifying Target Location

The debriefing also begins the process of fully identifying the location where contraband is believed to be possessed. All that is required of police is that the description of the targeted structure be detailed enough that the officer assigned to execute the search warrant can, with reasonable effort, identify the place intended to be searched.[51] For example, the Cincinnati Police Department requires the officer acting as the affiant to personally see the exact location the informant entered to make the purchase of evidence.[52]

Yet the frequency of wrong-door raids[53] illustrates the obvious: verifying the exact address does not always occur[54]:

> A Colorado woman was hospitalized after eight Drug Enforcement Administration (DEA) agents forced open her door, cursed her, and beat her to the ground—before realizing they were at the wrong house. The man they were really after was later charged with amphetamine manufacture. In a letter to the District Attorney (DA), the Wheat Ridge Mayor wrote, "drug manufacturers must be controlled but not by people who cannot even get the address for the raid correct."[55]

During the planning stage, the informant should be taken into the field by the control agent to point out the exact location where the purchase is going to take place. If the buy is to be made from a duplex or an apartment building with multiple doors, the CI must point out to the agent which door he will use. Remarkably, these steps are often ignored.

The process need not expose the CI's role. He can be driven to the location in a surveillance vehicle with darkened windows. The investigator will then be able to obtain both a physical address[56] and a physical description[57] of the targeted location.

10.3.5 Identify Suspects

A thorough debriefing[58] assists in fully identifying the trafficker before the buy occurs. The informant may not know the suspect's full name but only refer to him by a nickname or an alias. The nickname may be recognized by the interviewer,[59] allowing for full identification of the subject. Other officers may recognize both the nickname and the address as having a reputation for criminal activity. Their knowledge can serve to corroborate the informant's account in assessing whether the case should move forward.[60]

The informant may also have a residential telephone number or cellphone number for the suspect. Subscriber information[61] can be obtained through a crisscross directory. Nonpublished telephone numbers and toll records can be obtained from the service provider with a subpoena.[62]

When the exact address is determined, utility companies can be contacted to determine the name of the individual paying for services. A subpoena may be required to obtain the information and a copy of the original credit application.[63] Although the named applicant may not be the suspect, the information often provides investigative leads. Once a verifiable name and date of birth for the subject is obtained, photographs also become available. Law enforcement agencies can request copies of the color photograph taken for a driver's license. Targets of investigation without licenses may have identification cards or arrest photographs on file with a local police agency. On receipt of the photograph, the informant is given the opportunity to identify the subject from a group of photos.[64]

The CI should also be questioned about vehicles the subject has been seen driving or that are routinely located at the target location. Agents can conduct surveillance[65] and obtain license numbers of vehicles frequenting the residence or business.[66] The information can serve to further corroborate the source's accounts of criminal activity.[67] The Supreme Court has recognized the value of corroborating the informant's tip by independent investigation.

10.3.6   Contraband to Be Seized

To maximize the effectiveness of a search warrant, the informant must be thoroughly questioned regarding the illegal items he has observed while inside the premises. Obviously, in a narcotics search warrant, the objects to be searched for are drugs. Because drugs are easily concealed, agents are allowed wider latitude in the extent of their search.[68]

Agents often get tunnel vision in their debriefing approach. A detective assigned to recover stolen motorcycles may debrief his informant only about the location of the stolen vehicles. The informant should also be questioned about other contraband items used or possessed within the premises to be searched.[69] A warrant directing agents to search only for motorcycles would not allow officers to open desk drawers.[70] If the informant reports having observed narcotics[71] on the premises in addition to the stolen motorcycles, drugs[72] should be listed as items to be seized.[73]

A thorough debriefing can also elicit information that will ensure that items having evidentiary value that might be overlooked will be included as items to be seized. Many criminal enterprises utilize traditional paper files or personal computers to track their business activity. Those items need to be identified as objects of the search.[74]

10.3.7   Officer Safety Issues

The full inquiry of what was observed inside the premises by the informant addresses valid officer safety issues. Many residences used for drug dealing are heavily fortified. Steel doors, bars across ordinary doors and windows, and booby traps are common. The entry team needs to be aware of any impediments to a fast, safe, and effective entry. A no-knock search warrant may be necessary[75] (see Appendixes 10B and 10C).

Some agencies have forms that include a full range of questions for the interviewing detective to ask the informant. The questions, combined with the detective's experience, can illicit far more detailed information than a rambling interview.

It must be determined what the informant's relationship with the suspect is and for how long they have been associated. The length of the relationship and type of relationship will have a bearing on the credibility of the informant's information. A live-in paramour should know more about a targeted residence than an occasional visitor.[76]

10.3.8   Search of Informant and Vehicle

A thorough search of the informant prior to the buy is the only method that reasonably ensures he does not supply the contraband himself. The size of the item the informant is instructed to purchase dictates the extent of the search. Many agencies require only a pat-down.[77] Others require a strip search, particularly when the informant is purchasing a concealable amount of drugs or other small item.[78] If that is the case, and policy dictates, body cavities should be checked: they can be used to conceal remarkable amounts of contraband.[79] An officer of the same sex as the CI should conduct the search.[80]

Many agents do not like strip-searching informants. Some agents resist the process because it is time-consuming. Others find the procedure distasteful. Officers have committed perjury when called to testify about the extent of their search, claiming a strip search was conducted when only a pat-down or less was employed. A former detective convicted of perjury in the Johnston murder testified, "I have never seen anyone searched before they go into a house [in a controlled buy]. I've never seen that done."[81]

The CI should be required to surrender the content of pockets or purse to the control agent until after the buy is completed.[82] Unless specifically authorized, the informant should not be allowed to carry a firearm during a controlled buy or while performing any police-supervised activity.[83]

Informants do not like to be searched. CIs with a "police buff" mentality find the procedure degrading. Some object to the search because it makes it either difficult or impossible to supply the drugs themselves instead of making the purchase from the target.[84]

A Schenectady, New York, county sheriff department informant was caught on an in-store video surveillance camera planting crack cocaine in a targeted smoke shop during a controlled buy. The camera caught him retrieving the drugs from his back pocket immediately before photographing their location with his cell phone for awaiting surveillance officers.[85] The store owner was arrested and held for three weeks before convincing prosecutors to view the video. The same informant had been used in seven earlier investigations, two resulting in convictions. A lawsuit filed by the store owner for unspecified damages is pending at this writing.

The informant's vehicle, if used to drive to the buy location, must also be thoroughly searched.[86] Agents should make every effort to determine whether there are concealed compartments in the vehicle.[87]

Probable cause requires the affiant to provide enough information, so there exists a fair probability of the existence of criminal activity at the location to be searched. The search of the informant and his vehicle serves to further that probability.[88] It allows the magistrate to make a practical, commonsense decision whether, given all the circumstances set forth in the affidavit, there is a fair probability that contraband or evidence of a crime will be found in a particular place.[89]

10.3.9   Funds Provided for the Purchase of Evidence

The case agent provides the informant with the funds for the purchase of evidence. The informant should sign a receipt for the money. The term *marked money* is often mistakenly used to describe the buy money. The currency is not marked. The serial numbers are recorded on a paper or memorialized in a report. Some agencies simply xerox the notes.[90]

Buy money, or official advanced funds (OAF),[91] is serialized for two purposes. During a search warrant, all funds discovered in the premises or on the person of the target are seized. The serial numbers on the seized funds are compared with the prerecorded notes used during the controlled buy. The discovery of official advanced funds during the execution of the search warrant is extremely damaging evidence.

The notes are also serialized to assist in recovery efforts in the event of theft by either the informant or the target of the investigation. Robbery is a common occurrence during a controlled-buy operation.[92] It is not unusual for informants to steal some or all of the official funds intended for the purchase of evidence or to keep some of the purchased drug evidence for themselves to use or to resell.

10.3.10   Recording Devices and Body Wires

The informant may be required to wear either a concealed recorder or a transmitter during the controlled buy.[93] The recording produced during the purchase is maintained as evidence. When properly utilized, concealed recorders produce a far superior recording than that produced via a concealed transmitter.

Generally, transmitters are used for the security of the individual wearing the device. The equipment allows monitoring agents to hear what occurs during the undercover meeting and to react accordingly. Unfortunately, body bugs are notoriously unreliable,[94] and if a recording is produced, it may be unintelligible.

Many informants are reluctant to wear body wires or recorders. They argue that the devices, if discovered by the target of the investigation, place them in a life-threatening situation. However, advances in technology have made the devices nearly undetectable.[95]

10.3.11   Suspect Searches Informant

If the suspect does conduct a search of the informant, he will not find a gun. Most agencies have policies that strictly ban informants from carrying a gun during an undercover operation. In the face of danger, CIs are entirely dependent on the body wire, their own wits, and the control agent's savvy for ensuring their survival.

An extremely close call for one informant was detailed in an article written by a journalist with the *Lexington Herald-Leader*:

A Richmond, Kentucky, police informant Tory Williams[96] was probably feeling pretty confident when his control agent wired him up with a concealed recorder in December 2008. He was being sent to make a third crack buy from Gus Thompson. His control agent was probably lulled into an unjustifiable comfort zone, since the other two buys had gone without incident.

There is no explanation for why Thompson became suspicious. Almost immediately after the CI entered the apartment he tore open the CI's shirt and discovered the recorder.[97]

Thompson pistol-whipped the CI, split open his head, broke a finger on one of his hands, and broke the other hand completely. The CI was beaten to the ground, where Thompson put the gun to his head, asking, "Tell me why I shouldn't shoot you?" The gun was loaded. According to the CI, Thompson racked two rounds through the chamber, making sure it was ready to fire.[98]

The CI testified that while on the floor he managed to pull his jacket over his head to help blunt the continuing blows. Somehow he managed to retrieve his cell phone and called his control agent,[99] who was surveilling the apartment a short distance away.

Police subdued Thompson without a shot being fired. He was sentenced to 150 months in prison: 18 months for each drug deal, 7 years for use of a firearm during a dope deal and a bonus 48 months for the violence of the attack against a government informant.

The prosecutor had urged the court to impose the extra four years because such "senseless violence could have a chilling effect" on the recruitment of informants. The sentencing judge agreed with the recommendation saying "Examples have to be made in some situations."[100]

10.3.12 Observe the Informant Entering and Exiting the Location

Once the informant and his vehicle have been searched, both must be surveilled until the operation is completed. Constant surveillance eliminates the possibility that the informant obtained contraband from any place other than the targeted location. The informant must be directed to make no stops en route to the buy location.[101]

The surveillance team should personally observe the informant prior to the buy. If that is not possible, they should be provided with a photograph of the CI. Surveillance agents are often given little more than a clothing and physical description of the informant. It is a mistake that can undermine the investigation.

Members of the control agent's team should establish pre-buy surveillance of the targeted address. The agent following the CI to the buy location is directed to maintain radio or cell-phone communication with the surveillance team. It is his job to alert them of the CI's impending arrival. The surveillance team must make every effort to observe the informant enter the targeted location.[102]

Agents must maintain surveillance of the premises until the informant exits. The CI should then be followed from the buy location to the predetermined meeting place. The surveillance team verifies that the informant met with no one from the time he departed the targeted address until the post-buy meeting occurs.[103]

Following the informant's departure, at least one agent should maintain short-term surveillance of the buy location. Accomplices and sources of supply are often identified through post-buy surveillance.[104]

The events observed during the surveillance should be memorialized in a report for the case file. The surveillance report should identify which agent observed each event during the controlled buy.[105]

10.3.13 Post-Buy Meeting and Informant Search

Upon arrival at the post-buy meeting, the informant is ordered to surrender the evidence and electronic equipment to the control agent.[106] Original containers holding drugs or other evidence may be submitted to the agency's laboratory for latent fingerprint examination.[107]

Once again, the informant must be thoroughly searched.[108] It is not unusual for informants to attempt to steal some of the buy money or evidence.[109] If the informant's vehicle was used to travel to the buy location, it should also be thoroughly searched.

10.3.14 Follow-Up Informant Debriefing and Statement

The informant must be debriefed following the purchase.[110] Obtaining the names and/or physical descriptions of all persons present and participating in the transaction is essential.

The amount and location of contraband observed during the controlled buy must be determined. The information assists in assessing the immediacy for obtaining the search warrant. Undue delay may allow the information to become stale[111] or for evidence to be sold or moved.

Many law enforcement agencies require the informant to provide a written statement. The practice memorializes in the informant's own words the events that occurred during the undercover purchase. The statement makes it more difficult for the recalcitrant CI to claim "witness amnesia"[112] in the unlikely event he is needed to testify at trial.

Federal law enforcement agencies each have their own policies on informant statements. As an example, the DEA requires a statement when the informant has provided information or has participated in any activity that may require his testimony. All relevant information must also be reported in the investigative report.[113] The DEA uses the following format[114]:

Heading: The heading should contain the informant's code number or code name, the date, time and location of the statement, the names of the agents taking the statement, and a brief description of the events covered.[115]

Body: The body of the statement should be in the informant's own words. If prepared by the agents for the informant, it should be reported in the body of the statement.[116]

Conclusion: The conclusion should state that the informant has read the foregoing statement consisting of __ pages, that he has initialed each page and all corrections, that it is true and correct to the best of his knowledge and belief, and that he gave the statement freely and voluntarily, without threats, coercion, or promises.[117]

Signatures: The agents sign all copies; the informant signs only the original.[118]

Agents routinely prepare statements for informants who are unable to write their account. The original statement should be signed by the CI and witnessed by two agents. The original is held in the informant's file.

State and local agencies have promulgated their own policies regarding informant statements. The practice appears more prevalent among departments that have become more sophisticated in the use of informants or have experienced difficulties in their use.[119] Informant statements and required undercover purchase procedures serve to inhibit if not prevent the rare police practice of inventing a CI for probable-cause purposes.

10.3.15   Search Warrant Affidavits

Each application for a search warrant is supported by a written affidavit prepared by the officer and signed and sworn to before an issuing magistrate. The affidavit requires the following information:

1. State the name and department, agency, or address of the affiant.
2. Identify specifically the items or property to be searched for and seized.
3. Name or describe with particularity the person or place to be searched.
4. Identify the owner, occupant, or possessor of the place to be searched.
5. Specify or describe the crime that has been or is being committed.
6. Set forth specifically the facts and circumstances that form the basis for the affiant's conclusion that there is probable cause to believe that the items or property identified are evidence or the fruit of a crime, or are contraband, or are expected to be otherwise unlawfully possessed or subject to seizure, and that these items or property are expected to be located on the particular person or at the particular place described.
7. Provide a brief summary of affiant's experience, education, and training.
8. If a "nighttime" search is requested (i.e., 10 p.m.–6 a.m.),[120] the affiant must provide additional reasonable cause for seeking permission to search in the nighttime.[121]

It is the job of the magistrate to determine whether the affiant officer has provided enough probable cause to support the issuance of the search warrant. Since 1983, the "totality of the circumstances test" remains the benchmark for Fourth Amendment purposes when determining whether probable cause exists based on an informant's information.[122] However, the constitutional law of some states is stricter. Those states require application of the *Aguilar-Spinelli*[123] two-prong test of an informant's knowledge and veracity when determining whether sufficient probable cause exists for the issuance of a search warrant. The basis of knowledge or "underlying circumstances" is the first prong, and reliability or veracity is the second prong of the test. Logging past instances of the reliability of the informant is essential in those jurisdictions (see Appendix A).

10.3.16   Attacking the Search-Warrant Affidavit: *Franks* Hearings

In 1978, the U.S. Supreme Court held in *Franks v. Delaware*[124] that defendants could challenge the veracity of affidavits for search warrants. Before that time, a defendant's ability to challenge the affiant's veracity in the affidavit in support of a search warrant varied from jurisdiction to jurisdiction.

Under *Franks*, there is a two-step process. First, the defendant must provide enough evidence to convince the court that a hearing is necessary. If the defendant satisfies the initial burden, a hearing is held. If the defendant shows intentional or reckless falsehoods that, if stricken from the affidavit, remove probable cause, then the search warrant must be voided and the fruits of the search excluded. The Supreme Court in *Franks* explained the standard this way:

> In the event that at that hearing the allegation of perjury or reckless disregard is established by the defendant by a preponderance of the evidence, and, with the affidavit's false material set to one side, the affidavit's remaining content is insufficient to establish probable cause, the search warrant must be voided and the fruits of the search excluded to the same extent as if probable cause was lacking on the face of the affidavit.[125]

In *Franks,* the Court limited the attack on false affidavits, stating, "The deliberate falsity or reckless disregard whose impeachment is permitted today is only that of the affiant, not of any non-governmental informant."[126] When a defendant seeks a *Franks* hearing, the issue is the good faith of the affiant.

When a police officer is furnished false information by a CI and that information is later discovered to be false, there is no violation of *Franks*.[127] As long as the affiant is not aware of the falsity of the informant's statement, nor has any reason to doubt the accuracy of the information, there is no recklessness or intentional deceit on the part of the affiant. Thus, the "substantial preliminary showing" required for a *Franks* hearing is not established.[128]

However, police cannot insulate themselves from falsehoods. For example, in a pre-*Franks* case, the Supreme Court held that "the police could not insulate one officer's deliberate misstatement merely by relaying it through an officer affiant personally ignorant of its falsity."[129]

The court in *United States v. Cortina*[130] was confronted with a search that occurred only because a Federal Bureau of Investigation agent lied to the magistrate. The district court had determined that the agent's testimony was "incredible" and that "J. Edgar Hoover would be rolling over in his mausoleum if he heard that man in this courtroom."[131]

The court found that

> When he lied to the magistrate, he committed two offenses: one against the constitutional guarantee against unreasonable searches, and a second against

326 Informants, Cooperating Witnesses, and Undercover Investigations

the judicial system. In addition to the consequences flowing from the lack of probable cause, this second injury to the judiciary itself requires this court to guarantee that none of the tainted evidence reaches the courtroom. Our responsibility to uphold the integrity of the judicial system therefore requires the suppression of all the evidence resulting from the search as to all defendants.[132]

Even more troublesome to the court was that the agent's offense was committed against the court itself. "The violation here is particularly insidious because it is difficult to uncover misrepresentations in an affidavit underlying a search warrant. The information needed to prove such assertions false is peculiarly within the hands of the government."[133]

In 1986, the court held in *United States v. Reivich*[134] that, based on *Franks*, an individual might challenge a facially insufficient affidavit on the ground that it contains deliberate or reckless falsehoods or deliberate omissions. To prevail, however, the challenger must show

1. That the police omitted facts with the intent to make, or in reckless disregard of whether they thereby made, the affidavit misleading.
2. That the affidavit if supplemented by the omitted information would not have been sufficient to support a finding of probable cause.[135]

Omissions of facts are not misrepresentations unless they cast doubt on the existence of probable cause.[136]

10.4 Non-Traditional Search Warrants

10.4.1 Telephonic Search Warrants

Telephonic search warrants, as the name implies, are obtained with an oral affidavit taken under oath and recorded for later transcription. They are generally obtained at night when courts are closed or when an issuing magistrate is otherwise unavailable.

Parties to the recorded telephone call are usually an assistant state attorney, the officer/affiant, and the judge. Some jurisdictions permit the use of fax or e-mail to obtain the warrant.

10.4.2 Anticipatory Search Warrants

Anticipatory search warrants are issued conditioned upon the happening of a particular event or triggering condition. They are frequently used in controlled deliveries of drugs to a particular address.[137] "[T]he fact that the contraband is not 'presently located at the place described in the warrant' is immaterial, so long as 'there is probable cause to believe that it will be there when the search warrant is executed'."[138] In the case of a controlled delivery, the triggering condition is the delivery of the package. Agents generally wait for a short period after the delivery to allow the recipient to open or try to conceal the package to demonstrate scienter or guilty knowledge.

10.4.3 Sneak-and-Peek Search Warrants

A sneak-and-peek search warrant, also called a covert-entry search warrant or a surreptitious-entry search warrant, is a search warrant authorizing the law enforcement officers executing it to effect physical entry into private premises without the owner's or the occupant's permission or knowledge and to clandestinely search the premises. Executing a sneak-and-peek warrant usually requires a stealth entry that is authorized by the warrant.[139] To obtain a sneak-and-peek warrant, the government must give the court reasonable cause to believe that providing notice of the search would have an adverse result.[140] Jurisdictions vary on whether items may be seized or only noted, photographed, or copied.[141]

10.5 Keeping the Confidential Informant Confidential

In *Roviaro v. United States*, the U.S. Supreme Court articulated the following balancing test to dictate when the government must disclose the identity of the CI:

> We believe that no fixed rule with respect to disclosure is justifiable. The problem is one that calls for balancing the public interest in protecting the flow of information against the individual's right to prepare one's defense. Whether a proper balance renders nondisclosure erroneous must depend on the particular circumstances of each case, taking into consideration the crime charged, the possible defenses, the possible significance of the informer's testimony, and other relevant factors.[142]

The Supreme Court further emphasized that protecting an informant's identity serves an important public interest in that it encourages citizens to supply the government with information concerning criminal activity.[143] A defendant may satisfy his burden and overcome the privilege by demonstrating that the informant is a material witness or that his or her testimony is crucial to his case. "That the government has this privilege is well established, and its soundness cannot be questioned."[144]

Appendix 10A: Affidavit for Search Warrant

AFFIDAVIT FOR SEARCH WARRANT
Commonwealth of Virginia   VA. CODE § 19.2-54

The undersigned Applicant states under oath:

1. A search is requested in relation to an offense substantially described as follows:

[ ] CONTINUED ON ATTACHED SHEET

2. The place, person or thing to be searched is described as follows:

[ ] CONTINUED ON ATTACHED SHEET

3. The things or persons to be searched for are described as follows:

[ ] CONTINUED ON ATTACHED SHEET

(OVER)

FORM DC-338 (MASTER, PAGE ONE OF TWO) 07/12

FILE NO.

AFFIDAVIT FOR SEARCH WARRANT

APPLICANT:

NAME

TITLE (IF ANY)

ADDRESS

Certified to Clerk of .... Circuit Court

CITY OR COUNTY

on ....
        DATE

....
TITLE   SIGNATURE

Original Delivered [ ] in person [ ] by certified mail
[ ] by electronically transmitted facsimile
[ ] by use of filing/security procedures
defined in the Uniform Electronic Transactions Act

to Clerk of .... Circuit Court
CITY OR COUNTY WHERE EXECUTED

on ....
        DATE

....
TITLE   SIGNATURE

Complete only if different than above:

Copy delivered [ ] in person [ ] by certified mail
[ ] by electronically transmitted facsimile
[ ] by use of filing/security procedures
defined in the Uniform Electronic Transactions Act

to Clerk of .... Circuit Court
CITY OR COUNTY OF ISSUANCE

on ....
        DATE

....
TITLE   SIGNATURE

4. The material facts constituting probable cause that the search should be made are:

5. The object, thing or person searched for constitutes evidence of the commission of such offense.

6. [ ] I have personal knowledge of the facts set forth in this affidavit OR

7. [ ] I was advised of the facts set forth in this affidavit in whole or in part, by a person whose credibility or the reliability of the information may be determined from the following facts:

The statements above are true and accurate to the best of my knowledge and belief.

_____
APPLICANT

_____
TITLE OF APPLICANT

Subscribed and sworn to before me this day.

_____
DATE AND TIME

[ ] CLERK   [ ] MAGISTRATE   [ ] JUDGE

FORM DC-338 (MASTER, PAGE TWO OF TWO) 10/11

Appendix 10B: DEA Raid Execution Process

The DEA Tactical Training Unit currently teaches a raid execution technique that is referred to as the "snake" method, and that generally involves a six-person entry team (not including the perimeter team). This technique—or similar variations of it—has been adopted by many law enforcement agencies for use in drug raids because of its simplicity, safety, and effectiveness. For most raid situations, the DEA Tactical Training Unit advocates the use of speed, surprise, and "violence of action" in order to secure as much of a structure as possible within approximately six to ten seconds after gaining entry. After about ten seconds have elapsed—or at any earlier point in time that the entry team knows or believes that they have lost the element of surprise (thereby affording occupants time to gather weapons or to hide)—we suggest that the raid process *slow down* and that the remainder of the structure be cleared methodically by moving from one area to another using all available cover/concealment and applying fundamental room clearing tactics (e.g., "slicing the pie," "quick peeks," "limited penetration," and the use of portable mirrors and ballistic shields if necessary). The success of this technique is dependent upon a greater degree of teamwork and "raid discipline" than has historically been applied in many raids conducted by drug law enforcement agents. Simply stated, raid execution tactics *must* improve in order to overcome the challenge of drug traffickers who are becoming increasingly willing to resist and/or to kill law enforcement personnel.

The "snake" technique is based upon a very fundamental principle: each entry team member covers the person in front of himself/herself, and team members never work alone.

The following is a synopsis of each member's role in the "snake" formation:

The #1 person on the entry team primarily dictates the team's pace and direction of travel throughout the structure and, therefore, can be thought of as the "head" of the snake.

The #1 is the first person to enter each area/room and must aim his/her weapon at "danger areas" upon approaching and entering them (which includes the approach to the initial entry point). Note: If team members 2 through 6 cannot safely aim their weapons at danger areas (e.g., when moving along a narrow hallway behind #1), they should carry weapons in the "low ready" position (pointed *downward)*. All entry team members *must* keep their fingers off the triggers of their weapons until they *intend* to fire at a threat.

The #2 person follows #1 into *all* areas/rooms to be cleared. Person #2 simply keys off of #1 and covers in the direction that #1 does *not* cover. For example, if #1 dynamically (rapidly) enters a bedroom and turns toward the right, then #2 follows immediately and turns/covers toward the left. This procedure eliminates the need to "predetermine" which direction #1 and #2 will turn/cover upon entering rooms.) Unless silence is required, #2 should loudly announce, "Clear … coming out!" prior to exiting rooms that other team members have not accessed.

The #3 person covers #2. Person #3 must decide, based upon the configuration of the structure, where to position himself/herself to assist #2 and to cover other uncleared areas. For example, #3 might choose to enter a bedroom with #1 and #2, and then cover the exterior hallway from within that room. Note: *All* entry team members should avoid positioning themselves in hallways and stairways without sufficient cover and must *never* stop or hesitate when moving through doorways.

The #4 person in the formation is the agent in charge of the entry team ("team leader"). Person #4 covers #3 and is primarily responsible for announcing the raid team's identity and purpose (e.g., "DEA … search warrant!") as they enter and move throughout the structure and ensures that the team clears all potential danger areas. After the entire structure has been secured, the team leader is responsible for notifying the perimeter team (by portable radio or some other means) that the location is secure and/or that the entry team is exiting the structure. (No perimeter team member shall enter prior to this notification; the use of multiple entry points is strongly discouraged.)

The #5 person may be a breacher at the entry point (if #6 needs assistance in gaining entry), may be called upon for handcuffing, searching, or controlling occupants, and covers #4. Note: Agents should apply the "contact/cover" principle when arresting occupants. (One agent should cover an arrestee with a weapon, while one or more agents holster their weapons and physically control, handcuff, and search an arrestee.)

The #6 person is the primary breacher at the entry point, may also be called upon for the handcuffing, etc., of occupants, covers #5, and may be responsible for rear security.

Note: After #6 has breached the initial entry point, he/she should step aside (moving the entry tool, if any, out of the doorway) and allow #1 through #5 to enter the structure ahead of himself/herself. Note: If feasible, agents should consider attempting ruses to gain entry. (For example, by simply knocking on the door and awaiting a response, an occupant may open the door. This will allow the entry team to immediately detain/arrest one occupant and also gain entry more easily.)

The six-person entry team moves (whether it be quickly or slowly) only in the direction that #1 dictates, generally clearing all danger areas along the way. If, for example, a potential danger area is bypassed, the agent in charge may stop the team and direct them to clear that area. This procedure prevents the separation of the entry team within a structure, thereby eliminating the possibility of team members unexpectedly confronting fellow agents and potentially discharging weapons at each other. As with any technique or tactic, the "snake" method can be adapted depending upon varying factors, such as the number of agents available to conduct the raid, the nature of the situation, the size or characteristics of the structure to be raided, or the number of occupants inside the location. (For example, it may be necessary to increase/decrease the number of agents assigned to the entry team or to "target" a specific room within a structure to quickly secure it prior to clearing the remaining areas.)

The entry team should ideally consist of personnel who are familiar with each other and who have received similar raid execution training. All entry team members must follow the raid plan, be able to think and react quickly and appropriately under stress, be able to apply safe and effective raid tactics, and be highly proficient in the use of firearms and the application of defensive tactics. The group supervisor or agent in charge of conducting a raid should, as time permits, hold a postraid meeting so that entry and perimeter team members can discuss and constructively analyze the performance of the entire raid team.

Appendix 10C: Operational Plan Format

Date_____

I. SITUATION
  A. Type of operation (check appropriate area)
    1. Buy–Bust_____
    2. Search–Arrest Warrant_____
      a. Court/Judge_____
      b. Warrant #_____
    3. Surveillance_____
    4. Other_____
  B. Address of location (s)
    1. _____
    2. _____
    3. _____
    4. _____
  C. Description of location (s) (attached diagram)
    1. _____
    2. _____
    3. _____
    4. _____
  D. Suspect (s) (name, description, prior criminal background)
    1. _____
    2. _____
    3. _____

    E. Possible weapons (possessed or available to suspects)
        1. _____
        2. _____
    F. Countersurveillance (possible description of vehicles, etc.)
        1. _____
        2. _____

II. MISSION

    A. Background Information (obtained from informant, surveillances, investigation, etc.)

_____
_____
_____

    B. Brief overview of plan

_____
_____
_____

III. PERSONNEL INVOLVED

    A. Undercover personnel
        Name, Vehicle

_____
_____
_____

    B. Assisting personnel
        Name Vehicle Call Letters

_____
_____
_____

IV. PERSONNEL ASSIGNMENTS AND INSTRUCTIONS

    A. Assignments
        1. Containment Personnel (list name, specific locations, i.e., rear door, side, etc.)
            Names, Location

_____
_____
_____

        2. Entry personnel
            Names, Location

_____
_____
_____

3. Surveillance personnel
   Names, Location

   _____

   _____

   _____

B. Instructions (describe entire plan—duties of U/C, search team, entry team, money man, surveillance, etc.)

   _____

   _____

   _____

V. COMMUNICATION AND LOGISTICS
A. Communication
   1. Radio frequency_____, cell phone numbers
   2. Code designations (i.e., primary and secondary locations, etc.)

   _____

   _____

   3. Emergency signals (arrest signal, etc.)

   _____

B. Logistics
   1. Equipment required (raid jackets, protective vests, binoculars, etc.)

   _____

   2. Equipment issued (list items and to whom issued)

   _____

   _____

VI. ARREST PROCEDURES
A. Location of booking

   _____

   _____

B. Prisoner transportation (indicate who will transport)

   _____

   _____

Note: For security reasons, plans should be collected at the end of each operation and destroyed. File copies should be retained for inclusion in the case folder.

Endnotes

1. See *Ortega v. United States*, 897 F. Supp. 771, 780 (S.D.N.Y. 1995).
2. U.S. Const., Amend. IV.
3. Target offender: The person whom law enforcement personnel suspects will be implicated by the activities of a confidential informant.

4. *Guidelines For Florida State and Local Law Enforcement Agencies In Dealing With Confidential Informants (As Adopted By The Florida Police Chiefs Association, The Florida Sheriffs Association,* The State Law Enforcement Chiefs Association, and The Florida Department of Law Enforcement), March 2009.

5. See *Johnson v. United States,* 333 U.S. 10, 14, 68 S. Ct. 367, 92 L. Ed. 436 (1948).

6. See *Steagald v. United States,* 451 U.S. 204, 212–213 (1981).

7. Burkoff, J., *Search Warrant Law Deskbook* § 5.2 (West Group).

8. See *State v. Wiley,* 366 N.W.2d 265, 269 (Minn., 1985).

9. *Illinois v. Gates,* 462 U.S. 213, 238 (1983). See *Alabama v. White.* 496 U.S. 325 (1990); *United States v. Sokolow,* 490 U.S. 1, 7 (1989); *New York v. P.J. Video. Inc.,* 475 U.S. 868 (1986).

10. See *Shadwick v. Tampa,* 407 U.S. 345, 349 (1972). See also *United States v. Leon,* 468 U.S. 897, 914 (1984); *Connally v. Georgia,* 429 U.S. 245, 246 (1977).

11. Chief Magistrate, Cobb County, GA, quoted in M. Curriden, "Secret Threat to Justice," *Nat. L.J.* (February 20, 1995), p. 29.

12. See *People v. David,* 326 N. W.2d 485, 487–488 (Mich. Ct. App., 1982); *United States v. Guitterez,* 983 F. Supp. 905, 919 (N.D. Cat., 1998); *State v. Newton,* 489 S.E.2d 147, 151 (Ga. Ct. App., 1997); *United States v. Wagner,* 989 F.2d 69, 75 (2nd Cir., 1993); *People v. Broilo,* 228 N.W.2d 456, 458 (Mich. Ct. App., 1975); *State v. Gillespie,* 503 N.W.2d 612, 616 (Iowa Ct. App., 1993); *People v. Acevedo,* 572 N.Y.S.2d 101, 102 (App. Div., 1991); *State v. Spallino,* 556 So. 2d 953, 955 n.1 (La. Ct. App.1990).

13. *Sgro v. United States,* 287 U.S. 206, 210 (1932).

14. Cato Institute, "Botched Paramilitary Police Raids: An Epidemic of Isolated Incidents," November 30, 2006. See Aamot, G., "Botched Raid Terrorizes Minnesota Family," Associated Press, December 24, 2007.

15. Ibid.

16. See *Boyd v. United States,* 116 U.S. 616, 625 (1986).

17. *The Federal Bureau of Investigation's Compliance with the Attorney General's Investigative Guidelines,* U.S. Department of Justice, Office of the Inspector General (September 2005).

18. See Testimony from Professor Alexandra Natapoff before the House of Representatives Joint Hearing on Law Enforcement Confidential Informant Practices, July 19, 2007.

19. Benner, L.A. and Samarkos, C.T., "Searching for Narcotics in San Diego: Preliminary Findings from the San Diego Search Warrant Project," *California Western Law Review,* 36, 239, Spring 2000.

20. Visser, S., "Ex-Cop: Officers Routinely Lied to Obtain Search Warrants," *Atlanta Journal-Constitution,* May 8, 2008; Waren, B., "Prosecutors: Officers Admitted Lying about Botched Drug Raid," *Atlanta Journal-Constitution,* May 8, 2008.

21. Gaffney, S., "Police Sergeant Faked Drug Warrants," (McAllen, TX) *Monitor,* July 10, 2008; Curriden, M., "Secret Threat to Justice," *Nat. L.J.,* February 20, 1995 (examination of 1,212 warrants in four selected cities).

22. Visser, S., "Prosecution rests: FBI agent says police officer feared being labeled a rat," *Atlanta Journal-Constitution,* May 13, 2008.

23. Department of Justice Report, "Three Atlanta Police Officers Charged in Fatal Shooting of Elderly Atlanta Woman," April 26, 2007 (finding that police planted three baggies of marijuana in woman's home following shooting).

24. Cray, E., *The Enemy in the Streets: Police Malpractice in America*, Doubleday, New York, 1972.

25. Burkoff, J., Search Warrant Law Deskbook § 5.2 (West).

26. Informant Interaction: *Use of a CI to Make an Undercover Buy*, DEA Office of Training, Quantico, VA; See *United States v. Khownsavanh*, 113 F.3d 279, 285 (1st Cir. 1997), quoting *Terry v. Ohio*, 392 U.S. 1, 21–22 (1968).

27. Informant Interaction, *Use of a CI to Make an Undercover Buy*, DEA Office of Training, Quantico, VA.

28. *Narcotics Investigator's Manual, Undercover Operations* (1974), (Produced by U.S. Drug Enforcement Administration and Bureau of Operations and Research, International Association of Chiefs of Police.)

29. *Street-Level Narcotics Enforcement*, Bureau of Justice Assistance, April 11, 1990.

30. *Undercover Operations and Informant Handling Student Manual*, New York State Division of Criminal Justice, Section 3.5, December 2007.

31. Hight, J.E., "Avoiding the Informant Trap: A Blueprint for Control," *FBI Law Enforcement Bulletin*, November 1988.

32. *Informant Interaction, Use of a CI to Make an Undercover Buy*, DEA Office of Training, Quantico, VA.

33. Ibid.

34. Ibid.

35. Ibid.

36. Ibid.; See *United States v. Tirinkian*, 502 F. Supp. 620, 630 (D.N.D. 1980) (Officers corroborate informant by their own observations).

37. Ibid.

38. Ibid.

39. Ibid.

40. Ibid.

41. See *United States v. Sanchez*, 689 F.2d 508, 513 (5th Cir. 1982) (every detail corroborated).

42. See *Stanley v. State*, 19 Md. App. 507, 313 A.2d 847, 851 (1974).

43. See *United States v. Harris*, 403 U.S. 573 (1971); *People v. Cooks*, 141 Cal. App. 3d 224, 190 Cal. Rptr. 211, 261, *cert. denied*, 464 U.S. 1046 (1983); *State v. Burton*, 416 So. 2d. 73, 74–75 (La. 1982) (disapproved by *Illinois v. Gates*, 462 U.S. 213 reh'g denied (1983); *United States v. Bush*, 647 F.2d 357, 363 (3d Cir. 1981); *People v. Cooks*, 141 Cal. App. 3d 224, 190 Cal. Rptr. 211, 261, *cert. denied*, 464 U.S. 1046 (1983); *Showmaker v. State*, 52 Md. App. 463,451 A.2d 127, 134-35 (1982); *Commonwealth v. Salvaggio*, 307 Pa. Super. 385, 453 A.2d 637, 641 (1982); *People v. Kilmer*, 87 App. Div. 2d 949, 451 N.Y.S.2d 244, 245 (1982).

44. Snow, R.L., *Terrorists Among Us: The Militia Threat*, at 11, Da Capo Press (2002) (An unwritten but ironclad rule exists in law enforcement … never trust an informant); R. Settle, *Police Informers: Negotiation and Power*, at 196, Federation Press (Australia) (1995) (Never trust any criminal, more particularly, never trust an informant); Dorn, Nicholas, *Trafficker: Drug Markets and Law Enforcement*, at 23 Routledge Publishing 1992(Great Britain) (never trust an informant).

45. Denver Police Department Operations Manual, Section 307.08.

46. See Integrity Assurance Notes, Drug Enforcement Administration, Planning and Inspection Division, Vol. 1. No.1.

47. See *Thompson v. State*, 16 Md. App. 560, 298 A.2d 458 (1973); *United States v. Harris*, 403 U.S. 573 (1971); *People v. Rodriguez*, 52 N.Y.2d 483, 438 N.Y.S.2d 754, 420 N.E.2d 946 (1981); *State v. Lair*, 95 Wash. 2d 706, 630 P.2d 427 (1981).

48. *Thompson v. State*, 16 Md. App. 560, 298 A.2d 458, 461–62 (profit motive of CI provided circumstantial degree of reliability).

49. *Wesley v. State*, 162 Ga. App. 737, 293 S.E.2d 27, 28 (1982) (informant did not reveal how he knew facts he reported).

50. "2 More Sue City of Lowell Over Use of Informants," *Lowell Sun*, September 20, 2013.

51. See *Steel v. United States*, 267 U.S. 498, 503 (1925).

52. Cincinnati Police Department, *Confidential Informant Management and Control Manual*, 12. 131 M (1) (a).

53. "Commando Unit Mistake Leads to Terror for Minneapolis Family, Informant Got the Address Wrong," Associated Press, December 18, 2007.

54. Balko, R., Cato Institute Policy Paper, "Overkill: The Rise of Paramilitary Police Raids"; See also Cato Institute's interactive map of botched raids, www.Cato.org/raidmap/index.php?type=1.

55. *Denver Post*, July 16, 1993.

56. *United States v. Dancy*, 947 F.2d 1232 (5th Cir. 1991).

57. *United States v. Barnes*, 909 F.2d 1059, 1068 n.ll (7th Cir. 1990).

58. DEA Office of Training, Informant Interaction, Use of a CI to Make an Undercover Buy.

59. *United States v. Harris*, 403 U.S. 573 (1971) (the officer's own knowledge can serve to corroborate the informant's account).

60. See *United States v. Ventresca*, 380 U.S. 102, 110 (1965); *Illinois v. Andreas*, 463 U.S. 765, 771 n.5 (1983). See also *United States v. Tirinkian*, 502 F. Supp. 620, 627 (D.N.D. 1980).

61. *United States v. Ordonez*, 737 F.2d 793, 807 (9th Cir. 1984) (detective obtains telephone subscriber information).

62. 18 USC 2703(c).

63. 18 USC 2703(c).

64. See *People v. Simmons*, 569 N.E.2d 591 (Ill. App. 2d Dist 1991); *State v. Taylor*, 889 S.W.2d 124 (Mo. Ct. App. 1994); *Mayfield v. State*, 800 S.W.2d 932 (Tex. App. 1990).

65. See *United States v. Ordonez*, 737 F.2d 793, 808 (detective obtaining photograph through surveillance of suspect).

66. See *United States v. Luck*, 560 F.Supp. 258 (N.D. Ga. 1983) (officers may supplement tip by surveillance).

67. *Illinois v. Gates*, 462 U.S. 213, 241 (1983) (recognizing the value of corroboration of details by police investigation); See *Jones v. United States*, 362 U.S. 257 (1960); *Draper v. United States*, 358 U.S. 307 (1959); See *State v. Amerman*, 581 A.2d 19, 33–36 (Md. Ct. Spec. App. 1990); But See *People v. Paquin*, 811 P.2d 394, 398 (Colo. 1991) ("While police corroboration of significant aspects of an informant's tip is an important factor in the probable cause calculus ... it is not an indispensable component of the probable cause determination...").

68. See *Horton v. California*, 496 U.S. 128, 141 (1990); *Maryland v. Buie*, 494 U.S. 325, 330 (1990); *Arizona v. Hicks*, 480 U.S. 321 (1987); *Texas v. Brown*, 460 U.S. 730, 741–44 (1983); *Coolidge v. New Hampshire*, 403 U.S. 443, 466–71 (1971).

69. See *Stanford v. Texas*, 379 U.S. 476, 486 (1965); *Steel v. United States*, 267 U.S. 498, 504 (1925).

70. *United States v. Klein*, 565 F.2d 183 (1st Cir. 1977) (controlled substances); See *United States v. Rome*, 809 F.2d 665 (10th Cir. 1987).

71. See *United States v. Lunt*, 732 F. Supp. 599, 603 (W.D. Pa. 1990).

72. See *Morris v. United States*, 507 U.S. 988, 977 F.2d 677, 680–82 (1st Cir. 1992), *cert. denied*, 113 S. Ct. 1588 (1993).

73. *State v. Herbst*, 395 N.W.2d 399 (Minn. App. (1986) (warrant containing no description of narcotics to be seized found defective). See *Massachusetts v. Sheppard*, 468 U.S. 981 (1984).

74. *Searching and Seizing Computers in Obtaining Electronic Evidence in Criminal Investigations,* Computer Crime Section, Criminal Division, United States Department of Justice, July 2002.

75. See *United States v. Ramirez*, 118 S. Ct. 992 (1998) (The Fourth Amendment does not require a stricter standard for "no-knock" entries that result in the destruction of property).

76. *FBI Law Enforcement Bulletin*, September 1993, at 11.

77. See *Wright v. State*, 836 N.E. 2d 283 (Ind.App. 2005); *Flaherty v. State.* 443 N.E. 2d 340 (Ind. App. 1982); *Whirley v. State* 408 N.E. 2d 629 (Ind. App. 1980).

78. *Narcotics Investigator's Manual*, "Undercover Operations" Ch. 10, p.100. (Produced by U.S. Drug Enforcement Administration and Bureau of Operations and Research, International Association of Chiefs of Police, 1974)

79. Roach, M., *Gulp: Adventures in the Alimentary Canal*, Norton and Company, 2013; Describing the practice of hooping (inmates concealing contraband in their rectum) One inmate earned the nickname "OD," for Office Depot, by transporting (in his rectum) "two boxes of staples, a pencil sharpener, sharpener blades and three jumbo binder rings."

80. Olson, M., "14 More Baltimore Prison Officers Indicted in Jail Sex Scandal for Peddling Drugs and Phones for Notorious Gang by Smuggling Them in Their Vaginas," *Georgia Daily News*, November 24, 2013. See, Cincinnati Police Department, *Confidential Informant Management and Control,* and Ohio Revised Code 2933.32-Body Cavity and Strip Search.

81. Visser, S., "Ex-Cop: Officers Routinely Lied to Obtain Search Warrants," *Atlanta Journal-Constitution*, May 8, 2008

82. See *Iddings v. State*, 772 N.E. 2d 1006 (Ind. Ct. App. 2002).

83. See ATF, *Investigative Priorities, Procedures and Techniques Manual*, Ch. D, Section 36 (j) (for an example of informant firearm restrictions).

84. Department of Justice Press Release, September 5, 2002, "Former Dallas Police Department Drug Informant Pleads Guilty to Civil Rights Violations for Planting Fake Drugs." See Warren, Beth, "Prosecutor: Officer Admitted Lying about Botched Drug Raid," *Atlanta Journal-Constitution*, February 27, 2008.

85. Tucker, A., "Scotia Business Owner Cleared of Drug Charges by Surveillance Video, Informant Missing," *ABC News*, July 12, 2013.

86. See *United States v. Cuomo*, 479 F.2d 688 (2d Cir 1973).

87. See *United States v. Conception-Ledesma*, 447 F.3d 1307 (10 Cir. 2006).

88. *Illinois v. Gates*, 462 U.S. 213, 238, 246 (1983), *rejecting Aguilar v. Texas*, 378 U.S. 108 (1964), and *Spinelli v. United States*, 393 U.S. 410 (1969). See also *Massachusetts v. Upton*, 466 U.S. 727, 733 (1984). See, however, *Texas v.*

Brown, 460 U.S. 730,742 (1983) (plurality opinion of Rehnquist, J.) (probable cause "does not demand any showing that such a belief be correct or more likely true than false"); *United States v. Wayne*, 903 F.2d 1188, 1196 (8th Cir. 1990) (same).

89. See *Illinois v. Gates*, 462 U.S. 213, 238 (1983); See also *Alabama v. White.* 496 U.S. 325 (1990); *United States v. Sokolow.* 490 U.S. 1, 7 (1989); *New York v. P.J. Video.* Inc. 475 U.S. 868 (1986).
90. *Informant Interaction, Use of a CI to Make an Undercover Buy*, DEA Office of Training, Quantico, VA.
91. *DEA Agents Manual* Ch. 61.
92. Gootman, E., "Police Say Detective, After Drug Buy, Killed Man Trying to Rob Him," *New York Times*, October 21, 2000.
93. *On Lee v. United States*, 343 U.S. 747 (1952).
94. Portman, J., "Experts Examine Questionable Decisions that Left Rachael Hoffman Dead," *Tallahassee Democrat*, August 3, 2008 (concealed transmitter fails during drug buy, informant robbed and murdered).
95. DTC Communications Surveillance Technology website "Hear all Evil, See all Evil, Track all Evil."
96. Names changed.
97. Warren, J., "Richmond Man Gets 12½ Years in Prison for Pistol-Whipping Informant," *Lexington Herald-Leader*, July 2, 2009.
98. Ibid.
99. Ibid.
100. Ibid.
101. *Informant Interaction, Use of a CI to Make an Undercover Buy*, DEA Office of Training, Quantico, VA.
102. Ibid.
103. Fuer, A., "Officers Arrests Put Spotlight on Police Use of Informants," *New York Times*, January 27, 2008 (quoting NYPD Major Case Squad detective regarding controlled-buy procedures).
104. Ibid.
105. See *United States v. Hodge*, 539 F2d 898.
106. *Undercover Operations and Informant Handling Student Manual*, New York State Division of Criminal Justice, Section 3.5, December 2007.
107. *Latent Print Evidence Field Manual*, New Jersey State Police Special and Technical Services Section,V.4 (A)(B)(C) p.12.
108. See *United States v. McMillan*, 508 F.2d 101, 106 (1974).
109. Hepler, A., "Defendants: Informant Stole from Police," *Mount Vernon News*, January 4, 2008 (informant kept portion of buy money and drugs purchased from target).
110. *Informant Interaction, Use of a CI to Make an Undercover Buy*, DEA Office of Training, Quantico, VA.
111. See *United States v. Miles*, 772 F.2d 613, 616 (10th Cir. 1985), *cert. denied*, 476 U.S. 1158 reh'g denied, 478 U.S. 1032 (1986) (considering totality of evidence, warrant was not stale; property was shown to be stolen only 2 weeks before, so it was likely still there; omission of when informant saw it thus not fatal. Where the object held does not have a ready market or has an enduring personal use, the standards of staleness are somewhat relaxed. *Gerdes v. State*, 319 N.W.2d

710, 713 (Minn. 1982); *Evans v. State*, 161 Ga. App. 468, 288 S.E.2d 726, 729, appeal after remand, 166 Ga. App. 602, 305 S.E.2d 121 (1982). (that defendant was chopping up cars ten days ago was not stale); *United States v. McCall*, 740 F.2d 1331, 1336-37 (4th Cir. 1984) (two month delay in looking for gun; found to be close question, but nature of gun—being governmental property—made it probable it was still there); *United States v. Shomo*, 786 F.2d 981, 984 (10th Cir. 1986) (ten days in gun case not stale); *United States v. Batchelder*, 824 F.2d 563 (7th Cir. 1987) (information nine months old concerning the purchase of silencer was not stale since affiant indicated that of twenty-one similar searches, nineteen resulted in seizures).

112. *United States v. Di Caro*, 772 F.2d 1314 (7th Cir. 1985); dealing with "witness amnesia."

113. *DEA Agents Manual* Ch. 66.

114. Ibid.

115. Ibid.

116. Ibid.

117. Ibid.

118. Ibid.

119. See *People v. Lucente*, 506 N.E.2d 1269 (HI. 1987), (Court skeptical about detective abandoning informant records).

120. Jurisdictions vary on hours considered nighttime.

121. Pennsylvania Criminal Code, Rule 206, Contents of Application for Search Warrant.

122. *Illinois v. Gates*, 462 U.S. 213 (1983).

123. *Aguilar v. Texas*, 378 U.S. 108 (1964); *Spinelli v. United States*, 393 U.S. 410 (1969).

124. *Franks v. Delaware*, 438 U.S. 154 (1978).

125. *Franks v. Delaware*, 438 U.S. 154 (1978); See *United States v. Carlson*, 697 F.2d 231, 238 (8th Cir. 1983); *United States v. Hole*, 564 F.2d 298, 302 (9th Cir. 1977); *United States v. Botero*, 589 F.2d 430, 433 (9th Cir. 1978).

126. *Franks*, 438 U.S.171. See *Mosher Steel-Virginia v. Tieg*, 327 S.E.2d 87, 92 Va., 1985).

127. *United States v. Fawole*, 785 F.2d 1141 (4th Cir. 1986).

128. *United States v. McDonald*, 723 F.2d 1288, 1293 (7th Cir. 1983); *United States v. Southard*, 700 F.2d 1 (1st Cir. 1983).

129. *Rugendorf v. United States*, 376 U.S. 528 (1964).

130. *United States v. Cortina*, 630 F.2d 1207, 1213 (1980).

131. Ibid.

132. Ibid.

133. *Cortina*, 630 F.2d 1216.

134. *United States v. Reivich*, 793 F.2d 957, 960 (8th Cir. 1986).

135. Ibid.

136. See *United States v. Parker*, 836 F.2d 1080, 1083 (8th Cir. 1987).

137. See *United States v. Grubbs* 547 U.S. 90, 93–97 (2006).

138. *United States v. Lowe*, 575 F.2d 1193, 1194 (6th Cir. 1978); See *United States v. Dornhofer*, 859 F.2d 1195, 1198 (4th Cir. 1988).

139. From Georgia Defender September 2002; See Corr, "Sneaky But Lawful: The Use of Sneak and Peek Search Warrants," 43 *U. Kan. L. Rev.* 1103 (1995).

140. See Section 213 USA PATRIOT ACT: An "adverse result" is defined as (1) endangering a person's life or physical safety, (2) flight from prosecution, (3) destruction of or tampering with evidence, (4) intimidation of potential witnesses, or (5) otherwise seriously jeopardizing an investigation or unduly delaying a trial. See also *Dalia v. U.S.*, 441 U.S. 238 (1979), "covert entries are constitutional in some circumstances, at least if they are made pursuant to a warrant."
141. See *United States v. Freitas* (9th Cir. 1986) 800 F.2nd 1451; *United States v. Johns* (9th Cir. 1998) 851 F.2nd 1131, 1134–1135.)
142. *Roviaro v. United States,* 353 U.S., 62, 77 S. Ct. 628–629 (1957).
143. *Roviaro v. United States,* 353 U.S. 59, 77 S. Ct., 627 (1957); *United States v. Brown,* 3 F.3d 673, 679 (3rd Cir.), *cert. denied,* 510 U.S. 1017, 114 S. Ct. 615, 126 L, Ed. 2d 579 (1993).
144. *Roviaro,* 353 U.S., 64–65; *Monroe v. United States,* 943 F.2d 1007, 1012–1013 (9th Cir. 1991), *cert. denied,* 503 U.S. 971 (1992). *See United States v. Mathis,* 357 F. 3d 1200, 1208 (10th Cir. 2004).

Controlled Purchases of Evidence by Informants 11

11.1 Introduction

The undercover purchase of evidence by informants is an investigative technique routinely employed in drug, stolen property, and weapons investigations. Known as a controlled buy, it is the controlled purchase or attempted purchase of contraband, controlled substances, or other items material to a criminal investigation from the target offender.[1] The investigation is initiated, managed, overseen, and participated in by law enforcement personnel with the knowledge of the confidential informant (CI).[2]

Controlled buys are often planned as a buy-bust operation. A buy-bust is the prearranged arrest of suspects at the time of delivery of contraband to an undercover agent or informant.[3]

The investigative objective is to obtain evidence for a later prosecution of the individual selling the item to the informant. If that is the case, the target will be charged with the sale made to the informant. Once charged, the informant's identity will eventually be disclosed by the prosecutor.[4] If the case proceeds to trial, the informant will be named as a witness and called to testify.

In some instances, the purchase is used as a prelude to the introduction of an undercover agent by the informant to the target. The objective is to allow the agent to make a hand-to-hand purchase of drugs or other contraband from the target and to further develop the investigation. Doing so allows the agent to remove the informant from any future undercover purchases from the target. The initial purchase made by the informant may never be charged, and the informant may not be named as a witness. Although the process does little to protect the informant's involvement from the target, it reduces the chances that the informant may have to testify if a trial occurs.

Regardless of the investigative objective, many of the same steps used for undercover purchases made with the objective of obtaining a search warrant should be followed. The procedure assists in corroborating the informant's testimony and collecting damaging evidence.

Controlled buys are inherently high-risk undertakings. Informants are sent to meet with criminals who know they are arriving with money for the purchase. The targets of the investigation are arriving with an item of value.

Armed robberies are common occurrences in the illicit drug and gun trade. The following accounts illustrate the point:

> Firearms and Explosives (ATF) agents sent their wired informant to the mall with a $1,500 flash roll to buy five TEC-9 semiautomatic pistols.[5] The targets of the sting operation were Alphorns "Mack" Grady and James Roberts.[6] As agents kept their CI's green Lincoln Continental in view, they watched as the two gun dealers approached and got into the CI's vehicle.

> A Niagara Falls police investigator told reporters the deal "went bad, real quick."[7] When the informant showed Roberts the $1,500 flash roll, the gun sale turned into an armed robbery. According to the CI, "Roberts pulled out a gun and put it to the back of my head and said he was going to shoot me. He told Grady to take the money out of my pocket."[8] This is probably when the CI thought he would be saved by surveillance agents. Obviously, he thought, his control agent was hearing everything over the wire as it occurred. Apparently they did not.

> The CI described the shooting: "I yelled for help. Then Roberts leaned over and shot me in the left leg."[9] When agents heard the shooting, they finally moved in. Roberts fired three or four shots at the surveillance SUV. One of the slugs struck the SUV, narrowly missing the driver. The shooter was captured without agents firing a shot.

> Agents later learned from Grady that the deal had been a robbery from the start. He claimed to have set up the deal as a robbery for Roberts out of fear of being shot. Roberts had previously robbed and shot him and promised to shoot him again unless he produced another victim.[10]

11.2 Advance Planning

Agents, informants, and innocent bystanders have been killed or seriously injured during undercover drug purchases and buy-bust operations. The possible catalysts for an undercover operation to spin out of control are too long to list. If a list was possible to produce, armed robbery would be at the top. To reduce operational risk, the planning and execution stages of the investigation are critical.

During the planning stages of the operation, priority should be given to the safety of the officers and the informant, potential risk to innocent bystanders at the purchase/arrest location, security of official funds, and attainment of the investigative objectives. If any of these priorities cannot be met, the operation should not go forward.

At a minimum, the following should occur during the planning stages of the operation:

- Whenever possible, determine in advance the suspect's full identity, method of operation, associates, places frequented, vehicles utilized, and criminal histories.[11]

- Case agent or supervisor conducts a prebuy briefing of all surveillance agents. Suspect's name, description, and vehicle information are provided to all agents. Informant's description and vehicle information are also provided.
- Informant is given instructions by case agent on what is expected from him or her and ordered not to deviate from the plan. Informant (and vehicle, if used during buy) is thoroughly searched.
- A money list recording denominations and serial numbers will be prepared prior to making an undercover buy.[12] If a robbery occurs, the list will be used in the recovery of funds. If an arrest is made following the purchase, any funds seized will be compared with the original money list.
- Make provisions for adequate auditory and/or visual surveillance prior to, during, and after the purchase.[13]
- For reasons of corroboration and safety, avoid a situation in which an unaccompanied agent or informant makes the buy without adequate surveillance.[14]
- The informant may be ordered to wear either a concealed recorder or a transmitter during the controlled buy. The equipment should be tested in advance. Only a trained operator should be allowed to operate the receiver.
- Prearrange methods of communication and signals with the informant. Use of cellular telephones in undercover vehicles is strongly recommended.[15]
- Establish a postbuy meeting location with the informant.
- Informant and case agent meet at the postbuy meeting location for collection of evidence and search of informant.

11.3 Case Study: The Robbery and Murder of Informant Rachel Morningstar Hoffman

As a prospect for flipping, 23-year-old Rachel Morningstar Hoffman seemed ideal. She broke the mold for informants. She was a college-educated female from an upper-middle-class family. She drove a late-model Volvo; lived in an upscale Tallahassee apartment; and, perhaps most notably, was not a drug addict. Despite all that, she had a great deal in common with nearly everyone else facing arrest throughout America: fear of prosecution, fear of prison, and the hope of cutting a deal with police.

Fresh from her first arrest for possession of marijuana and resisting arrest in February 2007,[16] she had been given Florida's legal equivalent of a second chance. Represented by a private attorney, her case had been sent to drug court. In a break reserved for first offenders, the court offered Hoffman a deal: if she followed drug court rules for 1 year, the charges would be dropped. Her attorney could get the record expunged, and it would be almost as if she had never been arrested.

Drug court has strict rules: get arrested again, and prosecution goes forward. It's no secret that Florida's drug court dropouts are dealt with harshly—they can usually expect to do time for their original charges. Prison is a distinct possibility for those rearrested for drug offenses. Hoffman easily faced a few years in state prison if she reoffended.

It did not take long for Hoffman to draw the attention of the local police. According to Officer Roger Tate,[17] a patrol officer assigned to Hoffman's neighborhood, he had received reports of suspicious-looking characters coming and going from Hoffman's apartment. After checking out the apartment building, he inspected her garbage and discovered discarded records of drug transactions.

On April 17, 2008, Officer Tate and Detective Jim Baker[18] went to Hoffman's East Park Avenue apartment building to investigate. Several weeks earlier, the detective had received information from a CI that Rachel Hoffman was selling large amounts of marijuana from her residence. The CI had purchased from Hoffman in the past, but Hoffman had moved and the CI did not know her new address. The patrol officer's discovery renewed the detective's interest.

Baker, dressed in civilian clothes, decided to walk by Hoffman's apartment. He claimed to have immediately smelled the strong odor of fresh marijuana. Coupled with the report from his CI, Baker decided to get a search warrant for her residence. He left the uniformed officer with instructions to keep her apartment under surveillance.

There was no absence of details in the affidavit for the warrant to search Hoffman's apartment. It described suspicious-looking men with duffel bags leaving her door, odors of marijuana coming from the vicinity of her apartment, and drug records in her discarded garbage. The judge had no difficulty in determining that probable cause existed for a search of Hoffman's residence. A search warrant was issued.

While Baker was getting the warrant, Officer Tate observed Hoffman leaving her apartment and walking to her Volvo. He stopped her, advised her of her *Miranda* warnings, and told her that a search warrant was being prepared for her residence. She was extremely cooperative and admitted that there were marijuana, ecstasy, and Valium in her apartment.

When Baker returned with the search warrant, Hoffman continued to be cooperative. The officers seized 5 oz. of marijuana, ecstasy, Valium, and narcotics paraphernalia. During the search, Hoffman told Baker that she was selling between 10 and 15 lbs. of marijuana out of her apartment to friends each week.[19]

Baker explained to Hoffman that cooperating with police could make the case go away. By becoming a CI, she could work off the charges simply by making a few cases. He called it substantial assistance.

It was an offer she didn't refuse. Despite having a lawyer from her last arrest, she elected not to contact him for his opinion.[20] She never wanted to see the inside of a jail cell again. She became a CI.

Hoffman made an appointment for the following day at Tallahassee Police Headquarters. Baker, a 7-year veteran of the department and 18-month member of the Vice Unit, completed all of the necessary paperwork required to document her as an informant. He also gave her the standard informant agreement that contained a list of do's and don'ts to read and sign. (See Appendix 11A.) Violate any of the provisions, and the cooperation deal would be called off. Charges would be filed, and her prosecution would go forward. Hoffman signed the agreement and was assigned code number 1129.[21]

A circuit court judge, not a probation officer, supervised the Leon County drug court program that Hoffman had been ordered to complete. The program prohibited its participants from using or selling drugs or associating with known criminals. As informants are valued for their ability to associate with known criminals, Hoffman should have been disqualified from becoming an informant.

Hoffman's CI package was approved by Baker's sergeant. From almost the first day, it was apparent that Hoffman would be difficult to control. She immediately told her boyfriend that she'd become an informant. He later recalled that "the police told her all she had to do was one big deal; that's all she had to do." He told her, "Don't believe everything they tell you."[22]

She also confided to her best friend that she was working for the police as an informant. Her friend later explained: "They wanted her to turn in her friends, and she wouldn't do that. She said she wanted to get some grimy people off the street. She wanted to get the bad guys."[23]

It seemed as though she enjoyed her new role. That is not uncommon for many informants. Some seasoned detectives refer to it as the *James Bond* or *007 syndrome*. Almost overnight, a new informant begins living in a fantasy world based on what he or she has seen in the movies. Hoffman was an avid fan of the reality show *DEA*. The 007 informants are notoriously difficult to control.

Baker decided that Hoffman's first target would be Brian, her source of supply for ecstasy. She had given him the source's name during her initial debriefing. As instructed, Hoffman made a supervised recorded telephone call to the dealer and ordered $15,000 worth of the drug.[24]

As Hoffman was primarily a marijuana dealer, the target became immediately suspicious. It didn't help matters that Brian knew the police had searched her apartment. There are few people on the street who don't know about flipping. An unwritten rule treats a recently arrested person as an informant until he or she proves otherwise.

Hoffman's debut as a CI did not go well. When confronted by the ecstasy dealer, she confessed that she was working for the police. Remarkably, however, she convinced Brian to help her make cases so she could complete her commitment to police quickly.

All deals with Hoffman should have been off the table from that point forward. But her explanation to Baker—that she simply choked when confronted by the dealer—seemed plausible. The detective let it slide in the hopes of making a significant case.

It seemed Baker liked Hoffman. On one occasion, he examined her cell phone and discovered that his real name was listed as a contact. He instructed her to change it to "Pooh Bear."[25]

Brian, Hoffman's newly recruited surrogate informant, agreed to work for Baker provided the cases he made were credited to her. Baker completed the necessary paperwork and became the control agent of a new informant code numbered 1127.[26]

Brian delivered a case within a few days. It was a drug bust that resulted in the arrest of a street-level drug dealer. The case was counted toward Hoffman's substantial assistance agreement.[27]

Because Hoffman was only a marijuana dealer, her new partner Brian could help her put together a cocaine case against some real drug dealers. He knew two cocaine dealers who worked at a local car wash. Hoffman hoped that a big cocaine case might be all the substantial assistance she would ever need to provide.

In the next couple of weeks, Hoffman and Brian laid the groundwork for a big case: 2 oz. of cocaine, 1500 ecstasy tabs, and a handgun. It was to be the Tallahassee Police Department's (TPD) biggest buy-bust case ever conducted. It also demanded a record $13,000 flash roll.

With the exception of one telephone call, Baker had no contact with Hoffman from April 22 until May 5. In that call, she reported that she had met one of the cocaine dealers on the street and discussed the upcoming deal. She should have been instructed to never contact a target of investigation without the prior approval of her control agent.

Hoffman and Brian continued putting the deal together. They were left on their own and unsupervised by their control agent for 2 weeks. Hoffman was desperate to put together a big case that would set her free.

On May 5, Baker was ready for the deal to go down, even though he had yet to fully identify the dealer known only as "Flea." Hoffman was ordered to come to the police station and telephone Flea to get the deal rolling. Several attempts to reach him by telephone failed. Hoffman suggested that she go to the car wash where he worked to set up the deal. Baker agreed and wired her up with a recorder and transmitter and followed her to the business.

Flea wasn't at work. Instead, she met another man who said he was Flea's brother. Hoffman didn't get his name. He claimed that the two worked together selling drugs. He and Hoffman discussed the terms of the deal: 2 oz. of cocaine, 1500 tabs of ecstasy, and a .25-caliber handgun for $13,000. He gave Hoffman a phone number she could use to contact him.

On May 6, Baker received a call from Hoffman with news that Flea had called her the night before to say he was ready to do business and the deal could go down that afternoon at Flea's parents' home. Hoffman put him off, explaining that she was waiting for the people with money to arrive in Tallahassee the following day. The delay didn't appear to present a problem, and Flea promised to telephone her the next day at noon. Baker had not provided Hoffman with equipment to record the conversation.

On May 7 at approximately 10:00 a.m., Baker called Hoffman with instructions on what to tell Flea when he called. Once again, Hoffman was on her own and without a recorder.

At 10:30 a.m., Hoffman called Baker with news that she'd just received a call from Flea. He told her that he had the cocaine, ecstasy pills, and gun but was in a hurry and wanted to do the deal at 2:00 p.m. Once again, Hoffman had to put him off until she could talk to Baker. The detective wasn't present for the phone call, and it went unrecorded.

Baker finally instructed her to have no more contact with either dealer outside his presence. In the meantime, he began attempting to determine the identities of the two drug dealers. After a number of false starts, he finally came up with a name and driver's license photograph for Flea. He was Daneilo Bradshaw, and the photograph was positively identified by Hoffman.

Apparently, no one involved in the investigation ran Bradshaw's name through TPD records. Had any of the officers checked, they would have found that he was listed as the prime suspect in the theft of a .25-caliber handgun from a car at his car wash.

Flea's brother was still a John Doe. Much later, police would discern that he was Andrea Green, a convicted felon with a known history of violence.

Baker was running out of time. The 2-week-old investigation was needlessly turning into an emergency. He had apparently forgotten that without a buyer, namely Hoffman, there'd be no deal. His side should have been in control. Instead, the detective was allowing the dealers to call the shots.

The detective put together an operational plan that was to be distributed to all members of the surveillance team, yet it failed to fully identify both of the suspects or their vehicle and provided only one suspect's nickname. The dealers, not the police, had chosen to meet at the Super Wal-Mart. The success of the buy-bust operation was now being left to chance.

Meanwhile, Baker's supervisors were putting together a $13,000 flash roll and a 19-man surveillance team. It was the largest team ever assembled for a TPD buy-bust operation and included two Drug Enforcement

Administration (DEA) agents and one DEA surveillance aircraft. Members of the Leon County Sheriff's Department were conspicuously absent, the result of an apparent turf war. Because the deal might stray from the city into the county and no deputy sheriffs had been invited, one of the DEA agents hastily swore in the city officers as federal agents. That gave TPD officers jurisdiction if the case spilled over into the county.

At 5:57 p.m., Hoffman was instructed to make another call to Flea. This time, the call was recorded. In the course of the conversation regarding where the deal would take place, Hoffman explained her concerns to Bradshaw, "I'm a little Jewish girl. I need to be safe."[28]

Bradshaw told her that he had all the drugs and gun and would be driving a gray BMW. He changed the location where the deal was to go down to Forest Meadows Park. For Hoffman and the surveillance team, the Wal-Mart parking lot was far safer. Every drug deal holds the potential for an armed robbery. A crowded parking lot allows surveillance agents to mix easily with shoppers. Moving the deal to a secluded park made surveillance much more difficult. The dealers were minimizing their risk and were once again in control.

At approximately 6:00 p.m., Hoffman, equipped with a transmitter and her cell phone, was given the $13,000 flash roll. Baker suggested that an undercover officer accompany Hoffman. She declined, saying it would make her nervous.[29] Baker should have insisted; a second person in her car wouldn't have been unusual. In the uncontrolled meeting she had with the suspects, she'd had Brian with her. Hoffman had made a decision that should have been left to Baker.

Before leaving the police station, Baker's captain and the deputy chief of police cautioned Baker to not allow the $13,000 to leave his sight. So if the money didn't leave his sight, presumably Hoffman wouldn't leave his sight.[30]

At approximately 6:30 p.m., Hoffman was sent off alone in her Volvo to meet the dealers at Forest Meadows Park. She had never been there before and had to be given directions. Detective Baker and a DEA agent followed her in separate vehicles.

Hoffman was busy doing other things while driving to the park. She was text-messaging friends, receiving calls from Detective Baker, fielding calls from the two dealers, and trying to relay to Baker what they were telling her.[31]

At 6:34 p.m., as she was driving from the police station, she texted her boyfriend: "I just got wired up wish me luck I'm on my way."

Boyfriend to Hoffman: "Good luck, babe! Call me and let me know what's up."

Hoffman to boyfriend: "It's about to go down."[32]

Immediately following the message to her boyfriend, she texted her girlfriend who was already en route to Forest Meadows Park with a video camera. Unknown to Baker, Hoffman had asked the friend to videotape the buy-bust. It was all part of the real-life drama Hoffman was living. She wanted it documented for posterity.

Hoffman to friend: "Park off Meridian now."

Friend to Hoffman: "And Old Bainbridge?"

Hoffman to friend: "Its far ill call u after."

6:36 p.m.: Baker radios DEA agent telling him to "keep your eyes on her."

Detective Baker kept Hoffman in sight until the hastily planned operation began to fall apart. She made a wrong turn, and Baker and one of the DEA special agents briefly lost sight of her. It was becoming clear that Baker had taken on far more responsibility than he could handle. He was monitoring Hoffman's transmitter, a duty that should have been assigned to a qualified officer riding in the same car with him. He was the case agent and was supposed to be in communication with Hoffman. He was also supposed to be advising all units involved in the surveillance on what was transpiring over the wire and keeping abreast of what the surveillance units were observing. He had additionally decided to be one of the point men obligated to keep Hoffman in sight. The other point man was a DEA agent, not a TPD officer. The agent was basically along for support and to take joint credit for any arrests and seizures made that night. He really didn't have any stake in the outcome of the case and didn't know the area where the deal was set to go down.

At approximately 6:37 p.m., Hoffman called Baker, telling him she was lost. He explained to her how to get to Forest Meadows and saw her trying to pull out onto the highway. He stopped his car, waved his hand, and directed her to pull out in front of him. He allowed her to continue over a rise in the highway as he pulled into position to monitor her over the wire. They were finally in the vicinity of the Forest Meadows buy-bust location. That was the last time he saw her alive.

6:38 pm: Baker overhears via her transmitter a telephone conversation between Hoffman and one of the suspects. Hoffman to suspect: "Yeah … the residential side, yes it was, like, on the east side of the residential neighborhood, but um, right, so the, we're … alright. … so after I go, sorry, I'm going to go down this hill after Maclay and then I turned left on the Ox Bottom?"

6:39 pm: Baker advises all units that he is overhearing Hoffman's side of a conversation and that the suspect is attempting to send her to Ox Bottom Road.

6:40 pm: Investigator Baker advises all units he is approaching Maclay School. [According to reports filed later, he pulled into Maclay School to park and monitor Hoffman's wire. This would put him close enough to monitor the transmitter but not close enough to maintain visual surveillance of Hoffman].

6:41 pm: Transmission from Hoffman's wire. "Hey … he's telling me to go to his dad's nursery, or some shit, I'm not even sure; I'm going through Maclay right now if you see me. I'm actually going down this … Uh huh … alright, perfect, he told me to get in his car …. I'm going to go down this, on my left? Right here, turn left? Alright, I don't see the other car out there; I'll pull in here."

6:41 pm: DEA agent advises all units that Hoffman pulled into a baseball field.

6:41 pm: Baker calls Hoffman (1-minute, 37-second conversation).

6:42 pm: Baker advises all units that suspect is attempting to direct Hoffman to the nursery.

6:43 pm: Baker calls Hoffman (20-second conversation).

6:43 pm: Transmission from Hoffman's wire of telephone call between her and Baker: "You there? Alright. Ballpark … alright, call you right back."

6:43 pm: Baker advises all units that he is directing Hoffman to pull into Forest Meadows Park. She is to tell suspects that that is where she is.

6:45 pm: Hoffman speaks to suspect (2-minute, 45-second conversation). Transmission from Hoffman wire: "Hey, alright; I'm pulling into the park with the tennis courts right now, 'cause I have no idea where I am … [unintelligible] … all right, I'm in my Volvo." [Baker loses signal from Hoffman's wire].

6:45 pm: Baker attempts to call Hoffman. No answer.

6:45 pm: Baker asks units at Forest Meadows Park if they see her. They do not.

6:46 pm: Baker advises all units that he has lost Hoffman on the wire and cannot get her on the phone.

6:46 pm: Baker attempts to call Hoffman; no answer.

6:46 pm: DEA agent advises he has spotted a BMW occupied by two black males parked at the nursery with the vehicle's nose pointing toward the road. Baker radios the DEA agent, saying, "If we know where they are, at least we know where half of the deal is." The DEA agent did not maintain surveillance of the BMW.

6:46 pm: Baker advises units that he cannot get Ms. Hoffman by phone, has lost her on the wire and that they need to keep eyes on the suspect vehicle at the nursery.

6:47 pm: DEA agent advises he is turning around to get back to the nursery. It was too late; they had already left the nursery.

6:47 pm: The sergeant assigned to oversee the investigation advises units to get back with the suspect vehicle to ensure Hoffman does not pull in and make the deal outside their presence.

6:48 pm: Baker finally speaks to Hoffman by cell phone (42-second conversation).

6:48 pm: Baker advises all units that Hoffman is on Gardner Road following the suspects. He advises units to go to Gardner Road and move in immediately.[33]

Unfortunately, the surveillance team was composed of city police officers and one DEA agent. No one had any idea where Gardner Road was. Tree cover prevented the DEA surveillance aircraft from finding Hoffman. The sheriff's office, who would have known the area far better than anyone involved, wasn't there to help due to the turf war. The ground surveillance units weren't prepared for any changes to the original plan. Most of the surveillance team had done as instructed and were already in position in and around Forest Meadows Park.

The dealers were now fully in charge. Baker lost Hoffman again on the transmitter, and she wasn't answering his repeated cell phone calls. Baker finally received one more call from Hoffman saying she had followed the suspects from the nursery and they were on Gardner. Hoffman's last words were as follows: "It looks like the deal is going to go here. It's a dead-end street." Baker exclaimed: "I told you not to do that. Turn around! Turn around! Do not follow them!"

At 6:49 pm, all contact with Hoffman was lost.

At this point, only the police and Rachel Hoffman thought there was going to be a drug deal that night. Daneilo Bradshaw and Andrea Green had driven a stolen BMW to Tallahassee for an armed robbery. The only item they were bringing to the deal was the .25-caliber automatic Hoffman had ordered.

Baker later told internal affairs investigators, "I think she hung up on me. I think it was because she was in the heat of the deal, and the deal was about to go down."

Right up until the end, Hoffman probably wasn't worried about her situation. As far as she knew, the 19-man surveillance team and its aircraft were close by and ready to protect her. Earlier in the day, she had told concerned friends who knew about the deal not to worry; if anything goes wrong, "the police are going to swoop in and save me."[34]

Baker ordered all surveillance units to converge on Gardner Road. The problem was that most of the surveillance team had no clue where the rural street was. They had to be guided in by K-9 handler Officer Bill Herbert. He had a global positioning system.

On arrival at Gardner, the K-9 officer discovered one Reef Rider flip-flop sandal at a rise in the middle of the road. It was hours before anyone would recall that it was exactly like the ones Hoffman had been wearing.

Two live .25-caliber rounds and one shell casing were discovered much later that night. They were directly underneath where the K-9 car had been parked earlier in the evening. This was the crime scene where Rachel Hoffman had been executed.

Surveillance units heading for Gardner Road began asking Baker for the license plate number for Hoffman's Volvo. He didn't have it. Surveillance units requested the license plate number of the BMW. No one had managed to obtain it.

Hoffman probably didn't die quickly. Evidence revealed that the first two shots entered her right side. The shots were fired from the passenger side of her Volvo. The ejected rounds found at the scene indicated that at some point the gun jammed. She was still alive while the gunman was clearing the jam, sliding a live round into the chamber, and walking to the driver's side of her car. She was shot three more times in the head. She knew it was coming. The bullets passed through her wrist and fingers while she was trying to protect herself. Her body was driven from the scene by one of the suspects. She was later thrown into the woods in nearby Taylor County.

In the hours following Hoffman's disappearance, the surveillance team was clueless. Their behavior made it clear that recovering the flash roll was priority number one and that Hoffman was suspected of somehow being involved in its loss.

Around 9:00 p.m., Hoffman's boyfriend became worried and drove to her apartment building. He saw police cars but no sign of her car. The officers were searching her apartment.

At 2:00 a.m., police went to the home of the boyfriend's parents to check on his whereabouts.

At 2:30 a.m., two robbery detectives arrived at his apartment looking for Hoffman. He told them that he thought she was with them.

At 3:00 a.m., police wearing bulletproof vests went to another friend's house in search of Hoffman. The occupants told the police that they thought she was with them.[35]

Finally satisfied that Hoffman was among the missing, the search then focused on Flea and his accomplice.

Green and Bradshaw weren't hard to find. They had driven Hoffman's Volvo to Perry, Florida, where they bought bleach to try to remove bloodstains from her car. They had a friend take them to Orlando, where they went on a $750 shopping spree, buying clothes, shoes, and jewelry. They were arrested in the Macy's parking lot in Orlando approximately 36 hours after the murder.

Police quickly determined that Green, a.k.a. Flea, was the shooter. His discarded shoes were covered in blood. Bradshaw led the police to Hoffman's body. Jailhouse informants later testified that Green confessed to shooting Hoffman.

The media attention following the murder was intense. The *Tallahassee Democrat* and the *St. Petersburg Times* dispatched investigative reporters to cover the story.

Initially, the Tallahassee police chief blamed Hoffman for the events leading up to her murder. In a news conference, the chief claimed that she had failed to follow instructions and in essence was responsible for her own death. He later recanted, saying, "We were placing most of the blame on Rachel Hoffman. I regret that now. It made us look like we weren't taking responsibility for what happened."[36]

It wasn't long before Hoffman's murder received national attention. According to the Hoffman family attorney, "*60 Minutes* has called, *Dateline* has called, *20/20* has already been here and filmed. *Rolling Stone* was here to do a story. I can't tell you how many media representatives have called me. Agents, people that want to do books. I don't have enough time in the day for it all. The media interest has just been so intense." *20/20*, the national TV news show, got the exclusive. It devoted one hour to the events surrounding Rachel Hoffman's death.[37]

On December 30, 2008, Hoffman's parents filed a lawsuit against the City of Tallahassee under the Florida Wrongful Death Act.[38] The suit asked for damages in excess of the jurisdictional limit of $15,000.[39]

The Leon County Grand Jury investigated the circumstances surrounding how Hoffman was recruited by police, how she performed as an informant, and how she was murdered. It heard testimony from all the police officers involved in the investigation. The DEA agents involved were instructed by their agency not to testify.

The grand jury concluded in part as follows:

> We believe the command staff was negligent in its review of the OPS plan and supervision of this Transaction. The OPS plan does not reflect the terms of the deal or location of the Transaction in any way. The amount of drugs listed is wrong and the fact that a firearm was being purchased is never mentioned. With the exception of the sergeant who remained active in making decisions as matters developed during the course of the Transaction, the level of supervision was nonexistent.

> This transaction was the responsibility of T. P. D. However, it relinquished control to two convicted felons. Letting a young, immature woman get into a car by herself with $13,000, to go off and meet two convicted felons that they knew were bringing at least one firearm with them, was an unconscionable decision that cost Ms. Hoffman her life.

> There is no doubt that Andrea Green and Daneilo Bradshaw are the ones that brutally murdered Rachel Hoffman. But through poor planning and supervision, and a series of mistakes throughout the Transaction, T. P. D. handed Ms. Hoffman to Bradshaw and Green to rob and kill her as they saw fit.

> Based on the immaturity and poor judgment Ms. Hoffman used from the beginning of her relationship with T. P. D., she should never have been used as

a Confidential Informant. But if they were going to use her, they certainly had a responsibility to protect her as they assured her they would.

Less than fifteen minutes after she drove away from the offices of T. P. D., she drove out of the sight of the officers who assured her they would be right on top of her watching and listening the whole time. She cried out for help as she was shot and killed and nobody was there to hear her.

T. P. D. needs to require that their officers fully learn, understand and follow the procedures it writes. They should be more than pages in a book.

Confidential Informants should not be used in transactions of this magnitude without a long term working relationship in which they have demonstrated trust, credibility and an understanding of what is required to complete such work in a safe manner. Failure of the Informant to follow instructions on more than one occasion should result in the immediate termination of the C. I. Agreement.

Confidential Informants should not be allowed to make important decisions, such as whether an undercover officer will accompany them during the course of their work.

A Confidential Informant should never be sent alone to purchase a firearm.

T. P. D. should cease working with the D. E. A. unless the D. E. A. will require their officers to provide testimony regarding cases they are involved in. Otherwise, they are of no use to the investigation and actually a hindrance to the legal process.[40]

State Attorney Willie Meggs refuses to prosecute any cases brought by agents of the DEA. Meggs, in a letter to Florida Department of Law Enforcement Commissioner Gerald Bailey, wrote, "Due to recent events, please be advised the State Attorney's Office for the Second Judicial Circuit will no longer prosecute cases in State Court when agents from the DEA are involved. Should your agency join a task force or use federal DEA agents during your investigation, you should first contact the U.S. Attorney to make certain that the U.S. Attorney will take your case."[41]

On September 26, 2008, the City of Tallahassee released its 199-page internal affairs report concerning the death of Rachel Hoffman in a press release. The city announced the firing of Detective Baker.[42] It also reported that the city manager had issued a reprimand to the police chief to require a more stringent level of supervision from the top down.[43]

Hoffman's murder prompted an unprecedented debate in the state legislature regarding law enforcement's unregulated use of informants. Police departments throughout the state defended their use of CIs and rejected any effort to micromanage law enforcement. The president of the Florida Police

Chief's Association was willing to work with lawmakers to protect informants as long as law enforcement's ability to conduct undercover operations was not compromised.[44]

On May 8, 2009, the debate ended with the passage of legislation designed to rein in police practice regarding the recruitment and use of informants. Florida Governor Charlie Crist signed the legislation into law.[45] Known as Rachel's Law, it requires police agencies to take into consideration a prospective informant's age and maturity, emotional state, and the level of risk an undercover assignment presents to that informant. Police are prohibited from promising an informer more lenient treatment in exchange for cooperation. That power is reserved for prosecutors and judges.[46]

At the signing ceremony, Rachel's father, Irv Hoffman, said, "It's just a great day for Rachel's cause and memory."[47]

On April 10, 2010, the TPD issued the following press release:

> Police Chief Dennis Jones announced the reinstatement of Jim Baker[48] as a police officer with the Tallahassee Police Department.
>
> Baker was terminated September 30, 2008, following an Internal Affairs investigation that sustained policy violations against [Baker] in his role as a narcotics investigator.
>
> As part of a binding arbitration decision, and after fully considering the best interests of the Department and the citizens of Tallahassee, Officer [Baker] is being reinstated effective April 10, 2010.
>
> Chief Jones stated, "I respect the arbitration process and the Tallahassee Police Department will comply fully with the arbitrator's decision."

Baker wasn't returned to the Narcotics Division. He was reassigned as a uniformed officer assigned to the afternoon patrol shift.[49]

The lawsuit filed by Rachel Hoffman's parents was set to begin during the first week of January 2012. The attorneys representing the City of Tallahassee seemed determined to take the case to trial until jury selection was set to begin. That was when a $2.6 million settlement was offered by the city and accepted by Hoffman's family. The attorney representing the Hoffmans seemed to have anticipated the outcome, telling reporters, "Given all the circumstances, I'm not surprised. The negligence was so gross, the magnitude of the damages was so catastrophic."[50]

The size of the settlement, in excess of $200,000, required legislative approval. The authorizing bill was passed at the conclusion of the 2012 session. Florida Governor Rick Scott signed the bill on March 29, 2012.

Hoffman's parents issued the following statement to the press: "While it is true that no amount of money will ever fully compensate us for our mental pain and suffering, the claim bill was the only remedy available to us to right a terrible wrong. Today, the governor has helped ease our pain the only way he can."[51]

Daneilo Bradshaw was found guilty of first-degree murder and sentenced to life in prison. His lawyer offered a theory for what provoked the shooting during the trial. Hoffman had confessed to Green that she was an informant, which led Green to "flip out" and shoot her.[52] Andrea Green was sentenced to life in prison without possibility of parole. He smiled while being sentenced.

Appendix 11A: Tallahassee Police Department Confidential Informant Code of Conduct

Informant # _____

I, _____, the undersigned, understand that while I am cooperating and assisting the Tallahassee Police Department, agree to the following:

1. I may never search any suspect, person, house, papers or physical effects. I also understand that I may **not** affect **any** physical arrests for violations during my association with the investigating agency during my association with the investigating agency.
2. I further understand that I am **not** an employee of the Tallahassee Police Department or **any** participating agency, and that I may **not** use any documents or equipment that would identify me with a law enforcement agency. I fully understand that I am **not** a law enforcement officer and that I am **not** to use my association with the Tallahassee Police Department.
3. I further understand that I am **not** to carry a firearm or weapon of **any** type while working with the Tallahassee Police Department.
4. I further agree to keep in constant contact with the Tallahassee Police Department Narcotics Unit while assisting them.
5. I further understand that I **may** be required to testify in court cases in which I am involved. I agreed to tell the whole factual truth when testifying. I agree to inform the court and the Tallahassee Police Department Narcotics Unit, of any change in my address for subpoena service, and to make myself available for court, depositions or any other action that the court may require.
6. I understand I am **not** being asked to create crime. I further understand that I am only working to interrupt ongoing criminal activity.

7. I will **not** ask anyone to commit crimes that they are not already doing or capable of doing.
8. I understand I am **not** to use sexual enticement or promises of future sexual acts to get someone to commit a criminal act.
9. I understand that I will not be allowed to beg, pressure, or threaten anyone to commit a criminal act they ordinarily would not do.
10. I completely understand that the Tallahassee Police Department is **not** interested in investigating innocent people. They are only interested in people that I know are committing crimes and intend to commit crimes in the future.
11. I further understand that I may **not** engage in any illegal or improper conduct so long as I am working with the Tallahassee Police Department.
12. If an investigation which I take part results in a seizure and/or forfeiture of property or money, I understand that I will **not** receive any money or property based on a percentage of the property or money seized or forfeited.
13. Further, I understand that any violations arising from my actions in violation of the aforementioned circumstances will result in an investigation of the matter. If the charges are substantiated, appropriate action, to include the possibility of criminal prosecution, will be taken.
14. I agree to cooperate with the Tallahassee Police Department on my own free will, and **not** as a result of any intimidation or threats.
15. I agree **not** to simultaneously act as a confidential source for any agency without the prior permission of the Tallahassee Police Department.
16. I understand that I **may** be requested during any investigation, to submit to drug screen urine analysis, polygraph, stress analysis tests or other test designed to ensure my effectiveness and credibility as a confidential source. I agree to submit to any such examination immediately upon request.
17. I understand I **may** be subject to search during my meeting with an investigator. I further consent to a search of my belongings and vehicle (if applicable). I fully understand that any illegal contraband found subsequent to the search **may** be used as evidence against me in court.
18. I understand that if lodging is provided for me by the Tallahassee Police Department, I am consenting to search of the premises and my person by an investigator at any time.
19. While working as a confidential source for the Tallahassee Police Department, I will take _____ as an assumed name for

security purposes. I understand that the assumed name will **not** be used to sign any documents or official paperwork.

20. I hereby release the City of Tallahassee, the State of Florida, the Tallahassee Police Department, its officers, agents, affiliates and any other cooperating law enforcement agency, from any liability or injury that may arise as a result of this agreement.

Informant's Signature _____ Date _____
Investigator's Signature _____ Date _____
Supervisor's Signature _____ Date _____

Appendix 11B: Guidelines for Florida State and Local Law Enforcement Agencies in Dealing with Confidential Informants

(As Adopted By The Florida Police Chiefs Association, The Florida Sheriffs Association, The Florida State Law Enforcement Chiefs Association, and The Florida Department of Law Enforcement March, 2009)

I. Policy Statement

The utilization of confidential informants is lawful and often essential to the effectiveness of properly authorized criminal investigations or intelligence-gathering activities. At the same time, such utilization carries with it special challenges and risks that warrant prudent and responsible efforts. Those adopting or utilizing these Guidelines acknowledge that special care must be taken to carefully evaluate and closely supervise the use of confidential informants. Due to the inherent dangers associated with the investigations of drug-related crimes and other serious offenses, or similar concerns in any situation in which the use of a confidential informant is anticipated, a priority of such operations is the safety of the persons involved, including the confidential informant, agency personnel, target offender(s), and the public. Law Enforcement agency operational decisions and actions regarding the use of confidential informants must keep the safety of involved persons a top priority, and agency personnel should exercise the utmost care and judgment in order to minimize the risk of harm to all persons involved.

II. Purpose

The purpose of these statewide guidelines is to promote among the state and local law enforcement agencies utilizing confidential informants the development and maintenance of comprehensive policies and procedures addressing the recruitment, selection, and utilization of confidential informants and to articulate minimum training expectations for those agencies. Compliance with these guidelines will enhance the goal of establishing more uniform practices throughout the state and promote the safety of those involved in operations involving confidential informants. These statewide guidelines are intended to assure, to the greatest extent possible, uniformity of policy and procedure regarding the use of confidential informants by state or local law enforcement agencies throughout the state.

III. Principles

The following principles shall be incorporated within the policies and procedures of any state or local agency involved in the utilization of confidential informants—

A. The first priority in agency operational decisions and actions regarding the use of confidential informants is to preserve the safety of the confidential informant, law enforcement personnel, the target, and the public.

B. Factors to be considered in assessing the suitability of a confidential informant prior to the informant's utilization shall include, but are not limited to:

1. The informant's age and maturity;
2. The risk the informant poses to adversely affect a present or potential investigation or prosecution;
3. The effect upon agency efforts that the informant's cooperation becoming known in the community may have;
4. Whether the person is a substance abuser, has a history of substance abuse, or is known by the lead investigator or officer to be involved in a court-supervised drug treatment program or drug-related pretrial intervention program;
5. The risk of physical harm that may occur to the person, his or her immediate family, or close associates as a result of providing information or assistance, or upon the person's assistance becoming known in the community;
6. Whether the person has shown any indication of emotional instability, unreliability, or of furnishing false information;
7. The person's criminal history and/or prior criminal record;
8. Whether the nature of the matter being investigated is such that the use of the informant is important to, or vital to, the success of the investigation.

C. Each state or local agency utilizing confidential informants shall establish policies for the recruitment, control, and use of confidential informants that shall, as a minimum, contain the following requirements:

1. Articulation of standards related to maintenance of information regarding confidential informants, detailing what information shall be maintained on confidential informants, and standards stating general guidelines for the handling of confidential informants;

2. Articulation of the agency's process to assure the confidential informant is advised of conditions, restrictions, and procedures associated with his or her participation in the state or local agency's investigative or intelligence-gathering activities;

3. Establishment of a clearly designated supervisory and/or command-level review and oversight in the utilization of any confidential informant;

4. Limiting or restricting off-duty association or social relationships by agency personnel involved in investigative or intelligence-gathering with confidential informants;

5. Articulation of guidelines for the deactivation of confidential informants, to include necessary deactivation communications to the informant.

6. Articulation of the level of supervisory approval required prior to the utilization of any juvenile as a confidential informant.

D. Any person who is requested to act as a confidential informant shall, upon request, be afforded the opportunity to consult with legal counsel prior to agreeing to perform any activities as a confidential informant.

E. Each state or local law enforcement agency utilizing confidential informants shall ensure that when utilizing a confidential informant who is facing criminal charges, agency personnel clearly indicate to the informant that the agency cannot make promises or inducements such as a grant of immunity, dropped or reduced charges, or reduced sentences or being placed on probation, and that the value (if any) of the confidential informant's assistance and any effect that assistance may have on pending criminal matters can only be determined by the appropriate legal authority.

F. Each state or local agency utilizing confidential informants shall ensure that all involved or otherwise appropriate personnel are trained in the agency policy requirements and procedures, and shall keep documentation demonstrating the date of all such training.

G. Each state or local agency utilizing confidential informants shall establish written records security procedures that, as a minimum:
 1. Provide for the secured retention of any records related to the agency's confidential sources, including access to files identifying the identity of confidential sources;
 2. Limit availability to those records to those within the agency or law enforcement community having a need to know or review those records, or to those whose access has been required by court process or order;
 3. Require notation of each person who accesses such records (including date of access),
 4. Providing agency review and oversight to assure the security procedures are followed, and
 5. Define the process by which confidential informant records (if any) may be lawfully destroyed.
H. Each state or local agency utilizing confidential informants shall perform a periodic review of actual agency confidential informant practices to assure conformity with the agency's policies, procedures and these Guidelines.
 I. These Guidelines, and their adoption by organizations or agencies do not create a substantive or contractual right, or entitlement for any person.

APPENDIX—Definitions

Confidential Informant (CI):
Any person who, by reason of his or her familiarity or close association with suspected or actual criminals or

1. who can make a controlled buy or controlled sale of contraband, controlled substances, or other items material to a criminal investigation; or
2. can or does supply regular or constant information about suspected or actual criminal activities to a law enforcement agency; or
3. can otherwise provide information important to ongoing criminal intelligence gathering or criminal investigative efforts and who is, through such efforts, seeking to improve his or her status in the criminal justice system.

A person's improved status in the criminal justice system may include, but is not limited to, avoiding an arrest, a reduction or modification of a sentence imposed or to be recommended to be imposed upon him or her, or a reduction or modification of charges pending or anticipated to be placed against him or her and whose association or cooperation with law enforcement must remain unknown to those about whom the information is provided or with whom one or more transactions occur.

Controlled Buy: The purchase (or attempted purchase) of contraband, controlled substances, or other items material to a criminal investigation from a target offender which is initiated, managed, overseen, or participated in by law enforcement personnel with the knowledge of the confidential informant.

Controlled Sale: The sale (or attempted sale) of contraband, controlled substances, or other items material to a criminal investigation to a target offender which is initiated, managed, overseen, or participated in by law enforcement personnel with the knowledge of the confidential informant.

State or local law enforcement agency: As used in these Guidelines, a state or local law enforcement agency is an agency having a primary mission of preventing and detecting crime and the enforcement of the penal, criminal, traffic or highway laws of the state and that in furtherance of that primary mission employs law enforcement officers as defined at Section 943.10, Florida Statutes.

Target Offender: The person whom law enforcement personnel suspects will be implicated by the activities of a confidential informant.

Appendix 11C: Florida's Confidential Informant Law: "Rachel's Law"

Title XLVII CRIMINAL PROCEDURE AND CORRECTIONS

Chapter 914 WITNESSES; CRIMINAL PROCEEDINGS

SECTION 28

Confidential informants.

914.28 Confidential informants.—

1. This section may be cited as "Rachel's Law."
2. As used in this section, the term:
   a. "Confidential informant" means a person who cooperates with a law enforcement agency confidentially in order to protect the person or the agency's intelligence gathering or investigative efforts and:

      i. Seeks to avoid arrest or prosecution for a crime, or mitigate punishment for a crime in which a sentence will be or has been imposed; and

     ii. Is able, by reason of his or her familiarity or close association with suspected criminals, to:

        A. Make a controlled buy or controlled sale of contraband, controlled substances, or other items that are material to a criminal investigation;

        B. Supply regular or constant information about suspected or actual criminal activities to a law enforcement agency; or

        C. Otherwise provide information important to ongoing criminal intelligence gathering or criminal investigative efforts.

  b. "Controlled buy" means the purchase of contraband, controlled substances, or other items that are material to a criminal investigation from a target offender which is initiated, managed, overseen, or participated in by law enforcement personnel with the knowledge of a confidential informant.

  c. "Controlled sale" means the sale of contraband, controlled substances, or other items that are material to a criminal investigation to a target offender which is initiated, managed, overseen, or participated in by law enforcement personnel with the knowledge of a confidential informant.

  d. "Law enforcement agency" means an agency having a primary mission of preventing and detecting crime and the enforcement of the penal, criminal, traffic, or highway laws of the state and that in furtherance of that primary mission employs law enforcement officers as defined in s. 943.10.

  e. "Target offender" means the person suspected by law enforcement personnel to be implicated in criminal acts by the activities of a confidential informant.

3. A law enforcement agency that uses confidential informants shall:

  a. Inform each person who is requested to serve as a confidential informant that the agency cannot promise inducements such as a grant of immunity, dropped or reduced charges, or reduced sentences or placement on probation in exchange for serving as a confidential informant.

  b. Inform each person who is requested to serve as a confidential informant that the value of his or her assistance as a confidential informant and any effect that assistance may have on pending criminal matters can be determined only by the appropriate legal authority.

c. Provide a person who is requested to serve as a confidential informant with an opportunity to consult with legal counsel upon request before the person agrees to perform any activities as a confidential informant. However, this section does not create a right to publicly funded legal counsel.

d. Ensure that all personnel who are involved in the use or recruitment of confidential informants are trained in the law enforcement agency's policies and procedures. The agency shall keep documentation demonstrating the date of such training.

e. Adopt policies and procedures that assign the highest priority in operational decisions and actions to the preservation of the safety of confidential informants, law enforcement personnel, target offenders, and the public.

4. A law enforcement agency that uses confidential informants shall establish policies and procedures addressing the recruitment, control, and use of confidential informants. The policies and procedures must state the:

a. Information that the law enforcement agency shall maintain concerning each confidential informant;

b. General guidelines for handling confidential informants;

c. Process to advise a confidential informant of conditions, restrictions, and procedures associated with participating in the agency's investigative or intelligence gathering activities;

d. Designated supervisory or command-level review and oversight in the use of a confidential informant;

e. Limits or restrictions on off-duty association or social relationships by agency personnel involved in investigative or intelligence gathering with confidential informants;

f. Guidelines to deactivate confidential informants, including guidelines for deactivating communications with confidential informants; and

g. Level of supervisory approval required before a juvenile is used as a confidential informant.

5. A law enforcement agency that uses confidential informants shall establish policies and procedures to assess the suitability of using a person as a confidential informant by considering the minimum following factors:

a. The person's age and maturity;

b. The risk the person poses to adversely affect a present or potential investigation or prosecution;

c. The effect upon agency efforts that the disclosure of the person's cooperation in the community may have;

d. Whether the person is a substance abuser or has a history of substance abuse or is in a court-supervised drug treatment program;

    e. The risk of physical harm to the person, his or her immediate family, or close associates as a result of providing information or assistance, or upon the disclosure of the person's assistance to the community;

    f. Whether the person has shown any indication of emotional instability, unreliability, or of furnishing false information;

    g. The person's criminal history or prior criminal record; and

    h. Whether the use of the person is important to or vital to the success of an investigation.

6. A law enforcement agency that uses confidential informants shall establish written security procedures that, at a minimum:

    a. Provide for the secured retention of any records related to the law enforcement agency's confidential sources, including access to files identifying the identity of confidential sources;

    b. Limit availability to records relating to confidential informants to those within the law enforcement agency or law enforcement community having a need to know or review those records, or to those whose access has been required by court process or order;

    c. Require notation of each person who accesses such records and the date that the records are accessed;

    d Provide for review and oversight by the law enforcement agency to ensure that the security procedures are followed; and

    e. Define the process by which records concerning a confidential informant may be lawfully destroyed.

7. A state or local law enforcement agency that uses confidential informants shall perform a periodic review of actual agency confidential informant practices to ensure conformity with the agency's policies and procedures and this section.

8. The provisions of this section and policies and procedures adopted pursuant to this section do not grant any right or entitlement to a confidential informant or a person who is requested to be a confidential informant, and any failure to abide by this section may not be relied upon to create any additional right, substantive or procedural, enforceable at law by a defendant in a criminal proceeding.

History.—s. 1, ch. 2009-33.

Endnotes

1. The person who is a law enforcement personnel suspect will be implicated by the activities of a confidential informant as defined in *Guidelines for Florida State and Local Law Enforcement Agencies in Dealing with Confidential Informants*, March 2009. (Hereinafter *Guidelines*.) (See Appendix 11B.)
2. *Guidelines*.

3. *North Carolina State Bureau of Investigation Policy and Procedure Manual.*
4. See *United States v. Davila-Williams*, 496 F.2d 378 (1st Cir.1974).
5. Pfeiffer, R., "Courts: Wal-Mart Shooter Pleads Guilty," *Niagara Gazette*, November 13, 2008.
6. Names changed.
7. Pfeiffer, R., "Courts: Wal-Mart Shooter Pleads Guilty," *Niagara Gazette*, November 13, 2008.
8. Ibid.
9. Ibid.
10. Ibid.
11. *DEA Agent's Manual*, Subchapter 662, Undercover Activities.
12. Ibid.
13. Ibid.
14. Ibid.
15. Ibid.
16. Ross, B., *20/20* (ABC News Internet Ventures), July 26, 2008.
17. Name changed.
18. Ibid.
19. Leon County Grand Jury Presentment, August 1, 2008.
20. Poltilove, J., "Johnny Devine, Hoffman's Attorney, Said Police Should Have Spoken with Him," *Tampa Tribune*, May 13, 2008.
21. Portman, J., "The Left Turn Rachel Hoffman Didn't Make," *Tallahassee Democrat*, October 5, 2008.
22. Portman, J., "Friends Provide a Glimpse into Rachel Hoffman's Final Night," *Tallahassee Democrat*, July 13, 2008.
23. Ibid.
24. Tallahassee Police Department Internal Report regarding the Rachel Hoffman murder.
25. Portman, J., "Friends Provide a Glimpse into Rachel Hoffman's Final Night," *Tallahassee Democrat*, July 13, 2008.
26. Tallahassee Police Department Internal Report Regarding the Rachel Hoffman Murder.
27. Ibid.
28. Frank, J., "Jury Delays Decision in Rachel Hoffman Murder Case," *St. Petersburg Times*, December 16, 2009.
29. Portman, J., "The Left Turn Rachel Hoffman Didn't Make," *Tallahassee Democrat*, October 5, 2008.
30. Ibid.
31. Timeline that follows is taken from Tallahassee Police Department Internal Affairs Report S.I. 08-21.
32. Ibid.
33. Chronology obtained from Leon County Grand Jury Presentment, August 1, 2008.
34. Portman, J., "Friends Provide a Glimpse into Rachel Hoffman's Final Night," *Tallahassee Democrat*, July 13, 2008.
35. Post-shooting timeline from Portman, J., "Friends Provide a Glimpse into Rachel Hoffman's Final Night," *Tallahassee Democrat*, July 13, 2008.

36. Portman, J., "Tallahassee Police: We Shouldn't Have Blamed Rachel Hoffman," *Tallahassee Democrat*, September 27, 2008.

37. Clark, C., "National Media Interest Intense over Hoffman Case," *Tallahassee Democrat*, July 20, 2008.

38. Chapter 768.28, Florida Statutes. (See Appendix 11C.)

39. *Irving Hoffman and Marjorie Weiss v. The City of Tallahassee*, filed December 30, 2008.

40. Excerpt from "Leon County Grand Jury Report, In Re: Homicide of Rachel Morningstar Hoffman, Conclusion Section, Submitted August 1, 2008."

41. Burlew, J. and Portman, J., "Meggs Says He Won't Prosecute DEA Cases Because of Hoffman Case," *Tallahassee Democrat*, August 7, 2008.

42. Corbett, N., "Tallahassee Police Chief Defends Firing Decision in Rachel Hoffman Case," *Tallahassee Democrat*, September 26, 2008.

43. "City Takes Disciplinary Actions in TPD Case; Changes Implemented," www.talgov.com, September 26, 2008.

44. Portman, J., "Legislature, Law Enforcement at Odds over Rachel's Law," *Tallahassee Democrat*, January 9, 2009.

45. Leary, A., "Gov. Charlie Crist Signs Rachel's Law Putting Police Use of Informers under Tighter Rules," *St. Petersburg Times*, May 8, 2009.

46. Fla. Stat. § 914.28 (2010). See *Guidelines to Be Used by Florida State and Local Agencies in Dealing with Confidential Informants* as adopted by FPCA, FSA, SLECA, and FDLE in March, 2009.

47. "Governor Charlie Crist Signs 'Rachel's Law' Protecting Police Informants," *Tampa Bay Tribune*, May 7, 2009.

48. Name changed.

49. Montanaro, J., "Officer Reinstated to Tallahassee Police Department," *WCTV News Tallahassee*, April 2, 2010.

50. Cotrell, B., "Scott Signs Hoffman Settlement," www.tallahassee.com, March 30, 2012.

51. Ibid.

52. Frank, J., "Jury Delays Decision in Rachel Hoffman Murder Case," *St. Petersburg Times*, December 16, 2009.

Undercover Investigations

12

Reversals and Sting Operations

12.1 Introduction

An undercover investigation or operation is a series of related undercover activities occurring over a period of time that requires undercover law enforcement agents,[1] informants, or other persons working with the law enforcement agency to temporarily assume a fictitious role or identity. The operatives conceal their purpose and methods of detecting crime or obtaining evidence from third parties to prosecute those engaged in illegal activities.

Undercover law enforcement investigations range from simple in plan to extremely complex. They often demand more than casual encounters between undercover agents and targets of investigation. Some, like an undercover purchase of narcotics, can take a few minutes. Other operations can take years before attaining their goals. Long-term undercover operations are tightly choreographed, can often be dangerous, and can be costly undertakings.[2]

The Immigration and Customs Enforcement (ICE) has identified four types of undercover assignments based on duration, complexity, and the demands placed on the undercover agent.

12.2 Casual Undercover

Agents are frequently called on to perform what are described as casual undercover activities.[3] The assignment can be accomplished with or without fictitious identification; requires no change in appearance or personal habits; and requires only indirect contact with violators or potential violators, such as undercover telephone calls or performing surveillance duties, which require little or no contact with suspects.

12.3   Moderate Undercover

An assignment that involves,

- Assuming a fictitious identity, which may or may not involve a change in appearance or personal habits
- A limited number of short-duration, face-to-face contacts with violators or potential violators at an ICE-controlled covert location or an alternate location

12.4   Long-Term Undercover

An assignment that involves

- Assuming a fictitious identity with significant changes in appearance or personal habits to regularly meet with violators or potential violators with the intention of the assignment continuing for a period greater than 6 months
- Frequent and repetitious contact with the same violators or potential violators in covert locations, over an extended period of time, during which the undercover operative maintains an independence from the targeted group

12.5   Deep Undercover

A long-term undercover assignment that also involves

- Assuming a fictitious identity with significant changes in appearance or personal habits in order to infiltrate a criminal organization
- Working in a covert location or in a business enterprise operated by the targeted group or any other situation that requires regular and continuous face-to-face contacts with violators or potential violators

12.6   Training and Risk Management

Many agencies require agents and supervisors assigned to work in any undercover capacity to receive specialized training.[4] For example, the Drug Enforcement Administration (DEA)'s Practical Applications Unit (TRDP) provides all undercover and surveillance training for special agents.

The training utilizes practical exercises to present real-life scenarios that agents can expect to encounter during an undercover operation.

The TRDP also conducts two in-service courses on contemporary issues in the undercover process and risk management. The "Contemporary Issues in the Undercover Process" course is a 3-day advanced class that addresses undercover issues with a combination of classroom lectures, tabletop, and practical exercises. The risk-management course is given to special agents attending the Advanced Agent Course and Group Supervisor Institute. This course exposes the attendees to the principles of risk management as they apply to undercover operations, search warrants, and confidential sources.[5]

ICE also operates undercover-related training curriculums at its training facility. They include the Undercover Operatives School for agents assigned to undercover investigations. The Undercover Manager School is for supervisors placed in charge of an undercover operation. The Field Undercover Liaison Coordinator School is for those assigned responsibilities for selection of agents assigned to an undercover operation and monitoring the progress of undercover operations. Finally, the Undercover Record Keeper School is for individuals responsible for recording all financial transactions that occur during a certified undercover operation.[6]

12.7 Undercover Operation Proposal

Undercover investigations should only be initiated upon the approval of the case agent's immediate supervisor.[7] Protracted or sensitive investigations require approval from those further up the chain of command. DEA's Undercover Review Committee (URC) is the body responsible for reviewing proposals for undercover activities that involve sensitive circumstances.[8]

It is management's responsibility to determine whether the proposed investigative methods are reasonably necessary to develop evidence of criminal conduct and can be accomplished lawfully and under departmental guidelines. The case agent advancing the proposed operation should be required to submit an operational plan that should address the questions discussed in Sections 12.7.1 through 12.7.6.[9]

12.7.1 Preliminary Activities

Briefly summarize the case activities that have occurred to date. What is the nature and extent of undercover activities that have already occurred? Include a brief description of the operational targets, and discuss the focus of the operation. If possible, identify a particular case number that best describes the criminal activities of the subjects under investigation.

374 Informants, Cooperating Witnesses, and Undercover Investigations

12.7.2 Potential

Illustrate the potential for success. Specifically, who are the current identified targets? Describe the undercover scenarios and the evidence that is anticipated to result from them. Describe the goals that can be achieved over the next 6 months. What strategies will be employed to achieve them? What objectives must be met before the operation is concluded, and when is this likely to occur?

12.7.3 Security

In light of the previous activities of the investigation, has the operation been compromised in any way so far? How can the project continue without being compromised?

12.7.4 Safety

Describe the nature and frequency of undercover activities and the risk of personal injury, property damage, financial loss, or harm to innocent third parties. How long has the investigation been active?

What actions will be taken to ensure the physical and psychological well-being of the operatives and innocent third parties, if applicable? Have the undercover agents attended the required training, and are they certified to conduct undercover work?

12.7.5 Significance

Summarize the investment of resources (financial and personnel) that will be devoted to this operation. Demonstrate how the investment is warranted in light of the importance of the identified targets of the operation and the investigative priorities of the agency. Specifically identify the investigative priorities that relate to the operation.

12.7.6 Sensitive Circumstances

What sensitive circumstances are likely to occur in the operation? Identify them and briefly describe what they will involve.

12.8 Prosecutor Concurrence

Before allowing the operation to move forward, a supervisor should consult with the prosecutor and discuss the operational plan. The American Bar Association Standards on Prosecutorial Investigations[10] recommend that the prosecutor should consider the potential risks presented by the undercover investigation proposal including the following:

1. Physical injury to law enforcement agents and others
2. Lost opportunity if the operation is revealed
3. Unnecessary intrusions or invasions into personal privacy
4. Entrapment of otherwise innocent persons
5. Property damage, financial loss to persons or businesses, damage to reputation, or other harm to persons
6. Interference with privileged or confidential communications
7. Interference with or intrusion on constitutionally protected rights
8. Civil liability or other adverse impact on the government
9. Personal liability of the law enforcement agents
10. Involvement in illegal conduct by undercover law enforcement agents or government participation in activity that would be considered unsuitable and highly offensive to public values and that may adversely impact a jury's view of a case
11. The possibility that the undercover operation will unintentionally cause an increase in criminal activity[11]

12.9 Informants and Otherwise Illegal Activity

Informants working for the Federal Bureau of Investigation (FBI), DEA, and Bureau of Alcohol, Tobacco, Firearms, and Explosives (ATF) participating in undercover operations, particularly reverse undercover operations and money laundering sting investigations, are often given official authorization to commit crimes necessary to attain the goals of the investigation. Internally, the crimes are referred to as "otherwise illegal activity" (OIA). Allowing an informant to engage in OIA is reserved for those cases where it would be impossible to obtain the information or evidence needed for a successful prosecution and when the expected benefits outweighs the risks of allowing the source to commit a crime. Strict authorization procedures are supposed to be followed with final authority being granted by the agency special agent in charge. State and local law enforcement agencies who engage in similar conduct are guided by statute and internal guidelines.[12]

12.9.1 Tier 1 and Tier 2

"Tier 1 Otherwise Illegal Activity"[13] is any activity that

1. Would constitute a misdemeanor or felony under federal, state, or local law if engaged in by a person acting without authorization; and
2. Involves

376 Informants, Cooperating Witnesses, and Undercover Investigations

a. The commission, or the significant risk of commission, of any act of violence by a person or persons other than the confidential informant

b. Corrupt conduct, or the significant risk of corrupt conduct, by senior federal, state, or local public officials

c. The manufacturing, importing, exporting, possession, or trafficking of controlled substances in a quantity equal to or exceeding those quantities specified in United States Sentencing Guidelines § 2D1.1(c)(1)

d. Financial loss, or the significant risk of financial loss, in an amount equal to or exceeding those amounts specified in United States Sentencing Guidelines § 2B1.1(b)(1)(I)[14]

e. A confidential informant providing to any person other than a Justice Department law enforcement agency (JLEA) agent any item, service, or expertise that is necessary for the commission of a federal, state, or local offense, which the person otherwise would have difficulty obtaining; or

f. A confidential informant providing to any person other than a JLEA agent any quantity of a controlled substance, with little or no expectation of its recovery by the JLEA

"Tier 2 Otherwise Illegal Activity" is any other activity that would constitute a misdemeanor or felony under federal, state, or local law if engaged in by a person acting without authorization.

If the OIA is approved for the informant, at least one JLEA agent, known as the case agent, and an alternate agent must review special written instructions with the confidential informant that the confidential informant must sign or initial and date. The instructions must address the limits of the authority; the specific conduct authorized; the time period specified; prohibitions on certain behavior, including acts of violence and obstruction of justice; and the consequences to the confidential informant of operating outside the authority granted. In addition, if the OIA is extended past the initial authorized time period, the informants must receive and sign the instructions pertaining to the OIA every 90 days.[15]

Federal criminal prosecution of JLEA informants can result from the informant's unauthorized criminal conduct or from situations in which the informant exceeds the scope of his or her authority to engage in OIA. In such cases, the informants often claim in defense that the government authorized or immunized their crimes. An Office of Inspector General (OIG) report described the following examples:

An informant who was prosecuted for possession of child pornography claimed "entrapment by estoppel,"[16] asserting that he reasonably believed he was lawfully permitted to download the pornography as long as he sent it on to law enforcement.[17] The court rejected the defense, ruling that while the FBI contact agent had initially approved the defendant's possession of child pornography, the agent had later clarified that "the FBI no longer required his assistance and that possession of child pornography was illegal."[18]

One of the more notorious OIA cases was the Stephen "Rifleman" Flemmi and James "Whitey" Bulger scandal. Both were "top echelon" confidential informants for the FBI's Boston office. Along with four codefendants, they were indicted for racketeering, conspiracy, extortion, and bookmaking charges. Bulger was tipped off by his control agent, FBI Special Agent John Connolly, to his pending arrest. Bulger evaded law enforcement and remained a fugitive until 2012. When the government prosecuted Flemmi, he claimed that the FBI had authorized the crimes for which he was indicted.[19] The court disagreed. Flemmi, facing multiple murder charges, became a key government witness in several subsequent trials. His testimony helped to convict Whitey Bulger of murder.

Similarly, an "authorization" defense arose in the prosecution of Jackie Presser, a Teamsters official who was charged with embezzling over $700,000 in union funds. Presser asserted as an affirmative defense that he had been an FBI informant for 10 years and was authorized by the FBI to hire "phantom" or "no-show" employees. When Presser's FBI handlers testified under oath, they confirmed the assertions supporting Presser's defense. The government thereafter declined to prosecute Presser and consented to vacating earlier convictions of two phantom employees. A report by the staff of the Senate's Permanent Subcommittee on Investigations, one of three committees that investigated the matter, concluded that the Department of Justice (DOJ) had failed to adequately monitor the FBI's informant system and should have required the FBI to disclose information about its informants.[20]

Although authorizing confidential informants to engage in OIA can facilitate their usefulness as a source of information to the government, it may also have adverse consequences. As illustrated by the Bulger–Flemmi and Presser cases, the confidential informant's criminal activity can hinder prosecution of the informant's coconspirators by prompting defenses of public authority or entrapment. Moreover, OIA authorizations may have unforeseen consequences. For example, a decision to authorize a confidential informant to engage in bookmaking may create difficulties in prosecuting the informant or coconspirators if he or she engages in unauthorized criminal activity.[21]

12.9.2 Reporting Otherwise Illegal Activity

Tier 1 and 2 OIAs committed by FBI confidential human sources (CHSs) must be reported to the Justice Department annually. There is no similar requirement for the DEA or ATF. In 2012, the FBI disclosed that its 56 field offices authorized CHSs to commit at least 5939 crimes. This was up slightly from the 5658 crimes committed by CHSs in 2011.[22] There was no indication of how many unauthorized crimes were committed by FBI CHSs during the same period.

12.9.3   Informants Profiting from Otherwise Illegal Activity

The CHS's case agent and supervisors are responsible for closely monitoring the OIA and ensuring that innocent citizens are not adversely impacted. Because many OIAs involve high-profit crimes such as money laundering, it is also the responsibility of the case agent to determine whether the CHS is realizing undue profits from the OIA. It is unclear how much profit is too much profit, and undue profit is taken up in Section 12.14, when churning investigations are examined.

12.10   Reverse Undercover Drug Investigations

The DEA defines "reverse undercover" as a generic term for any variation of the traditional role of undercover personnel as the "buyer" of an illegal product or service such that the role is one of seller of illegal products or services.[23] For example, a DEA undercover agent becomes a drug dealer instead of occupying the traditional role of drug buyer.[24]

The DEA pioneered reverse undercover drug investigations during the early 1970s. One of the first cases hatched by agents assigned in the Miami and New York City field divisions had a confidential informant introduce three French "heroin smugglers" to members of the Mafia with an offer to "sell" 20 kg of heroin. The targets were two well-documented Mafia figures with records for both heroin trafficking and homicide. The undercover officers were two French detectives assigned to the DEA from the Sûreté (French National Police) and a French-speaking DEA agent.

Prosecutors initially opposed the sting operation for fear that the defendants would successfully argue that they had been entrapped by federal agents. However, the case agents eventually persuaded them otherwise, and the sting went forward. The drug purchasers brought their cash to Shea Stadium, tested a sample of heroin, and the transaction took place. Arrests were made and cash was seized. The trial resulted in convictions.[25]

A reverse undercover drug operation is fairly straightforward with few deviations. An informant locates an individual in the market for a significant quantity of narcotics. The informant contacts his control agent and gives him as much information as possible about the prospective buyer.

Once the control agent gives the go-ahead, the informant arranges another meeting, often referred to as a dry run, with the buyer in a public place to negotiate quantity and price. The informant is usually outfitted with a concealed body transmitter, and the meeting is heavily surveilled by undercover agents.

Quite often, the informant is instructed to use this meeting as an opportunity to introduce the undercover agent/seller to the buyer. Once the seller/buyer introduction takes place, the informant is no longer a part of the operation, and that should be the last the buyer will see of the informant. The purpose of cutting the informant out at this point in the investigation is twofold:

1. The informant won't be present during the dangerous part of the operation when the drugs and money come together and the arrest is made.
2. The informant may not be needed as a witness when and if the case goes to trial.

Once the quantity and price is decided on, a time and place for the transaction is set, usually a mall parking lot or a rented warehouse. The surveillance/team arrives well in advance. Because a reverse drug operation normally requires having a large quantity of controlled substance to complete the transaction, the supervisor in charge of the operation will ensure that all necessary precautions are taken to prevent an armed robbery. For example, the North Carolina Bureau of Investigation requires the special agent in charge or an assistant special agent in charge to be present during all reverse operations.[26]

When the buyer arrives, he is shown the narcotics and may be allowed to test the drug. Agencies differ on policies regarding undercover agents providing samples. Departmental manuals generally provide guidance. For example, the DEA distinguishes between supplying a controlled substance to a violator in an amount sufficient only for testing purposes and supplying an amount sufficient for redistribution. If the amount of the substance provided for testing realistically could not be redistributed by the violator, providing a sample does not constitute a sensitive investigative activity requiring headquarters' approval.[27]

The Rhode Island attorney general's reverse undercover guidelines treat samples a bit differently. The guidelines define "furnish" as giving a controlled substance to a violator. Under their guidelines, "in extraordinary circumstances where a small amount of drugs are given to a violator, there must be a clear indication that this approach will implicate the individual(s) involved and that the controlled substances furnished shall only be a small sample sufficient to test or necessary to establish the bona fides of the undercover officer."[28]

Once the buyer is satisfied with the quality of the drugs, the transfer of drugs and money is initiated. When the money and drugs are exchanged, the undercover agent gives a "takedown" signal, and the arrest is made by the arrest team. Undercover agents should not participate in the arrest unless absolutely necessary. The restriction is not to preserve the agent's undercover identity; instead, the restriction is in place for officer safety considerations. Armed undercover agents participating in arrests have been shot by tactical officers assigned to raid teams who were unaware of the agent's identity.

The DEA advises its agents against using the reverse undercover tactic as a general "advertisement," with little idea as to who may appear. It is to be used only against identified, significant traffickers, ideally preselected class I or II violators, the DEA's highest-quality targets.[29]

12.11   Blue-on-Blue Reversals

The DEA also recommends its agents to focus on identified targets to decrease the probability of robberies and operating at cross-purposes with other law enforcement agencies. Although attempted robberies are common during reversals, it is not unusual for undercover agents from one law enforcement agency to unknowingly engage in undercover negotiations with undercover agents from a neighboring police department. Armed confrontations between competing police agencies have occurred during "blue-on-blue" confrontations.[30] To preclude the chance of two undercover operations clashing with each other, it is important for reverse undercover operations to be coordinated with appropriate law enforcement agencies operating in the area.[31]

State and local law enforcement agencies have addressed the blue-on-blue issue. The State of Rhode Island Department of Attorney General requires the following precaution be taken before a reverse undercover operation can go forward:

> In order to prevent reverse undercover operations from clashing with each other, it is essential that reverse operations be coordinated with other state, local, and federal law enforcement agencies operating in an area. To prevent separate law enforcement organizations from targeting the same individuals and to prevent a law enforcement agency from conducting reverse stings on undercover officers from another law enforcement agency, all Rhode Island law enforcement organizations must first notify the Attorney General of the pending reverse operation. The controlling law enforcement agency and the Attorney General will then coordinate with other agencies insofar as possible without compromising or sacrificing the security of the proposed reverse operation.[32]

12.11.1 Case Study: Reversals and Robbery

Reverse undercover operations, while extremely lucrative, are also an extremely high-risk investigative tactic. The large quantity of drugs offered for sale by police in reversals is meant to bring in correspondingly large sums of money for forfeiture. The risk of an armed robbery occurring during the operation is always present. Criminals run sting operations of their own, posing as drug dealers and purchasers, with armed robbery as their only objective.

Like many local police agencies, the Chandler, Arizona, Police Department has a robust forfeiture program. Of the 35 forfeiture cases made in 2009, 20 were reverse undercover operations. Chandler police seized $3.2 million during that year. Reversals brought $2.7 million.

On the morning of July 28, 2010, a Chandler police informant located a man in the market for 500 pounds of marijuana. The trafficker, known only as "Chris," represented himself as working for a group of buyers with "cash on hand" and ready to do business.[33] The informant quoted a price of $250,000 for 500 pounds. He alerted his handlers and was told to confirm that the men Chris represented had the money. He did as instructed, set up a meeting in a parking lot, and reported being shown a bag stuffed with bundles of $100 bills.

The show of money set the stage for the production of a sample of the marijuana by the undercover agents. The informant arranged the meeting for the same parking lot. This time he was accompanied by two undercover agents with a bale of marijuana. The buyers were pleased with what they saw and the deal moved forward. The informant would be eligible for a reward based upon how much money the officers might seize later that day.

The location for the transaction was set by the buyers. It would take place at a residence located in an area of west Phoenix known for drug trafficking. A check of a regional intelligence-sharing database by the Chandler case agent did not indicate any police activity by other law enforcement agencies planned for the location. There would be no risk of engaging undercover officers from another agency in a blue-on-blue confrontation.

Neither the Phoenix Police Department, nor the DEA was invited to participate in the operation. There would be no need to share the funds set for seizure with any other agency.

A hastily prepared reverse undercover operation was now in its final phase. All of the events leading up to the sting would transpire in one day.

During the late afternoon of the 28th, surveillance agents observed several vehicles at the residence. Accounts vary, but as many as twelve men may have been at the house as the sting was about to take place. None of the individuals, including middleman "Chris," had been fully identified.

When the lead undercover agent arrived at the house, a disagreement over the showing of money and delivery of the marijuana had to be resolved before the drug deal moved to a conclusion. Once settled, the lead undercover agent called for the two agents in the delivery vehicle to bring the marijuana to the house. That gave the undercover team a total of three men to set the arrest phase in motion. A tactical team of officers was awaiting the bust signal from the lead undercover agent's concealed transmitter. Once the signal to move in was received, the raid team's estimated time of arrival was between 30 and 60 seconds.

A short time later the two undercover agents with the load of marijuana arrived, pulling the load vehicle into the garage. The money end of the transaction moved into the living room. The purchasers showed their money. The agents did not count it. Without warning a man burst into the room and opened fire with an automatic rifle. All three undercover agents were hit but two were able to return fire. Two of the officers survived their wounds. One died at the scene, having been hit four times in the chest. Two suspects were shot to death. Middleman Chris was seriously wounded.

The $250,000 never existed. The "purchasers" had prepared stacks of one dollar bills with counterfeit $100 dollar bills on top of each stack. The total amount seized was $999.

Chris, the man who set the transaction in motion with the Chandler informant, was charged with three counts of felony murder for his role in the robbery and the death of the detective and the two gunmen. While being treated for his wounds, Chris told detectives that he was a DEA informant. He claimed DEA had ordered him to set the drug deal in motion.

A DEA spokesperson later told reporters "DEA does not, as a matter of policy, confirm or deny the existence of any potential sources of information." Phoenix detectives confirmed that Chris had worked for DEA in Phoenix.[34] They also learned that he had been deactivated after agents declared him unreliable.[35]

According to the press, Chris was a veteran drug trafficker. He had been convicted in Kentucky of engaging in organized crime and drug trafficking while in possession of a firearm in 2002, and sent to prison for 15 years. He was paroled in 2006 but arrested again in Phoenix for fraud in 2008. He became a cooperating witness for the U.S. Attorneys Office and was promised that charges would be dropped if he fulfilled the terms of his agreement.[36] In securing his release prosecutors assured the judge that

> A violation of his [Chris'] plea agreement will both result in a lengthy sentence in this case and a parole violation for his Kentucky case. In the final analysis, [the defendant] has a substantial incentive to comply with the terms of his plea and remain law abiding.

Through his attorney, Chris maintained that he was working for DEA at the time of the shooting. Federal prosecutors responded, "Although [the defendant] had provided the government with information related to his involvement in a mortgage fraud scheme, he had no authority from the U.S. District Court judge, his supervising pretrial officer, his parole officer, or the U.S. Attorney's Office to work in any capacity as an undercover informant in a drug transaction or any other criminal activity. Any position to the contrary is not accurate."[37]

At this writing, Chris is awaiting trial.

12.12   State and Local Reverse Undercover Operations

State and local law enforcement agencies have followed the lead of their federal counterparts and also conduct reverse undercover operations. Many states have enacted laws that specifically allow for reverse undercover operations.[38]

Reverse undercover operations can be extremely profitable undertakings. The city of Sunrise, Florida, a bedroom community north of Miami, seized nearly $6 million selling cocaine during reverse undercover operations conducted in 2011 and 2012. One of their informants was paid over $800,000 for helping to arrange reverse drug transactions.[39]

Critics call reversals policing for profit. An attorney who has defended more than 100 sting cases told a journalist, "This has become a very sophisticated, very dangerous and very high revenue-generating speed trap. That's really all it is. You are taking a less effective, more problematic law enforcement technique and choosing that because of the money it generates."[40]

In the case of Sunrise, the *Sun Sentinel* obtained city payroll data and found that a dozen undercover narcotics officers since 2010 have collectively earned $1.2 million in overtime pay. A sergeant who supervises the stings collected more than $240,000 in overtime during that 3.5-year period.[41]

12.13   Reversals and the Entrapment Defense

The key ingredient to an effective sting operation is deception. Undercover agents and agents controlling informants should use caution as they develop a criminal case to avoid entrapment issues, but this is not always the case. Agent training on the issue varies from agency to agency.

The tightly choreographed nature of reverse undercover operations allows the collection of substantial amounts of recorded video and audio evidence. When the defendant is arrested, he or she is literally caught in the act of committing a crime. The evidence leaves the defense attorney with little else to argue but the entrapment defense.

12.13.1   Legal Standard

In enacting federal criminal statutes, Congress intended that otherwise innocent people should not be convicted if they were enticed or entrapped by the government into violating the law. If the evidence in the case establishes that the defendant was predisposed to commit the offense, however, the defense of entrapment will be defeated.[42]

The government may not originate a criminal design, implant in an innocent person's mind the disposition to commit the crime, and then induce its commission so that the government can prosecute that individual.[43] By such conduct, the government oversteps the line between setting a trap for the "unwary innocent" and the "unwary criminal."[44]

Unless the individual is predisposed to commit the crime for which he was arrested, the government may not induce him to commit it and obtain a lawful conviction. Predisposition must have existed before and independently of the government's efforts directed at the individual.

Entrapment is an affirmative defense.[45] The defendant bears the burden of proof to demonstrate that the government initiated, or induced, the crime. Once that burden is satisfied, the burden shifts to the prosecution to prove, beyond a reasonable doubt, that the defendant was predisposed to commit the crime for which he is being prosecuted.[46]

Predisposition can be established by many different types of evidence, as long as the conduct is similar to the crime for which the defendant is currently charged. To meet its burden of proving predisposition, the government may establish it with evidence of the following:

1. An existing course of criminal conduct, similar to the crime for which the defendant is charged
2. An already formed design on the part of the accused to commit the crime for which he is charged
3. A willingness to commit the crime for which he is charged as evidenced by the accused's ready response to the inducement[47]

The government must also prove that the defendant was disposed to commit the criminal act before he or she was first approached by government agents.[48] The defendant's predisposition must be "independent and not the product of the attention that the Government had directed at [the defendant]."[49] A defendant's ready and unhesitating acceptance of the government's offer to commit a crime is substantial evidence that he or she was predisposed to do so.

12.13.2 Outrageous Government Conduct

The courts have held that fundamental fairness will not permit a defendant to be convicted when the conduct of informants or agents was outrageous.[50] This differs from the entrapment defense as the conduct of the government, rather than the predisposition of the defendant, determines if the defense is available.

According to the U.S. attorney's *Criminal Resource Manual*, the court must determine that the conduct of an agent or informant was "so outrageous that due process principles would absolutely bar the government from invoking judicial process to obtain a conviction."[51] Thus, the outrageous government conduct defense is not really a defense at all. Rather, it is a claim that the institution of the prosecution suffers from a purely legal defect; as such, the claim is waived unless raised prior to trial.[52]

The *Criminal Resource Manual*[53] also notes that the Supreme Court has never held that the government's mere use of undercover agents or informants, or the use of deception by them, gives rise to a due process violation. The requisite level of outrageousness can only be reached when government conduct is so fundamentally unfair as to be "shocking to the universal sense of justice."[54]

12.13.3 Sentencing Entrapment and Sentencing Manipulation

Reversals also encourage the defense to advance claims of sentencing entrapment. The difference between sentencing entrapment and entrapment is that entrapment is a complete defense to the crime charged. The defense of sentencing entrapment may only lower a defendant's sentence.

Sentencing entrapment is defined as "[e]ntrapment of a defendant who is predisposed to commit a lesser offense but who is unlawfully induced to commit a more serious offense that carries a more severe sentence. It is also referred to as sentencing manipulation."[55] The defense makes the argument that during the undercover investigation, the police manipulated the defendant into a course of criminal conduct that would allow prosecutors to charge an offense that on conviction would result in a higher mandatory sentence.

The United States Sentencing Guidelines offer an example of sentencing entrapment: "if in a reverse sting the court finds that the government agent set a price for the controlled substance that was substantially below the market value of the controlled substance, thereby leading to the defendant's purchase of a significantly greater quantity of the controlled substance than his available resources would have allowed him to purchase except for the artificially low price set by the government agent, a downward departure in sentence may be warranted."[56]

A journalist described one of the Sunrise Police Department reversals in a 2013 article that fit the definition of sentencing entrapment:

> [Defendant] flew from New Jersey to Sunrise to do a deal for five kilos in 2012, but had only enough money for one, a police report states. Police agreed he could take one for $25,000 and have four more for only $1,000 each; repaying the debt once he sold the coke in New York and New Jersey. He was arrested when he took possession of the purported five kilos of cocaine.[57]

12.14 Case Study: The ATF and Churning Investigations

The ATF also engages in reverse undercover investigations using informants authorized to engage in authorized illegal activity. Some of these investigations generate huge sums of cash. The ATF calls these cases "churning investigations."

Income-generating undercover operations are relatively new territory for the ATF. In 2004, the existing law allowing such operations was amended to grant ATF the same authority that was previously extended only to the FBI and the DEA. It allows these agencies to use the proceeds of its undercover operations to support its investigative work. Specifically, the ATF was authorized, in the context of undercover investigative operations, to use appropriated funds to lease or purchase real property, establish and operate a proprietary business on a commercial basis, and deposit funds and proceeds generated during the operation in a financial institution.[58]

Under the new regulations, the ATF is also permitted to use the proceeds of the operation to offset necessary and reasonable expenses incurred in an undercover operation. The authority, which ATF refers to as "churning authority," may be exercised only if the proposed activity is certified by the director of the ATF and the attorney general as necessary conduct of the undercover operation.[59] The ATF, FBI, and DEA are now the only DOJ components with churning authority.

Between February 2006 and June 2011, the ATF approved 35 investigations using churning authority to investigate tobacco diversion. In those undercover investigations, the ATF purchased cigarettes from manufacturers and then agents or informants sold them to criminal targets at or below wholesale cost. The targets allegedly transported the contraband cigarettes to a high-tax state, where they were sold without collecting the proper state and local taxes. Of the 36 churning investigations conducted by the ATF between February 2006 and June 2011, 20 generated total reported revenues of nearly $162 million.

One churning investigation sold approximately $15 million worth of cigarettes in an 18-month period. The confidential informant utilized in the case was allowed to keep more than $4.9 million of the $5.2 million of gross profit generated from sales of tobacco to criminal targets. The undercover operation was never authorized by the ATF Headquarters or the DOJ.

An OIG investigation reported that according to ATF records, the confidential informant was allowed to keep that amount to cover his business expenses. However, the ATF did not ensure the reasonableness of the expenses claimed, nor did it require the informant to provide adequate documentation to support or justify those expenses. OIG investigators found that the $4.9 million covered more than just the business expenses related to ATF activity. It covered 100% of the confidential informant's total business operating overhead and more than $2.3 million in profit.[60]

12.15 Money Laundering

One of the ironies of the cocaine business is the sheer volume of bulk cash that drug sales produce. It is noted that 1 kg of cocaine (2.2 pounds) generates nearly 7 pounds of bulk cash. To put it into perspective, a mere $5 million in $100 bills if stacked would produce a pile 20 ft high. Considering that the drug trade is a multibillion-dollar-a-year industry, the logistics of getting the proceeds out of the United States is monumental. Money laundering sting operations have become the weapon of choice for law enforcement agencies targeting dirty money.

In the late 1970s and early 1980s, there was no shortage of U.S. banks and businesses willing to take dirty money. By 1982, an estimated 44 of Miami's banks were licensed to make international transactions. At least 36 foreign banks established branches on Miami's prestigious Brickell Avenue. All were laundering dirty money.

In 1986, Congress passed the most comprehensive and aggressive anti–money laundering law in history with the Money Laundering Control Act of 1986. Overnight, it began choking off the flow of dirty money into financial institutions. The act

- Established money laundering as a federal crime
- Prohibited structuring transactions to evade Cash Transaction Report filings
- Introduced civil and criminal forfeiture for Bank Secrecy Act (BSA) violations
- Directed banks to establish and maintain procedures to ensure and monitor compliance with the reporting and recordkeeping requirements of the BSA

Drug trafficking organizations drowning in cash proved resilient and began avoiding financial institutions. They began paying cash for real estate, jewelry, luxury automobiles, and yachts. Congress responded and passed the Anti-Drug Abuse Act of 1988 and redefined the term *financial institution*. The act

- Expanded the definition of financial institution to include businesses such as car dealers, jewelers, and real estate closing agencies. It required them to file reports on large currency transactions
- Required the verification of identity of purchasers of monetary instruments over $3000

The new laws criminalized money laundering with penalties of up to 20 years in prison and significant fines.[61] They also introduced the money laundering sting provisions.

12.15.1 Money Laundering Sting Operations: Operation Swordfish

Operation Swordfish was the DEA's first money laundering sting operation. It all started with a well-connected walk-in informant. He was a middle-aged

Cuban exile, a Bay of Pigs veteran, and trained by the Central Intelligence Agency. He had the right connections and big-time tax problems after taking a beating in the real estate market. He needed the DEA's help with the IRS.

With the exile as Swordfish's centerpiece informant, the DEA created a dummy corporation known as Dean Investments International. Their Miami Lakes storefront became money laundering central and would implicate the brother of the president of Colombia. The bogus investment firm washed over $19 million for drug traffickers. Swordfish led to the indictment of 61 money launderers.[62] Money laundering sting operations soon became one of law enforcement's primary tools for attacking drug dealers where it hurt most—their profits.

The documents authorizing the operation allowed for the use of funds generated by the undercover operation—the commissions—for "reasonable and necessary expenses" incurred by the operation. Money laundering stings quickly became self-funding undercover operations. Informants are paid in part from the proceeds of the investigation.

Generating commissions is not the purpose of Swordfish-style money laundering investigations. The objective is to identify domestic and offshore bank accounts used by drug traffickers. Informants are deployed into the field claiming to have connections that can move dirty money through legitimate bank accounts and businesses.

12.15.2   Sensitive Activities Review Committee Investigation

The success of Swordfish inspired similar money laundering sting operations. Although not routine, they have become a staple in the world of reverse undercover law enforcement. They have also proved to be controversial high-stakes cases that often have transnational implications. The investigations, known as Attorney General Exempt Operations, are tightly controlled and considered crucial in helping to determine how drug trafficking organizations move their money and in identifying high-value suspects.[63]

Federal money laundering sting proposals are put together by a federal agent with the aid of an assistant U.S. attorney. Approval requires a thorough review of an operational plan by the DOJ Sensitive Activities Review Committee (SARC) before authorization to go forward is granted. The sting operations are often referred to as SARC investigations.

In SARC operations, law enforcement agents are authorized by the attorney general to engage in what would otherwise be an illegal activity: in this case, money laundering. Testimony from a DEA supervisor described how the attorney general's exemption works:

> Basically, it was permission from the Attorney General of the United States to do a number of things which would normally be considered criminal

activities. Laundering the money is a criminal activity. Not filing the IRS forms when you make a transaction of $10,000 or more is a criminal activity. There's a Congressional prohibition against budget augmentation. In other words, I was in essence augmenting the established Congressional budget for the Agency by doing what I was doing. I had the permission to do all of these things, which normally would have landed me in jail.[64]

12.15.3   Operation Casablanca

Operation Casablanca was the most significant drug money laundering sting in the history of U.S. law enforcement. It also disturbed relations between the United States and Mexico. Agents seized $103 million in currency and indicted 26 Mexican bankers and three Mexican banks. Of Mexico's largest 19 banks, 12 were involved in the money laundering activities. Bankers from two Venezuelan banks were also indicted.

An agent involved in the case described for PBS how Casablanca worked:

Can you describe the operation?

Casablanca originally was targeted at Cali cartel brokers, currency brokers, people who were the contact people to launder money. As that investigation proceeded, we ended up working on the Juarez cartel people. The Cali cartel and the Juarez cartel had one thing in common: they collected a lot of money in the United States, and they didn't know what to do with all that cash. And they needed to move it back to where they could spend it in a clean traceless way. As we proceeded in that investigation, and in other investigations, I might add, we ended up with an undercover money laundering organization, set up to approach these people and to identify their sources of money in the United States. During that phase of the investigation, we legitimately stumbled into some bankers in Mexico. And the bankers actually asked us, hey, we know what's going on, so why don't you cut us in. So we ended up targeting the banks because they had approached us. And as we started with one bank, going to two banks, we actually were besieged, and I use that term guardedly, but we were besieged by bankers who heard from their friends that there were big profits to make. And as we proceeded, we ended up two bankers, four bankers, six, and the numbers just kept going up. And during that operation we laundered over $100 million of traffickers' money through those banks down into—ultimately most of it went to Colombia. And we would actually bring these people in the operation, and with undercover cameras, they would sit and brag and talk for hours about how much money they were going to make, and that they clearly knew it was drug money, and didn't care. As long as they didn't touch the drugs themselves, they didn't care. It was all about money, and it was all about lining their own pockets. It was probably the best lesson in greed you could see on television.

How did you collect the money and what did you do with it once you had it?

We actually did pickups in various manners. Some monies were brought to us. Others, we would meet couriers in parking lots. We would deposit some of the monies in the banks in the United States. And then we would move some of it electronically to the banks in Mexico. In other cases, we would actually move the bulk cash to a bank in Mexico. So there were various ways that the money was moved into Mexico in those banks.

U.S. Customs agents would drive the money into a Mexican bank? How did you do it?

Actually, the informant took money across the border, in at least one case that I know of. The majority was by electronic transfer. In some cases we used Caribbean banks that we had set up. And the money would move from Los Angeles to the Caribbean bank. From the Caribbean bank to Mexico, it would then either move back to the United States in converted form into Mexican bank drafts, and be deposited in various accounts that we stipulated, or it would move from those accounts, to other accounts sometimes offshore in the Caribbean. Or it could be transferred directly out of the Mexican bank to Colombia. And in some cases it would go not just to an individual bank account, but yet be laundered a second time in Colombia through a peso or currency exchange. So its identity became further remote.[65]

12.15.3.1   Informant Reward

According to press reports and court records, the lead informant (there were several confidential informants) in Operation Casablanca received $2.3 million and was eligible for another $7.5 million in rewards, depending on the outcome of forfeiture proceedings and spin-off investigations.[66] No one outside Customs will ever know just how much he was finally paid.[67] However, it's interesting to note that during the Operation Casablanca trial testimony was elicited from agents that his substantial rewards did not make him their highest-paid informant.[68]

On the floor of the U.S. Senate, Senator Charles E. Grassley of Iowa stated: "Drug traffickers are bad enough. But their financial advisers and bankers are truly despicable. Thus, the Customs' undercover operation that exposed some of these lowlifes is to be celebrated. My hat is off to the agents and informants involved with 'Operation Casablanca' that risked their lives to help defend our institutions and bring these pinstriped bandits to justice." Commentators noted that it was possibly the first time informants were praised on the floor of the Senate.[69]

The lead informant's control agent was awarded a $10,000 bonus and a certificate of merit from Customs Commissioner Raymond Kelly.[70] The bonus was added to the agent's five-figure salary for income tax purposes.

12.15.4   Operational Results

From financial year 2005 through March 2011, the DEA stripped approximately $17.7 billion in revenue from drug trafficking organizations. Money laundering stings and their informants figured prominently in the seizures.[71]

12.15.5   Equitable Sharing of Proceeds

In the early days of money laundering stings, the best that state and local law enforcement agencies could hope for was to participate as a member of a federal money laundering task force. Passage of the Comprehensive Crime Control Act of 1984 authorized the sharing of federal forfeiture proceeds with cooperating state and local law enforcement agencies. Today, there are scores of federal statutes that allow for the equitable sharing of forfeited property with task force partners. (See Appendix 7C.)

It has been a profitable partnership. By March 1994, the DOJ Asset Forfeiture Fund had shared over $1.4 billion in forfeited assets with more than 3000 state and local law enforcement agencies. From 1999 through September 30, 2004, equitable sharing allocation levels averaged $232,017,000. In 2005, this number grew to $270 million.[72] In 2012, $681 million was shared with local law enforcement agencies. As of 2013, the Asset Forfeiture Fund balance was $4.4 billion.[73]

As evidence of the program's appeal to local police agencies, the Monroe County, Florida, Sheriff's Office (the Florida Keys) received a check for $25 million as their share of forfeitures resulting from a money laundering investigation. The county law enforcement agency had been a member of a high-intensity drug trafficking joint task force responsible for the investigation.[74] The funds were shared in accordance with the memorandum of understanding (MOU) governing the operation. (See Appendix 12A.)

12.16   State and Local Money Laundering Task Forces

12.16.1   South Florida Impact Task Force

Local law enforcement agencies saw the cash potential of money laundering sting operations and became anxious to shed their federal partners. Doing so would allow the agencies to keep all of the proceeds of the sting operations. New laws enabled state and local agencies to engage in the stings.[75]

In 1993, the South Florida Impact Task Force was created. Located in Coral Gables, Florida, the task force was staffed by 50 officers assigned from 13 state and local police agencies. It was a law enforcement entity new to local policing: it paid for itself. Its only funding came from money it was able to take off the streets through sophisticated money laundering investigations and cash taken from money stash houses during what are known as knock-and-talk investigations.[76]

Impact's money laundering cases were clones of extremely successful FBI, DEA, and Customs money laundering sting operations such as Casablanca. They too focused on the Achilles' heel of the drug trade: cash. The unprecedented success of Impact was directly attributed to its stable of highly paid confidential informants. The confidential informants were promised 15% of the net value of anything seized as a result of their information.

In 1996, Impact seized $9.3 million and identified as many as 2000 bank accounts used as money laundering fronts. "Drug Czar" Barry McCaffrey considered Impact a law enforcement success story.[77] By 2000, its agents had seized $140 million, 30 tons of cocaine, and over 6 tons of marijuana.[78] Money seized by Impact was divided among the state and local police agencies participating in the task force after overhead expenses and the 15% rewards to its informants were paid out.

Impact soon became the focus of investigative reporters from the *Miami Herald*.

In 2000, the U.S. Attorney's Office in Miami and the Florida Department of Law Enforcement investigated the South Florida Impact Task Force. In sum, their investigation revealed a loosely run operation with extremely well-paid leaders. One manager received $625,000 for his work and a contract calling for a percentage of liquidated forfeited property.[79]

12.16.2   South Florida Money Laundering Strike Force

The investigation resulted in the creation of the South Florida Money Laundering Strike Force. A 15-agency enterprise,[80] it is a tightly operated law enforcement entity. Its MOU outlines its goals:

> The Strike Force is to effect dedicated and intensive investigative, preventative, and general law enforcement efforts primarily with regard to the investigation of illegal money laundering and drug trafficking operations and related crimes, and in efforts to dismantle and disrupt the organizations committing such violations. The principal goal of the Strike Force shall be the coordinated investigation of, and successful prosecution of perpetrators of such crimes, with particular emphasis on efforts designed to identify and dismantle organized criminal enterprises. Such efforts shall include, but are not limited to, undercover operations designed to detect illegal activity and to identify those involved in such activity including those directing or otherwise controlling such activity, interception of communications related to such activity as may be authorized by law, the arrest and prosecution of those involved (utilizing state and federal or other prosecutions, as appropriate); the seizure and forfeiture of assets of those engaged in such activity or otherwise supporting such activity

(utilizing state and federal forfeiture options, as appropriate); the prosecution of regulatory and civil actions designed to end such criminal activity, as appropriate; and the referral of investigative leads and intelligence to such other federal, state, foreign or local law enforcement authorities as may be required and appropriate under the Strike Force's operations. In recognition that such efforts transcend jurisdiction limits, it is the intent of this voluntary cooperation agreement to assure the continued functioning of law enforcement in areas where such limits might otherwise thwart major law enforcement efforts.

(See Appendix 12B.)

12.16.3   Tri-County Money Laundering Task Force, Bal Harbour, Florida

In October 2012, investigative reporters for the *Miami Herald* revealed that the Village of Bal Harbour, Florida, Police Department, a 27-officer force located on the northern tip of Miami Beach, seized nearly $49.7 million in little more than 3 years. The department is the leader of the Tri-County Money Laundering Task Force. It is not a member of the South Florida Money Laundering Strike Force. It was founded by one of the leaders of the defunct Impact Task Force.

Nearly all of the Tri-County Task Force's stings took place outside Florida. No local prosecutions resulted. After covering expenses and sharing the proceeds with task force partners, the village police department netted more than $8 million. Part of the proceeds was used to purchase a 35-ft speedboat, a mobile command center, trucks, and computers.

The cases responsible for the cash seizures were informant driven. *Herald* reporters followed the money and learned that task force informants were paid over $600,000 for their efforts.

The *Herald* labeled the task force a rogue operation, reporting that seized money was used to pay for beach parties and prohibited first-class airline travel by police officers.[81] An OIG investigation agreed with the *Herald*.[82] A September 2012 report concluded that the task force had violated rules governing the federal equitable sharing guidelines. It was ordered to turn over more than $4 million to the Justice Department.

12.17   Controlled Deliveries

Not often thought of as an undercover operation, controlled deliveries employ many of the ploys found in traditional sting operations. Also known as a convoy delivery,[83] it is an undercover investigative technique that allows illicit shipments of contraband, usually drug shipments, to pass out of, through, or into one or more states. The delivery is made under the tight supervision of law enforcement authorities to suspects who are anticipating receipt of the shipment.[84]

The shipments are usually those discovered at a point of entry by a Customs inspector during a routine inspection. With more than 13,000 trucks crossing into the United States from Mexico every day,[85] the seizures are becoming an everyday occurrence. So are controlled deliveries.

12.17.1   Controlled Delivery with a Cooperating Individual and Blind Mules

Immediately after a drug shipment is detected at a port of entry by an inspector, ICE agents are called to further the investigation. The driver is interviewed and usually arrested. Deals offered to the driver at this stage vary. If he is unaware of the illegal contents of his truck and is able to convince the agents of his unwitting role, he is considered a "blind mule"[86] and he may not face charges. However, the unwitting explanation is almost always advanced and the driver's legal fate often depends on his willingness to assist agents. If he is willing to cooperate, he remains in custody and the shipment is allowed to continue to its intended destination.

The cooperating driver plays an important role in furthering the investigation. He may have been previously directed to make scheduled stops or phone calls en route to the final destination to assure the recipients that the load was undetected. Agents may delay arrests en route to the final destination to identify as many members of the trafficking network as possible. Their objective is to arrest those involved at a point where the most valuable evidence is most readily available.

The technique can be very effective in identifying, arresting, and prosecuting the managers of criminal organizations. The tactic has proved extremely effective in the investigation of transnational organized criminal activity including trafficking in drugs, weapons, and humans.[87]

12.17.2   Cold Convoys: Controlled Deliveries with a Noncooperating Violator

Cold convoys are an investigative technique employed when law enforcement agents discover contraband in the course of Customs inspection without being noticed by the driver. The controlled substances are allowed to proceed from the border or port of entry (POE) to the intended destinations within the United States without the violators being aware that the controlled substances have been discovered.

The noncooperating driver is not under arrest, is not in custody, and has not agreed to assist the agents in the delivery of the controlled substance.

In most instances, the agents are not aware of the actual destinations of the controlled substance within the United States.

12.17.3   Controlled Importation: Transportation Cases

Controlled importation investigations are also referred to as transportation cases. They are close cousins to traditional reverse undercover operations. A transportation case generally involves an undercover agent with the assistance of a confidential informant providing a transportation service for the source of a controlled substance (who may be located in a foreign country) and making delivery of the controlled substance to a specifically identified intended destination and target within the United States.

Transportation cases typically have the agent or informant providing the vehicle, vessel, or aircraft and serving as the driver, captain, or pilot. The undercover operatives are paid by the owner of the drugs for services rendered. Variations in roles and services occur, but the investigative objective remains the same. In the case of drug shipments, the contraband is brought into the United States under the supervision of surveillance agents and delivered to the intended destination. The delivery is choreographed by agents in hopes that only high-quality targets are arrested.

12.17.4   Controlled Exportation

Also referred to as a controlled delivery from the United States to a foreign country, this technique involves the delivery of controlled substances to a location outside the United States to a suspect violator who is the subject of a criminal investigation.

12.17.5   Labor-Intense Operations

Controlled deliveries and transportation cases require significant planning, including approval from ICE headquarters and coordination with law enforcement agencies whose jurisdictions the controlled delivery is expected to pass. The cases also demand substantial personnel and equipment commitments. Surveillance activities can be lengthy and geographically broad, often requiring sophisticated tracking equipment and aircraft support to ensure the security of the contraband while it is in transit to its destination.

Controlled deliveries do not always go as planned. Recipients often become suspicious as the shipment moves across country, and they do not accept delivery. It is not unusual for low-level members of the organization to receive the shipment and effectively insulate their boss. Shipments have been completely lost. In such cases, the Office of Internal Affairs takes over the investigation.

12.18   Terror Stings and Proactive Preemption

Traditional reactive investigative techniques have proved fruitless in uncovering terror plots. Instead, the FBI has chosen to take a proactive approach to fighting the war on terror through sting operations and what it refers to as proactive preemption: making an arrest before an act of terror can be carried out.[88]

Public gathering places including houses of worship have become the focus of FBI attention. According to the FBI's former counterterrorism chief, "What matters to the FBI is preventing a massive attack that might be planned by some people … using the mosque or church as a shield because they believe they're safe there. That is what the American people want the FBI to do. They don't want some type of attack happening on U.S. soil because the FBI didn't act on information."[89]

Surveilling and infiltrating mosques is nothing new. In the early 1990s, a plan to blow up New York City landmarks was foiled by a Muslim informant who spent months inside a New Jersey mosque. The investigation led to the 1995 life sentence for the Egyptian cleric Sheik Omar Abdel Rahman, the so-called "blind sheik." He was said to be the spiritual leader of the men convicted in the 1993 bombing of the World Trade Center.[90] The informant was paid more than $1 million for his work.[91]

The prosecutor in that case defended sending an informant into the mosque: "A lot of what happened was planned in the mosque. The recruiting went on in the mosque, a lot of the instruction went on in the mosque, we even had gun transactions in there."[92]

It's no secret to the American Muslim community that it is the target of federal, state, and local police attention. When a stranger arrives at a mosque, it's often assumed that he is an informant.

12.18.1   Oracle and Operation Flex

In June 2007, the Council on American–Islamic Relations (CAIR) took the unusual step of calling the FBI to report a suspicious and frequent visitor at the Islamic Center of Irvine, California. He went by the name Farouk Al-Aziz. CAIR had concerns that the man was a possible terrorist.[93] No FBI action was taken on the complaint. CAIR had a restraining order issued to keep Aziz away from the mosque.

The man who prompted CAIR's action was an Anglo male, a 47-year-old veteran FBI informant code-named Oracle. From 2004 until 2008, he had assisted the FBI in narcotics, bank robbery, and murder-for-hire investigations.[94] In 2009, he was sent to the FBI's Orange County Joint Terrorism Task Force for an anti-terror assignment.

Oracle became the centerpiece of an anti-terror investigation code-named Operation Flex. The informant claimed he was given authority to "engage in jihadist rhetoric, including but not limited to conducting terrorist operations, possessing weapons, and initiating conversations to further terrorist acts against the United States."[95]

Little if anything would be known about Oracle had he not filed a $10 million civil rights lawsuit against the FBI.[96] He fell out of favor with the FBI following his arrest by Irvine police detectives for allegedly distributing steroids and lying to investigators. The FBI immediately deactivated him.

The publicity surrounding the Oracle lawsuit exacerbated the already strained relations between the Muslim community and the FBI. The executive of the Islamic Shura Council of Southern California was blunt: "We suspected this was happening. What these guys have done is create an environment where every person begins to suspect the other and with the infighting and inward suspicion, the community becomes its own victim."[97]

FBI Director Robert Mueller defended the tactic: "We don't investigate places, we investigate individuals. To the extent that there may be evidence or other information of criminal wrongdoings, then we will ... undertake those investigations. We will continue to do it."[98]

Muslim informants usually find themselves taking commanding roles in the FBI's counterterrorism investigative tool of choice: sting operations. Borrowed from the war on drugs, stings have become the centerpiece of the FBI's war of proactive preemption waged against domestic terrorists.

12.18.2 Fantasy Terror Operations and Entrapment

Entrapment is often the only viable defense that can be raised by defendants who've fallen for a terror sting. "It was the informant's idea, not mine" is often claimed at trial as a defense. But the defendants almost never win in court. Indeed, it's rare to find a drug-enforcement sting operation in which the subject of the investigation has no prior arrests for trafficking. Because the entrapment defense requires the defendant to prove that he had no predisposition to violate the law, a lengthy criminal record usually guarantees a conviction.

Ferreting out jihadists through sting operations has proved to be a bit more challenging than capturing drug dealers through a ruse. Almost without exception, the terrorists delivered to their FBI handlers by informants as sting targets have clean records. They are often unknown to authorities beyond their immigration records.

At trial, proving predisposition to beat the entrapment defense can be a tough hurdle for prosecutors. It's usually overcome by introducing lengthy transcripts of tape-recorded conversations between the informant and the purported terrorist where he is heard espousing jihadist rhetoric.

In 2011, a federal judge handed down a 25-year sentence after a jury found a defendant guilty of conspiring to blow up two Bronx, New York, synagogues. The informant in this case was a low-level drug dealer who was paid $250,000 and "immigration benefits" for his work. The judge called the case a "fantasy terror operation." She added that "only the government could have made a terrorist out of the [defendant], whose buffoonery is positively Shakespearean in its scope."[99]

The University of California, Berkeley's Investigative Reporting Program and political magazine *Mother Jones* examined the FBI's terror/sting case success ratio. Of the 508 terrorism suspects arrested since 9/11, 158 were the product of a sting operation. Of those defendants, 49 were informant-driven undercover operations. Only three of the highly touted terror cases made by the FBI during the last decade were made without an informant or a sting.[100]

12.18.3   Liberty City Seven

Following 9/11, the FBI made terrorism investigations their number one priority. Every FBI agent in the United States was ordered to get to work and recruit terror informants and start making terrorism cases.

Miami FBI agents were no exceptions. But where to start? The city, usually associated with anti-Castro activity, was never regarded as a terrorism hot spot. That was until June 22, 2006 when Attorney General Alberto Gonzales announced the arrest of the Liberty City Seven. According to Gonzales, the group was planning to destroy Chicago's Sears Tower and the FBI building in Miami. They also planned to blow up the Empire State Building. FBI Director Robert Mueller referred to the success of the operation in a speech entitled "Protecting America from Terrorist Attack: The Threat of Homegrown Terrorism."

The case got started when an eccentric Haitian–American known as Batiste had the misfortune of striking up a conversation with a Middle Eastern convenience store clerk. Batiste, a longtime resident of Miami's primarily black Liberty City section, was viewed by most residents as a bit odd. Relatives described him as a "Moses-like" figure often seen roaming the neighborhood wearing a robe and carrying a crooked wooden cane. He fancied himself the leader of the local Seas of David religious sect known as the Universal Devine Saviors and was always on the lookout for young men to convert.[101] At the moment, there were six in his flock.

The store clerk was a 22-year-old Yemeni snowbird from Brooklyn, New York. He was also a former New York Police Department (NYPD) drug informant, cross-trained by the police on how to make terrorism cases.

He moved to Miami Beach, Florida, in 2004 where he was almost immediately jailed for domestic violence. Unable to post bail, he contacted his NYPD control agent for help. The NYPD put him in touch with a Miami FBI agent who arranged for his release. The New Yorker was documented as a Miami FBI terror informant and put to work. Recruiting a Yemeni informant in Miami was a rare occurrence.

The FBI teamed their new informant with a Chicago FBI informant who had recently arrived from Lebanon. The two informants were directed to make a terrorism case against Batiste and his six followers. His flock of six was unemployed and could be found in a vacant Liberty City warehouse talking about religion. When the two informants entered their lives, talk quickly turned to terrorism. The informants seemed able to finance a terror plot. The Sears Tower, Empire State Building, and Miami FBI Office were decided on as the targets.

Just before Christmas 2005, Batiste gave the informants a list of supplies that he needed to carry out his jihad plot. It included boots, uniforms, machine guns, and vehicles. He provided the boot sizes for himself and his six followers. A week later, he requested radios, binoculars, bulletproof vests, and $50,000 in cash.

Hundreds of hours of video and audiotapes were made. Most notable was a March 2006 ceremony in which Batiste and his followers swore an oath of loyalty to al-Qaeda administered by the informants. The seven were arrested on June 22, 2006, accused of being a homegrown terror cell.

The arrests were made before the alleged terrorists struck any of their targets. The strategy of arresting suspects before the crime occurs is called preemptive prosecution. It's risky for the prosecutor. A conviction almost always relies on a jury believing the testimony of informants.[102]

In a rare turn of events, Batiste decided he would testify in his own defense. He explained to the jury that all he and his men were doing was trying to con the two informants out of their $50,000. It must have been persuasive testimony. One of the accused was acquitted by the jury. The judge declared a mistrial.[103]

The loss didn't deter the government. They took the case to trial again. The second jury didn't buy the government's case either. The jury was hung, but it also acquitted one more of the defendants. He was returned to his cell. The government would take action to deport the acquitted man along with his other freed codefendant.

It was now the Liberty City Five. The third trial resulted in convictions. Batiste and four of his remaining "soldiers" were convicted. Sentences ranged from 13 years for Batiste and 9, 8, 7, and 6 years, respectively, for his four remaining followers.

The government had said it was ready to take the case to trial a fourth time if necessary. The New York Times interviewed a veteran former Miami U.S. attorney who said, "If you sledgehammer the square peg three times, eventually you're going to blast it into the round hole. This isn't a terrorism case; it's an overcharged gang case."[104]

An interview with family members summed up why the government had, up until then, so much trouble proving their case:

> [A] lot of show has been made about the militaristic boots that they had ... It turns out ... the FBI bought them the boots. If you look at the indictment, the biggest piece of evidence ... is that the group may have taken pictures of a bunch of targets in South Florida. But the guys couldn't afford their own cameras, so the federal government bought them the cameras ... The federal government rented them the cars that they needed to get downtown in order to take the pictures. In addition ... the men provided the FBI informant with a list of things they needed in order to blow up these buildings, but in the list they didn't include any explosives or any materials which could be used to make explosives. So now everyone in Liberty City is joking that the guys were going to kick down the FBI building with their new boots, because they didn't have any devices which could have been used to explode ... .[105]

The jury never heard that the FBI paid the Yemeni informant $40,000 and the Chicago informant $80,000 for their work. Nor did they learn that the Yemeni informant had failed a polygraph test while working with the FBI in Chicago.

A retired 35-year veteran FBI agent hired by the defense team to testify as an expert witness in the use of informants was surprised by the government's conduct: "What I found to be startling was the fact that the Bureau had used an informant who had been found to be deceptive in a prior operation. I'm just shocked because it appears to me they violated Attorney General's Guidelines. The single most important factor when evaluating an informant's suitability is truthfulness." The jury never heard the opinion of the expert. The judge excluded him as a witness before he could take the stand.[106]

On November 1, 2011, the Eleventh Circuit Court of Appeals upheld the Liberty City Seven conviction.[107]

Appendix 12A: Application for Authorization to Conduct an Undercover Operation[108]

Date Submitted:
Name of Operation:
Programmatic Area: [Targeted Criminal Activity]
Location:
Group Supervisor: [and contact telephone number]
Operation Program Manager: [UC Schools dates 00/00]
Case Agent(s):
Undercover Operative(s):   [UC Schools dates 00/00]

Financial Record Keeper:	[UC Schools dates 00/00]
Exemption Requested:	[the exemptions should be listed, 1,2,3,4][109]
Prosecutor:	[attach letter from Prosecutor]
Offsite Location:	[Yes or No]
Internet Web Site:	[Yes or No]
Sensitivity:	
Funding Requested:	[appropriated funding needed]
Expenditure Authorization Requested:	[spending ceiling requested (w/ proceeds)]
DEA Designated ASAC:	[only if appropriate and contact telephone no]
Related Cases:	[list case numbers - current active cases]
Foreign Offices Contacted:	[If applicable, Yes or No]

PRELIMINARY ACTIVITIES:

Briefly summarize the case activities which have occurred to date. What is the nature and extent of undercover activities that have already occurred? Include a brief description of the operational targets and discuss the focus of the operation. If possible, identify a particular case number which best describes the criminal activities of the subjects under investigation.

POTENTIAL:

Illustrate the potential for success. Specifically, who are the current identified targets? Describe the undercover scenario(s) and the evidence that is anticipated to result from them. Describe the goals that can be achieved over the next six months. What strategies will be employed to achieve them? What objectives must be met before the operation is concluded and when is this likely to occur?

SECURITY:

In light of the previous activities of the investigation, has the operation been compromised in any way so far? How can the project continue without being compromised?

SAFETY:

Describe the nature and frequency of undercover activities and the risk of personal injury, property damage, financial loss, or harm to innocent third parties. How long has the investigation been active?

What actions will be taken to ensure the physical and psychological well being of the operative(s) and innocent third parties if applicable.

Have the undercover agents attended and are they certified to conduct undercover work (U/C Operative School)? If not, a request for a waiver to work in an undercover capacity must be submitted.

SIGNIFICANCE:

Summarize the investment of resources (financial and personnel) that will be devoted to this operation.

Demonstrate how the investment is warranted in light of the importance of the identified targets of the operation and the investigative priorities of the agency.

Specifically identify the investigative priorities that relate to the operation.

EXEMPTIONS:

List certifications for exemptions [under applicable law] necessary for the conduct of the operation. Provide justifications for each of the exemptions requested.[110]

SENSITIVE CIRCUMSTANCES:

List which sensitive circumstances are likely to occur in the operation? Identify them and briefly describe what they will involve.

OTHER AGENCIES:

If other agencies are involved, provide the following information:

- What is the role and degree of involvement of other agencies in this operation?
- Has this operation been reviewed through another agency's under-cover process? If so, what was the result?
- Who is responsible for determining investigative strategies among the agencies involved?
- What MOUs are applicable to this operation and have there been operational issues related to them?
- What arrangements have been made regarding prosecutions relating to the operation?
- Who will present the cases to the Prosecutor's Office?
- What violations will be considered for prosecution?
- What arrangements have been made with other agencies regarding payment for expenses of the operation?

- What agreements have been reached with other agencies regarding proceeds of the operation?

If this operation is directly related to HIDTA or OCDETF, attach a copy of the proposal to this application.

FOREIGN TRAVEL:

If foreign travel is anticipated, provide the following information:

- Describe any foreign travel anticipated and indicate that appropriate undercover documentation, i.e. undercover identification, required to accomplish the objectives, set forth in the proposal, will be (or have been) identified. If no foreign travel is anticipated put non-applicable (n/a) under this section. (This will not preclude an operation from traveling foreign if circumstances develop during the course of the operation which necessitate foreign undercover activity).

BUDGET:

Estimate the budget for six months. Also explain any unusual or costly expenses. In this section list any recoverable funds, however, do not include this amount in the total expenditures.

INFORMANTS:

Provide a list of the informants (by source number) who are currently involved in the operation. For each informant, provide the following information:

- What is the CI number?
- Is the informant a defendant or possible defendant in a criminal matter?
- What is the role of the informant in the operation?
- How has the informant demonstrated their reliability?
- What is the motivation of the informant?
- Who is controlling the informant?
- List by date the payments made to the informant in the last 12 months by any law enforcement agency for any purpose and show who made each payment?
- Place an asterisk by payments that relate directly to this operation.
- List total amount paid to the informant in this operation.
- List any other income derived by the informant from this operation and explain the circumstances for earning it.
- Attach a copy of the written Personal Assistance Agreement (PAA), if applicable, for the informant.[111]

Appendix 12B: Memorandum of Understanding Between the Bureau of Alcohol, Tobacco, Firearms and Explosives (ATF), and Local Police Department

This Memorandum of Understanding (MOU) is entered into by and between the Bureau of Alcohol, Tobacco, Firearms and Explosives (ATF) and Local Police Department as it relates to the Violent Offender Task Force (herein referred to as the "Task Force").

AUTHORITIES

Offenses investigated and enforced pursuant to this MOU are those falling within ATF's jurisdiction 28 U.S.C. sec. 599A; 27 CFR sec. 0.130. Specifically, the Gun Control Act of 1968, 18 U.S.C. §§ 921 et. seq. and the National Firearms Act, 26 U.S.C. §§ 5861 et. seq.

PURPOSE

The Task Force will perform the activities and duties described below:

a. Investigate firearms trafficking
b. Investigate firearms-related violent crime
c. Gather and report intelligence data relating to trafficking and firearms
d. Conduct undercover operations where appropriate and engage in other traditional methods of investigation in order that the Task Force's activities will result in effective prosecution before the courts of the United States and the State of [XXX].

The mission of the participating Agencies is to conduct in-depth investigations of arson-related crimes; to identify and target for prosecution the perpetrators of such crimes (i.e., outlaw motorcycle organizations, street gangs, armed career criminals and armed narcotic traffickers); and to achieve maximum coordination and cooperation in bringing to bear the combined resources of the participating Agencies aimed at reducing the most violent criminal activity within the community.

MEASUREMENT OF SUCCESS

The success of this initiative will be measured by the participating agencies' willingness to share certain information, (i.e., crime statistics) for the purpose of measuring the success of the task force as well as its performance:

• Reduce the risk to public safety caused by the criminal possession and use of firearms

PHYSICAL LOCATION

Officers/troopers/agents assigned to this Task Force by their employer shall be referred to as task force officers (TFOs). TFOs will be assigned to the ATF _____ Field Office and will be located at _____.

SUPERVISION AND CONTROL

The day-to-day supervision and administrative control of TFOs will be the mutual responsibility of the participants, with the ATF Special Agent in Charge or his/her designee having operational control over all operations related to this Task Force.

Each TFO shall remain subject to their respective agencies' policies, and shall report to their respective agencies regarding matters unrelated to this agreement/task force. With regard to matters related to the Task Force, TFOs will be subject to Federal law, Department of Justice (DOJ) and ATF orders, regulations and policy, including those related to standards of conduct, sexual harassment, equal opportunity issues and Federal disclosure laws.

Failure to comply with this paragraph could result in a TFO's dismissal from the Task Force.

ATF agrees to designate the Resident Agent in Charge, [XXXX] Field Office, as ATF's coordinator of this agreement. The Police Chief and/or designee will serve as the department's coordinator.

The coordinators have overall responsibility for the policies and guidelines affecting this MOU.

Operational problems encountered between ATF and Police Department will be mutually addressed and resolved by the coordinators.

PERSONNEL, RESOURCES AND SUPERVISION

To accomplish the objectives of the Task Force, ATF will assign Special Agents to the Task Force. ATF will also, subject to the availability of funds, provide necessary funds and equipment to support the activities of the ATF Special Agents and officers assigned to the Task Force. This support may include: office space, office supplies, travel funds, funds for the purchase of evidence and information, investigative equipment, training and other support items.

Each participating agency agrees to make available to their assigned task force members any equipment ordinarily assigned for use by that agency. In the event ATF supplies equipment (which may include vehicles, weapons or radios), TFOs must abide by any applicable ATF orders or policy, and may be required to enter into a separate agreement for their use.

All TFOs shall qualify with their respective firearms by complying with ATF's Firearms and Weapons Policy.

SECURITY CLEARANCES

All TFOs will undergo a security clearance and background investigation, and ATF shall bear the costs associated with those investigations. TFOs must not be the subject of any ongoing investigation by their department or any other law enforcement agency, and past behavior or punishment, disciplinary, punitive or otherwise, may disqualify one from eligibility to join the Task Force. ATF has final authority as to the suitability of TFOs for inclusion on the Task Force.

DEPUTATIONS

ATF, as the sponsoring Federal law enforcement agency, may request at its sole discretion that the participating agency's TFOs be deputized by the U.S. Marshals Service to extend their jurisdiction, to include applying for and executing Federal search and arrest warrants, and requesting and executing Federal grand jury subpoenas for records and evidence involving violations of Federal laws. Such requests will be made on an individual basis as determined by ATF.

The participating agencies agree that any Federal authority that may be conferred by a deputation is limited to activities supervised by ATF and will terminate when this MOU is terminated or when the deputized TFOs leave the Task Force, or at the discretion of ATF.

ASSIGNMENTS, REPORTS AND INFORMATION SHARING

An ATF supervisor or designee will be empowered with designated oversight for investigative and personnel matters related to the Task Force and will be responsible for opening, monitoring, directing and closing Task Force investigations in accordance with ATF policy and the applicable United States Attorney General's Guidelines.

Assignments will be based on, but not limited to, experience, training and performance, in addition to the discretion of the ATF supervisor.

All investigative reports will be prepared utilizing ATF's investigative case management system (N-Force), and utilizing ATF case report numbers. The participating agency will share investigative reports, findings, intelligence, etc., in furtherance of the mission of this agreement, to the fullest extent allowed by law. For the purposes of uniformity, there will be no duplication of reports, but rather a single report prepared by a designated individual which can be duplicated as necessary. Every effort should be made to document investigative activity on ATF Reports of Investigation (ROI), unless otherwise agreed to by ATF and the participating agency(ies). This section does not preclude the necessity of individual TFOs to complete forms required by their employing agency.

Information will be freely shared among the TFOs and ATF personnel with the understanding that all investigative information will be kept strictly confidential and will only be used in furtherance of criminal investigations. No information gathered during the course of the Task Force, to include informal communications between TFOs and ATF personnel, may be disseminated to any third party, non-task force member by any task force member without the express permission of the ATF Special Agent in Charge or his/her designee.

Any public requests for access to the records or any disclosures of information obtained by task force members during Task Force investigations will be handled in accordance with applicable statutes, regulations, and policies pursuant to the Freedom of Information Act and the Privacy Act and other applicable federal and/or state statutes and regulations.

INVESTIGATIVE METHODS

The parties agree to utilize Federal standards pertaining to evidence handling and electronic surveillance activities to the greatest extent possible. However, in situations where state or local laws are more restrictive than comparable Federal law, investigative methods employed by state and local law enforcement agencies shall conform to those requirements, pending a decision as to a venue for prosecution.

The use of other investigative methods (search warrants, interceptions of oral communications, etc.) and reporting procedures in connection therewith will be consistent with the policy and procedures of ATF. All Task Force operations will be conducted and reviewed in accordance with applicable ATF and Department of Justice policy and guidelines.

None of the parties to this MOU will knowingly seek investigations under this MOU that would cause a conflict with any ongoing investigation of an agency not party to this MOU. It is incumbent upon each participating agency to notify its personnel regarding the Task Force's areas of concern and jurisdiction. All law enforcement actions will be coordinated and cooperatively carried out by all parties to this MOU.

INFORMANTS

ATF guidelines and policy regarding the operation of informants and cooperating witnesses will apply to all informants and cooperating witnesses directed by TFOs.

Informants developed by TFOs may be registered as informants of their respective agencies for administrative purposes and handling. The policies and procedures of the participating agency with regard to handling informants will apply to all informants that the participating agency registers. In addition, it will be incumbent upon the registering participating agency to maintain a file with respect to the performance of all informants or witnesses it registers. All information obtained from an informant and relevant to matters within the jurisdiction of this MOU will be shared with all parties to this MOU. The registering agency will pay all reasonable and necessary informant expenses for each informant that a participating agency registers.

DECONFLICTION

Each participating agency agrees that the deconfliction process requires the sharing of certain operational information with the Task Force, which, if disclosed to unauthorized persons, could endanger law enforcement personnel and the public. As a result of this concern, each participating agency agrees to adopt security measures set forth herein:

a. Each participating agency will assign primary and secondary points of contact.
b. Each participating agency agrees to keep its points of contact list updated.

The points of contact for this Task Force are
        ATF: RAC _____
        Participating Agency: _____ _

EVIDENCE

Evidence is maintained by the lead agency having jurisdiction in the court system intended for prosecution. Evidence generated from investigations initiated by a TFO or ATF special agent intended for Federal prosecution will be placed in the ATF designated vault, using the procedures found in ATF orders.

All firearms seized by a TFO must be submitted for fingerprint analysis and for a National Integrated Ballistics Information Network (NIBIN) examination. Once all analyses are completed, all firearms seized under Federal law shall be placed into the ATF designated vault for proper storage. All firearms information/descriptions taken into ATF custody must be submitted to ATF's National Tracing Center.

JURISDICTION/PROSECUTIONS

Cases will he reviewed by the ATF Special Agent in Charge or his/her designee in consultation with the participating agency and the United States Attorney's Office and appropriate state's attorney offices, to determine whether cases will be referred for prosecution to the U.S. Attorney's Office or to the relevant state's attorney's office. This determination will be based upon which level of prosecution will best serve the interests of justice and the greatest overall benefit to the public. Any question that arises pertaining to prosecution will be resolved through discussion among the investigative agencies and prosecuting entities having an interest in the matter.

In the event that a state or local matter is developed that is outside the jurisdiction of ATF or it is decided that a case will be prosecuted on the state or local level, ATF will provide all relevant information to state and local authorities, subject to Federal law. Whether to continue investigation of state and local crimes is at the sole discretion of the state or local participating agency.

USE OF FORCE

All fulltime TFOs will comply with ATF and the Department of Justice's (DOJ's) use of force policies, unless a TFOs agency's Use of Force policy is more restrictive, in which case the TFO may use their respective agency's use of force policy. TFOs must be briefed on ATF's and DOJ's Use of Force policy by an ATF official, and will be provided with a copy of such policy.

MEDIA

Media relations will be handled by ATF and the U.S. Attorney's Office's public information officers in coordination with each participating agency. Information for press releases will be reviewed and mutually agreed upon by all participating agencies, who will take part in press conferences. Assigned personnel will be informed not to give statements to the media concerning any ongoing investigation or prosecution under this MOU without the concurrence of the other participants and, when appropriate, the relevant prosecutor's office.

All personnel from the participating agencies shall strictly adhere to the requirements of Title 26 United States Code, § 6103. Disclosure of tax return information and tax information acquired during the course of investigations involving National Firearms Act (NFA) firearms as defined in 26 U.S.C., Chapter 53 shall not be made except as provided by law.

SALARY/OVERTIME COMPENSATION

During the period of the MOU, participating agencies will provide for the salary and employment benefits of their respective employees. All participating agencies will retain control over their employees' work hours, including the approval of overtime.

ATF may have funds available to reimburse overtime to the State and Local TFO's agency, subject to the guidelines of the Department of Justice Asset Forfeiture Fund. This funding would be available under the terms of a memorandum of agreement (MOA) established pursuant to the provisions of 28 U.S.C. section 524. The participating agency agrees to abide by the applicable Federal law and policy with regard to the payment of overtime from the Department of Justice Asset Forfeiture Fund. The participating agency must be recognized under State law as a law enforcement agency and their officers/troopers/investigators as sworn law enforcement officers. If required or requested, the participating agency shall be responsible for demonstrating to the Department of Justice that its personnel are law enforcement officers for the purpose of overtime payment from the Department of Justice Asset Forfeiture Fund. This MOU is not a funding document.

In accordance with these provisions and any MOA on asset forfeiture, the ATF Special Agent in Charge or designee shall be responsible for certifying reimbursement requests for overtime expenses incurred as a result of this agreement.

AUDIT INFORMATION

Operations under this MOU are subject to audit by ATF, the Department of Justice's Office of the Inspector General, the Government Accountability Office, and other Government designated auditors. Participating agencies agree to permit such audits and to maintain all records relating to Department of Justice Asset Forfeiture Fund payments for expenses either incurred during the course of this Task Force or for a period of not less than three (3) years and, if an audit is being conducted, until such time that the audit is officially completed, whichever is greater.

FORFEITURES/SEIZURES

All assets seized for administrative forfeiture will be seized and forfeited in compliance with the rules and regulations set forth by the U.S. Department of Justice Asset Forfeiture guidelines. When the size or composition of the item(s) seized make it impossible for ATF to store it, any of the participating agencies having the storage facilities to handle the seized property agree to store the property at no charge and to maintain the property in the same condition as when it was first taken into custody. The agency storing said seized property agrees not to dispose of the property until authorized to do so by ATF.

The MOU provides that proceeds from forfeitures will be shared, with sharing percentages based upon the U.S. Department of Justice Asset Forfeiture policies on equitable sharing of assets, such as determining the level of involvement by each participating agency. Task Force assets seized through administrative forfeiture will be distributed in equitable amounts based upon the number of full-time persons committed by each participating agency. Should it become impossible to separate the assets into equal shares, it will be the responsibility of all the participating agencies to come to an equitable decision. Should this process fail and an impasse result, ATF will become the final arbitrator of the distributive shares for the participating agencies.

DISPUTE RESOLUTION

In cases of overlapping jurisdiction, the participating agencies agree to work in concert to achieve the Task Force's goals and objectives. The parties to this MOU agree to attempt to resolve any disputes regarding jurisdiction, case assignments and workload at the lowest level possible.

LIABILITY

ATF acknowledges that the United States is liable for the wrongful or negligent acts or omissions of its officers and employees, including TFOs, while on duty and acting within the scope of their federal employment, to the extent permitted by the Federal Tort Claims Act.

Claims against the United States for injury or loss of property, personal injury, or death arising or resulting from the negligent or wrongful act or omission of any Federal employee while acting within the scope of his or her office or employment are governed by the Federal Tort Claims Act, 28 U.S.C. sections 1346(b), 2672-2680 (unless the claim arises from a violation of the Constitution of the United States, or a violation of a statute of the United States under which other recovery is authorized).

Except as otherwise provided, the parties agree to be solely responsible for the negligent or wrongful acts or omissions of their respective employees and will not seek financial contributions from the other for such acts or omissions. Legal representation by the United States is determined by the United States Department of Justice on a case-by-case basis. ATF cannot guarantee the United States will provide legal representation to any State or local law enforcement officer.

Liability for any negligent or willful acts of any agent or officer under-taken outside the terms of this MOU will be the sole responsibility of the respective agent or officer and agency involved.

DURATION

This MOU shall remain in effect until it is terminated in writing (to include electronic mail and facsimile). All participating agencies agree that no agency shall withdraw from the Task Force without providing ninety (90) days written notice to other participating agencies. If any participating agency withdraws from the Task Force prior to its termination, the remaining participating agencies shall determine the distributive share of assets for the withdrawing agency, in accordance with Department of Justice guidelines and directives.

The MOU shall be deemed terminated at the time all participating agencies withdraw and ATF elects not to replace such members, or in the event ATF unilaterally terminates the MOU upon 90 days written notice to all the remaining participating agencies.

MODIFICATIONS

This agreement may be modified at any time by written consent of all participating agencies. Modifications shall have no force and effect unless such modifications are reduced to writing and signed by an authorized representative of each participating agency.

NO PRIVATE RIGHT CREATED

This is an MOU between ATF and the Police Department and is not intended to confer any right or benefit to any private person or party.

The MOU is hereby accepted as setting forth the general intentions and understandings of the undersigned authorized officials for their respective agency.

By_____ Date_____
Special Agent in Charge

By_____ Date_____
Local Official

Appendix 12C: South Florida Money Laundering Strike Force Voluntary Cooperation Mutual Aid Agreement

(September 2012)

**SOUTH FLORIDA MONEY LAUNDERING STRIKE FORCE
VOLUNTARY COOPERATION MUTUAL AID AGREEMENT**
(September 2012)

WHEREAS, the below subscribed law enforcement agencies have joined together in a multi-jurisdictional Strike Force (hereinafter referred to as the Strike Force) intended to combat illegal money laundering, drug trafficking and other drug law violations, and related criminal violations and to disrupt organizations engaging in such activity through coordinated and long-term investigative, forfeiture, and prosecution efforts; and

WHEREAS, the undersigned agencies agree to utilize applicable state and federal laws to prosecute criminal, civil, forfeiture, and regulatory actions against identified violators, as appropriate; and

WHEREAS, the participating agencies desire to utilize the Strike Force as the sole method of facilitating state and local money laundering investigations that are not otherwise part of a joint federally-directed effort within their respective jurisdictions; and

WHEREAS, the undersigned agencies have the authority under Part 1, Chapter 23, Florida Statutes, "the Florida Mutual Aid Act," to enter into a voluntary cooperation agreement for cooperation and assistance of a routine law enforcement nature that crosses jurisdictional lines; and

WHEREAS, the undersigned agencies acknowledge and recognize that they have been operating under the existing agreement and modifications thereto, that the agreement has continued in full force and effect, and express their present intent to renew and refine the original agreement and subsequent renewals thereof in order to better reflect the continued and present focus of the efforts of the agencies in this Strike Force;

NOW THEREFORE, the parties agree as follows:

Each of the undersigned law enforcement agencies approve, authorize and enter into this Agreement at the request of the Miami-Dade State Attorney's Office (SAO) to implement within the jurisdictional and other limits as noted herein the Money Laundering Strike Force for the purposes and goals indicated.

Parties To This Agreement:

--The Office of the State Attorney of the Eleventh Judicial Circuit of Florida,
--The City of Coral Gables Police Department,
--The City of Miami Police Department,
--The City of Miami Shores Police Department,
--The City of Miami Beach Police Department,
--The City of Hallandale Police Department,
--The City of Golden Beach Police Department,

--The Village of Indian Creek Police Department,
--The City of North Miami Police Department,
--The City of Fort Lauderdale Police Department,
--The City of Davie Police Department,
--The City of Hialeah Police Department,
--The Town of Surfside Police Department,
--The City of Doral Police Department,
--The Monroe County Sheriff's Office.

A party other than those listed on page one may, at the request of the SAO and with the approval of the Strike Force Steering Committee, enter into this Agreement as evidenced by its signing of this Agreement. Any party may cancel its participation in this Agreement upon delivery of written notice of cancellation to the Executive Director of the South Florida Money Laundering Strike Force (Strike Force Director), who shall immediately notify other participating parties of the cancellation.

NATURE OF LAW ENFORCEMENT ASSISTANCE AND VOLUNTARY COOPERATION TO BE RENDERED:

1. The Strike Force is to effect dedicated and intensive investigative, preventative, and general law enforcement efforts primarily with regard to the investigation of illegal money laundering and drug trafficking operations and related crimes, and in efforts to dismantle and disrupt the organizations committing such violations. The principal goal of the Strike Force shall be the coordinated investigation of, and successful prosecution of perpetrators of such crimes, with particular emphasis on efforts designed to identify and dismantle organized criminal enterprises. Such efforts shall include, but are not limited to, undercover operations designed to detect illegal activity and to identify those involved in such activity including those directing or otherwise controlling such activity, interception of communications related to such activity as may be authorized by law, the arrest and prosecution of those involved (utilizing state and federal or other prosecutions, as appropriate); the seizure and forfeiture of assets of those engaged in such activity or otherwise supporting such activity (utilizing state and federal forfeiture options, as appropriate); the prosecution of regulatory and civil actions designed to end such criminal activity, as appropriate; and the referral of investigative leads and intelligence to such other federal, state, foreign or local law enforcement authorities as may be required and appropriate under the Strike Force's operations. In recognition that such efforts transcend jurisdiction limits, it is the intent of this voluntary cooperation agreement to assure the continued functioning of law enforcement in areas where such limits might otherwise thwart major law enforcement efforts.

2. The Parties to this Agreement are contributing personnel and resources in support of the Strike Force efforts, with the operations of the Strike Force being coordinated by the SAO and other Strike Force members. No agency will participate in the Strike Force unless it provides resource contributions and operates within the operational parameters related to Strike Force efforts as required of it by the Steering Committee or the SAO.

3. Nothing herein shall otherwise limit the jurisdiction and powers normally possessed by an employee as a member of the employee's Agency. Nothing herein shall otherwise limit the ability of participating Strike Force members to provide, as provided by or allowed by law, such assistance in any enforcement action unrelated to Strike Force operations as may be lawfully requested by a law enforcement officer having jurisdiction over any such incident, crime or matter under consideration. However, extension of jurisdiction under the authority of this Agreement shall occur only as provided below.

EXTENSION OF PARTICIPANTS' JURISDICTION; COMMAND AND SUPERVISORY RESPONSIBILITY; STEERING COMMITTEE; NOTIFICATION REQUIREMENTS

1. The principal sites of Strike Force activity are Miami-Dade County, Broward County and Monroe County but Strike Force activities may occur elsewhere within the State of Florida consistent with the purpose and terms of this Agreement. As provided by Section 23.127(1), Florida Statutes, a Strike Force member engaged in an authorized Strike Force operation outside the member's jurisdiction but inside the State of Florida that is pursuant to, and consistent with, the purpose and terms of this Agreement shall have the same powers, duties, rights, privileges, and immunities under the laws of the State of Florida as if the member was performing duties inside the member's jurisdiction as provided by the "Florida Mutual Aid Act" and this Agreement.

2. Whenever Strike Force activities outside of Miami-Dade County, Broward County or Monroe County have resulted in an arrest or seizure of property, the Sheriff of the County or the Chief of Police of the municipality in which such activities have occurred shall be notified of the Strike Force's actions within the sheriff's or chief's jurisdiction.

3. Members of the Strike Force operating outside their normal jurisdictions recognize that their extra-territorial powers and authority are, unless otherwise supported by law, derived by and through this Agreement. Activities shall be considered authorized and under the authority of this Agreement when the activities have been approved and are under the overall direction of the Deputy Director, Deputy Commander or command designee assigned to the Strike Force. No extension of jurisdiction or authority is granted solely by reason of this Agreement for law enforcement activities unless they are approved and supervised as provided herein and are related to Strike Force operations, or have been encountered directly incident to an approved and supervised Strike Force operation.

4. a. A participating agency can work other money laundering investigations outside investigations handled under this agreement and through the Strike Force only upon approval by the Steering Committee. Absent such specific approval, all participating agencies agree to utilize the Strike Force as the exclusive means to engage in state or local investigations of all money laundering cases conducted by their agency personnel other than investigations conducted as part of a federally-directed joint operation. Notwithstanding this provision, an agency encountering money-laundering incidental to another investigation may initially continue its investigative efforts until such time as the Strike Force accepts the investigation or approval for the agency to work the case outside the Strike Force is granted. If the Strike Force Steering Committee declines to include a particular state or local money laundering investigation within its operations, a Strike Force participating agency will be free to independently pursue the investigation within the parameters of law. Any such independent investigation will be outside the scope of the Agreement and will not benefit from the extension of jurisdiction conferred by this agreement. All money laundering investigative efforts incidental to another investigation conducted by an agency prior to acceptance of the money laundering investigation by the Strike Force are outside the scope of this Agreement and will not benefit from the extension of jurisdiction conferred by this agreement. In the event that an agency's participation in a "federally directed joint money laundering operation" could reasonably be construed as conflicting with a Strike Force investigation, the participating agency must promptly notify the Strike Force Director and the Steering Committee. The Chair of the Strike Force will convene a Steering Committee meeting as soon practical to discuss the conflict and the appropriate resolution.

b. Any Strike Force participating agency that becomes aware of an investigation in violation of the limits imposed by this clause shall immediately report it to the Chair of the Strike Force Steering Committee. The Chair shall bring the matter to the attention of the Strike Force Steering Committee as soon as practical. Violation of the commitment under this clause may result in sanctions against the violating agency, which may include, but are not limited to, permanent reduction in the offending agency's share of forfeiture proceeds obtained from Strike Force efforts or suspension or dismissal from the Strike Force.

5. The Steering Committee consists of command level representatives from the signatory agencies to this agreement. The Steering Committee shall have plenary supervisory authority over Strike Force planning and direction. The Steering Committee shall assure that the Strike Force remains dedicated to its mission and primary goal of dismantling organized money laundering organizations operating within Florida. The Strike Force Steering Committee will meet quarterly or as otherwise required to maintain an ongoing and

active oversight role. The Steering Committee shall select a Chairman and Vice-Chairman from the signatory agencies. The Chairman shall serve one year. The Vice-Chairman shall assume the Chair upon the expiration of the term of the current Chairman. The Steering Committee shall select a new Vice-Chairman whenever the position becomes vacant.

6. The Strike Force Director will provide quarterly reviews to the Steering Committee and the SAO reporting Strike Force investigative, intelligence and forfeiture activity. The Steering Committee shall periodically, no less than twice yearly, assure that its meeting includes as the main agenda item a review the objectives and accomplishments of the Strike Force, a review of the success of the Strike Force in meeting its primary goal of dismantling organized money laundering organizations within Florida, and shall issue directives and cause such changes as may be necessary to assure the Strike Force efforts remain productive and focused on the Strike Force's primary missions.

7. Each participating agency shall contribute personnel and resources to the Strike Force in such numbers as are agreed to by the participating agency and the Strike Force Steering Committee. Participating agencies shall assign personnel to the Strike Force based upon their investigative experience and the operational needs of the Strike Force. Final acceptance of personnel assigned to the Strike Force shall rest with the Strike Force Director.

8. The Steering Committee shall regularly receive performance reports to review whether resource contributions of participating agencies and funding are adequate to assure Strike Force efforts are effective. The Steering Committee will also review and approve the Strike Force's annual operational budget and administrative expenses and financial status report.

9. Actual law enforcement operations of the Strike Force will be supervised and directed by sworn law enforcement officers of the Strike Force agreed upon by the Strike Force Director to serve in an overall supervisory role. The Strike Force second-in-command should be the rank of lieutenant or the operational equivalent to that rank. No person shall serve as second-in-command who is not a full-time, certified officer with his or her employing entity. The Strike Force Director may designate a team leader for specific field operations. The team leader may be any sworn member of a signatory agency to this agreement. Each Strike Force member participating in a Strike Force operation shall follow and adhere to, and is presumed to be following and adhering to, the supervision and direction given by the designated supervisor of the operation. If at any time the Deputy Director, Deputy Commander or designated team leader determines that the Strike Force operation should be terminated, all actions related to said operation as authorized by this Agreement are to be promptly terminated in a manner assuring the safety of all involved law enforcement officers. However, Strike Force-assigned officers or agents who are within their normal territorial jurisdiction(s) may, acting unilaterally as officers or agents of their employing agency, engage in continued investigative or enforcement actions as authorized by their agency supervisor(s). Any such actions shall not be considered the operations of the Strike Force and shall not fall within the privileges and obligations of this Agreement. Nothing in this paragraph shall modify or relax the restrictions against unilateral money laundering investigations by Strike Force participating agencies as addressed in Paragraph 4 herein.

10. Upon any termination of Strike Force operations, the supervisor shall document the circumstances of the termination, including whether there appears to have been an agency's unilateral continuation of investigative or enforcement activity, and the Strike Force shall retain the documentation. The Strike Force and its member agencies are not responsible for the actions of any participating agency or its officers or agents conducted after the Strike

Force operation has been terminated or otherwise performed outside the scope of this Agreement.

11. The Strike Force shall maintain a listing of Strike Force personnel serving as supervisors or designated supervisors. Documentation shall be maintained by the Strike Force that will reflect the involvement of sworn members in each Strike Force operation or investigative activity and the assigned supervisor or designated leader for each such operation or activity. No member of the Strike Force shall engage in Strike Force related activities that are unauthorized, unreported or otherwise unknown to the assigned Strike Force supervisor or designated leader and which are not documented as provided herein.

12. Any officer or agent participating in Strike Force operations shall promptly report to any Strike Force supervisor any suspected unauthorized, unreported, undocumented, or unsupervised investigative or enforcement activity of Strike Force personnel.

13. Any agency head of a party to this Agreement may request that a particular agency's member of the Strike Force no longer be allowed to participate in the Strike Force. Upon receiving the request, the Strike Force Director shall temporarily suspend the member's active participation in Strike Force efforts. At its next meeting, the Steering Committee shall determine whether the request should be honored on a permanent basis. Upon receipt from the Steering Committee of a request to no longer allow a particular agency member's participation in the Strike Force, the employing Agency shall promptly terminate the member's participation in the Strike Force. Absent an objection by any other Party to this Agreement, a Party to this Agreement may otherwise add, substitute, reinstate, or replace any of its sworn or support employees participating in the Strike Force. If a Party objects to any such action, the Steering Committee shall determine whether the action may proceed or be maintained.

14. If a conflict arises between an order or direction provided by the assigned supervisor or designated leader and a Strike Force member's employing Agency's rules, standards, or policies, the conflict shall be promptly reported to the supervisor or leader when circumstances safely allow a concern to be raised. The supervisor or team leader, in conjunction with available members of the governing board as may be necessary, shall attempt to resolve the conflict in a manner to allow the Strike Force operation to continue appropriately. No officer or agent shall be required to knowingly violate the policy of his or her employing agency while participating in Strike Force operations.

15. The Parties to this Agreement may, by a written memorandum of understanding or written attachments to this Agreement, identify or further define particular guidelines, policies, or procedures to be utilized by members of the Strike Force when engaged in Strike Force operations, provided that all such guidelines, policies and procedures are consistent with Florida law and Florida or federal forfeiture guidelines and the terms of this Agreement. However, Strike Force members' jurisdiction as provided under this Agreement may not be altered by any such written attachment. In the absence of a written memoranda of understanding or attachments, the policies and procedures to be utilized by Strike Force members shall be clearly identified by the Strike Force supervisor, or if a supervisor is unavailable, by a Strike Force team leader as designated by the supervisor. Written guidelines, policies, or procedures adopted for use by the Strike Force as provided herein may not be waived or abandoned by Strike Force supervisors or participants. However, when engaged in Strike Force operations no Strike Force member will be expected or required to violate or otherwise fail to maintain the member's employing Agency's standards of conduct, or be required to fail to abide by restrictions or limitations as may be imposed by law, or the member's employing Agency's rules, standards, or policies.

PROCEDURE FOR REQUESTING AND AUTHORIZING ASSISTANCE

Officers assigned to Strike Force operations pursuant to this agreement shall be empowered to render enforcement assistance and take enforcement action in accordance with the law and the terms of this Agreement. Execution of this agreement and continued participation by the SAO and one or more Strike Force member agencies shall constitute a general reciprocal, continuing request for and granting of assistance between the members of the Strike Force which shall be considered authorized in accordance with the provisions of this Agreement. No additional or specific formal request for assistance is required.

USE AND DISTRIBUTION OF SEIZED FUNDS AND PROPERTY; STRIKE FORCE ADMINISTRATIVE EXPENSES:

1. The Parties to this Agreement recognize that law enforcement is the principal objective of all asset forfeiture and that, as mandated by Section 932.704(11)(a), Florida Statutes, as enacted by Chapter 95-265, Laws of Florida, the Strike Force's operations and each Party's use of property, currency, or proceeds received by reason of state forfeiture actions are to conform with "Florida's Forfeiture Guidelines" as developed and adopted by the Florida Department of Law Enforcement, the Florida Sheriff's Association, and the Florida Police Chiefs Association, a copy of which are incorporated herein as Attachment C. In the case of federal forfeitures, applicable federal guidelines apply.

2. All Parties recognize that they are to avoid the appearance of impropriety in the acquisition, sale, retention or transfer of any forfeited property, currency or proceeds derived from such forfeiture, and that forfeiture funds may not be used to meet normal law enforcement agency operating expenses of each Party unless otherwise provided by Florida law.

3. All participating parties acknowledge that the Strike Force has no independent spending authority and is not empowered to encumber, grant, donate, or expend funds independently. Authorizations for expenditures must be consistent with law and authority granted to participating agencies and in support of the mission of the Strike Force and in accordance with the approved budget. A participating Strike Force agency shall function as the administrative agent for Strike Force operational expenditures. The City of Coral Gables Police Department as empowered by the City of Coral Gables is currently responsible for handling the administrative and support expenses incurred by the Strike Force in its operations and is acting as the Strike Force's current administrative agent. If properly authorized by law and the party's governing body, any other party to this Agreement may be authorized by the Steering Committee to assume the role of Administrative Party.

4. Parties acknowledge that the Strike Force is not a permanent operation and could be terminated at any time. Accordingly, the Strike Force shall avoid long-term commitments via leases or rental agreements unless such agreements reasonably provide for cancellation prior to their scheduled expiration dates.   The Strike Force shall endeavor to limit administrative expenses as much as reasonably possible, in order to maximize the flow of forfeiture proceeds to the individual participating agencies. Administrative expenses for which expenditure may be authorized may include, but are not limited to, expenses incurred in the storage of seized funds pending forfeiture, expenditures for rent of Strike Force facilities, rental of vehicles utilized in Strike Force investigative activity, providing phones, desks, office supplies and equipment in support of Strike Force operations, plaques and other recognition awards for exiting members, food and refreshments for Strike Force meetings and the payment of the salaries of a limited number of Strike Force administrative

and operational support personnel. Use of Strike Force resources to provide "percs" or benefits beyond that which personnel assigned to the Strike Force would not otherwise be entitled or provided by the employing agency of the personnel is expressly prohibited. Use of Strike Force phones, accounts, equipment, vehicles, or other resources for other than incidental personal purposes is prohibited.

5. Administrative expenses do not include the salaries or overtime compensation, in excess of 64 hours per month, of officers, agents, analysts, or other employees of Party agencies assigned to the Strike Force, or the purchase of regular or special equipment or resources by a Party agency that may be or are utilized in support of Strike Force operations. Compensation for such costs is the sole responsibility of the employing agency, and may, if authorized by law and applicable forfeiture guidelines, be paid from forfeiture funds received by the agency.

6. Anticipated administrative expenses for an administrative agent (currently the Coral Gables Police Department) during a budget year are to be identified by the administrative agent as a Strike Force operational budget item, and are to be approved for reimbursement by the Steering Committee in the Strike Force operational budget for the fiscal year. The Steering Committee may approve all or a portion of the proposed administrative expenses. Once approved, the administrative expenses may be reimbursed to the administrative agent in the manner noted below. The administrative agent is not obligated to expend resources in administrative support of the Strike Force if the Steering Committee does not approve the expenses for reimbursement via the budget process. All Parties acknowledge that the Strike Force itself has no authority to independently authorize the expenditure of seized or forfeited funds, or to make grants from such funds to others. As a result, reimbursement to the Administrative agent (currently the Coral Gables Police Department) for its administrative expenditures shall be done by a voluntary deferral of each Party's equitable share of forfeiture funds otherwise due to it in the manner set forth below.

7. Florida and Federal forfeiture laws allow multiple agencies participating in the seizure and forfeiture of property to equitably proportion the distribution of such property upon successful conclusion of the forfeiture. Distribution of the proceeds from successful forfeiture actions shall be equitable among the Parties to this Agreement and shall take into account their relative roles in support of the efforts of the Strike Force unless an alternate distribution allocation among the Parties has been agreed to.

8. Participating agencies agree that each agency should contribute a fair share toward the annual administrative costs of the Strike Force. Such contributions will be effected by deferring portions of forfeiture proceeds an Agency would otherwise be entitled to receive to the benefit of the agency operating as administrative agent to cover the proportionate share of the administrative expenses as noted herein. Such deferrals are to fairly and appropriately reimburse, not enrich, the administrative agent agency. To reasonably address the additional expenses incurred by the administrative agent for the administrative and support expense role described herein and approved by the Steering Committee in its operational budget, the other Parties agree that their respective proportionate share in the distribution of forfeited funds will be reduced as approved by the Steering Committee in such manner and amount to effect an increase in the share of forfeitures received by the administrative agent (currently, the Coral Gables Police Department) for the extra administrative expenses so incurred.

9. All Parties have an equitable ownership in the funds seized for forfeiture and interest earned on those funds pending perfection of ownership via final order of forfeiture. However, to further address the additional expenses incurred by the Administrative agent for the

administrative and support expense role described herein and approved by the Steering Committee in its operational budget, the Parties have agreed that all interest earned yearly on funds seized and pending forfeiture up to a maximum amount set by the Steering Committee at the time the yearly budget is approved shall be distributed to the Administrative agent upon final order of forfeiture in a manner consistent with this Agreement and law, with such funds to be applied to the approved administrative and support expenses. Any interest earned yearly in excess of the maximum amount set by the Steering Committee shall be included in the funds to be equitably distributed among the Parties to this Agreement and shall take into account their relative roles in support of the efforts of the Strike Force unless an alternate distribution allocation among the Parties has been agreed to.

10. The Steering Committee may approve on a case-by-case basis the adjustment of one or more distributions of forfeiture funds to Strike Force participating agencies to specifically increase a Party's share of forfeiture distribution funds for an unusual or substantial expense incurred by the Party directly associated with its participation in Strike Force activities. In order for such reimbursement to occur, the expenses must have a substantial nexus with the Strike Force's operations and mission. The Strike Force members acknowledge they have no independent authority by reason of this Agreement to disburse funds other than as authorized by law and as approved by each party's governing entity.

11. Each participating agency is solely responsible for assuring its use of distributed forfeiture funds is in compliance with state law and mandatory state and federal forfeiture guidelines. By continued participation in the Strike Force, each participating agency warrants it is operating in compliance with state law and mandatory guidelines. The Steering Committee shall assure regular training of Strike Force officers and agents as required by the State Guidelines occurs and is documented. Upon request of the SAO, a participating agency will provide documentation or certification demonstrating such compliance. Any participating agency found not to be operating within applicable forfeiture law and guidelines shall be suspended from Strike Force participation and forfeiture fund distribution until such time as the Agency demonstrates it is in compliance with law and guidelines.

12. The Parties to this Agreement acknowledge that under federal guidelines, funds derived from federal forfeitures are not to be commingled with funds derived from state forfeitures, and are to be maintained in a separate trust fund account, to be expended only in a manner as allowed by applicable federal guidelines. All Parties agree to file in a timely fashion all reports or accountings of receipts or expenditures of forfeiture funds as are required by state or federal law or applicable guidelines.

PROPERTY SEIZURE AND FORFEITURE CONSIDERATIONS:

1. No funds or other property seized by Strike Force operations are to be utilized by any Strike Force agency prior to successful forfeiture or until title or interest in the funds otherwise lawfully vests in one or more Strike Force agencies. Forfeiture actions based upon seizures made by the Strike Force may be pursued in either state or federal actions. Actions shall be based upon current statutory and case law, and shall be consistent with applicable state or federal forfeiture guidelines. The Parties agree that the Office of the State Attorney of the Eleventh Judicial Circuit, through its attorneys, will be primarily responsible under this Agreement for pursuing all Strike Force forfeiture actions on behalf of all of the Parties in state court in Miami-Dade County and through out the State of Florida. The Office of the United States Attorney, Southern District of Florida, will be primarily responsible for federal forfeiture actions. However, this provision shall not preclude the use of other forfeiture

attorneys or personnel as needed on particular matters and as authorized by the Steering Committee and agreed to by the above-noted primary entities responsible for forfeiture litigation.

2. Any Party to this Agreement or any prosecutor handling the criminal prosecution of Strike Force cases may request copies of forfeiture complaints and pleadings filed by reason of Strike Force seizures and such copies shall be promptly provided to the requester. Forfeiture actions are to be coordinated with criminal prosecutions. If any legal dispute or concern as to the form or sufficiency of forfeiture actions or other action proposing to vest the interest of Strike Force agency(ies) in seized cash or property is raised by any of the Parties to this Agreement, an attempt to resolve the issue through informal discussion and contact shall be made. In the event any Party responsible for filing and handling a forfeiture action believes there is an insufficient basis upon which to pursue the forfeiture of particular seized cash or property, and the concerns cannot be resolved, no forfeiture action on behalf of the Strike Force is to be filed.

3. All options available under law to state and local law enforcement agencies with regard to unclaimed evidence or abandoned property, gifts and plea agreements are available to the Strike Force, provided the property under consideration otherwise qualifies under law for such consideration.

4. Pursuant to Section 932.704(7), Florida Statutes, when a claimant and the Strike Force agree to settle the forfeiture action prior to the conclusion of the forfeiture proceeding, the settlement agreement shall be reviewed, unless such review is waived by the claimant in writing, by the court or a mediator or arbitrator agreed upon by the claimant and the seizing law enforcement agency. If the claimant is unrepresented, the settlement agreement must include a provision that the claimant has freely and voluntarily agreed to enter into the settlement without benefit of counsel. A copy of the settlement agreement is to be retained in the investigative case file giving rise to the forfeiture and settlement.

GUIDELINES FOR MONEY PICKUPS, TRANSFERS AND SECURITY; AUDITS AND REVIEWS:

1. The Parties to this Agreement recognize that substantial sums of cash will be seized by reason of Strike Force operations, and are committed to assuring that all such seizures are done with the greatest degree of security and integrity possible. The Strike Force will utilize procedures established by written directive of the Strike Force relating to the seizure of property for forfeiture and the seizure of contraband. At no time shall a Strike Force participant seize, handle, transport or count seized funds alone. Pursuant to Section 932.704(11)(b), Florida Statutes, the determination of whether to seize currency must be made by Strike Force supervisory personnel. Such determination must be documented in a manner to indicate the supervisory personnel providing such authorization. The attorney assigned to handle Strike Force forfeitures must be notified as soon as possible. In the absence of, or unavailability of that attorney, notification shall be made to the Strike Force Director.

2. No investigative money laundering by the Strike Force or its participating agencies may occur unless it is a means to an investigative end, rather than an end in and of itself. Authorized laundering may only be conducted as part of reverse sting or as an interim step reasonably expected to lead to the seizure of drugs, illicit funds, and/or arrests of those engaged in unlawful money laundering consistent with Section 896.105, Florida Statutes.

3. The Strike Force will utilize procedures established in writing by the Strike Force relating to the handling of evidence. A copy of Strike Force Directive 1.3, relating to forfeitures and seizures, is attached as Attachment A to this Agreement. A copy of Strike Force Directive 1.4, relating to the handling of evidence, is attached as Attachment B to this Agreement. Both of these Directives currently apply to Strike Force operations. The Parties to this Agreement acknowledge in signing this Agreement that they have reviewed the Attachments.

4. The Strike Force may modify, supplement or substitute written guidelines, provided that any modification, supplementation, or substitution assures as a minimum that all non-cash property coming into the custody of Strike Force members shall be treated as evidence, utilizing standard and commonly-accepted means of securing and handling same, and that all seizures of cash shall be done with appropriate checks and balances implemented to assure that all cash seized is accounted for, and properly secured until such time as title or interest in such funds lawfully vests in the seizing agency(ies) and the Strike Force. Copies of written guidelines or directives shall be provided any Party upon request.

5. The Steering Committee will determine the type, nature and extent of audits or reviews pertaining to Strike Force efforts, to include as a minimum an audit of Strike Force finances once every two years. In addition, the SAO may at any time order a review and audit by an auditor designated by the SAO of Strike Force operations with regard to the seizure and handling of all evidence, property or cash, use and disposition of property, currency or proceeds received by any Party by reason of a forfeiture, or any other aspect of Strike Force operations. The Strike Force Director or the Steering Committee by majority vote may request at any time that such a review and audit be performed by the SAO. The Parties agree to cooperate in any such audit by allowing full access to documents, personnel and facilities necessary to perform the audit function. The Parties agree to cooperate in any federal audit of Strike Force forfeiture activities as may be required or requested by the United States government.

COMPLAINTS AGAINST STRIKE FORCE MEMBERS:

1. Each person assigned to the Strike Force shall promptly report any suspected criminal activity or violation of rule or policy of any other member of the Strike Force or any person with whom the Strike Force is conducting business.

2. Whenever a complaint has been lodged as a result of Strike Force efforts, a designee of the SAO shall ascertain at a minimum:

   The identity(ies) of the complainant(s) and an address where the complainant(s) may be contacted, the nature of the complaint any supporting evidence or facts as may be available, including the names and addresses of witnesses to that which has been complained about, the identity(ies) of the Strike Force participant(s) accused and the employing Agency(ies) of the participant(s) accused.

3. The SAO will promptly provide to each affected employing Agency the above information for administrative review and appropriate handling or disposition. Each affected employing Agency shall, upon completion of said review, promptly notify the SAO of its findings and any actions taken.

4. Upon assignment to the Strike Force, and once yearly, each person assigned to the Strike Force shall be provided notification that he or she is obliged to report any wrongdoing or

impropriety by any Strike Force personnel. A local method of reporting such shall be provided, and the name, email address and phone number of the SAO Investigations Division shall also be provided as an option for making any such report, whose phone number is (305) 547-0669.

INTERPLAY WITH FEDERAL AND OTHER AUTHORITIES:

1. The Parties to this Agreement recognize that the federal law enforcement authorities have requested that the efforts of the Strike Force be closely coordinated with federal authorities having interests in money laundering investigations. The Parties recognize that federal agents will, as necessary, be co-located at the Strike Force headquarters or otherwise provided access to Strike Force operations and planning.

2. **International movement of funds:** No direct movement of funds internationally, or transactions which are known by the Strike Force to be an interim step prior to a specifically planned, expected, or known international transfer of funds shall occur unless the federal agent(s) assigned to work with the Strike Force are provided prior notice and federal approval and participation is secured. If a federal agency has an objection to any proposed operation of the Strike Force involving international movements of money, the operation is not to proceed until the federal objections are resolved, giving federal interstate and international responsibilities and concerns appropriate deference. The Strike Force shall not directly or knowingly indirectly engage in international movements of funds without securing authorization and participation from at least one federal agency having appropriate jurisdiction.

3. **Interstate movement of funds within the United States:**
    (a) **Federal notification:** A federal agent with appropriate jurisdiction assigned to work with the Strike Force (normally, a DEA Agent) must receive notification of any intended interstate movement of funds prior to the actual movement of the funds. The federal agent, upon receiving notification as provided herein, shall coordinate the Strike Force's efforts with other federal law enforcement agencies and make appropriate notification of the proposed transaction(s). If a federal agency objects to a proposed interstate movement of funds, no movement shall occur until the federal objections are resolved. The date of original federal agent notification and the absence of objection shall be specifically documented on the funds transfer authorization form. In the event of exceptional circumstances that do not allow timely prior notice to the federal agent, funds may be moved interstate upon the approval of the Director of the Strike Force, or in the absence of the Director, his/her designee. The notice required by this section shall occur as soon as practicable, but in no case longer than 48 hours after the interstate movement of funds has begun.

    (b) **Recipient or involved state notification:** Strike Force interstate movements of money not otherwise involving the active participation of a federal agency shall be in coordination with law enforcement agencies in the recipient or involved other states. In operations not actively involving a federal agency, the Strike Force shall not unilaterally conduct money transfers in another state, without notifying the appropriate state, or local law enforcement agencies of the proposed activities. Nothing in this Agreement provides Strike Force members with jurisdiction beyond the geographic limits of the State of Florida. Strike Force operations are to be performed in a manner to minimize and avoid conflict with the actions of, and mission of, federal agencies and other states' law enforcement agencies.

    (c) **Domestic security:** Recognizing that money laundering is an important tool of domestic and international terrorist organizations, no transfer of funds by the Strike Force shall occur until the Strike Force has checked available law enforcement intelligence databases, including, but not limited to, FDLE's "In-Site" to assure there is no believed connection between the proposed transfer of funds and terrorism. If there is a reasonable belief that the funds will be utilized by a terrorist organization, no transfer shall occur. Notwithstanding this prohibition, if the transfer of funds is essential to an investigation of the terrorist organization, and will substantially assist in the detection and apprehension of terrorists, or the interference with their planned objectives, upon approval of the Steering Committee, and with the approval of the primary agency investigating the terrorist organization, a transfer may occur.

POWERS, PRIVILEGES, IMMUNITIES, COSTS, LIABILITY AND RELATED ISSUES; STRIKE FORCE SUPPORT CONSIDERATIONS:

Each Party engaging in any mutual cooperation and assistance pursuant to this Agreement agrees to assume its own liability and responsibility for the acts, omission, or conduct of such Party's own employees while such employees are engaged in rendering such aid, cooperation and assistance pursuant to this Agreement, subject to the provisions of Section 768.28, Florida Statutes, where applicable. All personnel assigned to the Strike Force remain ultimately accountable to their respective employing agencies. In turn, each employing agency remains responsible for such employees and assumes any liability for the actions of its employees while assigned to the Strike Force. Each agency is individually responsible for securing supplemental insurance as may be desired to cover potential losses or liabilities associated with the Strike Force operation. With regard to the rental or lease of vehicles for use by the Strike Force personnel, the participating Law Enforcement Agencies of the South Florida Money Laundering Strike Force hereby agree to the extent permitted by Law to indemnify from any liability and hold harmless the other participating Law Enforcement Agencies of the South Florida Money Laundering Strike Force for any negligent acts or negligent omissions committed by their respective personnel while acting within the scope of their employment. Therefore, in consideration of the mutual terms and conditions contained herein, the parties agree as follows:

Each participating Law Enforcement Agency of the South Florida Money Laundering Strike Force hereby agree to secure or otherwise maintain its own automobile liability insurance or maintain a self-insuring fund for the term of this Agreement in the amounts determined by each participating Law Enforcement Agency to adequately insure each participant's liability derived from the use of the leased or rental vehicles assumed herein, but in no event shall such coverage be less than the amount of statutory waiver of sovereign immunity.

Each Party to this Agreement agrees to furnish necessary personnel, property, police equipment, vehicles, resources and facilities to render services to each other Party to this Agreement in order to effect the purposes of the Strike Force and agrees to bear the cost of loss or damage to its equipment, vehicles, or property so provided. Parties understand and agree that they will be responsible for their own liability and bear their own costs with regard to their property and resources, or personnel expenses incurred by reason of death, injury or incidents giving rise to liability. This provision shall not preclude, as otherwise authorized herein, the purchase of administrative support property or resources.

Each Agency furnishing aid pursuant to this Agreement shall compensate its employees during the time such aid is rendered and shall defray the actual expenses of its employees while they are rendering such aid, including any amounts paid or due for compensation due to personal injury or death while such employees are engaged in rendering such aid. The privileges and immunities from liability, exemption from laws, ordinances, and rules, and all pension, insurance, relief, disability, workers' compensation, salary (including overtime compensation or compensatory time), death and other benefits that apply to the activity of an employee of an Agency when performing the employee's duties within the territorial limits of the employee's Agency shall apply to the employee to the same degree, manner, and extent while such employee acts under this Agreement. This provision shall not preclude payment by a Party of compensation (including overtime compensation) to the Party's officers, agents, analysts, or other personnel assigned to the Strike Force, if allowed by Florida or federal law and applicable state or federal guidelines, through the use of legally vested Strike Force funds if the Party has obtained the necessary approval and authorization for such payment from the Party's governing commission or (if a state agency) the Legislature.

The privileges and immunities from liability, exemption from laws, ordinances, and rules, and pension, insurance, relief, disability, workers' compensation, salary, death, and other benefits that apply to the activity of an employee of an agency when performing the employee's duties within the territorial limits of the employee's agency apply to the employee to the same degree, manner, and extent while engaged in the performance of the employee's duties extraterritorially under the provisions of this Agreement. Each participating Party shall bear its own liability arising from acts undertaken under the Agreement except as may be otherwise allowed under Chapter 23, Florida Statutes, and any agreement by a participant to the contrary is void. The Administrative Agency may request purchase of optional insurance or other reasonable actions by the other Parties as a means of helping reduce the Administrative Agency's exposure to claims or liability incurred solely by reason of its role as Administrative Agency in renting automobiles or entering into contractual agreements on behalf of the Strike Force. Such requests shall be approved by the Steering Committee, but if not approved, the Administrative Agency shall not be obligated to enter into any particular rental or contractual obligation on behalf of the Strike Force.

OBLIGATION TO COORDINATE WITH PROSECUTOR'S OFFICE:

1. **A principal goal of this Strike Force is the successful prosecution of criminal violators.** Successful prosecution requires close coordination with prosecuting authorities, both in the state and federal courts. Members of the Strike Force are obligated to coordinate their efforts in such a way as to support the efficient prosecution of cases, including, but not limited to, prompt responses to requests from prosecutors for information or assistance in handling Strike Force generated cases, and reasonable availability for pretrial conferences with prosecutors, discovery depositions, pretrial hearings and trials. Civil or administrative actions derived from Strike Force operations are likewise to receive coordinated support efforts from Strike Force members.

2. Strike Force supervisors shall monitor the efforts of Strike Force members in support of criminal prosecutions, civil actions, administrative actions and forfeiture cases. Such monitoring shall include regular contact with assigned prosecutors or attorneys pursuing actions on behalf of the Strike Force to assure the expected level of support from Strike Force members is occurring. Failure by a member of the Strike Force to support such efforts on a routine and regular basis in the manner set forth herein shall constitute grounds for suspension or removal from the Strike Force and reduction or elimination of the agency's share of forfeiture proceeds derived from Strike Force operations.

PRIMARY STRIKE FORCE EFFORTS; SEMIANNUAL PROGRESS ASSESSMENT:

1. The Strike Force has as its prime mission these primary areas of activity:

   ✓ Money laundering investigations, including the seizure and forfeiture of funds derived from drug or other criminal activity and the investigation and prosecution of those involved in such activity;
   ✓ Criminal investigation and prosecution of those involved in organized drug trafficking enterprises and those involved in other drug related criminal activity, and efforts to disrupt and dismantle organizations involved in such illegal activity.

2. The Parties agree to provide sufficient and continued support and personnel resources to each of the above areas of activity, in a manner and to an extent determined and approved by the Steering Committee, or as may be requested by the SAO.

3. The Steering Committee no less than twice yearly review and evaluate the progress and success of efforts in each of the primary areas of activity. To the extent resources are available, they shall be reallocated to address observed deficiencies or to otherwise better assure the balanced success of the primary Strike Force efforts.

INTERPLAY OF STRIKE FORCE AGENCIES WITH FLORIDA VIOLENT CRIME AND DRUG CONTROL COUNCIL FUNDED INVESTIGATIVE EFFORTS

The mission of the Florida Violent Crime and Drug Control Council includes providing matching funding of significant drug and money laundering investigations within the state. To the extent that any investigation funded by the Council develops leads related to significant money laundering affecting investigative efforts of any participating Strike Force agency, the Agency shall relate the leads to the Strike Force Steering Committee, and the Steering Committee shall determine whether the money laundering aspect of the Council-funded investigation warrants inclusion as a Strike Force investigation.

COPY TO EACH PARTICIPATING STRIKE FORCE MEMBER:

When this Agreement is fully executed, a copy shall be provided to each Strike Force member so that each member may be fully aware of the powers, limitations, and expectations applicable to Strike Force members and operations.

TERM AND EFFECT OF AGREEMENT; OBLIGATION TO TIMELY RATIFY; MEANS OF CANCELLATION; AUTOMATIC EXTENSION; INTERIM CLARIFICATIONS OR MODIFICATIONS:

1. This Agreement is the successor agreement to the original Agreement first establishing the predecessor Strike Force, known as the Multi-Agency Money Laundering and Anti-Drug Trafficking Strike Force ("IMPACT") and all subsequent renewals thereof. It shall be effective as to the executing Parties upon execution by the SAO and at least one other participating Agency. As each additional Party executes this Agreement, it shall be

effective as to the newly executing Party. Upon execution, this Agreement supersedes previous versions of the agreements. Failure by a Party to secure a timely ratification of this superseding agreement will result in said party's participation in the Strike Force being suspended until such time as the Party executes the Agreement.

2. This Agreement shall remain in full force as to all participating Parties until September 1, 2015, unless earlier canceled in writing by the SAO as to all or separate Parties, or as canceled in writing by an individual Party as related to that Party as provided herein. In order for the Strike Force to continue operations beyond September 1, 2015, this Agreement must be renewed in writing by the participating Parties.

3. The terms of this Agreement may be clarified or modified, consistent with state and federal law and guidelines, by supplemental Memoranda of Understanding signed by the participating parties. Any such Memorandum shall incorporate by reference this Agreement, and shall become a part of this Agreement by inclusion as an Exhibit hereto. All such Exhibits are to be sequentially lettered and labeled as an attachment. Master copies of the current Agreement will be maintained by the SAO, the FDLE Office of Mutual Aid Coordinator and by the Strike Force Director.

4. This Agreement may be duplicated for dissemination to all Parties, and such duplicates shall be of the same force and effect as the original. Execution of this Agreement may be signified by properly signing a separate signature page, the original of which shall be returned to the attention of:

> Executive Director, SFMLSF
> 11200 NW 20th Street
> Suite 300
> Miami, Florida 33172

Upon receipt, originals will maintained by the Strike Force Director. Any written cancellation or extension shall be forwarded to the SFMLSF at the same address.

5. By signing the agreement, each representative of a party represents that he or she is fully authorized to enter into this agreement, and that the Party for which the representative is signing accepts the terms, responsibilities, obligations and limitations of this Agreement, and agrees to bound thereto to the fullest extent allowed by law.

(Rest of this page intentionally left blank.)

*
*
*
*
*
*
*
*
*
*
*
*
*

Party's Acceptance of the September 2012 SOUTH FLORIDA MONEY LAUNDERING STRIKE FORCE VOLUNTARY COOPERATION MUTUAL AID AGREEMENT

Pursuant to F.S. 23.1225(3), this agreement may be entered into by a sheriff, a mayor or chief executive officer of a municipality or county on behalf of a law enforcement agency, if authorized by the governing body of the municipality or county. By signing below, an indication of such authorization is being made.

Any signatory may attach to this signature page any further evidence of authorization you wish to remain on file at the SAO along with this signature page.
****

I hereby acknowledge that I have been authorized by the governing body of the municipality to enter into this Agreement on behalf of the Monroe County Sheriff's Office.

_____
Signature

_____
Print or Type Name

Title:
- Sheriff
- Chief Executive Officer, to wit: _____

Date: _____

_____
Sheriff (if above signed by Chief Executive Officer of County)

Date: _____

Party's Acceptance of the September 2012 SOUTH FLORIDA MONEY LAUNDERING STRIKE FORCE VOLUNTARY COOPERATION MUTUAL AID AGREEMENT

Pursuant to F.S. 23.1225(3), this agreement may be entered into by a sheriff, a mayor or chief executive officer of a municipality or county on behalf of a law enforcement agency, if authorized by the governing body of the municipality or county. By signing below, an indication of such authorization is being made.

Any signatory may attach to this signature page any further evidence of authorization you wish to remain on file at the SAO along with this signature page.
****

I hereby acknowledge that I have been authorized by the governing body of the municipality to enter into this Agreement on behalf of the Golden Beach Police Department.

_____
Signature

_____
Print or Type Name

Title:
- Sheriff
- Chief Executive Officer, to wit: _____

Date: _____

Party's Acceptance of the September 2012 SOUTH FLORIDA MONEY LAUNDERING STRIKE FORCE VOLUNTARY COOPERATION MUTUAL AID AGREEMENT

Pursuant to F.S. 23.1225(3), this agreement may be entered into by a sheriff, a mayor or chief executive officer of a municipality or county on behalf of a law enforcement agency, if authorized by the governing body of the municipality or county. By signing below, an indication of such authorization is being made.

Any signatory may attach to this signature page any further evidence of authorization you wish to remain on file at the SAO along with this signature page.
****

I hereby acknowledge that I have been authorized by the governing body of the municipality to enter into this Agreement on behalf of the Hallandale Beach Police Department.

_____
Signature

_____
Print or Type Name

Title:
■ Sheriff
■ Chief Executive Officer, to wit: _____

Date: _____

Party's Acceptance of the September 2012 SOUTH FLORIDA MONEY LAUNDERING STRIKE FORCE VOLUNTARY COOPERATION MUTUAL AID AGREEMENT

Pursuant to F.S. 23.1225(3), this agreement may be entered into by a sheriff, a mayor or chief executive officer of a municipality or county on behalf of a law enforcement agency, if authorized by the governing body of the municipality or county. By signing below, an indication of such authorization is being made.

Any signatory may attach to this signature page any further evidence of authorization you wish to remain on file at the SAO along with this signature page.
****

I hereby acknowledge that I have been authorized by the governing body of the municipality to enter into this Agreement on behalf of the Village Of Indian Creek Police Department.

_____
Signature

_____
Print or Type Name

Title:
■ Sheriff
■ Chief Executive Officer, to wit: _____

Date: _____

Party's Acceptance of the September 2012 SOUTH FLORIDA MONEY LAUNDERING STRIKE FORCE VOLUNTARY COOPERATION MUTUAL AID AGREEMENT

For the Office of the State Attorney of the Eleventh Judicial Circuit of Florida (In and For Miami-Dade County, Florida):

_____
Signature

Katherine Fernandez-Rundle
State Attorney

Date: _____

---------------------------------------*End of Signature Pages, Attachments Follow*---------------------------------------

<table>
<tr><td>ATTACHMENT A:
Strike Force Forfeitures and Seizures Directive (Rev. 10/06)</td></tr>
</table>

A.   FORFEITURE - means anything that is taken into custody by the SFMLSF investigators that falls under the Florida Forfeiture and Contraband Act. In general, all Asset Forfeitures will be conducted under Coral Gables Police Department procedures.

    1.   All property that is taken under forfeiture will be:

        a.   Placed into the Coral Gables Police Department Property Unit or, as in case of vehicles, recorded on Coral Gables Police Department Vehicle Storage Reports after inventory search. (See attached Coral Gables Police Department Policy number #050)

        b.   All property will be listed in the Coral Gables P.D. Case Report and copies forwarded to the appropriate forfeiture attorney by 5pm the next business day.

B.   SEIZURE OF CONTRABAND - means taking into custody anything illegal to possess. (See Currency Handling Procedures)

    1.   All seizures will be placed in the Coral Gables Police Department Property Unit or applicable seizing agency.

    2.   All property that is taken into custody will be:

        a.   Fully documented on Coral Gables Police Department Property Receipt.

        b.   All seizures will be listed in the Forfeiture/ Confiscation's Report and copies sent within 24 hours to the Dade County SAO Forfeiture Attorneys and the Confiscation Unit.

    3.   In all instances where controlled substances are seized that are in the amount which warrants trafficking charges or instances where monies are seized in excess of $1,000, the SFMLSF will assign at least three investigators to the custody of the contraband or monies. The investigators will maintain custody until the controlled substance or monies are placed into the Coral Gables Police Department Property/Evidence room or applicable seizing agency.

    4.   In all seizures, it is required to complete the SFMLSF ZY Entry Form. This   form is to be completed by the case agent.

ATTACHMENT B
Strike Force Evidence Directive

A. Each investigator is responsible for the evidence he or she has the occasion to purchase or seize. All controlled substances are to be treated in a very thorough and careful manner.

B. All evidence will be turned in to the Coral Gables Police Department Property/Evidence Unit as soon as possible after its seizure.

C. Evidence will not be stored in any facility other than the Coral Gables Police Department Property Unit (i.e., desk, lockers, etc.). Controlled substances will always be checked into the Coral Gables Police Department Property Unit prior to the end of the investigator's tour of duty.

D. Tests of controlled substances to establish probable cause will be done at the scene by the impounding investigator and the results documented in the SFMLSF Report.

E. Chemical analysis of controlled substances will be performed by the Miami-Dade Crime Lab or other facility as determined by the Task Force Deputy Director. The investigator is responsible for:

  - Coral Gables Property Receipt
  - Miami Dade County Lab Analysis Form
  - Miami Dade County Property Receipt with Miami Dade County Case number.

F. Three` investigators are required when handling trafficking amounts of controlled substances or amounts of currency in excess of $1,000.

G. When an arrest for a controlled substance is made, the arresting investigator will be responsible for maintaining the integrity of the evidence, until it is turned in to the Coral Gables Property/Evidence unit.

*   As the Coral Gables Police Department is our primary evidence repository see attached Coral Gables Police Department SOP #050 (Evidence and Property) in order to comply with those regulations.

Guidelines and Training Procedures
To Be Used By State and Local Law Enforcement Agencies
And State Attorneys in Implementing
The Florida Contraband Forfeiture Act

I. Policy Statement

The Florida Contraband Forfeiture Act, Sections 932.701 through 932.707, Florida Statutes, (Act) authorizes law enforcement agencies to seize and forfeit real and personal property, including currency, vehicles, aircraft, and other contraband articles that are used in violation of the Act.

The Act also allows seizure and forfeiture of any controlled substance as defined in Chapter 893, Florida Statutes, or any substance, device, paraphernalia, or currency or other means of exchange that was used, was attempted to be used, or was intended to be used in violation of any provision of Chapter 893, Florida Statutes if a nexus can be clearly demonstrated between the article(s) seized and the narcotics activity, whether or not the use of the contraband article(s) can be traced to a specific narcotics transaction.

It is the policy of the State of Florida that law enforcement agencies shall utilize the provisions of the Act to deter and prevent the continued use of contraband articles for criminal purposes while protecting the proprietary interests of innocent owners and lien holders and to authorize such law enforcement agencies to use the proceeds collected under the Act as supplemental funding for authorized purposes. The potential for obtaining revenues from forfeitures must not override fundamental considerations such as public safety, the safety of law enforcement officers, or the investigation and prosecution of criminal activity.

It is also the policy of this state that law enforcement agencies ensure that, in all seizures made under the Act, their officers adhere to federal and state constitutional limitations regarding an individual's right to be free from unreasonable searches and seizures, including, but not limited to, the illegal use of stops based on a pretext, coercive consent searches, or a search based solely upon an individual's race or ethnicity.

The Act provides procedural safeguards for those claiming or having an interest in the seized property, including bona fide lien holders, lessors, and innocent co-owners. The Act complements the other options available to Florida law enforcement agencies in addressing criminal activity, is a valuable tool of law enforcement to be used by Florida law enforcement agencies to assist their law enforcement mission, and is to be preserved and wisely used as a valuable weapon in Florida's law enforcement arsenal.

II.   Purpose

The purpose of these Uniform Standards is to provide statewide guidelines for law enforcement policies and procedures used in seizing, maintaining, and forfeiting property under the Act and to provide training procedures to be used by state and local law enforcement agencies and state attorneys in implementing the Act. Compliance with these Standards will enhance the goal of establishing more uniform forfeiture practices throughout the state. These Uniform Standards are to be interpreted in a manner to assure that to the greatest extent possible there is uniformity of policy and procedure throughout the state. It is not the intent or purpose of these Standards to create new rights of parties or new defenses to forfeiture actions. All rights and actions are defined by the substantive provisions of the Act itself or other applicable law.

III.   Principles

The following principles should be incorporated within the policies and procedures of any state or local law enforcement agency involved in the seizure and forfeiture of property under the Act-

A.   **LAW ENFORCEMENT IS THE PRINCIPAL OBJECTIVE OF ASSET FORFEITURE.**   The potential for obtaining revenues from forfeitures must not override fundamental considerations such as public safety, the safety of law enforcement officers, the investigation and prosecution of criminal activity, and respect for the rights of individuals as provided by law.

B.   The employment, salary, promotion or other compensation of a law enforcement officer or attorney should not depend on obtaining a quota of seizures.

C.   Agencies should ensure, through the use of written policy and procedures and training, compliance with all applicable legal requirements regarding seizing, maintaining, and forfeiting property under the Act.

D.   When property other than currency is seized for forfeiture, the probable cause supporting the seizure should be promptly reviewed by a supervisor who is not directly involved in making the seizure. The determination of whether to seize currency must be made by supervisory personnel.   The agency's legal counsel must be notified as soon as possible of all seizures.

E.   The determination of whether an agency will file a civil forfeiture action should be made by the agency head or other command level designee who is not directly involved in making the seizure.

F.   Every seizing agency should have policies and procedures promoting, when there is no other legitimate basis for holding seized property, the prompt release of such property as may be required by the Act or by agency determination.   To help assure that property is not wrongfully held after seizure, every agency shall have policies and procedures ensuring that all asserted claims of interest in seized property are promptly reviewed for potential validity.

G.   A seizing agency may not use the seized property for any purpose until the rights to, interest in, and title to the seized property are perfected in accordance with the Act.   This does not prohibit the use or operation necessary for reasonable maintenance of seized property.   Reasonable efforts shall be made to maintain seized property in such a manner as to minimize loss of value.

H.   Settlement of any forfeiture action shall be consistent with the mandates of the Act and in compliance with agency policy or directive.

I.   All forfeited property retained for law enforcement use should be maintained and utilized in accordance with the Act, and should be subject to the same controls with regard to property acquired through the agency's normal appropriations process.

J.   Any agency receiving forfeiture proceeds should maintain such moneys in a special fund as provided by law, which is subject to normal accounting controls and financial audits of all deposits and expenditures.   If the seizing agency is a county or municipal agency, the proceeds and interest thereon may not be used to meet normal operating expenses of the law enforcement agency.   Seizing agencies must file reports as required by the Act.

K.   Each state or local law enforcement agency that seizes property for the purposes of forfeiture shall periodically review the agency's seizures of property, as well as settlements and forfeiture proceedings initiated by the agency to determine whether such seizures, settlements and forfeitures comply with the Act and these Standards.   Such review should occur at least annually.   If the review suggests deficiencies, the agency shall promptly move to ensure the agency's compliance with the Act and these Standards.

L.   Agencies should avoid the appearance of impropriety in the acquisition, sale, retention, or transfer of any forfeited property or proceeds derived from such property.

M.   Agency personnel involved in the seizure of property for forfeiture shall receive periodic training as noted in Section IV, below.

IV.   Training Procedures

Each state or local law enforcement agency shall ensure that its officers involved in seizing property for forfeiture under the Act receive basic training and continuing education as required by the Act. Each agency shall maintain records demonstrating an officer's compliance with these training requirements. A portion of such training must address legal aspects of forfeiture, including search and seizure, or other constitutional considerations.

(End of Mandatory Forfeiture Guidelines).

End Of September, 2008 Mutual Aid Agreement and Attachments

Endnotes

1. An undercover law enforcement agent is an employee of a government agency working under the direction and control of a government agency in a criminal investigation, whose true identity as a law enforcement agent involved in the investigation is concealed from third parties. (Definition taken in part from the *ICE Manual* [for information only, date of issue and accuracy cannot be verified, herein after *ICE Manual*]; *DEA Agents Manual;* and ABA Standard 2.3, Use of Undercover Law Enforcement Agents and Undercover Operations).
2. See *The Federal Bureau of Investigation's Compliance with the Attorney General's Investigative Guidelines*, Special Report, Office of the Inspector General, September 2005.
3. Taken in part from the *ICE Manual*.
4. Casual undercover is generally exempted from training requirements.
5. www.justice.gov/dea/.
6. *ICE Manual*.
7. *DEA Agents Manual*, Chapter 66.
8. See *FBI Undercover Operations Guidelines Manual,* Section IV (C)(2) and *DEA Agents Manual* Ch. 66 (dates of issue unknown, included as historical reference).
9. Taken in part from the *ICE Manual*.
10. Standard 2.3, ABA Criminal Justice Standards, February 2008.
11. Ibid.
12. See Joh, E., "Breaking the Law to Enforce the Law: Undercover Police Participation in Crime," *Stan. L. Rev.* 155, December 2009. Participation in other illegal activities has been well documented. See, *Anchorage v. Flanagan,* 649 P.2d 957, 959 (Alaska Ct. App. 1982) (engaged in sexual acts with prostitutes); Ross, J.E., *Impediments to Transnational Cooperation in Undercover Policing: A Comparative Study of the United States and Italy*, 52 AM. J. COMP. L. 569, 569-70 (2004) (stole fine art); Alan, D., *Sting II: Police Departments Get into the Act*, Boston Herald, June 25, 1982, at 25 (commissioned and financed an "obscene film"); see *Hampton v. United States*, 425 U.S. 484 (1976) (supplied heroin to defendant and participated in its sale to another government agent); *Shaw v. Winters*, 796 F.2d 1124 (9th Cir. 1986) (sold food stamps and claimed they were stolen); *United States v. Parisi*, 674 F.2d 126, 127 (1st Cir. 1982) (provided the food stamps that formed the very basis of the conviction for improper use of food stamps).
13. *The Attorney General's Guidelines Regarding the Use of Confidential Informants* (hereinafter CI Guidelines); see *FBI Confidential Human Source Policy Manual*, P0L07-0004-D1, revised September 5, 2007, Section 4 Instructions to be Discussed with a Confidential Human Source; see also *Confidential Human Source Validation Standards Manual*, 0258PG, March 26, 2010.
14. The references to particular United States Sentencing Guidelines (USSG) sections are intended to remain applicable to the most closely corresponding USSG level in subsequent editions of the USSG manual in the event that the cited USSG provisions are amended. Thus, it is intended that subsection (iii) of this paragraph will remain applicable to the highest offense level in the Drug Quantity Table in future editions of the USSG manual and that subsection

(iv) of the paragraph will remain applicable to dollar amounts that, in future editions of the USSG manual, trigger sentencing enhancements similar to that set forth in the current section 2B1.1 (b) (1) (I).

15. CI Guidelines, § III.C.4; see *FBI Confidential Human Source Policy Manual*, P0L07-0004-D1, revised September 5, 2007, Section 4 Instructions to Be Discussed with a Confidential Human Source; see also *Confidential Human Source Validation Standards Manual*, 0258PG, March 26, 2010.

16. See *United States v. Burrows*, 36 F.3d 875, 882 (9th Cir. 1994); *United States v. Hedges*, 912 F.2d 1397, 1405 (11th Cir. 1990); *United States v. Clegg*, 846 F.2d 1221, 1222 (9th Cir. 1988); *United States v. Tallmadge*, 829 F.2d 767, 773-75 (9th Cir. 1987).

17. See *United States v. Hilton*, 257 F.3d 50 (1st Cir. 2001).

18. *The Federal Bureau of Investigation's Compliance with the Attorney General's Investigative Guidelines, Chapter Three: The Attorney General's Guidelines Regarding the Use of Confidential Informants* (Redacted), Office of the Inspector General, September 2005.

19. Ibid.

20. *The Federal Bureau of Investigation's Compliance with the Attorney General's Investigative Guidelines, Chapter Three: The Attorney General's Guidelines Regarding the Use of Confidential Informants* (Redacted), Office of the Inspector General, September 2005; see Staff Study in *Overview of Government's Handling of Jackie Presser Investigation*: Hearing Before the Permanent Subcommittee on Investigations of the Senate Government Affairs Committee, 99th Cong. 75 (1986).

21. Ibid.

22. Reilly, R.J., "FBI Allowed Informants to Commit More Crimes in 2012 Than Year Before," *Huffington Post*, December 27, 2013.

23. Author's note: In general, law enforcement officers engaging in reverse stings are not operating at risk of being charged with a crime. Drug dealing and drug possession are specific intent crimes requiring the requisite mental state to commit a crime. An undercover agent participating in a reverse undercover drug operation lacks the specific intent to commit the crime, and criminal liability does not attach.

24. *United States v. Gomez*, 103 F.3d 249, 252 n.1 (2d Cir. 1997).

25. See Levine, M., "Reverse Undercover: Boon for Police or Bust for the Justice System," *Police News*, November 7, 2013.

26. *North Carolina State Bureau of Investigation Policy and Procedure Manual*, Procedure 16, July 1, 2002.

27. *DEA Agents Manual*, Chapter 66.

28. Rhode Island Department of Attorney General, *Rules and Regulations for Reverse Undercover/Proprietary Operations*, Section II (B).

29. *DEA Agents Manual*, Chapter 66.

30. Scoville, D., "Blue-on-Blue Shootings," *Police Magazine*, June 20, 2000.

31. *DEA Agents Manual*, Chapter 66, Coordination with Other Agencies.

32. Rhode Island Department of Attorney General, *Rules and Regulations for Reverse Undercover/Proprietary Operations*.

33. Flatten, M. "Risk vs. Reward: Chandler Police Raise Risk to Officers as They Chase Lucrative Out-of-Town Drug Deals," Goldwater Institute, March 14, 2011.

34. See Maricopa County Superior Court Case No: 2010-007912-005-DT.

35. Affidavit filed by Maricopa County Prosecutor, March 29, 2011.

36. Flatten, M., "Suspect in Deadly Reverse Sting Drug Bust Was Federal Informant," The Goldwater Institute, August 28, 2011.

37. Ibid.

38. See North Carolina State Bureau of Investigation Policy and Procedure Manual, Procedure 16, July 1, 2002. The North Carolina State Bureau of Investigation requires agents requesting authorization for a reverse operation to submit a written plan and/or justification to the appropriate special agent in charge, who will evaluate the merit of the proposal. The plan should be detailed to include the following:
    a. Description of violator or violators, criminal history, if armed, information to support drug dealing, and so on.
    b. Date and location of proposed transaction to include complete description of location.
    c. Law enforcement personnel involved in the investigation. Plan should describe location of law enforcement personnel, indication they will be wearing clearly identifiable law enforcement clothing, marked vehicles utilized, take-down signal, and so on.
    d. Amount of drugs and where drugs are to be obtained.
    e. Contact with the appropriate district attorney and U.S. attorney by the special agent in charge or assistant special agent in charge to determine whether the prosecutor has any objection to the proposed investigation and whether the prosecutor will prosecute any individuals arrested as a result of a reverse operation.

39. O'Matz, M., "Cops, Cash, Cocaine: How Sunrise Police Make Millions Selling Drugs," *Sun Sentinel*, October 21, 2013.

40. Flatten, M., "Undercover Cop's Death Highlights High Risk/Reward of Reverse Stings," *East Valley Tribune*, March 21, 2011.

41. O'Matz, M., "Cops, Cash, Cocaine: How Sunrise Police Make Millions Selling Drugs," *Sun Sentinel*, October 21, 2013.

42. *FBI Legal Handbook for Special Agents—Informants and Entrapment*, Section 8-3.5 Entrapment.

43. See *Sorrells v. United States*, 287 U.S. 435, 442 (1932).

44. *Sherman v. United States*, 356 U.S. 369, 372 (1958).

45. See *United States v. Williams*, 23 F.3d 629, 635 (2d Cir. 1994).

46. See *United States v. Brand*, 467 F.3d 179, 189 (2d Cir. 2006); *United States v. Bala*, 236 F.3d 87, 94 (2d Cir. 2000).

47. *United States v. Brand*, 467 F.3d at 191; *United States v. Valencia*, 645 F.2d 1158, 1167 (2d Cir. 1980); *United States v. Viviano*, 437 F.2d 295, 299 (2d Cir.) cert. denied, 402 U.S. 983 (1971).

48. *Jacobson v. United States*, 503 U.S. 540, 549 (1992).

49. Ibid at 550.

50. See *U.S. v. Twiggs*, 588 F.2d 373 (3rd Cir. 1978).

51. *United States v. Russell*, 411 U.S. 423, 431-32 (1973).

52. Fed. R. Crim. P. 12(b)(1) and (b)(2). See *United States v. Henderson-Durand*, 985 F.2d 970, 973 & n. 5 (8th Cir.), cert. denied, 510 U.S. 856 (1993); *United States v. Duncan*, 896 F.2d 271, 274 (7th Cir. 1990); *United States v. Nunez-Rios*, 622 F.2d 1093, 1099 (2d Cir. 1980).

53. USAM, Title 9, *Criminal Resource Manual* 648.

54. USAM, Title 9, *Criminal Resource Manual* 648. at 432; see *United States v. Pedraza*, 27 F.3d 1515, 1521 (10th Cir.) (not outrageous for government "to infiltrate an ongoing criminal enterprise, or to induce a defendant to repeat, continue, or even expand criminal activity."), cert. denied, 115 S. Ct. 347 (1994).

55. Black's Law Dictionary.

56. USSG § 2D1.1, cmt. n.14, 2001 edition.

57. O'Matz, M., "Cops, Cash, Cocaine: How Sunrise Police Make Millions Selling Drugs," *Sun Sentinel*, October 21, 2013.

58. 28 U.S.C. § 533 note (explaining that Public Law 108–447, div. B, title I, § 116 extended to ATF the same authority previously granted to the FBI and DEA in Public Law 102–395 § 102(b) and in effect pursuant to Public Law 104–132 § 815(d)).

59. Pursuant to 28 U.S.C. § 510, the attorney general may also delegate certifying authority to specified individuals as appropriate.

60. Audit of the Bureau Of Alcohol, Tobacco, and Firearms and Explosives' Use of Income Generating Undercover Operations, U.S. Department of Justice Office of the Inspector General Audit Division, Audit Report 13-36, September 2013.

61. 18 U.S.C. §§ 1956 and 1957.

62. Rothchild, J., *Swordfish: A True Story of Ambition, Savagery, and Betrayal*, Pantheon, New York, NY, 1993.

63. Thompson, G., "Congressman Voices Doubt on Oversight of DEA," *New York Times*, January 27, 2012, "Both the D.E.A. and the Justice Department have defended the so-called Attorney General Exempt Operations, saying that they are tightly controlled, and that they are crucial in helping determine how drug-trafficking organizations move their money and in locating high-value suspects."

64. *SGS-92-X003 v. U.S.*, N0. 97-579C, January 27, 2009; also known as the DEA Princess case, it is a suit brought by a DEA money laundering informant for damages.

65. Interview from PBS Frontline, Drug Wars.

66. Berthelson, C., "Three Mexicans Are Convicted in Money Laundering Case," *The New York Times*, June 11, 1999.

67. Smith, M., "Rampant Use of Informants and Drug Cases Coming under Fire," *Houston Chronicle*, August 6, 2000.

68. Sheptycki, J., *Issues in Transnational Policing*, Routledge Press, London, 2000, p. 158.

69. Congressional Record, June 10, 1998, pp. S6011–6012.

70. Ed Bradley interview, *60 Minutes*, CBS, April 2000.

71. DEA home page.

72. DOJ Office of Inspector General Comments on Asset Forfeiture Fund, December 15, 2013.

73. Ibid.

74. High-intensity drug trafficking areas task forces are staffed by federal, state, and local law enforcement officers. The task forces are administered by the Office of National Drug Control Policy. There are 40 high-intensity drug trafficking areas task forces located in major cities throughout the United States.

75. Florida Statute 896.105: Penalty provisions not applicable to law enforcement. The penalty provisions of this chapter, including those directed at reporting violations or the conduct or attempted conduct of unlawful financial transactions, the unlawful transportation or attempted transportation of monetary

instruments, and the concealment of unlawful proceeds or their ownership are not applicable to law enforcement officers who engage in aspects of such activity for bona fide authorized undercover law enforcement purposes in the course of or in relation to an active criminal investigation, active criminal intelligence gathering, or active prosecution.

76. Knock and talk: Tactic employed by police who wish to gain entry into a dwelling without a search warrant. The officer knocks on the door, engages the occupant in conversation, and obtains permission to search without a warrant. Tactic frequently used when a house is suspected of being used to conceal large sums of currency or drugs.

77. Keynote address to the American Bankers Association and the American Bar Association, Washington, DC, November 5, 1997.

78. Kaplan, D.E., "A Case Study in Policing for Profit: A Model Drug Task Force Comes under Fire," *US News & World Report*, July 10, 2000.

79. Ibid.

80. The Office of the State Attorney of the Eleventh Judicial Circuit of Florida,
    — The City of Coral Gables Police Department
    — The City of Miami Police Department
    — The City of Miami Shores Police Department
    — The City of Miami Beach Police Department
    — The City of Hallandale Police Department
    — The City of Golden Beach Police Department
    — The Village of Indian Creek Police Department
    — The City of North Miami Police Department
    — The City of Fort Lauderdale Police Department
    — The City of Davie Police Department
    — The City of Hialeah Police Department
    — The Town of Surfside Police Department
    — The City of Doral Police Department
    — The Monroe County Sheriff's Office

81. "Bal Harbour Cops Spent Lavishly with Seized Drug Loot," *Miami Herald*, December 15, 2012.

82. U.S. Department of Justice Office of Inspector General Report, Case # 2012-005018.

83. *North Carolina State Bureau of Investigation Policy and Procedure Manual*, Procedure 16, July 1, 2002.

84. See memorandum of understanding between the DEA and the USC to implement Title 21 cross designation policies and procedures (2003), defining controlled deliveries.

85. Federal transportation statistics.

86. Levine, M., "Blind Mules: Fiction or Fact", *Law Enforcement Executive Forum*, June 2006.

87. Article 2 (i), The Draft UN Convention Against Transnational Organized Crime (A/AC. 254/36): Controlled Deliveries.

88. Making an arrest before an act of terror can be carried out. See *Journal of Conflict Resolution*, Vol. 49, No. 2, April 2005 183-200 DOI: 10.1177/0022002704272863.

89. Flaccus, G., "California Case Highlights Use of Mosque Informants," Associated Press, March 1, 2009.

90. Perez, R., "The Terror Conspiracy: The Security; U.S. Steps Up Precautions at Its Offices and Airports," *New York Times*, October 2, 1995.

91. Bernstein, R., "Bomb Informant Tapes Give Rare Glimpse of FBI Dealings," *New York Times*, October 31, 1993; see also Ragavan, C., "Tracing Terror's Roots: How the First World Trade Center Plot Sowed Seeds for 9/11," *US News & World Report*, February 16, 2003.

92. Ibid.

93. "Mosque Informants Infuriate US Muslims," *Islam Online*, February 28, 2009.

94. Hernandez, S., "Informant Files $10 Million Suit against FBI," *Orange County Register*, January 22, 2010.

95. Ibid.

96. Case #SACV10-00102-JVS, U.S. District Court, Central District of California.

97. "Mosque Informants Infuriate US Muslims," *Islam Online*, February 28, 2009.

98. "FBI Chief Defends Use of Informants in Mosques," Associated Press, June 8, 2009.

99. Shipler, D., "Terrorist Plots, Hatched by the FBI," *New York Times*, April 28, 2012.

100. Aaronson, T., "The Informants," *Mother Jones*, September /October 2011; Aaronson, T., "Inside the Terror Factory," *Mother Jones*, January 11, 2013.

101. Norman, B., "Liberty City Seven Trial Travesty: The Case against Miami 'Terrorists' Is Mired in Greed and Falsehoods," *Miami New Times*, November 24, 2007.

102. Ripley, A., "The Fort Dix Conspiracy," *Time Magazine*, December 17, 2007.

103. "Judge Declares Mistrial in the Liberty City Seven," *Miami News*, December 13, 2007.

104. "Five Convicted in Plot to Blow Up Sears Tower," *New York Times*, May 12, 2009.

105. "Aspirational Rather Than Operational," *Democracy Now*, June 26, 2006.

106. "A Trial Too Far: Is a Federal Prosecutor Seeking Justice or Trying to Save Face in Miami Terrorism Case," *Washington Post*, May 2, 2008.

107. *U.S. v. Augustin*, U.S. Court of Appeals, 11th Cir., No. 09-15985, Nov. 1, 2011.

108. Format obtained in part from *ICE Manual*.

109. See Section 12.15.2 regarding Sensitive Activities Review Committee and Attorney General Exempt Operations.

110. Ibid.

111. See Appendix 7D.

Controlling Informants and Institutional Ethics 13

13.1 Introduction

Police officers and federal agents face two major occupational hazards or risks during their careers: physical risks to their personal safety and professional risks stemming from decisions they make that may compromise their career path and integrity.[1] The operation of informants holds both the potential for physical danger to the officer and can lead to unethical conduct and corruption.[2]

The volumes of rules and regulations developed by federal and local law enforcement agencies governing the control of informants dramatically illustrates official recognition of the risks informants pose to agents and the public. The driving motive behind the policies is to minimize that risk by imposing institutional control over the agent–informant relationship.

Effectively managing confidential sources requires the law enforcement agency to constantly assess the risk associated with each source it operates. The continual identification and analysis of relevant adverse factor associated with an informant must be weighed against the potential benefit of using the source.[3] Failure to do so has undermined costly long-term investigations,[4] destroyed the careers of prosecutors and law enforcement officers,[5] and caused death[6] and serious injuries[7] to innocent citizens and police.[8] In many cases, the sequence of events leading to disaster began during the selection and recruitment[9] of the informant and were exacerbated by failures in control and supervision.

13.2 Informants, Agent Integrity, and Corruption

Failure in the management of cooperating individuals has proven to be one of the most prevalent causes of serious integrity problems in law enforcement.[10] The DEA, one of the leading "consumers" of informant services, investigated integrity problems stemming from the operation of CIs. Professional responsibility investigators listed ten of the most common violations committed by agents in their supervision and handling of informants; seven involved money, gifts, and gratuities:

- Socializing with informants and/or their families[11]
- Becoming romantically involved with CIs
- Purchasing items from CIs[12]

- CIs purchasing items from DEA employees
- Borrowing money from CIs
- Receiving gifts or gratuities from CIs
- Entering into business relationships with CIs
- Contacting CIs alone
- Paying CIs without benefit of witnesses
- Encouraging CIs to sign blank receipts for cash payments

The Office of Professional Responsibility investigators concluded that "many, if not most, such integrity problems could not have occurred without some lapse in supervisory or management oversight procedures." The study concluded that "in order to remedy these shortcomings, strong, consistent management needs to enforce all current requirements contained in the DEA manual."[13]

13.3   Supervisory Oversight

Many police departments and federal agencies have mid-level managers directly overseeing informant operations. They found it necessary because all too often, a close, symbiotic relationship[14] develops between an informant and his handler. The relationship leads to a corresponding loss of objectivity on the part of the informant handler. A mid-level manager who has no immediate personal stake in the operation of the informant can step in when necessary to enforce departmental procedures impartially.[15]

There is ample evidence that the use of informants is a catalyst for corruption. Regardless, the seductive nature of the informant–agent relationship is ever present. A former assistant director of the Federal Bureau of Investigation's (FBI's) Inspection Division described the problem. "You have to keep in mind it is a business relationship. On the other hand, if you have a good asset, it is hard not to develop a friendship. The stakes are extremely high, and if you have a valuable asset, it is hard not to go beyond an arm's-length relationship."[16]

A police inspector deciding the professional fate of one of his officers charged with violating informant handling procedures tried to define the officer–informant relationship:

The nature of any association that exists between a detective and a police informer is necessarily one incapable of precise definition. I do not believe I could possibly define the perimeters within which any such association could be said to be proper, or define any area outside of which that association could be labeled as improper, nor do I in these general remarks, purport to make any such definition. Every case that involves this sort of relationship must particularly be an individual case in which the circumstances are the only relevant guide. It is obvious, however, that such an association, while valuable information is coming, needs to be nurtured carefully. An informer's interest in continuing to be a reliable source is to be encouraged. That encouragement may no doubt take a variety of forms. It may include, as here, the provision of money. It may even, as here, include the provision of some measure of material within the police knowledge. It may include reaching a degree of familiarity which otherwise would be totally unacceptable. It all depends on the circumstances."[17]

13.4   Deadly Consequences

The informant will use every ploy imaginable to undermine the dominant role of the agent to accomplish his or her own goals. They can be treacherous. If the informant is able to undermine or compromise the integrity of his or her control agent, the informant–agent relationship is turned upside down.

Special Agent John Coleman,[18] a married father of two, was assigned to a small town outside Lexington, Kentucky. He found himself being manipulated by Susan Daniels Smith, his 27-year-old paid informant. She was a destitute, divorced mother of two young children with information concerning an auto theft ring. They ended up sleeping together.

According to Coleman, "We were in the car one night, Susan and I talking, and she sensed that I was down, and we just came together right there. I knew right at that point that I had compromised everything that I had worked for, because I broke the first rule of an FBI agent–informer relationship: Never sleep with your informant."[19]

Their affair spanned nearly 2 years and became complicated after she said she had become pregnant. She threatened to expose Coleman, ruining both his career and marriage.

On June 8, 1989, 30-year-old Coleman took Smith for a drive into the hills of Kentucky to discuss her demands of marriage. He strangled her during a quarrel. Coleman apparently offered to adopt the child, but Smith wanted him to leave his wife. He disposed of her body in an area of abandoned coal mines 9 miles outside of town.

Coleman returned to work, but Smith's disappearance did not go unnoticed. The local sheriff became convinced Coleman was responsible for the informant's disappearance. It took a year for the sheriff to crack the case. The FBI agent was arrested for murder.

Coleman worked out a deal with prosecutors. In return for a plea to a charge of manslaughter, the state would not bring charges for murder. According to the indictment returned by the Pike County grand jury, Coleman killed Ms. Smith "while under extreme emotional duress."[20] An autopsy of Smith's body failed to reveal any trace of a fetus.[21]

Coleman was sentenced to 16 years in prison, the first FBI agent in history to be sent to prison for a homicide. He wasn't going to be the last.

13.5   Pressure to Recruit Informants

Inexperience on the part of the control agent is often the cause for an informant-related scandal. Institutional pressure to produce cases compounds the problems presented by an inexperienced informant handler.

Immediately following graduation from training, FBI agents are expected to recruit and operate informants. The pressure to produce informants often forces the agent to choose between following the guidelines and job security. Agents are told:

> Each Agent involved in investigative activity is obligated to develop and operate productive informants. Those Agents who cannot develop productive informants must overcome the lack of informants through some other substantial contribution, such as the continued development during investigative assignments of Cooperative Witnesses. The proper operation of informants is a basic skill that requires dedication and ingenuity. The success each Agent enjoys normally depends on the strength of the Agent's personality and resourcefulness exercised in obtaining information.[22]

Pressure to develop informants,[23] coupled with lack of training and inexperience, resulted in the indictment by a state grand jury of an FBI agent for burglary. The charges were the result of the utilization of an untested informant who committed burglaries and auto theft with the permission of an FBI agent who was unable to control his informant.[24] During one of the burglaries, the informant went so far as to ask the agent to act as a "lookout" during the commission of the crime. Demonstrating the impact that the lack of control over an informant and pressure to develop informants can have, the agent testified:

> Colvin was the first informant in my career who began giving information of criminal activity after just appearing at the office. His information and his conversations with me over a period of time indicated that he had the information concerning the activities of several individuals in the Kentucky/Indiana area. His information to me was always that *someone else was the moving force in the criminal activity*. As an informant, he told me that his relationships with people would allow him to get close to and report on these individuals. Since I had been in the division for 18 months and had not developed a quality informant, *I suppose I was overwhelmed by what it appeared he could do*. He started providing me with information and it was in the context of "so and so is going to do this and we will be able to make a case."[25]

13.6   Control and the War of Wills

The majority of informants are criminals skilled in capitalizing on any personal weakness, regardless of the activity they are engaged in. Most have built their lives by violating the norms society imposes. The Court in *United States v. Bernal-Obeso* made this observation about the character of informants:

> By definition, criminal informants are cut from untrustworthy cloth and must be managed and carefully watched by the government and the courts to prevent them from falsely accusing the innocent, from manufacturing evidence against those under suspicion of crime, and from lying under oath in the courtroom.[26]

The dynamics involved in the agent–informant relationship constantly present opportunities for a skilled informant to resist efforts to control his activities. If successful, the informant is able to guide an investigation in the direction he wishes it to take, contrary to the instructions given him by the control agent. In doing so, he is also able to advance his own agenda. The absence of effective supervision of the control agent exacerbates the problem.

The Drug Enforcement Administration (DEA) identifies control as the most important aspect in successful confidential informant (CI) management. Agents are instructed that the informant must never be allowed to run the investigation regardless of how insistent or argumentative they may become. He or she must know that the ultimate decision maker during the case is the Special Agent.[27] Likewise, the Bureau of Alcohol, Tobacco, Firearms, and Explosives cautions that Special Agents must make certain that it is he or she, not the informant, who directs the investigation.[28]

The motivation for an informant to dominate an investigation ranges from simple to complex. The defendant informant who is "working off a charge" may be attempting to fulfill his substantial assistance commitment without actually producing the results desired by his control agent. He may be attempting to produce an alternative target and not burn any bridges. It may be that he never was able to deliver the target he promised.

Informants faced with a specific time frame in which to produce a case may become desperate and view attempts to control their activity as contrary to their own best interests. In *United States v. Medina-Reyes*,[29] the informant was given specific individuals as targets. His cooperation and plea agreement conspicuously stated that if his obligations were "not completed within 30 days of the signing of this agreement, for whatever reason, the defendant [informant] will not be entitled to any recommendations of leniency by the State."[30]

Throughout the period of the informant's "cooperation," he repeatedly violated the terms of his cooperation agreement. Two of the major contacts he claimed to have had with targeted individuals were initiated by the CI "on his own without the direction of law enforcement officers."[31] The informant also continued to engage in drug trafficking while operating as a CI. During the period that he was assisting agents, officers at the Des Moines Airport detained him and seized $20,000 in drug money from him.

In granting a motion to suppress evidence obtained during the execution of a search warrant obtained as a result of the informant's information, the *Medina-Reyes* court was extremely critical of the informant's conduct.

> [S]uch a dark shadow is cast on the reliability of the confidential informant, that probable cause cannot be found. He had no past track record as an informant demonstrating reliability; he was seriously flawed by his own drug dealing, drug usage, lies to [his control agent] and violations of the *control provision* of his cooperation agreement; and he was *under heavy pressure to make* a prosecutable case against [the targets]. One cannot reasonably conclude that information from such a person rose to the level of probable cause.[32]

13.7   The Levine Memorandum: Agents Working for an Informant

The use of informants and the methods used to control them is a clandestine activity. It does not routinely expose itself to close examination by those outside of law enforcement circles.[33] It is not until a case spins seriously out of the control of the case agent or the prosecutors that even a partial analysis is permitted.

A U.S. Customs drug case provided a rare opportunity for the court to examine an investigation driven by a manipulative informant.[34] The CI was successful in both determining the course of an investigation and pitting the Customs Service against the DEA. The story was contained in a hidden government memorandum, withheld when the government violated both *Brady*[35] and *Jencks*[36] by failing to disclose its existence.

The informant had been involved in illegal drug operations for 25 years, far longer than his Customs agent handlers had been employed. The path to becoming an informant in the case was a typical one. Following his arrest for possessing 1 kg of cocaine, the informant was able to convince a Customs agent that he could lead the U.S. Customs Service to high-level Mexican government officials involved in drug trafficking.[37] A substantial deal was set in motion.

The agent arranged for the informant's release from jail, and a "sting operation" was initiated, targeting traffickers in Mexico and Bolivia. The primary target named by the CI was a Mexican general he claimed provided protection for shipments of cocaine smuggled into the United States by aircraft. Throughout the course of the investigation, the informant was successful in preventing agents from either meeting with or tape recording conversations with the general, and he thwarted other opportunities to gather crucial evidence.[38]

A 42-page memorandum by DEA supervisor Michael Levine chronicled the control problems he observed and the influence the CI had over Customs agents and the government's investigation.[39] The memorandum was an indirect result of the informant's allegations of agent misconduct, including claims by the informant that he had bribed DEA agents. Originally withheld from the defense at trial, *de novo* review by the appellate court concluded that there was "a reasonable probability that had the [Levine Memorandum and attachments] been disclosed, the result of the proceeding would have been different such that [our] confidence in the outcome is undermined."[40]

Excerpts from the Levine Memorandum describe the lack of control over the informant when compared to prescribed handling techniques follow:

> I noticed that when Customs officers were talking about [the informant] it was almost as if they were in awe of him. They were ecstatic [sic] at the results of his cooperation to that point …

> The [Customs Undercover agent] later confided in me [DEA Group Supervisor Levine] that he often found himself pitted between his "bosses" (who preferred to follow [the informant's] suggestions) and me. He also stated that … he was very "uncomfortable" with the latitude and freedom the informant had been given, but being a new agent in Customs … he had felt often "trapped" in his role

> There was much uncontrolled [sic] telephone contact between [the informant] and the violators [some of the defendants]. He often, without consulting or coordinating with the DEA control agent … or myself, would speak to the violators telling them "Luis said …" This utilizing my undercover identity to manipulate the case the way he [the informant] saw fit. Weeks later I had to overcome many statements he attributed to "Luis" (my undercover identity). He was constantly allowed to operate in this fashion *throughout the investigation,* unless I was present. I made it clear, when I was present, that it was a drug case and that I was a DEA Agent, and that it would be done my way—which [the informant] never ceased to fight against

> The points of the various arguments [with the informant] were usually not as important as the control they signified. The issue was that the CI [the confidential informant] was out of control, in that he believed himself on an equal par with the investigating agents. Being an outsider in a case, I still did not think it my place to "rein him in."

> As a further demonstration of [the informant's] influence during the investigation, Levine observed: In the San Diego Customs office [the informant] seemed to have full run of the place, using telephones and desks at his will and was on a first name "kidding" basis with many of the agents and secretaries. He was extremely familiar with those "controlling" him, often joking about matters private and personal to each. He, in fact,—while no violators were present—not only had the full run of the undercover house, but the keys to all the leased undercover cars, which he utilized at his whim.

> Commenting exclusively on the behavior of his own agents Levine described the operation as "a nightmarish, failed, buy/bust operation in Panama during

which DEA functioned at its absolute worst." According to Levine, government agents involved in the undercover operation "were too drunk to deal with on a logical basis," thereby jeopardizing not just the investigation, but perhaps the lives of agents involved in the investigation.

The defense capitalized on the government's lack of control over the informant. Some of their arguments were described by the court as "insightful." They further illustrate the impact of lack of control.

[Millions of dollars are talked about but not one speck of cocaine shows up at any time and not one sample is gathered by the government and nothing really is seen except, surprise, surprise, surprise, that which [the informant] says he saw ...

The Government, the individuals involved in this case, through their trust and through their misguided confidence in [the informant], ignored by choice or by lack of wisdom points throughout this whole investigation that if they had been reviewed under even the most glancing of considerations would have revealed that this was all a scam.

What is incredible is that this man was essentially placed in charge of the investigation. We have 10, 15 agents milling around in the background, but the person who led this investigation throughout it was a convicted criminal who had not [had] verified any of the truths that supposedly he had told the government.[41]

We have [the informant] and unfortunately in this screenplay of a case, [the informant] was producer, director, screenwriter and actor. Not one of the agents involved in this case really supervised what this man did.[42]

The court agrees with the defendants that [the informant's] deliberate thwarting of Levine's attempt to tape-record a telephone conversation with the General [was] critically important. The informant's actions in deliberately acting contrary to instructions by Levine to bring the defendants to an undercover meeting so that a telephone call to the General could be made gave rise to the suspicion the informant knew or suspected that there was no General to call.

13.8   Prosecutors Falling in Love with Rats

Agents are not the only members of the criminal justice system to be manipulated by informants. Prosecutors have proven they are not immune from the seductive and corruptive influence of informants and cooperating witnesses (CWs).

The temptation for a prosecutor to wrap his case around the testimony of an informant or CW is dangerously seductive. Ethics are often thrown to the wind. A recent Benjamin N. Cardozo School of Law study took a close look at the nearly hypnotic powers wielded by CWs over prosecutors.

Researchers found that some prosecutors actually "fall in love with their rats."[43] One prosecutor quoted in the study described the experience: "You are not supposed to, of course. But you spend time with this guy; you get to know him and his family. You like him. The reality is that the cooperator's information often becomes your mind-set."[44]

13.9 Case Study: The El Rukn Prosecution

The El Rukns case,[45] an extremely high-profile, headline-grabbing Chicago gang prosecution, illustrates the devastating effect that the love-affair syndrome in tandem with a win-at-all-costs mindset of some prosecutors can have. The government's case depended heavily on the testimony of six former gang leaders turned CW who hoped to have their sentences drastically reduced in return for their testimony.

The prosecution alleged racketeering acts, as many as 20 murders, 12 attempted murders, 11 conspiracies to murder, large-scale drug distribution, kidnapping, and witness intimidation and retaliation. Following 4 years of litigation and trials, the cases resulted in 37 convictions and 16 guilty pleas. Five defendants were sentenced to life and two other defendants to 50-year sentences.[46]

Defense attorneys do not like losing cases any more than prosecutors do, and there was no shortage of defense lawyers outraged by the case's outcome. They alleged that federal prosecutors intentionally concealed damaging evidence bearing on the credibility of at least two of the gang leaders turned CWs who testified at trial.

Following the testimony of 29 witnesses at a posttrial hearing, the district court granted the convicted defendants a new trial. In a 137-page ruling, the judge found that the government had knowingly allowed the two primary CWs to perjure themselves. The court also found that prosecutors withheld evidence that during the trial, all six CWs being held at the Metropolitan Correctional Center (MCC) had used illegal drugs and received unlawful favors from prosecutors and their staff.[47]

Drug use was tame compared to what else the court learned. The ensuing investigation found a case where prosecutors were alleged to have allowed their CWs to run amok.

The prosecutors were alleged to have permitted the CWs to have "contact visits" with visitors both at the U.S. Attorney's office in the federal courthouse and in the Bureau of Alcohol, Tobacco, Firearms, and Explosives (ATF) office adjacent to the courthouse. Most of the visitors were women; there was seldom supervision by agents or attorneys. The visits were permitted, even though officers at MCC had revoked visitation privileges after finding one of the witnesses having sex with his visitor on the floor of the visiting room.[48]

Another CW had sex with his wife on several occasions while being guarded by ATF agents.[49]

The CWs were observed by other prisoners snorting cocaine and using heroin while in MCC. A fellow inmate reported that one of the CWs was "high on drugs from almost the time he arrived."[50] The drugs were believed to have been passed during the unsupervised contact visits at the government's offices.

Prosecutors were alleged to have given their prisoner witnesses unlimited and unsupervised telephone privileges while they were in government offices. Prosecutors, paralegals, and secretaries also accepted "hundreds" of collect telephone calls from the informants and forwarded the calls to other parties.[51] One of the forwarded informant telephone calls was to his drug supplier complaining about the poor quality of the drugs brought to him during a "contact visit."[52]

A prosecutor's paralegal was seduced by one of the CWs. She allegedly developed a personal relationship with him and engaged in "phone sex" during the trial.[53] The paralegal admitted to giving presents to the CWs, supplying beer to them during a party at the U.S Attorney's Office while celebrating a conviction, and smuggling contraband for them into the MCC.[54]

The CWs were allowed to move about freely within the U.S. Attorney's Office while participating in debriefings and pre-indictment preparation. Lack of supervision allowed them to steal pre-indictment prosecution memoranda and other materials relating to the El Rukns cases. Those materials were transported back to the MCC, where they were provided to other witnesses in the case.[55] It was alleged that one of the lead prosecutors allowed himself to be named as one of the CW's beneficiaries to his property, second only to his mother.[56]

Another prosecutor was alleged to have approached one of the informants about co-authoring a book about the El Rukns. The business discussions occurred during the prosecution of one of the cases, which called for the testimony of the CW.[57]

Three federal district judges reversed 13 of the El Rukn convictions, accusing the lead prosecutor of misconduct. The U.S. Attorney's Office agreed to sharply reduce sentences for 23 defendants, and charges were dropped against 4 others.

In April 1996, the lead prosecutor was fired from his $98,500-per-year position. The Justice Department said in its letter of termination that he knew or should have known about two government witnesses who tested positive for drugs while in custody. In 1998, however, an administrative judge supported the prosecutor's contentions that the lead prosecutor had never seen the drug-test results and that a conversation with a fellow prosecutor about the drug use never took place. He was awarded back pay with interest and reinstated.[58]

13.10   Government Liability for Torts Committed by Informants

Generally, the federal government has been successful in avoiding liability for torts committed by its employees, particularly for crimes committed by the employee's informants. That was until nearly $2 billion in wrongful death lawsuits related to the scandal surrounding a corrupt FBI agent's handling of informant James "Whitey" Bulger made their way into federal court.[59]

A major part of the government's success of avoiding law suits is owed to the Federal Tort Claims Act (FTCA).[60] By relying upon the "discretionary function" of the FTCA, the government has successfully argued that because the use of informants is discretionary (i.e., left up to the decisions of the individual law enforcement agency) rather than ministerial, there should be no liability on the government for torts committed by an employee because the government, under the FTCA, did not waive immunity for discretionary acts.

Before the passage of the FTCA, victims of torts committed by federal employees had to seek relief through a private relief bill from Congress.[61] The FTCA's basic purpose was to relieve Congress of the burden of considering these bills and to entrust their consideration to the courts. Enacted as part of the Legislative Reorganization Act of 1946, the FTCA was meant to provide for increased efficiency in the legislative branch of government.

13.10.1   Scope of Employment

For the government to be liable, the FTCA requires that the government employee's conduct fall within the scope of his or her employment as determined by state law.[62] For example, Massachusetts uses a three-pronged test to determine the scope of employment. The conduct must be (1) of the kind the employee was hired to perform; (2) occur within authorized time and space limits; and (3) motivated, at least in part, by an intent to serve the employer.[63]

13.10.2   Everything Secret Degenerates: James "Whitey" Bulger and Stephen "The Rifleman" Flemmi[31]

On June 11, 2009, a federal judge hearing a lawsuit brought by the family of a man murdered by FBI informant James "Whitey" Bulger in Boston began writing one of the final chapters in the FBI's most deadly, embarrassing, and costly informant scandals.[64] The case he was deciding, and other Bulger cases to follow, would make the federal courts more accessible to individuals and families of those injured or killed by rogue informants seeking money damages.[65]

James "Whitey" Bulger and Stephen "The Rifleman" Flemmi were informants for the FBI's Boston office at various times for more than 25 years.

They were considered particularly valuable sources for the FBI's high-priority investigation of the Boston branch of La Cosa Nostra (LCN). Bulger and Flemmi were both high-ranking members of South Boston's notoriously violent Winter Hill Gang, an LCN competitor. Local police regarded them as South Boston's most dangerous criminals.[66]

Flemmi was first recruited in 1964 by H. Paul Rico, an FBI supervisor in the Boston FBI Organized Crime Squad.[67] Bulger was recruited in 1971 by Special Agent John "Zip" Connolly. Bulger later explained to one of Connolly's supervisors that he became an FBI informant in part because he had a close feeling toward Connolly. They both grew up in the same neighborhood and had mutual childhood problems as well as a deep hatred for LCN.[68]

When Rico was transferred to another FBI office, Connolly inherited responsibility for Flemmi. Connolly, at this point, owned two of Boston's most productive CIs. If they stayed out of jail and continued to make cases, his career was secure and promotions were assured.

In a rare and risky move, the FBI made a tactical decision to make a team out of the two informants. This resulted in an astounding succession of unprecedented intelligence coups against the LCN. Countless Mafiosi from Capos to mid-level mobsters in the Northeast were convicted as a result of the team's information. The mobsters had no idea where the FBI was getting its intelligence. The Bureau was crippling the Northeast faction of the Mafia.[69]

As a result of all the convictions, the two CIs earned the coveted designation of Top Echelon informants. They became a deadly tag team, operating under the protection of the FBI. While the LCN reeled under the unrelenting FBI pressure, Bulger and Flemmi's gang grew even stronger and prospered, as did Agent Connolly's career.[70]

The alliance between the FBI and the snitches blossomed. They were invited to dine periodically with members of the FBI Boston Organized Crime Squad.[71] In violation of FBI regulations, not to mention common sense, some of the dinners were held both at Agent Connolly's house and in the home of John Morris, his boss. The guest of honor at one of the dinners was Special Agent Joe Pistone,[71] the FBI agent from New York who became famous for his infiltration of the Bonanno crime family as "Donnie Brasco."[72]

In 1985, at a dinner at Morris's home and in Connolly's presence, Morris gave Flemmi and Bulger the equivalent of a free pass to continue to commit crime. He told the informants, "You can do anything you want as long as you don't 'clip' anyone."

They did not follow his advice. During their duel careers as crime bosses and informants, they killed or ordered the killings of more than 20 people. At the same time, Bulger and Flemmi's criminal enterprise flourished, remarkably untouched by law enforcement. It was not due to lack of effort by local police, DEA, and Customs, who were constantly receiving information about the pair. But every time a criminal case against the two would begin to gel, the informants providing the information turned up dead or disappeared.

FBI agent handler John J. Connolly Jr., with assistance from his supervisor John Morris, leaked the identities of at least four informants to Bulger and Flemmi. It was a matter of career survival. Both agents had achieved nearly star status within the FBI, having received both promotions and bonuses. Their success was based almost solely on information given to them by Bulger and Flemmi. If the informants were arrested, the flow of information would cease; so would the bonuses and promotions.

Like all FBI offices, Boston's had a constant rotation of supervisors. When one became suspicious of the close relationship between Agent Connolly, Flemmi, and Bulger, he recalled warning Connolly to keep his dealings with his informants professional: "I told him information goes one way. Informants are not consultants. They are not friends, they are informants. And the agent remembers that and treats them accordingly."[73] Connolly did not heed the advice. Flemmi later recalled that Connolly and Morris treated him and his partner as equals. Connolly maintained contact with both of his informants following his retirement in 1990.

In 1995, Connolly learned from active FBI agents that Bulger and Flemmi were going to be arrested for extortion and racketeering. He promptly warned both men they were about to be picked up.[74]

Bulger immediately fled Boston and was rumored to have gone to Europe with his longtime girlfriend, Catherine Greig, with enough false identities and assets to sustain them for life. The FBI put him at the top of its Ten Most Wanted list with a $2 million reward. Hew was bumped to number two only when Osama bin Laden made the list in 2001.

Unfortunately for Flemmi, he was arrested before making an escape. When it became clear the FBI was not going to save him, he looked to the defense attorneys for rescue.[75]

Flemmi's lawyers argued that due to his status as a top-echelon FBI informant, he was immune from prosecution for the crimes he was being charged with. Flemmi testified that in return for their services, the FBI had given him and Bulger a free pass to commit crime. For a time, the FBI and prosecutors stonewalled the judge's demand for disclosure of Flemmi's informant file and refused to confirm or deny that he had ever been an informant.

The government's position changed when Judge Mark Wolf threatened the Deputy U.S. Attorney General with contempt of court if the files were not produced. The Flemmi informant file was finally released, with much of it made public at trial.

Ultimately, Wolf did not buy Flemmi's claim to immunity from prosecution based on his status as an FBI informant. In his 661-page decision,[76] the FBI was blasted for its nearly 40-year cover-up of crimes related to its informant program. Wolf wrote, "From the FBI's perspective, exposure of its agents' conduct had the foreseeable potential to reveal an extraordinary effort to protect Bulger and Flemmi that involved serious impropriety, if not illegality."[77]

In 2001, Flemmi was sentenced to 10 years in prison.[78] Because he had been exposed as an FBI informant, he was housed at one of the Federal Bureau of Prisons Protective Custody Units (PCU). The PCUs are secure units within a federal prison that are only used to house WITSEC inmates. The Bureau of Prisons operates seven PCUs located throughout the country.

Flemmi would not be allowed to rest easy for very long, however, as his unmasking brought new informants out of the woodwork. They were ready to settle scores and cut deals of their own. He was now facing at least two murder charges, with more on the horizon.

In 2004, Flemmi once again became a government witness. Part of the immunity deal saving him from the death penalty required that he give a complete accounting of all of the murders he had committed. Flemmi pled guilty to 10 murders and directly implicated John Connolly, his FBI agent handler, in at least 2 of the killings.[79] The Bulger–Flemmi duo was alleged to have collectively committed 22 murders. Flemmi was sentenced to life in prison.[80]

In sworn testimony at Connolly's 2008 murder trial in Florida, Flemmi claimed that while working for the FBI, he and his partner had paid Connolly $235,000 from money set aside in what they called the "X fund."[81] Each time the two would have a sudden in-flow of cash from a score, a percent was set aside for payoffs. The money paid to the agents came in the form of $10,000 Christmas gifts, $5,000 at vacation time, and bonuses of up to $25,000 at the conclusion of big dope deals. On one of his paydays the agent exclaimed, "Hey, I'm one of the gang."[82]

Flemmi recalled Connolly being carried away with his newfound wealth. According to the informant, "One time we gave him money, he went and bought a boat. Jim Bulger was upset about that. He had to sell the boat. I mean FBI agents weren't making much money back in those days. He was the best-dressed agent in the office and people would start looking at him. That was a concern."[83]

FBI agents working with Connolly also made comments about his dress and demeanor. There was a joke in the Boston office that Connolly was beginning to look like the Mafioso he investigated. They nicknamed him Cannoli.[84]

Flemmi's revelations have resulted in nearly $2 billion in lawsuits filed[85] against the FBI. Connolly was convicted of second-degree murder and sentenced to 40 years in prison. On March 2, 2011, the agent's conviction was upheld following an appeal.[86]

Flemmi's information and testimony gave some measure of closure to the families of the 22 people the informants had killed.[87] The cold case files on five murdered informants were finally closed, and lawsuits finally went forward.

13.11   Informants Murdering Informants: Wrongful Death Lawsuits

13.11.1   The Castucci Murder

Richard Castucci was a Top Echelon FBI informant. He was a Boston strip club owner, bookie, and friend of Frank Sinatra, Sammy Davis Jr., and Muhammed Ali.[88] A Boston FBI agent was operating Castucci with no ties to Agent Connolly. While no direct proof exists, it was believed that Supervisor Morris became aware of Castucci's information posed a threat to Bulger and Flemmi.

During trial, Flemmi testified that he learned from Agent Connolly in 1976 that Castucci had tipped off the FBI to the existence of a Winter Hill Gang safe house in New York City. By Flemmi's account, on December 30, 1976, he and Bulger had lured Castucci to a Somerville apartment, where hit man John Martorano put a bullet into Castucci's head.[89] His body was wrapped in a sleeping bag and stuffed into the trunk of his car.[90] His son was present when the body was found by police.

In the wake of Flemmi's cooperation deal, the family filed a wrongful death lawsuit against the government. Castucci's son testified during the trial. He tearfully recalled: "I saw my father in a sleeping bag with his head blown off. It was horrible."[91]

At trial, government lawyers defending against the suit argued that because Castucci never paid taxes on his illegal income, if the government was forced to pay compensation to his family for his lost earnings, then "we're being victimized twice."[92]

U.S. District Judge Reginald C. Lindsay did not see it that way. On June 11, 2009, he awarded the family $6.2 million. The judge ruled that the FBI was negligent in its handling of Bulger and Flemmi.[93]

13.11.2   The Wheeler Murder

On March 27, 1981, Bulger and Flemmi's run as top informants almost came to a close when millionaire businessman Roger Wheeler was murdered in Tulsa, Oklahoma. Wheeler was chairman of World Jai Alai, a Connecticut- and Florida-based gambling franchise. Flemmi and Bulger's former FBI handler, H. Paul Rico, had landed a retirement job as chief of security for World Jai Alai.[94]

Bulger had been shaking down John Callahan, the president of World Jai Alai. Roger Wheeler fired Callahan, put some of his own people in key positions, and begun an audit. Callahan was not happy. He went to Bulger and Flemmi for help in eliminating Wheeler in a bid to get his job back.[95] Flemmi later claimed that he and Bulger had conspired with Rico to prevent Wheeler from exposing their money-skimming scheme at World Jai Alai.

Bulger offered the hit to one of their enforcers, Brian Halloran. Because Halloran was already facing murder charges, he turned down the offer.[96]

In May 1981, Bulger dispatched hit man John Martorano to Tulsa, Oklahoma, to kill the executive. Flemmi's former handler, retired Special Agent Rico, gave Bulger all the logistics for the hit, including a physical description of Wheeler and the car he would be driving.[97]

Martorano waited in the parking lot of Tulsa's Southern Hills Country Club while Wheeler played golf. As Wheeler approached his car, Martorano calmly walked up to him and shot him between the eyes.[98]

It was one of Tulsa's highest-profile murder cases.[99] From the early days of the investigation, Tulsa homicide detectives complained that the Boston office of the FBI thwarted their efforts to nail Bulger and Flemmi for the hit.[100]

13.11.3   The Callahan Murder

FBI agents and Oklahoma City law enforcement officers almost immediately drew a link between John Callahan, a Wheeler associate, and Whitey Bulger. The information came from FBI informant and Winter Hill Gang member Edward Halloran, a close friend of Callahan's.

Authorities were seeking to question Callahan, a Winchester business-man with ties to Boston's underworld, about his role as an intermediary in the murder of Wheeler, but Callahan had disappeared. Agent Connolly alerted Bulger, telling him "Callahan was a weak link not able to withstand the pressure of an FBI interrogation."[101] Connolly's tip was like a death warrant.[102]

On July 31, 1982, Callahan fled to South Florida to avoid questioning by local cops. Martorano was not far behind. Somewhere between Fort Lauderdale and Miami, he shot Callahan twice in the head, put his body in the trunk of the victim's silver Fleetwood Cadillac,[103] and placed a dime on his chest—a subtle warning for others who might consider "diming out" the Winter Hill Gang.[104]

Martorano then drove to Miami International Airport and left the Cadillac in the parking lot. After several days of intense Miami heat, the foul odor emanating from the trunk became strong enough for police to investigate.[105]

Like the other murders, Callahan's was a cold case until the Flemmi revelations. It took nearly a decade to put together a murder case against Connolly, and the star witnesses at his trial were Flemmi and Martorano. Martorano struck a remarkable deal with prosecutors: In exchange for his testimony against Connolly, he served only 12 years and 2 months, despite having admitted to 20 murders.[106]

On January 14, 2009, a judge in Miami sentenced retired FBI agent Connolly to 40 years in prison for his role in the Callahan murder.[107]

13.11.4 The Halloran Murder

In January 1982, Agent Connolly learned that Brian Halloran was talking to other FBI agents in the Boston office about his star informants. Halloran had told the agents how he met with Bulger and Flemmi at Callahan's apartment and was offered $25,000 to kill Wheeler. Halloran had been placed in an FBI safe house on Cape Cod with his wife and two children while he was being debriefed.[108] Connolly alerted Bulger to the threat.

Halloran, Irish to the core, made the mistake of leaving the safe house for a few hours to visit one of his favorite South Boston pubs. Upon leaving the bar, he asked a friend, Michael Donahue, for a ride home. Donahue was a hard-working family man, not a criminal. Bulger and Winter Hill enforcer Brian Meeks[109] were waiting for Halloran. Donahue was just in the wrong place at the wrong time.[110]

As the two drove away, Meeks followed their car. Bulger fired a burst from his machine gun into the vehicle.[111] Witnesses said the two occupants were waving their arms wildly as bullets penetrated the car. Donahue was struck in the head and died instantly. As the car came to rest on the side of the road, Halloran ran from the vehicle with Bulger in pursuit, still firing his machine gun.[112] He was hit 22 times and bled to death on his way to the hospital. His widow testified that the FBI agents who had put the family in the safe house never told her that her husband had been murdered. Her sister-in-law and a state trooper brought her the news 5 hours after the killing.[113]

Once again, the two murders were cold cases until Flemmi began cooperating. The Halloran and Donahue families both filed wrongful death lawsuits.

After 27 years of government denials, the families were vindicated, but not before government lawyers took a parting shot at Donahue's widow. A Justice Department Civil Division attorney barked the question to Mrs. Donahue, "You're not seeking funeral expenses in this case are you?" She replied, "I don't know."[114] It had cost the mother of three children $1,100 to bury her husband.

On May 1, 2009, U.S. District Judge William G. Young awarded the families of the two men a total of nearly $8.5 million. In announcing his decision, Judge Young said it was "next to inconceivable that our government, through negligence, inattention, self-interested hubris, and outright corruption" was the direct cause of the murders of Michael Donahue and Edward Halloran.[115]

The government appealed the award and won. The court agreed with the defendant (the FBI) that the suit was barred by the statute of limitations. In other words, the family should have read the papers closer and filed their suit in the previous decade when Bulger's role as an informant first made it into the newspapers.[116]

Following Whitey Bulger's 2013 conviction, he asked the court to give the $822,000 seized from his apartment to the Donahue and Halloran families.[117] At this writing no decision has been made regarding the funds. Procedure requires it be forfeited to the U.S. Government and deposited into the Asset Forfeiture Fund.

13.11.5   The McIntyre Murder

John McIntyre was a 32-year-old fisherman who had built and repaired boats in Quincy, Massachusetts, since his discharge from the army. His life span was shortened considerably when he began working for Joe Murphy,[118] leader of a South Boston gang and an associate of Bulger and Flemmi.

In the fall of 1984, Murphy assembled a crew for a weapons-smuggling venture using a ship called the *Valhalla*. McIntyre joined the crew as the engineer. The vessel departed Gloucester, Massachusetts, loaded with weapons and ammunition destined for the Irish Republican Army (IRA).[119]

The *Valhalla* traveled to the coast of Ireland, where it was met by an Irish ship, the *Marita Ann*, and off-loaded its cargo before returning to Massachusetts. The *Marita Ann*, however, was seized before it reached port by Irish authorities acting on an IRA informant's tip. A crew member on the *Marita Ann* provided authorities with the name of the mother ship they had met for transfer of the weapons, with the information forwarded to the U.S. Customs Service. A search for the vessel ensued.

U.S. Customs patrol officers located the ship at anchor in Boston Harbor with two crewmembers onboard: one was John McIntyre. The vessel was seized and both men were detained.

Facing arrest, McIntyre took one of the Customs patrol officers aside and asked to speak with a Customs agent: He wanted to cooperate. Special Agent Patrick O'Malley[120] was dispatched to interview McIntyre.

McIntyre told O'Malley that he was already cooperating with DEA agents and a local cop in exchange for help with a misdemeanor prosecution. Now facing a federal smuggling prosecution by Customs, he was eager to cut another deal. Both men were released on the spot. O'Malley made arrangements to meet with McIntyre the following day for a debriefing.

On October 17, 1984, McIntyre met twice with law enforcement. During the first short meeting, O'Malley informed McIntyre that he would no longer be working with the DEA; he now belonged to U.S. Customs. The Boston Customs office was no different from any other in the United States. They were in a bitter rivalry with the DEA, particularly when it came to landing quality informants like McIntyre.[121]

Later that day, McIntyre again met with Agent O'Malley and two FBI agents assigned to Boston's Joint Federal Drug Task Force. The task force consisted of representatives from Customs, the Internal Revenue Service, and the FBI.

The meeting on the afternoon of October 17 was a full-blown debriefing. All of McIntyre's cards had to be on the table if he was going to escape prosecution. McIntyre detailed his 3-year association with Murphy, the *Valhalla* operation, and an upcoming drug shipment planned by Murphy, using the vessel *Ramsland*.

McIntyre confessed that Murphy was responsible for sending the *Valhalla* to Ireland and that he had helped load the weapons onto the ship in Gloucester and had been a member of the crew on the trip to Ireland.

McIntyre was the first person to provide links between Joe Murphy, the *Valhalla*, and Whitey Bulger. He recalled overhearing that "an individual named Whitey who operates a liquor store in South Boston became partners with Joe Murphy." At the time of the debriefing, Customs agent O'Malley had no inkling that Bulger was an FBI informant.

Unbeknownst to McIntyre or O'Malley, Bulger and Flemmi had provided some of the weapons for the *Valhalla* shipment. Furthermore, Bulger and cohort Brian Meeks had acted as lookouts while the *Valhalla* was being loaded in Gloucester.

At the conclusion of the debriefing, it became clear that McIntyre was the key to nailing Murphy, Bulger, and Flemmi and to seizing the *Ramsland* load. In return for his cooperation, Customs would not arrest McIntyre for his role in the *Valhalla* venture. His testimony would probably be needed to nail the organization if the *Ramsland* was seized. It was clear to O'Malley that McIntyre was petrified of the people he was working for.

Following the debriefing, O'Malley met with McIntyre every few days. His new informant kept him advised as the Murphy gang finalized the logistics for the *Ramsland* shipment.

On the basis of information provided by McIntyre, U.S. Customs and the FBI established surveillance of Boston Harbor, lying in wait for the vessel's arrival. On November 14, 1984, the *Ramsland* entered the harbor and was greeted by a team of heavily armed federal agents. McIntyre was onboard as a member of the "substitute crew" that had replaced the ship's English crew at the mouth of the harbor.

The ship contained 30 tons of marijuana, one of Boston's largest marijuana seizures. The press was all over the story. When the Customs Special Agent in Charge of Boston was interviewed, he lied to the press and explained the ship was spotted on a zigzag course and was stopped by authorities for inspection. O'Malley thought it was a "stupid transparent lie," which managed to alert Murphy to the existence of an informant within their crew.

The loss of the *Ramsland* was a devastating blow to the Murphy gang. Bulger and Flemmi were outraged. Flemmi later testified that he, Bulger, and Meeks each expected to receive $1 million from the shipment. After the seizure, McIntyre reported to O'Malley that Murphy suspected someone in the substitute crew was an informant; Murphy vowed to kill the person responsible for their loss.

The fact that there was an informant in the Murphy gang was an open secret at the Boston FBI Office. Sometime between October 17 and November 22, 1984, Connolly alerted Bulger that one of the two people taken off the *Valhalla* was an informant. Connolly later repeated the claim in Flemmi's presence. Before being tipped off by Connolly, neither Bulger, nor Flemmi, nor Murphy had proof that any member of the crew was cooperating with law enforcement.

Connolly never mentioned a name when he warned Bulger and Flemmi, but he conveyed sufficient information to identify McIntyre. At some point after Connolly's leak, Bulger told Flemmi that he believed McIntyre was the weak link.

Bulger and Flemmi developed a plan to confront McIntyre to confirm whether he was the informant responsible for the loss of the *Ramsland*. They decided to lure him to a meeting with them by offering him the opportunity to invest $20,000 in an upcoming smuggling venture.

On November 22, 1984, McIntyre advised O'Malley that Bill Riley,[122] a Bulger associate, had told him about the investment opportunity. Agent O'Malley recommended that McIntyre accept the offer. It was an incredible opportunity to get his informant deeper into Boston's drug trafficking hierarchy. It took the agent a week to put together an operation plan and get approval to front $20,000.

On November 29, 1984, McIntyre was given the $20,000. That same day, McIntyre was surveilled by his control agent as he delivered the money to Riley. It was the last time O'Malley saw McIntyre.

The following day Bulger associate Riley brought McIntyre to 799 East Third Street in South Boston, a house owned by his brother. They arrived around noon. Bulger and Flemmi had arrived earlier in the day with a bag they dubbed the duffel bag of death.[123] It contained rope, handcuffs, chains, a Mac-11 machine gun, and a .22 rifle with a silencer.

McIntyre came to the house carrying a case of beer, anticipating a social gathering with fellow investors. Instead, when he walked into the kitchen, Bulger stepped out from behind a refrigerator and pressed a submachine gun into his chest. McIntyre stumbled backward. Meeks immediately grabbed him by the throat and shoulders and slammed him to the floor.

McIntyre was dragged to his feet and pushed into a kitchen chair. Flemmi handcuffed and chained him to the chair. Bulger began what he thought would be a long and painful interrogation. Instead, McIntyre confessed almost immediately that he was cooperating with Customs. Meeks later testified that his confession came within 2 minutes into the questioning; Flemmi stated that it took only 30 seconds.

McIntyre told them everything, including that the $20,000 he had given Riley the day before had come from U.S. Customs. It was part of their plan to make a case on Bulger and Flemmi.

He apologized to Bulger, explaining that he had cooperated because he was weak. He was clearly terrified; as Flemmi later testified: "Look at the position he was in. I mean, who wouldn't be [frightened] under those circumstances? Of course he was in fear. The mental anguish."

Murdering McIntyre was not the original plan. Bulger and Flemmi discussed various options; they talked about the possibility of sending him to South America to cool off and keep him out of the reach of Customs. Another option was sending him into the grand jury with a "script" that would draw attention away from the Winter Hill Gang.

At some point during the day, Bulger made the decision that McIntyre had to be eliminated—he could not be trusted not to cooperate again. According to Flemmi, "That was [Bulger's] decision. Naturally I went along with it."

Bulger, Flemmi, and Meeks moved McIntyre to the basement. McIntyre was placed in a chair, still handcuffed, with the chains wrapped around his body. Bulger placed a boat rope around McIntyre's neck and began to strangle him. McIntyre struggled desperately for 1 or 2 minutes, gagging, gurgling, and vomiting, but he did not lose consciousness.

Bulger realized strangling McIntyre was not effective. "This ain't working," he said, and asked McIntyre, "Do you want one in the head?" McIntyre said yes. Bulger obliged and shot him in the head. Flemmi bent down to feel McIntyre's pulse and reported that he was still alive. Flemmi then grabbed McIntyre by the hair and pulled his head up, and Bulger shot him a few more times, saying, "He's dead now."

Bulger, exhausted, went upstairs and left Flemmi and Meeks with the dirty work. They stripped McIntyre's clothes off his body and, using pliers, pulled out and crushed his teeth, hoping to make his body unidentifiable. They drove McIntyre's pickup truck to a bar in the Quincy area and left it there.

McIntyre's mother filed a missing persons report with the police. It was as if he had dropped off the face of the earth. There was speculation in the press that he had been kidnapped and killed by the IRA.

McIntyre was buried in the basement alongside Arthur "Bucky" Barrett, the legendary safecracker and bank robber who had run afoul of the Winter Hill Gang. He had been kidnapped, tortured, and killed in August 1983 in what Flemmi said was a scheme by him and Bulger to steal Barrett's share of a bank heist. As with McIntyre, Flemmi pulled Barrett's teeth.

A few days after McIntyre's murder, Bulger, Flemmi, Meeks, and Riley divided the $20,000 of U.S. Customs money among themselves in equal shares. Bulger remarked to Meeks, "Customs must be upset—they lost their witness and their money."

In early 1985, Deborah Hussey, the daughter of one of Flemmi's girlfriends, accused him of molesting her when she was 13. Before she could go to the police, Bulger and Flemmi strangled her with a rope, stripped her, pulled out her teeth, cut off her fingers and toes, and buried her alongside McIntyre and Barrett.[124]

On Halloween night in 1985, when it appeared that the house at 799 East Third Street would be sold, Meeks and others disinterred the remains of Barrett, McIntyre, and Hussey and reburied them near Florian Hall in the Dorchester section of Boston.

13.11.5.1   *The McIntyre Lawsuit*

Following Flemmi's conversion to government witness in 1999, Emily McIntyre, John's mother, filed a wrongful death suit against the FBI. Once again, the government fought the suit with every tool it had. Justice Department lawyers denied any liability for McIntyre's. The judge did not see it that way. He found that disclosure of McIntyre's identity was in keeping with both the deferential treatment Bulger and Flemmi regularly received from all levels of the FBI and the kind of conduct Connolly undertook on other occasions with seeming acquiescence from his superiors.

In announcing his decision, Judge Reginald Lindsay showed a degree of empathy seldom seen in federal court. The judge told government lawyers and onlookers that McIntyre "had suffered more than physical pain." If, as Flemmi testified, McIntyre suffered mental anguish even before any attempt was made to kill him, the anguish he experienced as the attempt began and progressed must have intensified dramatically. He was terrified; he knew his tormentors would kill him. He had been an informant, and he would pay the price. He knew there would be no time for saying goodbyes or getting his affairs in order, as he would not leave that basement alive. It is difficult to imagine a more distressing set of circumstances—physically and mentally—than those encountered by McIntyre during the minutes preceding his death. It was, as Emily McIntyre said, "torture."

Said Judge Lindsay, "I infer that, for McIntyre, the one to two minutes of physical and mental pain were an eternity. It is not surprising, therefore, that when Bulger offered him the opportunity of a swifter death by a gunshot to the head, McIntyre pleaded for that gruesome, but quick relief from his suffering. It is his 'yes, please' that is the most certain evidence of his conscious suffering. It is difficult, of course, to ascribe a dollar value to conscious suffering: Converting feelings such as pain, suffering, and mental anguish into dollars is not an exact science. Under the circumstances described above, however, I find that a reasonable award is $3 million."[125]

13.11.5.2   *The Fallout*

When former FBI supervisor H. Paul Rico was asked by a member of the congressional committee investigating the Boston FBI scandal if he felt remorse for his behavior, he replied, "Remorse—for what? Would you like tears or something?"[126] He died in jail awaiting trial for the murder of Roger Wheeler.

Connolly has always maintained that he never sold his badge or caused the deaths of any of Bulger and Flemmi's victims. He was only doing his job. Now he is doing life in prison.

During the years since Bulger and his girlfriend Catherine Greig fled Boston, the FBI was pummeled with false leads. Some put the fugitives in faraway, exotic places. Boston journalists who had covered the story for more than a decade opined the Bureau did not want to capture Bulger, at least not alive. The prevailing theory was that the former informant just might put more FBI agents behind bars once he was put in handcuffs.

In early 2011, the Bureau began airing public-awareness television spots in Europe with photographs of what Bulger and his girlfriend might look like today. Figuring prominently in the spot was the $2 million reward for Bulger and $100,000 for his girlfriend.

Whitey Bulger and his paramour never went to Europe. They were hiding in plain sight in Santa Monica, California, as Charlie and Carol Gaskell. Regardless, the overseas television spots paid off. A woman visiting from Iceland had befriended the couple, initially taken by their kindness toward a stray cat named Tiger. The tourist soon became friends with the woman she knew as Carol Gaskell.[127]

After she returned to Iceland, the woman saw the FBI's enhanced photographs of the two fugitives and promptly called the FBI.[128] On June 22, 2011, Bulger was arrested without incident. A search of his apartment yielded 30 firearms and $822,000 hidden in a wall.[129] The FBI made the tourist a millionaire 4 months later when they paid her the $2,100,000 reward.[130]

It is unknown whether Bugler provided investigators with information that will put more Connolly-era FBI agents behind bars.

On November 14, 2013, Bulger was sentenced to two life terms plus 5 years. The sentencing judge told him, "The scope, the callousness, the depravity of your crimes, are almost unfathomable. The testimony of human suffering that you and your associates inflicted on others was at times agonizing to hear and painful to watch."[131] Throughout the course of the trial, the defense claimed that Bulger was never an FBI informant.

In an NPR interview, Massachusetts congressman William Delahunt, an outspoken critic of the U.S. informant system, was clearly embarrassed by what had occurred in his state. He was extremely critical of the government's use of killers as informants: "I think we've been remiss in not pushing the kind of oversight necessary. Because what we have discovered is, in too many cases, these informants have a free pass, if you will, to commit serious acts of violence, including murder. And that is not what justice is about, and that's not what the American people would ever approve of."[132]

As a remedy, the congressman advocated stricter guidelines governing the use of informants. He recommended harsh punishment for agents who fail to follow the rules for informant-handling.[133]

Delahunt was shortsighted. Any meaningful attempt to put a stop to informant scandals would require a completely new mind-set, a rewritten playbook if you will, for agents and prosecutors to follow. As it stands now, informants remain an integral part of our criminal justice system's infrastructure.

Endnotes

1. *Guidelines for Establishing and Operating Gang Intelligence Units and Task Forces*, Gang Intelligence Strategy Committee Global Justice Information Sharing Initiative, October 2008.
2. Crous, C., "Managing Covert Human Intelligence Sources: Lessons for Police Commanders," *Australasian Policing*, Volume 3, Issue 2, Summer 2011. The development of formal covert human intelligence source management includes the formulation of new policies and directives governing the relationship between police and informants to mitigate the risk of unethical behavior.
3. *Executive Summary, The DEA's Payments to Confidential Sources*, USDOJ, Office of Inspector General, Audit Division, May 2005, found that the agency could improve its risk management in the following areas: (1) initial suitability reporting and recommendations, (2) categorization of confidential sources, (3) continuing suitability reporting and recommendation, (4) review of long-term confidential sources, and (5) maintenance of impeachment information.
4. See *United States v. Boyd*, 55 F.3d 239 (7th Cir. 1995).
5. See *Commonwealth v. Lewin*, 405 Mass. 566, 542 N.E.2d 275 (1989).
6. *Vaughn v. United States*, Eastern District of Kentucky, Case #93-9.
7. See *Ostera v. United States*, 769 F.2d 716, 85 A.L.R. Fed. 843 (11th Cir.), *reh'g denied, en banc, 715* F.2d 304 (11th Cir. 1985).
8. See *Commonwealth v. Lewin*, 405 Mass. 566, 542 N.E.2d 2275 (1989).
9. See *United States v. Bernal-Obeso*, 989 F.2d 331, 333 (9th Cir. 1993). See also Hight, J.E., M.P.A., "Avoiding the Informant Trap, a Blueprint for Control," *F.B.I. Law Enforcement Bull.*, November 1998, pp. 1–5.
10. Integrity Assurance Notes, Drug Enforcement Administration, Planning and Inspection Division, Vol. 1, No. 1 (August 1991). See *DEA Agents Manual*, Ch. 66, Management and Review of Informants. See also *United States v. Gardner*, 658 F. Supp. 1573, 1575 (W.D. Pa., 1987).
11. Lehr, D., "Agent, Mobster Forge Pact on Southie Ties," *Boston Globe*, July, 1998.
12. *Attorney Generals Guidelines Regarding the Use of Confidential Informants*, III, A, 2, a.
13. Ibid.
14. A close, prolonged association between two or more different organisms of different species that may, but does not necessarily, benefit each member; a relationship of mutual benefit or dependence.
15. New South Wales. Independent Commission Against Corruption 1993, *Police Informants: A Discussion Paper on the Nature and the Management of the Relationship between Police and their Informants*, ICAC, Sydney, Australia.
16. Krikorian, G., "When Sources Go Bad," *Los Angeles Times*, July 9, 2003.

17. Decision, *Commissioner of Police v. Rogerson*, New South Wales Police Tribunal July 28, 1986, pp. 10–11).
18. Name changed.
19. From 1993 jailhouse interview with ABC-TV, quoted in Krikorian, G., "When Sources Go Bad," *Los Angeles Times*, July 9, 2003.
20. "Ex-FBI Agent Admits Slaying and Get 16 Years," Associated Press, June 13, 1990; See Jones, A., *FBI Killer*, Pinnacle Books, New York, 1992.
21. Breed, A.G., "Victim's Sister Haunted by Slaying a Year after FBI Agent Confessed," *Los Angeles Times*, July 7, 1991.
22. *FBI Manual of Investigative Operations and Guidelines (MIOG)*, § 137-2(3).
23. Lehr, D., "Agents Gave Bulger Starring Role in Mafia Case—But Was It Real?" *Boston Globe*, July 20, 1998.
24. See Freedberg, S.P., "FBI Allegedly Shielded Suspects in Miami Murder," *Miami Herald*, August 2, 1998.
25. *Kentucky v. Long*, 837 F.2d 727, 731 (6th Cir. 1988). See also Raab, S., "Charges Against FBI Agent Threaten a Major Mob Case," *New York Times*, June 14, 1997.
26. *United States v. Bernal-Obeso*, 989 F.2d 331, 333 (9th Cir. 1993).
27. *Seven Steps to Successful Informant Management*, DEA Informant Interaction, U.S. Drug Enforcement Administration, Office of Training, Quantico, VA.
28. *ATF Manual.*
29. *United States v. Medina-Reyes*, 877 F. Supp. 468, 472 (S.D. Iowa 1995).
30. Ibid.
31. *Medina-Reyes* at 475.
32. *Intelligence, Surveillance and Informants: Integrated Approaches*, Police Research Group, Crime Detection and Prevention Series: Paper No. 64, London Home Office, Crown Copyright 1995.
33. See *United States v. Brumel-Alvarez*, 976 F.2d 1235 (9th Cir. 1992).
34. *Brady v. Maryland*, 373 U.S. 83, 87, 83 S. Ct. 1194, 1196, 10 L. Ed. 2d 215 (1963).
35. *Jencks v. United States*, 353 U.S. 657 (1957)
36. *United States v. Brumel-Alvarez*, 976 F.2d 1239, 1239 (9th Cir. 1992).
37. Ibid.
38. *U.S. v. Salemme*, 91 F.Supp.2d 141 (D. Mass. 1999) Section 19, "Dining with Donnie Brasco."
39. Levine Memorandum, written by DEA Group Supervisor, Michael Levine, (Retired) [hereinafter Levine Memorandum].
40. *United States v. Brumel-Alvarez*, 976 F.2d 1239, 1239 (9th Cir. 1992).
41. Ibid. at 1242.
42. Ibid. at 1247.
43. Study conducted by Professor Ellen Yaroshefsky, quoted in *Bait and Snitch: The High Cost of Snitching for Law Enforcement*, Natapoff, A.; See also "*Cooperation, Punishment and Atonement*," 56 *Vand. L. Rev.* 1, (2003).
44. Ibid.
45. *U.S. v. Burnside*, 824 F.Supp.1215 (1993); *U.S. v. Andrews*, 824 F.Supp. 1273 (1993).
46. Ibid.
47. Stern, A., "U.S. Prosecutor, Fired Over Gang Trials, Exonerated," *Reuters*, July 24, 1998. Administrative judge supported AUSA's contentions that he had never seen the drug test results and that a conversation with a fellow prosecutor about the drug use never took place. He was awarded back pay with interest.

48. *U.S. v. Andrews*, 824 F.Supp. 1273, 1286-87 (1993).

49. *U.S. v. Burnside*, 824 F.Supp. at 1242.

50. Ibid.

51. *U.S. v. Andrews*, 824 F.Supp. at 1286.

52. *U.S. v. Burnside*, 824 F.Supp. at 1246.

53. Ibid.

54. *U.S. v. Boyd*, 55 F.3d 239, 244 (7th Cir. 1995); paralegal testified under immunity at the motion for a new trial.

55. *U.S. v. Burnside*, 824 F.Supp. at 1244.

56. *U.S. v. Andrews*, 824 F.Supp. at 1285.

57. *U.S. v. Boyd*, 874 F.Supp. 179, 181 (N.D. 111. 1994).

58. Stern, A., "U.S. Prosecutor, Fired Over Gang Trials, Exonerated," *Reuters*, July 24, 1998.

59. See Butterfield, F., "Ex-FBI Agent Sentenced for Helping Mob Leaders," *The New York Times*, September 17, 2002.

60. Federal Tort Claim Act, 28 USC § 1346

61. Ibid.

62. 28 U.S.C. § 1346(a)–(b)(1) (2006) (allowing private individuals to bring suit against United States in narrow set of circumstances). Congress enacted the FTCA in 1946 as a limited waiver of sovereign immunity. See *Román-Cancel v. United States*, 613 F.3d 37, 41 (1st Cir. 2010). This limited waiver permits suits when the plaintiff has suffered personal injury, death, or property damage, and the plaintiff's harm was caused by the negligent or wrongful act or omission of a government employee acting within the scope of his employment. See 28 U.S.C. § 1346(b) (2006). This waiver of sovereign immunity is hedged by statutory conditions explained in other sections of the FTCA. See 28 U.S.C. § 2680 (2006) (enumerating exceptions to liability under FTCA).

63. *Pinshaw v. Metro. Dist. Comm'n*, 402 Mass. 687, 694 (Mass. 1988).

64. Mitchell, P., "Judge Awards Family $8 Million to Family of Slain FBI Informant," *Los Angeles Times*, June 14, 2009.

65. Two theories have evolved in FTCA cases growing out of Bulger and Flemmi cases. The "emboldening" theory suggests that the FBI placed a protective shield around the two mobsters, in effect giving them carte blanche to commit crimes at will. See, *U.S. v. Rakes*, 442 F.3d 7 (2006). In contrast, the "leak" theory focuses on the wrongful disclosure of confidences, such as informants' identities, to the mobsters.

66. Author's note. Facts supporting the account regarding the Bulger and Flemmi scandal were found in *U.S. v. Salemme*, 91 F.Supp.2d 141 (D. Mass. 1999) (Wolf, J.) and articles produced by investigative journalists.

67. *U.S. v. Salemme*, 91 F.Supp.2d 141 (D. Mass. 1999) (Wolf, J.) (hereinafter *Salemme*), Section 2, Rico and Flemmi at p. 77.

68. *Salemme*, Section 4, "The Development of Bulger as an Informant."

69. *Salemme*, Section 5, "The FBI Forges the Flemmi-Bulger Partnership."

70. *Salemme*, Section 32: "Connolly had enjoyed a very successful career as an FBI agent, based largely on his handling of top echelon informants, and at times received unusually favorable treatment by the Bureau."

71. *Salemme*, Section 16, "Greenleaf Becomes SAC and Ring Become Supervisor of the Organized Crime Squad." Connolly's supervisor had the opportunity to

"observe and evaluate Connolly's interactions with Bulger and Flemmi and did not like what he saw."

72. *Donnie Brasco*, 1997 film starring Al Pacino and Johnny Depp dramatized the career of FBI agent Pistone.

73. Temple-Raston, N., "Bulger Case Changed FBI's Role with Informants," NPR, September 1, 2008, quoting retired FBI supervisor Jim Ring.

74. *Salemme*, Section 32, "The Investigation of Flemmi and Bulger." Connelly "was the source of the tip to Bulger concerning the indictments on or about January 10, 1995." Connolly told Supervisor Morris "that what Flemmi and Bulger wanted from their relationship with the FBI was a 'head start.'"

75. Ibid.

76. *U.S. v. Salemme*, 91 F.Supp.2d 141 (D. Mass. 1999) (Wolf, J.); See Murphy, S., "Death, Deceit, Then Decades of Silence," *The Boston Globe*, July 27, 2007.

77. Mahony, E., "FBI Protection of Informants Condemned in Mob Ruling," *Hartford Courant*, September 16, 1999; See *U.S. v. Salemme*, 91 F.Supp.2d 141 (D. Mass. 1999) (Wolf, J.).

78. *U.S. v. Salemme*, 195 F.Supp.2d 243 (D. Mass. 2001).

79. Murphy, S., "Flemmi Ties Connolly to Two Slayings, Gangster Admits to 10 Murders in Plea Deal," *The Boston Globe*, October 15, 2003.

80. "Bulger's Associate No Stranger to Justice System," WHDH.com, June 23, 2011.

81. "Mobster: Ex-FBI Agent Got Protection Money," Associated Press, September 22, 2008.

82. Murphy, S., "Flemmi: FBI Agent Joked He Was 'One of the Gang,'" *The Boston Globe*, September 22, 2008.

83. "Flemmi: Connolly Said 'Hey, I'm One of the Gang,'" mafia-news.com, September 22, 2008.

84. Cannoli: an Italian pastry desert.

85. Butterfield, F. "Ex-FBI Agent Sentenced for Helping Mob Leaders," *The New York Times*, September 17, 2002.

86. Murphy, S., "Convicted FBI Agent Connolly Loses Fla. Appeal," *The Boston Globe*, March 2, 2011.

87. Donn, j., "FBI's Bargain Written in Blood, Blind Eye Turned to Mob Informers," Associated Press, July 28, 2002.

88. Sweet, L.J., "Rat Pack Pal's Kin Seeks Money in Whitey Bulger Hit," *Boston Herald*, May 18, 2009.

89. "From Flemmi's Lips: A Sordid Tale of Intimidation and Murder," Boston.com, October 15, 2003.

90. Murphy, S., "Slain Club Owner's Children Recall His Generosity," *The Boston Globe*, June 10, 2009.

91. Ibid.

92. Murphy, S., "U.S. Ordered To Pay $6.2 Million to Family in 1976 Mob Killing," *The Boston Globe*, June 12, 2009.

93. Ibid.

94. *Salemme*, Section 13, "The Wheeler, Halloran and Callahan Murders."

95. Phillips, R., "Rogue FBI Agent Sentenced to 40 Years in Mob Hit," CNN, January 15, 2009.

96. *Salemme*, Section 13, "The Wheeler, Halloran and Callahan Murders."

97. Lawrence, J.M., "At 78, Rico Dies Under Guard: Former G-man Was To Be Tried for Murder," *Boston Herald*, June 18, 2004.
98. "Longtime Fugitive 'Whitey' Bulger Suspect in Tulsa Man's Murder Nabbed after 16 Years," *Tulsa World*, June 24, 2001.
99. Gelzinis, P., "Dad's Execution Mystery No More to Anxious Son," *Boston Herald*, May 12, 1998.
100. "FBI Blamed for Tulsa Probe Snag; Mob Quest Thwarts Roger Wheeler Murder Investigation, Report Says," Associated Press, November 10, 1997.
101. *McIntyre v. U.S.* 477 F.Supp.2d 54, 88 (D. Mass. 2006); LEXIS 63217.
102. Murphy, S., "Despite Sentence, Connolly's Legal Fight Not Over," January 15, 2009; Connolly sentenced to 40 years for second-degree murder.
103. *McIntyre v. U.S.* 477 F.Supp.2d 54, 98 (D. Mass. 2006); LEXIS 63217.
104. Carr, H., *The Brothers Bulger*, Warner Books, New York, 2006.
105. Freedberg, S.P., "Detectives Say FBI Shielded Mobster in Miami Murder Case," *Miami Herald*, August 2, 1998.
106. Murphy, S., "Ex-Hit Man Looks To Lead Quiet Life," *The Boston Globe*, March 20, 2007.
107. Phillips, R., "Rogue FBI Agent Sentenced to 40 Years in Mob Hit," CNN, January 15, 2009.
108. Anderson, K., "Widow of Alleged Whitey Bulger Victim Breaks Silence," WBZ-TV, November 18, 2011.
109. Name changed.
110. Barry, D., "A Voice for Those Silenced in Mobster's Reign," *The New York Times*, July 15, 2001.
111. Sweet, L., "Gangland Slaughter Detailed," *Boston Herald*, March 11, 2008.
112. Weeks K., and Karas, P., "Brutal: Untold Story of My Life inside Whitey Bulger's Irish Mob," HarperCollins, New York, 2006.
113. Murphy, S., "Government Never Told Widow of Husband's Slaying," *The Boston Globe*, March 13, 2008.
114. Murphy, S., "Kin Recount Loss after '82 Slayings," *The Boston Globe*, March 11, 2008.
115. Murphy, S., "Families of Whitey Bulger Victims Win Nearly $8.5 Million in Suit," Boston.com, May 1, 2009.
116. Cullen, K., "Court on wrong side of law," Boston.com, October 7, 2011.
117. Lavoie, D., "Bulger wants seized $822,00 to go to victim's families," *Boston CBS*, August 2, 2013.
118. Name changed.
119. Account of McIntyre's cooperation with U.S. Customs from *McIntyre v. U.S.* 447 F.Supp.2d 54 (D. Mass. 2006); differing accounts available in Lehr, D., "Mob Underling's Tale of Guns, Drugs, Fear," *The Boston Globe*, February 27, 2000.
120. Author's note: The agent's name is changed for privacy purposes.
121. 477 F.Supp.2d 54,100: "He's now an informant for Customs … exclusively, and any information he's supposed to give to us."
122. Name changed.
123. Fitzpatrick, R., and Land, J., *Betrayal: Whitey Bulger and the FBI Agent Who Fought to Bring Him Down*, Macmillan, New York, 2012.
124. "Bulger Victims' Families Get Wrongful Death Payments, Families of Two Southie Women Brought Suit," WCVB.com, April 9, 2012.

125. 447 F.Supp.2d 54, 120.

126. Testimony before the House Government Reform Committee.

127. Mann, T., "Whitey Bulger's Downfall: Saving a Stray Cat with Miss Iceland," *Atlantic Wire*, October 10, 2011.

128. Dwindell, J., "FBI Pays Out $2.1M Whitey Bulger Reward," *Boston Herald*, September 23, 2011.

129. Swain, J., "James 'Whitey' Bulger Was Turned In by Former Miss Iceland," *The Telegraph*, October 9, 2011.

130. Dorning, A., "Former Miss Iceland Got Cool $2 Million for Whitey Bulger Tip," ABC News, October 10, 2011.

131. Murphy, S., "Whitey Bulger, Boston gangster found responsible for 11 murders, gets life," Boston.com, November 14, 2013.

132. Kahn, C.,"Critics Blast Informant System Cloaked in Secrecy," NPR, February 12, 2010.

133. Ibid.

Witness Security Program
Falling Off the Face of the Earth

14

14.1 Introduction

Until now, little has been written about the U.S. Marshals Service (USMS) Witness Security Program's inner workings.[1] Better known as WITSEC, it is perhaps the most secretive layer of the federal criminal justice system. Those with the most knowledge of the program, marshals given the title of inspector, sign nondisclosure pledges before being given their coveted assignment. They are held to secrecy for life. WITSEC inspectors are among the lowest paid, most overworked, and least appreciated federal law enforcement officers in the Justice Department.[2]

The program is run by the Department of Justice and administered by the U.S. Marshals Service. WITSEC is supposed to be a program of last resort, reserved for those sources who become witnesses for the prosecution and face danger as a consequence. In some cases, admittance has come to be used as an enticement for those who are undecided about becoming an informant or a cooperating witness.

Entrance to the program is extremely selective.[3] Unlike in the European Union, where witnesses are guaranteed protection,[4] in the United States admittance to the program is strictly discretionary.[5]

The population of WITSEC is smaller than what might be expected. From its inception in 1971 until 1988, WITSEC protected, relocated, and provided new identities to no more than 5000 principal witnesses (the individuals targeted for retaliation).[6] By 2000, 7137 primary witnesses and 9091 family members had entered the Witness Security Program.[7] As of 2006, the last year that official numbers were released, approximately 8,000 primary witnesses and nearly 10,000 family members have been accepted into the program.[8]

WITSEC has proved to be one of the most potent weapons used in America's wars against organized crime, drugs, and terror. The program provides informant recruiters the power to offer a lifetime of protection in exchange for cooperation and truthful testimony.

The program is not without its critics. Some believe it poses a danger to unsuspecting communities. One attorney summed up his feelings about

WITSEC: "The federal government is busy renaming and relocating violent career criminals to peaceful suburban neighborhoods across this country. Maybe your new next-door neighbor killed 20 people but you'll never know it unless he wakes up one day and decides to shoot your wife, rape your daughter and slit your throat. That's when Americans will start to pay attention to what the federal witness program is really up to."[9]

The program is necessarily cloaked in secrecy: without WITSEC, informants and cooperating witnesses would be without its safety net.

WITSEC has also become part of the American pop culture. In an episode of *the Simpsons*, the cartoon characters were relocated to Terror Lake as the Thompson family, with Homer wearing a "Witness Relocation Program" T-shirt.[10] Novelty stores sell T-shirts bearing a mock-up WITSEC logo and the caption "You Don't Know Me." In 2007, National Public Radio interviewed an author who was convinced that Elvis Presley is alive and in the Witness Security Program, a rumor that has persisted since Presley's death in 1977.[11] Hollywood has produced several movies using WITSEC as the central theme.[12] Combined, they've left a confusing and often romanticized impression of a government program intended as a last resort for witnesses marked for murder. WITSEC is traumatic, not romantic, and has become an extremely costly informant-recruiting tool.

WITSEC is not a safe haven for the virtuous. The program should be called the Informant Protection Program, as 97% of WITSEC participants have extensive criminal records.[13]

The Federal Bureau of Investigation (FBI); Drug Enforcement Administration (DEA); Bureau of Alcohol, Tobacco, Firearms, and Explosives (ATF); Immigration and Customs Enforcement (ICE); and Central Intelligence Agency (CIA) each have a "program" tailored to protect informants who either refuse to or cannot enter WITSEC. Several states, including California, Connecticut, Illinois, New York, and Texas, administer their own version of WITSEC.[14]

Prior to the creation of the federal Witness Security Program, the protection of witnesses was the responsibility of the federal law enforcement agency bringing a case for prosecution. If an FBI witness was threatened, it was the FBI's duty to protect the witness. Unfortunately, most agencies were without the resources, skills, or patience to accomplish the task. Agencies that did offer protection did so only on a short-term basis, with the protection ceasing immediately after the witness testified. Long-term protection often consisted of little more than a bus ticket to another city.

From 1961 to 1965, the Department of Justice Organized Crime Program "lost" more than 25 informant witnesses. Hundreds of prosecutions reportedly did not go forward because of prospective witnesses' fears of being murdered.[15]

In 1966, President Lyndon Johnson's Crime Commission responded to the problem of safeguarding witnesses by delegating the responsibility to the USMS. This was not a simple task for an agency whose primary responsibility was to provide security to the courts and the judiciary. Witness protection efforts went nowhere. The Crime Commission had no authority to allocate funds.

In its early stages, a series of "safe houses"[16] strategically located throughout the United States were established to protect witnesses. Marshals were assigned to protect each witness 24 hours a day at the safe house until the witness testified. This method proved to be a shortsighted approach to a problem that could literally last for the witness's lifetime. The program, short on staff and seriously underfunded, needed drastic changes.

In 1970, Congress passed the Organized Crime Control Act.[17] Title V of the act granted the attorney general authority to expend funds for the protection of threatened witnesses being used in "organized crime prosecutions."[18] The USMS was officially named as the agency with the sole responsibility for developing an effective witness protection program.[19]

The Comprehensive Crime Control Act of 1984[20] repealed Title V of the Organized Crime Control Act of 1970. It had provided for the protection of *only* organized crime witnesses in *federal* cases. Dramatically expanding the original law, it now allowed for the protection of those testifying against individuals accused of *other serious offenses* in both *federal* and *state* courts,[21] including organized crime and racketeering, drug-trafficking offenses, and other serious federal felonies for which a witness may provide testimony. It also provided protection for witnesses in state court cases similar in nature to those covered under federal law.

The Witness Security Program appears to be achieving its stated goals: no witness who has followed the security rules of the program has been injured or killed.[22] The USMS claims a 90% conviction rate of the defendants whom participants in the program have testified against.[23] Witnesses feel safe to speak out against their confederates, and in the majority of cases they go on to live normal, law-abiding lives.[24] Only one in five protected witnesses goes on to commit new crimes, which is nearly half the rate of ordinary prisoners reentering society.[25]

According to former USMS director Frank Skorski, "It does work. The bottom line is: Witnesses get to court, they testify, they convict people, they go back home and they lead normal lives."[26]

However, those who resist the program's rules are at high risk of violent fallout. The Marshals Service estimates that about 30 witnesses who walked away from WITSEC have been murdered.

On paper, WITSEC is meant to be a program of last resort.[27] By law, it can be offered only by a federal prosecutor and must be approved by the Justice Department's Office of Enforcement Operations (OEO).[28] However, promises of entry into the program are liberally issued by agents, often made to people reluctant to cooperate with the government. Agents are not authorized to make promises regarding admittance into the program.

WITSEC's motto, "Truthful Testimony = Lifetime Protection," is one of the few facts the Marshals Service will confirm. Witnesses and their family accepted into the program are protected, given new identities, relocated to another U.S. city, and provided with a stipend until they become self-sufficient. Those without job skills are provided educational opportunities and assisted in finding jobs. Aside from this, nearly all other questions regarding the program are met with a standard answer: "The USMS will neither confirm nor deny … ."

14.2   Getting into the Program

The Justice Department's OEO is in charge of admittance to the Witness Security Program. OEO is staffed by pinstripe-suited lawyers, not agents, who have never worked on the streets.

Federal agents and prosecutors are not authorized to make representations or promises to witnesses regarding admission, funding, protection, or other Witness Security Program services.[29] Representations or agreements, including those contained in plea agreements concerning the program, are not authorized and will not be honored without specific authorization from the lawyers at OEO.[30] The internal guidelines for prosecutors are contained in the *United States Attorneys Manual*[31] and the *Criminal Resource Manual*.[32] There is little if anything left to question regarding the program that is not covered in one of the two manuals.

To facilitate the processing of a request by a government attorney for a witness's acceptance into the Witness Security Program, OEO's Witness Security Unit has designed an application form that requests the specific information needed to support the witness's need for protection. The form requires a summarization of the testimony to be provided by the witness and other information evidencing the witness's cooperation, the threat to the witness, and any risk the witness may pose if relocated to a new community.

It can take years from the day it's determined that a witness's life may be in jeopardy to the day he actually appears in court and testifies. It's quite possible that the witness may have a change of heart during that period, particularly if he finds that the rigors of the Witness Security Program are more than he can bear.

The OEO has that base covered:

> In order to make certain that each application for entry of a witness into the Program is both appropriate and timely, the witness should, prior to his/her acceptance into the Program, either appear and testify before the grand jury or in some other manner have committed themselves to providing testimony at trial. This requirement relates to the commitment of the witness to testify,

and is intended to ensure that the witness's testimony is available at the time of trial. It is equally as important a requirement that the prosecutor intend to have the witness testify, and that the witness' testimony be significant and essential to the success of the prosecution.[33]

Locking in the testimony makes it impossible for a witness to recant, back out, or otherwise change his story without serious legal repercussions.

14.3   Threat Assessment

Although providing testimony in a criminal trial may expose a witness to potential danger, the level of exposure to harm must be evaluated before admittance to the program can be considered. A witness does not have to be threatened to reach this stage of the admittance procedure. If the criminal or the criminal organization the witness is testifying against has the record or reputation for violence, or intelligence information obtained from other informants or wiretaps indicate the capability of the criminal organization to launch an attack against the witness, the witness and his family are recommended for WITSEC.

In the past, WITSEC has been liberal in its approach to whom the primary witness can bring with him into the program. A witness against the Panamanian dictator Manual Noriega, a former Panamanian military official and pilot, brought 20 family members, including a nanny, into the program.[34] Another witness was allowed to bring his wife, mistress, and mother into the program. One witness wanted to bring his mistress but not his wife. WITSEC would not permit the substitution.[35]

14.4   Risk Assessment

Some protected witnesses with new identities have unleashed crime waves on their unsuspecting new communities. One witness went on a cross-country murder rampage. The Justice Department has set aside a $1 million fund for the families of WITSEC murder victims, not to exceed $50,000 per family.[36] The Justice Department will also pay for the victim's funeral. If the victim's family received insurance benefits, that amount is deducted from the $50,000.[37]

In the early days of the program, prospective admittees passed little more than a gut-feeling test by agents, prosecutors, and the OEO. It was based almost exclusively on the pitch for admittance made by local prosecutors and agents using the witness. The lax standards for admittance proved to have disastrous consequences.

In 1978, while doing time in the Atlanta Federal Penitentiary for his second bank robbery, one of Marion Albert "Mad Dog" Pruett's cell mates was murdered.[38] It was one of a string of murders that made the institution look like a killing field, and the warden was desperate to prove that he, and not the inmates, was in charge.

Pruett got word to the warden claiming that he had witnessed the latest killing. Prison authorities investigated his account, and it matched the evidence: Pruett became the government's key witness at the murderer's trial.

In return for his testimony, Pruett was admitted to WITSEC. His name was changed to Charles "Sonny" Pearson, and he and his common-law wife were relocated to New Mexico to start a new life. Marion Albert Pruett no longer existed. Neither did his criminal record. Sonny Pearson had a clean slate.

The couple's new life in Rio Rancho was by no means domestic bliss. In little less than 2 years, Pruett lapsed back into crime to support a $4000-a-day cocaine habit.[39]

When, a few months later, more than one of his wife's friends noticed that she was missing, the local sheriff turned his attention to the man he knew as Charles Sonny Pearson.

Pearson was interviewed and did his best to convince the sheriff that he knew nothing about his wife's whereabouts. Yet all of the sheriff's instincts told him that Pearson was his man: despite having the bearing of a bad guy, he had an inexplicably crystal-clean record. Pruett was also experienced enough to know that the sheriff wasn't going to rest until he nailed him for the murder.

Pruett fled and went on a cross-country armed robbery and murder rampage. He killed at least five women in the course of his robberies, one in Mississippi, two in Colorado, one in Arkansas, and one in Florida. And his wife? It was later found that he had beaten her to death with a hammer, then chopped her body into the smallest pieces possible and spread her remains in the desert miles away from their home. Finally, he had soaked the pieces in gasoline and cremated the remains.

He received life sentences for all but the Arkansas killing. On October 12, 1981, he was sentenced to death. It took nearly 18 years to execute him. Pruett later told authorities that he had killed his Atlanta penitentiary cell mate and set up a fall guy for the murder. It was all part of his master plan to get out of prison and into WITSEC.

Pruett didn't go quietly. Over the years while exhausting appeals, he was interviewed by Geraldo. While on death row, he contacted a Mississippi newspaper with an incredible offer: for $20,000 he would give the paper the location of his Mississippi victim's engagement ring. The newspaper turned down the offer. About 2 weeks before his execution, he appeared on A&E Television Network's *American Justice*.

The Pruett case was the secretive WITSEC's first experience with bad press. The then associate attorney general Rudolph Giuliani pledged to tighten up the program: WITSEC would be reserved for high-priority witnesses in only the most significant of cases. There would be no more repetitions of the Pruett nightmare.

14.4.1 Arthur Katz and the Stock Market Crash of 1987

Attorney Arthur Katz, a Kansas City, Missouri, attorney, was indicted along with several physicians and lawyers in 1978 for his role in an insurance fraud automobile accident scheme. Knowing how to play the justice system, he was the first to offer to cooperate in return for a reduced sentence. He testified against doctors and several other lawyers engaged with him in the scheme. He also testified in a Philadelphia stock-manipulation conspiracy case with apparent links to the mob.[40]

His testimony was potent enough to elicit threats that were verified by the government.[41] Katz was quickly placed in the Witness Security Program. He was disbarred and sentenced to 2 years in prison. He did only 6 months in a halfway house before being relocated by U.S. Marshals to Miami, Florida. Arthur Katz was now Arthur Kane.

The Marshals Service assisted him in obtaining a midlevel job with the Social Security Administration. His coworkers described him as a mild-mannered mid-level bureaucrat. Kane was extremely adept at investing in the stock market, growing a modest nest egg that he brought along to Miami into what some estimated was worth more than $7 million.[42]

Life was good for the new Mr. Kane until the stock market crash of October 1987 occurred. Like most in the market, he took a beating. Unlike most, however, the crash pushed him over the edge. He purchased a .357 magnum, went directly to his stock broker's office, and opened fire. One broker was killed and one severely wounded before Kane turned the gun on himself.

When word hit D.C., WITSEC managers were shocked. They had been involved in the government's effort to persuade Katz and his wife to enter WITSEC. The head of WITSEC recalled, "If you had asked me to pick from the thousands of witnesses I knew, the most docile criminal I had ever encountered, I would have instantly named Arthur Katz. I would have sworn he was as safe a choice I could have possibly made when it came to putting a criminal into the program."[43]

14.4.2 James Allen Red Dog

It was another inmate murder that earned James Allen Red Dog admission into WITSEC. In 1987, while serving time at the maximum-security federal penitentiary in Marion, Illinois, Red Dog became an accomplice with two fellow prisoners in poisoning another inmate. With four murders under his belt, Red Dog had experience. His wife smuggled the white powder poison into the prison. The targeted inmate snorted the powder, thinking it was cocaine, and died almost instantly.

Red Dog became a witness and testified against his two fellow inmates. In return, he was placed in a Protective Custody Unit to serve a reduced sentence in return for his testimony. His wife was admitted to WITSEC; given a new identity; and relocated to Wilmington, Delaware.

On release, Red Dog joined his wife. She introduced him to their new neighbors, a middle-aged woman and her son. Unfortunately, suburban life didn't suit Red Dog.

In 1991, during a drunken rage he slit the neighbor's son's throat with a hunting knife. The attack was so brutal that the victim was nearly decapitated.[44] He then kidnapped the mother, raping her multiple times before she was able to escape. Investigators later learned that Red Dog took off his cowboy boots during the knife attack so that his victim wouldn't bleed all over them.

He pleaded no contest to charges of murder, kidnapping, and rape; he testified that he was drunk and did not remember the killing. He was allowed to have a Sioux medicine man perform final rights before he was executed.[45]

The year 1991 was a bad one for the program, bringing more demands for WITSEC reform. WITSEC and the Justice Department tightened up procedures governing admittance to the program, with particular focus on psychological screening of the criminals being thrown at the OEO by prosecutors in the field.

Before authorizing any witness to enter the Witness Security Program, the OEO arranges for psychological testing and evaluation for each prospective witness and all adult (18 years of age and older) members of the witness's household who are also to be protected. The testing, to the extent possible, determines whether the individual may present a danger to the relocation community.[46]

If the witness and his family make it through the initial psychological hurdle, the risk assessment moves forward. The potential risk the protected witness might pose to his relocation community must be evaluated. All WITSEC participants undergo careful vetting before being admitted into the program, including a complete psychological evaluation and consideration of the witness's value to the underlying prosecution, nature of the threat against the witness, and potential risk to the relocation community. A witness is admitted only if relevant federal law enforcement officials have determined that the witness is suitable for the program and the need to admit the witness outweighs any potential risk to the public. Those officials include the FBI or some other sponsoring law enforcement agency investigating the underlying criminal conduct; U.S. attorney for the district prosecuting the underlying criminal conduct; USMS; and OEO, which oversees WITSEC.[47]

14.5 Memorandum of Understanding

If the witness makes it through the preliminary psychological evaluation and the threat and risk assessment, the witness and members of the family must enter into a memorandum of understanding" (MOU) with the government. It is the document that spells out what is expected from the witness once he enters the program. It is also the document that the government puts in the witness's face when ejection from the program is contemplated. The MOU includes the following:

- The agreement of the person, if a witness or potential witness, to testify in and provide information to all appropriate law enforcement officials concerning all appropriate proceedings.
- The agreement of the person not to commit any crime.
- The agreement of the person to take all necessary steps to avoid detection by others.
- The agreement of the person to comply with legal obligations and civil judgments against that person.
- The agreement of the person to cooperate with all reasonable requests of officers and employees of the government who are providing protection under this chapter.
- The agreement of the person to designate another person to act as agent for the service of process.
- The agreement of the person to make a sworn statement of all outstanding legal obligations, including obligations concerning child custody and visitation.
- The agreement of the person to disclose any probation or parole responsibilities, and if the person is on probation or parole under state law, to consent to federal supervision. (The MOU also contains a clause providing for resolution of grievances.)[48]

14.6   Falling Off the Face of the Earth: Entering the Program

There is little in the life experience of any family, perhaps even of the most hardened criminal's, to prepare them for entry into the Witness Security Program.[49]

The trauma begins in a variety of ways for WITSEC participants. A wiretap or a tip from an informant may reveal that a witness has been targeted for imminent execution. The witness and his family are scooped up from their residences and evacuated by their case agent to a remote location, usually a hotel in a distant city—it is almost as if they dropped off the face of the earth. Once in a neutral site, the witness and his family are guarded around the clock by at least two armed special agents until they can be turned over to the U.S. Marshals.[50]

Criminal organizations are sometimes blindsided and don't see the betrayal coming. There is no imminent threat, and the extraction is methodically planned. The witness and his family are allowed to pack their belongings and given a date when marshals will be sent to pick them up. But even then it's difficult. One witness's wife recalled the day she left home forever. She had put everything she and her children were allowed to take with them into seven suitcases: "I thought I was going to be totally ready for it … until the last minute." She remembered looking back at her father as the marshals drove her away: "He just watched us disappear."[51]

14.7   Safe Site and Orientation Center

Since 1988, protected witnesses have been formally processed through the Safe Site and Orientation Center, a secret location in the metropolitan Washington, DC, area. A new alternative Safe Site and Orientation Center is under construction and expected to be completed in 2014.[52]

The Marshals Service operates its own air fleet, informally known as Con Air. It includes three Boeing 727s, two DC-9s, several smaller jet aircraft, and helicopters.[53] The witness is usually flown to the Washington, DC, area, arriving at Dulles, National, or any of the smaller regional airports. Extremely high-risk arrivals and departures use one of the surrounding military air bases.

The protected witness is driven from the airport to the center in an armored vehicle with draped windows.[54] Witnesses never see the exterior of the building and enter through a garage. The extreme security measures are designed not only to protect the individual in transit from harm but also to keep the witness honest: he can't give up the secret location. The tight security is also intended to thwart efforts by criminal organizations to monitor the movement of witnesses to and from the center.[55]

The physical complex itself is described by the USMS as "a secure area within a secure area."[56] The outer perimeter is patrolled while the actual grounds of the center, which are enclosed by a physical barrier, are under constant electronic surveillance. The security network is managed by a cadre of witness security inspectors who direct the movement of all personnel and witnesses within the center's grounds. There is never a time when a witness will see another witness while at the Safe Site.[57]

The facility contains six fully equipped apartments for nonprisoner witnesses and their families. Witnesses are never allowed to leave their living quarters unescorted. The apartments have walled exterior courtyards. The Orientation Center also has four holding cells for incarcerated witnesses. A polygraph room, interview rooms, and full medical and dental examination facilities are also located within the site.[58]

The witness is met at the Safe Site by a witness security inspector. The position is unique to federal law enforcement. The inspector not only is the participant's link to WITSEC but also becomes the witness's "protector, support system and confidant"[59] as he moves the witness through the system. There are approximately 135 witness security inspectors[60] stationed throughout the United States whose only responsibility is to protect and assist the program's participants.

All inspectors are required to sign secrecy agreements. This wasn't the case in the early years of the program. Today's inspectors are bound for life to keep what they know about the program and those they have protected confidential.

Organizationally, the program is operated from three levels: Marshals Service Headquarters; nine regional offices; and Metro units, which have a witness security inspector assigned to provide assistance to witnesses and to serve as an advisor to the local marshal on witness security matters. The witness security inspectors are supported by 150 deputy U.S. marshals who share their regular field assignment with WITSEC.[61]

Shortly after the witness's arrival, a special team of security specialists from Marshals Service Headquarters begins the task of determining where to relocate the witness. This decision follows a detailed interview in which extensive background information is collected and assessed. The participant's ultimate destination is based on the witness's ethnic background, where he has lived and visited in the past, any special medical or educational requirements for him or his family, the availability of employment, and where the Marshals Service can best service him.[62]

One mobster gave his version of how WITSEC picks the relocation area: "You tell them [at the orientation center] where your relatives are and where you did coke deals and where your racketeering was, and they won't put you in those states. They put you in a place where you don't know anybody. You stick out like a sore thumb and you don't know what to say to people when they ask, 'Where are you from? What do you do?'" He refers to the areas that the marshals relocate witnesses to as "somewhere out in Wahoo-land."[63]

Once the city is picked, admittees are given volumes of material to review regarding their new hometown. They are also coached on creating a cover story. While they are at the Orientation Center, participants undergo a second battery of psychological examinations. They also receive a thorough physical and dental examination. Counseling to prepare them for the move and the challenges it will present is also part of the process.[64]

The center gives the participants the opportunity to begin the redocumentation of identity procedure, starting with the selection of a new name. The only restriction is that the new name must not be a family name, like a grandmother's maiden name.[65] According to a former inspector, "There are some names we would not go along with and many that we would go along with."[66] Taking the name of a movie star or famous athlete is not allowed: Michael Jackson and Michael Jordan have been repeatedly turned down as new witness names.

Deciding to take a new first name "goes to an individual's own personal paranoia."[67] Although keeping the same initials and the same first name is encouraged, it is not mandatory.

WITSEC does not provide for plastic surgery. If a witness thinks it is necessary and is willing to pay for the procedure, WITSEC supports the decision. "Sammy the Bull" Gravano is one of the few known WITSEC participants to undergo plastic surgery. According to Gravano, "I asked the doctor if I could look like Robert Redford, do it. But he said no."[68] Ironically, 2 years after the surgery Gravano collaborated in a tell-all book with a color picture of his new face on the cover.[69]

Before leaving the Orientation Center, witnesses are provided with new driver's licenses, social security cards, birth certificates, and school and medical records. The name changes go through the courts but are kept under seal. An inspector described the process as being so complete that when the witness leaves the center he "ceases to exist under his old name, and the old record shows he never existed."[70]

All records are designed to be verifiable and able to stand even the closest scrutiny. No participant receives educational documentation or work history that puts him in either a better or a worse position professionally. The marshals do not provide false references or résumés.

Conversely, a noncriminal witness forced into the program because of what he had seen and testified to countered: "They call it 'the program of last resort' and they're right. It's just a little bit better than being dead. They take all your ID, you're in a strange place, and you're teaching your kids to lie about where you're from. It's very uncomfortable."[71]

Once the witness is relocated, a WITSEC security inspector assists the family in finding permanent housing, enrolling the children in school, locating doctors and dentists, and attending to the multitude of other tasks related to moving into a new community.

"There is a unique trauma involved when a family is uprooted and moved to an entirely new community," said one witness security inspector. "Remember your own feelings—if you have ever moved to a new city where you know no one—the adjustment was somewhat difficult, particularly hard on your spouse and your children. Now, think of that same situation, but imagine giving up the name you have known since birth and not being able to tell anyone back home—even your relatives and closest friends—where you are."[72]

In the early days of the program, arrangements were made to securely move the family furniture and personal belongings from the danger area to their new home. Today, the practice has been replaced by purchasing new furniture at WITSEC's expense. The resettlement must not only be accomplished without drawing attention to the family but also to avoid any connection to the witness's danger zone or the past. Once the family is settled, the inspector stays in touch with the family.[73]

"Some witnesses experience a big change in lifestyle after they enter the program," says an inspector who has been with the program since its inception. "They may have had a very affluent lifestyle, driving new cars and living in a big house with maids. But their lives are drastically different once they enter the WITSEC program. The witness may now have to rent an apartment and drive a used car. The transition into the program can take some time."[74]

Relocating presents many unexpected sacrifices for the protected family. All ties to the family's previous community must be severed. Witnesses can continue to stay in contact with friends and relatives but only by mail forwarded through secure channels of the Marshals Service. Phone calls to close family members not in the program are made through secure telephone channels. E-mailing has presented WITSEC inspectors with a host of predictable challenges and admittees with predictable temptations to reunite with their past lives.

Many participants are divorced and custodial parents. Nonparticipant parents are still entitled to visitation of children, presenting costly logistical hurtles for the USMS to overcome.[75] Inspectors reportedly average arranging between 15 and 18 visits per child per year.[76] Obviously, the visits must take place away from the participant's danger zone and the city of relocation to ensure the integrity of the program.[77]

14.8   Employment as a WITSEC Member

Witnesses receive a monthly stipend until they are gainfully employed or become self-sufficient through other means. Monthly payments are based on the Department of Labor cost-of-living indexes.[78] No consideration is given to restore a participant to an opulent lifestyle he once may have enjoyed. This doesn't sit well with former mob big shots. One inspector describes the watered-down lifestyle of WITSEC: "The worst ones are the guys who were in prison first, because they've had a couple years to sit around and listen to the war stories of other prisoners about what you can get out of the program. They think they know everything because Sammy the Horse or whoever they were in jail with said you could get triple pay if you fight for it."[79]

Subsistence terminates 6 months following the first payment. There are provisions for a 90-day extension of benefits for circumstances outside the control of the participant.[80]

Lengthy trials and multi-trial appearances often delay the employment process and require an extension of the subsistence allowance. "Jimmy the Weasel" Fratianno was on and off the witness stand for more than 10 years. He appeared before 12 grand juries, several congressional hearings, 1 presidential commission, and 15 criminal trials. His testimony put 37 mobsters away.[81] He allegedly never took a job during his entire time in WITSEC.

Many WITSEC participants never held a job in their lives. According to a former mobster and WITSEC admittee, "I know bookmaking and shakedowns. There were no ads in the paper for that." A former WITSEC inspector seemed to sympathize with his plight: "If you did nothing but sell drugs for 20 years, where do you work? The night shift at Burger King?"[82]

The Marshals Service is responsible for providing only one job opportunity to the witness after relocation. If the participant has a valid reason for not accepting the position, one more job opportunity is offered.[83] The USMS has a network of more than 300 employers in the United States that accept WITSEC participants.[84] The employment offer should be in a field compatible to the participant's work history.

According to a former WITSEC inspector, "You go to the head of the corporation and you say, 'This guy has been convicted of blah blah blah.' You tell him the crimes. You have that obligation. But you're not going to get a bank robber a job as a teller."[85]

For those without transferable skills, there are provisions for job training. Participants are also free to fulfill their own career goals. WITSEC has helped admittees start their own businesses. It is only failure to seek or resist employment that terminates their subsistence payments.

However, the participant is expected to become self-sufficient as soon as possible after admission to the program. Internal regulations explain that under no circumstances will the witness be considered "entitled" to subsistence payments until he has testified.[86]

14.9   Witness Rewards

Participants in the program are entitled to reward monies from the agency that had control over their activities. For example, if an informant was responsible for the government seizing a piece of property worth $1 million, he's eligible for a reward. But forfeiture cases take time to process while the witness is tucked away in his new home. The agency headquarters paying the reward must coordinate the payment through the OEO and the USMS for the disbursement of the funds. Cutting a U.S. government check for a significant sum could easily compromise the witness's new identity. Consequently, the reward is often disbursed in cash through U.S. Marshals Headquarters.[87] Rewards for incarcerated protected witnesses are handled in much the same fashion but coordinated with the Bureau of Prisons.

14.10   Hiding in Plain Sight

The success of WITSEC is due in large part to the nation's population to swallow up a threatened witness and his family. Once the witness is relocated to a safe location, he is no longer provided physical protection by members of the Marshals Service; it falls on the witness to preserve the secrecy of his new identity and new place of residence. Disclosing either is grounds for expulsion from the program.

One witness explained how she and her husband coped: "You must be constantly aware of what role you're playing. You're constantly clicking on and clicking off. We remind each other, 'Remember, you're this, not that.'"[88]

In the early stages of relocation, the witness is visited twice a week and called every other day by his assigned inspector. If the witness is experiencing problems, the inspector is available 24 hours a day. Some witnesses make the transition seamlessly. Some are nothing but headaches for their inspector. According to one inspector, "Everything is a hassle. You're always dealing with problems. You get people on dialysis, you get people on methadone. You have to deal with their teenage daughters' pregnancies. You have to deal with every problem in society, compounded by the fact that they're in the program."[89]

14.11 Children: The Weak Link

The children of relocated witnesses, particularly school-aged children, are the weak link in the program. It's WITSEC's policy to inform a high-ranking member of the school system of the new student's situation, but individual teachers are not informed.

Some children can't maintain secrecy. An inspector recalled, "All of a sudden you get a neighbor come to the door and say, 'My daughter Susie says you're a Mafia guy the government moved here.' Boom! You've got to move them again. Immediately. You've got to start all over. And the second move is much worse than the first because the kids are settled, they're in school, they're making friends. And now they've got to do it all over again with a third name."[90]

The family is then uprooted and moved to one of the seven other so-called Safe Sites located in large metropolitan areas throughout the United States. The relocation process begins all over again.[91]

Safe Sites are described by the Marshals Service as "self-contained, secure housing units designed and maintained by the Marshals Service to provide witnesses and their families maximum protection in a hotel setting. The units are complete with dining, exercise, and entertainment facilities and the latest in closed-circuit television networks, intruder alarm systems, and radio and telephone communication systems." Deputy U.S. Marshals are assigned at Safe Sites to protect the witnesses from harm. The locations are also used to house witnesses when they return to the danger area to testify.[92]

14.12   WITSEC Participants as Informants

Informants who enter the Witness Security Program and begin a new life do occasionally resurface as informants.[93] They can also reenter the WITSEC program if necessary.[94]

This practice was evidenced in the 1994 high-profile FBI arrest of Malcolm X's daughter in a murder-for-hire case.[95] The informant used in the case had previously participated in the investigation of a militant group who had planned to bomb an Egyptian government tourist office in New York in 1978. Following that case, he was placed in the Witness Security Program and was relocated with a new identity.[96]

The Reuters News Service quoted him as saying that he expected to receive $45,000 from the FBI for his latest services. He said that he was paid $34,000 and expected to receive the balance plus expenses as "compensation for having to relocate and adjust to a new life in the witness protection program he reentered after the indictment of the target of the investigation."[97]

In an interview with *Newsweek*, the informant was asked a series of questions about his involvement in the case. His answers provide a commentary on the realities of WITSEC:

> Q. Maybe you just wanted an easy life in the federal witness-protection program?
> A. I'd been in the program before [after the 1978 case]. I knew what a horrible life it was. I did not leave my friends and loved ones willingly. The $45,000 the government paid me was calculated to equal six months of my salary at the job I'd have to leave. Would you take six months' salary to leave everyone and everything you know?
> Q. What's it like?
> A. Short of a jail cell, this is the hardest existence I can fathom. Imagine sitting in a Sleepy 8 motel room for months when your only social contact is the Domino's delivery man. Since January, I think I've lived in six cities, give or take. Last week, after the settlement, I saw my girlfriend for the first time in almost four months. We were allowed to embrace for 15 minutes, with six federal marshals standing nearby.[98]

The DEA has historically viewed admission into WITSEC as permanent, and the informant will not be utilized again. The prohibition extends to any family member who is relocated as a result of the informant's cooperation. The *DEA Manual* acknowledges that the Department of Justice may waive the prohibition.[99]

The OEO does not foreclose utilizing a protected witness as an informant. Instead, it acknowledges an "ongoing relationship" between the witness and the department.[100] The consent of OEO is required before a currently protected witness, anyone relocated because of a witness's cooperation, or a former protected witness can be used as an informant.

14.13   Ejection from WITSEC

The MOU signed by the witness at the Safe Site and Orientation Center contains the commandments that admittees must live by. The two that top the list are an agreement not to commit any more crimes and to take all necessary steps to avoid detection.[101] Officially, WITSEC is a one-strike program: violate the rules and you're out. Unofficially, it depends on the value of the witness.

James Martinelli[102] put WITSEC rules to the test. He was a witness in the 1987 prosecution of "Teflon Don" John Gotti. Gotti had earned the nickname because through the years each time the government brought him to trial the charges wouldn't stick. The juries found him not guilty.

Under cross-examination, Martinelli proved to be more valuable to the defense than the prosecution. When asked what he was getting from the government in return for his testimony, he answered truthfully: he had been promised immunity for four murders; would be given a new identity and $10,000 in cash; and would be relocated. When asked what he thought about the deal, he replied, "I think I made a fantastic deal."[103] The jury didn't miss a word.

Once again, Gotti was acquitted by the jury. Shortly after the trial, one of Gotti's codefendants who had been merely suspected of being an informant was shot to death in a hail of 18 bullets. According to homicide detectives, "The first bullet was enough to kill him. The rest were for effect."[104] Despite Martinelli's dismal performance on the witness stand, he had to be protected.

Martinelli, now 40 years old, was sent to a Protective Custody Unit to serve a few years for his four murders. Upon release, he was relocated to Oklahoma City to start a new life under WITSEC.

He didn't stay in the program very long. He violated parole and told his girlfriend his life story—including WITSEC. In clear violation of his MOU, he was ejected from the program. But he didn't go quietly.

Martinelli donned a sandwich board sign that read "Marked to die by the Justice Department" on one side and "Mob Star Witness" with a bull's-eye on the other. He picketed the federal courthouse in Albuquerque, New Mexico, and was all over television news and newspapers nationwide.[105]

A couple of weeks later, Martinelli appeared on CNN's *Larry King Live* complaining that the government had exposed him to danger and had reneged on its promise to protect him. During the interview, he said he had been warned not to fly to Washington.

Martinelli returned to Albuquerque the following day and was arrested for violation of parole.[106] He hasn't been seen or heard from since. The Marshals Service will "neither confirm nor deny" if he is back in the program.[107] One account is that Martinelli got a WITSEC second chance and was relocated.[108]

14.14   Terror Witnesses: New Challenges

The face of WITSEC participants is constantly changing. Entrants reflect which crime the government is currently battling. Since the late 1970s, when the War on Drugs heated up, it's been drug traffickers of all stripes who populate WITSEC. They range from Hispanic mules to gritty outlaw motorcycle gang members to Colombian and Mexican cartel kingpins.

The war on terror occupies the twenty-first-century center stage. It's producing an odd mix of recruits with new languages, ethnicities, customs, and immigration headaches for WITSEC.[109] The lack of U.S. Marshals with Middle Eastern language capabilities has also proved to be a challenge.

According to a 2013 Office of Inspector General's report,[110] former known or suspected terrorists admitted into the program have provided invaluable assistance to the United States and foreign governments in identifying and dismantling terrorist organizations and disrupting terror plots.[111] Among other investigations and prosecutions, WITSEC participants have provided essential cooperation and testimony regarding the following: the 1993 World Trade Center bombing and "blind sheik" prosecutions, 1995 bombing of the Alfred P. Murrah Federal Building in Oklahoma City, 1998 East Africa Embassy bombings, 2000 Millennium terror plot, 2007 plot to bomb the John F. Kennedy International Airport, and 2009 New York City subway suicide bomb plot. Each of the prosecutions resulted in the conviction of individuals responsible for committing or attempting to commit terrorist attacks against U.S. citizens.[112]

In July 2012, the USMS reported that it was unable to locate two former WITSEC participants identified as known or suspected terrorists. Through its investigative efforts, it concluded that one individual was, and the other individual was believed to be, residing outside the United States. An Office of Inspector General investigation ensued.

The OIG reported as follows:

To help protect witnesses from the persons and organizations against whom they testify, the USMS provides a WITSEC participant and his or her dependents with a new name and necessary identity-related documentation. We found that the Department was not authorizing the disclosure to the Terrorist Screening Center (TSC)[113] of the new identities provided to known or suspected terrorists in the WITSEC Program. The TSC's consolidated terrorist watch list is exported to various screening databases to include the Transportation Security Administration's (TSA) No Fly and Selectee lists, which are used to identify known or suspected terrorists attempting to fly on commercial airlines. Individuals placed on the TSA's No Fly list are prohibited from flying on commercial planes and individuals on the TSA's Selectee list require additional screening procedures in order to board a commercial aircraft.

As a result of the Department not disclosing information on these known or suspected terrorists, the new, government-provided identities of known or suspected terrorists were not included on the government's consolidated terrorist watch list until we brought this matter to the Department's attention. Therefore, it was possible for known or suspected terrorists to fly on commercial airplanes in or over the United States and evade one of the government's primary means of identifying and tracking terrorists.[114]

The Office of the Deputy Attorney General responded as follows:

> The Government generally cannot choose its witnesses. This is particularly true in cases involving terrorism, where witnesses are often former known or suspected terrorists, or individuals who are close enough to terrorists to have information about them, their organizations, and their plans, but whose cooperation is necessary to successfully prosecute those who pose the most significant threat to our national security. Regardless of the prosecution's target, however, no witness—in a terrorism case or otherwise—is admitted into the Program without being subject to an intensive vetting by: the FBI or other sponsoring law enforcement agency investigating the underlying criminal conduct; the United States Attorney for the district prosecuting the underlying criminal conduct; the USMS, which protects and monitors witnesses who require a change of identity and relocation services; and OEO, which oversees the WITSEC Program. Thus, as noted above, national security stakeholders such as the FBI have been deeply involved in the Program admission process—often as the party sponsoring a terrorism-linked witness's admission into the Program—even before the Department began implementing changes to the Program's treatment of terrorism-linked witnesses. Indeed, of the identified universe of terrorism-linked witnesses, the FBI sponsored nearly 80% of these witnesses into the Program.[115]

14.15   Immigration Benefits

Foreign-born informants facing danger due to their cooperation and testimony stand to receive significant immigration benefits. In addition to the basic WITSEC protection, relocation, and new identity, noncitizen entrants receive the coveted S-5 visa: only 200 are issued annually. Terror informants from abroad move to the head of a very elite visa line. They are issued an S-6 visa: only 50 are allotted each year. Both visas have proved to be invaluable informant recruiting tools. The S-5 and S-6 visas enable each member of the informant's family to receive a visa.[116]

14.16   Alternatives to WITSEC

The Justice Department uses WITSEC as a program of last resort. For a variety of reasons, many informant witnesses either cannot or will not enter the program.

Some agencies offer an alternative measure of protection through a less formal relocation than that demanded by WITSEC. The DEA offers financial assistance for its informants' relocation from the agency's internal expense budget.[117] These monies can be used to pay for moving an informant's household goods, apartment lease, and transportation.

An alternate method compensates for the cost of relocation when determining the amount of reward to be paid to the cooperating witness.[118] The informant is given a "lump-sum" payment, which includes the cost of relocation and instructions on how to obtain assistance for housing and rent.[119]

14.16.1   Federal Bureau of Investigation

The FBI has been known to enter into written agreements with witnesses and informants who are unwilling or unable to enter the Witness Security Program. Known as a Witness Security and Relocation Plan, the agreement resembles and in effect is a contract between the cooperating witness and the FBI. It is not a casually drafted document. It is prepared by an FBI contracting officer with the assistance of the witness's control agent and designed to meet the needs peculiar to the individual witness and his family.

One of the first bases covered in the relocation plan is a pledge by the witness to maintain secrecy. If the witness participated in a sensitive investigation or one that grabbed headlines and could embarrass the bureau, he must promise not to profit from the case. Specifically, he must agree not to publish or participate in the publication or dissemination of any information or material without the prior express written authorization of the FBI. In other words, there should be no book contracts or screenplays.

If the informant disregards this provision, any profits or royalties become the property of the U.S. government. More significantly, it will constitute a bad-faith breach of the agreement. This can be a significant loss, as the witness security relocation plans can be extremely generous. Some include life insurance, compensation for lost wages, and financial assistance for the purchase of a residence.

14.16.2   Drug Enforcement Administration

When former hit man and DEA informant John Martorano was released from prison in 2008, he was given a lump sum payment of $20,000 cash to help start a new life. Martorano served 12 years for 20 murders. He was released early for testimony that helped nail a retired, corrupt FBI agent for murder. The payment worked out to $1000 per murder—his sentence represented a little over 6 months for each murder.

An assistant U.S. attorney saw nothing wrong in the payment to Martorano: "It's not unusual for an individual like Martorano, who was in the Witness Security Program while incarcerated and who opted not to accept placement as a civilian, to receive a small sum of money to assist him in starting his life again."[120]

Martorano moved back to Boston, Massachusetts, home to several family members of his victims.

14.16.3 Bureau of Alcohol, Tobacco, Firearms, and Explosives

The ATF maintains a "source of highly confidential funds which are available for use in exigent circumstances. The account … enables the Bureau to meet its responsibilities to those informants and witnesses whose cooperation with ATF results in an immediate threat to their lives."[121] Known as the Emergency Expense Fund, the monies allow ATF the flexibility of providing short-term protection and immediate relocation of a witness. It is a remedial measure compared to the Witness Security Program but effective in the short term.[122]

14.16.4 Immigration and Customs Enforcement

ICE has a short-term protection program similar to the ATF and DEA. It produces short-term results but does not come without risk.

14.16.4.1 Case Study: Informant Murders Relocated Informant

It was in late 2008 when Daniel Gonzalez-Galeana, a lieutenant in the Juarez drug cartel faction known as *La Compania*, found himself running for his life and in need of protection. His fate changed overnight after the arrest of his boss, "the Tiger." His arrest was followed by a Mexican army raid on one of his cocaine warehouses.[123] It was a rare and highly publicized success in Mexico's battle against the cartel.

The Tiger's arrest put La Compania on alert. They had an informant in their midst. Gonzalez-Galeana was inexplicably identified as the informant responsible for the Tiger's arrest. Orders were immediately issued by the cartel for Gonzalez-Galeana's abduction, torture, and execution.

Gonzalez-Galeana immediately dropped out of sight. His only chance was to defect to one of the U.S. law enforcement agencies known in Mexican trafficking circles as *tres letras*, or "three letters": the DEA, FBI, and ICE. He resurfaced barely 3 mi. away from Juarez at the El Paso office of Immigration and Customs Enforcement. He agreed to become an informant in exchange for protection for himself and his family.

ICE officials provided their new informant and his family with S visas. Better known as "snitch visas," the documents allowed them to remain in the United States for as long as the former drug boss continued to work for ICE.[124]

ICE didn't relocate Gonzalez-Galeana to another part of the United States for safety. He and his family weren't admitted into the U.S. Marshals' Witness Security Program and given new identities. Instead, he was housed in an upscale El Paso neighborhood. The El Paso chief of police lived a few houses away from Gonzalez-Galeana's home but was never told of his new neighbor's value to ICE or the danger he faced.[125]

The informant and his family successfully avoided detection in El Paso for nearly a year. He was keenly aware that the Juarez cartel had put out a contract on his life. Regardless, he ran a freight business from his house.[126] Police later alleged that he also continued to coordinate drug shipments for another trafficking organization while working for ICE.[127]

The Juarez cartel assigned one of its enforcers, known as "Dorado," the task of hunting down Hidalgo. Tracking men marked for death by La Compania had become Dorado's specialty.[128] He immediately put together a hit team: a U.S. Army private as the shooter, a getaway-car driver, and a look-out.[129] All were trusted members of Dorado's burglary and truck-hijacking ring. The shooter would be paid $7500 for the hit; the others would receive $5000 each.[130]

On the evening of May 15, 2009, Dorado located his prey on the west side of El Paso, where he had been visiting relatives. The team, communicating with cell phones, followed Gonzalez-Galeana to the east side of the city. He eventually led them directly to his home on Pony Trail Drive.[131]

As Gonzalez-Galeana walked toward his front door, the army private jumped from his car. He shot the informant eight times at point-blank range with a .45-caliber semiautomatic pistol. Neighbors reported hearing shouting in Spanish just before the shots were fired, so it's clear that he knew what was coming. The shooter was so close to Hidalgo that two of the eight slugs had enough power left over to rip through his chest and exit his body. One bullet embedded itself in the wall of a neighbor's home. Another struck a parked car.[132] The chief of police heard the shots from his backyard. According to the chief, "He got shot up close. Whoever did it wanted to make sure it was known that it was for payback."[133] Gonzalez-Galeana earned the distinction of being the first Mexican cartel boss to be assassinated on U.S. soil.[134]

Gonzalez-Galeana's wife did as instructed by her husband at the beginning of their ordeal. He had programmed a number into her cell phone with instructions that it should be called in the event that something happened to him.[135] Only after calling that number was she to dial 911.[136] While her husband was bleeding to death on the street, she did exactly as she had been told.

Weeks later, an investigative journalist covering a pretrial hearing recounted testimony from officers responding to the shooting. A uniformed officer testified that on arrival at the scene he found Gonzalez-Galeana's wife on the telephone. She was talking to a man who identified himself to the officer as an ICE agent in Washington, DC.[137] A police lieutenant testified that as homicide detectives were responding to the scene of the shooting a team of ICE agents also showed up.[138]

Later that evening, Gonzalez-Galeana's ICE control agent telephoned the El Paso homicide detective in charge of the case. He explained that the victim was an ICE informant with ties to the Juarez cartel. The ICE agent also promised to provide assistance in the murder investigation.[139]

A total of 3 days went by before the lead detective investigating Gonzalez-Galeana's murder met the ICE control agent. The agent produced a group of mug shots of individuals he regarded as possible suspects. A Texas ranger present for the display recalled that the agent had also shown him a similar photo spread earlier—but this time, one picture was missing. The agent had no explanation for the missing picture.[140]

The ICE agent's next contribution to the investigation into the murder of his informant came 3 days later. This time, he put the nickname "Mayer" to the missing photograph, claiming that he was an ICE informant who might have information regarding the identity of the shooter.[141] He'd make the informant available to the detective for an interview.

The detective conducted two interviews of Mayer in the presence of the ICE agent. The agent never offered Mayer's nickname: Dorado.

The detective concluded that the ICE informant was not reliable.[142] That was the last time the detective would receive assistance from the ICE agent regarding the murder of Gonzalez-Galeana.[143]

The El Paso Police Department solved the case without help from ICE. Several days after the murder, Dorado and his crew were arrested after trying to hijack a 53-ft trailer load of televisions by towing it away with an SUV.[144] The story and mug shots of the suspects made the *El Paso Times*. All three thieves were released on bail.

An investigator assigned to the Hildalgo case recognized the mug shot of Dorado accompanying the *El Paso Times* article reporting the television caper. It was the photo of the missing man from the initial ICE photo display of suspects.[145]

It took several weeks of old-school detective work mixed with new-age technology and luck for the police to put together their case against Dorado. They were able to use cell phone records of the phones used by Dorado's hit team while Gonzalez-Galeana was being followed home. The records put the suspects near the scene of the murder.[146]

About 2 months following the murder, the police had the shooter, the getaway-car driver, and Dorado all in custody. Each faced charges of capital murder. The driver[147] and the shooter[148] later cooperated with prosecutors to escape the death penalty.

Dorado's interrogation was barely under way, however, before he revealed his identity as an ICE informant to the homicide detective. He wanted him to contact his ICE handler. The detective soon learned that both his victim and his suspect were working for the same ICE control agent.[149]

Whether Dorado capitalized on his ICE connections in the hunt for Hidalgo has yet to be determined. Why the ICE control agents misled homicide investigators is left to speculation. In 2009, the lead homicide detective in Gonzalez-Galeana's murder offered his opinion. In an interview with an Associated Press reporter, he expressed his frustration with ICE, saying, "Some agencies don't take murder as seriously as drugs."[150]

14.17   CIA Defector Program: National Resettlement Operations Center

As in Chapter 2, Section 2.4.5.1, the CIA refers to the informants it operates overseas as "assets." When an asset faces danger in his home country as a result of his work for the United States, the CIA is able to bring him into the United States for protection and relocation. When he makes landfall in the United States, he is referred to as a "defector."

The CIA aggressively recruits assets from hostile nations with the promise of substantial monetary rewards, protection, and resettlement in the United States. It is part of the CIA's "brain drain" program, designed to entice scientists and military officers from countries like Iran and North Korea to defect.[151]

The CIA version of the Witness Security Program is operated by an extremely secretive division within the CIA called the National Resettlement Operations Center (NROC). Staffed by NROC officers, the center facilitates the process of providing false identities, résumés, references, and resettlements for defectors. Unlike in WITSEC, defectors are allowed to choose where they want to resettle.[152] Much like the success of WITSEC, NROC's success depends on the United States' geographic size and population to hide defectors in plain sight.

The dangers that defectors face are palpable. In November 2006, the world watched defector Alexander Valterovich Litvinenko, a former Russian Federal Security Service agent and former Soviet KGB agent, die in a London hospital.

Following his defection to Great Britain, Litvinenko had become a journalist and an extremely vocal critic of Vladimir Putin. Litvinenko claimed that the Chechen Moscow theater hostage crisis was orchestrated by the Russian Federal Security Service. He became ill following a day of meetings and interviews with former KGB agents. It took him 23 days to die. Extensive tests determined that he had been poisoned with radioactive polonium-210.[153]

In April 2008, defector Oleg Gordievsky, one of Britain's most successful Russian double agents in the 1980s, was poisoned at his home in Surrey. According to Gordievsky, "I've known for some time that I am on the assassination list drawn up by rogue elements in Moscow."[154] In recognition of his Cold War service, Gordievsky was made a Companion of the Most Distinguished Order of St. Michael and St. George, the same honor awarded to the fictional spy James Bond.[155]

In 1978, Bulgarian defector Georgi Ivanov Markov, another Cold War defector to Britain, became posthumously famous as the victim of a killer dubbed "The Umbrella Assassin." A BBC World Service journalist and fierce critic of the Soviet Bulgarian regime, Markov's son survived three kidnapping attempts. His wife was nearly killed when her car was deliberately forced off the road.[156]

Markov was shot with a poison pellet on the back of his right thigh while crossing London's Waterloo Bridge. The pellet was discharged from an umbrella.[157] Markov saw his assailant drop and then retrieve his umbrella immediately after what he described as feeling like a bee sting.[158] He recounted the incident to a co-worker at the BBC. The wound looked like a pimple, and he soon fell into a fever. The defector died three days later.[159] The cause of death was listed as poisoning from a ricin-filled pellet. In the wake of the Litvinenko murder, Markov's cold case, referred to as "The Umbrella Murder," was reopened.[160] At this writing the case remains unsolved.

The process of resettling a defector presents a whole different range of challenges than those faced by the average WITSEC participant. The differences in culture, language, and ideology make integrating the resettlee extremely difficult. A retired CIA case officer recalled as follows: "They just don't integrate well. It's always a goddamn mess, always, always, always. The defector who can land on his feet is a rare one."[161]

In 2009, a high-value Iranian nuclear scientist defected to the United States. He is believed to be one of the sources for the 2007 National Intelligence Estimate regarding Iran's nuclear ambitions. He was resettled in Tucson, Arizona, and was promised $5 million as part of a CIA benefits package. The money was put into a trust of sorts, administered by a financial firm outside the CIA's control.[162]

In an interview with MSNBC, a former CIA case officer revealed that an arrangement like the Iranian scientist's deal was not extraordinary: "$5 million is really not that much when you consider it's not a one-time payment, it's building a new lifestyle for someone coming into the United States." Another source told the journalist that money paid to defectors is often paid out over a long period of time—upward of 20 years—and is designed to create an incentive for defectors to leave their countries, and sometimes their families, to relocate in the United States. It provides a base for them as they buy a home and attempt to create a new livelihood.[163]

In July 2010, the scientist abruptly redefected to Tehran. One U.S. official quoted by ABC attributed his departure in part to homesickness. He "wanted to see his family again. Defectors are human beings. In this country, they make their own choices. He made up his mind; and in the United States, at least, he has that right."[164]

On his return to Iran, the former defector became the focus of media attention. He offered an interesting story claiming that he had been kidnapped while on a pilgrimage to Saudi Arabia by the CIA and Saudi agents and flown to the United States, where he was tortured and interrogated.[165]

As for the $5 million, one official put it this way: "Anything he got is now beyond his reach, thanks to the sanctions against Iran. We got his information and the Iranians have him." Another official said, "He's gone but the money is still here."[166]

A former CIA case officer who worked with defectors wasn't surprised at the Iranian's redefection: "This happens all the time. Defectors come across, they think it's a good idea, they get paid a lot of money. Then once the boredom sets in and the loneliness, they realize it's a huge mistake."[167]

Others believe that the scientist was a double agent sent to the United States by the Iranian intelligence service. His mission was to mislead the CIA in its attempts to penetrate Iran's nuclear program.[168] He wouldn't be the first to put one over on the CIA.

In 1985, Vitaly Yurchenko, a 25-year veteran KGB agent, defected to the United States while on an assignment in Rome. He outed two American intelligence officers as KGB agents.

Three months into his defection, while having dinner with his CIA case officer at a Washington, DC, restaurant he casually got up from the table and said, "I'm going for a walk. If I don't come back, it's not your fault."[169] He didn't return. Two days later, he called a press conference at the Soviet Embassy. He claimed to have been kidnapped while visiting the Vatican, drugged, and taken to the United States for interrogation. On return to the Soviet Union, he was awarded the Order of the Red Star for successfully infiltrating the CIA.[170]

Officially, the NROC program is known as PL-110—its name drawn from the original public law number that created the CIA.[171] Participants in the program are informally referred to as "resettlees."[172] There is no position within the CIA equivalent to the Marshals Service's sought after position of WITSEC inspector. The NROC has been called a babysitting assignment and a dumping ground for troubled case officers. Most have limited experience overseas and no knowledge of the culture or language of the defectors assigned to their charge.[173]

The program is as old as the CIA itself. Anticipating the need to both entice and protect defectors, the law provides the following:

Whenever the Director [of Central Intelligence], the Attorney General, and the Commissioner of Immigration and Naturalization shall determine that the admission of a particular alien into the United States for permanent residence is in the interest of national security or essential to the furtherance of the national intelligence mission, such alien and his immediate family shall be admitted to the United States for permanent residence without regard to their inadmissibility under the immigration or any other laws and regulations, or to the failure to comply with such laws and regulations pertaining to admissibility: Provided, that the number of aliens and members of their immediate families admitted to the United States under the authority of this section shall in no case exceed one hundred persons in any one fiscal year.[174]

The CIA's concern for secrecy and the safety of its spies has deep-seated roots. In 1777, General George Washington told an aide, "The necessity of procuring good intelligence is apparent and need not be further urged—all that remains for me to add is that you keep the whole matter as secret as possible."[175] In 1779, Washington cautioned members of his intelligence service that the identities of their spies "should be kept profoundly secret, otherwise we not only lose the benefits desired from [their espionage], but may subject him to some unhappy fate."[176]

14.17.1   Defector Lawsuits and the Totten Doctrine

Like WITSEC, the NROC has had its share of bad press. In 2002, the *Washington Post* ran an article that was extremely critical of the program. It quoted a former CIA case officer as saying, "Even in very high-profile cases, the handling of these individuals [defectors] has been downright atrocious."[177]

The biggest complaint of resettlees is that the government doesn't live up to the promises made during the initial recruiting pitch. Most complaints focus on the amount of the reward paid or the cancellation of a stipend that resettlees believed was meant to last a lifetime.[178]

Dissatisfaction among defectors is nothing new. In 1988, the Helms Committee[179] was formed to allow defectors to appeal what they claimed were breaches of promise. The panel is composed of three former high-ranking CIA officials. An attorney representing two defectors before the panel called it a "kangaroo court" that refused to provide him with any regulations governing the panel's procedures. He recalled that when the panel recommended that his clients should receive an additional year's benefits CIA lawyers demanded that the defectors should sign a waiver relinquishing any future claims.[180]

Defectors seeking redress in the federal courts have had no success. A former Soviet diplomat defector and his wife filed suit against the CIA in federal court in Seattle, Washington, as John and Jane Doe.[181] The couple had tried, and failed, to resolve a dispute over benefits that had been withdrawn by the CIA. In a letter from the CIA that refused to reinstate their benefits, an agency lawyer wrote as follows: "We sympathize with the situation you find yourself in but regret that due to our budget constraints, we are unable to provide you with additional assistance." The CIA lawyer added, "We want you to know that this office has great respect for the people we serve and we remain grateful for your past service to this country. We continue to be concerned for your security and welfare and would hope to be flexible should you require assistance in the future. Again, we wish you and your family every success."[182]

In court, the Does testified that they had been promised a lifetime of financial support and that the CIA had failed to live up to its obligation. A $27,000-a-year stipend and health benefits were at stake. The resettlees claimed that both benefits had been promised for life but had been withdrawn. Mr. Doe was in his late sixties, was ill, and had been laid off and unable to find work. He needed the stipend to be reinstated to survive. The judge ruled in favor of the CIA.

In 2005, the Does' case made its way to the U.S. Supreme Court. In a unanimous decision, the court ruled in favor of the CIA.[183] Justices relied on an 1875 decision often referred to by the CIA and the courts as "the *Totten Doctrine*."[184] The Supreme Court sent the Does back to Seattle destitute.

In the Totten case, the estate of William A. Lloyd, a spy hired by President Abraham Lincoln to gain information on Confederate troops during the Civil War, brought suit in the Court of Claims to recover compensation in the amount $9753. Lloyd had been promised, under a secret agreement with President Lincoln, to be paid $200 a month for his services. The president was assassinated, and the spy was never paid.[185]

The Supreme Court explained that the case was not justiciable for the following reasons:

> The service stipulated by the contract was a secret service; the information sought was to be obtained clandestinely, and was to be communicated privately; the employment and the service were to be equally concealed. Both employer and agent must have understood that the lips of the other were to be forever sealed respecting the relation of either to the matter. This condition of the engagement was implied from the nature of the employment, and is implied in all secret employments of the government in time of war, or upon matters affecting our foreign relations, where a disclosure of the service might compromise or embarrass our government in its public duties, or endanger the person or injure the character of the agent. If upon contracts of such a nature an action against the government could be maintained, whenever an agent should deem himself entitled to greater or different compensation than that awarded to him, the whole service in any case, and the manner of its discharge, with the details of dealings with individuals and officers, might be exposed, to the serious detriment of the public. A secret service, with liability

to publicity in this way, would be impossible; and, as such services are some-times indispensable to the government, its agents in those services must look for their compensation to the contingent fund of the department employing them, and to such allowance from it as those who dispense that fund may award.[186]

One former CIA case officer voiced the sentiments of many of his col-leagues: "It's hard enough to recruit people. As word spreads that you don't keep your word, it's going to be even harder."[187]

Appendix 14A: 18 U.S. Code § 1512 - Tampering with a witness, victim, or an informant

(a)
(1) Whoever kills or attempts to kill another person, with intent to—
   (A) prevent the attendance or testimony of any person in an offi-cial proceeding;
   (B) prevent the production of a record, document, or other object, in an official proceeding; or
   (C) prevent the communication by any person to a law enforce-ment officer or judge of the United States of information relat-ing to the commission or possible commission of a Federal offense or a violation of conditions of probation, parole, or release pending judicial proceedings; shall be punished as pro-vided in paragraph (3).
(2) Whoever uses physical force or the threat of physical force against any person, or attempts to do so, with intent to—
   (A) influence, delay, or prevent the testimony of any person in an official proceeding;
   (B) cause or induce any person to—
      (i) withhold testimony, or withhold a record, document, or other object, from an official proceeding;
      (ii) alter, destroy, mutilate, or conceal an object with intent to impair the integrity or availability of the object for use in an official proceeding;
      (iii) evade legal process summoning that person to appear as a witness, or to produce a record, document, or other object, in an official proceeding; or
      (iv) be absent from an official proceeding to which that person has been summoned by legal process; or
   (C) hinder, delay, or prevent the communication to a law enforce-ment officer or judge of the United States of information relat-ing to the commission or possible commission of a Federal offense or a violation of conditions of probation, supervised

      release, parole, or release pending judicial proceedings; shall be punished as provided in paragraph (3).

  (3) The punishment for an offense under this subsection is—

      (A) in the case of a killing, the punishment provided in sections 1111 and 1112;

      (B) in the case of—

         (i) an attempt to murder; or

         (ii) the use or attempted use of physical force against any person; imprisonment for not more than 30 years; and

      (C) in the case of the threat of use of physical force against any person, imprisonment for not more than 20 years.

(b) Whoever knowingly uses intimidation, threatens, or corruptly persuades another person, or attempts to do so, or engages in misleading conduct toward another person, with intent to—

  (1) influence, delay, or prevent the testimony of any person in an official proceeding;

  (2) cause or induce any person to—

      (A) withhold testimony, or withhold a record, document, or other object, from an official proceeding;

      (B) alter, destroy, mutilate, or conceal an object with intent to impair the object's integrity or availability for use in an official proceeding;

      (C) evade legal process summoning that person to appear as a witness, or to produce a record, document, or other object, in an official proceeding; or

      (D) be absent from an official proceeding to which such person has been summoned by legal process; or

  (3) hinder, delay, or prevent the communication to a law enforcement officer or judge of the United States of information relating to the commission or possible commission of a Federal offense or a violation of conditions of probation, supervised release, parole, or release pending judicial proceedings; shall be fined under this title or imprisoned not more than 20 years, or both.

(c) Whoever corruptly—

  (1) alters, destroys, mutilates, or conceals a record, document, or other object, or attempts to do so, with the intent to impair the object's integrity or availability for use in an official proceeding; or

  (2) otherwise obstructs, influences, or impedes any official proceeding, or attempts to do so, shall be fined under this title or imprisoned not more than 20 years, or both.

(d) Whoever intentionally harasses another person and thereby hinders, delays, prevents, or dissuades any person from—

(1) attending or testifying in an official proceeding;

(2) reporting to a law enforcement officer or judge of the United States the commission or possible commission of a Federal offense or a violation of conditions of probation, supervised release, parole, or release pending judicial proceedings;

(3) arresting or seeking the arrest of another person in connection with a Federal offense; or

(4) causing a criminal prosecution, or a parole or probation revocation proceeding, to be sought or instituted, or assisting in such prosecution or proceeding; or attempts to do so, shall be fined under this title or imprisoned not more than 3 years, or both.

(e) In a prosecution for an offense under this section, it is an affirmative defense, as to which the defendant has the burden of proof by a preponderance of the evidence, that the conduct consisted solely of lawful conduct and that the defendant's sole intention was to encourage, induce, or cause the other person to testify truthfully.

(f) For the purposes of this section—

(1) an official proceeding need not be pending or about to be instituted at the time of the offense; and

(2) the testimony, or the record, document, or other object need not be admissible in evidence or free of a claim of privilege.

(g) In a prosecution for an offense under this section, no state of mind need be proved with respect to the circumstance—

(1) that the official proceeding before a judge, court, magistrate judge, grand jury, or government agency is before a judge or court of the United States, a United States magistrate judge, a bankruptcy judge, a Federal grand jury, or a Federal Government agency; or

(2) that the judge is a judge of the United States or that the law enforcement officer is an officer or employee of the Federal Government or a person authorized to act for or on behalf of the Federal Government or serving the Federal Government as an adviser or consultant.

(h) There is extraterritorial Federal jurisdiction over an offense under this section.

(i) A prosecution under this section or section 1503 may be brought in the district in which the official proceeding (whether or not pending or about to be instituted) was intended to be affected or in the district in which the conduct constituting the alleged offense occurred.

(j) If the offense under this section occurs in connection with a trial of a criminal case, the maximum term of imprisonment which may be imposed for the offense shall be the higher of that otherwise provided by law or the maximum term that could have been imposed for any offense charged in such case.

(k) Whoever conspires to commit any offense under this section shall be subject to the same penalties as those prescribed for the offense the commission of which was the object of the conspiracy.

Source: From 18 U.S.C. § 1512—Tampering with a witness, victim, or an informant, www.law.cornell.edu.

Endnotes

1. The author has provided Department of Justice–funded WITSEC training to post-Soviet counties seeking to develop their own WITSEC programs. He has received WITSEC training by members of the USMS while serving in Eastern Europe. He is credited with being instrumental in the creation of the first post-Soviet WITSEC in Lithuania.
2. Observation by author during 40 years of criminal justice experience.
3. The procedure for designation of a person as a protected witness is set forth in the Department of Justice Offices, Boards and Divisions Order 2110.2, "Witness Protection and Maintenance Policy and Procedures." This order places with the U.S. Marshals Service the responsibility for the security of these witnesses and their families.
4. Witness Protection Programmes: EU Experiences in the International Context, Library of the European Parliament, January 28, 2013.
5. EU Standards in Witness Protection and Collaborators with Justice, Institute for International Research on Criminal Policy, Ghent University (JAI/2004/AGIS/077).
6. Director's message, the Witness Security Program, Stanley E. Morris.
7. USMS Pub. 4/29/99 supplementing USMS, Financial Management Branch Witness Security Division, January 1996; see also statement of Gerald Shur, senior associate director, Office of Enforcement Operations, Criminal Division, Before the Subcommittee on Crime and Criminal Justice, Committee on the Judiciary, U.S. House of Representatives Concerning Witness Intimidation, presented on August 4, 1994.
8. Goodman, B.M., "An Inside Look at Witness Protection: U.S. Marshals Give Rare Glimpse into a Successful, Secretive Program," CBS News, July 18, 2006. See Interim Report Of the Department Of Justice's Handling of Known or Suspected Terrorists Admitted into the Federal Witness Security Program, U.S. Department of Justice, Office of Inspector General, Report 13-23, May 2013.
9. *Philadelphia City Paper*, May 31–June 7, 2001, "Witness Protection: Sometimes, Bad Guys in Hiding Stay Bad," quoting Attorney Robert F. Simone, author of *The Last Mouthpiece: The Man Who Dared to Defend The Mob*, Camino Books, Philadelphia, PA, 2001.
10. *The Simpsons*, "Cape Feare" episode, 1993.
11. Beaubien, J., "Preacher Selling Elvis Museum on EBay," NPR, November 7, 2007 (Beaubien's theory: Elvis helped the FBI with a mob sting; the Mafia got angry and tried to kill him, so Elvis staged his own funeral and went into the witness security program); see Beeny, B., *Elvis' DNA Proves He's Alive*, Branden Books, Wellesley, MA, 2005.
12. *Eraser 2005*, starring Vanessa Williams and Arnold Schwarzenegger; *Bird on a Wire*, starring Mel Gibson and Goldie Hawn; *My Blue Heaven*, starring Steve

Martin and Joan Cusack; *Nowhere to Hide*, starring Scott Bakula and Rosanna Arquette; *Witness Protection*, made-for-television movie starring Tom Sizemore and Forest Whitaker, based on Sabbag, R., "The Invisible Family," *The New York Times*, February 11, 1996.

13. *The Pentacle* (official USMS newsletter obtained through FOIA, date of issue not provided, hereinafter *The Pentacle*).
14. California Witness Relocation and Protection Program (CAL WRAP), California Bureau of Investigation, California Department of Justice, Office of the Attorney General. (FY 2009/2010 Budget $4,855,000). The 2010 California Witness Relocation and Assistance Program (CAL WRAP) Annual Report to the Legislature summarizes the fiscal year (FY) reporting period of July 1, 2009, to June 30, 2010. During this reporting period, the CAL WRAP serviced 870 cases: 495 previously approved cases and 375 new cases. As of June 30, 2010, the program closed 434 cases, leaving 436 cases active. The CAL WRAP resides within the Division of Law Enforcement's Bureau of Investigation and Intelligence.

    The 375 new cases opened during FY 2009–2010 provided services for 418 witnesses and 689 family members, who testified against 670 violent offenders. Of the 375 new cases, 304 were gang-related. Other case types identified were high risk (56), domestic violence (9), and narcotics trafficking (6). Charges of homicide and attempted homicide were the precipitating charges on 73.9% of the cases, and assault accounted for 9.6%. The remaining 16.5% of cases involved rape, kidnapping, robbery, threats, narcotics, home invasion, carjacking, and criminal conspiracy.
15. Commentary on WITSEC by Gerald Shur, senior associate director, Office of Enforcement Operations, U.S. Department of Justice.
16. Ibid.
17. Pub. L. No. 91-452.
18. Ibid at Title V.
19. *The Pentacle*, at 3.
20. Pub. L. No. 98-473.
21. Witness Security Reform Act of 1984 Part F.
22. See also statement of Gerald Shur, senior associate director, Office of Enforcement Operations, Criminal Division, Before the Subcommittee on Crime and Criminal Justice, Committee on the Judiciary, U.S. House of Representatives Concerning Witness Intimidation, presented on August 4, 1994.
23. Goodman, B.M., "An Inside Look at Witness Protection, U.S. Marshals Give Rare Glimpse into a Successful, Secretive Program," CBS News, July 18, 2006, interviewing Maureen Killion, U.S. Department of Justice, Office of Enforcement Operations.
24. McShane, L., "Witness Protection Is an Offer That More Can Refuse; Informants Find Less to Fear from Today's Mafia," *Seattle Times*/Associated Press, January 2, 2000.
25. Goodman, B.M., "An Inside Look at Witness Protection: U.S. Marshals Give Rare Glimpse into a Successful, Secretive Program," CBS News, July 18, 2006, quoting Maureen Killion, U.S. Department of Justice, Office of Enforcement Operations, citing a study conducted by the U.S. Marshals Service.
26. Ibid.

27. Early, P. and Shur, G., *WITSEC: Inside the Federal Witness Protection Program*, Bantam Books, New York, 2002, p. 340–341.
28. *U.S. Marshals Service Administration of the Witness Security Program*, March 2005, Office of the Inspector General.
29. See *Doe v. Civiletti*, 635 F.2d 88, 96 (2d Cir. 1980). DEA agent and AUSA lacked actual authority to bind the government.
30. *U.S. Attorneys Manual* § 9.21 (hereinafter *USAM*).
31. *USAM* § 9.21.
32. *U.S. Attorneys Criminal Resource Manual* §701.
33. *USAM* § 9.21.
34. Moushey, B., "Cloaked in Secrecy, the Witness Protection Program Loses Its Innocence," *Pittsburgh Post-Gazette*, June 15, 1996; a former pilot for Noriega pilot, admitted to smuggling 1000 kg of cocaine worth $25 million and faced a sentence of life plus 145 years in prison until he helped prosecutors with Noriega. He was released after only 2 years in a protected witness unit, which was followed by 3 years of parole. The government paid $211,681 for his living expenses, including the purchase of a car.
35. Goodman, B.M., "An Inside Look at Witness Protection," CBS News, July 18, 2006.
36. The Victim Compensation Fund was established by Section 1208 of the Comprehensive Crime Control Act (Title II of P.L. 98-473). The fund is used by the attorney general to "pay restitution to, or in the case of death, compensation for the death of any victim of a crime that causes or threatens death or serious bodily injury and that is committed by any person during a period in which that person is provided protection under this chapter." In the case of death, an amount not to exceed $50,000 may be paid to the victim's estate. Moreover, the act authorizes payment of an amount not to exceed $25,000 to the estate of any individual whose death was caused by a protected witness before the enactment of this law.
37. 18USC § 3525(d).
38. See *Marion Albert Pruett v. Larry Norris*, director, Arkansas Department of Corrections, 153 F.3d 579 (8th Cir.1998) for details used in account regarding Pruett's release and related crimes.
39. "New Mexico Killer Set to Die in Arkansas," *Albuquerque Tribune*, April 11, 1999.
40. Carlson, P., "Joe Dogs/Jimmy the Weasel/Sammy the Bull/John Dean: Protected Witnesses Sometimes Do Strange Things with Their New Identities. The US Marshals Service Tells No Tales, But Others Do," *Washington Post*, December 6, 1998.
41. Nordheimer, J., "Investor-Slayer Led Double Life," October 28, 1987; see Earley, P. and Shur, G., *WITSEC: Inside the Federal Witness Protection Program*, Bantam Books, New York, 2002.
42. Carlson, P., "Joe Dogs/Jimmy the Weasel/Sammy the Bull/John Dean: Protected Witnesses Sometimes Do Strange Things with Their New Identities. The US Marshals Service Tells No Tales, But Others Do," *Washington Post*, December 6, 1998.
43. Early, P. and Shur, G., *WITSEC: Inside the Federal Witness Protection Program*, Bantam Books, New York, 2002, p. 16.

44. Moushey, B., "Cloaked in Secrecy, the Witness Protection Program Loses Its Innocence," *Pittsburgh Post-Gazette*, June 15, 1996

45. "Condemned Indian Gains Special Right," *The New York Times*, February 28, 1993.

46. *USAM* § 9-2.

47. Press release, Department of Justice, Office of Public Affairs, Statement Regarding Inspector General Report on the Handling of Former Known or Suspected Terrorists Admitted into the Federal Witness Security Program, May 16, 2013.

48. 18 U.S.C. §3521.

49. Mass, P., "My Secret Talks with Sammy the Bull," *Parade*, April 1997: "Sammy Gravano has elected to leave the constrictions of the Witness Protection Program." See also McShane, L., "Witness Protection Is an Offer That More Can Refuse," *Seattle Times*/Associated Press, January 2, 2000: "Attorney Ron Kuby represents the families of the brutal Mafiosi's 19 murder victims, they are suing Gravano for any profits made from his Peter Mass penned biography, *Underboss*."

50. Mass, P., *Underboss: Sammy The Bull Gravano's Story of Life in the Mafia*, HarperCollins, New York, 1997; see Sabbag, R., "Disappearing, The Invisible Family," *New York Magazine*, February 11, 1996: "Jess Brewer and his family ceased to exist at 9:00 on the morning of July 18, 1994. That was when the marshals from the Federal Witness Protection Program showed up at their door."

51. Sabbag, R., "The Invisible Family," *New York Times*, February 11, 1996.

52. Program Increase—USMS Alternative Safe Site and Orientation Center: $6.0 million and 0 positions. The USMS has identified and highlighted operational security risks relating to the integrity, security, and location identity of the Witness Security Program's sole orientation center, which has existed since the 1980s. Phased construction of a new alternative safe site and orientation center will be completely funded through existing resources to ensure the continuity of security within the Witness Security Program. USMS's FY 2014 current services for the protection of witnesses are 0 positions and $38.8 million.

53. USMS Pub. No. 17, April 27, 1999. In 1995, the air fleets of the U.S. Marshals Service and the Immigration and Naturalization Service merged to create the Justice Prisoner and Alien Transportation System.

54. Earley, P. and Shur, G., *WITSEC: Inside the Federal Witness Protection Program*, Bantam Books, New York, February 2002.

55. Ibid.

56. *The Pentacle*.

57. Sabbag, R., "The Invisible Family," *The New York Times*, February 11, 1996.

58. Ibid.

59. *The Pentacle*.

60. USMS, Administration of the Witness Security Program, U.S. Department of Justice, Office of the Inspector General, Executive Summary, March 2005.

61. *The Pentacle*.

62. *The Pentacle*.

63. Carlson, P., "Joe Dogs/Jimmy the Weasel/Sammy the Bull/John Dean: Protected Witnesses Sometimes Do Strange Things with Their New Identities. The US Marshals Service Tells No Tales, But Others Do," *Washington Post*, December 6, 1998.

64. *The Pentacle*.

65. Carlson, P., "Joe Dogs/Jimmy the Weasel/Sammy the Bull/John Dean: Protected Witnesses Sometimes Do Strange Things with Their New Identities. The US Marshals Service Tells No Tales, But Others Do," *Washington Post*, December 6, 1998.

66. Ibid.

67. Ibid.

68. Wagner, D., "Mobster Sammy the Bull Reveals Life in Arizona," *The New York Times*, July 18, 1999.

69. Maas, P., *Underboss: Sammy the Bull Gravano's Story of Life in the Mafia*, HarperCollins, New York, 1997.

70. Sabbag, R., "The Invisible Family," *New York Times*, February 11, 1996.

71. Carlson, P., "Joe Dogs/Jimmy the Weasel/Sammy the Bull/John Dean: Protected Witnesses Sometimes Do Strange Things with Their New Identities. The US Marshals Service Tells No Tales, But Others Do," *Washington Post*, December 6, 1998.

72. *The Pentacle*.

73. Ibid.

74. Ibid.

75. See *Prisco v. United States Dep't of Justice*, 851 F.2d 93 (1988) (federal government interfered with noncustodial parent rights by accepting child into the federal Witness Security Program, resulting in claim of deprivation of parental relationship with child, cert. denied, 490 U.S. 1089 [1989]).

76. *The Pentacle*.

77. Ibid.

78. See The United States is currently divided into eight D.O.L. regions, each with different cost-of-living indexes.

79. Carlson, P., "Joe Dogs/Jimmy the Weasel/Sammy the Bull/John Dean: Protected Witnesses Sometimes Do Strange Things with Their New Identities. The US Marshals Service Tells No Tales, But Others Do," *Washington Post*, December 6, 1998.

80. *U.S. Attorneys Criminal Resource Manual* §706.

81. Carlson, P., "Joe Dogs/Jimmy the Weasel/Sammy the Bull/John Dean: Protected Witnesses Sometimes Do Strange Things with Their New Identities. The US Marshals Service Tells No Tales, But Others Do," *Washington Post*, December 6, 1998.

82. Ibid.

83. *U.S. Attorneys Criminal Resource Manual* §707.

84. *The Pentacle*.

85. Carlson, P., "Joe Dogs/Jimmy the Weasel/Sammy the Bull/John Dean: Protected Witnesses Sometimes Do Strange Things with Their New Identities. The US Marshals Service Tells No Tales, But Others Do," *Washington Post*, December 6, 1998.

86. *U.S. Attorneys Criminal Resource Manual* §706.

87. *USAM* § 9-21.

88. Sabbag, R., "The Invisible Family," *The New York Times*, February 11, 1996.

89. Carlson, P., "Joe Dogs/Jimmy the Weasel/Sammy the Bull/John Dean: Protected Witnesses Sometimes Do Strange Things with Their New Identities. The US Marshals Service Tells No Tales, But Others Do," *Washington Post*, December 6, 1998.

90. Ibid.
91. *The Pentacle.*
92. Ibid.
93. Moushey, B., "Deals with the Devil, Protected Witness," *Pittsburgh Post-Gazette*, May 26–31, 1996: "The Federal Witness Protection Program often gives freedom and riches to heinous criminals …. Once in the program, some can't resist the temptation of returning to the criminal life."
94. *U.S. Attorneys Manual* 9-21.800.
95. "Shabazz Informant Says He Was Paid," *Miami Herald*, March 24, 1995.
96. Ibid.
97. Ibid.
98. Cormick, J.M., "I Was in It to Save Lives," *Newsweek*, May 15, 1995.
99. *DEA Agents Manual* at 6612.73(k).
100. *U.S. Attorneys Manual* at 9-21.800.
101. 18USC §3521.
102. Name changed.
103. May, A., "John Gotti, the Last Mafia Icon," TruTv Crime Library.
104. James, G., "Man Linked to John Gotti Is Slain on Brooklyn St.," *The New York Times*, August 30, 1988.
105. "Gotti Witness Protests Withdrawal of Protection," *Orlando Sentinel*, April 25, 1990.
106. "Mob Witness Jailed after Appearance on TV," *Orlando Sentinel*, May 21, 1990.
107. Carlson, P., "Joe Dogs/Jimmy the Weasel/Sammy the Bull/John Dean: Protected Witnesses Sometimes Do Strange Things with Their New Identities. The US Marshals Service Tells No Tales, But Others Do," *Washington Post*, December 6, 1998.
108. Early, P. and Shur, G., *WITSEC: Inside the Witness Protection Program*, Bantam Books, New York, 2002.
109. National security stakeholders such as the FBI and DEA may be involved in the WITSEC program admission process as sponsoring agencies. A sponsoring agency provides WITSEC program personnel with information on the witness, including a threat assessment and a risk assessment. The threat assessment evaluates the threat to the witness for cooperating with the federal government, whereas the risk assessment reports on potential risks to the public caused by the witness's enrollment in the WITSEC program.
110. *Interim Report on the Department of Justice Handling of Known or Suspected Terrorists Admitted into the Federal Witness Security Program*, U.S. Department of Justice Audit Division, Report 13-23, May 2013.
111. The Office of Inspector General Interim Report claims that "of the identified universe of terrorism-linked witnesses, the FBI sponsored nearly 80% of these witnesses into the Program."
112. E.g., *In re Terrorist Bombings a/U.S. Embassies in East Africa*, 552 F.3d 93 (2d Cir. 2008); *United States v. Rahman*, 189 F.3d 88 (2d Cir. 1999); *United States v. McVeigh*, 153 F.3d 1166 (10th Cir. 1998); *United States v. Ibrahim*, No. 07-CR-543 CDLI), 2011 WL 4975291 CE.D.N.Y. October 19, 2011); see also *United States v. Medunjanin*, No. 10 CR 019, 2012 WL 1514766 (E.D.N.Y. May 1, 2012).
113. The TSC is managed by the Federal Bureau of Investigation (FBI) and was established to serve as the U.S. government's consolidation point for information about known or suspected terrorists.

114. Office of the Deputy Attorney General, Response to Office of Inspector General WITSEC Interim Audit Report, May 6, 2013; the department stated that as of March 2013, (1) the FBI had completed all but one of the threat assessments on WITSEC program participants disclosed to them as having a potential nexus to terrorism, and (2) none of these individuals have revealed a threat to national security at this time.

115. Ibid.

116. *U.S. Attorneys Criminal Resource Manual.*

117. *DEA Agents Manual*, Ch. 61; money known as PE/PI funds, purchase of evidence/payment for information, can be expended for informant/witness security expenses.

118. Ibid.

119. See U.S. Department of Housing and Urban Development. Notice PIH 96-16, "One Strike and You're Out" Screening in Eviction Guidelines for Public Housing Authorities; Congress has made witness relocation one of the eligible activities under the Section 8 rental certificates program.

120. Murphy, S., "US Paid Hit Man $20,000 on Release from Prison," *The Boston Globe*, January 16, 2008.

121. *Investigative Priorities, Procedures and Techniques*, Ch. 45, Bureau of Alcohol, Tobacco and Firearms.

122. Ibid.

123. "U.S. Soldier Charged in Mexico Cartel Killing," Associated Press, August 11, 2009.

124. Booth, W., "Mayhem Crosses the Border with Informers," *Washington Post*, August 27, 2009.

125. Caldwell, A.A., "Slain Cartel Leader Said to Be U.S. Informant," Associated Press, July 27, 2009.

126. "U.S. Soldier Charged in Mexico Cartel Killing," Associated Press, August 11, 2009.

127. Chávez, A.M., "Trial Starts for Man Accused of El Paso Cartel Slaying," *El Paso Times*, February 25, 2013.

128. "U.S. Soldier Charged in Mexico Cartel Killing," Associated Press, August 11, 2009.

129. Chávez, A.M., "Trial Starts for Man Accused of El Paso Cartel Slaying," *El Paso Times*, February 25, 2013.

130. Chávez, A.M., "El Paso Drug Cartel Killing: Victim Was Stalked," *El Paso Times*, February 26, 2013.

131. Ibid.

132. Caldwell, A.A., "Slain Cartel Leader Said to Be U.S. Informant," Associated Press, July 27, 2009.

133. "Juarez Cartel Member Murdered in El Paso," KTSM News, El Paso, July 28, 2009.

134. "U.S. Soldier Charged in Mexico Cartel Killing," Associated Press, August 11, 2009.

135. Chávez, A.M., "El Paso Cartel Shooting Trial: Judge Slams Feds in Slaying of Informant," *El Paso Times*, March 8, 2013.

136. Caldwell, A.A., "Immigration Agents Mishandle Informants, Documents Show," Associated Press, October 26, 2009.

137. Chávez, A.M., "El Paso Cartel Shooting Trial: Judge Slams Feds in Slaying of Informant," *El Paso Times*, March 8, 2013.
138. Ibid.
139. Caldwell, A.A., "Immigration Agents Mishandle Informants, Documents Show," Associated Press, October 26, 2009.
140. Ibid.
141. Ibid.
142. Chavez, A.M., "El Paso Cartel Shooting Trial: Judge Slams Feds in Slaying of Informant," *El Paso Times*, March 8, 2013.
143. Caldwell, A.A., "Immigration Agents Mishandle Informants, Documents Show," Associated Press, October 26, 2009.
144. "U.S. Soldier Charged in Mexico Cartel Killing," Associated Press, August 11, 2009.
145. Caldwell, A.A., "Immigration Agents Mishandle Informants, Documents Show," Associated Press, October 26, 2009.
146. Chávez, A.M., "El Paso Drug Cartel Shooting: Man on Trial over '09 Death Cited Fear," *El Paso Times*, March 1, 2013.
147. Chávez, A.M., "Man Pleads Guilty in East El Paso Cartel-Tied Killing," *El Paso Times*, January 23, 2013.
148. Chávez, A.M., "El Paso Drug Cartel Killing: Victim was Stalked," *El Paso Times*, February 26, 2013.
149. Chávez, A.M., "Trial Starts for Man Accused of El Paso Cartel Slaying," *El Paso Times*, February 25, 2013.
150. Caldwell, A.A., "Immigration Agents Mishandle Informants, Documents Show," Associated Press, October 26, 2009.
151. Miller, G., "CIA Has Recruited Iranians to Defect: The Secret Effort Aims to Undermine Iran's Nuclear Program," *Los Angeles Times*, December 9, 2007; see also Sherwell, P. and Lowther, W., "CIA Suspects Iranian Nuclear Defector Who Returned to Iran Was a Double Agent, *Sunday Telegraph* (UK), August 25, 2010.
152. Miller, G., "CIA Says It Moved Iranian Scientist, Second Informant to US over Safety Concerns," *Washington Post*, July 17, 2010.
153. "Russian Authorities Likely behind Litvinenko's Death, His Wife Says," *International Herald Tribune*, December 10, 2006. See Cowell, A., *The Terminal Spy: A True Story of Espionage, Betrayal and Murder*, Random House, New York, 2008.
154. Taylor, M., "Former KGB Defector Claims He Was Poisoned by Russians," *Guardian*, April 7, 2008.
155. Taylor, M., "Former KGB Defector Claims He Was Poisoned by Russians," *Guardian*, April 7, 2008.
156. See "How the CIA exploited and then disowned their own agent," www.borislorczak.com.
157. "Secrets of the Dead: The Umbrella Assassin," PBS, October 9, 2011.
158. Lax, A.J., *The Cunning of Bacterial Poisons*, Oxford University Press, Oxford, UK, 2005.
159. Ibid.
160. Brown, J. "Poisoned Umbrella Murder Cases Reopened," *The Independent*, June 20, 2008.

161. McCartney, R., "Inside the CIA Slush Fund for Informants: US Intelligence Sets Aside Millions Every Year to Pay Defectors," MSNBC, July 16, 2010, quoting former CIA agent.
162. Miller, G., "CIA Says It Moved Iranian Scientist, Second Informant to US over Safety Concerns," *Washington Post*, July 17, 2010.
163. McCartney, R., "Inside the CIA Slush Fund for Informants: US Intelligence Sets Aside Millions Every Year to Pay Defectors," MSNBC, July 16, 2010, quoting former CIA agent Bob Baer.
164. Cole, M., "Iran Nuke Defector Left Behind $5 Million in CIA Cash," ABC News, July 15, 2010, quoting unnamed U.S. official familiar with the defection.
165. Sherwell, P. and Lowther, W., "CIA Suspects Iranian Nuclear Defector Who Returned to Tehran Was Double Agent," *The Telegraph* (UK), July 17, 2010.
166. Ibid.
167. Cole, M., "Iran Nuke Defector Left Behind $5 Million in CIA Cash," ABC News, July 15, 2010, quoting former CIA case officer.
168. "CIA Suspects Iranian Nuclear Defector Who Returned to Tehran with a Double Agent," *Sunday Telegraph* (UK), August 25, 2010.
169. Kessler, R., *The CIA at War: Inside the Secret Campaign Against Terror*, St. Martin's Press, New York, 2003.
170. Kessler, P., *Undercover Washington: Where Famous Spies, Lived, Worked and Loved*, Capital Books, Washington, DC, 2005.
171. Central Intelligence Act of 1949; 50 U.S.C. § 403h.
172. Savage, C., "Disgruntled Ex-Spy Sues the CIA," *The New York Times*, January 13, 2005.
173. Pasternak, D., "Squeezing Them, Leaving Them: Some Defectors Say Washington Isn't Always Good about Keeping Its Word," *Washington Post*, June 30, 2002.
174. Central Intelligence Act of 1949; 50 U.S.C. § 403h.
175. Letter from George Washington written 8 mi. east of Morris Town, July 26, 1777, www.cia.gov.
176. Fleming, T., "George Washington, Spymaster," *American Heritage Magazine*, February/March 2000, Vol. 51, Issue 1.
177. Pasternak, D., "Squeezing Them, Leaving Them: Some Defectors Say Washington Isn't Always Good About Keeping Its Word," *Washington Post*, June 30, 2002.
178. See *Tenet v. Doe* No. 03-1395, 544 U.S. 1 (2005) 329 F.3d 1135, reversed.
179. Named after former DCI Richard Helms.
180. Loeb, V., "Soviet Defectors and Former Spies Accuse CIA of Betrayal/Ex-Diplomat, Wife Left Out in Cold over Pay, Benefits," *Washington Post*, July 21, 2000.
181. No. 01-35419 and CV-99-01597-RSL.
182. See *Tenet v. Doe* No. 03-1395, 544 U.S. 1 (2005) 329 F.3d 1135, reversed.
183. Ibid.
184. *Totten v. United States*, 92 U.S. 105 (1876).
185. *Tenet v. Doe.*
186. Ibid.
187. Adair, B., "Spy vs. CIA: It's a Shot in the Dark," *St. Petersburg Times*, January 10, 2005.

Index

informants, 46, 61
persons apprehended at a border while
    smuggling drugs, 189–190
raid execution process, 330–332
source of information, 33–34
Drugs
  dangerous, 181–183
  exchange of, weapons, 192
  for information, 221
  laboratories, 179
  obtaining or moving, 180
  persons apprehended at a border while
    smuggling drugs, 189–190
  sources, 178–179
  transportation and storage, 179–180
  war on, 18
Drug trade, involvement of terrorist and
    insurgent groups in, 192
Drug trafficking, 32, 36, 175–181, 288, 449
  foreign government involvement in, 192
  high-intensity, 391
  illegal money laundering and, 392
  multibillion-dollar business of, 2
  organizations, 387, 388

E

E-communications, 279
Ego, motivations for cooperation, 56–57
Electronically stored information,
    corroboration through, 279–280
Electronic data, analysis of, 300
El Rukn prosecution, 453–454
Entrapment defense, 397
  reversals and, 383–385
Eugene Vidocq, from informant to chief of
    French Sûreté, 4–5
Evidence, TFO, 408
Export Administration Act, 227

F

False Claims Act (FCA), 7, 237–239
  relator share guidelines, 246–247
Family Jewels, CIA, 90–91
FBI, see Federal Bureau of Investigation
FCA, see False Claims Act
Fear
  cooperation, motivations for, 47
  of deportation and VISAs, 57
Federal Bureau of Investigation (FBI), 29,
    107, 127, 207–209, 446, 494

confidential human sources, 30–31
counterterrorism, 273
as global counterintelligence
    organization, 86–87
informant recruitment, 70–71
recruiting guidelines, 71–72
whistle-blowers, 31–32
Federal Bureau of Prisons Protective
    Custody Units (PCU), 458
Federal False Claims Act (FCA), 31
Federal human trafficking investigations,
    T visas and, 82
Federal investigative agencies, statutes
    enforced by, 224–227
Federal law enforcement agencies
  drug enforcement administration,
    32–34
  emergence of, 8–9
  FBI, 29–32
Federal prisoners, 33
Federal prosecuting attorney (FPO), 207
Federal Tort Claims Act (FTCA), 411, 455
Field Intelligence Groups (FIGs), 284
Financial records, 277–278
5K1 sentence, 114–115
  and Cartel of Snitches, 126–129
Flex, 396–397
Florida, 26–27
Florida drug smuggling conspiracy, 268
Florida's Confidential Informant Law,
    364–367
Florida State, guidelines for confidential
    informants, 360–363
Fluttering, 273
FOIA, see Freedom of Information Act
Ford, Gerald, 11–12
Forfeitable assets, state and local pressure
    for, 219
Forfeiture awards, 208–209, 212
  calculating informant, 216–217
  civil and criminal, 214–216
  Department of Justice (DOJ) Asset,
    213–214
Forfeitures/seizures, of Task Force,
    410–411
Fourth Amendment, 254, 278
  trash pull, 278
  video surveillance, 272
FPO, see Federal prosecuting attorney
Freedom of Information Act (FOIA), 16, 91
  Privacy Act, 407
FTCA, see Federal Tort Claims Act